William M. Cave
Mark A. Chesler
UNIVERSITY OF MICHIGAN

Sociology of Education:

An Anthology of Issues and Problems

Macmillan Publishing Co., Inc.
NEW YORK
Collier Macmillan Publishers
LONDON

Macmillan Publishing Co., Inc.
866 Third Avenue, New York, New York 10022

Collier-Macmillan Canada, Ltd.

Library of Congress Cataloging in Publication Data

Cave, William M   comp.
  Sociology of education.

  Includes bibliographical references.
  1. Educational sociology—Collected works.
I. Chesler, Mark A., joint comp. II. Title.
LC191.C37   301.5'6   73–13171
ISBN 0–02–320400–1

Printing: 1 2 3 4 5 6 7 8   Year: 4 5 6 7 8 9 0

Preface

This book deals with issues and problems in the sociology of education. It encompasses many of the traditional areas of sociological inquiry: the sociocultural context of education; education as a social institution; education as a major socializing force; education as a reflection of the social structure; and the management of differences and conflict in schools and classrooms. We are concerned with an analysis of the society's dominant cultural values and the structural avenues through which these values are transmitted. Our book attempts to identify and describe the ideological underpinnings of educational practices and to analyze the mechanisms of control that support the maintenance of certain kinds of educational differences and the subordination of cultural variations.

There are some important differences that we feel distinguish this book from others and that we hope will wrest us and the reader from the shackles of conventionality. First, we have devoted an entire section of this book to programs and problems of educational change. Most texts in the sociology of education do not explicitly deal with change, but tend to bury change-oriented articles under traditional sociological categories. Why do they do so? Perhaps because they wish to maintain the fiction of value-free scholarship, uncommitted to any particular educational plan or picture? Perhaps because to delineate current controversies tends to date a book? Perhaps because members of the scientific elite are committed to schools as they are and to service to school managers as they currently operate? Who really knows why? But the gap is important, and it is critical to see that our focus is different.

Next, our perspective is necessarily a sociological one. Hence, the concepts and tools of sociology, together with a complex social analysis, are brought to bear on the educational institution and its social systems. The result is to provide a more comprehensive picture and understanding of the educational system and the change processes. Crucial to this understanding is recognition of the political roles of schools and the political nature of education itself. Schools are seen as governing their affairs in ways that reflect choices between priorities, which in turn indicate value preferences. Further, schools support certain ideologies and proceed to implement them in educational practices.

Finally, departing from convention, we sought to establish internal logic in the selected readings by introducing the three major sections of the book through introductory essays that represent the point of view held by the authors with respect to each of the three areas. Thus, you, the reader, can read with a full understanding of our own values, and perhaps yours as well. We are cognizant of the likely criticisms that may ensue from such an approach, but at the same time, we are convinced that the authors' value preferences should be made clear to the reader. The myth of objectivity in the social sciences is superseded only by the larger myth of value-free research.

ACKNOWLEDGMENTS

We are indebted to Nancy Schafer, who so capably assisted us in the search for relevant materials, and to Lydia Drelles, who carried a lion's share of the administrative detail. We also wish to express our gratitude to the secretaries in the Sociology Department for their invaluable assistance. Finally, thanks to our colleagues on the Educational Change Team of the University of Michigan from whom many of our insights and understandings are derived.

W. M. C.

M. A. C.

Contents

PART I
The Societal Context of Education 1

A. Socialization 18
   1. Our Educational Emphases in Primitive Perspective
      MARGARET MEAD 18
   2. The Development of the Self in Social Interaction
      GEORGE HERBERT MEAD 27

B. Cultural and Social Structural Background 37
   1. The Ethos of Industrial America
      DONALD G. MCKINLEY 37
   2. Social Inequality
      CHARLES H. ANDERSON 53

C. Educational Systems and Culture 73
   1. Traditional Values and the Shaping of American Education
      MERLE L. BORROWMAN 73

2. The Education of Immigrants in the United States:
Historical Background
RICHARD G. DURNIN 93

3. Institutional Racism: The Crucible of Black Identity
JAMES A. GOODMAN 103

D. Educational Systems and Social Structure 121
1. Equality of Educational Opportunity (The Coleman Report)
U.S. OFFICE OF EDUCATION 121

2. Socioeconomic Position and Academic Underachievement
RICHARD A. CLOWARD 134

3. Counselor Bias and the Female Occupational Role
JOHN J. PIETROFESA AND NANCY K. SCHLOSSBERG 148

PART II
The Institutional Fabric of Education 151

A. Ideologies and Norms—Myths and Realities 166
1. Compensatory Education and Contemporary Liberalism
in the United States: A Sociological View
D. C. MORTON AND D. R. WATSON 166

2. The Political Functions of the Educational System
HARMON ZEIGLER AND WAYNE PEAK 183

B. Systemic Controls on Education 207
1. School Desegregation and School Decision Making
ROBERT L. CRAIN AND DAVID STREET 207

2. An Analysis of Curriculum Policy Making
MICHAEL W. KIRST AND DECKER F. WALKER 221

C. Control and Communication Systems in Schools 252
1. Students and Schools: Some Observations on
Client Trust in Client-Serving Organizations
CHARLES E. BIDWELL 252

2. Institutional Paternalism in High School
BUFORD RHEA 278

3. Variations on the Theme of Primary Groups: Forms
of Social Control Within School Staffs
DONALD I. WARREN 288

D. Managing Differences and Conflict   309
    1. Culture Conflict and Mexican-American Achievement
       NEAL JUSTIN   309

    2. The Present Failure to Educate the American Indian
       ROBERT B. KAPLAN   313

    3. Sexism in the Elementary School
       CAROL JACOBS AND CYNTHIA EATON   323

E. The Nonschool Socializing System   327
    1. The Generation Gap
       EDGAR Z. FRIEDENBERG   327

    2. The Socialization Community
       RONALD LIPPITT   338

PART III
Programs and Problems of Change   363
A. Retraining Personnel—Attitudes and Role Behavior   378
    1. Helping Teachers Improve Classroom Group Processes
       RICHARD A. SCHMUCK   378

B. Organizational Change   404
    1. Changing Schools Through Student Advocacy
       MARK A. CHESLER AND JOHN E. LOHMAN   404

    2. People-Changing Institutions: The Transformed Schools
       MORRIS JANOWITZ   434

    3. Desegregation or Integration in Public Schools?
       The Policy Implications of Research
       IRWIN KATZ   440

C. Client or Community Development   454
    1. Participation, Decentralization, Community Control,
       and Quality Education
       MARIO D. FANTINI   454

    2. Firing the Staff: How to Get Rid of Incompetent
       Teachers, Principals and Supervisors
       ELLEN LURIE   468

    3. Mobilization: Gettin' the Students Together
       JOHN BIRMINGHAM   474

D. Social Policy Restructuring 490

   1. Reslicing the School Pie
      JOHN E. COONS, STEPHEN D. SUGARMAN, AND
      WILLIAM H. CLUNE III 490

   2. The Detroit School Decision
      STEPHEN J. ROTH 498

   3. Schools for Scandal—The Bill of Rights and
      Public Education
      IRA GLASSER 504

E. Alternative Educational Patterns 513

   1. Open Education: Its Philosophy, Historical Perspectives,
      and Implications
      EWALD B. NYQUIST 513

   2. After Deschooling, What?
      IVAN ILLICH 520

   3. Alternative Systems of Education
      JESSIE E. WRAY 533

   4. Mississippi's Freedom Schools: The Politics of Education
      FLORENCE HOWE 537

Part I

The Societal
Context
of Education

Educational systems are universal
phenomena in organized society. Their
content and character vary tremendously in
different cultures, but they exist,
nevertheless. The universality of these
arrangements can be attributed to the need
for all human societies to preserve their
cultural heritage, and to inculcate their
young with the thought patterns, formal
customs and proprieties of that culture.

Every culture has its own definition, for instance, of what it means to be human, as well as what it means to be "American" or "Rhodesian" or "Cambodian." And this definition, with its concomitant rules and roles, must be passed on. What is preserved, and therefore passed on or transmitted, is a function of the content of cultural values, artifacts, and symbols. How this material is transmitted, and therefore inculcated into the young, or learned, may vary considerably according to the particular culture or the part of the culture we observe.

In the American society formal schooling has emerged as one of the major repositories of our dominant cultural heritage. Moreover, our school systems have been officially charged with the responsibility for mass transmission of this content. Some of the most explosive issues confronting American education relate to the nature of this content. Difficult and searching questions often boil down to this: Whose heritage should be transmitted? What values should be taught and what skills learned? Whatever their source, these questions are best understood within the ideological and cultural framework of American society.

The mechanisms for transmission of this material are also at the center of much public debate and controversy. Some of the obvious and important questions in this regard are these: How is specific material best transmitted, best learned? Where is the locus of decision making for education in a local community? What will the schools do that parents and churches can not do, and the reverse? The fact that we Americans have relied primarily upon a mass, public, and universal system of education indicates our commitment to the preservation of our culture in ways that try to unify our diversity and stabilize our changing society.

In Part I of this book we explore the relations between the nature of the cultural and social systems in America and its educational institutions. In the initial chapter, "Socialization," our concern is to demonstrate the ways in which young people become humanized or become part of a culture. This process is universal, although as we have indicated, its form and content vary by culture. The acculturation of the young is, of course, also a means whereby the society passes on and preserves its heritage.

In the next chapter, "Cultural and Social Structural Background," we focus upon the nature of this society and culture, and thus on the backdrop for our educational system. In particular, we review unique aspects of American ideologies or belief systems. Our purpose is to demonstrate how knowing the cultural and social structure may help us understand an educational system. This examination should provide us with a clear perspective on the ideological functions of schooling and the societal need to acculturate and organize the uninitiated—the young and especially those who appear to be different.

A central concern of the third chapter, "Educational Systems and Culture," is the role of the cultural context and social values in the direct shaping of the educational process. The basic cultural modalities, as well as conflicts among them, can be seen in the content of education and in the norms or values of the school. The history of cultural conflict is a key analytical tool here.

The final chapter in Part I, "Educational Systems and Social Structure," provides us with insight into the means by which the objectives and procedures of education stay congruent with those of other agencies and institutions in the social order. The school reinforces the demands and expectations of elite political and economic groups in the ways it channels and instructs various groups of students. Operating as a primary preparation system for the socioeconomic system, the school is largely responsible for perpetuating the myths associated with education, income, and social role and the resultant social class and status divisions.

We view the issues and problems that arise in Part I as rooted in historical, cultural, and social structural patterns. Attempts to deal with current educational issues in the absence of these concerns and contexts are likely to prove superficial. Here is where we must all start. The reader who knows he disagrees considerably with what is said here can expect to differ with us in later portions of this book.

SOCIALIZATION

In the broadest sense of the term, education is the society's formal mechanism for the transmission of its culture. Despite the wide variety of human cultures, and despite considerable variance within any society, this does appear to be the fundamental function of the educative process. For the society, the schools preserve the cultural heritage; for the individual the schools pass on or inculcate the cultural heritage. Thus the broad meaning of *education* is in many ways similar to the meaning of *socialization*, the process whereby persons are acculturated into a human community. The manifest aim of schooling is to produce human beings who, at best, will perpetuate and improve the present society or who, at worst, will not destroy the society, its values and structures.

The concept of culture assumes a key position in the analysis of education irrespective of whether that analysis is made at the formal or informal level of social system dynamics. For instance, some scholars limit their use of *education* to the formal schooling apparatus and use *socialization* as a broader term encompassing all that is learned—overtly and covertly. But whether formally acknowledged or not, the culture seeps through all aspects of the society and the school system. Educational systems cannot be abstracted from the embracing culture and social structure; rather they can best be understood as part and parcel of it.

We may characterize culture as a uniquely human product of social interaction, consisting of material and nonmaterial symbols having meaning for persons. Further, technological media and material artifacts also have varied functions and meaning for individuals. As a result of these shared meanings, members of a society assume certain regularities in thought as well as actions. Common meaning systems or thought patterns can be attributed to the culture's common symbols and expectations or prescriptions for acceptable use and behavior.

The institution of education assumes a pivotal role both in inculcating the individual with the ways of the social order and in developing his ability to adopt new and emerging patterns of behavior. Accordingly, the educative process must deal simultaneously with common historic meanings and with the discontinuity of change. Thus we have a continuing debate whether the "true purpose" of education is to teach about the past or to prepare for the future, whether schools are conservers of historic tradition or agents of change. Probably either of these choices is more or less satisfactory depending upon the particular observer's biases at the moment. We all want some things to change and others to stay the same.

The primary socialization process begins with the young person's discovering parts of himself in others and parts of others in himself. The learned ability to know what is happening to another is clearly a product of empathic human interaction. With this skill one can also adopt or play the role of the other person. In so doing one can see himself as others see him. And thus he develops self-reflective behavior, the key to human interactions among individuals. *The selection by George Herbert Mead, "The Development of the Self in Social Interaction," describes this process in illuminating terms.*

A prime medium of self–other socialization in human cultures has been the family. Here, presumably, the problems of self-constraint and conformity with others are more tolerable because they are presented by intimates, and the transition from childhood to adulthood is thought to meet with a minimum of conflict. The family is, after all, the first prolonged and intimate interaction system the individual encounters. In this context he discovers humanness and moves from primitive biogenetic instincts to learned social responses. Here are learned the rudiments of social interaction.

The things that members of a given family can know are limited by that family's experience. But all that is known is usually shared within the system. The acquisition of this knowledge by the child is sought, is rewarded, and is a clear requisite to adult or peer status. Although conflict may be minimal in these systems, so is pluralism. But considerable tension still does arise from adult control of this process as well as from disparities between the ideal and real patterns of behavior. As contact with others grows, the alternatives for new behaviors inevitably increase, and so does the conflict among preferred alternatives.

It is typical in more heterogeneous or industrialized societies that the areas of technical knowledge increase enormously; thus necessary information can no longer be shared by all, certainly not by all families. The relative homogeneity and tranquillity of the socialization process is disturbed by the presses of other value systems. This ambiguity is heightened by a number of sociological factors: shifts in basic interaction patterns, the rapidity of social change, demographic shifts, increased social mobility, specialization, and so on. Dramatic increases in the number and influence of contacts with people who are different further complicate the issue.

Increasingly, the primary socialization family tends to relinquish its historic functions to secondary institutions, the chief ones being the school and often the church, or the state-church. Roles once performed exclusively by the family become absorbed by the school. Adult intimates formerly in charge of the socialization process are replaced by professionals, adults expert in the acculturation of large numbers of young people without the biases of intimate connections. Activities that once went on in relatively small groups now occur in larger and more complex settings. *Margaret Mead discusses some of the changes that occur in schools as the major structures of society change or differ.*

The content of necessary socialization activities is technically rationalized into a curriculum—a formal ideology and a set of carefully prescribed practices. Clearly, what parents could do by instinct professionals must do with clear regulations and justifications. Practical courses (such as sewing, cooking, and industrial arts) are introduced and justified on the basis that these skills are no longer learned in the family circle. Courses particularly characterized by moral and ideological overtones (family living, sex education, and social studies) are rationalized on the premise that the traditional strongholds of these values are rendered incapable by the external forces of change of transmitting them effectively. School activities (termed extracurricular), rationalized as participatory character-building pursuits, also are devised. The *latent* function of these is to segregate the adult world from that of the child, controlling the young and minimizing the inevitable generational conflict. Of course that conflict often surfaces anyway.

The data indicate that all these programs and activities provide differential socialization. They segregate the young along certain lines, setting up classes, races, and age statuses in opposition to each other, establishing youth–adult lines of conflict as well. Thus the school reflects and encourages the conflict manifest in every portion of this nation. The school replicates the struggles of the larger social order and thus catapults itself into the maelstrom of the political arena. What is taken for granted as the natural social order now becomes a matter of debate. The school's "neutral" posture, never a reality, becomes even more openly partisan under these circumstances.

Not only the content but the characteristic modes of socialization and education are themselves political in nature. The process of role learning and role taking is not just general and whole; we also learn specialized roles, one or several out of an entire range of possibilities. The actual roles we learn are consistent with our assumptions about the culture in which we live and our experiences with the social structure we encounter. What is learned is usually what is required for the individual to assume the status of adulthood in a given culture. And this is a function of the culture's values, which, in turn, reflect the society's ideological commitment and social structure.

The instructional or transmission processes further stress mass conformity and carefully regulated peer experiences under bureaucratic rule. Clearly, schools are selective in the value domain and, as we shall indicate later, are committed to an ideological and operational base that is both tolerant of the political order and reinforcing of the economic structure.

Cultural and Social Structural Background

The processes of socialization are tuned to the particular nature of the cultural and social structure for which one is being prepared. As these systems differ, so will the content and operations of socialization systems. In an effort to understand how these processes occur in the American society we must attend to the distinctive context or backdrop within which, or against which, our educational systems operate.

The core of a society's culture is reflected in its dominant values, values generally shared by most members of the society or of its major subgroups. These values help to interpret, integrate, and channel the organized activities of a society, providing direction and guidance for its members. From this process follows the implied close relationship between preferred values and norms, or standards and expectations for behavior.

Specific values are also closely linked to broader ideologies, whose content consists of patterns of beliefs and concepts (both factual and normative) that explain complex social phenomena. Such interpretations or explanations of the world help simplify and direct the sociopolitical choices facing individuals and groups. It is always difficult to see our own ideologies clearly because we are so embedded in them and in the culture under which they are subsumed. But one good test is to examine what we take for granted, what looks or feels unassailable. That test often gives the signal when we are in touch with a core ideological principle.

In periods of rapid change and societal upheaval the common cultural or core values often are in disarray and are not tightly integrated. During such critical periods, there is an absence of normative cohesion in the society and its members appear to agree on less of the ideological core. Frequently, conflict in dominant values or ideologies arise as different reactions to the same situations increase substantially. Ralph Linton refers to newly emerging ideologies as alternative values, or those that are shared by certain individuals but are not common to all members of the society or even to all members of any one of the socially recognized categories.

Karl Mannheim presents somewhat the same point of view in another way. He contrasts the current ideology of a social system with its newly developing images of utopian organization. These interpretations of the relationship between current core values of a society and its utopian alternatives are often useful in the attempt to decipher conflicts between various social groups—blacks and whites, the young and the old, the rich and the poor, professional educators and lay community members, the privileged and the oppressed. Different groups in a society, occupying different positions and statuses, will have different values or different shades of preferences within core values. The social structure thus helps explain lines of conflict within a common cultural system.

The major ideological and structural attributes of the American society clearly will affect the character of the educational system. Thus it is worth our while to try to piece out, in brief, some aspects or highlights of our own system. One predominant attribute is an ideology of capitalism and the firm belief that all other economic systems are inferior. Our forms of economic organization thus stress private property holdings and try to take profitable advantage of various economies of scale. The resultant stress on maximal profit motivations has led to larger and larger organizational forms in all sectors of our economy. The commitment to capitalist economic organization also brings with it divisions among the populace, as some are private owners of our productive capacities and others are privately hired employees working within these systems.

The capitalist ideology also triggers a value system that has as a chief component the value of achievement. We confer on achievement the unusual distinction of being both a means to important ends and an end in itself. Thus it is through the medium of competitive achievement that meaning and purpose are derived for much of the population; and it is through competition for achievement that individuals attain a degree of material comfort and success. A focus on achievement inevitably engenders systems of inequality; in some cases it creates inequality and in other cases it occurs the other way around. *Charles H. Anderson's article, "Social Inequality," examines American inequality in detail, locating its roots in our economic organization.*

Successful competition requires a greater and greater concentration of resources, especially power, to take and hold an advantageous position with regard to peer organizations. In the American political economy the result is the establishment, over time, of great concentrations of economic resources in the hands of a relatively small number of people. And the corollary is the parallel concentration of political power. As more economic and political power accrues to an individual or organization, he, she or it is in a better position to compete successfully, and the cycle continues.

Still dominant as a value system, and exhibiting remarkable resiliency in the midst of rapid cultural change, is the Protestant ethic. *The article by Donald G. McKinley, "The Ethos of Industrial America," traces varied elements of American Protestantism and their implications for the historical development of our capitalist, achievement-oriented industrial system.* Usually cited as the central core of the value system responsible for America's industrialization, the Protestant ethic remains a salient value among high achievers in society and thus continues to figure prominently in educational and occupational success. Protestant individualism, stemming from the religion's emphasis upon each individual's personal belief and relationship with God, provides a secular support for individual rights and dignity. It is an important support for our political system of liberty and freedom. At the same time its rhetoric supports an image of independence and autonomy that flies in the face of the reality of social interdependence. The consequent stress on privatism and self-restraint clearly affects the kinds of interpersonal and organizational patterns in the society at large. Impersonal bureaucracies rather than intimate groupings serve this ideology, as does the corporate tendency toward bigness and scale.

Rationalism as an intellectual attribute and rationality as an economic attribute stress the role of technique and intellectual discipline as organizing principles for our economic system and for organizational functioning. Hard work is seen as its own reward in this system, originally as a form of glorification of God as well as the self, and those who escape hard work—whether because of their own indigence, lack of good health, or their choice of a life of the mind or soul—are deviants. Waste is worst, and the stress on efficiency has led to a reliance on advanced technology and highly structured forms of social organization. The role of the technical expert, the professional, thus becomes a most highly valued organizational role.

The American society also is characterized by institutional patterns and ideologies reflecting and justifying racial injustice and oppression of minorities. Blacks, Chicanos, native Americans, and other non-Anglo minority groups are systematically denied access to major social opportunities and rewards. Preceding and succeeding from this state of affairs is an elaborate self-justifying ideology of racism that explains why these patterns are all right. Whether couched in biogenetic determinism or sociocultural deficit, the white American culture has many explanations for why minorities are incapable or unworthy of full membership in the society. These ideologies also serve to justify the majority's efforts to maintain power and control over the minority—in economic, political, and cultural spheres. The existing political structures, the distribution of political power, and the laws governing the relationships of those with divergent racial and cultural backgrounds are major determinants of the kinds of racial and ethnic contacts and interpersonal relations that exist at any moment in history. And racism is a form of power that is used to maintain societal control in the hands of white elites.

Several key structural forms may be distinguished as means for establishing control over minority–majority relations, and they stem from differential cultural assumptions. In the early eighteenth century in America, white Anglo-Protestants established the dominant cultural pattern. Later, as immigration increased, Anglo-Americans became alarmed by the possibility that their manner of life would be disrupted by the impact of foreign culture groups. The Anglos resorted to devious measures in defense of the supremacy of their cherished position and used their own pattern of life as the American way: "It became popular for Anglos to believe that non-Anglos transplanted inferior modes of living, perpetuated lower-class folk-ways, and yielded easily to the corruptive influences of political machines." * This belief was later transplanted to the American Black population, which soon replaced non-Anglo Europeans as the prime target for acculturation practices.

One outcome of this conformity creating process was that nonconformers had little room for mobility, especially if they could not, or would not, pass as members of the majority. And the majority continued to reject and isolate the nonconforming minorities, a second form of racist organization. The majority had the power to segregate the minority, and as the minority lived within forced economic and geographic segregation, more and more limited contact between different groups ensued.

The term *melting pot* refers essentially to the process of social assimilation that goes beyond negotiated conformity. The history of intergroup rhetoric indicates that the melting pot, or the ideology of assimilation, has been potent throughout a large portion of American history. However, it is decisively less dominant in current social practices and policies. Other powerful forces have functioned simultaneously to reinforce group differences as well as to encourage social assimilation. Some ethnic groups have cherished their distinctiveness, whereas others have emphasized intercultural homogeneity. Over-all, dominant Anglo groups have managed to control the content of the melting pot, although Italian spaghetti, Polish sausages, and Chinese chow mein seem to have become well mixed in.

Genocide has taken many forms within the history of intercultural relations throughout the world and within our own society. Some forms of genocide are explicitly physical in nature and are aimed at the elimination of a race or culture through violent warfare or murder. This was the early American posture toward the native inhabitants of the new American territories. When direct warfare was seen as too brutal a form of genocidal treatment, our social policies reflected a more subtle program for gradual elimination via deprivation of food, shelter, and clothing, which encouraged "nature" to take its course. The incarceration of races or cultural groupings may represent another form of genocidal treatment, which we have used in our attempt to confine the Indians to reservations and in our World War II imprisonment of Japanese-Americans, American citizens of Japanese descent. Attempts to eradicate the cultures of certain groups can be seen in calculated white ignorance of minority cultures, in their exclusion from our compendiums of cultural heritages and works.

Advocates of pluralism believe that the era of the arbitrary domination of minorities has passed. In its place, they endorse a live-and-let-live policy—a policy that decrees that each ethnic and racial group should respect the other's rights and encourage the maximum freedom of all groups within the democratic value system. Payne portrayed the concept of cultural pluralism as follows:

* G. Steward and Mildred W. Cole, *Minorities and the American Promise* (New York: Harper & Row, Publishers, 1956), pp. 135–136.

No culture contains all favorable elements, but each group that makes up the total American population has unique values, and the nation will be richer and finer in its cultural makeup if it conserves the best that each group has brought. The theory assumes, furthermore, that the minority groups have been so thoroughly conditioned by their heritages that the historic past could not be sacrificed even if they chose to forget the past experiences. Their natures, characters, and personalities are built out of cultures different from our own, and the method of effective cultural transmission requires that the fundamentals of their heritages be preserved for generations.*

It would not be difficult to demonstrate the relatively low level of pluralism throughout American society. In practice, pluralism has often been a mask for subtle attempts at Anglo-conformity.

We have insisted that in order to fathom the American educational scene, one must be conversant with the historical background of American education and its cultural context. But knowledge of the historical and cultural backgrounds of American education is not enough; one must be aware of the forces that govern it and the mechanisms that control it.

The issue, then, is not whether America's schools have a "point of view" and aggressively pursue it, but why that point of view is clothed in a masquerade of neutral or nonpolitical curricula, activities, events, and special codes all designed to deny its existence. The subtleties involved in transmitting an ideology and orienting one to a social structure may be partially explained by the reluctance of those in control to admit that schools are not impartial, that they are not prone to examine all points of view, and that, in fact, they do indoctrinate their students in partisan ways. There do exist a central core of values and a set of norms taught by the schools through the socialization process. And there exist unequal patterns of success and opportunity for access to the social structure that are made available by the schools. We now turn to the particular shape of these patterns.

Educational Systems and Culture

As in all major social institutions, the character and structure of the educational institution reflect the culture itself. For example, problems of education are less complicated in small or homogeneous societies at the preindustrial stages of development. In these societies well-institutionalized processes of socialization occur in the family and in organized relations between the generations; both the necessary instruction in basic economic skills and induction into a relatively homogeneous social life are provided. But for us the problems and issues are different:

Thus, in primitive societies, the educational problem is that of individual

---

* E. George Payne, "Education and Cultural Pluralism," F. J. Brown and J. S. Roucek, eds., *One America* (New York: Prentice-Hall, Inc., 1951).

socialization in the interest of consensus and integration: and an anthropologist interested in education in these societies is concerned with relations between the generations wherever they occur, but especially within the family, and with substructures such as age-sets and religious fraternities carrying socialising functions. The focus of attention for the sociologist working in industrial and technological societies, however, must be on formal and specialised educational institutions. His concern is with the social forces which create and mould pedagogical aims and educational policies and the institutions in which they are embodied; and also with these institutions themselves, and with their functions as, in some measure, independent parts of a wider and changing social structure.*

Different formal institutions may emphasize varied and often opposing cultural values, but public schools presumably extract the core norms of the entire public society for transmission to the young. In practice, however, the values represented in the school reflect a rather narrow band of the cultural spectrum. For the most part, this is owing to the nature of external control over the school, which limits its ideological perspective to that which is acceptable to the more influential segments in society, a perspective that, in effect, supports the values of the dominant economic and political structures. In "Traditional Values and the Shaping of American Education," Merle L. Borrowman suggests ways in which these value systems are reflected in the curriculum.

We have already discussed the competitive norms and values of the American society developed from an ideology of capitalism and achievement-oriented protestantism. These values are reflected in our schools in a clear emphasis upon academic achievement and performance. Peer collaboration in academic tasks obviously is curtailed in favor of an atomistic and individualistic approach to knowledge, individualism in a mass form for purposes of efficiency and orderliness. Such operational guidelines thus shape the nature of the instructional process and justify concerns for better human relations. Good social relations are not seen as matters of personal enjoyment but as a criterion of good adjustment and an effective standard for future role success. Social relations may even be competively graded!

The ideology of efficient bureaucracy, already evident in the corporate economic form, is further standardized in the professional monopoly of knowledge and control in the school. Expertise is reflected in an ideology of professionalism, a commitment to the expert's hoarded supply of technical information. The school relies on the society's commitment to a priestly class of technocrats who advise and rule the young.

A multiplicity of school activities, academic and otherwise, are organized around traditional virtues. Testing programs, curricular distinctions, "tracking," award ceremonies and rituals, and organized athletics are among the more prominent elaborations on these values. So ingrained are they that

* Jean Floud and A. H. Halsey, "Education and Social Structure: Theories and Methods," in A Trend Report and Bibliography, Current Sociology, VII, No. 3 (1958), p. 171.

failure to achieve in any one or more of these school activities often consigns one to failure in the larger society. Clearly the emphasis on achievement and competition leads many who deviate from these values to be seen as casualties. The rejection of achievement goals, whether based on inability, psychic reaction, or cultural difference, has left as its residue a large number of marginal and alienated youth who have been denied an early and important badge of success in the system.

Psychic conflict among youth also arises from inconsistencies and disparities rooted in society that are reflected in the school in its everyday operations. For instance, our transmission system, like our culture, is fraught with disparities between stated ideals and actual behavior, between expressed and practiced values, between achievement and equality, and between individualism and conformity. If such inconsistencies were clearly identified as conflicts and potential choices they might be used fruitfully. But when their existence is denied, inconsistencies can only lead to serious value confusion for some; for others, to oppression of their own alternatives.

Friedenberg likens the school's performance in the value domain to that of promoting a Darwinian selection process. For instance, the school

> endorses and supports the values and patterns of behavior of certain segments of the population providing their members with the credentials and shibboleths needed for the next stages of their journey, while instilling in others a sense of inferiority and warning the rest of society against them as troublesome and untrustworthy.*

The dominance of certain cultural prescriptions is reflected in and strengthened by the development of educational systems whose geographic as well as cultural boundaries are politically determined and whose classroom patterns reflect the stratified character of society. The sustenance of these systems has depended on the priorities of those having economic and political power and the real or apparent threat these people posed to the school structure. This dependence is particularly true of schools whose geographical location reflects large demographic shifts and transitory populations. Here the lack of independent political leadership on the part of school authorities has helped increase the vulnerability of the school to external forces and controls.

Under such circumstances, the schools have become the mechanism by which the minds—fears, hopes, assumptions—of the society's oppressed are controlled. Predictably, schools have been rendered incapable of acting as agents of ideological change, at least of change in the direction resisted by prevailing elites.

Concurrent with this perspective has been an ideology of cultural relations that has further established the school as a major socializing force. For it has been the public school's lot to acculturate the immigrants and to "American-

---

* Edgar Z. Friedenberg, *Coming of Age in America* (New York: Random House, Inc., 1963), p. 49.

ize" their children and mold them into society's conception of the good citizen. *The article "The Education of Immigrants in the United States: Historical Background," by Richard G. Durnin, explicitly reviews these processes with regard to the acculturation of immigrant groups through the schools.* Persons who could not or would not adapt to these "goods" have been seen as unadjusted, provincial, or clannish. Some groups or religious sects have created their own schools, and others have sought to influence the cultural content of the school via social control over the curriculum and the social composition of the teaching staff. Ironically, significant demographic movements in the society at large have triggered a mass exodus of the more affluent to the suburbs and have served to strengthen the middle-class and "Waspish" culture of their schools. The exodus to the suburbs has not only reinforced the segregation patterns of society but has created a new system of publicly supported private schools—private in the sense of cultural homogeneity, exclusiveness, and inaccessibility to others.

The current reflection of cultural racism is clear in the content and organization of our schools. Our curriculum reflects a white view of American history and social studies, and the major symbols and school artifacts similarly dispute any pretense at pluralism. Educators participate in an embracing ideology that explains the school failures of Black, Chicano, and native American students in terms of their inadequacies—usually created elsewhere. The various forms of this ideology have been clearly visible in the plethora of ignominious attempts at local, state, and national levels to socialize America's minorities into the ways of a society whose values they may not share fully, the acceptance of which would seriously impair their cultural integrity. *James A. Goodman's selection, "Institutional Racism: The Crucible of Black Identity," details ways in which these practices affect the education of Blacks—a prototype analysis for other examples of cultural oppression as well.*

Whereas a political solution to racist ideology has been called for by the exigencies of the mid Twentieth century, we have witnessed instead an outpouring of technical programs largely hatched by the educational establishment and financed by the government. Many of the terms used to describe the programs and their clientele—for example, *culturally deprived* and *disadvantaged*—are merely new jargon to clothe the old racist ideology. We have been led to believe that: "The poor aren't motivated to learn; the blacks incapable of learning." "Slum families are disorganized, ridden by social pathology." "Inner-city neighborhoods reflect the worst in American urban life." It has been expected and justified, therefore, that amidst such depraved and deranged environmental conditions education could accomplish little except perhaps to socialize the few that are vulnerable or willing into middle-class values.

The ideology of racism has been combined with the value bases of individualism to form the idea that individuals, not cultural and social structures, are responsible for their own status. Thus these ideological frameworks, aided and abetted by the professional mythology of expertise and service, have been used to avoid blaming school failure on the schools. Rather, failure is a fault of the individuals or cultures being served. Ryan has referred to this intellectual legerdemain as a new liberal scientific ideology of "blaming the victim." *

Surprisingly, in the face of overt hostility toward and loss of confidence in the public school, America's poor and other minorities still cling to their faith in the institution of education as the avenue for equality and social justice—perhaps because they have no other recourse in a society that so highly values these technical credentials. Or is this faith perhaps attributable to the efficiency of the public school in transmitting the prevailing ideology and perpetuating the myth surrounding the value of education? Presumably, both of these interpretations carry strains of validity. But the ideology of schooling has not been bought completely, nor without continued cost. The cultural conflicts between rhetoric and reality, or ideology and practice, are reflected in the disorder and disruption occurring almost daily in America's schools and communities. For the young and the minorities the schools have become the institutional battlefield for waging a cultural "war" (for racial and economic justice) that the society refuses to acknowledge.

EDUCATIONAL SYSTEMS AND SOCIAL STRUCTURE

The cultural values of a society and the social structures of society are both forms of basic organization. It is a moot question as to which determines which, but it is clear that these grand systems interreact closely. In like fashion, the societal structure is reflected in the organization of the school. As we have discussed the close relationship between cultural values and ideologies and the nature of the school, so can we now review the relation between the social structure and the school.

Social structures are ways of operating, mechanisms for organizing production, consumption, and survival in ways consistent with, or generative of, prevailing ideologies. Structure is the composition, arrangement, and balance of components or units; social structure consists of the parts of social life and the manner in which they are arranged. Generally speaking, social structure includes three kinds of phenomena: (1) the statuses, roles, or positions that people occupy in social life; (2) groups, organizations, or clusters of persons in certain status positions that have definable similarities; and (3) institutions or large systems of interrelated groups and organizations that serve basic purposes in social life. The idea of structure is important for many of the same reasons that regularity in social life is important—people do not behave in accidental, random ways but in certain observable patterns and forms of relationships.

Industrialization and other forms of increased complexity and hetero-

* William Ryan, *Blaming the Victim* (New York: Pantheon Books, Inc., 1971), pp. 299.

geneity place new burdens on the socialization processes. One result is an attenuation of the relationships between the individual and the wider social structure. Thus the educational system, as a secondary structure, comes to occupy a strategic role as a central determinant of the individual's relation to other economic, political, and social institutions.

There seems to be little question that the nature of the educational system influences a person's role in the social structure. Moreover, it often does this in ways that belie its official rhetoric and lay naked the underlying ideologies we have already discussed. *"Counselor Bias and the Female Occupational Role," by John J. Pietrofesa and Nancy K. Schlossberg, illuminates a common example of just one way this is accomplished—and accomplished over generations of experience—to reinforce male chauvinism.*

An even broader example of the controlling effects of ideology and social structure is the very stress on schooling itself. It matters little now whether the schooling experience is intrinsically meaningful. We give it extrinsic meaning by relying on it and using it as a gateway to employment, college entrance, and other opportunity systems. It also matters greatly that we do not have to reckon with sizable numbers of youth roaming the street, competing for scarce jobs and other resources, and potentially becoming a nuisance. The school, in this instance, functions as an internal safety valve, imprisoning youth for extended periods of time and prolonging their entry into the external adult world.

Judging by the reported school dropout rates (one can not empirically arrive at the psychological dropout rate!), a substantial number of students find the experience intolerable. For the seekers of high-status occupations, their capitulation enables them to qualify for entry into college and professional schools. For those who cannot, for whatever reason, tolerate the system, ambitions are scaled down and expectations adjusted accordingly. In this context, Lasch makes the following observation:

> Those who had no aptitude for school, who could not afford it, or who merely hated it, tailored their expectations accordingly. In this way the school system came to serve the function . . . of limiting the number of aspirants to high-status jobs—jobs that are widely believed (not without reason, but with less reason than is commonly supposed) to depend on schooling. Educational credentials came to serve as "a legitimate device for rationing privilege" in a society "that wants people sorted and graded but does not know precisely what standards it wants to use." *

As Jencks points out, schools select, sort out, and distribute students into various roles and futures.† This process has the latent and unacknowledged function of meeting the economic and social needs of society without

---

* Christopher Lasch, "Inequality and Education," *The New York Review of Books,* Vol. XX, No. 8 (May 17, 1973), p. 22.
† Christopher Jencks and others, *Inequality: A Reassessment of the Effect of Family and Schooling in America* (New York: Basic Books, Inc., 1972), p. 399.

seriously altering the social structure. At the level of public rhetoric, this socioeconomic filtering realizes the democratic ideology; it provides opportunity for social and economic mobility by selecting and training the most able and industrious youth for higher-status positions. In practice, however, the system perpetuates an elitist ideology by maintaining existing class distinctions and ensuring that those who start life with advantages will advance further and achieve more than those who don't.

This outcome is made possible as well as legitimate via the ingenious labeling and tracking system of the schools. Essentially, this mechanism provides the means whereby the privileges accorded in society are replicated in the school. The school preserves the status quo by placing children of similar social status together in the same tracks, thus reinforcing existing social class differences in apparent "ability." To the extent that race and social class overlap, these operations also maintain the economic and political oppression of Blacks, Browns, Native Americans, and other third-world minorities. In fact, given the related character of ethnicity and class in American economic life, the school also helps keep the less affluent from advancing.

Given the assumption that opportunity for mobility is limited and that not everyone will "succeed" in life (in achievement terms, of course), the failure of some children in school seems inevitable, if not necessary. If, as Colin Greer suggests, the latent function of the public school system is to rechannel those whom the higher levels of the employment structure cannot absorb—whose class and ethnic origins consign them to a marginal economic position—then rigged failure in school relegates a portion of the population to failure in life.* The conditions of upward mobility are thus governed by the school, and blocked mobility patterns and declining aspiration levels in society are reinforced by the very institution originally purported to open them up. *In "Socioeconomic Position and Academic Underachievement," Richard A. Cloward clearly delineates this state of affairs and examines the relation between class background and life opportunities in school.*

Perhaps the other end of this mutual influence system is the dominance that powerful political and economic elements of the American social structure has exerted over the common school—both in the areas of social control and in the fostering of racism and class elitism. *The summary of the Coleman Report (U.S. Office of Education) presents a brief synopsis of the outlines of that process and of its outcome in terms of school performance.*

From the middle of the nineteenth century, when universal compulsory education won general acceptance, the American school system has served well the special interests of dominant economic and political groups. The interconnections of the public school with the business community are of long standing. The origins of efficiency, "business methods" of management

---

* Colin Greer, *The Great School Legend: A Revisionist Interpretation of American Public Education* (New York: Basic Books, Inc., Publishers), 1972, pp. 206.

and accounting, and skill training are all linked historically to common ideological principles of economic organization. The culture of capitalism, as well as its organizational form, clearly leads to certain kinds of preferred results in terms of public school graduates' values, information, skills and behavioral styles.

If Michael Katz's thesis is valid, "that by about 1880 American education had acquired its fundamental structural characteristics, and that they have not altered since," * then we should not be surprised at the failure of subsequent reform movements. With rare exceptions, attempts at school reform have been largely programmatic adaptations within an unaltered political and economic system. Little effort has been directed toward change that does not serve existing social structures. And in those cases in which serious attempts have been made, the efforts have generally faltered from lack of nourishment. Clearly, efforts to change schools significantly would require and lead to changes in the surrounding social structure. Without the agreement and the collaboration of the ruling elites in these systems, changes in schools simply have not come about.

SUMMARY

The task of any educational system is to transmit the values, knowledge, skills, and behavior required by the society for the individual to perform adult roles. There are, of course, wide cultural variations in educational systems—variations related to the degree of formality, the amount of education, the control of education, and the degree of unification with other segments of the society.

Generally, large-scale industrial societies tend to have educational systems characterized by formalization, specialization, and a delayed process of secondary socialization. These systems also tend to develop elaborate and complex ideologies and operating bureaucracies that permit them to perpetuate the myth that schools perform vital functions not capable of being performed by other institutions. What these functions are may never be clear, but the belief in the mind of the lay public that they exist and may be important further enhances the power and status of schools.

Traditionally, formal education has been the prerogative of the favored and has served to perpetuate the ideology of elite superiority. In democracies this process has been less visible and acceptable, but it is accomplished, nevertheless. It is accomplished through the acquisition of social and verbal skills that have functioned to distinguish the elite from other strata and by the selection and training of the elite for leadership roles in society. Thus schools have become the chief accessory to the maintenance of the unequal division of status, power, and other rewards.

* Michael B. Katz, *Class, Bureaucracy, and Schools* (New York: Praeger Publishers, Inc.), 1972, p. XIX.

This process seems to be circular. Maintenance of the status quo is an important and compelling focus of the educational system, because the society has established schools as its means for preserving its own cultural heritage, or what is selected as "the" cultural heritage of a pluralistic society. If we find this a distressing definition and description of the roles of educational systems, it is because we are committed to alternative ideologies and structures for the American society—we would like to see schools serve these alternative ends. As we both discuss these alternative images and further document our own and other writers' perspectives on the "failings" of traditional schooling, we hope that the reader will be better able to take his or her own stance on the proper roles, functions, directions, and practices of American schooling.

A. Socialization

Our Educational Emphases in Primitive Perspective

MARGARET MEAD

In its broadest sense, education is the cultural process, the way in which each newborn human infant, born with a potentiality for learning greater than that of any other mammal, is transformed into a full member of a specific human society, sharing with the other members a specific human culture. From this point of view we can place side by side the newborn child in a modern city and the savage infant born into some primitive South Sea tribe. Both have everything to learn. Both depend for that learning upon the help and example, the care and tutelage, of the elders of their societies. Neither child has any guaranty of growing up to be a full human being should some accident, such as theft by a wolf, interfere with its human education. Despite the tremendous difference in what the New York infant and the New Guinea infant will learn, there is a striking similarity in the whole complicated process by which the child takes on and into itself the culture of those around it. And much profit can be gained by concentrating on these similarities and by setting the procedure of the South Sea mother side by side with the procedure of the New York mother, attempting to understand the common elements in cultural transmission. In such comparisons we can identify the tremendous potentialities of human beings, who are able to learn not only

FROM *The American Journal of Sociology*, Vol. 48, No. 6 (May 1943), pp. 633–39. Reprinted by permission of The University of Chicago Press.

to speak any one of a thousand languages but to adjust to as many different rhythms of maturation, ways of learning, methods of organizing their emotions and of managing their relationships to other human beings.

In this paper, however, I propose to turn away from this order of comparison—which notes the differences between human cultures, primitive and civilized, only as means of exploring the processes which occur in both types of culture—and to stress instead the ways in which our present behavior, which we bracket under the abstraction "education," differs from the procedures characteristic of primitive homogeneous communities. I propose to ask, not what there is in common between American in 1941 and South Sea culture which displays in 1941 a Stone Age level of culture, but to ask instead: What are some of the conspicuous differences, and what light do these differences throw upon our understanding of our own conception of education? And, because this is too large and wide a subject, I want to limit myself still further and to ask a question which is appropriate to this symposium; What effects has the mingling of peoples—of different races, different religions, and different levels of cultural complexity—had upon our concept of education? When we place our present-day concept against a backdrop of primitive educational procedures and see it as influenced by intermingling of peoples, what do we find?

I once lectured to a group of women—all of them college graduates—alert enough to be taking a fairly advanced adult-education course on "Primitive Education" delivered from the first point of view. I described in detail the lagoon village of the Manus tribe, the ways in which the parents taught the children to master their environment, to swim, to climb, to handle fire, to paddle a canoe, to judge distances and calculate the strength of materials. I described the tiny canoes which were given to the three-year-olds, the miniature fish spears with which they learned to spear minnows, the way in which small boys learned to calk their canoes with gum, and how small girls learned to thread shell money into aprons. Interwoven with a discussion of the more fundamental issues, such as the relationship between children and parents and the relationships between young children and older children, I gave a fairly complete account of the type of adaptive craft behavior which was characteristic of the Manus and the way in which this was learned by each generation of children. At the end of the lecture one woman stood up and asked the first question: "Didn't they have any vocational training?" Many of the others laughed at the question, and I have often told it myself as a way of getting my audience into a mood which was less rigidly limited by our own phrasing of "education." But that woman's question, naive and crude as it was, epitomized a long series of changes which stand between our idea of education and the processes by which members of a homogeneous and relatively static primitive society transmit their standardized habit patterns to their children.

There are several striking differences between our concept of education today and that of any contemporary primitive society; [1] but perhaps the most important one is the shift from the need for an individual to learn something which everyone agrees he would wish to know, to the will of some individual to teach something which it is not agreed that anyone has any desire to know. Such a shift in emphasis could come only with the breakdown of self-contained and self-respecting cultural homogeneity. The Manus or the Arapeth or the Iatmul adults taught their children all that they knew themselves. Sometimes, it is true, there were rifts in the process. A man might die without having communicated some particular piece of ritual knowledge; a good hunter might find no suitable apprentice among his available near kin, so that his skill perished with him. A girl might be so clumsy and stupid that she never learned to weave a mosquito basket that was fit to sell. Miscarriages in the smooth working of the transmission of available skills and knowledge did occur, but they were not sufficient to focus the attention of the group upon the desirability of teaching as over against the desirability of learning. Even with considerable division of labor and with a custom by which young men learned a special skill not from a father or other specified relative but merely from a master of the art, the master did not go seeking pupils; the pupils and their parents went to seek the master and with proper gifts of fish or octopus or dogs' teeth persuaded him to teach the neophyte. And at this level of human culture even close contact with members of other cultures did not alter the emphasis. Women who spoke another language married into the tribe; it was, of course, very important that they should learn to speak the language of their husbands' people, and so they learned that language as best they could—or failed to learn it. People might compliment them on their facility or laugh at them for their lack of it, but the idea of assimilating them was absent.

Similarly, the spread of special cults or sects among South Sea people, the desire to join the sect rather than the need to make converts, was emphasized. New ceremonies did develop. It was necessary that those who had formerly been ignorant of them should learn new songs or new dance steps, but the onus was again upon the learner. The greater self-centeredness of primitive monogeneous groups (often so self-centered that they divided mankind into two groups—the human beings, i.e., themselves, and the nonhuman beings, other people) preserved them also from the emphasis upon the greater value of one truth over another which is the condition of proselytizing. "We (human beings) do it this way and they (other people) do it that way." A lack of a desire to teach them our ways guaranteed also that the we group had no fear of any proselytizing from the they groups. A custom might be imported, bought, obtained by killing the owner, or taken as part of a marriage payment. A custom might be exported for a price or a consideration. But the emphasis lay upon the desire of the importing group to obtain the new skill or song and upon the desire of the exporting group for profit in

[1] This discussion, unless otherwise indicated, is based upon South Sea people only.

material terms by the transaction. The idea of conversion, or purposely attempting to alter the ideas and attitudes of other persons, did not occur. One might try to persuade one's brother-in-law to abandon his own group and come and hunt permanently with the tribe into which his sister had married; physical proselytizing there was, just as there was actual import and export of items of culture. But, once the brother-in-law had been persuaded to join a different cultural group, it was his job to learn how to live there; and you might, if you were still afraid he would go back or if you wanted his cooperation in working a two-man fish net, take considerable pains to teach him this or that skill as a bribe. But to bribe another by teaching him one's own skill is a long way from any practice of conversion, although it may be made subsidiary to it.

We have no way of knowing how often in the course of human history the idea of Truth, as a revelation to or possession of some one group (which thereby gained the right to consider itself superior to all those who lacked this revelation), may have appeared. But certain it is that, wherever this notion of hierarchical arrangements of cultural views of experience appears, it has profound effects upon education; and it has enormously influenced our own attitudes toward education. As soon as there is any attitude that one set of cultural beliefs is definitely superior to another, the framework is present for active proselytizing, unless the idea of cultural superiority is joined with some idea of hereditary membership, as it is among the Hindus. (It would indeed be interesting to investigate whether any group which considered itself in possession of the most superior brand of religious or economic truth, and which did not regard its possession as limited by heredity, could preserve the belief in that superiority without proselytizing. It might be found that active proselytizing was the necessary condition for the preservation of the essential belief in one's own revelation.) Thus, with the appearance of religions which held this belief in their own infallible superiority, education becomes a concern of those who teach rather than of those who learn. Attention is directed toward finding neophytes rather than toward finding masters, and adults and children become bracketed together as recipients of conscious missionary effort. This bracketing-together is of great importance; it increases the self-consciousness of the whole educational procedure, and it is quite possible that the whole question of methods and techniques of education is brought most sharply to the fore when it is a completely socialized adult who must be influenced instead of a plastic and receptive child.

With social stratification the possibility of using education as a way of changing status is introduced, and another new component of the educational idea develops. Here the emphasis is still upon the need to learn—on the one hand, in order to alter status and, on the other, to prevent the loss of status by failure to learn. But wherever this possibility enters in there is also a possibility of a new concept of education developing from the relationship between fixed caste and class lines and education. In a static society members of different caste or class groups may have been teaching their children different standards of behavior for many generations without any essential difference between their attitudes toward education and those of less complex societies. To effect a change it is necessary to focus the attention of the members of the society upon the problem, as conditions of cultural contact do focus it. Thus, in present-day Bali, the high castes are sending their daughters to the Dutch schools to be trained as schoolteachers because it is pre-eminently important that learning should be kept in the hands of the high castes and profoundly inappropriate that low-caste teachers should teach high-caste children. They feel this strongly enough to overcome their prejudices against the extent to which such a course takes high-caste women out into the market place.

As soon as the possibility of shift of class position by virtue of a different educational experience becomes articulately recognized, so that individuals seek not only to better their children or to guard them against educational defect but also to see the extension of restriction of educational opportunity as relevant to the whole class structure, another element enters in—the relationship of education to social change. Education becomes a mechanism of change. Public attention, once focused upon this possibility, is easily turned to the converse position of emphasizing education as a means toward preserving the status quo. I argue here for no historical priority in the two positions. But I am inclined to believe that we do not have catechumens taught to say "to do my duty in that state of life into which it has pleased God to call me" until we have the beginning of movements of individuals away from their birth positions in society. In fact, the whole use of education to defend vested interests and intrenched privilege goes with the recognition that education can be a way of encroaching upon them. Just as the presence of proselytizing religions focuses attention upon means of spreading the truth, upon pedagogy, so the educational implications of social stratification focus attention upon the content of education and lay the groundwork for an articulate interest in the curriculum.

Movements of peoples, colonization, and trade also bring education into a different focus. In New Guinea it is not uncommon to "hear" (i.e., understand without speaking) several languages besides one's own, and many people not only "hear" but also speak neighboring languages. A head-hunting people like the Mundugumor, who had the custom of giving child hostages to temporary allies among neighboring people, articulately recognized that it was an advantage to have members of the group be well acquainted with the roads, the customs, and the language of their neighbors, who would assuredly at some time in any given generation be enemies and objects of attack. Those who took the hostages regarded this increased facility of the Mundugumor as a disadvantage which had to be put up with. But the emphasis remained with the desirability of learning. Today, with the growth of pidgin English as a lingua franca, bush natives and young boys are most anxious to learn pidgin. Their neighbors, with whom they could trade and communicate more readily if they knew pidgin, are not interested in teaching them. But the European colonist is interested. He sees his position as an expanding, initiating, changing one; he wants to trade with the natives, to recruit and indenture them to work on plantations. He needs to have them speak a language that he can understand. Accordingly, we have the shift from the native who needs to learn another language in order to understand, to the colonist who needs someone else to learn a language so that he, the colonist, may be understood. In the course of teaching natives to speak some lingua franca, to handle money, to work copra, etc., the whole focus is on teaching; not, however, on techniques of teaching, in the sense of pedagogy, but upon sanctions for making the native learn. Such usages develop rapidly into compulsory schooling in the language of the colonist or the conqueror, and they result in the school's being seen as an adjunct of the group in power rather than as a privilege for those who learn.

Just as conquest or colonization of already inhabited countries brings up the problems of assimilation, so also mass migrations may accentuate the same problem. This has been true particularly in the United States, where education has been enormously influenced by the articulate need to assimilate the masses of European immigrants, with the resulting phrasing of the public schools as a means for educating other peoples' children. The school ceased to be chiefly a device by which children were taught accumulated knowledge or skills and became a political device for arousing and maintaining national loyalty through inculcating a language and a system of ideas which the pupils did not share with their parents.

It is noteworthy that, in the whole series of educational emphases which I have discussed here as significant components of our present-day concept of "education," one common element which differentiates the ideas of conversion, assimilation, successful colonization, and the relationship between class-caste lines and education from the attitudes found in primitive homogeneous societies is the acceptance of discontinuity between parents and children. Primitive education was a process by which continuity was maintained between parents and children, even if the actual teacher was not a parent but a maternal uncle or a shaman. Modern education includes a heavy emphasis upon the function of education to create discontinuities—to turn the child of the peasant into a clerk, of the farmer into a lawyer, of the Italian immigrant into an American, of the illiterate into the literate. And parallel to this emphasis goes the attempt to use education as an extra, special prop for tottering continuities. Parents who are separated from their children by all the gaps in understanding which are a function of our rapidly changing world cling to the expedient of sending their children to the same schools and colleges they attended counting upon the heavy traditionalism of slow-moving institutions to stem the tide of change. (Thus, while the father builds himself a new house and the mother furnishes it with modern furniture, they both rejoice that back at school, through the happy accident that the school is not well enough endowed, son will sit at the same desk at which his father sat.) The same attitude is reflected by the stock figure of the member of a rural school board who says, "What was good enough for me in school is good enough for my children. The three R's, that's enough."

Another common factor in these modern trends of education is the increasing emphasis upon change rather than upon growth, upon what is done to people rather than upon what people do. This emphasis comes, I believe, from the inclusion of adults as objects of the educational effort—whether the effort comes from missionaries, colonizers, conquerors, Old Americans, or employers of labor. When a child is learning to talk, the miracle of learning is so pressing and conspicuous that the achievement of the teachers is put in the shade. But the displacement, in an adult's speech habits, of his native tongue by the phonetics of some language which he is being bullied or cajoled into learning is often more a matter of triumph for the teacher than of pride for the learner. Changing people's habits, people's ideas, people's language, people's beliefs, people's emotional allegiances, involves a sort of deliberate violence to other people's developed personalities—a violence not to be found in the whole teacher-child relationship, which finds its prototype in the cherishing parent helping the young child to learn those things which are essential to his humanity.

We have been shocked in recent years by the outspoken brutality of the totalitarian states, which set out to inculcate into children's minds a series of new ideas which it was considered politically useful for them to learn. Under the conflicting currents of modern ideologies the idea of indoctrination has developed as a way of characterizing the conscious educational aims of any group with whom the speaker is out of sympathy. Attempts to teach children any set of ideas in which one believes have become tainted with suspicion of power and self-interest, until almost all education can be branded and dismissed as one sort of indoctrination or another. The attempt to assimilate, convert, or keep in their places other human beings conceived of as inferior to those who are making the plans has been a boomerang which has distorted our whole educational philosophy; it has shifted the emphasis from one of growth and seeking for knowledge to one of dictation and forced acceptance of clichés and points of view. Thus we see that the presence of one element within our culture—a spurious sense of superiority of one group of human beings over another, which gave the group in power the impetus to force their language, their beliefs, and their culture down the throats of the group which was numerically, or economically, or geographically handicapped—has corrupted and distorted the emphasis of our free schools.

But there has been another emphasis developing side by side with those which I have been discussing, and that is a belief in the power of education to work miracles—a belief which springs from looking at the other side of the shield. As long as the transmission of culture is an orderly and continuous process, in a slowly changing society, the child speaks the language of his parents; and, although one may marvel that this small human being learns at all, one does not marvel that he learns French or English or Samoan, provided that this be the language of the parents. It took the discontinuity of educational systems, purposive shifts of language and beliefs between parents and children, to catch our imagination and to fashion the great American faith in education as creation rather than transmission, conversion, suppression, assimilation, or indoctrination. Perhaps one of the most basic human ways of saying "new" is "something that my parents have never experienced" or, when we speak of our children, "something I have never experienced." The drama of discontinuity which has been such a startling feature of modern life, and for which formal education has been regarded in great measure as responsible, suggested to men that perhaps education might be a device for creating a new kind of world by developing a new kind of human being.

Here it is necessary to distinguish sharply between the sort of idea which George Counts expressed in his speech, "Dare the Schools Build a New Social Order?" and the idea of education as creation of something new. Dr. Counts did not mean a new social order in the sense of an order that no man had dreamed of, so much as he meant a very concrete and definite type of society for which he and many others believed they had a blueprint. He was asking whether the teachers would use the schools to produce a different type of socioeconomic system. His question was still a power question and partook of all the power ideas which have developed in the long period during which men in power, men with dominating ideas, men with missions, have sought to put their ideas over upon the other men. His question would have been phrased more accurately as "Dare the schools build a different social order?" The schools of America have these hundred years been training children to give allegiance to a way of life that was new to them, not because they were children to whom all ways were new, not because the way of life was itself one that no man had yet dreamed of, but because they were the children of their parents. Whenever one group succeeds in getting power over the schools and teaches within those schools a doctrine foreign to many of those who enter those doors, they are building up, from the standpoint of those students, a different social order. From the standpoint of those in power, they are defending or extending the old; and, from the moment that the teachers had seriously started to put Dr. Counts's suggestion into practice, they would have been attempting by every method available to them to extend, in the minds of other people's children, their own picture, already an "old" idea, of the sort of world they wanted to live in.

It is not this sort of newness of which I speak. But from those who watched learning, those who humbly observed miracles instead of claiming them as the fruits of their strategy or of their superior teaching (propaganda) techniques, there grew up in America a touching belief that it was possible by education to build a new world—a world that no man had yet dreamed and that no man, bred as we had been bred, could dream. They argued that if we can bring up our children to be freer than we have been—freer from anxiety, freer from guilt and fear, freer from economic constraint and the dictates of expediency—to be equipped as we never were equipped, trained to think and enjoy thinking, trained to feel and enjoy feeling, then we shall produce a new kind of human being, one not known upon the earth before. Instead of the single visionary, the depth of whose vision has kept men's souls alive for centuries, we shall develop a whole people bred to the task of seeing with clear imaginative eyes into a future which is hidden from us behind the smoke screen of our defective and irremediable educational handicaps. This belief has often been branded as naive and simple-minded. The American faith in education, which Clark Wissler lists as one of the dominant American culture traits, has been held up to ridicule many times. In many of its forms it is not only unjustified optimism but arrant nonsense. When small children are sent out by overzealous schoolteachers to engage in active social reforms—believed necessary by their teachers—the whole point of view becomes not only ridiculous but dangerous to the children themselves.

Phrased, however, without any of our blueprints, with an insistence that it is the children themselves who will some day, when they are grown, make blueprints on the basis of their better upbringing, the idea is a bold and beautiful one, an essentially democratic and American idea. Instead of attempting to bind and limit the future and to compromise the inhabitants of the next century by a long process of indoctrination which will make them unable to follow any path but that which we have laid down, it suggests that we devise and practice a system of education which sets the future free. We must concentrate upon teaching our children to walk so steadily that we need not hew too straight and narrow paths for them but can trust them to make new paths through difficulties we never encountered to a future of which we have no inkling today.

When we look for the contributions which contacts of peoples, of peoples of different races and different religions, different levels of culture and different degrees of technological development, have made to education, we find two. On the one hand, the emphasis has shifted from learning to teaching, from the doing to the one who causes it to be done, from spontaneity to coercion, from freedom to power. With this shift has come the development of techniques of power, dry pedagogy, regimentation, indoctrination, manipulation, and propaganda. These are but sorry additions to man's armory, and they come from the insult to human life which is perpetuated whenever one human being is regarded as differentially less or more human than another. But, on the other hand, out of the discontinuities and rapid changes which have accompanied these minglings of people has come another invention, one which perhaps would not have been born in any other setting than this one—the belief in education as an instrument for the creation of new human values.

We stand today in a crowded place, where millions of men mill about seeking to go in different directions. It is most uncertain whether the educational invention made by those who emphasized teaching or the educational invention made by those who emphasized learning will survive.

But the more rapidly we can erase from our society those discrepancies in position and privilege which tend to perpetuate and strengthen the power and manipulative aspects of education, the more hope we may have that that other invention—the use of education for unknown ends which shall exalt man above his present stature—may survive.

The Development of the Self
in Social Interaction
GEORGE HERBERT MEAD

In our statement of the development of intelligence we have already suggested that the language process is essential for the development of the self. The self has a character which is different from that of the physiological organism proper. The self is something which has a development; it is not initially there, at birth, but arises in the process of social experience and activity, that is, develops in the given individual as a result of his relations to that process as a whole and to other individuals within that process.

It is the characteristic of the self as an object to itself that I want to bring out. This characteristic is represented in the word "self," which is a reflective, and indicates that which can be both subject and object. This type of object is essentially different from other objects, and in the past it has been distinguished as conscious, a term which indicates an experience with, an experience of, one's self. It was assumed that consciousness in some way carried this capacity of being an object to itself. In giving a behavioristic statement of consciousness we have to look for some sort of experience in which the physical organism can become an object to itself.[1]

When one is running to get away from someone who is chasing him, he is entirely occupied in this action, and his experience may be swallowed up in the objects about him, so that he has, at the time being, no consciousness of self at all. We must be, of course, very completely occupied to have that take place, but we can, I think, recognize that sort of a possible experience in which the self does not enter. We can, perhaps, get some light on that situation through those experiences in which in very intense action there appear in the experience of the individual, back of this intense action, memories and anticipations. Tolstoi as an officer in the war gives an account of having

REPRINTED from Mind, Self and Society by George Herbert Mead by permission of The University of Chicago Press. Copyright © 1934 by The University of Chicago Press.

[1] Man's behavior is such in his social group that he is able to become an object to himself, a fact which constitutes him a more advanced product of evolutionary development than are the lower animals. Fundamentally it is this social fact—and not his alleged possession of a soul or mind with which he, as an individual, has been mysteriously and supernaturally endowed, and with which the lower animals have not been endowed—that differentiates him from them.

pictures of his past experience in the midst of his most intense action. There are also pictures that flash into a person's mind when he is drowning. In such instances there is a contrast between an experience that is absolutely wound up in outside activity in which the self as an object does not enter, and an activity of memory and imagination in which the self is the principal object. The self is then entirely distinguishable from an organism that is surrounded by things and acts with reference to things, including parts of its own body. These latter may be objects like other objects, but they are just objects out there in the field, and they do not involve a self that is an object to the organism. This is, I think, frequently overlooked. It is that fact which makes our anthropomorphic reconstructions of animal life so fallacious. How can an individual get outside himself (experientially) in such a way as to become an object to himself? This is the essential psychological problem of selfhood or of self-consciousness; and its solution is to be found by referring to the process of social conduct or activity in which the given person or individual is implicated. The apparatus of reason would not be complete unless it swept itself into its own analysis of the field of experience; or unless the individual brought himself into the same experiential field as that of the other individual selves in relation to whom he acts in any given social situation. Reason cannot become impersonal unless it takes an objective, non-affective attitude toward itself; otherwise we have just consciousness, not *self*-consciousness. And it is necessary to rational conduct that the individual should thus take an objective, impersonal attitude toward himself, that he should become an object to himself. For the individual organism is obviously an essential and important fact or constituent element of the empirical situation in which it acts; and without taking objective account of itself as such, it cannot act intelligently, or rationally.

The individual experiences himself as such, not directly, but only indirectly, from the particular standpoints of other individual members of the same social group, or from the generalized standpoint of the social group as a whole to which he belongs. For he enters his own experience as a self or individual, not directly or immediately, not by becoming a subject to himself, but only in so far as he first becomes an object to himself just as other individuals are objects to him or in his experience; and he becomes an object to himself only by taking the attitudes of other individuals toward himself within a social environment or context of experience and behavior in which both he and they are involved.

The importance of what we term "communication" lies in the fact that it provides a form of behavior in which the organism or the individual may become an object to himself. It is that sort of communication which we have been discussing—not communication in the sense of the cluck of the hen to the chickens, or the bark of a wolf to the pack, or the lowing of a cow, but communication in the sense of significant symbols, communication which is directed not only to others but also to the individual himself. So far as that type of communication is a part of behavior it at least introduces a self. Of course, one may hear without listening; one may see things that he does not realize; do things that he is not really aware of. But it is where one does respond to that which he addresses to another and where that response of his own becomes a part of his conduct, where he not only hears himself but responds to himself, talks and replies to himself as truly as the other person replies to him, that we have behavior in which the individuals become objects to themselves.

The self, as that which can be an object to itself, is essentially a social struc-ture, and it arises in social experience. After a self has arisen, it in a certain sense provides for itself its social experiences, and so we can conceive of an absolutely solitary self. But it is impossible to conceive of a self arising outside of social experience. When it has arisen we can think of a person in solitary confinement for the rest of his life, but who still has himself as a companion, and is able to think and to converse with himself as he had communicated with others. That process to which I have just referred, of responding to one's self as another responds to it, taking part in one's own conversation with others, being aware of what one is saying and using that awareness of what one is saying to determine what one is going to say thereafter—that is a process with which we are all familiar. We are continually following up our own address to other persons by an understanding of what we are saying, and using that understanding in the direction of our continued speech. We are finding out what we are going to say, what we are going to do, by saying and doing, and in the process we are continually controlling the process itself. In the conversation of gestures what we say calls out a certain response in another and that in turn changes our own action, so that we shift from what we started to do because of the reply the other makes. The conversation of gestures is the beginning of communication. The individual comes to carry on a conversation of gestures with himself. He says something, and that calls out a certain reply in himself which makes him change what he was going to say. One starts to say something, we will presume an unpleasant something, but when he starts to say it he realizes it is cruel. The effect on himself of what he is saying checks him; there is here a conversation of gestures between the individual and himself. We mean by significant speech that the action is one that affects the individual himself, and that the effect upon the indi-vidual himself is part of the intelligent carrying-out of the conversation with others. Now we, so to speak, amputate that social phase and dispense with it for the time being, so that one is talking to one's self as one would talk to another person.

This process of abstraction cannot be carried on indefinitely. One in-evitably seeks an audience, has to pour himself out to somebody. In reflective intelligence one thinks to act, and to act solely so that this action remains a part of a social process. Thinking becomes preparatory to social action. The very process of thinking is, of course, simply an inner conversation that goes on, but it is a conversation of gestures which in its completion implies the expression of that which one thinks to an audience. One separates the significance of what he is saying to others from the actual speech and gets it ready before saying it. He thinks it out, and perhaps writes it in the form of a book; but it is still a part of social intercourse in which one is addressing other persons and at the same time addressing one's self, and in which one controls the address to other persons by the response made to one's own gesture. That the person should be responding to himself is necessary to the self, and it is this sort of social conduct which provides behavior within which that self appears. I know of no other form of behavior than the linguistic in which the individual is an object to himself, and, so far as I can see, the individual is not a self in the reflexive sense unless he is an object to himself. It is this fact that gives a critical importance to communication, since this is a type of behavior in which the individual does so respond to himself.

We realize in everyday conduct and experience that an individual does not mean a great deal of what he is doing and saying. We frequently say that such an individual is not himself. We come away from an interview with a realization that we have left out important things, that there are parts of the self that did not get into what was said. What determines the amount of the self that gets into communication is the social experience itself. Of course, a good deal of the self does not need to get expression. We carry on a whole series of different relationships to different people. We are one thing to one man and another thing to another. There are parts of the self which exist only for the self in relationship to itself. We divide ourselves up in all sorts of different selves with reference to our acquaintances. We discuss politics with one and religion with another. There are all sorts of different selves answering to all sorts of different social reactions. It is the social process itself that is responsible for the appearance of the self; it is not there as a self apart from this type of experience.

A multiple personality is in a certain sense normal, as I have just pointed out. There is usually an organization of the whole self with reference to the community to which we belong, and the situation in which we find ourselves. What the society is, whether we are living with people of the present, people of our own imaginations, people of the past, varies, of course, with different individuals. Normally, within the sort of community as a whole to which we belong, there is a unified self, but that may be broken up.

The unity and structure of the complete self reflects the unity and structure of the social process as a whole; and each of the elementary selves of which it is composed reflects the unity and structure of one of the various aspects of that process in which the individual is implicated. In other words, the various elementary selves which constitute, or are organized into, a complete self are the various aspects of the structure of that complete self answering to the various aspects of the structure of the social process as a whole; the structure of the complete self is thus a reflection of the complete social process. The organization and unification of a social group is identical with the organization and unification of any one of the selves arising within the social process in which that group is engaged, or which it is carrying on.

The phenomenon of dissociation of personality is caused by a breaking up of the complete, unitary self into the component selves of which it is composed, and which respectively correspond to different aspects of the social process in which the person is involved, and within which his complete or unitary self has arisen; these aspects being the different social groups to which he belongs within that process.

We find in children . . . imaginary companions which a good many children produce in their own experience. They organize in this way the responses which they call out in other persons and call out also in themselves. Of course, this playing with an imaginary companion is only a peculiarly interesting phase of ordinary play. Play in this sense, especially the stage which precedes the organized games, is a play at something. A child plays at being a mother, at being a teacher, at being a policeman; that is, it is taking different rôles, as we say. We have something that suggests this in what we call the play of animals: a cat will play with her kittens, and dogs play with each other. Two dogs playing with each other will attack and defend, in a process which if carried through would amount to an actual fight. There is a combination of responses which checks the depth of the bite. But we do not have in such a situation the dogs taking a definite rôle in the sense that a child deliberately takes the rôle of another. This tendency on the part of the children is what we are working with in the kindergarten where the rôles which the children assume are made the basis for training. When a child does assume a rôle he has in himself the stimuli which call out that particular response or group of responses. He may, of course, run away when he is chased, as the dog does, or he may turn around and strike back just as the dog does in his play. But that is not the same as playing at something. Children get together to "play Indian." This means that the child has a certain set of stimuli which call out in itself the responses that they would call out in others, and which answer to an Indian. In the play period the child utilizes his own responses to these stimuli which he makes use of in building a self. The response which he has a tendency to make to these stimuli organizes them. He plays that he is, for instance, offering himself something, and he buys it; he gives a letter to himself and takes it away; he addresses himself as a parent, as a teacher; he arrests himself as a policeman. He has a set of stimuli which call out in himself the sort of responses they call out in others. He takes this group of responses and organizes them into a certain whole. Such is the simplest form of being another to one's self. It involves a temporal situation. The child says something in one character and responds in another character, and then his responding in another character is a stimulus to himself in the first character, and so the conversation goes on. A certain organized structure arises in him and in his other which replies to it, and these carry on the conversation of gestures between themselves.

If we contrast play with the situation in an organized game, we note the essential difference that the child who plays in a game must be ready to take the attitude of everyone else involved in that game, and that these different rôles must have a definite relationship to each other. Taking a very simple game such as hide-and-seek, everyone with the exception of the one who is hiding is a person who is hunting. A child does not require more than the person who is hunted and the one who is hunting. If a child is playing in the first sense he just goes on playing, but there is no basic organization gained. In that early stage he passes from one rôle to another just as a whim takes him. But in a game where a number of individuals are involved, then the child taking one rôle must be ready to take the rôle of everyone else. If he gets in a baseball nine he must have the responses of each position involved in his own position. He must know what everyone else is going to do in order to carry out his own play. He has to take all of these rôles. They do not all have to be present in consciousness at the same time, but at some moments he has to have three or four individuals present in his own attitude, such as the one who is going to throw the ball, the one who is going to catch it, and so on. These responses must be, in some degree, present in his own make-up. In the game, then, there is a set of responses of such others so organized that the attitude of one calls out the appropriate attitudes of the other.

This organization is put in the form of the rules of the game. Children take a great interest in rules. They make rules on the spot in order to help themselves out of difficulties. Part of the enjoyment of the game is to get these rules. Now, the rules are the set of responses which a particular attitude calls out. You can demand a certain response in others if you take a certain attitude. These responses are all in yourself as well. There you get an organized set of such responses as that to which I have referred, which is something more elaborate than the rôles found in play. Here there is just a set of responses that follow on each other indefinitely. At such a stage we speak of a child as not yet having a fully developed self. The child responds in a fairly intelligent fashion to the immediate stimuli that come to him, but they are not organized. He does not organize his life as we would like to have him do, namely, as a whole. There is just a set of responses of the type of play. The child reacts to a certain stimulus, and the reaction is in himself that is called out in others, but he is not a whole self. In his game he has to have an organization of these rôles; otherwise he cannot play the game. The game represents the passage in the life of the child from taking the rôle of others in play to the organized part that is essential to self-consciousness in the full sense of the term.

We were speaking of the social conditions under which the self arises as an object. In addition to language we found two illustrations, one in play and the other in the game, and I wish to summarize and expand my account on these points. I have spoken of these from the point of view of children. We can, of course, refer also to the attitudes of more primitive people out of which our civilization has arisen. A striking illustration of play as distinct from the game is found in the myths and various of the plays which primitive people carry out, especially in religious pageants. The pure play attitude which we find in the case of little children may not be found here, since the participants are adults, and undoubtedly the relationship of these play processes to that which they interpret is more or less in the minds of even the most primitive people. In the process of interpretation of such rituals, there is an organization of play which perhaps might be compared to that which is taking place in the kindergarten in dealing with the plays of little children, where these are made into a set that will have a definite structure or relationship. At least something of the same sort is found in the play of primitive people. This type of activity belongs, of course, not to the everyday life of the people in their dealing with the objects about them—there we have a more or less definitely developed self-consciousness—but in their attitudes toward the forces about them, the nature upon which they depend; in their attitude toward this nature which is vague and uncertain, there we have a much more primitive response; and that response finds its expression in taking the rôle of the other, playing at the expression of their gods and their heroes, going through certain rites which are the representation of what these individuals are supposed to be doing. The process is one which develops, to be sure, into a more or less definite technique and is controlled; and yet we can say that it has arisen out of situations similar to those in which little children play at being a parent, at being a teacher—vague personalities that are about them and which affect them and on which they depend. These are personalities which they take, rôles they play, and in so far control the development of their own personality. This outcome is just what the kindergarten works toward. It takes the characters of these various vague beings and gets them into such an organized social relationship to each other that they build up the character of the little child.[2] The very introduction of organization from ouside supposes a lack of organization at this period in the child's experience. Over against such a situation of the little child and primitive people, we have the game as such.

The fundamental difference between the game and play is that in the latter the child must have the attitude of all the others involved in that game. The attitudes of the other players which the participant assumes organize into a sort of unit, and it is that organization which controls the response of the individual. The illustration used was of a person playing baseball. Each one of his own acts is determined by his assumption of the action of the others who are playing the game. What he does is controlled by his being everyone else on that team, at least in so far as those attitudes affect

---

2 ["The Relation of Play to Education," *University of Chicago Record*, I (1896–97), 140 ff.]

his own particular response. We get then an "other" which is an organization of the attitudes of those involved in the same process.

The organized community or social group which gives to the individual his unity of self may be called "the generalized other." The attitude of the generalized other is the attitude of the whole community.[3] Thus, for example, in the case of such a social group as a ball team, the team is the generalized other in so far as it enters—as an organized process or social activity—into the experience of any one of the individual members of it.

If the given human individual is to develop a self in the fullest sense, it is not sufficient for him merely to take the attitudes of other human individuals toward himself and toward one another within the human social process, and to bring that social process as a whole into his individual experience merely in these terms: he must also, in the same way that he takes the attitudes of other individuals toward himself and toward one another, take their attitudes toward the various phases or aspects of the common social activity or set of social undertakings in which, as members of an organized society or social group, they are all engaged; and he must then, by generalizing these individual attitudes of that organized society or social group itself, as a whole, act toward different social projects which at any given time it is carrying out, or toward the various larger phases of the general social process which constitutes its life and of which these projects are specific manifestations. This getting of the broad activities of any given social whole or organized society as such within the experiential field of any one of the individuals involved or included in that whole is, in other words, the essential basis and prerequisite of the fullest development of that individual's self: only in so far as he takes the attitudes of the organized social group to which he belongs toward the organized, co-operative social activity or set of such activities in which that group as such is engaged, does he develop a complete self or possess the sort of complete self he has developed. And on the other hand, the complex co-operative processes and activities and institutional functionings of organized human society are also possible only in so far as every individual involved in them or belonging to that society can take the general attitudes of all other such individuals with reference to these processes and

[3] It is possible for inanimate objects, no less than for other human organisms, to form parts of the generalized and organized—the completely socialized—other for any given human individual, in so far as he responds to such objects socially or in a social fashion (by means of the mechanism of thought, the internalized conversation of gestures). Any thing —any object or set of objects, whether animate or inanimate, human or animal, or merely physical—toward which he acts, or to which he responds, socially, is an element in what for him is the generalized other; by taking the attitudes of which toward himself he becomes conscious of himself as an object or individual, and thus develops a self or personality. Thus, for example, the cult, in its primitive form, is merely the social embodiment of the relation between the given social group or community and its physical environment—an organized social means, adopted by the individual members of that group or community, of entering into social relations with that environment, or (in a sense) of carrying on conversations with it; and in this way that environment becomes part of the total generalized other for each of the individual members of the given social group or community.

activities and institutional functionings, and to the organized social whole of experiential relations and interactions hereby constituted—and can direct his own behavior accordingly.

It is in the form of the generalized other that the social process influences the behavior of the individuals involved in it and carrying it on, i.e., that the community exercises control over the conduct of its individual members; for it is in this form that the social process or community enters as a determining factor into the individual's thinking. In abstract thought the individual takes the attitude of the generalized other [4] toward himself, without reference to its expression in any particular other individuals; and in concrete thought he takes that attitude in so far as it is expressed in the attitudes toward his behavior of those other individuals with whom he is involved in the given social situation or act. But only by taking the attitude of the generalized other toward himself, in one or another of these ways, can he think at all; for only thus can thinking—or the internalized conversation of gestures which constitutes thinking—occur. And only through the taking by individuals of the attitude or attitudes of the generalized other toward themselves is the existence of a universe of discourse, as that system of common or social meanings which thinking presupposes as its context, rendered possible.

What goes to make up the organized self is the organization of the attitudes which are common to the group. A person is a personality because he belongs to a community, because he takes over the institutions of that community into his own conduct. He takes its language as a medium by which he gets his personality, and then through a process of taking the different rôles that all the others furnish he comes to get the attitude of the members of the community. Such, in a certain sense, is the structure of a man's personality. There are certain common responses which each individual has toward certain common things, and in so far as those common responses are awakened in the individual when he is affecting other persons he arouses his own self. The structure, then, on which the self is built is this response which is common to all, for one has to be a member of a community to be a self. Such responses are abstract attitudes, but they constitute just what we term a man's character. They give him what we term his principles, the acknowledged attitudes of all members of the community toward what are the values of that community. He is putting himself in the place of the generalized other, which represents the organized responses of all the members of the group. It is that which guides conduct controlled by principles, and a person who has such an organized group of responses is a man whom we say has character, in the moral sense.

---

[4] We have said that the internal conversation of the individual with himself in terms of words or significant gestures . . . is carried on by the individual from the standpoint of the "generalized other." And the more abstract that conversation is, the more abstract thinking happens to be, the further removed is the generalized other from any connection with particular individuals. . . .

I have so far emphasized what I have called the structures upon which the self is constructed, the framework of the self, as it were. Of course we are not only what is common to all: each one of the selves is different from everyone else; but there has to be such a common structure as I have sketched in order that we may be members of a community at all. We cannot be ourselves unless we are also members in whom there is a community of attitudes which control the attitudes of all. We cannot have rights unless we have common attitudes. That which we have acquired as self-conscious persons makes us such members of society and gives us selves. Selves can only exist in definite relationships to other selves. No hard-and-fast line can be drawn between our own selves and the selves of others, since our own selves exist and enter as such into our experience only in so far as the selves of others exist and enter as such into our experience also. The individual possesses a self only in relation to the selves of the other members of his social group; and the structure of his self expresses or reflects the general behavior pattern cf this social group to which he belongs, just as does the structure of the self of every other individual belonging to this social group.

There is one other matter which I wish briefly to refer to now. The only way in which we can react against the disapproval of the entire community is by setting up a higher sort of community which in a certain sense outvotes the one we find. A person may reach a point of going against the whole world about him; he may stand out by himself over against it. But to do that he has to speak with the voice of reason to himself. He has to comprehend the voices of the past and of the future. That is the only way in which the self can get a voice which is more than the voice of the community. As a rule we assume that this general voice of the community is identical with the larger community of the past and the future; we assume that an organized custom represents what we call morality. The things one cannot do are those which everybody would condemn. If we take the attitude of the community over against our own responses, that is a true statement, but we must not forget this other capacity, that of replying to the community and insisting on the gesture of the community changing. We can reform the order of things; we can insist on making the community standards better standards. We are not simply bound by the community. We are engaged in a conversation in which what we say is listened to by the community and its response is one which is affected by what we have to say. This is especially true in critical situations. A man rises up and defends himself for what he does; he has his "day in court"; he can present his views. He can perhaps change the attitude of the community toward himself. The process of conversation is one in which the individual has not only the right but the duty of talking to the community of which he is a part, and bringing about those changes which take place through the interaction of individuals. That is the way, of course, in which society gets ahead, by just such interactions as those in which some person thinks a thing out. We are continually changing our social system in some respects, and we are able to do that intelligently because we can think. . . .

B.   Cultural and Social Structural Background

The Ethos of Industrial America

Donald G. McKinley

Christian wouldst thou in grace excel?
Wouldst thou enlarge thy store?
Use what thou hast with liberal zeal,
and God will give thee more.

Let not thy sacred talents lie
concealed beneath the ground.
But bless thy fellow Christian by
the Treasures thou hast found.

—Eliza Ellis, 1831
Framed sampler, Homestead Hotel, Evanston, Ill.

THE DOMINANT CULTURE AND ITS HISTORICAL ROOTS

Our position is that the ranking of people in society by a certain set of standards and the resulting differences in how they are rewarded both have a significant influence on how the individuals of the different classes act. What is the dominant cultural standard in America, an industrial society, by which individuals are judged and rewarded? In the present chapter we shall try to answer this and to discuss briefly some of its history. . . . It will give us added understanding concerning who is at the top and why—and why others are in the lower strata of society. It will also allow us to predict the particular pattern of responses characteristic of a class, given the cultural standards or ethos of the society.

The Basic Theme

Our view is that the basic theme of the American cultural system is control of the social and physical environment and the manifestation of this mastery in high productivity. This includes not simply maximization of production of material goods but of personal services, skills, and satisfactions. Traditions, specific moral norms, ascribed roles, and traditional allocations of rewards are all sacrificed in the interest of rational and efficient production in great quantity of a large number of resources. For American society the word "freedom" conveys this rational pursuit of a large number of relatively unspecified goals. According to this ethos, "freedom" also implies that there are few institutionalized restrictions on *who* may pursue these goals and on what *means* they may use to pursue them.

It might be protested that if individuals can pursue so many different values in so many different rational ways there is no general theme. It appears to this analyst, however, that the pluralism is itself a general principle. That is, the fact that there are relatively few limitations on who can pursue what and on the means of pursuit, except for the expectation that the pursuit be efficient and directed toward the goal of maximizing the amount of resources available to the society, is itself an ethos. Our morality "forces" us to be free.

This position should not be given an extreme interpretation. Thus, Durkheim's discussion (1933) of the ethical basis within which business contracts must be developed has significance here: it is recognized that there are very binding moral conditions within which this rational activity must be conducted. Relative to other societies, however, the conditions are fewer in number and less specifically outlined.

In achievement-oriented (that is, oriented toward bringing about increasingly efficient mastery over the physical and social environment) American society, this ethos seems to derive from Protestantism. This is Protestantism not as Americans now think of it but as it was proposed by early European spokesmen for that religious movement. Let us discuss its historical roots and its relationship to capitalism and the American cultural system in the twentieth century.

Pre-Reformation Elements

In our understanding of the central importance of Protestantism in Western industrial society, we are greatly indebted to Weber (1930). His analysis of the relationship between capitalism and Protestantism reveals that Protestantism was not simply a parochial religious protest but actually a culmination of several broad cultural trends or threads in Western thought.

There are important elements of Greek philosophy and values in Christianity in general, and these seem to have been emphasized in Protestantism. The emphasis in Greek thought on rationality in science and theology and the focus on rational mastery of oneself and the environment were brought over into Protestantism.

Such themes as the imperatives to go beyond passive obedience to God's will, to actively work to change this world, and to bring about the Kingdom of God on earth are Protestant manifestations of this approach to life (Bellah, 1959, and Weber, 1930).

Greek philosophical thought, especially Platonic philosophy, fostered a view which sharply separated the domains of the spirit and of the flesh. Not only was there this rather sharp dichotomy, but the view was that the latter as a realm of being and as a realm of human activity and interest was much more base. In Christianity and especially ascetic Protestantism this developed into a view that the pleasures of the flesh were evil and the instrument of the devil.[1] Pleasure was therefore to be replaced by work and the accomplishment of God's will. This suggests the concept of sublimation and Freud's forceful insight that civilized achievement is gained at the expense of "eros" or libidinal pleasure. Though Freud's insight probably has universal application, it is perhaps much truer in Western society and much less true in those societies where civilized activity consists of inherited traditions and a refinement of libidinal pleasure itself.

Judaism is also an inextricable part of Protestantism. The Judaic focus on one supreme God who is personally aware of one's deeds and misdeeds contributes to the modern emphases on devotion to higher callings and on responsible self-control in daily activities. Not merely aware, the Judaic God punishes and rewards, not according to chance or personal impulse, but according to one's actions and devotion to God's commands. God, much like the rational market system, is just.[2]

Though Protestantism was a rejection of many aspects of Catholicism, it was still basically Christian, and thus, it derived many of its principles from early Christianity. Perhaps most relevant for our interest here was the emphasis on the equality and fate of each individual soul. This posture both in early Christianity and in Greek thought probably paved the way for individualism in later developments of Western society. It is this individualistic interpretation of life and afterlife that makes it possible for the person "freely" to choose his own goals and his own means of achieving these goals.[3] This approach seems characteristic of American society, and is alien to an ascriptive, traditional, and unchanging approach to the choice of means

---

[1] It is interesting to see how such broad and abstract themes of life get translated into moral standards of parental action. Thus Miller and Swanson (1958), in a review of American child-rearing literature, found that fairly severe sanctions and restraints were recommended to parents to prevent genital fondling by their young children in the eighteenth and nineteenth centuries. By the middle of the twentieth century, however, some change had occurred, and mothers were advised to distract the child with a toy or some activity whenever such behavior was observed. Generally, this would be interpreted as more permissive (and more likely to lead to development of a healthier attitude toward body pleasure). This writer, however, wonders if such antiseptic parental behavior is really wise, since it may almost define out of psychic existence the realms of body pleasure and psychosexuality for the child. One wonders, then, if the same puritanical attitudes and themes are not still at work in modern disguise.

[2] This interpretation of God seems also to structure our psychiatrically influenced definition of the good parent. Even in such intimate spheres of life as parenthood, personal desire should be replaced by rationality and justice. Kohn (1959) finds that middle-class American parents do punish in a manner parallel to this conception of God. Working-class parents punish like gods dominated by personal impulse.

[3] It is this individualistic ethos in American society that has probably impeded the development of theories of social systems. In contrast, the psychology of the individual has considerable popular support, and even sociology tends to have an individualistic bent. It should be pointed out that Protestantism, especially in its early Calvinistic form, does not unqualifiedly accept the idea of freedom for the individual soul. Rather, the individual soul has a predestined and unchangeable fate.

and goals. It is an approach which allows the individual to act to an important degree in his own interest. But in so doing, ideally he brings about changes in society which maximize the resources made available to society.

The contribution of classical Rome to the development of rational society and Protestantism was its system of secular laws. It emphasized that the state was composed, to an important extent, of free and unincorporated individuals. As citizens they were equally subject to a universally applicable set of laws. This relatively greater standardization of expectations and sanctions, which Western society has inherited, makes possible the development of innovating and contractual agreements or exchanges between any two individuals or units in the social body. Ideally, no special rules impede maximum freedom in the development of rational agreements which will maximize production and mastery of the environment.

As an outgrowth of this view, and probably not only for humanitarian reasons but also in the interests of efficiency, American society, especially its more liberal elements, judges some types of discrimination in public and economic activities to be reprehensible. Racial discrimination does, after all, introduce "irrational" elements into what would otherwise be rational and efficient contractual arrangements between individuals of whatever color.

Thus the cultural heritage of European society provided values similar to American views, and it provided several crucial elements in the development of a near-Protestant ethic: the concept of a supreme God who was personally aware of one's devotion to His laws and who rewarded justly; an emphasis on rational thought as a tool in an active effort to understand and thus control oneself and the environment; an attitude of respect toward universal legal rules before which all were equally judged ("government by law"); and the interpretation that individuals' essential beings are equal in ways independent of their position in the corporate state.

Calvinist Elements

Given these conditions, what special position did Protestantism offer, and how does it relate in its secular form to modern American values? Weber (1930) and many sociological analysts of the values of modern industrial society view Calvin's statement of Protestantism as the most crucial one in the origin of capitalism and the development of a rationalistic approach to everyday activities. Much of the core of Calvinistic Protestantism was not truly new to Christian theology. Rather, it was the stress on certain views and the motivational implications of their unique combination by Calvinists that gave it force. These views are clearly stated in this quotation:

> The propositions are, schematically, as follows: (1) There is a single, absolutely transcendental God, creator and governor of the world, whose attributes and grounds of action are, apart from Revelation, completely beyond the reach of finite human understanding. (2) This God has predestined all human souls, for reasons totally beyond possible human comprehension, either to eternal salvation or to "eternal sin and death." This

decree stands from and for eternity and human will or faith can have no influence on it. (3) God for His own inscrutable reasons has created the world and placed man in it solely for the increase of His glory. (4) To this end He has decreed that man, regardless of whether predestined to salvation or damnation, shall labor to establish the Kingdom of God on Earth, and shall be subject to His revealed law in doing so. (5) The things of this world, human nature and the flesh, are, left to themselves, irreparably lost in "sin and death" from which there is no escape except by divine grace. (Parsons, 1949, p. 522.)

The orientation tends to project the personal isolation and responsibility characteristic of secular individualism onto the cosmic level. Just as one cannot really lose oneself in others, so also the individual exists on the fleshly and human level and cannot expect spiritual union with God. Passive meditation and obedience will not link him with the Holy Spirit. Instead, he must actively work to bring about the Kingdom of God on this earth. Two choices have then been made: (1) active mastery of the natural and social environment rather than passivity, and (2) a concern for this world and its everyday challenges rather than for the world of the spirit or the afterlife.

Since God cannot be "intuited" by spiritual union he can only be served as a willing and effective worker. Effective service requires a knowledge of God's works. This theological position leads to a secular emphasis on empirical "facts" and general laws of nature and human behavior rather than of intuited wisdom, on education rather than on meditation, and on various forms of science (Merton, 1949, pp. 329–346). A choice has been made in a third area of human concern.

In Calvin's view the individual's mortal fate was predetermined by God. One's soul was either of the elect or of the damned. The individual could not, either by good works or by sacred ritual, change his destiny; a kind of fatalism could have resulted had the moral posture allowed passivity and submission. The general interpretation is that predestination when combined with a demand for active mastery had certain results: great anxiety and strong motivations arose to understand one's fate.

The anxiety led to a modification of Calvinistic theology by Calvin's followers: an interpretation emerged which stated that though a person's fate was predetermined he could gain knowledge of this fate by looking for signs of his destiny. Success in secular activities, which would bring about God's Kingdom on Earth, was taken as divine evidence and reassurance of one's good standing among the elect. Thus one must constantly strive, through rational control of personal desires and knowledge of natural laws, toward this-worldly success.

These attitudes were combined with a kind of individualism which was in some degree peculiar to Protestantism but which also derived from early Christianity. This individualism emphasized a fear of others who might be of the damned or who might seduce one into sinful actions which would be evidence that the actor himself was damned. It also emphasized the moral imperative that the serious demands of God take precedence over personal motives of pleasure or pride, as well as over the traditionally meaningful loyalties to friends, family, and community. This produced an anxious inner loneliness which neither "many acquaintances but few friends" nor success seemed (nor presently seems) to still.

One must serve God rationally and in an informed manner, he must reject or place in a lower order of importance the demands of self and others. He must act consistently to bring about God's Kingdom on Earth and to re-affirm his elect position by success in individualistic enterprises. In Weber's interpretation success in the rationally organized and serious business of business seemed ideally suited to salve the anxious psychological conse-quences of Calvinism.

Success meant material affluence, but this was a wealth that could not be used for charity, for the fate of the poor was evidence of their own slothful-ness, their damned souls, and God's will.[4] Also, compassion for the poor was dangerously close to passion and other forms of impeding human emotional ties. Nor could this wealth be used for the dangerous pursuit of pleasure. Unlike Catholicism in its position of some tolerance and understanding toward the weaknesses and delights of the senses, Protestantism looked upon pleasure as in nearly constant conflict with God's work and will. Pleasure could not be allowed, for it might reveal that one's soul was damned. Economic resources could only be accumulated and reinvested. In this way, economic power was constantly available for further economic development (mastery and change of the natural environment and economic organization).

In summary, certain choices were made which led to anxiety about one's real worth, questioning of the value and/or morality and trustworthiness of intimate quasi-erotic loyalties and of compassion, deemphasis of most human institutions and the community in its various forms. There resulted a strong focus on the economic institution and an emphasis on the maximization of individual success and "productivity" in bringing about the good society (God's earthly Kingdom).

Secularization of Protestant Elements

Does this adequately characterize the cultural values of industrial Ameri-can society? Taken by itself and without qualifying explanations it may seem a rather extreme statement. The position taken here is that compared with the cultures of other societies (for instance, of traditional India or Spain), these choices in a secular form characterize the dominant ethos of our industrial society. An examination of some aspects of American society in its beginnings will help us understand how these choices have been modified in America.

---

[4] A later secular statement in the form of Social Darwinism held that the poor were poor as a consequence of the operation of natural laws (survival of the fittest); in this manner the neglect of the needy was rationalized.

The basic modification of the moral standard has been its secularization. Part of the secularization took place in Europe itself. The economic views and political philosophies to support these views developed by Adam Smith, John Locke, and the Utilitarians provided an explicitly theology-free statement of the moral importance of rationality, individualism, free enterprise, and hard work. John Locke, particularly, spelled out the moral and political consequences of rationality and individualism. These ideas became the progressive ideas of the time of the American Revolution (Northrup, 1947, esp. pp. 66–164). They gave justification for and structure to the new American society.

In Locke's view, society and the government were composed of innately independent individuals.

> . . . all men are naturally in . . . a state of perfect freedom to order their actions, and dispose of their possessions and persons as they think fit, within the bounds of the law of Nature, without asking leave or depending upon the will of any other man. (Locke, 1887, p. 192.)

But societies and governments do arise, for

> [Man is] willing to quit [the state of Nature] which, however free, is full of fears and continual dangers; and it is not without reason that he seeks out and is willing to join in society with others who are already united, or have a mind to unite for the mutual preservation of their lives, liberties, and estates, which I call by the general name—property. (p. 256.)

From this perspective a commonwealth is created for "the preservation of property" and to protect the individual from others. Thus, society, rather than being given and structured from the very beginning by man's *ascribed* biological nature and psychosocial dependency (the view of Aristotle and modern sociology), was *achieved* through the rational efforts of originally independent persons in order to protect their private interests.

Another perspective held by Locke led to an emphasis on and provided intellectual and moral justification for personal choices, tolerance of varying minority views, and a deemphasis of political organization in the new society. Because each individual was innately free and rational and reached his "truth" by way of direct communication between his inner mental being and God, all must recognize the views and needs of others.

This was certainly a philosophical position favorable to the needs of a society moving in the direction of high economic and cultural development and diversification. This general position also provided a favorable base for American political values, which maintain that "all men are born free and equal" and that the government originates in "the consent of the governed." The state's function is not to bring into fruition, through power and coordination, a people's noblest goals. Its primary purpose, rather, is to constrain and inhibit both private offenses and a high concentration of public power. Absolute power corrupts, and it must be divided to create various fairly autonomous sources of power (the Federal system) and the three branches of government.

Though these secular ideas developed in a bourgeois Protestant Europe, their acceptance and resulting influence were more marked in America. Having come alive at this intellectual and philosophical point in Western culture, America was at the same time saturated by this perspective and then somewhat isolated from later moderating and reacting ideas which developed in Europe after Locke and the Utilitarians. In America no powerful working tradition of society as an organic hierarchically structured system existed to dilute this cultural theme. Further, this individualistic emphasis on economic effort and rational mastery was particularly suited to an economically under-developed and potentially wealthy nation of successful individuals.

The rather specifically Protestant definition of the "will of God," "God's laws," and predestination required secularization because America's newly recruited citizens were not largely ascetic Protestants who would accept these parochial teachings. They were often the religiously alienated, members of persecuted religious sects and Jews, Roman Catholics, Eastern Ortho-dox, and various nonascetic Protestants. The Kingdom of God on Earth became "democracy" and the "American way of life." Responding to God's calling came to mean responding secularly to the morality of success.

The deemphasis of traditional norms, of the organic social body, of the compassionate and quasi-erotic primary group ties, of the mystery and beauty of the inner spirit; and the emphasis (to a greater extent than in industrial Europe) on impersonal mastery, rational economic endeavor, and success was and is probably a consequence of the migration of particular individuals to America. They were, after all, individuals who were largely willing to give up the highly developed and subtle values of Europe. They were also willing to give up the intimate ties to country, village, friends, and family in the pursuit of a "better way of life." It was a way of life which had few binding traditions, statuses, and goals compared with the European way of life, and it was the way of life of a society which deemphasized personal ties and emphasized social and geographical mobility ("Go West young man") in the interest of economic progress. The ethos was probably exaggerated by some of the immigrants themselves and in response to them. Thus, in their attempt to prove themselves acceptable Americans the immigrants developed values which were caricatures of American values of rationality and indi-vidualistic goals. Also, coming as they did from diverse cultures, it was perhaps necessary, if sharp cultural conflict was to be avoided, for even greater tolerance and freedom in the choice of means and ends in the pursuit of the good life to be introduced into the American ethos.

The general picture we are trying to draw seems to be one seen by early European travelers in America. De Tocqueville in 1840 wrote:

To evade the bondage of system and habit, of family maxims, class opinions, and, in some degree, of national prejudices; to accept tradition only as a means of information, and existing facts only as a lesson used in doing otherwise and doing better; to seek the reason of things for one's self, and in one's self alone; to tend to results without being bound to means, and to aim at the substance through the form—such are the principal characteristics of what I shall call the philosophical method of the Americans. . . .

The practice which obtains among the Americans of fixing the standard of judgment in themselves alone leads to other habits of mind. As they perceive that they succeed in resolving without assistance all the little difficulties which their practical life presents, they readily conclude that everything in the world may be explained, and that nothing in it transcends the limits of the understanding. Thus they fall to denying what they cannot comprehend; which leaves them but little faith for whatever is extraordinary, and an almost insurmountable distaste for whatever is supernatural. (de Tocqueville, 1947, pp. 251–252.)

It may seem to the reader that certain salient themes of American society have been ignored. Such motifs as violence, other orientedness as opposed to the inner loneliness we spoke of, and the pursuit of pleasure and sensuality come to mind. We shall try to relate them all to the dominant ethos we have outlined, for they undoubedly exist in American society. It is the view here, however, that they manifest themselves in particular ways which can be fit into the position that the dominant ethos is productive mastery of the environment.

The Dominant Culture in Contemporary America

It is the dominant theme that we are interested in, for its values take precedence over or bring into question other values held; and it is the basic theme which is used by people to evaluate and reward. It also holds a position of legitimacy: individuals in positions of control are committed to it, and others not committed to it must generally deal with it and adjust to it. Our definition does not require that all or even most people accept it as their personal standard. Nearly all must, however, recognize its normative power in the society.

As it impinges on the adult male in American society, the value system seems to be this: each person must prove himself basically worthy of approval by acting as an instrument of some higher goal through productive effort—especially in his occupation—which will indirectly bring about a somewhat undefined better society or life for all. (Even the "good" society is undefined because it itself should remain a flexible instrument for achieving the "good life.") In an almost Calvinistic sense this effort is required of all, for no one is good (not even the white Anglo-Saxon Protestant of an old elite family) until he proves himself *productive*. And to be productive means to create resources which will allow individuals or groups in this complex and differentiated society to choose, fairly autonomously, their own goals.[5]

Behavior As a Consequence of This Value Orientation

This value posture may result in an anxious postponement in choice of goals ("Americans don't know how to enjoy life") and an anxious preoccupation with activity and productiveness ("Americans don't know how to relax"). For individuals without the required position and the know-how of productiveness, it may lead to goallessness and normlessness (Merton, 1949, pp. 125–149)—a rather thorough and hostile alienation from society. This is perhaps most characteristic of the lower levels of the urban proletariat (Meier and Bell, 1959).

The dominant orientation results in individuals behaving in a number of ways considered by informal observers to be typically American (busy, restless, rootless, driven, "materialistic," or better, "productivistic"). Let us give some formal order to these observations:

1. A person must *achieve* by "effort," which means *postponing* certain *pleasures* of the senses.
2. The person as an instrument of some future goal may indulge himself, but primarily with the idea of increased ability to produce. Thus leisure may be pursued actively, but it becomes recreative rather than simple pleasure. After all, all work and no play would make Jack unproductive.

In this way leisure is consumed and pleasure sought in a conspicuous and rather anxious manner in industrial America. The new emphasis on consumption may also reflect the institutionalization of productive norms. People now "just naturally" work hard within a very efficient social organization. This produces the affluence we see, and also the problem of what to do with the affluence (Galbraith, 1958). With our deemphasis on the general human community it is difficult to invest it in public needs (parks, schools, and public rituals); with our skepticism of the moral worth of compassionate charity it cannot be used too copiously to rehabilitate those "lost souls" at the bottom of the social heap. Nor can it all be reinvested economically, for that would only increase the wealth and postpone a solution. We have had to make an uneasy peace in the last twenty or forty years with consumption and pleasure. It must be not only a "healthy" and rehabilitating pleasure but one which will consume the products of the market and sustain the productive processes and motivations. Perhaps such

---

[5] That certain studies such as North and Hatt's ("Jobs and Occupations: A Popular Evaluation," *Opinion News*, September 1, 1947, pp. 3–13) show certain occupations such as state governor or Supreme Court Justice ranking higher than more "productive" occupations such as factory owner may only reflect the American political philosophy. This philosophy holds that the government is to act primarily as a moral referee and control over the dominant activity—the production and organization of goods and services. Holding this position of control would be given higher status, but primarily by virtue of the services provided to the economic activities.

expensive and vigorous leisure as skiing is most typical of this new trend. We "work" at pleasure (the mock drama and seriousness of sailing or baseball). Those directly interpersonal pleasures which might occupy leisure —such as goalless loafing, visiting, social rituals, and extrafamilial eroticism —seem either to be decreasingly indulged in or to be engaged in covertly and with considerable concern. Such libidinal and social pleasures seem less normatively organized and more ego-alien in our culture than in, say, traditional Latin cultures.

3. As an instrument of this future and general goal, the individual need not always respond to the needs and feelings of his kind or particular friends. (William F. Whyte's "college boys" recognize this, and thus are distinguished from his "corner boys.") He is a private individual answering a higher duty or more general value system. This does not mean that he can be antisocial or even asocial, for a productive role requires smooth and pleasant interaction. This obligation is found in such concepts as "other-directed" and "the organization man." He must not, however, love too much or hate too much, for such emotions are demanding and are personal indulgences. They can be disruptive and can impede efficiency. He must be pleasant, *well adjusted*, and cooperative.

And still there continues the haunting concern about one's basic good-ness or social worth, a concern which is a secular parallel to anxiety about the fate of one's immortal soul. Striving to contribute to the society through success in achieved roles helps allay this concern.

4. Devoted effort is not enough, however. A person must be rational, skilled ("a person needs an education"), and neither foolish nor senti-mental. This would seem to mean that a person must act to maximize resources even at the expense of certain traditional sentiments and beliefs which are ends in themselves but restrain productivity.

We are not saying that these are the personal values of all or a majority of the American population. They merely form the major measuring rod for all. Neither do we mean that they are the only values, for numerous ascriptive qualities act as evaluative bases, and many individuals pursue goals of a variant nature with some social support and reward (F. Kluckhohn, 1950).

Evidence in Support of This Statement
What kinds of contemporary evidence can we offer to support such a broad outline? The writer would first appeal to the reader's sense of the reason-ableness of the outline; that is, it fits in with numerous experiences and with literature, fictional and nonfictional, including the analyses of Western and American society and culture made by such writers as de Tocqueville, Weber,

Mead, Kluckhohn and Kluckhohn (1947), Handlin, and Parsons and White (1961).

Let us, however, present a line of thinking and then some evidence which will lend some precise empirical support to our position. Whatever social class and status may be, they seem to be a ranking of people from the most highly esteemed and rewarded to the least esteemed and rewarded. If we can determine the basis of this ranking in American society perhaps we will have a clue to the dominant values, the ethos.

We have maintained that efficient and productive activity for the development of a good society is the dominant value in American society. This activity is carried out in American society largely in the occupational role. If our position is correct, then the occupation held should be the major basis of class placement, for it is an indicator of the contribution of the individual to society.[6]

A study by Hollingshead and Redlich provides some evidence. They and their workers judged social class position on the basis of a large number of details gained through observation and interviews. These rankings correlated 0.94 with a combined index of education, residence, and occupation (Hollingshead and Redlich, 1958, p. 394). These rankings when correlated with each of the variables of the combination produced the figures in Table 1. We see occupation to be the most important contributor to the combination and to be the variable most highly correlated with placement.

TABLE 1

Judged Class Correlation with Individual Variables

Judged class with residence	.69
Judged class with education	.78
Judged class with occupation	.88

SOURCE: A. Hollingshead and F. Redlich, *Social Class and Mental Illness* (New York: John Wiley and Sons, Inc., 1958), p. 394.

Even Warner, who suggests (Warner and Lunt, 1942) that the importance of occupation and economic position in the stratification system has been overstated, gives evidence for the importance of occupation. He finds that occupation correlated 0.91 with social class as determined by "evaluated

---

[6] A critic might take the position that the occupational role only provides the best predictor of power and the resulting ability to change power to esteem. This esteem is not necessarily forced or "bought" through one's position but rather eventually becomes legitimized by an educational effort to change the basis of esteem to match the basis of power. Thus the bourgeoisie of Western Europe developed a value-base which rivaled and eventually dominated the landed aristocracy's.

participation," which took into account prestige and patterns of social inter-action. Correlation with the Evaluated Participation Index was increased to only 0.97 when education, source of income, amount of income, dwelling area, and house type were combined into an index (Warner et al., 1949, pp. 167–168).

Similarly, Centers, whose interests are devoted to revealing other types of relationships, says: .

> By far the largest differences in adolescent attitudes with respect to labor and collectivism are found in relation to parental occupational strati-fication, and the lower the occupational level, the greater is the incidence of pro-labor and collectivist views. (Centers, 1953, p. 369.)

A thorough study by Kahl and Davis (1955), using the method of factor analysis, shows the central importance of occupation among nineteen different measures of socioeconomic status. The factor which accounted for most of the variability in an individual's status was highly associated with or defined by several measures of the individual's occupation. Association of variability in status with education was slightly lower, and with such things as the interviewers' ratings of subject, residence, place of residence, etc., it was considerably lower. This detailed study is perhaps the most crucial for our thesis that the occupational role is the prime determinant of social status and therefore the focal role in the culture's standard of evaluation.

A study by Bott (1954) also gives supporting evidence, although the study was made in Great Britain. The opinions of the general population should not be taken as final verification of sociological concepts, but here again there was very strong agreement among her subjects that occupation was the most important factor in placing a person in a social class.

We would not take the position unequivocally that these values, with their emphasis on occupation, are directly and solely derived from the Protestant ethic. This ethic could reasonably be considered a *post facto* theological and religious organization of ideas originating in secular social and cultural conditions. As a catalytic statement it gave, in turn, further impetus to the trends which originally gave it birth. It may be that such a set of values— the focus on individualism, on productive work, on means, and on relatively undefined future ends—results from exposure to fluid social situations, from exposure to varying sets of values, from the development of expanding con-trol over the physical environment through science and technology, and as a consequence of liberation from ascriptive ties. These are generally the conditions of urban secular societies.

If we take the ranking of occupations as evidence of a nation's values, and if nations with different religions agree on the ranking of occupations, we then have evidence that a nation's religion is not crucial in determining its secular values. In fact, we observe that the populations of predominantly Protestant nations (Germany, Great Britain, New Zealand, and the United States) are in close agreement with the populations of non-Protestant (the

Soviet Union) and non-Christian (Japan) nations on the prestige ranking of a number of occupations (Inkeles and Rossi, 1956). The prestige scores or ranks given to comparable occupations in Japan and in the various Protestant societies all correlated over 0.90. This may indicate the emergence of a basic agreement between diverse industrialized societies with various religious pasts on the relative worth of diverse occupations. It is true that minor variations in ratings were obtained which were attributed to special cultural allegiances.

In terms of empirical evidence, in terms of detailed and sophisticated analyses, and in terms of everyday observation in this society, it appears reasonable, however, to regard a rather secularized Protestant ethic as the dominant value orientation in American society.

Contemporary Change of the Dominant Theme

There is a great deal of discussion in the literature on whether or not basic American values have changed. That is, has there been a movement from the nineteenth-century focus on the serious instrumental problems in life to a greater focus on problems of aesthetic expression, styles of life, and skills in consumption? In the writer's opinion, American society still evaluates its members in terms of, and gives control to those segments of the population who are concerned with, the "serious business" of production and the preparation and control of impulse necessary for this serious business. There may, however, be a new revolution in the offing. Individuals and groups like Frank Sinatra, the Beats, Ava Gardner, Elvis Presley, and a host of television, movie, rock 'n roll, and café society celebrities provide the "proletariat" not only with heroes and heroines, but also with skills for a new and gratifying way of life. These celebrities also teach the masses new skills which enable the latter as entertainers themselves to provide others with gratification. Their talent allows them, in turn, to accumulate considerable money and influence. Here one thinks of the numerous teen-age stars of lower-status ethnic group origin who have learned a particular skill by listening to and watching mass media. In a sense they may be the twentieth-century American parallel of Marx's progressive proletariat. That is, they have gotten hold of new abilities in the area that will count in the future just as the rising bourgeoisie "discovered" new skills that were to count for the future in industrial Europe.

This embryonic revolution may be abortive, however, for several reasons. First, it may not be possible for a society as complex and rationally organized as our own to operate effectively with a focus on expressive gratification. The affluence that makes possible these mass-produced and mass-consumed forms of expressive gratification also requires rationality and technical competence. (Of course, Americans may decide they are disinterested in mass-produced pleasure.) Second, the challenge of rising countries (the Soviet Union, China, etc.) which seem to be breaking out of an older era where traditional styles of life and not instrumental achievement were the focus, may make a dominant focus on this relaxation impossible.[7]

One might hypothesize that there is a circulation of elites within a society and a circulation of elite and powerful countries in terms of this instrumental-expressive dichotomy. As the lower classes within a society begin to focus on instrumental skills and become more powerful within the society, the country becomes relatively more powerful internationally. Meanwhile, the proletariat in other countries, bored with the instrumental focus of their societies, grasp new progressive skills in the expressive sphere and climb to positions of control. The country relaxes its attention to the pressing problems in the external and instrumental sphere and becomes less powerful internationally. One thinks here of "bread and circus" demands in classical Rome or Galbraith's analysis of America as an affluent society and its power position vis-à-vis the Soviet Union. In both cases, the general population might be viewed as weary of the trials and serious responsibilities of power and mastery of the environment. In the one case, refusal to attend to these matters and the focus on personal interests may have led directly to a diminution of imperial power. It could have similar results in the other.

Are America's values changing? With so broad a problem, and with so few well-controlled data, no answer comes easily. The truth of various interpretations may be determined, in the pragmatic American manner, more by their usefulness in explaining these and other problems.

Coda

We have at some length discussed what is considered here the dominant standard of evaluation in American society. It is a standard which influences American family behavior directly in the sense that the child is socialized by norms of parent-child interaction developed out of a moral climate permeated by this standard. He is also socialized to accept and work toward the goals defined by this ethos. That is, our emphases on equality of the spouses and permissiveness in child rearing (let him develop his own ways of doing things in a nonpunitive atmosphere) draw on the themes of freedom and equality. The emphases on being active, getting educated, and "doing better than his folks did" focus on the themes of success and productive rational mastery of the environment. This is spelled out in interesting detail by Miller and Swanson (1958), but is not our central concern.

Our general interest is in explaining the influence of status (as it is determined by this ethos) on the individual's motivation and behavior, on the modes of family behavior, and on the emergence of subcultures.

[7] The theme of expressive relaxation and consumption is now present, but that it can become the legitimately dominant one is another question. As stated earlier, this writer believes it now functions as an additional mode of achievement and mastery, as recreative in the interest of further and more productive effort, and as a solution to the excessively efficient institutionalized productivity of the society.

REFERENCES

Bott, Elizabeth. "The Concept of Class As a Reference Group." *Human Relations* (August, 1954), 259–86.

Centers, Richard. "Children of the New Deal: Social Stratification and Adolescent Attitudes," in Reinhard Bendix and S. M. Lipset (eds.). *Class, Status, and Power.* New York: Free Press of Glencoe, Inc., 1953, 359–70.

de Tocqueville, Alexis. *Democracy in America* (Richard D. Heffner, ed.). New York: Oxford University Press., Inc., 1947.

Durkheim, Emile. *The Division of Labor in Society.* Translated by George Simpson. New York: Macmillan Publishing Co., Inc., 1933.

Galbraith, John Kenneth. *The Affluent Society.* Boston: Houghton Mifflin Company, 1958.

Hollingshead, A., and Redlich, F. *Social Class and Mental Illness.* New York: John Wiley & Sons, Inc., 1958.

Inkeles, Alex, and Rossi, Peter H. "National Comparisons of Occupational Prestige," *Amer. J. Soc.* (January, 1956), 329–39.

Kahl, Joseph A., and Davis, James A. "A Comparison of Indexes of Socio-Economic Status," *Amer. Sociol. Rev.* (June, 1955), 317–25.

Kluckhohn, Clyde, and Kluckhohn, Florence. "American Culture: Generalized Orientations and Class Patterns," *The Conference on Science, Philosophy, and Religion.* New York: Harper & Row, Publishers, 1947, 106–28.

Kluckhohn, Florence R. "Dominant and Substitute Profiles of Cultural Orientation: Their Significance for Social Stratification," *Social Forces* (May, 1950), 376–93.

Kohn, Melvin L. "Social Class and the Exercise of Parental Authority," *Amer. Sociol. Rev.* Vol. 24, No. 3 (1959), 352–66.

Locke, John. *Two Treatises on Civil Government.* London: George Routledge & Son, 1887.

Meier, Dorothy L., and Bell, Wendell. "Anomie and Differential Access to the Achievement of Life Goals," *Amer. Sociol. Rev.* (April, 1959), 189–202.

Merton, Robert K. "Puritanism, Pietism, and Science," in *Social Theory and Social Structure.* New York: Free Press of Glencoe, Inc., 1949, 329–46.

————. "Social Structure and Anomie," in *Social Theory and Social Structure.* New York: Free Press of Glencoe, Inc., 1949, 125–49.

Miller, Daniel R., and Swanson, Guy E. *The Changing American Parent.* New York: John Wiley & Sons, Inc., 1958.

North, Cecil C., and Hatt, Paul K. "Jobs and Occupations: A Popular Evaluation," *Opinion News* (September, 1947), 3–13.

Northrup, F. S. C. *The Meeting of East and West.* New York: Macmillan Publishing Co., Inc., 1947.

Parsons, Talcott. *The Structure of Social Action.* New York: Free Press of Glencoe, Inc., 1949.

Parsons, Talcott, and White, Winston. "The Link Between Character and

Society," in S. M. Lipset and Leo Lowenthal (eds.). *Culture and Social Character*. New York: Free Press of Glencoe, Inc., 1961.

Warner, W. Lloyd, and Lunt, Paul S. *The Status System of a Modern Community*. New Haven: Yale University Press, 1942.

Warner, W. Lloyd, Meeker, Marcia, and Eells, Kenneth. *Social Class in America*. Chicago: Science Research Associates, Inc., 1949.

Weber, Max. *The Protestant Ethic and the Spirit of Capitalism*. Translated by Talcott Parsons. London: George Allen and Unwin, 1930.

Social Inequality

CHARLES H. ANDERSON

DEFINING SOCIAL INEQUALITY

Critics of social inequality, Marx among them, rarely argue that every member of a society should be equal to every other one in an absolute sense. But before we say any more about inequality and equality, we must ask the logically prior question, equality with respect to what? Education? Intelligence? Appearance? Prestige or status? Responsibility? Leisure? Power? Wealth and possessions? Because people vary greatly in terms of their physical makeup and their own priorities of value, only a monolithic totalitarianism, with the aid of highly sophisticated science, could even dream of approximating or imposing a condition of absolute social equality. Obviously, important genetic differences would have to be standardized by totalitarian scientists, and minds would have to be subjected to systematic conditioning from birth, as noted previously, almost a scientific fantasy for the foreseeable future.

While recognizing the highly variable nature of human propensities and values in any given society, the hard fact of the matter is that within any given society there exists a more or less shared common core of values. And values dealing with matters of disposable wealth in all likelihood hold about the highest consensus of any value area. Americans differ considerably (though far from randomly) in the kind of work they would like to do, the kind of education they might aspire to, what they prefer to do with their leisure, to what types of people they accord prestige, and even how much power they would like to exercise over others. But we differ much less on questions concerning the value of income and wealth. For it is precisely with income and wealth that we are able to seek how much and what kind of education we each desire for ourselves and our children, and hence, what kind of work we and our children might enter. Income and wealth set limits

REPRINTED with permission from Anderson, *Toward a New Sociology: A Critical View* (Homewood, Ill.: The Dorsey Press, 1971 ©), pp. 83–102.

on how we are able to express our leisure interests and the style of life we are able to set for ourselves. And quite clearly, our economic powers largely define our ability to exercise power over others. Thus, as both Marx and Weber have argued in slightly different ways, a person's economic standing is the keystone of his life; it literally determines his *life chances*. I do not intend to minimize here the importance of power. Although people may vary greatly in terms of their desire to control the behavior of others (power), most all of us would like as much self-determination and influence on events that directly affect us as possible. But to date, the extent of a person's self-determination and influence over events that directly impinge upon him has been largely set by the undemocratic "ability to pay." So we are again forced to return to income and wealth as the pivotal issues in the study of social inequality.

We should understand, however, that even equalitarians such as Marx are usually not primarily concerned that everyone could or should have exactly equal amounts of income and wealth. Marx, for example, believed that each of us should produce according to our abilities and consume according to our needs. Marx is referring to a type of relative economic equality in which there are no marked differences of wealth, but at the same time there is some variation in what each person or family is able to responsibly produce and reasonably consume. In socialist society, Marx foresaw no need or place for personal hoarding or superfluous and demeaning consumption; self-realization is achieved not by gorging oneself with externally produced goods, but by experiencing one's own creative powers and those of the group itself. Significantly, absolute equality of incomes *does* seem to be the stated goal of Fidel Castro for Cuban society: ". . . to the extent that we produce certain essential products in practically unlimited quantities—as a result of the development of agriculture—our policies in the coming years will move steadily toward equalization of income." And, "When we succeed in equalizing incomes, and establish free distribution of essential articles, we will have reached communism." [1] Castro adds that money per se will exist until the technological revolution (forces of production) allows free distribution of nonessentials. Castro here follows a line of argument explored and espoused by socioeconomist Robert Theobald.[2]

In short, social inequality, insofar as it implies voluntary differences in such things as work, education, leisure, life styles, and a plethora of other human diversities, does not tend to be challenged under a democratic ideology. By contrast, social inequality arising from marked or involuntary differences in income and wealth that sets unjust limits to individual aspirations in work, education, leisure, and life styles is being increasingly challenged by equalitarians and democrats everywhere.

[1] Saul Landau, "Socialist Democracy in Cuba: An Interview with Fidel Castro," *Socialist Revolution*, I (March–April 1970), p. 139.

[2] Robert Theobald, *Free Men and Free Markets* (New York: Doubleday & Company, Inc., 1965).

WHY SOCIAL INEQUALITY?

Unless otherwise specified, inequality shall henceforth refer to economic inequality, and by implication, the whole range of life chances and social privileges that stem from economic inequality. The historian Gabriel Kolko has stated the realities of inequality in the United States very succinctly: "The essential, primary fact of the American social system is that it is a capitalist society based on a grossly inequitable distribution of wealth and income that has not been altered in any essential manner in this century." [3] The extent of inequality will be examined in a moment. But before we do that, the theoretical question concerning the *necessity* of inequality must first be considered.

A school of thought in sociology known as functionalism includes among its several tenets the view that inequality serves a useful and essential function (nonfunctionalists, of course, may also believe in the necessity of inequality). Although the functionalist argument is similar to the kind the average person might present in defense of social inequality, Davis and Moore have stated the argument in more sophisticated and precise form.[4] It runs something like this: Every society must distribute its members into the various jobs within the division of labor and induce them to perform their work competently. If all positions were equally important and required equal skill, it would then make little difference as to what individuals performed what jobs; but such is not the case. Thus, a society must offer rewards, as incentives to acquire the skill level needed to perform important jobs. The greater the skill requirements and importance of the job, the greater must be the rewards "built into" that position. In the words of Davis and Moore, "Social inequality is thus an unconsciously evolved device by which societies insure that the most important positions are conscientiously filled by the more qualified persons." [5]

As Melvin Tumin has pointed out, the functionalist argument for the necessity of social inequality runs into a number of theoretical and empirical difficulties. In taking a straight look at the real world, we immediately see that people are not sifted and sorted into appropriate positions of privilege and disprivilege by some unseen hand of society. As we learned in Chapter 1, society itself is an abstraction from the concrete interests and interactions of individuals. The outstanding fact of social inequality is that people are *born*

---

[3] Gabriel Kolko, *The Roots of American Foreign Policy* (Boston: Beacon Press, 1969), p. 9.
[4] See Kingsley Davis and Wilbert E. Moore, "Some Principles of Stratification," *American Sociological Review*, 10 (April 1945), pp. 242–49. See their own and their critic's papers, especially Melvin Tumin's, as collected in Reinhard Bendix and Seymour Martin Lipset, eds., *Class, Status, and Power* (New York: The Free Press, 1966); see also the discussion and criticism by Milton M. Gordon, *Social Class in American Sociology* (Durham, N.C.: Duke University Press, 1958).
[5] Davis and Moore, "Some Principles of Stratification."

into family positions of privilege and disprivilege.[6] Granted, it is possible to move upward and downward in terms of privilege, but the probabilities governing where we end up are largely set from birth in even the most "open" societies. Rather than some sort of meritocracy where every individual begins the race (almost literally a race) from the same line, the starting blocks are so widely staggered that the runners in the rear have only a remote chance of catching up with those ahead, while those starting ahead must virtually quit to even begin to lose ground. In British sociologist T. B. Bottomore's evaluation, "Indeed, it would be more accurate description of the social class system to say that it operates, largely through the inheritance of property, to *ensure* that each individual *maintains* a certain social position, determined by his birth and *irrespective of his particular abilities*." [7]

But why in the first place do some families stand above others in terms of material wealth and thus transmit privilege to their children? Haven't more wealthy families attained their higher position through greater inherent capacity of intelligence? Assuming for the moment that people with greater inherent capacity have achieved greater wealth, on what scientific or moral grounds is it possible to argue that persons with greater intelligence deserve greater wealth? And inherent capacity for what? On what scientific or moral grounds is it possible to argue that people with an inherent capacity for business should have greater wealth than people with an inherent capacity to write poems?

However, there is no reason to even assume in the first place that there is any relation between native abilities and material success, or in functionalist language, that "the most important positions are filled by the most qualified persons." Sociological critics of this view such as George Homans and Gerhard Lenski perceive other grounds of social inequality: the *power* of various individuals and groups to self-designate and command for themselves wealth and economic privilege (and, of course, transmit and inherit it).[8] In Homans's view, "society" doesn't reward people, but rather people and groups with scarce resources, increasingly artificially preserved and self-designed, garner what they can, owing precisely to the economic power derived from the scarcity. By restricting the supply of a service, a skill, or a good, even a society with the productive and individual capacity to provide unlimited abundance can persist in

[6] Correctly enough, the most persistent problem in Michael Young's social science fiction book *The Rise of Meritocracy* (Baltimore: Penguin Books, Inc., 1961) is how to prevent the rich from passing on privileges to average or dull children. In the meritocracy, dull people are happy doing simple, dull work and bright people are commensurately happy doing challenging things.

[7] T. B. Bottomore, *Classes in Modern Society* (New York: Vintage Books, 1968), p. 11. Italics are mine to emphasize the precisely opposite description of the dynamics of inequality from that offered by Davis and Moore.

[8] George Homans, *The Nature of Social Science* (New York: Harbinger Books, 1967), p. 67, and Gerhard Lenski, *Power and Privilege* (New York: McGraw-Hill Book Company, 1966).

sharp stratification and inequality. In the modern era, argues Theobald, "it is precisely those groups who are most successful in restricting supply which are entitled to the largest quantity of resources" and "those who are willing to and able to preserve scarcity who will increase their claims on available abundance." [9] Inequality once based on the power to take scarce resources is thus increasingly based on the power to *artificially preserve* scarcity in an era of high literacy and automated abundance. Finally, as Homans points out, it is the scarcity that makes a person or group important, not some natural hierarchy of social importance.

Taking just one, albeit important, example of artificially preserved scarcity in the area of services, and hence power to command high reward, Martin Gross observes that the $44,000 a year which the average physician in the United States earns ". . . is a by-product of the doctor shortage and his ability to command a seller's market among the ill. . . ." [10] The self-designed nature of the doctor shortage is fairly obvious. The medical profession is for all practical purposes a semiclosed occupation: only so few openings in so few medical schools for so few sons of the affluent. And who has the evidence to demonstrate that the doctor who writes a drug prescription is more important than the pharmacist who fills it, the truck driver who transports it, the worker who produced it (I am not referring to the board of directors or big stockholders in the highly profitable drug companies, since the same logic applies to them, only much more so), or the chemist who discovered it? Without any one of these persons, the sick person would not safely get his drug. And what popular beliefs might be with regard to occupational importance may have no bearing at all on actual economic remuneration. A British survey disclosed that blue-collar workers such as drivers and dock workers were considered more important to the nation than accountants and civil servants, but the latter are about twice as well off economically as the former.[11]

The Davis-Moore argument for the necessity of inequality has a number of other difficulties besides the facts that privilege is inherited or artifi-

[9] Theobald, *Free Men and Free Markets*, pp. 62–63.

[10] Martin Gross, *The Doctors* (New York: Dell Publishing Co., Inc., 1967), p. 25. This explanation strikes some people as being too crude. Perhaps Samuelson's account is more suitable: ". . . suppose that (1) as many babies were born each year with the capacity necessary for a surgeon as with the capacity necessary for a butcher, (2) we knew how to train surgeons in no time at all, and (3) a surgeon's activities and responsibilities were not regarded as less pleasant or more taxing than those of a butcher. Then do you really think that surgeons would continue to receive higher earnings than butchers?"— Paul A. Samuelson, *Economics* (New York: McGraw-Hill Book Company, 1970), p. 557. Yes, I think so, because these factors are largely irrelevant to the observed income differences and total wealth holdings of surgeons and butchers. There are plenty of babies born with the capacity to do surgical work; once initiated a training program can turn out finished products on an annual or semiannual basis; and it is highly doubtful that a butcher has greater work satisfaction than a surgeon. Again we encounter the surgeon's infinitely greater capacity to control supply of services, compared to the butcher's.

[11] Mark Abrams, "Some Measurements of Social Stratification in Britain," in J. A. Jackson, ed., *Social Stratification* (Cambridge: Cambridge University Press, 1968), p. 139.

cially created and importance is entirely relative. For example, the argument neglects the fact that people work for reasons besides the promise of money, or prestige based on money. Ask yourself, Why am I choosing or will I choose to pursue one kind of work rather than another? (There are probably millions of American youth who have nonmaterial aspirations for which there currently exists no outlet. If you really had a full range of work alternatives, your answer might be different from what it *must* be.) I have asked large introductory sections of sociology exactly the same question, and the predominant inducements lie in the area of *work satisfaction* rather than material reward or prestige. Even a sizable percentage of business and engineering majors place strong emphasis on work satisfaction. One of the upshots and terrible ironies of social inequality is that the kinds of work which offer the greatest intrinsic satisfaction *also* tend to offer higher material rewards than the psychologically unrewarding kinds of work. Is it conceivable that a society could have a shortage of, or less competent, presidents, senators, executives, managers, scientists, professors, entertainers, or physicians (assuming the government, with a few of the billions it douses on the military, would build medical schools and provide free medical education for all who desired it) if, say, a $15,000 annual ceiling were placed on *all* spendable earnings? [12]

But, you say, hasn't the executive, scientist, or doctor sacrificed greatly while studying through many years of higher education and professional school? Doesn't he deserve much higher rewards for his sacrifice? Again, would you rather study in a university for several years or drive a city bus? Whatever the job in question may be, attending college and professional schools is a *privilege*, not a sacrifice. Fidel Castro captured well what we are saying here when he said ". . . it would not be fair if the one that you sent (to study) to be an engineer earned three times more than the one who had to remain working with a tractor in the field." [13]

I have tried to demonstrate the sociological difficulties encountered in any functional necessity of stratification. We might also note that the argument is politically conservative, for it accepts the status quo with all its injustices and inequities as given. Thus, J. P. Nettl declares that "The fundamental nature of modern reality is less and less in dispute, and attempts or claims on the part of sociology to change it do not even arise." [14]

[12] Even the "laws" of bourgeois economics are confounded by the direct increase of income with work satisfaction. The hypothesis of "equalizing differences" asserts that "Jobs that involve dirt, nerve strain, tiresome responsibility, tedium, low social prestige, irregular employment, seasonal layoff, short working life, and much dull training all tend to be less attractive to people. To recruit workers for such occupations you must raise the pay. On the other hand, jobs that are especially pleasant or attractive find many applicants, and remuneration is bid down."—Samuelson, *Economics*, p. 555. Surely this is an extremely plausible hypothesis, but as most empirical cases of work testify, the fact does not follow.

[13] Landau, "Socialist Democracy in Cuba: An Interview with Fidel Castro."

[14] J. P. Nettl, "Are Intellectuals Obsolete?" *The Nation*, March 4, 1968, pp. 303–4.

Sociologists are changing, but as a profession we have some distance to travel before we outlive such things as functionalism's unequal society.

A final word might be said regarding Gerhard Lenski's theory of inequality.[15] Lenski contends that as a society's surplus increases so does inequality (Chart 8). Elites tend to accumulate the surplus wealth. However, Lenski argues that the direct relationship between surplus and inequality *reverses* itself in advanced industrial society as elites increasingly make concessions so as to avoid discontent in the rest of society. Lenski seems to have confused the overall rise in the standard of living in advanced industrial society with a reduction in inequality. As we shall see presently, there has been no trend in the United States, at least, toward greater equality of wealth. The millionaires just become multimillionaires,

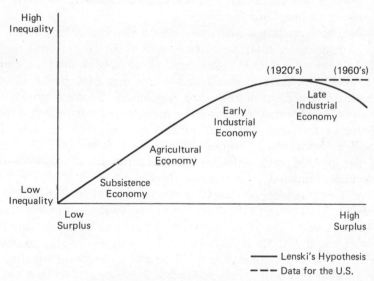

CHART 8.   Surplus and Inequality.

and the multimillionaires become centimillionaires and even billionaires, while millions of persons wallow in starchy poverty.

INEQUALITY IN THE UNITED STATES

Economic inequality among persons may be viewed from several perspectives. We shall examine four: total wealth, corporate wealth, income, and savings. Easily the most critical of these is corporate wealth; corporate wealth is not only the prime source of all large money incomes and great fortunes, but far more important, the source of the power to decide what the nation's resources will ultimately be spent for, or wasted upon. Let

15 Lenski, *Power and Privilege.*

us look first at the extent of inequality in the sphere of corporate wealth, then at wealth in general.

Wealth

Data dealing with the distribution of corporate wealth in the United States, though not in abundance and difficult to gather owing to the secrecy and subterfuge used in disguising possession of great wealth, reflects the careful study of both government and university economists.[16] The most striking fact about the distribution of corporate wealth is its almost unbelievable concentration in the hands of a miniscule percentage of the American people. The next most striking fact is that the extent of concentration has not changed much over the past decades. And a third salient point is that there has been marked continuity of corporate wealth among the same people or families.

The data on corporate wealth converge on the figures that about 1 percent of the American adult population owns about 80 percent of all publicly held corporate stock.[17] Since upward of $600 billion of corporate stock is held by or for individuals, this means that $480 billion is held by the wealthiest 1 percent of the adult population. Needless to say, within this group of people may be found the managers of our society. From the standpoint of spending units, 0.2 percent own over 65 percent of publicly held industrial stock, disproportionate by a factor of 325![18] And as Kolko has pointed out, estimates of concentration of stock ownership may be underestimated, as about one third of all stock is held in foundations and trusts, though ultimately controlled by top-bracket individuals.[19] In terms of absolute numbers, then, about two to three hundred thousand households possess most of the nation's vast corporate wealth. As of 1968, there were about 100,000 millionaires (153 centimillionaires) in America, or .049 percent of the population.[20] These and a couple of hundred thousand persons or so worth from one-third to a million dollars own the lion's share of corporate wealth. Significantly, about two thirds of the 200,000 top corporate wealth holders (1962) with a half million dollars worth of

[16] Research by Robert Lampman, Gabriel Kolko, the University of Michigan, and the government have been helpfully summarized and evaluated by Ferdinand Lundberg, *The Rich and the Super Rich* (New York: Bantam Books, Inc., 1969), Chapter 1. Lampman's research may be found in *The Share of Top Wealth-Holders in National Wealth* (Princeton, N.J.: Princeton University Press, 1962).

[17] Lampman, *The Share of Top Wealth-Holders in National Wealth*, p. 8. The careful investigations of C. Wright Mills revealed that 0.2 or 0.3 percent of the population hold the payoff shares of corporate wealth. *The Power Elite* (New York: Oxford University Press, 1956), p. 122.

[18] Data by Robert Heilbroner presented in G. William Domhoff, *Who Rules America?* (Englewood Cliffs, N.J.: Prentice-Hall, Inc., 1967), p. 45.

[19] Gabriel Kolko, *Wealth and Power in America* (New York: Frederick A. Praeger, Inc., 1962), p. 51.

[20] George Kirstein, *The Rich, Are They Different?* (Boston: Houghton Mifflin Company, 1968), p. 8.

stock counted *inherited* assets.[21] Millionaires are thus nearly all made from birth or from property. They do not earn their millions through salaried work.

With so much corporate wealth held by so few, we would obviously expect to find little such wealth in the rest of the population. Actually, 86 percent of all households (1960) owned no corporate wealth at all.[22] And of the remaining portion of the population who do hold corporate stock, all but 3 percent own less, most much less, than $10,000 worth.

Although corporate wealth underlies economic power and control in society at large, we should also consider total wealth, or that which includes nonindustrial wealth such as insurance policies, home and business ownership, bank deposits, and, especially, real estate. On the score of total wealth, 0.5 percent of the adult population accounts for at least one third of the nation's private-sector wealth, probably a larger proportion than the top one half of 1 percent owned in the 1920s.[23] Wealth is no more evenly distributed once you move beyond this circle, for the upper 11 percent of spending units account for 60 percent of the net worth of all private holdings. (We should keep in mind that about 20 percent of national wealth is government-owned.) Although Internal Revenue Service figures underestimate the concentration of wealth (an artifact of tax evasion by the rich), we gain a further idea of the extreme concentration of wealth from the fact that the 4,132 individuals reporting gross assets of $60,000 or more in 1962 had a net worth of $670 billion.[24]

As in the case of corporate wealth only, the extreme concentration of total wealth logically portends severe imbalances in the rest of society. The University of Michigan survey of 1963 disclosed that 11 percent of United States consumer units had a *deficit* net worth (assets less debt), 17 percent zero to $999 net worth, and another 17 percent $1,000 to $4,999 net worth.[25] Add another 15 percent with a net worth between $5,000 and $9,999, and we see that in 1963 an easy majority of the population held a net worth of less than $10,000. The largest percentage of the population (23 percent) fell in the $10,000 to $24,999 range. From there on up the percentages drop off sharply while wealth figures soar.

Returning to the top 1 percent of American adults and their one third of the nation's wealth, Lampman reports that in addition to the 80 percent of all corporate stock they own, this relatively small group counts among its total assets virtually all state and local government bonds (tax-exempt), almost 40 percent of federal bonds (what patriotism!), 36 percent of all mortgages and notes, and almost 30 percent of the nation's

21 Lundberg, *The Rich and the Super Rich*, 1968, p. 25.
22 *Ibid.*, p. 13.
23 *Ibid.*, p. 11.
24 U.S. Bureau of the Census, *Statistical Abstract of the United States: 1969* (Washington, D.C., 1969), p. 334.
25 Lundberg, *The Rich and the Super Rich*, p. 21.

cash.[26] In terms of net savings, the top income *tenth* has held around *three fourths* of the total since the 1920s, while the lowest tenth has been far in the hole.[27] Indeed, the entire bottom half of the income ladder has had *no* net savings or minus net savings. The second top-income tenth has held 20 percent of total savings, while the next two tenths have about held their own.

In summary, wealth, and particularly power-giving corporate wealth, is badly maldistributed in the United States, far exceeding what even the most devout sociological adherent to the theory of the necessity of inequality might think is necessary.

Income

The overwhelming majority of the population must rely on annual salaries, hourly wages, personal fees, or insurance-transfer payments for their incomes. As a rule, only salaries and fees will permit what Americans imagine as the Good Life complete, but they far, very far, from guarantee it. Usually, even the salaried middle-range businessman must rely heavily on company expense accounts and in-kind privileges to regularly enjoy the embellishments of the truly affluent life style. Ironically, but understandably, as one moves up into the higher salary brackets of $25 thousand, $50 thousand, $75 thousand, and beyond, the income in kind via expense accounts and company privileges increases commensurately. Expensive automobiles, small jet aircraft, posh restaurants, the "best" entertainment, topflight clubs, exclusive hunting and fishing resorts, and world travel are not obtainable (after family, clothing, and housing "essentials" are paid for) even on salaries that stagger the imagination of the camper-driving American. Such luxuries and privileges are "fringe" benefits which vastly augment actual income.

The best and only reliable way to make real big money is through large holdings of corporate stock, and especially through the purchase and sale of stock options, that is, the purchase of company stock at some fraction of market value and subsequent sale at inflated values. (Don't head for the nearest broker and ask him for a stock option; that's right, stock options are the prerogatives of corporate executives only. As some sage once said, "Those that have shall receive more"; perhaps even better, "Those that have shall *give* themselves more.") For example, U.S. Steel granted its executives stock options with a *face value* of $49 million in 1951, and in 1957 the stocks were worth $133 million.[28] This fantastic increase of wealth is appropriately called "capital *appreciation*" (not to be confused with dividends or interest, unlikely to make one wealthy unless he is already wealthy enough to own very large blocks of stock).

The median income in 1967 for white families was $8,274 and for non-

---

[26] *Ibid.*, p. 8.
[27] Kolko, *Wealth and Power in America*, p. 48.
[28] *Ibid.*, p. 42.

white families, $5,141 (Table 1). In that year, 11 percent of all white families and 27 percent of all nonwhite families had incomes under $3,000; conversely, 13 percent of white families and 5 percent of nonwhite (which includes Chinese and Japanese) reported incomes of over $15,000. Unrelated individuals, mostly senior citizens, exist at pathetically low standards. In terms of white-nonwhite income changes during the sixties, the rate of increase from 1960–65 was the same for both categories, while from 1965–68 the nonwhite rate of increase definitely exceeded that of whites.[29] (Low-income groups must realize larger annual percentage-point increases just to maintain the previous year's absolute dollar gap between themselves and the higher income groups. Identical rates of percentage increases between a low and high income group will usually mean an increase in the absolute dollar gap.) However, with unemployment rates now sharply rising among unskilled and nonwhite workers, the relative income growth rates are probably much less favorable for nonwhites than were those of 1965–68.

TABLE 1
Income Classes in the United States
(1967)

INCOME	PERCENT OF WHITE FAMILIES	PERCENT OF NONWHITE FAMILIES	PERCENT OF UNRELATED INDIVIDUALS
$15,000+	13%	5%	$\left.\begin{array}{c} \\ \\ \end{array}\right\}$ 5%
10,000–15,000	24	12	
7,000–10,000	25	17	8
5,000– 7,000	16	18	13
3,000– 5,000	12	22	17
Under $3,000	11	27	57
	100%	100%	100%
Median	$8,274	$5,141	$2,391

SOURCE: U.S. Bureau of the Census, *Statistical Abstract of the United States: 1969* (Washington, D.C., 1969), pp. 332–33.

Is personal income in the United States moving toward a more equitable or toward a less equitable distribution within the population? Government statistics suggest there have been no noteworthy changes in income distribution since 1944.[30] Since World War II, the highest fifth of family income units has received about 45 percent of the total personal money

[29] U.S. Bureau of the Census, *Statistical Abstract of the United States: 1969* (Washington, D.C., 1969), pp. xiii–xvii.
[30] See Herman P. Miller, *Rich Man, Poor Man* (New York: Signet Books, 1968), p. 52.

income (this is also the money-in-kind expense account category as well), the bottom fifth, only 5 percent. Table 2 provides the distribution of income by income tenths. The highest tenth receives almost three times its share, while the lowest tenth only one tenth of its share. In fact, we must move all the way up to around the 70th percentile before a family begins to receive an equitable share of the personal income pie. As we shall see in a moment, taxes have very slight redistributive effect.

TABLE 2

Income Inequality in the United States
(1967)

INCOME TENTHS (FAMILY UNITS)	SHARE OF TOTAL MONEY INCOME
Highest Tenth *	28%
9th	16
8th	13
7th	11
6th	9
5th	8
4th	6
3rd	5
2nd	3
Lowest Tenth	1

* Lowest income in this group is $15,400.

SOURCE: U.S. Bureau of the Census, *Statistical Abstract of the United States: 1969* (Washington, D.C., 1969), p. 321.

An undeniable fact concerning personal income in the United States is that there has been a marked increase of persons in the higher income brackets. The number of millionaires has grown by leaps and bounds over the past three decades, while the number of affluent Americans has risen sharply, even considering the bite of inflation on their paychecks. (Personal income has increased about 50 percent a decade, but inflation accounts for about 33 of these percentage points.) (Table 3.) However, it is extremely doubtful that the lower half of the population has experienced any real improvement in their standard of living since the mid-fifties. To be sure, for many people things may seem *relatively* worse, insofar as people they used to know have moved into higher income brackets and the whole income structure of the population has moved up. And currently, many people feel that they or the entire economic system may have reached an impasse. Certainly the majority are beginning to realize that a high standard of living cannot be purchased with personal income alone, as they witness the erosion of their cities and environment.

TABLE 3

Classes and Income Inequality
(share of total money income by income groups)

	1955	1967
$15,000	13%	30%
10,000–14,999	14	30
7,500– 9,999	15	17
6,000– 7,499	15	8
5,000– 6,000	13	5
4,000– 5,000	11	3
3,000– 4,000	9	3
2,000– 3,000	6	2
Under $2,000	4	2.5

SOURCE: U.S. Bureau of the Census, *Statistical Abstract of the United States: 1969* (Washington, D.C., 1969), p. 321.

The Effect of Taxes

"When all tax payments are taken into account, there is a real question as to whether taxes have a significant effect on the equalization of income." [31] So writes Herman P. Miller, government statistician-economist. Miller's Census Bureau figures disclose that the richest 5 percent of the population has its 20 percent share of personal income reduced by 2 percentage points by *federal* taxes, while the rest of the population moves only 1 percentage point in either direction. Conversely, the some 35 million persons living in families with incomes under $3,000 in the mid-sixties were being taxed a billion dollars a year. Federal tax legislation in 1970 has eased the burden of the low income groups but will accomplish little or nothing in the way of income redistribution.

Persons with incomes of *less* than $2,000 have been the *heaviest* taxed income group, paying 19 percent of their income to federal taxes and 25 percent to state and local, for a total of 44 percent of their income. [32] For income groups ranging from $2,000 to $15,000, the progressive federal tax takes 16 percent from the lower end and 19 percent from the upper end, while the regressive state and local taxes take 11 percent from the lower end and 9 percent from the upper end. Thus, the overall effective tax rate is around 27 percent for persons with incomes all the way from

[31] *Ibid.*, p. 53. Lipsey and Steiner, authors of a basic economics text, have an answer to Miller's question: "If the purpose of our tax structure has been to be neutral with respect to the over-all income distribution, it has been a success. If its purpose has been to be an instrument of general redistribution from rich to poor, it has not been a success." —Richard G. Lipsey and Peter O. Steiner, *Economics* (New York: Harper and Row, 1966), p. 508.

[32] Joseph Pechman, "The Rich, the Poor, and the Taxes They Pay," *The Public Interest*, 17 (Fall 1968), pp. 21–43.

$2,000 to $15,000. From persons with incomes over $15,000, the federal government takes 32 percent of income and state and local governments, 7 percent, for a total of 38 percent—less than persons with incomes under $2,000! The effective federal tax rates (excluding capital gains and dividends) for even the top 1 percent of tax units is only 26 percent.

What the figures suggest, then, is that millionaires tend to pay a percentage of their income taxes which is not much greater than that of an average white- or blue-collar wage worker. Indeed, millionaires pay much less in tax percentage than does the ordinary American, if we consider the chief sources of their wealth—capital gains. Law Professor W. David Slawson calculates that the wealthiest 1 percent of adults receive income of upward of $30 billion a year from capital appreciation (this does *not* include dividends), but this income produces only about $1 billion in tax —"a rate of only 3.3 percent despite the income's being received by persons most of whom are (or should be) in the 70 percent bracket." [33] Nor do inheritance taxes seem to be any more effective than income or capital gains taxes in achieving the goal of redistribution. The largest estates seldom pay more than 20 percent inheritance taxes, and frequently much less.[34] Thus, we have already noted the marked continuity of wealthy families in this century. How is it possible that, as President John F. Kennedy found, some $40 billion in taxes annually dodge the tax collector? The explanation lies in the fact that the rich simply deal themselves tax advantages and loopholes through a very compliant Congress. Of great significance is the fact that a very large group of congressmen are themselves millionaires eager to preserve their fortunes for themselves and their children.

Perhaps the most widely debated corporate tax privilege is that enjoyed by oil corporations, the depletion allowance (reduced from a long-standing 27.5 percent to 20 percent in 1970). Oil companies may pay little or no taxes at all as a result of the allowance. Among families, placing wealth in trust funds is another common tax avoidance procedure, also holding inheritance tax to a minimum. Although beneficiaries of trusts include widows and minor orphans, Lundberg notes that ". . . most of the beneficiaries are able-bodied adults, unwidowed, unorphaned and, as often as not, pleasantly idle." [35] The dividing of estates, gifts, family holding companies, and foundations all keep fortunes intact and minimize taxes. Among executives, deferred compensation plans, profit-sharing trusts, and stock options maximize income in the form of low-taxed capital gains or postpone disbursement until retirement. Whatever the tax dodges employed, they have been very effective in preventing any noteworthy redistribution of income. Tax burdens have fallen the heaviest on the shoulders of mod-

[33] W. David Slawson, "Moves to Patch the Loopholes," *The Nation*, June 16, 1969, p. 763. Unfortunately, the loopholes were not patched in 1970.

[34] Kolko, *Wealth and Power in America*, p. 32.

[35] Lundberg, *The Rich and the Super Rich*, p. 232.

erate to low income groups, and there is no reason to believe that there will be any changes in the near future. The property-owning class obviously intends to preserve its tax privileges and, hence, its wealth and income.

ECONOMIC CONDITIONS IN THE WORKING CLASS

We have already noted that half, perhaps a majority, of Americans are not now improving much upon their standard of living. Inflation, severe housing shortages, shoddy consumer goods, military waste, rising unemployment, excess population growth, and maldistribution and narrow uses of wealth and resources are all converging on the ordinary American. The frequently inept and narrow use of natural and human resources by the managers of American society have led Ferdinand Lundberg to write: "It would be difficult in the 1960's for a large majority of Americans to show fewer significant possessions if the country had long labored under a grasping dictatorship." [36]

The brunt of the economic pressures (the annual increases reported as the gross national product do not mean that the majority of the population is rising to ever greater economic heights) and social inefficiency has fallen upon the working class. By working class we mean people employed in blue-collar jobs, together with those in a fairly sizable sector of lower white-collar jobs, especially clerical and personal service workers. Indeed, the majority of persons in lower white-collar jobs themselves originated in blue-collar families. In the estimate of a sociologist Arthur Shostak, who has perhaps studied the working class more extensively than anyone else, "Blue-collar prosperity is precariously supported, maintained as it is largely by heavy installment debt and steadily declining purchasing power." Shostak continues, "Pathos and 'affluence' to the contrary blue-collarites today in America are *not* especially well off." [37] Since its peak in early 1966, the real-income purchasing power of the average American factory worker has been declining 1 percent a year.

There has been some debate as to whether the lower ranks of white-collar workers are as well off as the highest ranks of blue-collar workers, the craftsmen or skilled workers. Skilled workers definitely stand above semiskilled workers (operatives) in terms of income and job security. And skilled workers far outdistance unskilled and blue-collar service workers, who for some time have been losing ground to the rest of the working class.[38] Overall, the income of skilled workers has been slightly higher than that of lower white-collar workers. However, if only full-time, male lower white-collar workers are included in the comparison (skilled work-

[36] *Ibid.*, p. 1.
[37] Arthur Shostak, *Blue Collar Life* (New York: Random House, Inc., 1969), pp. 274–75.
[38] Miller, *Rich Man, Poor Man*, p. 63.

ers would not tend to compare themselves to white-collar females or part-time student workers), differences between the two occupational groups are insignificant.[39] If anything, the lower white-collar worker's income is slightly higher. Furthermore, persons in white-collar jobs usually desire and often think they have relatively good opportunities for both job and income promotions and many, in fact, are on the way up. By contrast, blue-collar workers usually hold slim hopes for promotion, banking mainly on occasional hourly wage increases to remain abreast of inflation. Full-time male white-collar fringe benefits and job security are often better than those of even the skilled wage worker, though not always.

Among the most hard-pressed, typically forgotten about members of the full-time, year-around male work force are the over 10 million white and black heads of households earning between $5,000 and $7,000 annually.[40] There are, of course, many full-time workers earning less than $5,000 to be added to this group. Nor is there any reason why we should stop at $7,000 for the hard-pressed category. How many luxuries are possible on even $10,000 in most large metropolitan centers?

The majority of the working class has moderate to serious economic problems. From 1960 to 1967, weekly after-tax take-home pay of an average factory worker with three dependents increased by 11 percent, but the cost of living for that size family rose by 24 percent.[41] In housing, health, diet, family necessities, and education, working-class people harbor considerable anxieties about the future and spend the large portion of their leisure moonlighting, bargain shopping, and doing home and auto repair. Minority-group workers are more precariously placed than whites. Labor unions have consistently called for national government action on matters of health, education, job and income security, and other worker benefits. Any gains in these areas would benefit the middle class and, of course, the very poor.

However, Shostak concludes his comprehensive review of working-class life by saying that the "American working class is one that fears to dare. . . ."[42] In the event of economic crises in the seventies, the working class—employed and unemployed, skilled and unskilled, white and colored—must learn to dare or be faced with the indignities of the existing welfare system. They and their white-collar allies might demand from America's unprecedented and unparalleled material base free education, from nursery to professional school; free health care, from dental fillings to death; recreational facilities and parks where they might take their children; low income

[39] See Richard F. Hamilton, "Income, Class, and Reference Groups," *American Sociological Review*, 29 (August 1964), pp. 576–79; and "The Marginal Middle Class," *American Sociological Review*, 31 (April 1966), pp. 192–99.

[40] See Dennis Duggan, "Still Forgotten: The Working Poor," *The Nation*, June 9, 1969, p. 726; and Al Bilik, "The Alienated Rank and File," *The Nation*, November 17, 1969, pp. 527–30.

[41] Shostak, *Blue Collar Life*, p. 29.

[42] *Ibid.*, p. 290.

housing in city, suburb, and town; the right to a respectable job; the right to a guaranteed income; and consumer price and quality protection against corporate profiteers. The working class and its allies might demand that idle and underutilized capital and human beings be put to work in the interest of all members of society, that their cities be made livable, that economic waste be eliminated, and that misused and maldistributed resources be put to constructive social purposes. Finally, and in conjunction with all of the above, workers of all stripes might demand something better from their income taxes than moon shots, faster jet fighters, bigger transport planes and bombers, missiles, antimissile missiles, and war. Why shouldn't an American worker (whose effective taxes are as high and country far wealthier) enjoy the economic security of a Scandinavian worker?

Inequality and Social Problems

So the United States has a rather marked degree of economic inequality. So what? Highly educated people have told the author that a more equitable distribution of income and wealth would solve only the poverty problem, implying that poverty sits in a corner unrelated to what might be considered other social problems and also that the poor require considerably more than a better share of the nation's wealth to set them straight. We shall deal with these questions at greater length in Chapter 7. Suffice it to point out here that the elimination of poverty and marked economic inequality would seem to deserve a higher rating than "only." With liberals viewing the problem so calmly it should not be surprising that the distribution of income has not changed during the past generation or two. While receiving a subsistence income when others are inheriting fortunes may seem like an "only" problem to the affluent, it ranks very high among the pressing problems of the white and black poor.

And is poverty and marked inequality of condition an isolated problem? I think not. The maldistribution of economic means (in a society that banks more heavily on personal than social spending) has tremendous relevance for educational inequality, the ghettoization of the city, discrepancies in health and diet, crime in the streets and against property, family dissolution and rising welfare costs, and a host of other things in the area of race relations and urban life. And at the top-heavy end of the distribution, economic inequality has steadily contributed to greater and greater concentration of social and political power. In combination, these discrepancies of wealth and power have threatened to destroy democratic sensibilities and have already impaired democratic functioning. Minimizing the importance of economic inequality strikes us as a diversion tactic of the well-to-do.

COMPARATIVE INEQUALITY

An argument might be made for the existence of greater income inequality in a traditional society in the *early* stages of industrialization than in a materially advanced industrial society. In a traditional society, leisure and consumption tended to hold greater value than extra work and capital accumulation, though long hours of work were usually required simply to live. A main key to industrialization is to accept capital accumulation as a prior value to leisure and consumption (see Chapter 14). Thus, industrializing societies might utilize cash rewards for individual willingness to exert greater productive effort sustained over long periods of time. The Chinese, for example, have made extensive use of material work incentives, especially piece rates, in both industry and agriculture.[43] If social esprit de corps is not a sufficient motivation, differential material incentives and progressive taxation are clearly preferable to exploitative or conscript labor as a means of capital accumulation. I am not implying that a sense of social duty or obligation cannot be a powerful incentive to personal sacrifice. Indeed, successful industrialization would seem quite impossible today without social esprit de corps. Where a sense of dedication to national goals is ubiquitous, differential material rewards lose their justification.

By saying differential material rewards may be of utility in an industrializing society we do not mean to imply that persons in different occupations must necessarily receive unequal incomes and privileges. As stressed before, occupations that customarily receive greater remuneration are those which are easiest to fill on the bases of work satisfaction, prestige, and desirability. Where a sense of dedication to national developmental goals is not ubiquitous and there remain sectors of society holding traditional economic values, differential material rewards may prove expeditious *within* industrial occupational categories. Any marked differences *between* types of industrial work would contribute nothing to industrialization, but rather would stem from the same type of preemption of privilege by elites that has been characteristic of Western capitalism. In some instances, as when traditional prestige is found in law and the arts when agricultural and industrial skills are in short supply, income differences between such occupations may be required. But the supply of labor into such areas may be partially controlled through admissions and funds in higher education.

In advanced industrial societies with a large material base, the chief problem is not capital accumulation (capital accumulation is a problem only if it continues to be the prime goal of the society) but rather how to achieve greater equality and cultural viability.

Some Operating Differences

How great is inequality in the United States as compared to other nations in the world? Comparisons of material reward on a cross-cultural basis are virtually impossible. In a country where child care, education, medicine, and dental care are free, an income of probably only half the size would be re-

[43] William T. Liu, *Chinese Society Under Communism* (New York: John Wiley & Sons, Inc., 1967), p. 295.

quired as in one where the individual must pay as he goes. Would a Swedish steel worker with an income of $5,000 trade life chances with an American steel worker earning $10,000? Probably only if the Swede were certain a personal injury, a layoff, unemployment, serious family illness, and a number of other life contingencies would not sink him into permanent poverty. The Swedish worker would also require that he could take his family into any city park or neighborhood day or night, he could get to work rapidly and cheaply on mass transit, and his children could attend college free. Finally, the Swede might also hedge over the fact that his American employer would probably be a millionaire receiving an annual salary 10 times larger than his own and a retirement stipend 25 times as great.

In the Soviet Union, income inequality was marked in the 1930s but, owing both to rising educational levels and central planning, has decreased greatly since that time. In the thirties, a Soviet factory director had an income of as much as 25 times more than an unskilled laborer,[44] while today the differential is more in the vicinity of 7 times greater.[45] Soviet differentials between the upper white-collar and blue-collar levels have been reduced continually since the thirties. Today an engineer receives about 50 percent more income than a factory worker, but not necessarily more than a skilled mechanic or miner.[46] Indeed, a Soviet skilled wage worker with a wife working as a saleswoman and a son in a factory earns as much as an engineer married to a doctor and with a son in a university.[47] A skilled blue-collar worker may earn twice as much as a doctor, the latter being in the same income bracket with teachers, legal officials, salesmen, and bureaucrats.[48] The unskilled worker, by contrast, earns but half as much as these white-collar workers.

In Communist China, a factory director typically earns about twice that of a skilled worker. In both China and the Soviet Union, professors and scientists earn more than managers of large factories, the discrepancy being a striking 300 percent (3 to 1) in China and about 33 percent in the Soviet Union.[49]

In the Third World, income differences between government bureaucrats and laborers are more marked than, say, in the Soviet Union or the United States. In areas where the civil service is the main channel of mobility, such as in West Africa, a young university graduate entering government service can expect to earn 10 times more than an urban laborer.[50] In areas such as

---

[44] Pierre Sorlin, The Soviet People and Their Society (New York: Frederick Praeger, Inc., 1968), p. 171.

[45] Murray Yanowitch, "The Soviet Income Revolution," in Celia S. Heller, ed., Structured Social Inequality (New York: Macmillan Publishing Co., Inc., 1969), p. 151.

[46] Ibid., p. 147.

[47] Sorlin, The Soviet People and Their Society, p. 233.

[48] Ibid., p. 233.

[49] C. H. G. Oldham, "Science and Education in China," in Ruth Adams, ed., Contemporary China (New York: Random House, Inc., 1966), pp. 292–93; and Yanowitch, "The Soviet Income Revolution," p. 151.

[50] P. C. Lloyd, Africa in Social Change (Baltimore: Penguin Books, Inc., 1967), p. 150.

Latin America, where aristocracies have accumulated vast landed wealth and a few foreigners and royalists have a grip on industry and commerce, inequality is usually even more extreme. The most notorious case was in Peru, where 30 families controlled 80 percent of the nation's wealth. In Brazil, 63 percent of the wealth is held by 17 percent of the population; in Venezuela, 50 percent by 12 percent; and in Colombia, 41 percent by only 5 percent.[51] Although a comparison between Latin America and United States populations on standard of living is scarcely possible, it is startling to discover that wealth is much more highly concentrated in the United States (about 1 percent owning 32 percent) than in most of Latin America. Income in Latin America is not much more equitably distributed than wealth; for instance, 16 percent of the Mexican population garners 56 percent of the nation's total income. In the Mexican case, income is concentrated in the upper fifth of the population to a greater extent than in the United States. However, comparisons of inequality between advanced industrial and underindustrialized societies must necessarily be misleading. The idea of relative deprivation simply isn't applicable when the parties are, to begin with, not even in the same economic league. And in the final analysis, comparisons between different industrial societies on matters of inequality can only be of the broadest and most general nature.

INEQUALITY IN RETROSPECT

Inequality may be of different kinds, but that which underlies most other varieties of inequality is inequality of income and wealth. Economic inequality sets the conditions for differences in health, education, work, leisure use, life style, and power, though these factors influence economic position in return. Feelings of inequality are importantly conditioned by a person's comparison reference group, but marked degrees of economic inequality such as exist in the United States present themselves so vividly to the unequal that reference groups are often unnecessary to experience deprivation. Arguments for the necessity of inequality may not hold much appeal to the unequal, and the arguments contain serious logical and empirical flaws whatever or to whomever their appeal.

Personal income, wealth, income in kind, and especially corporate wealth, the repository of all great personal wealth, all display very imbalanced distributions in the United States and have not been noticeably redistributed over the past generation or more. Taxation has slight effect on economic inequality and falls relatively heaviest on the bottom half of the class structure. The organized working class has faced increasing difficulties in preserving its position of the mid-sixties, while the unorganized and unskilled have dropped relatively further behind other blue- and white-collar workers over the past 15 years. And the view that giving a better balance to the distri-

[51] Irving Louis Horowitz, *Three Worlds of Development* (New York: Oxford University Press, 1966), pp. 199–201.

bution of economic means will solve no problems other than poverty seems to underestimate both the importance of poverty and its relation to other critical social problems.

Cross-cultural comparisons of national inequality are difficult to make, even between industrial societies, but especially between industrial and technologically underdeveloped societies because the latter have almost completely different economic status. Cross-cultural industrial comparisons are difficult owing to the differences in the amount of social spending for welfare, education, social insurance, transportation, health, and recreation, altering the significance of personal power of consumption.

One of the several sociological consequences of economic inequality is the creation of the conditions for the emergence of social classes. To an analysis of social class we turn next.

C. Educational Systems and Culture

Traditional Values and the Shaping of American Education

MERLE L. BORROWMAN

Discussion of educational values is usually derived from the commitments of formal religion, the folklore of democracy and capitalism, widely accepted ethical canons, and such specific educational traditions as humanism, scholasticism, and pragmatism. These are important reservoirs of moral capital. To explore their depths and appraise their content is important. Nevertheless, such appraisal and exploration, if carried on with traditional terminology, tends to degenerate into a battle of quickly recognized clichés around which patrons and educators rally. When time-honored guidons fly, it is not difficult to anticipate which armies will take the field.

In recent years, however, much educational debate has cut across conventional groups. The policies and practices which the public has been inclined to support or to resist indicate the operation of values that have not been clearly enough defined in normative (value) discussions to date. It would seem that certain inadequately recognized concepts have acquired sufficient emotional power to enter significantly into educational judgments. What follows is an attempt to supplement existing literature on educational values by making explicit a few of these concepts. Since, in a single essay, one cannot cover the entire range of such concepts, even if he adequately understands them all, this essay is intended merely to be suggestive. The concepts

FROM *Social Forces Influencing American Education,* 60th Yearbook, II, National Society for the Study of Education, 144–70. Copyright © 1961 by Herman G. Richey, Secretary. Reprinted by permission of National Society for the Study of Education.

with which we shall be concerned here are of community, work and play, authority, and human nature.

In one sense, of course, such concepts are not values at all; they are descriptive rather than normative terms. They enter the domain of values only when human emotion and preference become strongly attached to them; that is, when people feel that a community "ought" to have certain characteristics, that one set of relations between inferiors and superiors possesses moral superiority over another, that human nature "must" be viewed in a particular manner to avoid the risk of eternal or temporal damnation, and that "good" people have one attitude toward work and play while "bad" people have another.

The processes by which strong emotional support is brought to such concepts are several. It may be, as Erich Fromm implies in his books, e.g., *The Sane Society*, that the human animal is of such nature that some social conditions simply are satisfying while others are intolerably frustrating; and surely contemporary rhetoric moves some people emotionally to prefer particular alternatives. The process with which the historian is concerned, however, is that in which social re-enforcement over a long period of years conditions members of a particular human group to certain preferences. Only in a group which is somewhat isolated from alien influences, and in which considerable ideological homogeneity prevails, do the strongest of such preferences occur. When, as most Americans have done, an individual leaves a close-knit ideological group and encounters opposing views, it is difficult to predict his action.

The historian cannot, therefore, say that a particular value will actually enter the decision-making activity of a specific individual. Such is the province of other social scientists. As the geneticist can only say that among those who receive a specified biological inheritance one can anticipate the possible emergence of a particular trait, so the historian can only say that, since certain historical groups have held certain concepts long enough for them to have acquired normative significance, one can expect them to show up sooner or later in some form. This essay deals with a kind of heredity— that which one inherits from the culture into which he is born.

CONCEPTS OF COMMUNITY

The Puritan View

The kind of communal life which the Puritans sought to build and maintain in New England cradled our system of higher education and nurtured our common schools. Many Americans turn in nostalgia to certain of its characteristics, as did Louis Mumford in writing the text for the great documentary film, *The City*. To others, however, the term "Puritan" has become representative of community efforts to interfere in a most repressive and bigoted manner in the life of an individual. A study of the Puritan attitude toward community might, then, permit us to identify continuing normative issues.

The New England Puritan believed that ideological unity was essential, that a considerable degree of co-ordination and control of economic activities was necessary, and that political authority should seek to maintain both ideological conformity and economic efficiency. The economically unproductive citizen, the "squatter" who preempted land and was careless about the law, and the Quaker or Catholic who held unorthodox religious views were equally dangerous.

The Puritan did not believe that these functions should be sharply differentiated. To be sure, one could discriminate among the roles of the merchant, the elder, and the member of the General Court or town meeting. But so long as all were controlled by the oligarchy, the "elect" to use their term, no sharp conflict was conceivable.

The elect were divided between congregationalism and presbyterianism as forms of church government, and between town and colony as foci of political and economic power. In New England they formally adopted congregationalism, a system in which religious authority was vested in the local communion, but they hedged against the possibility of local congregations becoming heretical by adopting the principle of "consociation," a principle under which, as in presbyterianism, colony-wide meetings of elders and ministers met annually to adjudicate theological controversy. Though much political and economic responsibility was delegated to the town meeting, the General Court held the reins. As the colony spread geographically, the congregation and the town tended to gain power at the expense of synod and colony.

The New England Puritan lived with deep anxiety. Save for a brief period during Cromwell's regime in England, there was an ever-present threat that the Crown would so revise the Charter that the oligarchy would lose its power. For many years the economy operated so closely to the subsistence level that potential starvation was faced. Even though covenant theology gave the elect some assurance of salvation, which was denied them under a rigorous predestinarian theory, the Puritan was left in constant concern about the destiny of his immortal soul. These constant threats gave emotional support to the Puritan's feelings that a community "ought" to be characterized by ideological uniformity, regulated economic interdependence, and political authority exercised by an oligarchy in the interest of perpetuating a stable ideological and economic system.

Early Massachusetts school legislation was consistent with this view of the community. The laws of 1642 and 1647 explicitly affirm economic and political objectives as well as the more frequently cited religious ones. Characteristically, responsibility was delegated, so far as possible, to the local community where face-to-face relationships were easily maintained. Curricula were designed to insure conformity with the dominant ethos.

Separatist Religious Groups

Although the Puritans were, perhaps, the most influential immigrant group, their view of community was not totally unique. Other Protestant groups, particularly such pietistic sects as the Mennonites of Pennsylvania, Delaware, and New Jersey, had similar views. Because they did not have political control of any colony and because they had in most cases been persecuted minorities in their homeland, these groups became in some respects even more parochial than the Puritans.

Like the Pilgrims of Plymouth, these groups were separatists, committed to a congregational church polity and anxious to isolate themselves as much as possible from other social groups who might tempt their own members into error and sin. They came quickly to favor minimal government on the colonial level, preferring, instead, to keep controls within local, religiously homogeneous centers. It is small wonder, then, that such groups as the Mennonites resisted Penn's efforts to set up a colony-wide educational program in Pennsylvania. While such groups differed widely concerning the amount and kind of education they considered desirable, they were alike in viewing the local, usually parochial, school as a community center, designed, among other ends, to perpetuate ideological conformity and local community loyalty.

When in the nineteenth century the tradition of local control of public schools had become strongly entrenched, some separatist religious-ethnic groups came to the support of public schools, partly because they could completely dominate local school boards. Thus, for example, when the public school-parochial school controversy was raging among new Lutheran groups in the Old Northwest, some fascinating arguments were heard. At an 1869 conference in Wisconsin, ministers and laymen from the Lutheran state church insisted on parochial schools. Leaders of the pietistic groups, on the other hand, having been repelled by developments in the Lutheran states and in "high-church" Lutheranism, argued for public schools, noting that the public school could be controlled in the interest of the local community while parochial schools may be subordinated to the state and to state-church ministers. Particularly in the Midwest, and in Pennsylvania, school consolidation has met with especially virulent opposition in small communities where religious-ethnic homogeneity persists.

The Views of the Southern Gentry

Provincialism, a tendency to define values in terms of the interests and beliefs of the local oligarchy, was as marked in the southern tidewater communities as it was in New England. Here, too, a local aristocracy, which thought of itself as called to lead, quickly emerged. The same threat of English interference and exploitation, the same possibility of economic disaster, and the same fear that the influences of the frontier and the irresponsible classes would lead to barbarianism that plagued the Puritan were sharply felt by his southern counterpart. Here, too, they re-enforced the inclination of the gentry to concentrate power on the local level and to guard the seats of power from encroachment by undesirable elements. The southerner derived an ideal from an image of the English landed gentry, who in the spirit of *noblesse oblige* assumed the gentlemen's responsibility for the maintenance of high culture, the economic well-being of the community, and political stability.

But in the plantation areas there were no congregations of saints; the individual squire was likely to stand alone. To be sure, he met with his peers in Williamsburg or elsewhere to discuss common problems and colonial policies. As if father to the whole group of small farmers, artisans, indentured servants and slaves who lived nearby, however, he ministered to their economic needs, advised them on political matters, provided such education as many of them received, and tried to set a pattern of civilized life that would inspire them. That he tried very hard is attested by such volumes as the *Secret Diary of William Byrd II.*

In contrast to members of the New England oligarchy, the southern squires developed a way of life less dominated by theological considerations. Because of the episcopalian pattern of church government and the system of priestly ordination which prevailed in the southern, Anglican colonies, religious authority remained largely in England. Frequently the ministers were conceived almost as aliens. Since the layman did not participate in church government as fully as was the case in other colonies, he tended to define community mores in secular terms. Though he was not irreligious, the "southern gentleman" rather than the Puritan "saint" was his ideal.

Anticommunitarian Elements

It is interesting to note that colonial leaders in both Massachusetts and Virginia thought they saw in neighboring colonies examples of communities destroyed by rampant individualism and community irresponsibility. As early as 1729 William Byrd II, of Virginia, described the inhabitants of North Carolina as largely criminals, debtors, and run-away servants and slaves addicted to sloth and lapsing rapidly into savagery. Two centuries later Samuel Eliot Morison, distinguished, scholarly heir and defender of the Puritan tradition, scarcely concealed his delight in reporting that for many generations libertarian Rhode Island failed to create effective schools and other social institutions. To Morison's ancestors, Roger Williams and his kind had created a colony which epitomized anarchy and social degeneracy.

Every human community has its rebels, those who perceive the demands of organized society as designed to preserve special privilege and to destroy the legitimate aspirations of the less privileged or to stamp out personal idiosyncrasies. Among those who moved into frontier areas were many of these rebels. Folklore concerning such men as Daniel Boone, Davy Crockett, and John Sevier attests to their generally incorrigible tendencies and their desire to hold organized society at a distance. Probably the necessity for reliance on one's self and family, supported only by occasional short-term co-operative projects among the settlers of a given region, sharpened the anti-communitarian proclivities of the frontier's natural rebels.

As Louis Booker Wright points out in his *Culture on the Moving Frontier*, there were always on the edge of expansion those dedicated to building a community with the high culture and social organization of the older cities. But the ratio of such people to those who protested against, or were merely careless toward, community sentiment and organization was no doubt smallest in the frontier communities. It was against the frontier towns that the Massachusetts General Court most frequently brought action for carelessness in observing educational legislation; it was to the new Middle West and the Pacific coast that the missionary societies sent young men from Yale and Princeton carrying higher education.

However, most of the extreme individualists were silent men so far as the historical record is concerned. Unbounded by geography, religious background, or ethnic origins, they arose in every group, but were of none. The lonely trapper, the isolated farmer, the noncommunicative tradesman, the wealthy recluse remained anonymous. They were, however, temperamentally related to certain literary figures who, either because they had to write to know themselves or because basically they yearned for communion with others who would understand, wrote of their convictions.

Two spokesmen of extreme individualism who, although somewhat ignored in their own day, have since appealed to a considerable number of Americans were Henry Thoreau and Herman Melville. Neither was pleased with the direction in which American culture moved under the banners of co-operation and progress; each withdrew into himself. Thoreau was appalled at the growing power of the community over the individual, and he saw in the developing technology and the growing preoccupation with material goods a dire threat to the good life and to human dignity. But he remained in a sense optimistic, ever believing in human virtue and the eventual triumph of the good.

Melville, on the other hand, remained to the end deeply pessimistic. To him God was silent, evil was and would ever be present, and individual men were eternally doomed to fight in darkness and without hope for victory against it. The pride which men took in their social systems was purchased at the price of ignoring evil and thus, ultimately, of abandoning their destiny. Only the recluse, the lonely prophet and warrior, could be true to himself. Melville's pessimism was even more profound than that of the sin-obsessed Puritan who at least believed that God spoke clearly and who accepted the support and re-enforcement of the congregation of the elect.

In the older cities, some groups in opposition to the dominant community mores developed in such numbers that they could maintain themselves as islands of resistance. Within these islands they created as strong a sense of ideological unity and economic co-operation as was achieved by the dominant majority; but they lived in, and were not of, the larger community. When the number and strength of such groups were sufficient, they at times formed through temporary alliances concurrent majorities which could exert economic and political power. Illustrative of such an alliance was that of the Irish, the Jews, and the Italians in New York City. Such alliances as these were not opposed to community action as such, but, precisely because they were alliances, they were likely to combine for rather specific ends and to treasure a social system which allowed for maximum diversity in ways of living.

The Community and the Common School

Perhaps more thoroughly than that of any other person, Horace Mann's attitude toward community is imbedded in the traditions of the American common school. Mann's concept was a modification of the Puritan attitude; some of the same elements, with further modification, are found in the views of John Dewey and James B. Conant. As had his ancestors, Mann believed in the absolute necessity of ideological unity in a society. Like them, he conceived property and labor as being in a sense public; the property-holder was a steward, managing God's earth in trust for the well-being of the entire human race, and the laborer was "called" to serve in God's kingdom to the interest of all. Ideology, economics, and politics were, he thought, inseparable. The school, he argued, was the greatest instrument ever created to build a good society, and its central purpose was to create among all a common faith, a sharp sense of common interest, and love for a political order which served this faith and these interests.

But New England was no longer a community in the Puritan sense. What had been basic dogma in theology, economics, and politics was now at issue. A common ideology could be created only by emphasizing the beliefs shared by all Christian groups and all political-economic groups. The "common elements of Christianity" and the "common elements of republicanism" were, by implication, to become the important elements so far as the community and school were concerned. Issues on which fundamental disagreement existed were, as far as possible, to be kept out of the school. To restore a community of conviction, Mann thus excluded discussion of problems deeply concerning the public.

Mann reduced the ideological content of the public school faith to a minimum, and as non-Christian groups grew in power, and differences among Christian groups became more clear, even his "common elements" were subject to dispute. Yet, in Mann's approach to community-building through the schools were certain ideas to be emphasized by John Dewey. The first was to call into participation a wider range of communities—Dewey's term was "publics"; the second was to focus attention on the process of shared decision-making through political discussion and persuasion.

The Puritan community of belief in a detailed set of specific principles had become, with Dewey, a community bound only by a common commitment to the scientific processes of inquiry and the political processes of persuasion and legislation in which all interest groups participate. Where the Puritans had sought to prevent the development of ideological differences, and Mann had banned the discussion of such issues from the schools, Dewey found it essential that they be openly debated in the schools so that students might learn the processes on which his kind of ideal community depended. Confronted with Puritan-like community attitudes, the descendants of Dewey were to call in other groups as countervailing forces.

Neither Mann nor Dewey abandoned, however, the puritan conviction that only through close and active association on a face-to-face basis could a sense of community be built. In this they were to be joined by James B. Conant, who, while advocating ability grouping for the study of most subjects, still insisted that representatives of all groups and intellectual levels be periodically brought together for a discussion of basic social issues.

Yet, in the sixth decade of this century there were many who, like Roger Williams, Thoreau, and Melville before, found the community and its common schools oppressive. In the South, those who resented the intrusion of outsiders were in protest; in rural areas, groups sharing particular religious-ethnic backgrounds held out for small, easily controlled school districts; and, throughout the nation, powerful churches sought to expand schools in which loyalty to their religious community was a fundamental aim.

Work and Play

In discussing how emotion-laden attitudes toward work and play influence men's judgments of educational practices, it may be useful to note two ideal types, both extreme abstractions never found in their pure form among actual groups of people. Let us call these two stereotypes the "Hebraic-Puritan" and the "Hellenic-Romantic," since certain elements of the ideal types were in fact found among the groups whom these titles fit. But one need not literally have descended from the designated groups to have developed the attitudes to be described. The Western tradition has exposed all the well-educated to both views.

The Hebraic-Puritan Attitude

The Hebraic-Puritan attitude derives from the biblical tale of the fall of Adam and his expulsion from the Garden of Eden. It grants that the child's world of irresponsible play and naïveté is idyllic, that to which the natural man will aspire. The Garden is a child-centered world; the Father provides all that is required for a life of joy and comfort and spontaneity. Yet this world of play is one in which the temper runs free, and man's natural hankering for pleasure ever makes him subject to sin. Because Adam fell from grace, as inevitably would all his descendants, God justly condemned them to live in a vale of tears where they were to subsist by the sweat of their brow until redeemed. Henceforth, one who made of play a virtue and a goal was doubly sinful. He not only ignored a specific commandment of God but he continued to subject himself to the tempter.

The American Puritan never doubted that this life had justly been made one of suffering and hard work. Duty and obligation were his watchwords, and, next to pride, irresponsibility and frivolous consumption were the greatest sins. But he did not rely solely on the negative commandment that "thou shalt not play too freely"; he added positive sanctions for work and success. So long as it was the result of honest, frugal, and untiring effort, material success was viewed as evidence that one was of the elect. It seemed reasonable that God would inspire his chosen followers to behave in this manner and that prosperity would be the inevitable consequence of such behavior just as poverty inescapably followed from slothfulness. The able-bodied poor must obviously have yielded to the desires of the natural man, as all from whom God withheld the gift of grace would do. The prosperous could find great spiritual comfort in their work. Were they to forget, however, that success was ultimately due to God and attempt to use wealth for the gratification of physical appetites instead of in the interests of God and the human community, they would be guilty of the cardinal sin of pride.

This attitude did not begin with the New England Puritans, nor was it peculiar to them. It was rooted in the Hebraic tradition to which all Christianity was heir. In the nineteenth century it was secularized, as were many attitudes formerly based on theological premises. The most commonly cited secular sanction was the "survival of the fittest," as interpreted by the social Darwinists. Its influence ebbs and flows throughout our history. One suspects (a hypothesis worth testing through more extensive research) that, in times perceived as "times of trouble," a sense of guilt for having done something wrong pervades American thought and re-enforces the Hebraic-Puritan tendency. Certainly in recent years the critics of American education have emphasized the desirability of hard, even unpleasant, work and have stressed the student's duty to serve his society.

The Hellenic Attitude

The image of the classical Greek, with his games, his festivals, his gymnasiums, his poetry, and his sculpture is one of a people at play. Even when he spoke of his most serious business, politics, religion, and the pursuit of understanding, the literate Hellenist tended to stress leisure. His Gods were incessantly at play, and his most profound conversations often occurred over the banquet table. The vocations, the callings, worthy of a true man were thought of as liberal, that is, best carried out when one had leisure to play with ideas.

Though Plato, one among the most influential Greeks, is often described as condemning the masses to an unsatisfying life of drudgery and servitude, it seems reasonable to argue that this charge is unjust. His big "lie" is the literal story that some men are born of brass, others of silver, and others of gold. Behind this lie is what he considered the truth—that men find realization in different types of callings. What one who knows himself best would choose to do, the activity in which he does in fact find greatest satisfaction, is that to which Plato suggests he be assigned. That Plato denied the ability of all men to judge for themselves is true and warrants the charge that he was antidemocratic. It does not justify the claim that he believed men should be compelled to work at tasks which they found to be unsatisfying. Even the artisan was to engage in activities that followed his natural bent and were, therefore, playful in a sense. Plato remained a true Hellene.

Perhaps it was this element of Plato's which led Rousseau, the great eighteenth-century romanticist, to describe *The Republic* as the greatest pedagogical treatise ever written. Ever the exponent of following the unspoiled impulses of the natural child, Rousseau reversed the Hebraic-Puritan picture of play and work. Provided always that the man had not been corrupted by society, Rousseau believed that those activities in which the individual freely chose to engage out of his own self-interest, and which were therefore characterized by spontaneity, joy, and immediate satisfaction, were not only the more virtuous but also the more productive. Distaste for that which is usually called "work" was to him a function of the fact that it was imposed from without and entailed exploitation of the individual by others. In Rousseau's Garden of Eden, productive effort abounded and sin was absent.

In America the transcendentalists, the members of those religious groups which place great emphasis on "love" rather than sin and which have great confidence in human nature, the aristocracy of wealth not controlled by the Hebraic-Puritan ethos, a number of educational leaders in the romantic and pragmatic traditions, and certain industrial and labor leaders have, in greater or lesser degree, held a Hellenic-romantic attitude toward work. The influence of a philosophic tradition can be clearly seen in some instances. In other cases, people have acted as if adhering to this tradition although no literal influence can be established.

Thus, for example, the influence of Plato and Rousseau on Emerson and other transcendentalists was clear. Emerson's essay on *Education*, like Rousseau's *Emile*, was a plea that the child's natural genius, his native bent, be followed to the fullest. Were this done, Emerson argued, a vocation which was a true calling would emerge. This vocation would in time lead one to all truth, to an understanding of one's ideal relationship with both animate and inanimate nature, and, above all, to a knowledge and full realization of self.

Dewey and his followers parted company with Plato, Rousseau, and Emerson by rejecting the concept of the "enfolded," "natural" self. Their alternative was the social self of George Herbert Mead. But they continued to propose that one should start with those activities in which a presently lively interest existed, that he should work in terms of pleasurable activities, and that, as the student's interest took on the characteristics of a vocation, other necessary learnings could be provided as extensions in the social significance of the chosen calling. As had Plato, Rousseau, and Emerson, Dewey insisted that one's total life be integrated in terms of a calling, a vocation, viewed as a way of life sanctioned by the inter-relationships of an entire social system.

Partly under the leadership of such social psychologists as Elton Mayo, American industry has moved in a direction paralleling that proposed by Dewey. Just as the "whole child," learning through the study of economic and other social callings, was the concern of the Dewey school, the "whole worker" came to be of concern to management. Industry came increasingly to care for the morale of face-to-face working groups, to establish health and welfare plans, to sponsor company recreational activities, and even to be concerned with such matters as family counseling. Organized labor augmented this trend. In so far as workers could be led to organize their recreational, political, and welfare interests around their vocational roles, the significance of the union in their lives could be enhanced. Quite obviously, neither the pragmatists nor industrial and labor leaders came to this position solely and directly by way of the Hellenic tradition. Social scientific research gave new support, and sometimes a new rationale, to an older attitude.

Similarly, the "gentleman" class reached a position like that of the Hellenes through a devious route in which current social and economic conditions played a major part. Yet, the tradition of the landed gentry was partly shaped by the Renaissance view of the good life, a view rather directly derived from the literature of the classical era. The humanistic secondary school, like one of its descendants, the finishing school, was originally designed for a new leisure class. As had been the case in ancient society, this class had a vocation, that of governing, conducting military operations, and managing the economic system. Policy-making and negotiation, not immediate production of economic goods, were its major responsibilities.

The forum and symposium of classical times, the court and castle of the Renaissance, the salon of the enlightenment, and, perhaps, the country club of the twentieth century were the places in which this group conducted many of its vocational tasks. Pleasant, tactful conversation, shared recreational activities, inter-group loyalty, and leisure facilitated the performance of these tasks. Being a gentleman was a way of life, and, though the activities in which this group participated bore little resemblance to those of the proletariat, one ought not be blind to the vocational elements involved. For one to be accepted among those with whom he shared responsibilities, and therefore effective in his vocation, the ancient Greek had to be a skilled wrestler, the Italian courtier a talented fencer, and the twentieth-century manager a reasonably competent golfer. Just as Dewey's school child and Mayo's industrial worker were to find work pleasurable because of its integration into a way of life, those aristocrats not tormented by a Hebraic-Puritan conscience found tremendous satisfaction in their vocation.

There has, however, been an interesting paradox in the classical tradition. During Athens' "time of troubles," and increasingly through the Hellenistic period, philosophies of renunciation and restraint developed. One of the most important of these, Stoicism, flourished in ancient Rome. The Stoics who, it was alleged, "made their heart a desert and called it peace" profoundly influenced the classical tradition, particularly through Cicero and

Seneca. There have always been what Crane Brinton called the "spare humanists," those who emphasized the doctrine of restraint. These were easily accepted within the Hebraic-Puritan tradition, a fact which explains why the New England Puritans remained avid students of the classics.

Attitudes Outside the Hebraic-Puritan and the Hellenic-Romantic Traditions

Two further attitudes toward work and play should be noted. One, based on what Veblen called "instinct for workmanship," was similar to the Hellenic-romantic notion in that it made of work an inherently, almost instinctively, rewarding activity. Veblen and others viewed the skilled artisan, who worked largely with hand tools and converted raw materials by his own imagination and skill into finished products, as finding sufficient satisfaction in the work itself. Neither profit, nor duty, nor an elaborate scheme of planned social and welfare activity were primary motives to this kind of worker. As in the Hellenic-romantic tradition, work was viewed as a process of creative self-realization. Unfortunately, from the point of view of those holding this attitude toward work, the rise of the entrepreneur, the system of mass production, and the ethic of consumption led to such specialization of function that the inherent pleasure of a job well done was denied a large segment of the population. Indeed, as Veblen saw it, the instinct for skilful work was increasingly degenerating into a passion for consumption.

David Reisman, C. Wright Mills, and others, accepting as inevitable the trend which Veblen has observed, have suggested an attitude toward work which may well have dominated the thinking of most Americans throughout our history. This attitude views work as simple necessity, neither good nor bad, or rather both good and bad. One engages in it as a means of sustenance and seeks self-realization in his avocational pursuits: in religion, family activities, politics, art, and recreation. Work cannot, save for the fortunate few, be an end in itself.

Attitudes Toward Work and Attitudes Toward Education

At the price of over-simplification, it might be useful to suggest how the above-sketched attitudes toward work and play might affect people's judgment of educational practices. That of the Hellenic-romantic would seem clear; unless students are "playing" at school tasks—that is to say, approaching them with joy, spontaneity, self-direction, and enthusiasm—the Hellenist would suspect that the student is being exploited in terms of someone else's interests. If, on the other hand, the student is obviously "having fun," the Hebraic-Puritan would be suspicious, if not actually offended. The recent *Life* series on the "Crisis in Education" beautifully illustrates this conflict by contrasting the relaxed good humor of American students and schools with the austere severity of Soviet schools and students. The representative of American students, Stephen Lapekas, is characteristically pictured with a broad grin; his Soviet counterpart, Alexei Kutzkov, is never shown smiling.

Life's sympathies seem clearly to be with the Puritan atmosphere of the Soviet school, where duty is stressed, rather than with the "country-club" aura of the American school.

One would expect the Hellenist of the Deweyan variety to seek an integration of class activities with extracurricular projects. He might expect those of the Reisman persuasion, as loosely described here, to favor extracurricular activities but to expect students in class to get down to business and get the work done.

Since none of these attitudes has completely dominated a distinct historical group, one is likely to find many Americans who vacillate from one to another, or who accept one attitude toward their own work and play activities while advocating another for their children. There are duty-driven parents who want their youngsters to enjoy youth, just as there are adults who rationalize their play as "good business," or good for shop morale, while demanding long hours of homework for students.

AUTHORITY AND SUBMISSION

The problem to be examined here concerns feelings about the pattern of relationships that should characterize adult-child interactions. Anthropological and social psychological research has amply demonstrated a tremendous range of attitudes concerning the pattern and amount of deference the young are expected to show their elders, or the elders the young. Historical research, on the other hand, has not yet yielded enough evidence on this problem that trends can be clearly established. One suspects that further research will reveal in this case, and in the cases of values described above, that a simple scale of "traditional" and "emergent" attitudes used by such researchers as Spindler and Getzels will prove to be inaccurate. No one attitude appears to have been completely dominant in any era, and the pendulum stroke from one attitude to another appears too short to warrant the assumption of a long-term trend. It might be wiser to anticipate the entire range of attitudes in the school's public at any time and to calculate the relative strength of each set of values at the moment a controversial issue arises.

Let us consider, for example, the colonial and early national periods. Among the most popular of writers with early Americans was John Locke, who expressed in his *Thoughts Concerning Education* perhaps the dominant attitude so far as formal expressions of it are concerned. The first and most important habit which the child should develop, Locke believed, was that of unquestioned obedience to legitimate adult authority. The child was to be "seen and not heard," "silent unless spoken to." Only after he had thoroughly accepted the iron law of obedience could he be gradually admitted to a status of near equality to his elders.

American writers differed on how obedience was to be taught. The Puritans, for example, insisted that the child's "pride," his aspirations for complete independence, should be broken through a rather harsh discipline. As Cotton Mather argued in A *Family Well Ordered*, only one who had first learned to accept his dependence on, and the obligation to submit to, the authority of parents and other adults would easily accept his life-long, complete dependence on God. The same sinful nature which impelled an adult to rebel against God was thought to be at work in the child who resisted his elders.

The Puritan was not lacking in affection for children, as is widely believed, nor did he fail to reveal this affection. Love for their children was, in fact, a powerful motive to which Mather appealed in his advice to parents. Yet, the contrast between the method of the Puritans, for example, and that of the Moravian Christopher Dock is clear. Dock's appeal, like that of the Quakers and other pietistic groups, was to love, to the child's "better nature." Nevertheless, the ultimate necessity of obedience and submission to adult authority was accepted as completely by Dock as it was by Mather.

Children's textbooks, from the New England Primer through Webster's "Blueback Speller" to the McGuffey readers, echoed the themes of obedience and respect for elders. If one judges by these formal statements, it seems clear that the traditional American had no desire to live in a child-centered world.

Yet, paradoxically enough, foreign visitors to the American scene during the early centuries almost invariably commented on the liberties granted by American parents to their children. To the visitors, American children were bad mannered; to at least one American host, they were "sturdy young republicans." While Emerson had little tolerance for foolishness and horseplay, he noted with approval that in America boys were freely admitted and treated with affection everywhere.

Morison reminds us that among the reasons given by the Reverend Solomon Stoddard for the need of a new college in 1703 was the charge that indulgent, "fond and proud" parents had encouraged their sons to introduce frivolous and evil customs into Harvard life. And these were largely New England parents. A century later the parentally encouraged indulgences of southern students were the despair of college educators North and South. The formal emphasis on obedience and submission was evidently considerably softened by indulgence in practice.

The dominant tradition might, then, be characterized as one of continuous tension between an explicit ideal of child submissiveness and implicit delight in the children's assertions of independence from adult authority. Those who have grown up in this tradition will have a certain ambivalence. Perhaps, again, in times when the adult feels that the world, or his own personal life, is "getting out of control," we might expect him to be emotionally offended at the sight of a classroom in which the mantle of authority is lightly worn by adults. Those who feel more secure in their own lives may be expected to be more comfortable in the presence of educational practices which emphasize the initiative and freedom of the child.

An interesting variant of this tension in the dominant group can be found in the attitudes of certain more recent immigrant groups. Oscar Handlin, in *The Uprooted*, described conditions which could well have created ambivalence on the part of both adults and children in such families. The central tendency among societies from which these groups came was that of an authoritarian family, usually of the patriarchal sort. Yet, when the immigrant adult was placed in a strange culture late in life, confronted with incredible difficulties in making an adequate living, and denied educational opportunities which would have eased the transition, he often found himself dependent on the child as a mediator of the new culture. The child was, on the one hand, expected to give unquestioned obedience and deference to his elders. On the other hand, he was painfully aware of the parent's ineptness with American ways, of the ridicule to which the unacculturated immigrant was subject, and of his elder's dependence on him for help and advice. Since neither immigrant adult nor child lived according to a clearly defined and consistently operating concept of the proper relationships between adult and child, tension and vacillation could be expected. Anxiety about teacher-child relationships was perhaps the inevitable consequence.

HUMAN NATURE

Underlying all the concepts described above were concepts of human nature. The problem "what is man?" has concerned our greatest thinkers, and every judgment about whether to approve or resist a given educational practice involves one's sense of what is appropriate treatment for the kind of creature man is thought to be. Yet, of all the concepts here treated, this is the most complex; with all the speculation that has occurred we remain, perhaps, farthest from consensus on this issue.

The mere cataloguing of questions which those holding differing concepts of human nature will answer differently suggests the complexity of this particular problem: Ought man to regulate his life with reference to the achievement of certain temporal conditions or with reference to his individual eternal salvation? What are the relative effects of "grace," "will," genetic heredity, geographical conditions, social institutions, and historical accident on the behavior of an individual? Would the "natural" man tend toward love and altruism in his treatment of others, or would he be dominated by greed and brutality? Is reason capable of dominating the behavior of man or merely a tool which he uses to mediate between the demands of an insatiable *id* and an uncompromising *super-ego*? Does human nature never change, or is it, as Hocking suggests, "human nature to change itself"? Can virtue be taught? What are the limits of educability?

In *The Image of Man in America*, Don M. Wolfe discussed these and other questions as they have been implicitly or explicitly answered in the writings of such men as Jefferson, Holmes, Whitman, Mark Twain, Dreiser, Lincoln, and John Dewey. He concluded with a brief summation of recent anthropological, psychological, and biological research bearing on the nature of man and described this research as constituting barely a start toward a "science of man." He noted that even such tentative findings as those which suggest the tremendous plasticity of human nature and the determining effects of biochemistry and enculturation have not yet penetrated into the awareness of the average citizen. Education's public, therefore, remains under the control of traditional views, of which there are many. Let us sample them, utilizing, in several cases, portraits painted by Wolfe.

The Depravity of Man

At the head of a long stream of American writers who have been convinced that man is dominated by a sinful nature stood the founding fathers of New England. As one of them, John Winthrop, stated the case in his *Journal*, natural liberty, which man shares with the beasts, "makes men grow more evil, and in time to be worse than brute beasts. . . . [It] is that great enemy of truth and peace, that wild beast, which all the ordinances of God are bent against, to restrain and subdue it." Only the grace of God, supported by the well-organized society of saints, could enable a man to overcome this beastly nature.

Some generations removed from Winthrop and his own early New England ancestors, John Adams still described man as dominated by ambition, jealousy, envy, and vanity. Altruistic tendencies, the existence of which was granted, could, he argued, be expected to dominate only in the rarest of cases. Evil, he assumed, was ineradicably rooted in man's nature, and such social institutions as schools and governments were established primarily to control human passions. Though, through schooling, the passions might be harnessed by social control, their basic tendency could not be fundamentally altered.

At the end of the nineteenth century, one of John Adams's progeny, Brooks Adams, still held this view: "As I perceived that the strongest of human passions are fear and greed, I inferred that so much and no more might be expected . . . from any automation so actuated." The reform of social institutions might create the illusion of progress; for example, the growth of democracy yielded a small advance in altruism, but in the long run even democracy, according to Adams, promised only the triumph of greed and the surrender to passion.

For a time Mark Twain had been even more depressed over the depravity of human nature than Adams was. Among the most stinging denunciations of the human race and the God who created it was Twain's *The Mysterious Stranger*. Here, too, depravity was assumed to be innate. Later in his life, however, Twain mellowed somewhat. His *What Is Man?* suggests that so far as inheritance is concerned, man is morally neutral. What he becomes is a function of environment; one inherits possibilities, and the environment determines which of them will be realized. Twain thus came, in time, to a position similar to that later held by Clarence Darrow and Theodore Dreiser.

Few Americans studied the criminal mind more carefully than Darrow; few described men's surrender to evil more clearly than Dreiser. Both, however, maintained a high level of compassion based on the conviction that individual men were inescapably the products of environmental factors beyond personal control. Neither had great hope for the reform of social institutions to the point where the good would, in most cases, triumph. We must turn to the writings of Jefferson, Horace Mann, and John Dewey for a more optimistic view.

Meliorism and the Plasticity of Human Nature

Jefferson was no naïve optimist. He seldom used the popular enlightenment phrase, "the *infinite* perfectability of man." Though he considered great progress possible, he expected it to come much more slowly than did the more exuberant sons of the enlightenment. He did, however, maintain that man's behavior was the result of purely natural causes, of biological inheritance and of experience in the physical and social environment. Through the use of intelligence in the control and manipulation of these environmental factors, he believed that the natural man could be greatly improved.

This conviction, which Jefferson shared with other reformers, provided a major argument in the French and American campaigns for universal education. Education, it was claimed, would expand the use of intelligence in social affairs. As social institutions were reformed in light of new knowledge, the mind and character of man would be raised to new heights. The new man would then be capable of further institutional reform and the more effective utilization of natural forces and resources. Thus was the wheel of progress ever to turn.

Jefferson's belief in the existence of a natural aristocracy and his suggestion that the educational system be used to "rake from the rubbish" those capable of leadership are often cited as evidence that he was no egalitarian. The charge is valid if, by egalitarianism, one refers to a belief that all men are capable of the same kind and same order of behavior. Jefferson recognized that the biological inheritance of individuals differed, and he granted that such inheritance defined the bounds, however broad, within which subsequent development must occur. He was even inclined to believe that there existed racial differences in intellectual potentiality, although he was still suspending final judgment and seeking new evidence on this point to the end of his life.

Yet, in a way these differences were relatively insignificant for Jefferson. All men, he thought, were rational, all educable, and all possessed of sufficient basic talent to participate in the making of fundamental social decisions. There was none whose intelligence was so unmalleable that his capacity for more effective living could not be increased by education.

Jefferson did, however, remain convinced that man had an innate moral sense. The social instinct, the disposition to love and serve, exists, he thought, in every man. On this point Jefferson agreed with the romantics and the transcendentalists. Here, too, he anticipated the views of Horace Mann.

Few have had such confidence in the educability of mankind as did Mann. Human tendencies, even the innate moral sense, were, he was convinced, so easily shaped by experience that the nature of social institutions largely determined whether a specific individual would be noble or mean. Given proper institutions, and especially adequate schools, Mann expected poverty, crime, bigotry, and selfishness to disappear. If educational opportunities were widely enough distributed, Mann believed that highly significant differences in virtue and talent would no longer exist.

John Dewey, heir to both Jefferson and Mann, was more of an environmentalist than either. Though he, too, began his philosophical journey with a belief in man's innate moral sense, he came to believe that human nature was completely amoral at base. Indeed, he thought those characteristics considered most distinctively human, moral commitment and the capacity of rational thought, were the result of experience and learning. Though he ultimately parted company with the systematic behaviorists in psychology, he continued to assume that an infant could be made into almost any kind of a person desired by those who controlled his environment. He was always fearful of the mental-testing movement, since the limits revealed by testing under a specific set of conditions, and based on a particular kind of educative experience, were too easily taken as measures of innate potential. To Dewey, as to Jefferson and Mann, failure to have developed needed intelligence and skill pointed to the necessity of reconstructing the environment to which the young were exposed.

Neither Jefferson nor Dewey had quite the exalted faith in the power of the formal school that Horace Mann had possessed. Both agreed with him, however, that it was among the more effective forces for the improvement of human nature.

The belief that human nature is highly plastic and subject to being molded by culture into an almost infinite number of shapes has, of course, been shared by a great many social scientists and, particularly, by American anthropologists. This view has been shocking and frightening to many Americans, particularly when they perceive that the Communist world has, through "brain washing," used scientific knowledge to undermine values which Americans had thought to inhere in the soul and conscience of men. Whether belief in the plasticity of human nature has been rationalized as untrue because it is frightening to admit that beliefs held dear have no supernatural supports, or because adequate evidence concerning an innate and ineradicable moral sense is thought in fact to exist, cannot be determined as a generalization. One suspects, however, that a belief in the innate goodness of man is, in most cases, a psychological rather than a logical or scientific necessity. Nevertheless, there is a long tradition to support this belief.

The Natural Man As Virtuous

Among American Christian sects have been a number which assumed, as did Jefferson and Mann with qualifications, that the natural man was a man of virtue. The debate between these groups and those obsessed with man's depravity concerns, in religious terms, the relative strength of the spirit of God dwelling within and the sinful nature also believed to be present. The Quakers and the early Unitarians, for example, were willing to grant to their Calvinist compatriots that man was subject to acute temptation arising from his physical passions and social conditions. Nevertheless, they argued, the spirit of love, the God within the natural man, was sufficiently strong to lead most men on the path to righteousness.

In secular terms, Emerson nicely illustrates the popular faith in the natural goodness of man. To Emerson each individual was essentially a part of the great oversoul and his unspoiled inclination was to seek and maintain contact with the sublime. To be sure, he could be made a monster if others sought to constrain him to a life pattern not his own. Emerson believed, as had Rousseau, that all things, all men, came from nature essentially good. They were spoiled by the meddling of men. Though Emerson did from time to time praise the public school system, he was ever fearful that formal social institutions, even schools, would be destructive of the individual's natural genius, that which impelled him to live the good life. Attempts to mold the individual, as if he were clay, were, Emerson believed, offenses against nature. No good could come of them. Meliorism, the attempt to improve human nature through social reform, he considered a delusion.

Rational and Irrational Man

Cutting across the arguments concerning the virtue or evil of natural man, and the degree to which he can be molded by environmental factors, has been the question of his essential rationality. Tension between the mystic and the intellectual has been ever present throughout the Christian tradition. There have always been those who "felt" their way to truth as well as those for whom rational analysis was considered essential to understanding. The early argument between the rationally oriented Puritans and those who would exploit religious "enthusiasm" was but one of many conflicts on this issue. So, too, was the nineteenth-century frontier struggle between those churches that insisted upon a "learned ministry" and those stressing the simple faith of the relatively unlettered.

On the political front a related issue was spelled out by Justice Stone in his dissent on the Barnette (flag saluting) case. Justice Stone granted that a society was legitimately concerned with insuring reasonable loyalty among its members. He noted, however, that a choice of methods was available. One was the method of securing loyalty through emotionally charged rituals, making little direct appeal to reasoned judgment. The other was the slower, but he believed more just, method of disseminating information concerning the society's tradition and usages in the hope that a reasoned commitment would ensue.

With the growing acceptance of psychoanalytic theory in the 1920's, the old argument of the rational versus the nonrational took new form in its effects on attitudes toward education. Nowhere was the argument sharper than between two leaders of the progressive-education movement, John Dewey and Margaret Naumberg, the founder of Walden School. Their differences were partially concerned with the relative emphasis given to group activities and group loyalties. Behind this issue, however, was Miss Naumberg's conviction that the school should be primarily concerned with the child's emotional development. Under the influence of psychoanalytical theory, she apparently believed that learning and the development of rational powers would be a relatively simple matter if the child's emotional life were in order. Dewey, on the other hand, though not unconcerned with emotion, was never comfortable with the Freudian and neo-Freudian movements. He was far too much a rationalist.

Views on Human Nature and Attitudes Toward Education

The historian always finds it difficult to compare published views of intellectuals with those of people whose views are not published. Dependent on documentary evidence, he is compelled to base his conclusions on the study of an atypical population. In the present case many of the people whose points of view have been described were of groups which may have held consistently the positions set forth. It seems reasonable to assume that the Adamses, Mann, and Emerson represented significant portions of the old New England Congregationalist and Unitarian families. The religious traditions that have emphasized man's sinful nature, as well as those which have stressed man's natural virtue, can be identified. One can roughly describe the communities in which Jefferson, Dewey, and Naumberg were most popular. It remains true, however, that historical research has done very little to correlate attitudes toward human nature with identifiable social groups.

Moreover, one can only speculate on the way a given attitude toward human nature will enter as a value in educational judgments. It does seem reasonable to assume that one who has great faith in the plasticity of human nature will be uncomfortable in the presence of efforts to restrict educational opportunities; that one who considers students naturally evil, or at least rebellious, will favor a rather tightly organized classroom situation; that a Jeffersonian or Deweyan will be greatly concerned with group morale and will desire a curriculum organized around those disciplines which promise to extend control over the physical and social environment; that an Emersonian will favor a child-centered school, though not one of the Deweyan or Freudian sort; that the mystics and those who follow Mark Twain will have little confidence in the power of the formal school while a disciple of Horace Mann may expect the school to solve most acute social problems; and that a follower of Darrow will have great tolerance and compassion for the deviant student.

When educational conflict arises, the educational practitioner must determine on the spot what values actually enter in. A historical discussion of concepts of community, work and play, authority, and human nature can only alert him to certain factors which might be present.

The Education of Immigrants in the
United States: Historical Background
RICHARD G. DURNIN

Since America is a nation of immigrants, it would seem that a good portion of its history of education would concern the schooling offered to these newcomers and their children. The process of becoming an American, one that has persisted since the 17th century, is indeed a major theme in American social history. The historiography of education, dealing rather exclusively with schooling in this country, begins essentially with the early 20th century. The topic of the education of the immigrant seldom was treated as a discrete one.

The fact that America was, for the most part, an English-speaking land, with most people coming from a similar social-economic class in the British Isles in the 17th, 18th, and early 19th centuries, tended to erase the concept of these peoples as immigrants, in the latter 19th-century sense of the term. Presumably, these settlers were more or less quickly assimilated into the life of their towns and cities.

In whatever way the immigrants thought of themselves or were thought of by their contemporaries, the history of American education has not dealt with them and their schooling to any great degree. That Dutch settlements were extensive in New York and New Jersey, that German-speaking people made up a considerable portion of the population of the Province of Pennsylvania, that French Huguenots were present in several of the colonies, and that New York City always had a sizeable number of inhabitants of non-English language and culture have hardly concerned the educational historian seriously until recent years. It was, of course, the incursions of non-English speaking peoples during the second half of the 19th century that have affected American education the most.

Cubberley, in referring to the early immigrants—those who came during the 1840s—wrote glowingly: "All were from race stock not very different from our own, and all possessed courage, initiative, intelligence, adaptability, and self-reliance to a great degree. The willingness, good nature, and executive qualities of the Irish; the intellectual thoroughness of the Germans; the respect for law and order of the English; and the thrift, sobriety, and industry of the Scandinavians have been good additions to our national life." [1]

But, in the late 19th century, after 1882, there was a change in the nature of immigration. Cubberley wrote of these new people in strong and unfavorable terms. His observations and feelings, and no doubt those of many of his fellow Americans, were that these newcomers were "largely illiterate, docile,

FROM Brickman and Lehrer (Eds.), *Education and the Many Faces of the Disadvantaged* (New York: John Wiley & Sons, Inc., 1972), pp. 181–92. Reprinted by permission of John Wiley & Sons, Inc.

[1] Ellwood P. Cubberley, *Public Education in the United States* (Boston: Houghton Mifflin, 1919), p. 337.

often lacking in initiative, and almost wholly without the Anglo-Saxon conceptions of righteousness, liberty, law, order, public decency, and government. . . ." He believed that their coming "served to dilute tremendously our national stock and to weaken and corrupt our political life . . ." and observed, as a result, that "foreign manners, customs, observances, and language have tended to supplant native ways and the English speech. . . ." [2] Apparently holding the "melting pot" theory, he felt that the nation had suffered from "racial indigestion," and that the mission of public education had indeed been made more difficult from the last two decades of the 19th century on.

The public schools, especially in the cities, were faced with problems of crowding, non-English-speaking children (many illiterate in their own language), parents whose working conditions would not allow much concern with school progress, and alienation between parents and the educational establishment. But Cubberley's rather conclusive remarks about the immigrants themselves were written before much evidence became manifest and accepted regarding the enrichment of the American way: its cuisine, economy, language, literature, art, music, and life style in general. He lived through those years when the thrust of immigration was greatest, when its impact seemed almost overwhelming, and when restrictions on the movement of foreigners to America were being enacted into law.

It is interesting and pertinent to note that most of the disparaging characterizations directed at the late 19th-century immigrant have been said in recent decades (but perhaps not as often written) about the Negro, Puerto Rican, and Mexican-American in-migrant to our cities. The children and grandchildren of those European arrivals of the 1880s and 1890s are prospering in suburbia and usually form a bulwark of American "patriotism."

The early story of the education of immigrants in America is interwoven with the annals of the conventional pattern of American schooling. These immigrants were, for the most part, English-speaking, and so the transition was nominal. Much of the educational account of English-speaking immigrants, as well as for those from other cultures, in earlier periods has been blended into the chronicle of schooling in the city. Here the newcomers landed and many of them remained. Noninstitutional aspects of education (apprenticeships, ethnic mutual aid societies, the family, and self-study) were responsible for much of the adjustment to the new way of life. The history of immigrant education in America is often the history of schooling in the American city. Aside from being the place where they landed and where many remained, more provisions seem to have been made for them in the city and their educational experiences there are better documented.

The concept of the immigrant as "disadvantaged" or "deprived" is one that is closely associated with the study of specific immigrant groups in American history. A generalization can be made that all immigrants were

2 Ibid., p. 338.

disadvantaged to some degree, but not all were economically impoverished. The Huguenots who came to New York, Pennsylvania, and the Carolinas after the revocation of the Edict of Nantes in 1685 were skilled, industrious, and prosperous. The Immigration Act of 1965, abolishing the national quota system, admits new people who have the skills needed according to Department of Labor schedules. Inability to speak English, or to speak it sufficiently for employment, has served to make immigrants and in-migrants disadvantaged. To be "culturally disadvantaged" would seem to include the language problem (but not necessarily), lacking those skills needed in the society, and falling short of a life style (competitive spirit, hustle and bustle, prolonging of gratification, the Protestant ethic of hard work) generally associated with successful Americans.

The term "culturally disadvantaged" has not received favorable acceptance in very recent years by all cultural anthropologists, sociologists, and educators. And ethnic and racial groups, themselves, reject the concept. American Indians, Hispanic Americans, and, increasingly, Afro-Americans have been heard from regarding this view. Much more is likely to be said (and educational programs influenced) concerning subcultures in America and their relationship to the American way.

New York City has served as a haven for immigrants throughout its 300-year history. In its colonial period (1609 to 1783), Dutch, Walloons, Jews, French Huguenots, West African and West Indian Negroes, English, Scots, and Irish made up its diverse population. As for schooling provided for its children, with the exception of the school established by the Dutch Reformed Church and the Dutch West India Company in 1638 (now known as the Collegiate School), the "voluntary principle" associated with English educational policy and practice prevailed. The family, private tutoring, charity schools, proprietary schools, the apprenticeship system, and education provided by religious denominations served to instruct the young in the vernacular.

The Free School Society of New York City (renamed the "Public School Society" in 1826), chartered by the state in 1805, was concerned with the schooling of poor children who were not provided for by any religious society or by any of the existing charity schools. Although this charitable organization was only quasi-public in nature, it provided what was really the beginning of free, common school education on a large scale in the city. Its first school, opened in May, 1806, using the Lancastrian monitorial system of instruction, undoubtedly included among its early urchin-pupils, youngsters who were recent immigrants or whose parents were immigrants.[3] New York immigration, at this time, was made up heavily of English-speaking people.

Henry Bradshaw Fearon, an Englishman who came to America in 1817 to gather information for a book intended for British emigrants, paid some

[3] *An Account of the Free-School Society of New York* (New York: Collins and Company, 1814).

attention to the schools of New York City. The Free School Society's schools, with their Lancastrian methodology, were spoken of as being for "the lower orders," and Fearon felt that the monitorial system of instruction had not spread as widely here as in England due, perhaps, to its being less wanted by the common people themselves.[4]

The work of these schools, greatly expanded from their 1806 beginnings, and until they became a part of the public schools of the New York City Board of Education in 1853, provided schooling for many children of the poor and recently-arrived. Although the Scriptures were read daily in these schools, the trustees of the society represented most of the religious groups prominent in the city and those in charge of the schools were instructed to avoid inculcation of the tenets of any particular religious sect. But these schools remained Protestant Christian in orientation, even though their rolls showed Roman Catholic children. It was the alleged permeation of Protestant Christian thought in these charity schools, and later in the public schools, that in part led the Roman Catholic Church towards opening its own schools in the 1840s.

At about the time of the early period of the Free School Society, the Economical School gave instruction to children of refugees from the West Indies, and the Manumission Society (whose work had begun in 1785) schooled hundreds of children of New York City's Negroes. This latter group joined with the Free School Society (then known as the Public School Society) in 1834. Accordingly, separate colored schools were built into the system of schools handed over to the Board of Education in New York by the Public School Society in 1853.

In spite of these efforts to extend common schooling to those who could not afford to pay for it, not all city children by any means were receiving instruction. Compulsory school laws and child labor laws were many years away. And poor and immigrant families did not all make use of those limited facilities that were available, some because they could see little value in education and others because they needed the services of their young.

The opening of the West saw immigrants following. How did immigrants settling in the interior of the nation fare so far as education was concerned? The territory and later state of Minnesota, a popular Midwestern agricultural land, where many people of Irish, German, and Scandinavian blood settled, might epitomize a typical frontier settlement in the middle 19th century. Beginning about the 1850s, there were Yankees from New England, Irish, Germans, Norwegians, Swedes, and Czechs residing there. After statehood in 1858, the Homestead Act of 1862, the end of Indian troubles, and the end of the Civil War, many more of these people, essentially small farmers, came to Minnesota. By 1890, the population of the state had

---

[4] Henry Bradshaw Fearon, *Sketches of America: A Narrative of a Journey of Five Thousand Miles Through the Eastern and Western States of America* (London, 1819), p. 38.

reached 467,000, 215,000 of whom were Scandinavians.[5] The diverse population of Minnesota in that year can be shown by the presence of 39 foreign newspapers in that agricultural state.[6]

An immigrants' guidebook to the territory issued in 1856 boasted not only of the area's agricultural advantages, but made a strong point of stressing the provisions there for education, the prevalence of churches, and the "general intelligence of the people." By an Act of Congress, grants of land were made available in every township for the support of common schools. The guidebook informed its readers that, with regard to the villages, "nearly all have good district schools." A comparison was even made with New England's schools, generally accepted as among the best in the country: Minnesota's schools were only second to them, and "but a short time will elapse before they will be fully equal or superior. . . . never in the history of the West in so new a country as Minnesota, has so much attention been paid to the subject of education, or so deep an interest manifested in it." [7]

In the towns of Minnesota, Roman Catholic and Lutheran parishes often had their own parochial schools. As might be expected, they were highly ethnic in composition and no doubt often carried on the language pattern and other mores of the particular group for another generation. But there were those who spoke for more rapid Americanization. Georg Sverdrup, a Norwegian-Lutheran church leader in Minnesota in the 1870s, advocated public education for children of the newcomers: "Our children must grow into the language and history of this country." [8] There were ethnic associations and institutions, aside from the churches, that aided the immigrant in adjusting to the land. These were similar to the ones he would have found in the Eastern cities. The Czechs in Minnesota established the *sokol*, a Bohemian social, athletic, and educational organization, for their fellow countrymen. One Czech immigrant, Antonin Jurka, was teaching English to Czech children in the St. Paul public schools in the early 1870s.[9] With the exception of provisions such as those mentioned above, schooling available to the rural immigrant child was the same as that for the native-born.

There is little doubt that the prevalence of common schools in Minnesota and its advanced educational policy were important factors in helping its many foreign pioneer settlers to come into the mainstream of American life as quickly as most of them did. Of course, these immigrants prospered more in a land of good soil on independent farms, and in an absence of exploitation, than was the situation with so many others in the factory system of the

[5] Theodore Blegen, *Building Minnesota* (Boston: Heath, 1938), p. 370.
[6] Ibid., p. 374.
[7] *The Immigrants' Guide to Minnesota in 1856. By an Old Resident* (St. Anthony: W.W. Wales, 1856), p. 87.
[8] Theodore Blegen, *Minnesota: A History of the State* (Minneapolis: University of Minnesota Press, 1963), p. 414.
[9] Ibid., p. 370.

East. Certainly, the Germans, Irish, and Scandinavians (perhaps the Finns less so) amalgamated into American life more rapidly than did some of the immigrants coming to America from Southern and Eastern Europe in the late 19th and early 20th centuries.

The development of industry through the factory system in New England attracted Europeans from a variety of backgrounds in the 19th century. The public schools in the cities and larger New England towns began to be aware of the presence of foreign children in the 1850s. Beginning in the 1840s, the Irish predominated as an immigrant group.

The report on schools for the year 1849–1850, in Cambridge, Mass., stated that in one common school "nearly all the children attending are of foreign parentage." That there was some difficulty in reaching them with instruction is reflected in the comment that, "while many of them are intelligent and studious, and acquire a good standing as scholars, the results of instruction on another portion are less satisfactory." [10] At the annual examination, the school cited above ranked the lowest in reading and spelling accomplishment.

True to the 19th century attitude associating education and virtue, the School Committee of Cambridge concluded that, if all the children of its foreign population attended school (there were no means for compelling attendance), they would become virtuous youth and respectable citizens. Their absence would tend to direct their lives toward idleness and vagrancy.[11]

In Manchester, N.H., the School Committee took cognizance of the preponderance of Irish children in three of their primary schools. "Could they have equal advantages with our native children, and improve as they do in these schools, they would not be excelled by any," reported the committee.[12] Again, there was the concern with schooling as the route to goodness.

No arrangements seem to have been made in the mid-19th century in the schools of New England industrial towns and cities to provide any special tutelage for these youngsters of immigrants. The common school emphasis, aside from instruction in the three R's, was on improvement of moral character. This had supplanted, to some degree, the strong religious emphasis in the schools during the 17th, 18th, and early 19th centuries.

The influx of foreigners from other than the British Isles and Northern Europe, after 1882, shifted the school emphasis somewhat to that of loyalty to the Republic. People began to realize that free, public elementary schooling was essential for the newcomers as well as for the natives. There was fear regarding these strangers coming to America. They represented economic competition for many older Americans; they came from lands that

10 *The City of Cambridge: Report of the School Committee for the Municipal Year Ending April 1, 1850* (Cambridge: Metcalf, 1850), p. 11.

11 Ibid., p. 39.

12 *Report of The School Committee of the City of Manchester, for the Year 1854–5* (Manchester: Abbott, Jenks, 1855), p. 8.

were not democracies; they did not speak English; most were non-Protestant Christians—and many were not Christians at all; and they came from countries not having a heritage of free, public education. In some instances their loyalty was called into question. Cubberley, in referring to Massachusetts at this time, wrote of the "avalanches of foreign-born peoples who have corrupted her politics, diluted her citizenship, and often destroyed the charm of her villages." [13] The Americanization function of the public school began to be realized in the latter decades of the 19th century.

New York City bore the brunt of the influx of immigrants during the late 19th and early 20th centuries. The New York City system of public schools had come into existence in 1842 and had absorbed the charity schools of the Public School Society in 1853. There was no child labor law until 1886, nor a compulsory education law until 1894, and even then the enacted legislation was directed to factory labor of children under 13, and only required school attendance of youngsters from eight to 12 years (children over 12 and under 14 could go to work if they had attended school for 80 days during the year).

It was not the public schools of New York City, however, that geared themselves in philosophy or practice to handle the influx effectively. Indeed, it appears from a study of curriculum, textbooks used, sources of teachers, school regulations, evidence from students then in attendance, and other contemporary sources that the public schools of the city went on about their business in about the same manner as they had earlier in the century. Many of the children of immigrants and the poor were outside of the reach of public education. An 1868 source related that "there are forty thousand vagrant and destitute children in this section of the great city [The Five Points, Fourth, and Sixth Wards]. These are chiefly of foreign parentage. They do not attend the public schools, for they have not the clothes necessary to enable them to do so, and are too full of vermin to render them safe companions for other children." [14] Although the schools were public and free, the pupils (or their parents) were required to maintain habits of cleanliness and neatness. And for many this was hopeless.

Almost three decades later, another observer of the New York situation wrote that "Fifteen thousand homeless, hungry, cold, and naked children wander today in our streets, and as yet no agency has been found that meets their need, and the hands that would rescue are powerless. The city money jingles in Tammany pockets, and the taxpayers heap up fortunes for Tammany politicians, while these thousands of little ones are outcasts and soon will be criminals." [15]

But an agency had come into being that began to do something about

13 Cubberley, op. cit., p. 479.

14 Edward Winslow Martin, The Secrets of the Great City (New York: Jones Brothers, 1868), p. 191.

15 Helen Campbell, Darkness and Daylight; or Lights and Shadows of New York Life (Hartford: Hartford Publishing Co., 1896), p. 168.

the plight of poor and immigrant children in New York City, and before long it was more potent and of greater influence with regard to these youngsters than the public schools. It was the Children's Aid Society, a charitable organization founded in 1853, for the industrial education of young "street arabs" who attended no schools, that helped to meet this need. The mission of the society also embraced providing lodging houses for uncared-for children, providing foster homes for them in rural areas, and in transporting unwanted and surplus city children by the hundreds off to the American West.

This mass movement of excess and unwanted poor and immigrant young-sters to the new territories and states of the West has received very little attention from social and educational historians. This episode was, in a sense, a throwback to an earlier British practice of increasing the population of Canada, Australia, and South Africa by removing thereto thousands of children from the crowded cities of Britain. From 1853 to 1882, the Chil-dren's Aid Society sent 62,287 boys and girls from New York City west-ward.[16] Farmers, always in need of help, adopted them, and many a city urchin grew up along with the West and prospered. Letters came back to the Society from some of the transplanted youth, and these tended to support the emigration undertaking. "Once a New York pauper, now a Western farmer. . . . when I was twenty-four I married, and two years afterward I bought myself a farm of eighty acres. . . . have been out West seven years . . . was not contented, and I had four different homes before I made up my mind to settle down. . . . I like this country well, and I like my new home that I am in, and the people are very kind to me. . . ." wrote the boys and girls.[17] Cases on the Society's records showed that some of these redundant city children had received schooling through college, had married well, and had generally prospered in the upwardly mobile so-cial and economic life of the West.

The Children's Aid Society also was helpful especially in aiding in the education of recently-arrived Italian and German children. Three of the Society's 22 industrial schools were designated to serve Italian young people. Here instruction was given in carpentry, cooking, and sewing. By the 1890s, thousands of Italian-American youngsters were benefiting from these pro-grams. "Nothing has done more to make the Italian immigrant contented with New York than the industrial schools which are thronged with chil-dren," wrote Helen Campbell in commenting upon Italian life in the city.[18] The story was told of one pair who had landed at Castle Garden (point of disembarkation) at six in the morning and were found in line the same morning at the Children's Aid Society's industrial school—and they an-nounced that seven others would be there that afternoon.

[16] George C. Needham, *Street Arabs and Gutter Snipes* (Boston: D. L. Guernsey, 1884), pp. 327–328.
[17] Ibid., pp. 314, 328, 331, 337.
[18] Campbell, op. cit., p. 406.

Immigrant self-help organizations—almost every ethnic group had at least one—were vital in the process of adjusting to the harshness of the ghettos and to the new world in general. The Italian colony in New York had nearly 80 benevolent societies, several weekly papers, Italian banks, and a chamber of commerce by 1891.[19] Some ethnic groups attempted schooling on their own, but here the Roman Catholic Church was most successful with its large Irish population.

The public schools of Brooklyn, Queens, and Staten Island joined with those of Manhattan, in 1898, to make up the consolidated New York City school system, when those areas came together to make up greater New York. William H. Maxwell, who had been superintendent of schools in Brooklyn, became superintendent of the new enlarged system. It was under his leadership (1898 to 1914) that the public schools gave attention to the crying need of its immigrant population.

Before the time of Maxwell, there were practically no provisions made for the non-English-speaking child in the public schools. Morris Cohen (1880–1947), later to be an eminent professor and philosopher, arrived in America as an immigrant boy in 1892, and has left an autobiographical account of his experiences in the public schools of Manhattan and Brownsville, in Brooklyn, from the fall of 1892 until the spring of 1895.[20] He found no arrangements for the older or more advanced immigrant student. Young Cohen was precocious, a voracious reader, and he brought with him a heritage of Hebrew studies and a love of learning. And he was fortunate in meeting up with a few teachers who took a personal interest in him, encouraging him at the age of 15 to take the entrance examinations to the City College. But Morris Cohen was the exception among the throng of immigrant youth.

An extensive Federal investigation in 1908 and a subsequent massive report (42 volumes) in 1911 on the problems associated with immigration paid considerable attention to education. Among a mass of data, it reported that children of foreign-born parents left school at an earlier age; that only 4.7% of the high school enrollment was made up of students from foreign parentage; and that retardation of children of foreign parents was greater than that of those from native parents.[21] On the matter of retardation, the differences were not great, and they practically disappeared in the second generation. The backwardness of children from foreign descent appeared to be the result of language difficulties and of various conditions of home life.[22] John Haaren, an associate superintendent of

[19] Ibid., p. 410.
[20] Morris Raphael Cohen, A Dreamer's Journey (Boston: Beacon Press, 1949), pp. 70–84.
[21] U.S. Congress, Report of the Immigration Commission (Washington: Government Printing Office, 1911), Vol. II.
[22] Roland P. Falkner, "Immigration and Education," in Paul Monroe, ed., A Cyclopedia of Education, Vol. III (New York: Macmillan Publishing Co., Inc., 1912), pp. 390–396.

schools in New York City, warned against assuming that all immigrant children were culturally deprived. He pointed out that immigrants brought their particular contribution to enrich American civilization, and some of these additions might serve to soften the materalism so characteristic of life here.[23]

Before the advent of Maxwell as New York City's superintendent of schools, immigrant students were put into regular, lower-grade classes. Here, difficulty for the teacher, generally unable to speak the foreign tongue, as well as for the average student was brought about. Maxwell, between 1904 and 1905, instituted "C" classes for non-English-speaking students, "D" classes for slow students about to reach age 14, and "E" classes for late entrants who had the potential of doing several grades' work in a short time.[24] These endeavors marked the first, large-scale public school effort toward Americanizing recently arrived children and the children of immigrants. There was some homogeneity (ethnic segregation) in these classes due essentially to the language factor. One district superintendent, in referring to the separation, wrote that "the Jewish child is more ambitious than the Italian child" and that he found parent cooperation better from the former.[25]

Adult education in the Americanization of immigrants was undertaken by a number of agencies. The International Ladies Garment Workers' Union (providing students and encouragement) in conjunction with the New York City Board of Education (providing buildings and teachers) established 19 English classes between 1918 and 1919.[26] Attrition was high in the evening schools; the long hours of labor, fatigue, the necessity of changing clothes, lack of social life for the students, and the working-shift arrangement (causing attendance in alternate weeks) were factors limiting the success of this institution. But the desire for citizenship and to improve themselves economically kept many an immigrant at the task of getting an education.

At the outset of the 20th century, there was little or no research available on teaching English as a second language, on citizenship education, or on teaching the so-called culturally disadvantaged. There were no national funds available and few states offered a subsidy to towns and cities faced with the problems of immigrant education. But, by 1921, most states that had a substantial foreign-born population had provided facilities for Americanization classes. The greatest accomplishment attributed to the American public school has been the Americanization of hundreds of thousands of newcomers to this country in the late 19th and early 20th centuries.

[23] U.S. Bureau of Education. *Education of the Immigrant* (Washington: Government Printing Office, 1913), p. 19.
[24] Selma C. Berrol, "William Henry Maxwell and a New Educational New York," *History of Education Quarterly*, 8: 222, Summer, 1968.
[25] U.S. Bureau of Education, *Education of the Immigrant*, op. cit., p. 24.
[26] Frank V. Thompson, *Schooling of the Immigrant* (New York: Harper, 1920), p. 107.

In the 1960s, when the problems of economically disadvantaged in-migrants, mainly Negroes and Puerto Ricans, flocking to the cities have challenged every level of educational institutions, reference often is made to the American schools' experience with the immigrant. Irving Kristol has written that, had a conference been held 100 years ago on "The Crisis in Our Cities," it would have described conditions not too different from those in black and Puerto Rican ghettos today.[27] It is, however, fair to say from all evidence that conditions in the city slums were much worse a century ago.

Negroes are different from immigrants—indeed they are among the oldest of Americans. However, the literature about immigrant groups in the 19th and early 20th centuries—in terms of their disadvantaged status—has its counterpart in some of the writings by and about blacks today. Recognizing the racial factor, but not letting it block out everything else, it is Kristol's thesis that the tragedy of the recent, urban Negro is not that he is black or poor, but that he has come rather late into a highly technical and organized society. Writing as an assimilationist (he did not deal with the Black Power or the separatist movement), his prognosis is, on the whole, a sanguine one: that Negroes in large numbers are "making it" by virtue of their own efforts, and they are entitled to assistance from the society that has made them into the new immigrants.

[27] Irving Kristol, "The Negro Today Is Like the Immigrant Yesterday," *New York Times Magazine*, September 11, 1966, p. 50.

Institutional Racism:
The Crucible of Black Identity

JAMES A. GOODMAN

The individual's entry into the accepted roles and statuses of his society is highly complex. Given the nature of American culture, it becomes a task of immense magnitude to chart the specific steps of that journey. With respect to blacks, the social definition of race is a further complicating factor in any effort to unravel the process of identity formation.

Historically, blacks have been included in the general conceptualizations concerning identity development. However, there is growing awareness that the nature of the social patterns in our society have led to differing outcomes with reference to patterns of black and white identity. Specifically, how does discrimination on the individual or group level affect black self-identity? In this context, discrimination should be viewed more as a condition of being acted upon or attacked in the psychosocial sense rather than as ignored or neglected. Being black has many implications for the development of self-perceptions that are not consistently reflected in lower class membership.

Black people have to contend with the normal developmental tasks in addition to the survival factors associated with the fact of inheriting an inferior class status. Segregated housing, schools, and other facilities continually suggest a difference—an unacceptable one of inferiority. Recently, as an explanation for the behavior exhibited by whites towards blacks, the phrase "white racism" has become part of the daily language of a significant portion of the American public. These words join a long list of other shorthand phrases for a very comprehensive set of dysfunctional behaviors.

Racism is any individual or collective act which denies blacks access to positive identity factors in American society. However, it is of limited value to bandy this concept about in an unfocused manner. It would appear to be more useful to relate white racism to specific undesirable societal outcomes in order to provide an analytic as well as corrective frame of reference.

The focus of this discussion will be on the effects of racism in relation to the development of black identity. Black identity as an aspect of human socialization has many dimensions. We propose to look at some of the individual and group dimensions of identity as reflected in the black experience. We are particularly concerned with the experiences black people have within the educational systems of the nation.

An individual's notion of who he is contributes significantly to the development of his response pattern to the institutions of society. Further, the extent to which his notion of self is confirmed or rejected by others will be crucial to his vision of self. Personal identity, which is rooted in the processes of socialization, represents a person's search for relatedness to other individuals, groups, institutions, and practices which are sanctified in a particular cultural context. The manner in which the individual develops his personal identity statement depends both on the conditions for self-realization in the environment and the ability of the individual to perceive these conditions in objective terms. Depending upon the outcome, this may tend to enhance or impede the biological and psychological push from within that involves man's search for identity. When this inner thrust is counteracted, inner conflict may be seen as a function of the degree of awareness that the individual has. If limited alternatives are provided in the environment this conflict is likely to be expressed in "self" directed or "other" directed hostility. In order for an individual to feel a positive sense of selfhood, he must come to believe that the society in which he lives places value on his being.

SELF-IDENTITY

Some Theories

Definitions and theories abound as to what constitutes self-identity. As one begins to carefully scrutinize the definitions in this area, the concept seems to become less specific. Klapp puts it this way:

> Strictly, it includes all things a person may legitimately and reliably say about himself—his status, his name, his personality, his past life. But if his social context is unreliable, it follows that he cannot say anything legitimately and reliably about himself. His statements of identity have no more reliability than a currency which depends upon the willingness of people to recognize and accept it. We feel that we can count on our identity not only because of habit, but because we can count on people responding to it.[1]

Erikson approaches the subject matter of identity by letting the term *identity* speak for itself in a number of connotations. He refers to a conscious sense of individual identity, to an unconscious striving for a continuity of personal character, to a criterion for the silent doings of ego synthesis, and as a maintenance of inner solidarity with a group's ideals and identity.[2] He further evaluates the definition of identity as being a psychoanalytic term as well as a psychosocial one. A distinction is then made between the self and the ego aspects of identity formation. Erikson maintains that identity covers more than what has been called the self— it includes the ego's synthesizing functions which are concerned with the "genetic continuity" of self representation.[3] Ego functions of cognition, integration, defenses, and execution perpetuate and maintain one's "idea" of oneself.

Definitions provided by Sarnoff, McCandless, and Secord illustrate the self aspect of identity in their discussion of self-concept. Self-concept is "the idea one has of oneself." [4] Self-concept involves three components of attitudes toward oneself—the cognitive, affective, and behavioral.[5] The self-concept may be thought of as "a set of expectancies, plus evaluations of the areas or behaviors with reference to which these expectancies are held." [6] Role categories are seen to aid the stability of an individual's self and behavior. Perlman suggests that problems of identity are related to

---

[1] Orrin E. Klapp, *Collective Search for Identity* (New York: Holt, 1969), pp. 5–6.

[2] Erik Erikson, "Identity and the Life Cycle," *Psychological Issues* 1, no. 15 (1959), Monograph 1, p. 102.

[3] Erikson, ibid., pp. 147–149.

[4] Irving Sarnoff, *Personality Dynamics and Development* (New York: Wiley, 1962), p. 142.

[5] Paul Secord and Carl Backman, *Social Psychology* (New York: McGraw-Hill, 1964), p. 579.

[6] Boyd R. McCandless, *Children and Adolescents* (New York: Holt, 1961), p. 174.

some unmanageable or insufferable role difficulty.[7] The affective component of attitudes toward self and evaluation in terms of role expectancies ties in with Freud's references to self-esteem and to the ego's attitudes toward the self.[8]

The concept of identification is a crucial one in the establishment of self-identity. The developing individual incorporates and imitates the behaviors, beliefs, and values of those around him through this process. Parents serve as early models; siblings, peer groups, teachers, friends, and the larger society provide later examples. The individual's final identity is, however, more than any single input into his personality structure. The unity of self reflects the unique individual interpretation within the context of the social process.[9, 10]

Thus, self-identity in this essay will include both self and ego aspects, an idea of oneself that is perpetuated by ego functions. "Self-identity emerges from all those experiences in which a sense of temporary self-diffusion was successfully contained by a renewed and ever more realistic self-definition and social recognition.[11]

Personal and ego identity as described by Erikson are aspects of this self-identity:

> . . . the immediate perception of one's self-sameness and continuity in time; the simultaneous perception of the fact that others recognize one's sameness and continuity. . . . the awareness of the fact that there is selfsameness and continuity to the ego's synthesizing methods and that these methods are effective in safeguarding the sameness and continuity of one's meaning for others.[12]

In sum, self-identity is the relationship of oneself to oneself, to others, and to social institutions. It implies a continuity and sameness within the person (and perception that ego forces are effective in maintaining this) and the sharing of some essential character with others.

Not only does the individual identify with others in society, society also identifies the individual. The maturing individual soon realizes that society evaluates him, in large measure, in terms of his group identifications. Cooley posits the notion of the self as a looking glass with three related dimensions of one's self-concept: "the imagination of our appearance to the other person; the imagination of his judgment of that appearance; and some sort of self-feeling, such as pride or mortification." [13]

---

[7] Helen Harris Perlman, "Identity Problems, Role, and Casework Treatment," *Social Service Review* 37, no. 3 (September 1963).

[8] Erikson, op. cit., p. 147.

[9] George H. Mead, *Mind, Self, and Society* (Chicago: University of Chicago, 1934), Part 3.

[10] Charles H. Cooley, *Human Nature and the Social Order* (Glencoe, Ill.: Free Press, 1956), passim.

[11] Erikson, op. cit., p. 149.

[12] Erikson, ibid., p. 23.

[13] Cooley, op. cit., p. 184.

Self-identity as viewed by Freud and Erikson evolves through successive developmental stages. Conscious, preconscious, and unconscious factors influencing individual growth, experiences in early life that are basic to the individual's later adjustment, social learning in relation to others especially the family, ego capacities of cognition, defenses, integration, and action are all part of this developmental process that affects individual identity.

Every individual is thought to proceed through Freud's stages of psychosexual development (oral, anal, phallic, genital), either successfully or unsuccessfully. Erikson's "primary concern with the continuity of experience necessitates a shift to the function of the ego" [14] beyond these stages of Freud. Erikson rebuilds these phases so that "they lose many of their biosexual implications.[15] He stresses a wider social setting, and he focuses more upon healthy development. Erikson, then, describes eight developmental tasks that should be mastered successfully by the healthy individual. His fifth stage—achieving a sense of identity—when mastered, enables the individual to face the challenges of the adult world. His sense of identity begins to develop at birth and continues until death, but the identity crisis is in adolescence. Successful mastery of every other phase of development influences self-identity. A sense of basic trust, of autonomy, of initiative, of industry precede that of identity; and a sense of intimacy, generativity, and integrity follow. Whatever influences successful or maladaptive solutions to each crisis of development—and specifically in regards to the obtainment of a sense of identity—we know that the individual and his environment interact in all stages of the individual's development.

Certain factors influencing adaptive patterns in an individual's development are applicable to this particular subject. Forces within the individual respond to outside influences—especially those of other persons. As an infant the child's contact is generally with his family, primarily the mother. The child's experience with his environment will result in his perception of the world as basically comforting and secure or as basically hostile and fearful. What the child will "dare" in terms of new experiences will be much molded by his earlier experience. His own worth and ability is reflected by reactions of others toward him. While many authors indicate that the foundation of character is established by five years of age and that disordered relationships early in life may leave a nearly ineradicable scar, this writer agrees with Allport in his view that the child who "enjoys a normal affiliative groundwork" has established foundations of character only in the sense that he is then "free to become." [16] Erikson also has a more optimistic view of human growth as he emphasizes task resolutions throughout the life of the individual.

[14] Henry Maier, *Three Theories of Child Development* (New York: Harper & Row, 1965), p. 17.
[15] Maier, ibid., p. 17.
[16] Gordon Allport, *Becoming* (New Haven: Yale University, 1955), p. 33.

In sum, then, the process of identity formation in Erikson's formulation emerges as an evolving configuration:

> . . . it is a configuration gradually integrating constitutional givens, idiosyncratic libidinal needs, favored capacities, significant identifications, effective defenses, successful sublimations, and consistent roles.[17]

The interplay between the individual and his family as well as the larger society should permit the individual to establish a self-identity recognized mutually by that individual and his society.

Obviously, individuals are rewarded differentially on the basis of their memberships in various groups. Cultural patterns in the United States, for example, have long provided a basis for blacks to be evaluated as being different from, and outside of, the norms of society. Identity formation for blacks, with respect to the larger society, is rooted in a societal statement of scorn and disparagement. The black individual is taught that his selfhood must articulate a different imposed notion of who he is. Therefore, the black individual who identifies with the predominant cultural values risks accepting and ritualizing the very behaviors which place limits on what he may become.

In this country the black individual is given a consistent image of who he is by white society; black skin means that he is inferior and not quite human. The black individual comes to evaluate himself in the context of his significant holding groups with the knowledge that racial and ethnic groupings constitute the primary limits of his identity. The influence of membership in the black group, for instance, supersedes the consequences of memberships in all other groups.

Several other theories of socialization provide additional insight into the complex identity-formation processes. The contributions of learning theory are of particular usefulness to this discussion.

Learning Theory and Identity Development

Learning theory in relation to the development of self-identity is limited here primarily to the formulations of Robert Sears; his formulations have utilized analytic concepts and complement theories of psychoanalysis and ego psychology. "From the learning point of view, the self-concept is the apex—the culmination of all the social and personal experiences the child has had." [18] Conditioning and instrumental learning, primary and secondary generalization, reward and punishment, motives and drives, expectancies and probabilities, and conflicts all are involved in establishing identity. The satisfactions of fears experienced by the individual (throughout his total life experience—but most importantly in current reality) develop the framework for individual identity.

[17] Erikson, op. cit., p. 116.
[18] McCandless, op. cit., p. 172.

Environment shapes behavior; stress is placed upon parental child-rearing practices. Behavior is seen as self-motivated by its tension-reduction effect: every unit of behavior preceding a goal achieves a reinforcement potential. Primary drives are only instrumental for the beginning of behavior in a social world—socially learned (secondary motivational) systems eventually motivate all behavior. Since all behavior represents reinforced actions, development is viewed as a training process. Parents are seen as the most important reinforcing agents; Sears maintains that every "parent could do better if he knew better." [19] Parents must then have access to reinforcement procedures that would contribute to healthy development. Sears speaks also of the effect of learning beyond the family upon the socializing of the child. The individual then within a learning theory framework, would gain self-identity through reinforcement of behavior by others.

In addition, Sears mentions that identification influences behavior, which starts with the mother-child relationship and extends to others as the child becomes older. Identification rests neither upon trial-and-error nor child-rearing efforts—it evolves from the childs' own role playing. The child selects available others as models and imitates them. Reinforcement comes through recognition received from others for imitating and personal satisfaction in seeing the actions of others in one's own behavior.

Self-identity can then arise from satisfactions in perceiving of oneself, as behaving as another, and from responding to the expectations of behavior as conveyed by others.

Although Sears focuses much upon behavior, effective identity involves cognitive, affective, and action components. Self-identity also implies a continuity of identity as well as an awareness of (or idea of) identity. Therefore, Erikson's formulations including both ego and self aspects appear to this writer to integrate learning and analytic theories to successfully designate the process and definition of self-identity.

Unfortunately, the process of incorporating the societal statements about self and self-potential begin very early. Allport maintains that a child is capable of a sense of ethnic group identification as early as the age of five.[20] In a fairly extensive study of 253 black children between the ages of three and seven, Clark and Clark maintain that the period between four and five years of age may be the critical period in the development and outlining of racial attitudes towards oneself and others. These researchers posit: "At these ages these subjects appear to be reacting more uncritically in a definite structuring of attitudes which conforms with the accepted racial values and mores of the larger environment." [21]

[19] Maier, op. cit., p. 150.
[20] Gordon Allport, *The Nature of Prejudice* (Garden City: Doubleday, 1958), pp. 28–29.
[21] K. B. Clark and M. P. Clark, "Racial Identification and Preferences in Negro Children," T. M. Newcomb and E. L. Hartley, eds., *Readings in Social Psychology* (New York: Holt, 1947), pp. 169–178.

DEVELOPMENT OF BLACK IDENTITY

The black individual's concern with self-identity, unlike that of his white counterpart, is supposedly emotionally laden in all of its aspects. As Proshansky and Newton put it:

> . . . the young child acquires value-laden racial labels and fragments of popular stereotypes to describe his own and other racial and ethnic groups. Both Negro and white children learn to associate Negro with "dirty," "bad," and "ugly," and white with "clean," "nice," and "good." For the Negro child, these emotionally charged descriptions and judgments operate to establish the white group as vastly superior to his own racial group.[22]

Identification with the majority culture, it would seem, is not a method of survival for black people. At best it suggests accommodation to the status quo. It would appear that identification with the aggressor is a threat to healthy black self-identity.

A balanced view of self is the positive outcome of having access to a wide range of roles. The individual with this type of identity knows himself to be a full-fledged member of the communal culture. For blacks, however, the limited range of available roles affects the development of positive self-identity in direct relationship to the individual's reliance upon those cultural symbols which inevitably place him at odds with the reality associated with his blackness. In the Eriksonian model, identity versus identity diffusion is the choice to make when childhood proper comes to an end and youth begins. Growing and developing young people are then primarily concerned with attempts at consolidating their social roles. They are sometimes morbidly, often curiously preoccupied with what they appear to be in the eyes of others as compared with what they feel they are.[23]

It is within this struggle for self-acceptance that the black individual fares badly; the eyes of whites reflect back a nonexistent or limited sense of cultural continuity. The "old country" is stripped of all validity in terms that are meaningful to him. He has therefore found it convenient to define himself in terms that are alien to his personal frame of reference; his selfhood is related to a paradoxical statement: in order for black identity to have meaning it must exist only as a reaction to white identity.

The black father, the black mother—the sacred hosts of all black progeny—give mute testimony to the progression of genius shunted into meaningless and repetitive acts of mediocrity. These acts, these obscenities, give rise to the general cultural statement that blacks are completely incapable of self-realization outside the context of the white-oriented frame

[22] H. Proshansky and P. Newton, "The Nature and Meaning of Negro Self-Identity," M. Deutsch et al., eds., *Social Class, Race and Psychological Development* (New York: Holt, 1968), p. 186.
[23] David J. De Levita, *The Concept of Identity* (New York: Basic Books, 1965), p. 62.

of reference. This argument suggests that the peculiarities of the black subculture constitute a variant of the general societal pattern of identity development. Logically, however, one would expect that the process of black socialization would produce patterns of identity substantially different from those associated with whites.

Although the data concerning changing patterns of black identity are not fully available, it appears that blacks have begun to reject imposed definitions of self. Individual black identity thereby becomes a potent force in black group consciousness. Individuals begin to relate their selfhood to the blackness variable as a statement of group unity and cohesiveness. Arnold Rose defines group identification as a conscious recognition that one is a member of a group with a positive evaluation accorded such membership.[24] This identification or sense of unity in a minority group is created by pressure from outside the group.

In the instance of blacks, the myriad of negative symbols conjured up by the white society served as the locus for developing a different statement of selfhood. The concept that "black is beautiful" is merely the overt manifestation of the deeper process of trying on new, and previously denied, role patterns. The research by the Clarks makes it very clear that black youngsters in the past did not consider black as being beautiful. This research was conducted prior to the beginning of what is commonly referred to as the black revolution. The period of the sixties has seen an explosion of black pride which will have significance for the future development of black identity.

The future development of notions of selfhood by blacks will be more than a function of the black is beautiful phenomenon. However, as indicated earlier, identity is an outcome of an interactional process between the individual and society. The social process of confirming the black individual in society is enhanced in the primary social institutions of the society. Billingsley states:

> Racism is deeply imbedded within the institutional fabric of American society. All the major institutions including the political, economic, educational, social, and others have systematically excluded the Negro people in varying degrees from equal participation in the rewards of these institutions. None of them works as effectively in meeting the needs of Negro families as they do white families. The keys to the enhancement of Negro family and community life are therefore institutional keys.[25]

Obviously, the quality and function of social institutions can have impact upon the nature of black selfhood. If these outcomes are compatible with black societal prerequisites for survival as a viable cultural entity, there is no argument. It is when the institutional arrangements are such

[24] Arnold Rose, *Sociology: The Study of Human Relations* (New York: Knopf, 1965), p. 684.

[25] Andrew Billingsley, *Black Families in White America* (Englewood Cliffs, N.J.: Prentice-Hall, 1968), p. 152.

that black people have limited access to them, or upon relating to them find that they impede the development of positive black identity, that black social concern develops. This concern has to be translated into acts designed to alter the negative impact these institutions have on the growth and development of black identity.

It is quite clear that the institutional advantages enjoyed by whites create the general cultural assumption that blacks constitute a lower socio-economic group which is monolithic in character. This factor probably contributes most significantly to the white community's attitudes that it is superior to the black community in all areas. This form of racism, when translated into the historical quality of contacts between blacks and whites, also serves to reinforce the black individual's notions of personal and community inferiority.

Although it is true that blacks are more likely to be afflicted with the ills of poverty and low socioeconomic status than whites, it is equally true that blacks learn to cope in highly unique ways. Moreover, the effect of black people's perception of their class position as this affects identity has not been made clear. The basic question is: how can a wider range of coping strategies be provided while racist practices solidify the barriers against entry into the institutional life of the country? This question becomes the focal point for various strategies to be posed in the process of liberating blacks from the vortex of an identity rooted in the American way of life. For example, should blacks try to change the total society? Perhaps the focus should be upon key institutional practices. Because blacks are a diverse people, their responses to institutional racism will likely reflect this diversity.

Himes illustrates the nature of this issue for some:

> In the case of lower-class Negroes, the significant institutional precondi-
> tions include, among others, color segregation, material discrimination, in-
> ferior or collateral social status, disparaging social evaluation, chronic social
> frustrations, and a substantially distinct subculture. From socialization from
> such preconditions, the individual emerges as a functioning member of
> his social world. Certain dimensions of the functional adjustment to his
> effective social world, however, constitute cultural deprivation in terms
> of the standards and demands of the larger world from which he is more
> or less excluded.[26]

EDUCATIONAL INSTITUTIONS AND
BLACK SELF-CONCEPT

The major institution of socialization in this society in addition to the family is education. In many ways the family has given responsibility for the supervision of the child's development to the school. It is clear, there-

[26] Joseph G. Himes, "Some Work-Related Cultural Deprivations of Lower-Class Negro Youths," Louis A. Ferman et al., eds., *Poverty in America* (Ann Arbor: University of Michigan, 1965), pp. 384–385.

fore, that at least the school and the home share responsibility in varying degrees for the socialization of the child. As McNeil views it:

> The terms "education" and "socialization" should be considered synonymous in our society, for education is the primary means of socializing all children after they reach the age of five. Our children now spend the bulk of their time in groups of about 30 strange peers dominated by a professional teacher in a building specially erected for that purpose. This educational system socializes children by teaching them the knowledge and intellectual skills essential to full participation in society as well as the mores and habits of its members.[27]

Education must, therefore, reflect the nature of the total society if it is to prepare all individuals to live in their effective social worlds. This formulation implies an egalitarian approach within the educational delivery system. However, all segments of the population in the United States have never received the same quality of education. It is only recently that this inequality has been viewed as problematic. For a long time, Americans were content with the doctrine of "separate but equal" educational facilities for that part of its population considered inferior—the blacks. Because blacks were considered inferior, and therefore unteachable, it was thought that admitting them to white schools would lower the quality of education received by the whites. As a consequence of this type of thinking, separate schools for blacks were established; there was, however, limited concern for the quality of these schools. Since the school system in this country is undeniably an arm of the government, political pressure is the reason for each school being as it was and is now—good or bad.[28]

In 1954 the Supreme Court decided that separate but equal educational facilities were unconstitutional, and ordered the schools to desegregate. This decision reflected a growing awareness that educational goals for blacks were not being achieved in the facilities allocated to them. In a majority of cases their potential has not been realized because of environmental factors, such as family and neighborhood deprivation, differences in cultural tradition, and economic impoverishment.[29]

Educators have kept blacks from realizing their potential by assuming that they cannot expect much of them and by treating them condescendingly. The children find it natural and automatic to accept the school's structural inadequacies and to incorporate them, as it were, into their notions of self. Many of these youngsters actually begin to view themselves as biologically inferior to whites.[30]

[27] Elton B. McNeil, *Human Socialization* (Belmont, Calif.: Brooks/Cole, 1969), p. 138.
[28] Lydia Pulsipher, "The American School: A Legitimate Instrument for Social Change," *School and Society* 96 (March 30, 1968), p. 201.
[29] Regina Barnes, "Higher Horizons," *Clearing House* 40 (October 1965), p. 113.
[30] Jonathan Kozol, "Halls of Darkness: In the Ghetto Schools," *Harvard Educational Review* 37 (Summer 1967), p. 393.

More people gradually have come to accept the *ideal* of educational equality for all and to realize that our school system must compensate with a saturation of services that will rescue the culturally different (black) youngsters emotionally, provide them with direction, and above all, inculcate skills enabling them to function successfully both academically and vocationally.[31] But de facto segregation continues to exist. Because segregated schools often reflect patterns of segregated housing, many people feel that the schools cannot do anything unless whites and blacks are geographically integrated. Others suggest various bussing plans as a means of achieving quality education for all youngsters.

In the North, much of the effort of the civil rights movement has been directed toward the elimination of de facto school segregation through some form of modification in the traditional patterns of school districting. Implicit in the activities designed to alter these traditional patterns is the assumption that integrated education produces quality education for students without regard to their racial backgrounds. As Young puts it:

> . . . with integration Negroes will benefit from a better educational system, better materials, facilities, and teachers. But as I see it, there are precious benefits for both whites and Negroes. I do not believe education can be absolutely first rate without integration. To the extent that people say that integration of the schools has no relationship to the quality of education, they are, in fact, saying that separate but equal education is valid.[32]

A counter argument, of course, is that schools in all areas of the community should be brought to a single standard of excellence. Youngsters would then receive quality education without respect to their place of residence. On this point, however, Clark argues that, "the goals of integration and quality education must be sought together; they are interdependent. One is not possible without the other." [33] The validity of either argument has to be evaluated in terms of the functions of education. The mere presence of blacks and whites in the same classroom is not a guarantee that change will occur in the educational content provided. Stated differently, integration cannot of itself solve the problems associated with racial isolation. Integrated schools can, however, provide the opportunity for black and white youngsters alike to develop equal status contacts which alone can diminish the effectiveness of racially created antagonisms and distance producing behaviors.

From the vantage point of white society, the primary function of education is the maintenance of white culture. Ostrom makes the point in this manner:

---

[31] Ibid., p. 393.

[32] Whitney M. Young, Jr., *To Be Equal* (New York: McGraw-Hill, 1964), p. 110.

[33] Kenneth B. Clark, *Dark Ghetto: Dilemmas of Social Power* (New York: Harper & Row, 1965), p. 117.

Man's capacity to learn, to organize learning in symbolic forms, to communicate this learning as knowledge to other members of the species and to act on the basis of learning or knowledge is the source of all cultural phenomena. . . . Any culture and the civilization based upon that culture must depend upon the ability of the civilization to articulate and transmit its learning as semiautonomous, cognitive systems. These represent the accumulated knowledge in every field of inquiry and comprise the subject matter in all education. This is what we mean when we speak of the school's responsibility in transmitting a cultural heritage.[34]

Some Underlying Values and Assumptions

If there is ever going to be more general agreement about what is to happen when youngsters come together in designated educational space, the teaching content and methodology must not be based on the assumption that the white middle-class subculture is better than the black subculture. At best, each subculture is functional to the needs of the respective groups. The white-dominated educational system must recognize the particularized needs of the black student that evolve from the black subculture which previously has been ignored in planning educational activities. Ornstein [35] has suggested that the beginning of a solution is to do away with the strictly middle-class standards of the school. He feels that these standards do more harm than good in lower class schools.

The educational system must accept the disadvantaged on their own terms and work to achieve its goals by serving as an ego-supporting, meaningful institution which encourages diversity. This would enable the disadvantaged to become their best possible selves by utilizing their culture, not by trying to change it.

Basically, what is indicated for the educational system is the provision of a learning opportunity for black youngsters to gain a positive social identity. Social identity, in this context, refers to the expression of selfhood which is an external manifestation of the black individual's perception of who he is— of allowable social roles. In discussing this aspect of self we must be mindful that it does not contain the total statement of the individual's integrity. There are, as we suggested earlier, other aspects of identity. The holistic quality of personal identity is of great significance in relation to blacks because of the negative cultural statements regarding the black presence in the society. Society, which is generally benign toward people, deprives blacks of man's most fundamental right; that of self-determination through creative activity. This is only possible if the individual is accorded dignity so that he is free to make choices over a wide expanse of opportunities.

Schools, as primary agents of socialization, must help black youngsters

---

[34] Vincent Ostrom, "Education and Politics," B. Henry Nelson, ed., *Social Forces Influencing American Education* (Chicago: National Society for the Study of Education, 1961), pp. 10–12. Distributed by the University of Chicago Press.

[35] Allen Ornstein, "Reaching the Disadvantaged," *School and Society* 96 (March 30, 1968), p. 215.

attain a positive view of self at the internal level of identity. This inner quality of identity is the outcome of the responses to the cultural environment. This aspect of personal identity is highly critical; black inner identity is a result of the many responses to the cultural statement of black group identity.

Apart from its broad function of transmitting culture in a formal manner, education has a role in influencing the course of social change; determining the content of culture for future generations of students is of equal importance. There has to be greater recognition that the school is very much a part of society and must be criticized for not concerning itself with being implicated in the major social problems of our society. As a part of society, the school has been involved in discriminatory practices. It has perpetuated the racism which fostered segregation in all aspects of American life, including housing. When the courts order the schools to remedy the consequences of housing patterns, they are actually directing schools to make amends for past acts of commission and omission which have culminated in the ghettoization of American blacks.

Black schools are academically inferior because they reflect the cumulative inferiority of segregated education and the inevitable problems of a racist, segregated society which imposes upon lower-status individuals a debilitating, humanly destructive form of public education, both in the South and the North. Black schools are inferior because our society persists in not finding the commitment or the resources to provide high quality education for powerless black youngsters—because associated with this rejection, exclusion, and the dehumanizing aspects of racism, is the inevitable lowering of morale in any lower-status institution. Lower-status schools present crises in self-respect, nagging and gnawing feelings of inferiority, or deep and disturbing questions related to self-hatred. These types of schools add to the black youngster's rejection of self. Proshansky and Newton report empirical evidence that shows this tendency toward self-rejection:

> . . . Given a choice, a majority of both Negro and white children tend to choose a white doll in preference to a Negro one (Clark and Clark, 1947; Stevenson and Steward, 1958; Radke and Trager, 1950; Goodman, 1952; Morland, 1962; Landreth and Johnson, 1953). In a more recent study of 407 young children, Morland (1962) found that 60 percent of the Negro children, but only 10 percent of the white children, preferred to play with children of the other race; in comparison, 18 percent of the Negro children and 72 percent of the white children preferred playmates of their own race.[36]

These data and the attendant conclusions are bolstered by the fact that large numbers of Negroes use products which are designed to make them into imitation whites. In nearly all popular black magazines one encounters adver-

[36] Proshansky and Newton, op. cit., p. 187.

tisements for skin creams, bleaches, pomades, and other compounds designed to transform blacks into an acceptable white facsimile. This argument is not designed to suggest that the school is fully responsible for this set of circumstances. The school, however, continues to create the illusion that only middle-class white norms of behavior are acceptable. Therefore, the black child is forced to abandon his identity if he is to be rewarded by society. The white individual does not go unscarred in this process. Clark gives the following reasons why he also considers white schools inferior:

1. Education has become ruthlessly competitive and anxiety-producing, in which the possibility of empathy and the use of superior intelligence as a social trust are excluded from the educational process.
2. They have facilitated the reduction of the educational process to a level of content retention required for the necessary scores on college boards.
3. They have permitted elementary and secondary schools to become contaminated by and organized in terms of the educationally irrelevant factors of race and economic status.
4. They have watched in silence the creeping blight of our cities and the spawning of Negro ghettos.
5. They have remained detached and non-relevant to this major domestic issue of our time.[37]

It is clear that education performs a major socializing function in society, and that this is one of its primary functions. We may look to the schools to teach children reading, writing, and arithmetic, but we must admit that we also look to the schools for the inculcation of a particular civic culture. The schools are expected to instill a set of normative values which support, not challenge, the existing societal values.[38]

If, as we posit in our thesis, the normative values which the schools are expected to instill are middle-class and white-oriented, then schools socialize black youngsters into the existing societal values which are rooted in racism. The fact that the American educational delivery system has been designed for the youngsters of the white middle-class sector of America forces the black youngster to see himself as unimportant and therefore excluded. The black experience as part of the cultural statement emanating from the pluralistic nature of American society is conspicuous by its absence from the educational process. Black students, from kindergarten to graduate school, are expected to engage psychologically, culturally, and socially in an endeavor which is ostensibly designed for the purpose of broadening their horizons and providing them proper knowledge to better relate to the world. In truth, educa-

[37] Kenneth B. Clark, "Higher Education for Negroes: Challenge and Prospects," *Journal of Negro Education* 36 (Summer 1967), p. 200.

[38] Charles V. Hamilton, "Education in the Black Community: An Examination of the Realities," *Freedomways* 8 (Fall 1968), p. 319.

tional enterprises are unaccepting and essentially rejecting of the social and cultural backgrounds of black people.

Class and Family Considerations

Schools must serve as a bridge between the lower-class black family and the demands of potentially hostile white institutions. The family is consistently ascribed by most writers to be a major source of self-identification. The question arises: how does the identification process in lower-class black families differ from the largely white middle-class family?

With respect to class differences, the problem of just who is in the lower class needs clarification. For our purposes, Gans' and Miller's description of the lower-class subculture will be used.[39] There is disagreement not only about who is in the middle class, but also in regard to the values, child-rearing practices, and behavior which can rightfully be attributed to it.

Two basic views and sources of research stand out in regard to values. Writers such as W. Miller, L. Hyman, A. Davis, L. Empry, and O. Lewis indicate that the lower-class culture has a stable tradition with integrity of its own.[40] Others such as Rodman, Parsons, and Merton refer to the common value system in all of society.[41] Rodman talks about a lower-class value stretch and concludes that the lower class does share the values of the overall society, but by adapting to his circumstances, the lower-class person holds these values less strongly and also develops new values unique to the lower class. Recent writing has maintained that lower-class values are concerned:

1. with avoiding trouble, with toughness, smartness, excitement, fate, and autonomy
2. with lower levels of aspiration
3. with high education, but more in terms of improved income rather than satisfaction in work accomplished
4. with similar desires for leisure time and security
5. with adapting values to deprived circumstances [42]

Child-rearing practices of the lower class also continue to be questioned. However, lower-class families are viewed as:

1. more involved in punishment during toilet training
2. expecting lower educational achievements of their children

[39] Herbert J. Gans, "Subculture and Class," *Poverty in America*, Ferman et al., eds. (Ann Arbor: University of Michigan, 1965), pp. 302–311. See also: Walter Miller, as quoted in "Implications of Urban Low-Class Culture for Social Work," *Social Service Review* (September 1959), p. 230.

[40] See review in Hyman Rodman, "The Lower Class Value Stretch," *Poverty in America*, op. cit., pp. 270–285.

[41] Rodman, ibid., p. 270–285.

[42] W. Miller, op. cit., pp. 219–236. See also: "Focal Concerns of Lower-Class Culture," in *Poverty in America*, op. cit., pp. 261–270; L. Hyman and A. Davis, in *Poverty in America*, p. 273; Lola Irelan, ed., *Low Income Life Styles* (Washington, D.C.: H.E.W., Div. of Research, 1966), pp. 6–7.

3. more concerned with respectable behavior in children—obedience, neatness, and cleanliness—rather than developing self-reliance and independence
4. attuned primarily to maintenance functions
5. rigid and oriented to discipline in terms of roles and parent-child relations [43]

Lower-class behavior in contrast to middle-class behavior is said to be:

1. composed of more hostility, tension, and aggression
2. segregated as to sexes
3. more intolerant and authoritarian
4. given to resignation and fatalism
5. more prone to action
6. present rather than future-oriented
7. productive of more illegitimate birth—this situation is not condoned but is more prevalent in lower-class families
8. in a state of alienation—having feelings of powerlessness, meaninglessness, anomia, and isolation [44]

Family structure in the lower class is described as:

1. primarily female-based
2. having patterns of serial marriages
3. role of the male is marginal
4. emphasizing peer group relationships—grouped by age and sex
5. higher evaluation of female than male role
6. differing from both the working class, with its family-circle orientation (both parents and relatives) and the middle class, with participation in family and the larger society, by its (lower class) focus upon the mother and female relatives [45]

Although lower-class families often have a good deal of concern for one another, an ability to share, and less insistent valuation on conformity, achievement, and "success"; they often lack opportunities to expand their experiences. This lack of opportunity extends into the educational context. Levine sees the ineffectiveness of the school in teaching lower-class (black)

[43] Lola Irelan, op. cit., pp. 15–31. See also: R. Havighurst and A. Davis, "A Comparison of the Chicago and Harvard Studies of Social Class Differences in Child Rearing," *American Sociological Review* 20 (August 1955), pp. 438–442; E. Herzog, "Some Assumptions About the Poor," *Social Service Review* 37, no. 4 (December 1963), pp. 389–401.
[44] Herzog, op. cit., pp. 389–401; Irelan, op. cit., pp. 1–26; J. Pakter, "Out of Wedlock Births in New York City," *American Journal of Public Health* 51, no. 5 (May 1961), pp. 683–697.
[45] W. Miller, "Implications of Urban Low-Class Culture for Social Work," and *Poverty in America*, op. cit.; Herzog, op. cit. See also: "Is There a Breakdown of the Negro Family?" *Social Work* (February 1966), reprint from Anti-Defamation League of B'nai B'rith, New York; Gans, *Poverty in America*, op. cit., pp. 302–311.

youth as deriving not so much from its commitment to values which are foreign to the youth, as from its failure to provide the type of environment which would reinforce their groping and half-hearted attempts to live up to these goals.[46]

Clearly, the black individual's behavior in families is closely structured by adaptation to deprivation and lack of opportunity. Self-evaluation would obviously demonstrate lower-class categories. Lack of economic security, improper nutrition, poor housing, and less adequate clothing often produce and reflect a lowered self-image in comparison to the larger society.

Family feeling of powerlessness, fatalism, and fear of planning can limit individual goal-seeking. The middle-class child can more easily draw upon models from the school, from occupations other than [sic] the relatively isolated lower-class black child.

In relation to Erikson's formulations, one finds the black child at a disadvantage because the economic insecurity of his home often does not enable him to develop an adequate sense of societal trust. He is also less likely to develop a sense of autonomy and initiative because lower-class black families often have ambivalent attitudes toward child independence and fewer opportunities. More emphasis is placed on luck within the black family because a world controlled by fate that produces failure is often perceived.

Difficulties experienced in mastering each of these earlier stages also make self-identity a more complex task. Obviously, many lower-class black families can and do succeed in aiding the child to successfully master these phases of development. Ausubel has emphasized that "the consequences of membership in a stigmatized racial group can be cushioned in part by a foundation of intrinsic self-esteem established in the home." [47] However, lower-class black families (in common with all blacks) that have to overcome deprivations of poverty plus those of racism, do have the momentous task of aiding the child to establish a positive and healthy self-identity.

Because the school is such an integral part of society, because it places people in the reward system, it must develop the social as well as the individual man. The current concern with education of the culturally different (black) child is to make education relevant to his needs as an individual and as a social being.

[46] Daniel Levine, "Cultural Diffraction in the Social System of the Low Income School," *School and Society* 96 (March 20, 1968), p. 206.

[47] D. P. Ausubel, "Ego Development Among Segregated Negro Children," *Mental Hygiene* 42 (1958), p. 368.

D. Educational Systems and Social Structure

Equality of Educational Opportunity (The Coleman Report)

U.S. OFFICE OF EDUCATION

The great majority of American children attend schools that are largely segregated—that is, where almost all of their fellow students are of the same racial background as they are. Among minority groups, Negroes are by far the most segregated. Taking all groups, however, white children are most segregated. Almost 80 percent of all white pupils in 1st grade and 12th grade attend schools that are from 90 percent to 100 percent white. And 97 percent at grade 1, and 99 percent at grade 12, attend schools that are 50 percent or more white.

For Negro pupils, segregation is more nearly complete in the South (as it is for whites also), but it is extensive also in all the other regions where the Negro population is concentrated: the urban North, Midwest, and West.

More than 65 percent of all Negro pupils in the 1st grade attend schools that are between 90 and 100 percent Negro. And 87 percent at grade 1, and 66 percent at grade 12, attend schools that are 50 percent or more Negro. In the South, most students attend schools that are 100 percent white or Negro.

The same pattern of segregation holds, though not quite so strongly, for the teachers of Negro and white students. For the Nation as a whole the average Negro elementary pupil attends a school in which 65 percent of the teachers are Negro; the average white elementary pupil attends a school in which 97 percent of the teachers are white. White teachers are more predominant at the secondary level, where the corresponding figures are 59 and 97 percent. The racial matching of teachers is most pronounced in the South, where by tradition it has been complete. On a nationwide basis, in cases where the races of pupils and teachers are not matched, the trend is all in one direction: white teachers teach Negro children but Negro teachers seldom teach white children; just as, in the schools, integration consists primarily of a minority of Negro pupils in predominantly white schools but almost never of a few whites in largely Negro schools.

In its desegregation decision of 1954, the Supreme Court held that separate schools for Negro and white children are inherently unequal. This survey finds that, when measured by that yardstick, American public education remains largely unequal in most regions of the country, including all those where Negroes form any significant proportion of the population. Obviously,

FROM the Summary Report of the Survey, *Equality of Educational Opportunity*, U.S. Department of Health, Education, and Welfare (Washington, D.C.: U.S. Government Printing Office, 1966).

however, that is not the only yardstick. The next section of the summary describes other characteristics by means of which equality of educational opportunity may be appraised.

The Schools and Their Characteristics

The school environment of a child consists of many elements, ranging from the desk he sits at to the child who sits next to him, and including the teacher who stands at the front of his class. A statistical survey can give only fragmentary evidence of this environment.

Great collections of numbers such as are found in these pages—totals and averages and percentages—blur and obscure rather than sharpen and illuminate the range of variation they represent. If one reads, for example, that the average annual income per person in the State of Maryland is $3,000, there is a tendency to picture an average person living in moderate circumstances in a middle-class neighborhood holding an ordinary job. But that number represents at the upper end millionaires, and at the lower end the unemployed, the pensioners, the charwomen. Thus the $3,000 average income should somehow bring to mind the tycoon and the tramp, the showcase and the shack, as well as the average man in the average house.

So, too, in reading these statistics on education, one must picture the child whose school has every conceivable facility that is believed to enhance the educational process, whose teachers may be particularly gifted and well educated, and whose home and total neighborhood are themselves powerful contributors to his education and growth. And one might picture the child in a dismal tenement area who may come hungry to an ancient, dirty building that is badly ventilated, poorly lighted, overcrowded, understaffed, and without sufficient textbooks.

Statistics, too, must deal with one thing at a time, and cumulative effects tend to be lost in them. Having a teacher without a college degree indicates an element of disadvantage, but in the concrete situation, a child may be taught by a teacher who is not only without a degree but who has grown up and received his schooling in the local community, who has never been out of the State, who has a 10th grade vocabulary, and who shares the local community's attitudes.

One must also be aware of the relative importance of a certain kind of thing to a certain kind of person. Just as a loaf of bread means more to a starving man than to a sated one, so one very fine textbook or, better, one very able teacher, may mean far more to a deprived child than to one who already has several of both.

Finally, it should be borne in mind that in cases where Negroes in the South receive unequal treatment, the significance in terms of actual numbers of individuals involved is very great, since 54 percent of the Negro population of school-going age, or approximately 3,200,000 children, live in that region.

All of the findings reported in this section of the summary are based on responses to questionnaires filled out by public school teachers, principals, district school superintendents, and pupils. The data were gathered in September and October of 1965 from 4,000 public schools. All teachers, principals, and district superintendents in these schools participated, as did all pupils in the 3d, 6th, 9th, and 12th grades. First grade pupils in half the schools participated. More than 645,000 pupils in all were involved in the survey. About 30 percent of the schools selected for the survey did not participate; an analysis of the nonparticipating schools indicated that their inclusion would not have significantly altered the results of the survey. The participation rates were: in the metropolitan North and West 72 percent, metropolitan South and Southwest 65 percent, nonmetropolitan North and West 82 percent, nonmetropolitan South and Southwest 61 percent.

All the statistics on the physical facilities of the schools and the academic and extracurricular programs are based on information provided by the teachers and administrators. They also provided information about their own education, experience, and philosophy of education, and described as they see them the socioeconomic characteristics of the neighborhoods served by their schools.

The statistics having to do with the pupils' personal socioeconomic background, level of education of their parents, and certain items in their homes (such as encyclopedias, daily newspapers, etc.) are based on pupil responses to questionnaires. The pupils also answered questions about their academic aspirations and their attitudes toward staying in school.

All personal and school data were confidential and for statistical purposes only; the questionnaires were collected without the names or other personal identification of the respondents.

Data for Negro and white children are classified by whether the schools are in metropolitan areas or not. The definition of a metropolitan area is the one commonly used by Government agencies: a city of over 50,000 inhabitants including its suburbs. All other schools in small cities, towns, or rural areas are referred to as nonmetropolitan schools.

Finally, data for Negro and white children are classified by geographical regions. For metropolitan schools there are usually five regions defined as follows:

Northeast—(Using 1960 census data, this region contains about 16 percent of all Negro children in the Nation and 20 percent of all white children age 5 to 19).

Midwest—(containing 16 percent of Negro and 19 percent of white children age 5 to 19).

South—(containing 27 percent of Negro and 14 percent of white children age 5 to 19).

Southwest—(containing 4 percent of Negro and 3 percent of white children age 5 to 19).

West—(containing 4 percent of Negro and 11 percent of white children age 5 to 19).

The nonmetropolitan schools are usually classified into only three regions:

South—(containing 27 percent of Negro and 14 percent of white children age 5 to 19).
Southwest—(containing 4 percent of Negro and 2 percent of white children age 5 to 19).
North and West—all States not in the South and Southwest (containing 2 percent of Negro and 17 percent of white children age 5 to 19).

Data for minority groups other than Negroes are presented only on a nationwide basis because there were not sufficient cases to warrant a breakdown by regions.

Facilities

For the Nation as a whole white children attend elementary schools with a smaller average number of pupils per room (29) than do any of the minorities (which range from 30 to 33). In some regions the nationwide pattern is reversed: in the nonmetropolitan North and West and Southwest for example, there is a smaller average number of pupils per room for Negroes than for whites.

Secondary school whites have a smaller average number of pupils per room than minorities, except Indians. Looking at the regional breakdown, however, one finds much more striking differences than the national average would suggest: in the metropolitan Midwest, for example, the average Negro has 54 pupils per room—probably reflecting considerable frequency of double sessions—compared with 33 per room for whites. (Nationally, at the high school level the average white has one teacher for every 22 students and the average Negro has one for every 26 students.)

It is thus apparent that the tables must be studied carefully, with special attention paid to the regional breakdowns, which often provide more meaningful information than do the nationwide averages. Such careful study will reveal that there is not a wholly consistent pattern—that is, minorities are not at a disadvantage in every item listed—but that there are nevertheless some definite and systematic directions of differences. Nationally, Negro pupils have fewer of some of the facilities that seem most related to academic achievement: they have less access to physics, chemistry, and language laboratories; there are fewer books per pupil in their libraries; their textbooks are less often in sufficient supply. To the extent that physical facilities are important to learning, such items appear to be more relevant than some others, such as cafeterias, in which minority groups are at an advantage.

Usually greater than the majority-minority differences, however, are the regional differences. For example, 95 percent of Negro and 80 percent of white high school students in the metropolitan Far West attend schools with language laboratories, compared with 48 percent and 72 percent respectively, in the metropolitan South, in spite of the fact that a higher percentage of Southern schools are less than 20 years old.

Finally, it must always be remembered that these statistics reveal only majority-minority average differences and regional average differences; they do not show the extreme differences that would be found by comparing one school with another.

Programs

Just as minority groups tend to have less access to physical facilities that seem to be related to academic achievement, so too they have less access to curricular and extracurricular programs that would seem to have such a relationship.

Secondary school Negro students are less likely to attend schools that are regionally accredited; this is particularly pronounced in the South. Negro and Puerto Rican pupils have less access to college preparatory curriculums and to accelerated curriculums; Puerto Ricans have less access to vocational curriculums as well. Less intelligence testing is done in the schools attended by Negroes and Puerto Ricans. Finally, white students in general have more access to a more fully developed program of extracurricular activities, in particular those which might be related to academic matters (debate teams, for example, and student newspapers).

Again, regional differences are striking. For example, 100 percent of Negro high school students and 97 percent of whites in the metropolitan Far West attend schools having a remedial reading teacher (this does not mean, of course, that every student uses the services of that teacher, but simply that he has access to them) compared with 46 and 65 percent, respectively, in the metropolitan South—and 4 and 9 percent in the nonmetropolitan Southwest.

Principals and Teachers

One percent of white elementary pupils attend a school with a Negro principal, and 56 percent of Negro children attend a school with a Negro principal.

The average white student goes to an elementary school where 40 percent of the teachers spent most of their lives in the same city, town, or county; the average Negro pupil goes to a school where 53 percent of the teachers have lived in the same locality most of their lives.

Other characteristics which offer rough indications of teacher quality include the types of colleges attended, years of teaching experience, salary, educational level of mother, and a score on a 30-word vocabulary test. The average Negro pupil attends a school where a greater percentage of the teachers appears to be somewhat less able, as measured by these indicators, than those in the schools attended by the average white student.

The average white pupil attends a school where 51 percent of the white teachers would not choose to move to another school, whereas the average Negro attends a school where 46 percent would not choose to move.

Student Body Characteristics

The average white high school student attends a school in which 82 percent of his classmates report that there are encyclopedias in their homes. This does not mean that 82 percent of all white pupils have encyclopedias at home, although obviously that would be approximately true. In short, these tables attempt to describe the characteristics of the student bodies with which the "average" white or minority student goes to school.

Clear differences are found on these items. The average Negro has fewer classmates whose mothers graduated from high school; his classmates more frequently are members of large rather than small families, they are less often enrolled in a college preparatory curriculum, they have taken a smaller number of courses in English, mathematics, foreign language, and science.

On most items, the other minority groups fall between Negroes and whites, but closer to whites, in the extent to which each characteristic is typical of their classmates.

Again, there are substantial variations in the magnitude of the differences, with the difference usually being greater in the Southern States.

ACHIEVEMENT IN THE PUBLIC SCHOOLS

The schools bear many responsibilities. Among the most important is the teaching of certain intellectual skills such as reading, writing, calculating, and problem-solving. One way of assessing the educational opportunity offered by the schools is to measure how well they perform this task. Standard achievement tests are available to measure these skills, and several such tests were administered in this survey to pupils at grades 1, 3, 6, 9, and 12.

These tests do not measure intelligence, nor attitudes, nor qualities of character. Furthermore, they are not, nor are they intended to be, "culture-free." Quite the reverse: they are culture-bound. What they measure are the skills which are among the most important in our society for getting a good job and moving up to a better one, and for full participation in an increasingly technical world. Consequently, a pupil's test results at the end of public school provide a good measure of the range of opportunities open to him as he finishes school—a wide range of choice of jobs or colleges if these skills are very high; a very narrow range that includes only the most menial jobs if these skills are very low.

Table 1 gives an overall illustration of the test results for the various groups by tabulating nationwide median scores (the score which divides the group in half) for 1st-grade and 12th-grade pupils on the tests used in those grades. For example, half of the white 12th-grade pupils had scores above 52 on the nonverbal test and half had scores below 52. (Scores on each test at each grade level were standardized so that the average over the national sample equaled 50 and the standard deviation equaled 10. This means that for all pupils in the Nation, about 16 percent would score below 40 and about 16 percent above 60.)

With some exceptions—notably Oriental Americans—the average minority pupil scores distinctly lower on these tests at every level than the average white pupil. The minority pupils' scores are as much as one standard

TABLE 1

Nationwide Median Test Scores for First- and Twelfth-Grade Pupils

	RACIAL OR ETHNIC GROUP					
TEST	PUERTO RICANS	INDIAN-AMER-ICANS	MEXICAN-AMER-ICANS	ORIENTAL-AMER-ICANS	NEGRO	MAJOR-ITY
First grade:						
Nonverbal	45.8	53.0	50.1	56.6	43.4	54.1
Verbal	44.9	47.8	46.5	51.6	45.4	53.2
Twelfth grade:						
Nonverbal	43.3	47.1	45.0	51.6	40.9	52.0
Verbal	43.1	43.7	43.8	49.6	40.9	52.1
Reading	42.6	44.3	44.2	48.8	42.2	51.9
Mathematics	43.7	45.9	45.5	51.3	41.8	51.8
General information	41.7	44.7	43.3	49.0	40.6	52.2
Average of the 5 tests	43.1	45.1	44.4	50.1	41.1	52.0

deviation below the majority pupils' scores in the first grade. At the 12th grade, results of tests in the same verbal and nonverbal skills show that, in every case, the minority scores are *farther below* the majority than are the 1st graders. For some groups, the relative decline is negligible; for others, it is large.

Furthermore, a constant difference in standard deviations over the various grades represents an increasing difference in grade level gap. For example, Negroes in the metropolitan Northeast are about 1.1 standard deviations below whites in the same region at grades 6, 9, and 12. But at grade 6 this represents 1.6 years behind, at grade 9, 2.4 years, and at grade 12, 3.3 years. Thus, by this measure, the deficiency in achievement is progressively greater for the minority pupils at progressively higher grade levels.

For most minority groups, then, and most particularly the Negro, schools provide no opportunity at all for them to overcome this initial deficiency; in fact, they fall farther behind the white majority in the development of several skills which are critical to making a living and participating fully in modern society. Whatever may be the combination of nonschool factors—poverty, community attitudes, low educational level of parents—which put minority children at a disadvantage in verbal and nonverbal skills when they enter the first grade, the fact is the schools have not overcome it.

Some points should be borne in mind in reading the table. First, the differences shown should not obscure the fact that some minority children perform better than many white children. A difference of one standard deviation in median scores means that about 84 percent of the children in the lower group are below the median of the majority students—but 50 percent of the white children are themselves below that median as well.

A second point of qualification concerns regional differences. By grade 12, both white and Negro students in the South score below their counterparts— white and Negro—in the North. In addition, Southern Negroes score farther below Southern whites than Northern Negroes score below Northern whites. The consequences of this pattern can be illustrated by the fact that the 12th-grade Negro in the nonmetropolitan South is 0.8 standard deviation below— or in terms of years, 1.9 years behind—the Negro in the metropolitan Northeast, though at grade 1 there is no such regional difference.

Finally, the test scores at grade 12 obviously do not take account of those pupils who have left school before reaching the senior year. In the metropolitan North and West, 20 percent of the Negroes of ages 16 and 17 are not enrolled in school, a higher dropout percentage than in either the metropolitan or nonmetropolitan South. If it is the case that some or many of the Northern dropouts performed poorly when they were in school, the Negro achievement in the North may be artificially elevated because some of those who achieved more poorly have left school.

RELATION OF ACHIEVEMENT TO SCHOOL CHARACTERISTICS

If 100 students within a school take a certain test, there is likely to be great variation in their scores. One student may score 97 percent, another 13; several may score 78 percent. This represents variability in achievement *within* the particular school.

It is possible, however, to compute the average of the scores made by the students within that school and to compare it with the average score, or achievement, of pupils within another school, or many other schools. These comparisons then represent variations *between schools*.

When one sees that the average score on a verbal achievement test in School X is 55 and in School Y is 72, the natural question to ask is: What accounts for the difference?

There are many factors that in combination account for the difference. This analysis concentrates on one cluster of those factors. It attempts to describe what relationship the school's characteristics themselves (libraries, for example, and teachers and laboratories and so on) seem to have to the achievement of majority and minority groups (separately for each group on a nationwide basis, and also for Negro and white pupils in the North and South).

The first finding is that the schools are remarkably similar in the effect they have on the achievement of their pupils when the socioeconomic background of the students is taken into account. It is known that socioeconomic factors bear a strong relation to academic achievement. When these factors are statistically controlled, however, it appears that differences between schools account for only a small fraction of differences in pupil achievement.

The schools *do* differ, however, in the degree of impact they have on the various racial and ethnic groups. The average white student's achievement is less affected by the strength or weakness of his school's facilities, curricula, and teachers than is the average minority pupil's. To put it another way, the achievement of minority pupils depends more on the schools they attend than does the achievement of majority pupils. Thus, 20 percent of the achievement of Negroes in the South is associated with the particular schools they go to, whereas only 10 percent of the achievement of whites in the South is. Except for Oriental Americans, this general result is found for all minorities.

The conclusion can then be drawn that improving the school of a minority pupil will increase his achievement more than will improving the school of a white child increase his. Similarly, the average minority pupil's achievement will suffer more in a school of low quality than will the average white pupil's. In short, whites, and to a lesser extent Oriental Americans, are less affected one way or the other by the quality of their schools than are minority pupils. This indicates that it is for the most disadvantaged children that improvements in school quality will make the most difference in achievement.

All of these results suggest the next question: What are the school characteristics that account for most variation in achievement? In other words, what factors in the school are most important in affecting achievement?

It appears that variations in the facilities and curriculums of the schools account for relatively little variation in pupil achievement insofar as this is measured by standard tests. Again, it is for majority whites that the variations make the least difference; for minorities, they make somewhat more difference. Among the facilities that show some relationship to achievement are several for which minority pupils' schools are less well equipped relative to whites. For example, the existence of science laboratories showed a small but consistent relationship to achievement, and minorities, especially Negroes, are in schools with fewer of these laboratories.

The quality of teachers shows a stronger relationship to pupil achievement. Furthermore, it is progressively greater at higher grades, indicating a cumulative impact of the qualities of teachers in a school on the pupils' achievement. Again, teacher quality is more important for minority pupil achievement than for that of the majority.

It should be noted that many characteristics of teachers were not measured in this survey; therefore, the results are not at all conclusive regarding the specific characteristics of teachers that are most important. Among those measured in the survey, however, those that bear the highest relationship to pupil achievement are first, the teacher's score on the verbal skills test, and then his educational background—both his own level of education and that of his parents. On both of these measures, the level of teachers of minority students, especially Negroes, is lower.

Finally, it appears that a pupil's achievement is strongly related to the educational backgrounds and aspirations of the other students in the school. Only crude measures of these variables were used (principally the proportion of pupils with encyclopedias in the home and the proportion planning to go to college). Analysis indicates, however, that children from a given family background, when put in schools of different social composition, will achieve at quite different levels. This effect is again less for white pupils than for any minority group other than Orientals. Thus, if a white pupil from a home that is strongly and effectively supportive of education is put in a school where most pupils do not come from such homes, his achievement will be little different than if he were in a school composed of others like himself. But if a minority pupil from a home without much educational strength is put with schoolmates with strong educational backgrounds, his achievement is likely to increase.

This general result, taken together with the earlier examinations of school differences, has important implications for equality of educational opportunity. For the earlier tables show that the principal way in which the school environment of Negroes and whites differ is in the composition of their student bodies, and it turns out that the composition of their student bodies has a strong relationship to the achievement of Negro and other minority pupils.

*　　*　　*　　*　　*　　*　　*

This analysis has concentrated on the educational opportunities offered by the schools in terms of their student body composition, facilities, curriculums, and teachers. This emphasis, while entirely appropriate as a response to the legislation calling for the survey, nevertheless neglects important factors in the variability between individual pupils within the same school; this variability is roughly four times as large as the variability between schools. For example, a pupil attitude factor, which appears to have a stronger relationship to achievement than do all the "school" factors together, is the extent to which an individual feels that he has some control over his own destiny. The responses of pupils to questions in the survey show that minority pupils, except for Orientals, have far less conviction than whites that they can affect their own environments and futures. When they do, however, their achievement is higher than that of whites who lack that conviction.

Furthermore, while this characteristic shows little relationship to most school factors, it is related, for Negroes, to the proportion of whites in the schools. Those Negroes in schools with a higher proportion of whites have a greater sense of control. Thus such attitudes, which are largely a consequence of a person's experience in the larger society, are not independent of his experience in school.

Opportunity in Institutions of Higher Education

The largely segregated system of higher education in the South has made comparison between colleges attended mainly by Negro students and mainly by majority students easy in that region. Elsewhere it has not been possible in the past to make comparisons between educational opportunities because of the general policy in Federal and States agencies of not collecting data on race. In the fall of 1965, however, the Office of Education reversed this policy as a result of the interest of many agencies and organizations in the progress of minority pupils in gaining access to higher education. The racial composition of freshmen of all degree-seeking students was obtained from nearly all of the colleges and universities in the Nation.

These racial compositions have been cross-tabulated against a variety of characteristics of the institutions in the report itself. Over half of all Negro college students attend the largely segregated institutions in the South and Southwest. About 4.6 percent of all college students are Negro.

Whereas the bulk of the institutions (1104) have on the average 20 students per faculty member, those with predominantly Negro enrollment (96) have on the average 16 students per faculty member. Negro students are proportionally in colleges with lower proportions of Ph.D. faculty. This is generally but not always true in the various regions.

Negro students are in colleges with substantially lower faculty salaries. The institutions in the South and Southwest generally pay lower salaries than those in other regions, and the colleges serving primarily the Negro students are at the bottom of this low scale.

Other findings of the study are that—(1) in every region Negro students are more likely to enter the State College system than the State University system, and further they are a smaller proportion of the student body of universities than any other category of public institutions of higher education, (2) Negro students are more frequently found in institutions which have a high dropout rate, (3) they attend mainly institutions with low tuition cost, (4) they tend to major in engineering, agriculture, education, social work, social science, and nursing.

Future Teachers

Since a number of investigations of teacher qualification in the past few years have indicated that teachers of Negro children are less qualified than those who teach primarily majority children, this survey investigated whether there might be some promise that the situation may be changed by college students now preparing to become teachers. To this end, questionnaire and achievement test data were secured from about 17,000 college freshmen and 5,500 college seniors in 32 teacher training colleges in 18 States that in 1960 included over 90 percent of the Nation's Negro population. Some of the findings of this survey are:

1. At both the freshman and senior levels, future teachers are very similar to students in their colleges who are following other career lines. (It should be remembered that these comparisons are limited to students in colleges that have a primary mission in the training of teachers, and is not, of course, a random sample of all colleges.)

2. Majority students being trained at the college level to enter teaching have a stronger preparation for college than have Negro students; that is, they had more courses in foreign languages, English, and mathematics, made better grades in high school, and more often were in the highest track in English.
3. Data from the senior students suggest that colleges do not narrow the gap in academic training between Negro and majority pupils; indeed, there is some evidence that the college curriculum increases this difference, at least in the South.
4. Substantial test score differences exist between Negro and white future teachers at both freshman and senior levels, with approximately 15 percent of Negroes exceeding the average score of majority students in the same region. (This figure varies considerably depending on the test, but in no case do as many as 25 percent of Negroes exceed the majority average.)
5. The test data indicate that the gap in test results widens in the South between the freshman and senior years. The significance of this finding lies in the fact that most Negro teachers are trained in the Southern States.
6. The preferences of future teachers for certain kinds of schools and certain kinds of pupils raise the question of the match between the expectations of teacher recruits and the characteristics of the employment opportunities.

The preferences of future teachers were also studied. Summarized in terms of market conditions, it seems apparent that far too many future teachers prefer to teach in an academic high school; that there is a far greater proportion of children of blue-collar workers than of teachers being produced who prefer to teach them; that there is a very substantial number of white teachers-in-training, even in the South, who prefer to teach in racially mixed schools; that very few future teachers of either race wish to teach in predominantly minority schools; and finally, that high-ability pupils are much more popular with future teachers than low-ability ones. The preferences of Negro future teachers are more compatible with the distribution of needs in the market than are those of the majority; too few of the latter, relative to the clientele requiring service, prefer blue-collar or low-ability children or prefer to teach in racially heterogeneous schools, or in special curriculum, vocational, or commercial schools. These data indicate that under the present organization of schools, relatively few of the best prepared future teachers will find their way into classrooms where they can offset some of the environmental disadvantage suffered by minority children.

School Enrollment and Dropouts

Another extensive study explored enrollment rates of children of various ages, races, and socioeconomic categories using 1960 census data. The study included also an investigation of school dropouts using the October 1965 Current Population Survey of the Bureau of the Census. This survey uses a carefully selected sample of 35,000 households. It was a large enough sample to justify reliable nationwide estimates for the Negro minority but not for other minorities. In this section the word "white" includes the Mexican American and Puerto Rican minorities.

According to the estimates of the Current Population Survey, approximately 6,960,000 persons of ages 16 and 17 were living in the United States in October 1965. Of this number 300,000 (5 percent) were enrolled in college, and therefore, were not considered by this Census Bureau study. Of the remaining, approximately 10 percent, or 681,000 youth of 16 and 17, had left school prior to completion of high school.

About 17 percent of Negro adolescents (ages 16 and 17) have dropped out of school whereas the corresponding number for white adolescents is 9 percent. Most of this difference comes from differences outside the South; in the South the white and Negro nonenrollment rates are much the same.

The data suggest that the dropout rate is different for different socioeconomic levels, for whereas the nonenrollment rate was 3 percent for those 16- and 17-year-olds from white-collar families, it was more than four times as large (13 percent) in the case of those from other than white-collar families (where the head of household was in a blue-collar or farm occupation, unemployed, or not in the labor force at all). Furthermore, this difference in nonenrollment by parental occupation existed for both male and female, Negro and white adolescents.

The racial differences in the dropout rate are thus sharply reduced when socioeconomic factors are taken into account. Then the difference of 8 percentage points between all Negro and white adolescent dropouts becomes 1 percent for those in white-collar families, and 4 percent for those in other than white-collar families.

The largest differences between Negro and white dropout rates are seen in the urban North and West; in the nonurban North and West there were too few Negro households in the sample to provide a reliable estimate. In the South there is the unexpected result that in the urban areas, white girls drop out at a greater rate than Negro girls, and in the nonurban areas, white boys drop out at a substantially greater rate than Negro boys.

Effects of Integration on Achievement

An education in integrated schools can be expected to have major effects on attitudes toward members of other racial groups. At its best, it can develop attitudes appropriate to the integrated society these students will live in; at its worst, it can create hostile camps of Negroes and whites in the same school. Thus there is more to "school integration" than merely putting Negroes and whites in the same building, and there may be more important consequences of integration than its effect on achievement.

Yet the analysis of school effects described earlier suggests that in the long run, integration should be expected to have a positive effect on Negro achievement as well. An analysis was carried out to examine the effects on achievement which might appear in the short run. This analysis of the test performance of Negro children in integrated schools indicates positive effects of integration, though rather small ones. Results for grades 6, 9, and 12 for Negro pupils classified by the proportion of their classmates the previous year who were white show that in every case but one the highest average score is recorded for the Negro pupils where more than half of their class-mates were white. But the increase is small and often those Negro pupils in classes with only a few whites score lower than those in totally segregated classes.

Those pupils who first entered integrated schools in the early grades record consistently higher scores than the other groups, although the differences are again small.

No account is taken in these tabulations of the fact that the various groups of pupils may have come from different backgrounds. When such account is taken by simple cross-tabulations on indicators of socioeconomic status, the performance in integrated schools and in schools integrated longer remains higher. Thus although the differences are small, and although the degree of integration within the school is not known, there is evident even in the short run an effect of school integration on the reading and mathematics achievement of Negro pupils.

Tabulations of this kind are, of course, the simplest possible devices for seeking such effects. It is possible that more elaborate analyses looking more carefully at the special characteristics of the Negro pupils, and at different degrees of integration within schools that have similar racial composition, may reveal a more definite effect. Such analyses are among those that will be presented in subsequent reports.

Socioeconomic Position and
Academic Underachievement
Richard A. Cloward

What we do about a persisting social problem, such as poor academic achievement, depends in large part on our assumptions about the forces that produce it. Every approach to this problem is based on certain assumptions, explicit or implicit, about why the problem it is seeking to solve exists in the first place. In this paper, I shall set forth some ideas which I hope are helpful in accounting for the problem of poor academic performance among certain categories of children.

At the outset, I should like to note that the problem I have been asked to

MIMEOGRAPHED, December 1961, pp. 1–22. Reprinted by permission of the author. Footnote for table, p. 136, updated.

focus upon is that of the generally direct correlation between socioeconomic position and academic achievement. There are, of course, important qualifications which should be noted when this correlation is discussed. Although the correlation holds generally when the various strata of our society as a whole are compared, it may not necessarily hold for certain important sub-groupings; some ethnic groups may tend to perform well despite their low socioeconomic position; some groups may tend to perform poorly despite very high socioeconomic position. My point is not that the correlation is un-varying whatever the specialized status categories one compares, but rather that it tends to hold for very large aggregates of the population despite these internal variations. By defining the problem in these terms, it should be noted that I am excluding from consideration in this paper the problem of the low achiever as he may be found other than in the low economic segments of our population.

For all practical purposes, I am inclined to dismiss the possibility that this correlation can be accounted for in terms of native endowment, although I am aware that there are distinct differentials by income level in intelligence test performance. My objection here is the not uncommon one that such tests probably do not differentiate social influences from native endowment well enough, and thus probably measure achievement as well as endowment. Even if, by a process of selective social mobility, a correlation between endowment and social position does exist, then I would still be inclined to take the view, until contrary evidence is produced, that this factor alone is not enough to explain the general correlation between income level and academic achievement. I would still assume, in short, that the achievement-income correlation would persist, although perhaps in a weakened form, if native endowment were held constant.

The use of the term "under-achiever" may obscure more than it illumines. Like many other terms which designate gross social problems, such as juvenile delinquency, it is necessary to ask whether the term subsumes behavior which is all of a piece or whether discrete types of behavior are not otherwise lumped together. With respect to underachievement, I am inclined to believe that there are at least two general types: those whose under-achievement is not inconsistent with the beliefs, values and norms of those with whom they interact, and those whose underachievement *is* inconsistent with the beliefs, values and norms of those with whom they interact. In the first case, underachievement is socially structured; that is, high achievement does not receive strong support in the milieu of the actor. In the second case, however, underachievement is idiosyncratic; it is an isolated instance of aberrant behavior which receives no support and may be condemned in the milieu of the actor.

I have the distinct impression that these two forms of underachievement are differentially distributed in the social structure. If we ask how support for underachievement is distributed, we would probably answer that it is more likely to be found in the lower socioeconomic strata of our society, for a great deal of evidence suggests that there is less emphasis here upon educational performance than elsewhere in the society. Although education is widely valued in our society, it is not equally valued among the several social classes. Hyman has summarized a national survey in which a sample of youths were asked: "About how much schooling do you think most young men need these days to get along well in the world?" The results are shown below:

Class Differentials in Emphasis on the Need for College Education
(201 Males Aged 14 to 20)

SOCIOECONOMIC POSITION OF FAMILY	PERCENT RECOMMENDING A COLLEGE EDUCATION	NUMBER OF RESPONDENTS
Wealthy and prosperous	74	38
Middle Class	63	100
Lower Class	42	62

* H. H. Hyman, "The Value Systems of Different Classes: A Social-Psychological Contribution to the Analysis of Stratification," in Reinhard Bendix and S. M. Lipset, eds., *Class, Status and Power*, 2nd edition (Glencoe, Ill.: Free Press, 1966), p. 492.

These data, like others that Hyman presents, show that a sizable proportion of persons at each point in the social structure consider a college education desirable. Even in the lowest level of society, the proportion who emphasize the need for education is not small. But it is also true that there are strong differences from one stratum to another. In general, the proportion recommending higher education increases with each upward step in the socioeconomic hierarchy.

The task confronting the educational enterprise obviously differs greatly depending on which of these forms of underachievement it must overcome. In the case of socially-structured underachievement we probably face the more difficult task, for we must deal not only with an actor who deviates from official educational prescriptions but with a milieu which buttresses such behavior as well. Since the matter of social support may lie at the heart of lower-class underachievement, it is to some thoughts about this particular problem that I shall address myself. What I shall have to say, then, will not go to the important question of the more idiosyncratic forms of underachievement, for I do not believe that a single explanation can encompass the various forms of underachievement which confront us. It is one thing to ask why cultural values arise at certain points in the social structure which, if only inadvertently, tend to support underachievement; to the extent that the underachievement of a given person represents conformity with those values, the salient question then becomes one of explaining the origin of the values rather than the behavior of the individual. It is quite another thing to ask, however, why some persons fail to attain good academic records when the milieu in which they find themselves condemns such failure. Although I shall limit my remarks to the first question, the second also calls for answers.

Life Chances and Educational Achievement

Given the fundamental importance of education to social advancement, how are we to account for these class differentials in emphasis on the value of education? Why is it that a substantial proportion of lower-class males aged 14 to 20 do *not* orient themselves toward educational achievement? What are the special pressures impinging upon youth in city slums to which deviant patterns—such as educational failure—are a logical outcome?

It is my view that one very important pressure toward underachievement in this group arises from discrepancies between their social and economic aspirations and their opportunities to achieve these aspirations by legitimate means. The aspirations are the result of socialization in a society that places great emphasis on economic and occupational achievement and whose ideology stresses the possibility of achievement by all its members, irrespective of their ethnic or socioeconomic backgrounds. Members of low socioeconomic or minority groups, however, are subjected to discriminatory practices which have the effect of restricting access to the usual means (e.g., education) of rising in the social and occupational scale. Slum youth, therefore, share the aspirations of youth located elsewhere in American society but, for reasons largely beyond their control, are much less likely to achieve these goals.

The emphasis on upward mobility for all members is a unique characteristic of industrial societies. Something in the organization of life in such societies must therefore require that the members make a virtue of dissatisfaction, of discontent with their present positions. If we can identify this "something," we shall be on our way to understanding an important feature of American life, and, furthermore, we shall have taken an important step toward an explanation of lower-class patterns such as educational underachievement.

All societies, industrial or not, must solve the problem of perpetuating themselves or else disintegrate. In many societies it is enough that the young work alongside their parents, acquiring through these intimate associations the values and skills that will enable them to engage successfully in adult occupational and family activities. The occupational systems in such societies are relatively simple and undifferentiated; most of the major work roles can be passed directly from father to son. The transmittal of occupational skills is a more difficult problem in our society, with its vastly proliferated structure of extremely technical work roles. We cannot depend upon the vagaries of birth to determine who will occupy each role, for we cannot assume that the son of a physicist will be a competent successor to his father. Nor can we require the father to transmit highly specialized knowledge to his son in the context of the family, for this would divert the father's energies from the primary work role that he is supposed to perform. The family, in other words, is not a satisfactory environment for the learning of specialized occupational skills. The industrial society must organize itself in such a way that it can allocate people to roles more or less on the basis of merit and endowment rather than on the basis of social origins, and it must provide—outside the family—the formal learning experiences that are prerequisites to occupational performance.

A crucial problem in the industrial world, then, is to locate and train the most talented persons in every generation, irrespective of the vicissitudes of birth, to occupy technical work roles. Whether he is born into wealth or poverty, each individual, depending upon his ability and diligence, must be encouraged to find his "natural level" in the social order. This problem is one of tremendous proportions. Since we cannot know in advance who can best fulfill the requirements of various occupational roles, the matter is presumably settled through the process of competition. But how can men throughout the social order be motivated to participate in this competition? How can society generate the ambition and persistence that are necessary if the individual is to make his way in the occupational world? How can we persuade the young to invest their resources, time, and energies in acquiring specialized knowledge and complex skills? It is not enough for a few to make the race; all must be motivated to strive, so that the most able and talented will be the victors in the competitive struggle for high status.

One of the ways in which the industrial society attempts to solve this problem is by defining success-goals as potentially accessible to all, regardless of race, creed, or socioeconomic position. Great social rewards, it is said, are not limited to any particular segment or segments of the population but are available to everyone, however lowly his origins. The status of a young man's father presumably does not put an upper limit on the height to which the son may aspire; in fact, he is exhorted to improve his status over that of his father. The industrial society, in short, emphasizes *common* or universal success-goals as a way of ensuring its survival. If large masses of young people can be motivated to reach out for great social rewards, many of them will make the appropriate investment in learning and preparation, and a rough correlation between talent and ultimate position in the occupational hierarchy will presumably result.

One of the paradoxes of social life, however, is that the processes by which societies seek to ensure conformity sometimes result in nonconformity. If a cultural emphasis on unlimited success-goals tends to solve problems in the industrial society, it also creates new ones. A pervasive feeling of position discontent leads people to compete for higher status and so contributes to the survival of the industrial order, but it also produces acute pressure for aberrant behavior if large sectors of the population are denied equal opportunity to achieve high status.

Let us turn then to a discussion of barriers in access to educational facilities which confront low-income groups in our society.

Relationship of Educational Achievement to
Occupational Achievement

"Education," Lipset and Bendix have remarked, "has become the principal avenue for upward mobility in most industrial nations," particularly in the United States. The number of nonmanual occupations that can be fruitfully pursued without extensive educational background is diminishing and will doubtless continue to do so as our occupational structure becomes increasingly technical and specialized.[1]

It should be pointed out, however, that educational attainment does not necessarily enable the lower-class person to overcome the disadvantages of his low social origins.

> Thus workers' sons with "some college" education are about as well off [financially] as a group as the sons of nonmanual fathers who have graduated from high school but not attended college. Similarly, high school graduation for the sons of workers results in their being only slightly better off than the sons of nonmanual workers who have not completed high school.[2]

To the extent that one's social origins, despite education, still constitute a restraining influence on upward movement, we may assume that other objective consequences of social position intervene, such as the ability of one's family to give one a start in a business or profession by supplying funds or influential contacts.

The influence of social class as a deterrent to social mobility, despite the possession of education, becomes all the more important when coupled with influences stemming from race and nationality. It hardly needs to be said to an audience of this kind that race frequently acts as a major barrier to occupational mobility no matter what the educational achievement of the person involved. This situation is easing, to be sure, as progress in fair employment practices for all racial groups is slowly achieved. Nevertheless, it would be grossly inaccurate to say that a Negro youth in our society has the same chance as a white youth to become upwardly mobile given an equivalent level of education. It is not in the least uncommon to find Negro youth with college training forced to take employment in semi-skilled and lower white collar positions. Among the professions, only teaching and social work have been readily available to them.

The point is, of course, that the major inducement to educational achievement in our society is the promise of future occupational rewards. If, however, it is known in advance that these rewards will be largely withheld from certain socioeconomic and racial groups, then it is unlikely that high levels of educational achievement can be sustained in such groups. Thus academic performance may be devalued because the young in such groups see no relationship between it and the realities of their future.

[1] S. M. Lipset and Reinhard Bendix, *Social Mobility in Industrial Society* (Berkeley and Los Angeles, Calif.: University of California Press, 1959), p. 91.

[2] *Ibid.*, p. 99.

What we have been saying about the relationship between educational performance and occupational rewards assumes, of course, that discrepancies between the two tend to be perceived by low income and minority groups in our society. Generally speaking, the evidence available does suggest that perceptions of opportunity do accord with the reality. In this connection, Hyman summarizes data which show that there are distinct differentials by socioeconomic status in judgments regarding the accessibility of occupational rewards. Thus 63 percent of one sample of persons in professional and managerial positions felt that the "years ahead held good chances for advancement," while only 48 percent of a sample of factory workers gave this response. Furthermore, the factory workers were more likely to think that "getting along well with the boss" or being a "friend or relative of the boss" were important determinants of mobility; professional and executive personnel were more likely to stress "quality of work" and "energy and willingness." [3] Such findings suggest that low-income persons do indeed perceive the impact of social origins upon their life changes. If these are the perceptions of occupational mobility held by parents in such groups, it is hardly likely that children in such families would hold contrary views on a wide scale. Under such circumstances, the perception of the role of education as a determinant of mobility may fail to assume the importance which we might otherwise wish.

Equality in Access to Educational Facilities

It is doubtful that lower-class persons are unaware of the general importance assigned to education in our society or of the relationship between education and social mobility. But they are probably also very much aware of their limited opportunities to secure access to educational facilities. Educational achievement is not just a matter of favorable attitudes; opportunities must be available to those who seek them. For many members of the lower class, struggling to maintain a minimum level of subsistence, the goal of advanced education must seem remote indeed. In a family that can scarcely afford food, shelter, and clothing, pressure is exerted upon the young to leave school early in order to secure employment and thereby help the family. In a recent study of an extensive sample of adolescents in Nashville, Tennessee, Reiss and Rhodes found that most adolescents who quit school did so because they wanted to go to work immediately. Quitting school, their data show, is not necessarily a negative or rebellious response to compulsory-attendance laws but may be a necessary response to economic pressures.[4]

In the past few decades, a variety of studies have concluded that there are

[3] *Op. cit.*, p. 437.
[4] A. J. Reiss and A. L. Rhodes, "Are Educational Norms and Goals of Conforming and Delinquent Adolescents Influenced by Group Position in American Society?" *Journal of Negro Education* (Summer 1959), pp. 262–266.

marked class differentials in access to educational facilities.[5] The lower the social position of one's father, the less likely that one can take advantage of educational opportunities. Furthermore, class differentials in access to educational facilities are not explained by differences in intelligence. If children from various social classes who have the same general intelligence are compared, differentials in chances to acquire an education still obtain.

The influence of economic barriers to education can be inferred from studies of situations in which these barriers have been temporarily relaxed. Warner and his associates, for example, observed a "sharp increase in college and high school enrollment [resulting from] the establishing of the National Youth Administration student-aid program in 1935."[6] In a more recent study, Mulligan examined the proportions of students from various socioeconomic strata enrolled in a Midwestern university before and during the G.I. Bill of Rights educational program. Not surprisingly, his data show that as a result of the government-aid program a larger proportion of students were drawn from the lower echelons of the society. This strongly suggests that the lower class contains many persons who desire higher education but cannot ordinarily afford to acquire it.[7]

Commenting on financial barriers to high-school attendance, Warner and his associates note: "There is a substantial out-of-pocket cost attached to attendance at a 'free' high school. . . . Students can go to school and spend little or no money. But [the poor] are barred from many of the school activities, they cannot even take regular laboratory courses, and they must go around in what is to high-school youngsters the supremely embarrassing condition of having no change to rattle in their pockets, no money to contribute to a party, no possibility of being independent in their dealings with their friends."[8]

Aside from economic barriers in access to education, there is the further fact of inequality stemming from the organization of educational facilities for low-income youth. One problem is that of differentials in teacher turnover. For a variety of reasons, many teachers are reluctant to teach in the slum school. A study of the career patterns of Chicago public-school teachers documents the fact that teachers normally begin their careers in lower-class neighborhoods, where there are more vacancies, and transfer out as

[5] See W. L. Warner, R. J. Havighurst, and M. B. Loeb, *Who Shall Be Educated—The Challenge of Unequal Opportunities* (New York: Harper & Bros., 1944); Lipsct and Bendix, *op. cit.*; Elbridge Sibley, "Some Demographic Clues to Stratification," *American Sociological Review*, VII (June 1942), 322–330; and George F. Zuok, "The Findings and Recommendations of the President's Commission on Higher Education," *Bulletin of the American Association of University Professors*, XXXV (Spring 1949), 17–22.

[6] W. L. Warner *et al.*, *op. cit.*, p. 53.

[7] R. A. Mulligan, "Socio-Economic Background and College Enrollment," *American Sociological Review*, XVI, No. 2 (April 1961), 188–196.

[8] W. L. Warner *et al.*, *op. cit.*, pp. 53–54. For a further discussion of these and related matters, see A. B. Hollingshead, *Elmtown's Youth* (New York: John Wiley & Sons, 1949).

soon as they can.[9] Thus teachers in slum schools are generally less experienced.

The effect of this situation is especially unfortunate when one considers the characteristic instability of many slum communities, not to mention the economic uncertainties of slum youngsters' lives and the frequent changes in the composition of their families. It is important that the school, as represented by its teachers, be a constant, stable, omnipresent force in the community.

Because of the greater control problem posed by lower-class pupils and the greater turnover of teachers in slum schools, lower-class youngsters receive less actual instructional time than do school children in middle-class neighborhoods. Indeed, one study of a deprived-area school indicated that as much as 80 percent of the school day was devoted to discipline or organizational detail; even with the best teachers this figure never fell below 50 percent.[10] While these figures may be high, or unique to the particular school which was studied, problems in discipline and teacher turnover must inevitably limit instruction time in lower-class schools. In such instances, the role and self-image of the teacher may be transformed from instructor to that of monitor.

The generic problems of the school system—i.e., oversized classes, split shifts, inadequate staffing, the dearth of specialized services, etc.—are especially problematic for lower-class youngsters. For example, while an accepted New York State standard is 300 pupils to 1 guidance counselor in junior and senior high schools, ratios in New York City are 637 to 1 in the high schools, 1,710 to 1 in junior high schools. Still larger guidance loads are usual in elementary schools, with many such schools having no guidance person at all. In vocational high schools, which as a rule serve children from deprived backgrounds, counselors are assigned as many as 1,000 pupils each. Other specialties are similarly understaffed. In these and other ways, then, the accessibility of education is greatly influenced by socioeconomic factors. Inadequate educational performance among the poor can be understood in part as a response to restrictions in the availability of education and in part as a response to the inferior quality of the education which they do get.

If traditional channels to higher position, such as education, are restricted for certain categories of people, then pressures will mount for the use of alternative routes. Thus some lower-class persons orient themselves toward occupations in the fields of entertainment and sports. People of modest social origins who have been conspicuously successful in these spheres often become salient models for the young in depressed sectors

[9] Howard Becker, "The Career of the Chicago Public School Teacher," *American Sociological Review*, XVII, No. 7 (July 1952), 470–476.

[10] Martin P. Deutsch, *Minority Group and Class Status as Related to Social and Personality Factors in Scholastic Achievement* (New York: The Society for Applied Anthropology, Monograph No. 2, 1960), p. 23.

of the society. The heavyweight champion, the night-club singer, the base-ball star—these symbolize the possibility of achieving success in conventional terms despite poor education and low social origins. The businessman, the physicist, the physician, on the other hand, occupy roles to which the lower-class youngster has little access because of his limited educational opportunities. By orienting himself toward occupations which offer some hope of success in spite of poor social origins and education, the lower-class boy follows a legitimate alternative to traditional avenues to success-goals.

But the dilemma of many lower-class young people is that these alternative avenues to success-goals are often just as restricted as educational channels, if not more so. Of the many lower-class adolescents who go into the "fight game," hoping to win social rewards—money and glamor—by sheer physical exertion and stamina, a few succeed, but the overwhelming majority are destined to fail. For these lower-class youth there seems no legitimate way out of poverty. Thus they experience desperation born of the perception that their position in the economic structure is relatively fixed and immutable—desperation made all the more poignant by their exposure to a cultural ideology in which failure to orient oneself upward is regarded as a moral defect and failure to become mobile as proof of it. In a society that did not encourage them to set their sights high, they might more easily adjust to their impoverished circumstances; but since social worth is so closely identified with social position in American society, discontent and alienation are experienced by many youth in the lower reaches of the social order. Here, then, is one general source of a lack of emphasis among low-income people upon the value of education.

SOCIALIZATION AND EDUCATIONAL ACHIEVEMENT

Various elements in the socialization of lower-class youth also help to account for poor educational performance. In general, these elements stem from two related sources: the character of lower-class occupations and the content of various ethnic and nationality values found in large segments of the lower class. Both of these forces markedly influence the nature of socialization in the lower class and help to account for the lower emphasis upon education and for the relatively poorer academic performance found there.

Occupation and Inadequate Socialization

Low income produces inadequacies in socialization, and this in turn has implications for educational achievement. In the lower-class family, the need to concentrate upon economic survival severely limits the amount of attention parents can allocate to the "non-essential" activity of stimulating their children's intellectual growth or planning their educational future. Further, the crowding, lack of privacy, and disorder characteristic of family life in many slums are poor preparation for the quiet, orderly classroom. Differentials by social class in this respect have been described by the Institute for Developmental Studies: "The lower-class home seems to be characterized by a lot of noise and very little sustained verbal communication, while the middle-class environment seems to be almost the reverse. Thus, the lower-class child entering school is ill-prepared for the classroom setting in which he is continually called upon to speak or be spoken to." [11] With less demand made upon him in the home, the lower-class youngster has less need to develop a sustained attention span or a high degree of articulateness; since thought processes are dependent upon the use of language, the result is underdevelopment of abstract thinking processes.

Intellectual stimulation in the form of books, recordings, trips, and the like is lacking in the lower-class home, for purely economic reasons if not for others as well. The youngster who has seen his parents read books, as have most middle-class children, enters school identified with people who are literate. His lower-class counterpart is less often exposed to experiences that whet his intellectual curiosity.

The lower-class child is also handicapped educationally by the inexperience of his parents, which limits their ability to prepare their youngster for school success; for example, they often lack the knowledge as well as the time to help with homework. Shyness and suspicion further inhibit the lower-class parent from demonstrating his interest by visiting the school, discussing his child's progress, and, when necessary, intervening in the child's behalf. The child may therefore receive little support in his attempt to bridge these two adult worlds.

The problems in socialization for education characteristic of lower-class children generally are most acute in the very bottom economic groups. The lower class is not all of a piece; there are distinctive subgroupings within it, and the extent of the problem in these various groups differs.

From the standpoint of economic stability, it is possible to conceive of the lower class as being composed of two broad groupings. The first is composed of those who are more or less regularly employed (excepting severe recessions, strikes, and the like) and may be called the "stable working class." Persons in this category engage in manual occupations of a semi-skilled or skilled character. The second broad grouping consists of those who are irregularly employed—the transient, casual, intermittent, seasonal, and occasional workers who engage in essentially unskilled forms of employment.

[11] Institute for Developmental Studies, *Descriptive Statement* (New York: New York Medical College, 1960), p. 2. For some related essays on lower-class socialization and education, see the following:

Allison Davis, "What Are Some of the Basic Items in the Relation of Intelligence Tests to Cultural Background?" *Intelligence and Cultural Differences,* Eells *et al.,* eds. (Chicago: University of Chicago Press, 1951), p. 26; Donald Super, *The Psychology of Careers* (New York: Harper & Bros., 1957), p. 108; Robert J. Havighurst and Bernice Neugarten, *Society and Education* (Boston: Allyn and Bacon, 1957), p. 265; Martin P. Deutsch, *op. cit.,* p. 25.

One of the major consequences of these economic differences is the character of family structure in the two groupings. The stable working class generally exhibits a solidary, patriarchal, sometimes extended kinship system. By contrast, the large grouping of irregularly employed persons generally exhibits a female-centered household characterized by much illegitimacy and frequently transient adult males. Both groups exhibit a variety of values in common, including an emphasis on security rather than risk, expressive rather than instrumental orientations (including a strong person orientation rather than a task or function orientation), traditionalism, pragmatism and anti-intellectualism. It is important to note, however, that these emphases are found more strongly in the irregularly employed class than in the stable working class. Indeed, it would be accurate to say that the stable working class stands more or less midway between the transient labor subculture and the middle class.

The importance of this socioeconomic distinction stems from the observation that the irregularly employed subgrouping within the lower class contributes disproportionately to underachievement and drop-outs. Persons socialized in this group experience the greatest discrepancy between socially-induced aspirations and socially-structured life chances. They are least likely to have been exposed to familial systems which can successfully inculcate values and skills essential in achieving upward mobility. For example, boys socialized in this sector of society are not likely to have had stable father figures who held stable occupational positions, and thus opportunities for identification with occupational roles are limited if not absent. Such identification is crucial to achievement, and it is difficult to make such identification in the absence of appropriate role models. In view of these facts, frustrations ensuing from discrepancies between aspirations and life chances are acute, and alienation from the school and other middle-class institutions is the consequence.[12]

As these cultural patterns emerge in response to economic life circumstances, persons who are exposed to them become all the more unable to negotiate channels of mobility. In primary and secondary schools, for example, the children of the poor find themselves at a competitive dis-

---

[12] Work with the irregularly employed grouping within the lower class should not necessarily be aimed at opening channels for them to middle-class status. Perhaps some can make the transition, and they of course should be afforded the opportunity to do so. But it appears to be true that the movement of groups out of this unstable economic situation to the middle class occurs in stages, the most important of which is the formation of a stable working-class culture. To move into this intermediate stage depends upon educational opportunities to acquire some middle-class values and upon economic opportunities to form a stable monogamous kinship system. Once this stage of socioeconomic development has been achieved, a base for subsequent movement into the middle class then exists. From the standpoint of educational policy, therefore, it follows that goals or aspirations for differing socioeconomic groupings should vary. In the case of the least economically stable groups, the achievement of a stable working-class culture should be the aspiration. Programs leading to middle-class status, however, would seem realistic for those who already have been socialized in the working-class world, and they should be encouraged in such aspirations.

advantage with those from higher strata, for verbal fluency, a capacity for deferred gratification, a sustained attention span, and other attributes which facilitate academic achievement are more closely integrated with socialization in the middle-income than in the low-income strata of our society. The result is that many lower-income youngsters come to compare themselves invidiously with middle-income youngsters because the latter succeed more readily in school. Subsequently, some former adolescents may become estranged from the school and join the ranks of the dropouts. Continued exposure to the cultural patterns may even affect IQ scores adversely.

The major problem in dealing with self-defeating adaptations is that they generally become "functionally autonomous"—that is, once they come into existence, they tend to persist quite independent of the forces to which they were initially a response. The adaptation itself becomes elaborated and refined as a way of life into which people are directly socialized from birth. Hence they become carriers of the cultural system even before they have themselves experienced some of the frustrations discussed in the earlier part of this paper. Instead of developing a capacity to need and enjoy long-range accomplishments, for example, they may learn to need and enjoy immediate achievements; instead of developing satisfaction from risk-taking, they learn to derive satisfaction from successfully organizing their limited resources in a way that provides maximal security; instead of stressing instrumental skills, they may stress elaborate and stylized expressive modes of behavior. Once stabilized, in other words, these patterns of living become capable of maintaining themselves in part through the induction of the young who learn to satisfy their needs through them. When the children of the poor eventually come to experience dissatisfaction with their lot in life as the larger society reaches them and generates status discontent, they then find that they are imperfectly socialized for competition in the middle-class world. Although they may have high aspiration, they do not have the values and skills which would permit them to compete effectively in the middle-class world. The task, then, is to institute programs which will permit the effective re-socialization of such youth—effective in the sense that they will enable them to acquire traits useful in the exploitation of new opportunities.

DIFFERENTIAL SOCIALIZATION AND EDUCATIONAL ACHIEVEMENT

It would be a mistake, however, to say that the problem of socialization in some parts of the lower class is a problem simply because it is deficient, inadequate or incomplete. There is the further problem of differential socialization, and it may well be that we have been insufficiently attentive to the task of taking these differential values into account in the structuring of educational programs.

The problem of differential socialization vis-à-vis educational achievement can best be seen by looking at certain ethnic and nationality values. By and large, immigrant groups historically have entered our social structure at the bottom, and thus it is in the lower class that one finds the greatest impact of such values. In many of the groups which have come to this country, distinctive systems of values were already well established and thus tended to persist for a number of generations here. Although the more superficial aspects of the American middle-class value system may have been acquired rapidly, the more subtle and deeply embedded aspects of the Old World values were abandoned less readily. Indeed, there is good reason to think that many of these values continue to exert a profound influence upon the behavior of many persons in the second and third generation.

The point to be made about these persisting value orientations is that they do not always facilitate success in the school. Our system of education places a strong stress upon doing rather than being, upon a future orientation rather than an orientation toward the present or the past, upon the notion that man is superordinate to nature rather than in harmony with it or subjugated by it, upon the notion that man is flexible and plastic and capable of change rather than that he is essentially evil and perhaps immutably evil. A child who has not acquired these particular value orientations in his home and community is not so likely to compete successfully with youngsters among whom these values are implicitly taken for granted. In a number of ethnic and nationality groups, a strong emphasis upon the value of being, on the present and the past, and the like can be detected. These values are rooted in traditions many centuries old, and can be expected to be extinguished only through successive generations of assimilation in this culture. Although the values may, after several generations, be greatly weakened, they nevertheless continue to exert a subtle influence in many spheres of role behavior, including educational performance. Part of the problem of underachievement among some lower-class persons may therefore be attributed to the existence of these alternative value orientations to which the young are differentially socialized. This is a further sense, then, in which underachievement is supported in some ethnic and nationality subcultures in the lower class.

In conclusion, I would like to make a brief statement about the problem of equality of opportunity in education. I take it that there are at least three respects in which equality can be understood. First, equality means that equivalent educational facilities shall be available whatever the socioeconomic position of the child. Second, equality means that individual differences in learning patterns shall be taken into account. Finally, equality means that the educational system shall not be organized in such a way as to favor children who are socialized in one rather than another part of the social structure. Differentials in socialization, arising from socioeconomic position and ethnic origins, must, like individual differences in learning, also be adjusted to by the school system. If the educational enterprise is simply an extension of the middle-class home, then it follows that only middle-class children will tend to do well in it. If the school fails to practice equality in these several respects, then it can be understood as contributing to the very problem which it otherwise deplores.

Counselor Bias and the Female Occupational Role

JOHN J. PIETROFESA AND
NANCY K. SCHLOSSBERG

Even though a large percentage of women work, and a large percentage of workers are women, the startling fact is the decline in their position in recent years. [Women's] representation among professional workers has actually declined from 40 percent in 1950 to 37 percent in 1966. Furthermore, women receive proportionately fewer Master's degrees and Doctorates today than in the 1920s, and women hold proportionately fewer technical and professional positions today than in 1940. . . . Complicating the picture is the fact that each sex occupies different levels on the status hierarchy and the sexes are unevenly distributed as to field of endeavor. It has been substantiated that:

> American education is blighted by a sex-split in its curriculum. At present the whole field of knowledge is divided along tacit but well-understood sex lines. Those subjects given the highest status in American life are "masculine"; those given the lowest are "feminine" . . . thus math, the sciences . . . business administration . . . are men's subjects . . . and the humanities are relegated . . . "suitable to women." [1]

Since many high school and college women discuss their choice of major and occupation with counselors, the question arises—what do counselors feel the role of women should be? In discussing this question with counselors-in-training, they voice a partial egalitarian view—women should do whatever they want to do. Since actions speak louder than words, it was decided to study actual interviews of counselors-in-training with a female client who was deciding between a "feminine" and "masculine" occupational role. The assumption was that through careful analysis of verbatim interviews, the degree of counselor bias would be revealed. Thus, this study was conceived as an investigation of the counselor's bias in the

---

[1] K. Millett, *Token Learning: A Study of Women's Higher Education in America* (New York: National Organization for Women, 1968), p. 14.

JOHN J. Pietrofesa and Nancy K. Schlossberg, "Counselor Bias and the Female Occupational Role," in Nona Glazer-Malbin and Helen Youngelson Waehrer (Eds.), *Woman in a Man-Made World*, © 1972 by Rand McNally and Company, Chicago, pp. 219–21.

total process of role stereotyping of women. If counselors do display bias, the ramifications of such a fact would have to be taken into account in counselor-education programs.

The data suggest that counselors do hold bias against women entering a so-called "masculine" occupation. Female counselors, interestingly enough, displayed as much bias as did their male counterparts. The results tend to suggest that male and female counselors both display more statements "biased against females" than "biased for females." The three ratings combined showed a significant difference at the .01 level of confidence. Percentage results strongly reinforce the conclusion that counselors are biased against women entering masculine fields. Of the total bias statements, 81.3 percent are against women, whereas only 18.7 percent are biased for women.

A content analysis of the 79 biased statements made by the counselors in this study reveals that most negatively biased statements emphasized the masculinity of the field. Working conditions and promotional opportunity were a far second and third.

In order to tabulate the statements 10 categories were devised so that negative bias (NB) and positive bias (PB) statements could be classified as to content. The following examples of bias statements will give the flavor of the kinds of pressures counselors imposed.

Salary—Amount of monetary return
(NB) "Money isn't everything."
(PB) "You could make much more money as an engineer."
Status—Perception of self in vocation
(NB) "The status of a woman is higher in the field of teaching."
(PB) "There is more prestige in becoming an engineer."
Marriage and Family—Family Attachment
(NB) "Would your husband resent you being an engineer?"
(NB) "You would only be gone from home during school hours if you taught school."
(PB) "Being an engineer would not interfere with you becoming married."
Parents—Parental Support
(NB) "How do your parents feel about you entering engineering instead of education?"
(PB) "I am glad your parents want you to become an engineer."
Educational Time—Amount of time necessary for preparation to enter the vocational field
(NB) "Engineering would take five years and elementary education would be four years. . . . These are things you might want to consider."
(PB) "It may take longer to become an engineer but it is well worth it."
Educational Preparation—Classes one must take to enter the field and the kinds of classes already taken
(NB) "The course work in engineering would be very difficult."
(PB) "Your classwork up to now shows that you would do well as an engineer."

Promotional Opportunities—Advancement in position
 (NB) "There might be a holding back of you because you are a woman."
 (PB) "Your chances of promotion would be good in engineering."
Hiring—Opportunity to enter field
 (NB) "They are not supposed to discriminate against women, but they still get around it."
 (PB) "The opportunities for a woman in engineering are good."
Working conditions—Where, with whom, what kind of work, and/or under what conditions work is done
 (NB) "Engineering . . . it is very, you know, technical, and very, I could use the term 'unpeopled.' "
 (PB) "You could work at a relaxed pace as an engineer."
Masculine Occupation—Identification of occupation as masculine
 (NB) "You normally think of this as a man's field."
 (PB) "There is no such thing as a man's world anymore."

The implications of the study are quite clear—counselors, both male and female, hold biases against female counselees entering an occupation characteristically associated with males. Counselor-education programs must take this into account in their programs and attempt to bring into the open such biased feelings, so that counselors are able to control them, or better yet, remove them from their counseling and human encounters.

Women should have an equal opportunity to compete in the world of work with their male counterparts. Yet, discriminatory practices still exist. Further subtle pressures and influences against entering so-called "masculine" occupations by parents, as well as teachers and counselors, may do more harm than discriminatory practices by employers. Self-fulfillment for women is not an insubstantial and irrational dream; it can be achieved.

Part II

The Institutional
Fabric
of Education

The major priorities and patterns of the
American society are reflected in the nature
of its schools. But it is not enough to know
that this is the case; we must identify the
procedures responsible for this congruence
and the mechanisms by which the school
serves the society's priorities. This section
focuses upon such mechanisms in the nature
of schools as social institutions. Here we
review some of the ways in which schools
transmit and inculcate major aspects of the
American culture and social structure in
educating succeeding generations of
young members.

One of the major issues we examine is the *ideological character and content* of American schooling. We suggested earlier that the schools help transmit the ideology and norms of a society. Inasmuch as we can understand, from Part I, some of the primary ideological commitments or priorities of the American society, we can examine here how these positions are reflected in the mission and the operating procedures of schools. Ideologies are an important part of the goals and procedures of any social organization; they are especially crucial for a public institution whose job it is to train young people in the values and ways of the society.

A second major issue we examine is the way *the society*—national, state, or local—*controls* or *influences the educational process*. The school is an instrument of the State and is responsive to local norms, interest groups, and social pressures. Various groups contend with each other to affect the content and procedures of schooling.

A third major issue is the *internal pattern of communication and control* that is at work in most school organizations. All organizations must share information and use power to govern themselves and to manage their relations to other social systems. The particular procedures through which power is exercised in schools are important in determining why schools operate as they do. Some investigators have so avoided the political roles of schools that they refuse to look at this variable at all. Clearly we see schools as political entities—internally and externally. They select certain ideologies and support them in educational operations—this is an obvious act of political preference. They govern their affairs in ways that reflect choices between priorities, and thus they act politically. Different people, in different roles, have varying amounts of influence or control over the daily life of schools, and thus power determines the internal character of schools as well. Power is vital, and it must be understood. Whether the operation of power serves ideology or whether the invention of ideology serves current power patterns is a moot question the reader must determine for himself. They do go together, and the major value systems and power patterns are reflected in the structure of teaching-learning interactions.

A fourth key issue for any social organization is the *management of processes of differentiation and integration, balancing the need for consensus and conflict*. All organizations are composed of people and roles that are different from one another, and for survival all must maintain, meld, and manage these differences in integrated ways. This process varies among institutions and varies at times within any given institution. To the extent that a single public system seeks to serve diverse groups of persons and purports to deal with those persons and groups in ways that respect and/or advance their uniqueness and individuality, the school becomes a particularly important institution to examine in this respect. The school is also important because it strives to fulfill this function for the society at large, not only in its own internal workings. How differences are maintained, if indeed they are, and how different people and groups are brought together, if indeed they are, are among the key questions we pose.

A fifth major issue we examine is the *relation between the school and other organizations concerned about or dealing with youth.* The school is not the only part of the society focused upon youth, nor is it the only organization rather explicitly mandated or expected to help socialize and prepare youth for the adult community. How the school interfaces with these and other youth-serving or youth-controlling systems is an important problem. Do they compete with each other? Support each other? Support the same or different norms? Only in this context can we truly understand the totality of the functioning of educational systems. Too much research on schools seems to portray schools operating in a social vacuum. Here we deliberately try to overcome that bias and to restore some of the complexity of social reality to the review of schools and schooling.

IDEOLOGIES AND NORMS—MYTHS AND REALITIES

All social systems, large and small, are held together in part by their common beliefs, by their agreed-upon assumptions about the nature of the environment. The perceptions of the world held in common by a group of people become their definition of social reality, their notion of "the way things are." If groups of persons had widely divergent assumptions about social reality, it would be hard for them to agree on common ways of interpreting or evaluating events or on a common set of behaviors or actions. It is essential, then, for a social system to have some common assumptions or perspectives, and we label them the prevailing ideologies. Members who do not share these images of the world are considered deviant—in some cases wrong or misguided, in other cases "crazy" or sick. Error or misinterpretation is usually considered a voluntary and easily correctable form of deviance; "craziness" is usually considered involuntary and hard to ameliorate or control.

Because any social system requires some degree of consensus on major ideological frameworks as a basis for social action, it is important to understand how these images get passed from one generation to another and how they permeate members and organizations in all corners or at all strata of the society. Most institutions have only limited access to the broad spectrum of American society, inasmuch as their immediate clientele tends to represent a narrow stratum of the population. In fact, many social institutions (churches, clubs, neighborhood agencies) are fairly exclusive in character and include a very limited range of the American social structure. Schools, on the other hand, have greater potential for the diffusion of broad images because their clientele theoretically is representative of the total social structure. This potential ascribes to schools a far greater level of plural concern and influence than they actually possess, often posing difficulties not of their own making.

Schools are not the only social institutions serving to promulgate and gain loyalty to ideological frameworks; churches, family groupings, YMCA clubs, and certainly literature and mass media also play important parts. But the school does operate as the official societal mediator of major value systems and ideologies. It has a formal responsibility to translate and transmit the society's ideological perspectives and moral commitments to the next generation.

The major ideological commitments of a social system are not always clear; sometimes they are fuzzily concealed amidst a variety of moral priorities. Further, official rhetoric is not the same as prevailing ideology, and anyone who attempts to pass on the actual value system must understand the difference. Disparities between official verbalizations and underlying ideology are common to most social systems. Knowledge and acceptance of these disparities help reduce the tension that arises from subscribing to and trying to implement an ideal far distant from reality.

From another point of view, the school's attempt to pass on the prevailing ideology often illuminates the disparity between ideology and mere rhetoric. Nowhere is this disparity as clear as in the area of race, racial relations, and racism. The official American ideological system suggests that we are committed to egalitarianism and to a belief in the inherent worth and equality of persons regardless of race, and that we advocate equal opportunity for all. It is obvious that this is not our national practice; in fact, our institutions operate in ways that indicate a great disparity between our beliefs and our practices. Perhaps we never believed as a nation in an egalitarian ideology anyway; even our founding documents, such as the original federal Constitution, indicate compromises on this score. Whether our national practice has deviated from our original value pattern, or whether two competing ideologies were present from the start in the new nation, or whether we were committed to racism from the start with only a rhetorical bow to egalitarianism doesn't matter here. It is clear that the prevailing American ideology supports racism and that it provides a sophisticated and embracing belief and value system supportive of continued racial discrimination and oppression. And it is also clear that the school acts as one of the chief emissaries of this ideology. *In the selection "Compensatory Education and Contemporary Liberalism in the United States: A Sociological View," D. C. Morton and D. R. Watson suggest that even the so-called liberal attempts to equalize educational opportunity reflect individualistic assumptions as a mode for solving social problems.* The ideology of individualism serves racism by advancing the conviction that minorities' problems are rooted in individual skills and abilities rather than in the injust or discriminatory nature of the school or the social order. The selection is a case study of a sophisticated unmasking of social rhetoric.

We have suggested that the school is the formal institution entrusted with the responsibility for sharing and exhorting loyalty to preferred social ideologies. Moreover, as part of the total social system, and not apart from it, the school mirrors prevailing ideologies in its own moral order, social structures, and operating procedures. The actual espousement of an ideology is always sustained by other elements of social organization, which together demonstrate norms in practice, values in action. Students, and organizational members as well, learn from operational practice as well as formal pronouncements. *Harmon Ziegler and Wayne Peak's article, "The Political Functions of the Educational System," clearly indicates the extent to which the American educational system propagates a narrow set of consensual political values in its clientele.* They argue that the formation of attitudes consistent with the requisites of a pluralistic democracy are not enhanced by current instructional practices.

The highly technocratic and specialized nature of our advanced (some would say post-) capitalist society stresses the importance of adequate knowledge for institutional management and decision making. Thus we reward expertise, and in our schools we train people in narrow or specialized expertise that can be used most effectively in the industrial and governmental systems. Moreover, we operate our schools on the basis of professional expertise, as exemplified in the backgrounds and experiences of leadership cadres. Teaching, then, just like managing corporations, is seen as a learned technical skill, not as one element in a thoroughly human interaction between people. The skills to lead and the skills to teach are seen to lie in one person, and that person is supposed to direct the lives of others. As Mead so aptly points out, ". . . emphasis has shifted from learning to teaching, from the doing to the one who causes it to be done, from spontaneity to coercion, from freedom to power. With this shift has come the development of techniques of power, dry pedagogy, regimentation, indoctrination, manipula- • tion, and propaganda." *

The ideologies of specialized knowledge and of expert leadership so essential to a technocratic capitalism are mirrored in the major norms of the school. These norms are linked closely to the basic philosophical orientations of the American school and are buttressed by a set of assumptions regarding human nature, the concept of the child, appropriate teaching methods, the teacher's role, and the relation of the school to the community and the underlying social order.

Our studies of public education indicate that the traditional school remains the dominant American experience. Thus we may expect many of the more traditional belief systems to prevail: that things should proceed according to the concept of the "average child"; that children should not be trusted; that discipline is a major organizing principle; that punishment is a prime motivating force; that the teacher is expected to assign lessons and hear recitation; that memorization, the mastery of facts and skills, and the development of abstract intelligence represent basic outcomes; that the community as a vital educative force should largely be ignored; and that

* Margaret Mead, "Our Educational Emphases in Primitive Perspective," *The American Journal of Sociology,* Vol. 48 (May 1943), p. 639.

fitting the child into the existing social order should be a prime concern of the professional teaching staff.

In practice, our assumptions about the nature of man and the nature of young people strongly suggest that they must be held in check and protected against themselves and their expressive natures in order for them to accomplish their task. Essentially, students must be controlled, for their own good, or they will not learn. They will play, fool around, goof off, take advantage of the teacher—and this is their basic nature. Many adults see in young people the actualization of their own fantasies, their own fettered needs and vicarious desires. So young people must be controlled; and they must be taught the value of hard work, thrift, control of their emotions, and, in general, the traditional belief patterns of Protestant America. This view of the student's social nature has led to an ideology of teacher control over the educational process and the learning process. This ideology is parallel with other control-oriented assumptions made throughout American industry with regard to low-status workers and throughout governmental and welfare systems with regard to clients. Thus the stage is set—in ideological terms— for certain allocations of power and control in the society and the school that will inculcate these values.

The American priority of competition over cooperation, of individualism over communalism, also is played out in school. This priority provides the setting in which teachers encourage students to vie with each other for "best" academic performance, for top grades. It prevents peer collaboration on learning tasks and defines learning, as most work in life, as an individual task at which each one works for himself and his own advantage. Parenthetically, this modality also serves to pit students against each other and to prevent unification of students against the ruling patterns of adult educators. As such, it places a premium on achievement but orders activities in such a way as to prevent achievement for a significant portion of the student body.

Schools are a special kind of institution dedicated to providing a social service to the community and to promoting the general social welfare. As such, they have their own peculiar ideology, one giving form and meaning to the unique organizational arrangements and moral priorities incumbent upon a people-serving or people-processing institution. When a parent asks, for instance, why this subject is in the curriculum, or why the classroom is organized in this manner, or why teachers with these credentials are important, the school must have an answer defensible via recourse to a set of criteria. And these criteria, submerged in technical jargon or not, take the form of an ideology of education. In some cases social science may be brought in to support this ideology; then we purport to discuss theories of learning or theories of education. But fundamentally we are once again talking about ideology: a set of values and moral choices rooted in a framework of beliefs and/or assumptions about the world—about children, about the society, about the nature of learning, about the economic system the products of educational training will enter, about the world they will live in, in short, a circumscribed and selected set of beliefs about the nature of social reality.

SYSTEMIC CONTROLS ON EDUCATION

The system of public education is one portion of the total institutional arena of American life. Schools are affected by the nature of our federal system and by major political decisions regarding war and peace, economic concentration and reform, urban and metropolitan affairs, and the like. The character of the state is an important factor in educational operations as well. Not only do different states have different administrative systems for their schools but different financial resources, curricular concerns, and sometimes value priorities as well.

The fact that education is a public institution means that many varied interest groups legitimately contend for influence on school matters. Eventually the people control, but "the people" is divisible into numerous interest groups with their own priorities and concerns for educational outcomes and procedures. One of the most important "publics" that contends for school influence is the professional educational establishment itself and its many national, regional, state, and local components. The debates between professional and lay publics are ongoing features of our public school system. *The selection by Michael W. Kirst and Decker F. Walker, "An Analysis of Curriculum Policy Making," points out that curriculum decisions are seldom based on objective data or thoughtful decision techniques.* The decisional procedure gives full rein to varied groups intent upon influencing or controlling the educational system. It also provides a great deal of latitude for the professional staff to exercise authority in curriculum matters at the local level. This fact confirms our suspicion that many external and public matters tend to be implemented as internal issues, often unilaterally arrived at, provided a "low profile" is maintained.

The school is located in a local municipal context, as well as in a national or state social system. Because they are public institutions they are very vulnerable and responsive to the nature of the local civic community. Who the mayor is or what the political values of local elites are are very important questions in an understanding of school governance and educational operations. The economic character of the local urban or rural community and the way the community decides to allocate its economic resources have a tremendous impact on the financial status of local schools. These factors also affect the nature of the local job market and the employment opportunities available for graduates, in turn affecting the vocational orientation of the school curriculum.

Robert L. Crain and David Street's study, "School Desegregation and School Decision Making," suggests the extent to which individual school boards are both powerful and autonomous in their policy-making role. Of course, school board members are affected—and often elected—by local political forces and do represent partisan elements of the total local community. But they have considerable latitude in mediating local norms, distant judicial decrees, and the tenor of the times. This is especially clear with regard to issues such as desegregation, one of the most visible and important current arenas of local-national and intracommunity controversy over norms and social control.

CONTROL AND COMMUNICATION SYSTEMS IN SCHOOLS

The educational complex, like any major social system, manifests certain behavioral regularities that are instrumental in carrying on system functions. By explicating these regularities, it is possible to illumine a structure of social relations that determine the varying characteristics of different roles and status positions. Some individuals, upon examination, will be found to occupy certain statuses within the structure that ascribe to them the authority to render decisions affecting members who occupy lesser statuses. On the other hand, the statuses of others will have built into them few or no rights of leadership or of decision-making power. This hierarchical arrangement, common to all social systems, represents a built-in control mechanism enabling the social system to manage the problems of resource allocation and goal attainment and the internal ordering of relations and roles with a minimum of disequilibrium and disruption.

In any organization priorities must be set, procedures established, and all organizational components directed toward the essential purposes of existence. The exercise of organizational direction or control is an essential feature of all social systems—societies, school systems, schools, communities, and so on.

Our attempts to understand the mechanisms of organizational control usually revolve around two points: the nature of power and decision-making operations within an organization and between organizational elements; and the manner in which rules and regulations are maintained, or the ways in which the organization controls the lives of its members.

Formal organizations must develop formalized ways of making and implementing decisions. In American culture, the predominant form of social organization for managing the affairs of modern society has been bureaucracy. Unquestionably, structures of power and influence, patterns of job definition and performance, and systems of communication and interaction are organized into a complex bureaucratic form in the school. We have already alluded to the facts that bureaucracy and social structure are interrelated, that education is bureaucratically organized, and that this form of social organization represents a mode of social control that reflects both a class bias and the corporate interests of the economic structure.

The analogy of the bureaucratic school organization to that of business and industry may not be entirely accurate. Although it is appropriate to categorize the school as a bureaucracy, it is a bureaucracy different from others developed along an industrial or governmental model. The school is not only a public institution; it is to a degree accountable to the human individuals within it and served by it, as well as to the community. Moreover, it is staffed by professionals, persons desirous of and accustomed to working with each other and with supervisors as peers or colleagues, rather than as slotted subalterns. The output of this system is not a material product but a form of human services—in fact, humans themselves! Thus the school is a peculiar kind of bureaucracy, one with severe strains between collegial and humanistic ways of working and traditionally hierarchical and technocratic ways of working. *This observation is shared by Charles E. Bidwell in the selection "Students and Schools: Some Observations on Client Trust in Client-Serving Organizations."* Here the emphasis is directed toward the relationship between two orders in the membership of schools: teachers conducting their work and students responding to it. The scope and intensity of student trust is linked to the degree to which the professional staff and the staff-role system live up to the moral sentiments of a humanistic concern for their clients.

The professional staff of the school, the principal and teachers, exercise their authority in a variety of ways. At times they operate traditionally and with close adherence to universal rules and regulations. At other times they persuade and cajole, bending and interpreting regulations in more particularistic directions. In most cases the professional staff decide matters unilaterally, by themselves, with the major question being the division of authority between the principal and the teachers.

One of the assumptions underlying professionalism is that the personnel are competent as a matter of course. Principals, however, are usually not provided with any specialized training in how to run a school, in how to manage this complex human environment. The result is that they often are unsuited to and unprepared for this task, retreating to the more coercive aspects of the power of their office to rule a tenuous staff situation.

Teachers, too, are reluctant to shed their mask of competence and often find it difficult to ask for help from colleagues. A request for help may be interpreted as a sign of incompetence—especially because competence is assumed from the start and defended jealously against potential attack. So teachers are often lonely and rule their classrooms autonomously, but with discomfort. On the other hand, of course, some mechanisms must exist to counter this atomistic tendency, to integrate various staff members, and to organize the amount of diversity or deviance that exists. *In the selection "Variations on the Theme of Primary Groups: Forms of Social Control Within School Staffs," Donald I. Warren analyzes four mechanisms of social control in relationship to elementary school staffs.* He describes well how internal control mechanisms are employed to direct the staff toward a peer-oriented consensus on educational values and procedures.

Students are seldom engaged in making decisions about the content or processes of classroom instruction. Of course, in some instances their opinion is sought, in some cases they are permitted to offer advice. But substantial influence or decisional control is lacking almost universally. This pattern is present in the overall operations of the school—with regard to both policy and program—as well as in the classroom. Even in areas of student behavior itself students are systematically excluded from exercising control over their school lives. Student governments and student courts are hoaxes, mere showplaces of initiative and influence that make of self-government an exercise in bootlicking obeisance to authoritarian control from the wings. Even ostensibly student-operated newspapers are typically censored and controlled by faculty advisers and reviewers—all operating in the name of representing broad societal values and norms and concerned with preventing youth from making their own mistakes.

To the extent that adult school authorities make decisions for students, they control the young in school. To the extent that school life is pervaded by numerous rules and regulations about many aspects of daily behavior, the reins of adult control weigh heavily on students' shoulders. The current situation is so severe that several recent court cases have paved the way for judicial intervention in the schooling process to help guarantee to students some elementary constitutional protections. For instance, school life is rife with examples of administrative operations by fiat with regard to disciplinary hearings and the meting out of punishment. Unilateral and apparently arbitrary administrative action often denies students rights of due process, including the presentation of charges, the hearing of witnesses, the opportunity to defend oneself, and perhaps even access to legal representation. Obviously, the cloak of professionalism, which appears to serve students so well that they do not need to be protected against any excesses or actions not in their interests, has also hidden the possibilities of injustice. Prior censorship of student opinions, meetings, demonstrations, and expressions of free speech have also been held to be unconstitutional in several recent court cases. The orderly processes of education must be supported, but courts have ruled they must not be elevated to a position superior to students' constitutional prerogatives.

The concern with control of students is reflected not merely in values and ideologies, nor in patterns of communication and influence in schools. It is also present in the way the classroom is organized, the lessons are presented, and teachers' styles with students and curriculum are organized. As a means to reach certain formalized ends, the instructional system embodies most of the other assumptions of schooling. In all these areas the developing intellect and the young person are ordered and controlled in ways that prepare them for obedient performance in adult roles.

What options are left for students? Among the most traditional reactions to this situation is the passive acceptance of such control and the attempt to look for ways to slide through without rocking the boat. Another form of this reaction involves the manipulation of the myth of institutional paternalism, which allows students to provide meaning for bureaucratic activities by defining them as preparation for college or some distant, yet undefined goal. *Buford Rhea's article, "Institutional Paternalism in High School," addresses itself to this option—as a way to make it through school and seemingly to enjoy it as well.*

Still another reaction is the attempt to escape: to leave such constraining environs formally by dropping out, or to drop out spiritually on drugs. In recent years we have come to see two other major—and more interesting— reaction patterns. One is a continuation of dropping out and drug use but along with attempts to mold them to create new alternatives to schools, to escape the despair of control by others in new forms of self-control over one's own education outside of the formal system. Another major form of reaction is the directly political attack on the institutions' control mechanisms and the engagement in protests that wrest control out of the hands of adults and put power directly in the hands of students and members of the community. Of course these new forms require the development of new ideologies to justify such behavior, and the antischool proyouth ideology in vogue in some educational circles serves this movement well.

Managing Differences and Conflict

America is a nation of many peoples, of people from many different backgrounds. We are also a very complex society, with a substantial division of labor and economic strata that results in different life styles, opportunities, and outlooks on the world. And we are thoroughly imbued with the rhetoric of individualism, with a belief in the existence of differences in talent and life style and values among the population. In public schools, students representing all these traditions and situations come together under a common roof; they come together for a relatively common learning purpose; they also come together to be prepared for the same adult mores and general norms. Does this process allow for preexisting differences sufficiently to maintain their legitimacy? Their advocacy? Or does such a process necessarily require the assimilation of different cultures, the amalgamation of different desires and roles and outlooks, the punishment and control of difference and deviance?

Figuratively speaking, the schools provide a window into the homes, the families, and the communities of many variations in cultural styles and backgrounds. However, the schools' typical response to the pluralistic nature of their own clientele very often denies the existence of diversity itself. Thus, although the schools seem the perfect setting for the conflict accompanying pluralism, most operate as if consensus were the unchallenged mode and as if conflict among pluralistic groups were both unnecessary and inappropriate. Rather than seeing the confrontation among differences as bringing forth a new dialectic and a new synthesis, the schools seek to avoid that conflict via the imposition of an established consensus. This consensus is supported not just by ruling community political elites but by the weight of professional expertise, by which a set of distinctive norms appear to be the product of trained expertise rather than moral choice alone. Internal attempts, by either students or teachers, to alter this consensus in the absence of community support usually prove to be an exercise in futility.

We can see the effect of these tendencies in the ways in which schools deal with the cultural pluralism of our society, in both historic and contemporary context. The racism of the larger society finds expression in intellectual content and organizational procedures in school operations. The curriculum is, of course, one illustration of these value preferences. In terms of both what is omitted and what is retained we can see the effects of cultural dominance by Western, white, and Protestant thought. *The selections by Neal Justin, "Culture Conflict and Mexican-American Achievement," and by Robert B. Kaplan, "The Present Failure to Educate the American Indian," are provocative discussions of this cultural dominance and its tragic effects.*

Instructional procedures and patterns of classroom organization and control mirror similar priorities in behavior and the learning process. Teachers teach in standardized ways, ways they find comfortable in terms of their own styles, talents, and experiences. Essentially, they stress a highly verbal interactional form and control of body movement and expressions of emotions. Students who because of their own ethnic or social class background or personal style favor or are more comfortable with different forms of interaction are left out. In many of the teaching situations judged to be difficult or undesirable, the "clash of styles" is the root of the problem.

The selection of teachers from certain social class backgrounds, and in the past from white racial origins, has led to a rather homogeneous teaching population. Colleges, the recruiting and training grounds for new teachers, have played crucial roles in the development of these discriminatory patterns. The homogeneity of background, of training, and of peer socialization in the profession established an apparent consensus on the nature and conduct of schooling. This consensus is not merely a reflection of racism, and racial advantages for whites are by no means the only lines of challenge and strain for a consensus-oriented system amidst difference and conflict. We can see similar tendencies developed as a function of differences in social class membership. Although the school was originally conceived as a public trust to help youngsters overcome "accidents of birth"—including specifically class-biased opportunities—it has operated to maintain class divisions and ensure generational economic stability. Educational patterns in the curriculum, in staffing and instructional procedures, in patterns of control, and in the very organization of the student and student-adult system, all lead irrevocably to this effect. Formal tracking procedures merely solidify the informal distinctions and discriminations operative in most schools.

The problems and potentials of difference and conflict are not merely products of the organization of a local school. It is clear that entire educational systems are segregated by race and social class: often a town or a city will have a high school that is largely black and another (or several) that is largely white, or some largely lower class or poor and others largely middle class or affluent. The community itself obviously supports many of these distinctions—perhaps all the community, perhaps only the elite or the privileged white and affluent portions—perhaps consciously, perhaps not. But this discussion returns us to our prior review of the nature of ideologies or value systems and the mechanisms of control. The ideologies that we have reviewed in this section and the mechanisms of control that we have likewise reviewed operate to create and/or support the maintenance of certain kinds of educational differences and the subordination of various cultural, economic, and sex-role differences. *In their article, "Sexism in the Elementary School," Carol Jacobs and Cynthia Eaton demonstrate how sex roles and differences are fostered in elementary school experiences.*

The essential questions here are ones that face the entire society, of course. Ours is a society that has prided itself on the rhetoric of pluralism. But we have constantly opted for assimilation. And control of our major economic and political institutions rests in the hands of monocultural elites, not in any mass-based populations that are ethnically or racially diverse in origin and practice. For the school to deal productively with the possibilities of differences, for the school to utilize conflict creatively, would require a resource base and a mission markedly different from those of current operations. It would require a staff and a support system experienced with pluralism and differences and willing to take risks in order to achieve progress. And it would require an institutional commitment to remake our social order. For the school cannot operate for long at odds with major social ideologies and patterns of power. This dilemma is but another example of the problems of differences in the school. Without a clear moral focus, aside from contemporary societal norms, that is, the school is almost incapable of taking risky or controversial positions on moral issues, on issues of value preference or ideology. Thus it cannot itself in any way exploit societal pluralism for the purposes of educational advantage, instruction, or gain, let alone societal reform. It is caught in apparent neutrality, and because neutrality does not itself exist, the school is caught in adherence to traditional norms and the maintenance of a mythic social consensus.

THE NONSCHOOL SOCIALIZING SYSTEM

As we indicated earlier, the school is not an isolated organization. It does not set its own goals; neither does it have the mandate to implement them independently of the community social structure. Its operational structure is constantly beseiged by external forces, all attempting to influence the cultural transmission process in their own way. Accordingly, what occurs in the daily management of the school system may also be expected to work back to affect the values, sentiments, and operations of the tangential segments with which it interacts, that is, families, community agencies, and so on. Moreover, although the school is society's designated institution for the formal education and control of the young, it is not the only institution contributing to that mission. The similarities and differences between the schools and other youth-serving institutions should shed additional light on the peculiar mission and function of these systems.

The primary social unit that deals with the young is the family. In our culture, and indeed in most organized societies, the family is the first and most enduring arena for social interaction and the socialization of new members of the society. The family is an intimate social unit, one stressing close personal relations between all members. Clear role divisions do exist between adults and youngsters, males and females, but even these divisions are muted in the case of clear individual preferences or differences. The schools differ considerably from the family in their stress on mass relationships; this stress results both in more impersonal relations, characterized by distance rather than closeness, and in the use of universalist standards of evaluation and relationship. Role divisions not only are clear between adult and youth, they are maintained despite any individual's characteristics or preferences.

As a mass and public system, the school is obliged to counteract the particularism of the family. The school is secular where the family may be sacred, assimilationist where the family may prefer separatism or legitimate difference. Sometimes the school and the family stress the same norms or goals and values, sometimes they conflict. Given the nature of differences and the power to make societal decisions, the school and the family are most likely to be alike when the students (and family) are white and middle or upper middle class. In other cases we may expect conflict between home and school or between school and community or neighborhood. On occasion, the parties to the conflict may be student and school, with parents still in the background; on other occasions parents may be in the forefront.

The local community itself is another broad arena for the socialization of the young. Broad community norms are likely to be implemented through a variety of agencies, including local media, entertainment and recreational opportunities, churches, police and courts, youth clubs, and YM–YWCA's and YM–YWHA's. All of these agencies seek to realize the community's norms and values in their relations with youth. They seek to train youth to believe in and to act in accordance with the standards of the local community. Their business is not instruction; they are not educational in any strict sense of the word. However, they do engage in moral training. They also help plan the politicization of the young in directions sanctioned by the local community. Some schools seem to be in a constant state of warfare, primarily because of the nature of the lessons or values being taught in these youth-oriented systems. In some instances, for example, youth agencies have so opened young people's eyes to alternative futures they have become disaffected from the schools and have taken their schools to task on the inadequacy of their education. In other instances, outside groups have espoused particularistic sets of values that run counter to those the school seeks to maintain as the arbiter of a general consensus. *"The Socialization Community," by Ronald Lippitt, is an attempt to focus on the linkage between the characteristics of a "national culture" and the goals and techniques of parents and teachers.* The article avoids the usual emphasis on processes of interaction between socialization agents and children and focuses our attention on the relations among these socialization agents.

One subelement of the youth-serving community is the youth community or "youth culture" itself. Some scholars have argued that the youth of today have nothing coherent enough to be called a separate culture or movement. Be that as it may, we are drawn to a review of the youth revolt in its many and varied forms. In some cases a clear presentation of cultural and life-style alternatives, in other cases manifestly a political movement for reform or restructuring of schooling, more and more young people are establishing their own personal and collective priorities for schooling and education. Many scholars of educational systems and many professional educators continue to treat students as the product of educational operations, as passive entities to be acted upon or planned for. But changing times demonstrate the need for new conceptions that see youth truly as active components in the process. Such a view also requires new visions of educational systems that permit and encourage the development of youth consciousness. *"The Generation Gap," by Edgar Z. Friedenberg, suggests the possibility that the intergenerational conflict may, in fact, be an expression of a genuine class conflict between an exploitive older generation and a more politically and socially aware youth.* In this context youth-adult issues, and school issues, take on new political meaning.

In fact, this entire section may be seen as a series of explorations of the school and community conditions leading to the youth culture and youth "revolution" in school.

A. Ideologies and Norms—Myths and Realities

Compensatory Education and Contemporary Liberalism in the United States: A Sociological View

D. C. MORTON AND D. R. WATSON [1]

The greater the degree of internal structural and cultural differentiation of a society, the less likely it is that educational institutions will promote all groups' values "equivalently." As an established empirical generalization, it seems that in modern societies some groups' values and skills predominate over those of other groups. These groups, who have a consequent advantage in school, are those which have an economic and power advantage in modern society, i.e. the dominant groups.[2] This paper constitutes an attempt to demonstrate sociologically the full significance of this empirical generalization for the education of children from subordinate groups. First, we examine the concepts of "compensatory education" and "liberalism."

WHAT IS COMPENSATORY EDUCATION? [3]

During the past decade, increasing emphasis has been placed by educationists and applied social scientists upon the "disadvantage" and "deprivation" of children from certain socio-economic groups. This emphasis has been particularly marked in the USA, but is also increasingly noticeable in Britain. These concepts of "disadvantage" and "deprivation" are often ill-defined and diffuse, but seem to centre upon an alleged lack of "language development" in these children. Educational programmes have been developed to "compensate" for these perceived "deficits."[4] Most such "com-

[1] The authors wish to thank Mr. E. C. Cuff for his assistance in the proof reading of an early draft of this paper, and the Bernard van Leer Foundation of Holland and the New World Foundation of New York for their financial assistance.

[2] See, for example, the reader edited by A. H. Halsey, J. Floud and C. A. Anderson: *Education, Economy and Society*, New York: Free Press, 1961, for some of the material which established this empirical generalization.

[3] See E. W. Gordon: "Programs of Compensatory Education," in M. Deutsch *et al.*: *Social Class, Race and Psychological Development*, New York: Holt, Rinehart and Winston, 1968; H. L. Miller: *Education for the Disadvantaged*, New York: Free Press, 1967; A. H. Passow: *Education in Depressed Areas*, New York: Teachers College Press, 1963; H. Rees: *Deprivation and Compensatory Education*, New York: Houghton Mifflin, 1968.

[4] For an outline of the data cast in terms of these alleged deficits, see the social psychologist T. F. Pettigrew: *A Profile of the Negro American*, Princeton: Van Nostrand, 1964, Chapter 5. Pettigrew also makes reference to compensatory programmes in this chapter (see pp. 125–6).

FROM *International Review of Education*, Vol. 17, No. 3 (1971), pp. 289–307.

pensatory programmes" are related to the pre-school education of children, being rooted in psychological research into "early childhood development." In general, the emphasis upon linguistic and perceptual deficits in compensatory education programmes seems to have developed from the interests of psychologists, who sometimes came into this field of research from that of remedial education for mentally-handicapped children. The programmes generally aim at "compensating" children through pre-empting the growth of deficits by exposing the children to an "enriched," stimulating, pre-school environment. The main objective is to equip such children to compete with more "privileged" groups of children in the school system, from the earliest possible age. These programmes feed into dominant psychological theories of the development of skills and "intelligence" and their relatedness to success within the educational system, which in turn is supposed [5] to be causally related to success in the "wider society."

The Liberal Ideology

This ideology implies a view of society, as well as being a set of explicit political beliefs and directives, which we believe to be widespread in both the USA and Britain.[6] We shall be primarily concerned with the former aspect. The liberal ideology advocates social change in piecemeal fashion, within the existing framework of social institutions. It denies the need for basic institutional reorganization, upheaval or revolution. Thus the liberal ideology is in a sense a variety of conservative ideology rather than of radical-socialist ideology, although recognizing the "need" for limited institutional change. In the case of increasing claims for civil rights in the U S A ,[7] the extreme conservative argues that Negroes are in their present situation vis-à-vis other groups of Americans, because they "deserve to be," by virtue of their alleged inferiority, laziness, apathy and lax morality. The radical socialist claims that Negroes are in their present position because American social institutions are fundamentally racist, and that their plight is inevitable, given that type of social structure. His implied ameliorative action involves basic structural changes, such as the setting up of a separate black state founded upon Negro institutions and culture. The liberal adopts

[5] For a more cautious assessment of this widespread supposition, see C. A. Anderson: "A Sceptical Note on Education and Mobility," in A. H. Halsey, J. Floud and C. A. Anderson: op. cit., and S. M. Lipset and R. Bendix: Social Mobility in Industrial Societies, Berkeley: Univ. of California Press, 1959, chap. VII.

[6] Here we are really referring to the modern form of the liberal ideology, which, as will be seen, assumes certain relationships to the state and other powerful bureaucracies. Nineteenth century liberalism tended, relatively speaking, to be more anti-bureaucratic, anti-clerical and anti-elitist than its modern counterpart. In this section was stress the basic components of modern liberalism in ideal-type form.

[7] Of course, neither liberals in the general sense nor "compensatory educationists" concentrate solely upon a specific group (e.g., Negroes) as opposed to other "underprivileged" groups. We cite the case of "underprivileged Negroes" as one of many examples from groups of low socio-economic status upon which a political position may be assumed.

the position of the "reasonable man" by taking an allegedly middle path, which assumes the fundamental adequacy of American institutions and denies the need for radical change, but acknowledges that "something needs to be done" if the system is to function equitably.

The liberal ideology is epitomised by non-violent, constitutional, legal and administrative "solutions," whereas radical ideologies are often associated with violent and revolutionary "solutions." Thus Samuel Lubell [8] has claimed that "in the South the first need has long been to end all discrimination *by law.*" Karl Mannheim [9] has shown how the liberal perspective involves an identification with bourgeois groups, a humanistic morality (see Dr. M. L. King, Jr.'s statement below) and stresses individualism and the importance of rationality in social problem-solving—a rationality embodied in bureaucratic action and administrative routine.[10] Liberal solutions tend to avoid those sectors of society which are "emotionally-charged" or constituted of so many "contradictions" as to be unmanageable by bureaucratic-administrative rationality.

In the mid-1960's *laissez faire* conservatives and segregationists in Congress were finally overcome by the liberals on the civil rights and poverty issues. During the first half of the decade, poverty and related problems became more visible to the public.[11] Urban poverty in particular was increasingly viewed as a threat to the established social order. In Conant's dramatic words: "We are allowing social dynamite to accumulate in our large cities." [12] The civil rights movement came to be perceived, rightly or wrongly, as one of the primary sources of pressure for rapid social change. Civil rights commentators, protestors, and others stressed not only the high levels of poverty and unemployment of the largely Negro, urban centres, but also the part played by educational institutions in perpetuating such problems. Thus education became a prime concern of civil rights groups in the northern cities as well as in the segregated south.

[8] S. Lubell: *White and Black: Test of a Nation,* New York: Harper Colophon, 1964, pp. 190–1.

[9] K. Mannheim: *Ideology and Utopia,* London: Routledge and Kegan Paul, 1960.

[10] This administrative bias is by no means to be simply equated with governmental intervention. It also extends to "liberal" policies fostered by private enterprise, such as the Ford Foundation programmes. "The Ford Foundation," says C. E. Silberman, "which is sponsoring large scale 'gray area' programmes in five cities, plus a state-wide project in North Carolina, has bet millions on a grandiose fusion of paternalism and bureaucracy"; see his *Crisis in Black and White,* New York: Vintage Books, 1964, pp. 351–6.

[11] Among those who contributed to this was M. Harrington, through his book *The Other America,* New York: Macmillan Publishing Co., Inc., 1962.

[12] See J. B. Conant: *Slums and Suburbs: A Commentary on Schools in Metropolitan Areas,* New York: McGraw-Hill, 1961, p. 10. In relation to liberal policies of large-scale corporate bureaucracies in the private sector, see R. A. Cloward and F. Fox Piven's article "Corporate Imperialism for the Poor," *Nation,* 16 October 1967, pp. 365–7. Cloward and Piven attribute the efforts of large-scale department stores and insurance companies in this respect to their vested interests in establishing social order so as to reduce huge damage to their property in ghetto riots. See also A. Sinfield: "Poverty Rediscovered," *Race,* 1968, pp. 202–9, on the "special areas" approach.

In the light of growing public concern, more and more governmental officials came to see the institutions of education not only as a primary focus of civil rights workers' demands but also as a means of redressing many grievances through breaking "the cycle of poverty." P. Meranto [13] reports the then Secretary of Health, Education and Welfare as linking poverty, unemployment and poor education with rising crime and delinquency (that is with growing social disorder) [14] and as expressing the hope that better education would break these links. In this context, the 1965 Elementary and Secondary Education Act, which embodied the liberal ideology, provided Congress with a vehicle for at least partially satisfying the needs of the poor "without appearing to 'knuckle-under' to the demands of civil rights groups," and led to a dramatic increase in Federal aid to primary and secondary schools, from about $500 million in 1965 to $1800 million in 1966.[15]

As part of this movement towards accommodating these threats to order through adjusting the institutions of education, the function of compensatory education became more clearly and explicitly defined. As already indicated, the liberal accepts the legitimacy of the existing social order and defines those groups who implicitly or explicitly challenge the adequacy of the social system by their non-conformity to dominant norms and values, as being ill-equipped to maximise the advantages supposed to be available to them within the present system. Such non-conformity and expressions of discontent are often "explained" as being symptoms of maladjustment.[16] John Horton lucidly elaborates these criteria of maladjustment and points to their political implications.[17]

Because the liberal accepts the general inviolability of the social order, he often regards problems as being moral in nature, as in this passage by Martin Luther King, Jr.:

> By non-violent resistance the Negro can also enlist all men of goodwill in his struggle for equality. The problem is not a purely racial one, with Negroes set against whites. In the end it is not a struggle between people at all, but a tension between justice and injustice. Non-violent resistance

[13] See P. Meranto: *The Politics of Federal Aid to Education*, New York: Syracuse University Press, 1967, p. 36.

[14] Our insertion. For an account of how similar concerns for social order and discipline pervaded the movement towards providing universal secondary education in England, see D. V. Glass: "Education and Social Change in Modern England," in Halsey, Floud and Anderson, *op. cit.*, pp. 394–5.

[15] P. Meranto, *op. cit.*, p. 41.

[16] M. D. Fantini, in his article "Beyond Cultural Deprivation and Compensatory Education," *Psychiatry and Social Science Review*, 13, 1969, pp. 6–13, testifies to the prevalence of these "adjustment criteria" in the schools (pp. 6–8), but since he, unlike the present authors, is not explicitly concerned with an ideology analysis, he does not note the broad ideological roots of such an assumption. So he does not note the prevalence of its application to structural situations outside formal education.

[17] J. Horton: "Order and Conflict Theories of Social Problems as Competing Ideologies," *American Journal of Sociology*, May 1966, pp. 701–13. See also C. Wright Mills: "The Professional Ideology of Social Pathologists," *American Journal of Sociology*, XLIX, 1942, pp. 165–80.

is not aimed against oppressors but against oppression. Under its banner, consciences, not racial groups, are enlisted. . . . The way of non-violence means a willingness to suffer and sacrifice. It may mean going to jail . . . it may even mean physical death. But if physical death is the price a man must pay to free his children and his white brethren from a permanent death of the spirit, then nothing could be more redemptive.[18]

The liberal maintains his ideology with its implicit emphasis on the essential morality of the social order by adopting individualism as a sufficient mode of both understanding and solving the "social problems" and "social evils" which he perceives. Thus Samuel Lubell [19] asks "What are the conditions that are needed for racial peace to become attainable? The key requirement, I believe, is to replace racialism with individualism. What is indispensable is . . . that we restructure our own thinking to be able to treat each Negro as a recognisable individual and not as an anonymous black face . . . Until that comes to pass, the social framework for orderly evolutionary racial progress will be missing."

Morality and individualism are combined in the liberal's belief in the God-given or constitutionally-guaranteed "rights of the individual," and in his moral condemnation of those in the dominant group, such as some employers and landlords, who visibly deny such rights to members of minority groups. He regards all men as being created equal, with equal rights, but also extends this belief to the assumption that all men are similar. Thus he assumes that all Americans, whether Negro, Jewish, Puerto Rican, or Sioux Indian, can come to conform to and identify with the so-called "American Dream" of achievement and success. Since the liberal identifies himself with the image of social order embodied in the American Dream, he easily assumes that all men not only can, but should, so conform and identify.

THE RELATION OF LIBERALISM TO COMPENSATORY EDUCATION

It is our contention that the ideology of compensatory education is a specific expression of the liberal ideology. From this standpoint the formulation of social problems in psychological terms such as "maladjustment," "linguistic or sensory deprivation" and "poor motivation" can be seen as the scientific counterpart of the individualistic approach to social problems which characterises the liberal perspective. The technical terminology of psychology thus reflects the liberal's conviction that problems are rooted in individuals rather than in the overall social order.

Liberal convictions that the social order is both legitimate and right are

[18] Martin Luther King, Jr.: "The Meaning of Non-Violence," *Dialogue*, 1, 1968, 2, pp. 3–4.
[19] S. Lubell, *op. cit.*, p. 190.

buttressed by several other concepts which focus attention elsewhere. A common "ameliorative" policy advocated by liberals is the "special areas approach." By implying that "the problem," whether that of poverty or educational disadvantage, is limited to certain areas and to a small minority of the total population, such an approach tends to deflect attention from the full extent of the problem and its roots in the overall social system. This approach is exemplified by such concepts as "the inner city" and "educational priority areas," which together focus attention away from rural and small-town problems and the educational disadvantages encountered by working-class children everywhere.[20]

As a variant of conservative ideology, the liberal perspective involves an implicit identification with the dominant, privileged strata of society,[21] commonly referred to as "the Establishment."[22] For example, Bayard Rustin's address[23] to the Center for the Study of Democratic Institutions contains many transparent and explicit indications of his identification with "the leadership group," whom he distinguishes from "the simple people on the street." Such identification usually leads to the liberal's implicit acceptance of the dominant group's values and skills as those of society as a whole. The ethic of professionalism, which includes ideals of vocation, service and selflessness that are part of the moral position of liberalism, represents a major example of a dominant group value. Horton suggests that professionals, under the guise of "scientific neutrality" or "professional detachment," assume that their own particular group values and perspectives constitute the core values and perspectives of the majority of Americans. In particular, it is reasonable to assume that social workers and educators increasingly construe professional/upper middle-class values as the core values of society as a whole.[24] This general orientation is expressed in the use of such phrases as "culturally deprived."[25] In C. Wright Mills' parlance, the vocabulary and

[20] See A. Sinfield, op. cit., for a critique of the special areas approach, and see B. Bernstein and D. Young: "Social Class Differences in Conceptions of the Uses of Toys," Sociology, 1, 1967, pp. 131–40, and B. Bernstein and D. Henderson: "Social Class Differences in the Relevance of Language to Socialisation," Sociology, 3, 1969, pp. 1–20, among many other contributions testifying to the middle-class bias of the formal educational system, such as H. S. Becker: "Social Class Variations in the Teacher-Pupil Relationship," Journal of Educational Sociology, 25, 1952, pp. 451–65; A. V. Cicourel and J. I. Kitsuse: The Educational Decision-Makers, Indianapolis: Bobbs-Merrill, 1963.

[21] See the paradigm presented by J. Horton, op. cit., p. 706, and his comments on p. 705 and 709.

[22] See K. Mannheim, op. cit., p. 199.

[23] Tape-recording of B. Rustin: "The Negro Revolution," Center for the Study of Democratic Institutions.

[24] See P. Goodman's essay on vocational guidance in Utopian Essays and Practical Proposals, New York: Random House, 1962, for a critical attack upon social work policies based on such assumptions.

[25] That non-middle-class cultures exist and are widespread in American society is well documented by such studies as Oscar Lewis's La Vida, New York: Random House, 1966, and "The Culture of Poverty," Scientific American, 215, Oct. 1966, and B. Jackson: Working Class Community, London: Routledge and Kegan Paul, 1968.

assumptions of social pathologists are socially "situated" in the dominant groups of society.[26]

An important instance of the tendency of professionals to assume a widespread consensus with their own "establishment values" is the fact, noted by many observers, that seemingly objective and scientific IQ tests are far more "culture-bound" than "culture-fair." [27] Alfred Binet,[28] who developed the first scale of IQ tests in 1905, made it perfectly clear that by 1908 he was aware that his tests measured the effects of cultural training upon "intelligence" rather than "intellectual capacity," despite his efforts to avoid this danger. Professor F. L. Goodenough of the University of Minnesota, who in 1926 herself devised a widely-used performance test which she believed to be "culture-fair" has since admitted to being mistaken. Writing with D. B. Harris [29] in 1950 she stated ". . . the search for a culture-free test, whether of intelligence, artistic ability, personal-social characteristics, or any other measurable trait is illusory, and . . . the naive assumption that the mere freedom from verbal requirements renders a test equally suitable for all groups is no longer tenable." She even apologised for her own earlier study.

In effect, such tests implicitly over-generalise in that they assume that the norms, values, orientations and skills which constitute the intelligence of middle-class people are the only valid measurer of the intelligence of people of all groups in the society and therefore provide an "objective" basis for comparing all people. Professor Allison Davis [30] aptly crystallises this issue as follows:

> The lifelong process by which culture helps to guide, develop, limit and evaluate all mental problem-solving has not received sufficiently serious attention from either test-makers or educators. They continually make the error of regarding middle-class culture, and even more narrowly, middle-class school culture, as the "true" culture, or the "best" culture. More than 95% of our teachers and professors are middle-class in their socio-economic status. Like all other cultural groups, teachers and professors regard that particular version of culture (those mores, emotional patterns, and social values) which they have learned from their own families, friends, and teachers, as the "best" and only "true" culture. This attitude is powerfully reflected in school curriculums, in intelligence tests, and in teachers' judgments of their pupils.[31] It is an attitude which is fatal to

[26] See C. Wright Mills: "Situated Actions and Vocabularies of Motive," *American Sociological Review*, V, 1940, pp. 901–13; and "The Professional Ideology of Social Pathologists," *op. cit.*

[27] See K. Eells, A. Davis, *et al.: Intelligence and Cultural Differences*, Chicago: University of Chicago, 1951, p. 5 and 26, and O. Klineberg, *Race and Psychology*, Paris: UNESCO, 1958.

[28] See K. Eells, *et al., ibid.*, chapter V.

[29] See F. Goodenough and D. B. Harris: "Studies in the Psychology of Children's Drawings," *Psychological Bulletin*, Sept. 1950.

[30] See K. Eells, *et al., op. cit.*, p. 26, and C. E. Silberman, *op. cit.*, p. 267–8, for a very similar statement.

[31] See H. S. Becker, *op. cit.*, for validation of this point (our footnote).

the development of the full mental capacity of either the teacher or the pupil.

In what ways do the values and other elements of the culture of the middle-class become expressed in supposedly objective and fair tests? Among many general predisposing factors mentioned by Eells and his collaborators is the nature of the vocabulary and grammar taught and used in schools, which is that commonly used within middle-class groups, including the teaching profession, and which may be unfamiliar to the children of non-middle-class parents, amongst whom different "codes" and orientations to the use of language predominate. The work of Bernstein and his colleagues seems to substantiate this point.[32]

In spite of Binet's failure and Professor Goodenough's assertion, many testers continue to construct what they claim to be culture-free or culture-fair tests.[33] Many items which supposedly test apprehension of spatial relationships are often claimed to be culture-fair even when they rely heavily upon language in giving directions pertaining to the item. Eells points out that such directions often utilise abstractions with which a middle-class child is likely to be more familiar.[34] One such item, intended for nine year old children, is:

Mark the group of three letters that has the most loops:

BTB   DWD   FMF   HFL

Eells reports that proportionally twice as many low status group children made errors in answering this item, and gives scores of examples of similarly biased items. We suggest that the concepts and grammatical structure in the directions would be more familiar to a higher status nine year old.

Another test item which contains cultural bias is referred to by Klineberg.[35] In one portion of the National Intelligence Test the subject must supply the missing word in the following sentence: ". . . should prevail in churches and libraries"; the correct answer being "silence." As Klineberg points out: "Anyone who has visited an American Negro church in the south of the United States knows, however, that silence is neither the rule nor the ideal." On the basis of their experience, Negro children would be less likely than others to answer this item "correctly."

Bernstein's research into social class differences in the use of language and

---

[32] See B. Bernstein and D. Henderson, *op. cit.*

[33] Pettigrew, *op. cit.*, in his chapter on Negro American Intelligence plays down the questioning bias in IQ tests. Although paying lipservice to the "class linked" nature of IQ tests, Pettigrew treats the tests as being *to all intents and purposes* valid indicators of intelligence. M. D. Fantini also implicitly accepts IQ tests as valid measures of intellectual ability and development (*op. cit.*, p. 8).

[34] See K. Eells, *et al.*, *op. cit.*, pp. 285–6.

[35] See O. Klineberg, *op. cit.*, p. 12.

toys, during early childhood, indicates differences in the cultural meanings which are realised through language by different socio-economic groups. These differences favour the middle-class child, since the meanings and modes of realisation employed in school are those most familiar to the middle classes. Bernstein also claims that experiments and tests which lead to "unfavourable" comparisons of working-class with middle-class children tend to compare the groups solely in terms of the presence or absence of middle-class cultural elements. This gives rise to a "deficit-system" view of working-class children and the notion that they are in need of "compensation." [36] Bernstein finally attacks the concepts of compensatory education for focusing attention upon the child's home and "sub-culture" as the source of his educational "disadvantages," thereby distracting analytical and practical attention from the intrinsic bias of the school in favour of middle-class children.

POSSIBLE UNFORESEEN CONSEQUENCES OF THE IMPLEMENTATION OF LIBERAL POLICIES

This variety of "liberalism" may well contain many limitations. Let us trace what may be the wider social repercussions if compensatory education programmes advocated by liberals are successfully implemented. We can also draw some parallels with liberal policies outside education. Liberal educationists tend to overlook social institutions outside the bounds of formal education in their explanations of and solutions for the problems they address.[37] Other liberals, whilst still considering only formal institutions, often discuss a wider range of them.

As Rustin points out, the "technological revolution" in the USA, as shaped by the dominant groups,[38] is evidently leading to a general contraction of the labour force. At the same time, compensatory education programmes have the manifest aim of equipping people to compete more successfully for these contracting opportunities. Hence, it may well be that such programmes, if successful in increasing the numbers of qualified and highly motivated school-leavers, will also succeed in intensifying the struggle for increasingly scarce job opportunities. Robert K. Merton has already pointed out, in his essay on

[36] Liberals, in their ideologies and policies, often ignore factors relating to IQ tests that traditional conservatives stress—e.g. arguments for the genetic basis of IQ test performance. These contradict the liberals' heavy emphasis on "environmentalism," which is the assumption underlying most compensatory education programmes. On the alleged genetic basis of IQ test performance and possible implications for educational technique, see A. Jensen's: "How Much Can We Boost IQ and Scholastic Achievement?," *Harvard Educational Review*, 39, 1969, pp. 1–123.

[37] Fantini's article, *op. cit.*, is a good example of this myopia. He speaks of a "re-formed educational system."

[38] See B. Rustin, *op. cit.*, and R. K. Merton, "The Machine, the Worker and the Engineer" in R. K. Merton, *op. cit.*, on how the "technological revolution" is often used as a weapon by employers against the demands of workers.

anomie, the unforeseen consequences of limited opportunity structures in society. They engender large numbers of people whose aspirations have been "blocked," leading to various forms of crime, delinquency and rebellion, which, of course, are directly counter to the *manifest* aims of education as embodied in liberal ideology.

This increased competition for jobs may lead to the development of new patterns of racial prejudice and discrimination, or new adaptations of existing patterns.[39] As Merton and others have indicated, to imbue different groups of the population with the same qualities (e.g. the skills and motivation to compete for jobs), is not necessarily to remove intolerance, discrimination and other "irrational" barriers to equality.[40] It has been pointed out by the Political and Economic Planning Report on "Racial Discrimination in Britain" that discriminatory practices in employment tend to be greatest in the case of *highly-qualified* minority group members. Thus, what are, in the case of white Anglo-Saxon Protestants regarded as virtues ("ambition," "willingness to compete," "determination to make good," "self-confidence") became perceived vices when displayed by, say, Jews ("self-seeking," "cut-throat," "ruthlessness," "over-confidence," "superciliousness"). In this, and other more basic ways, the liberal "solutions" of assimilation and acculturation may not only leave white prejudice untouched, but also leave the Negro's hatred of the white man and the oft-postulated autonomous social and cultural identity of the Negro out of account.[41]

In many respects, therefore, the liberal educator's solution unwittingly implies many changes of a fundamental (or radical) nature in many institutional arrangements, such as the occupational structure and the provision for leisure, which fall outside the framework of formal educational institutions. For instance, if everyone is to "make good" occupationally within a context of full employment, then each individual's working week would have to be shortened and his leisure time increased, given the declining total demand for labour. Thus, liberal policies which purportedly tread a middle path in social change, ultimately imply many derivative changes which have been characterized as "radical" and recommended by such radicals as Paul Goodman—changes which the middle path is designed to avoid. Needless to

[39] See R. K. Merton's essay "Social Structure and Anomie" in Merton, *op. cit.*, and also L. Killian and C. Grigg, *Racial Crisis in America*, Prentice-Hall, 1964, p. 114, for a similar theme regarding segregation.

[40] See R. K. Merton's essay "The Self-Fulfilling Prophecy," in Merton, *op. cit.* Fundamentally conservative policies, in the past, have resolved this contradiction by educating subordinate groups to dominate group values, especially values recognizing the legitimacy of the existing overall social order and the legitimacy of the subordinate groups' "special," i.e. separate, lowly position in that social order. See, for example, J. Dollard: *Caste and Class in a Southern Town*, New York: Harper, 1949.

[41] As Silberman (*op. cit.*, p. 316) says, ". . . The Negroes' failure to 'acculturate' is due only partly to ignorance or indifference; they do not acculturate because they regard doing the things implied by that term as treason to their race—as 'going along with Mr. Charlie's program.'"

say, liberals do not follow through these implications.[42] Without these derivative changes, the "liberal solution" alone is little more than an articulated tokenism, the long-term short-comings of which have been attested to by Killian and Grigg: [43]

> White liberals may regard each token step as a gain for which all Americans should be thankful. But in the context of intergroup relations, each of these steps will be a victory for Negroes, and a defeat for the dominant white group. But such small symbolic victories will not signify the termination of the power struggle, either in the communities in which they occur, or in the larger American Society. In spite of temporary victories or temporary defeats, the drive of Negroes for identity will continue for a long time. There will be respites following periods of struggle and stress. Token victories will not eliminate the substratum of dissatisfaction which underlies the Negro's struggle, but they will encourage renewal of the struggle.

Hence, liberal values in education may not only be doomed to failure (in their own terms) but may actively produce results which liberals would regard as problems.

Some liberals, largely outside the field of education, perceive a need for the creation of jobs, and suggest that governmental agencies should assume this function. But many of these recommendations, when examined in detail, would, if implemented, merely tend to reinforce occupational stratification on ethnic group lines. For example, Bayard Rustin [44] suggests that young Negroes, who he alleges are sitting in Central Park, smoking marihuana and drinking wine, could be put to work by City Hall, renovating and maintaining the park. He also suggests employing Negroes as "assistant teachers," to take over the disciplinary, supervisory and custodial duties of the qualified professional teacher. This is only one step removed from the table-waiting, shoe-shining, Redcap image of the Negroes' place in society.

Perhaps the most telling limitation of the liberal position is that members of subordinate groups may, as Horton puts it, "have difficulty in recognizing themselves in the role in which they are cast by the liberal story." It may be that even Rustin's position, where he speaks of his solving the problems of

---

[42] Willard Waller, in his article "Social Problems and the Mores," *American Sociological Review*, 1, 1936, pp. 922–33, brings out the contradictions in such "liberal-humanitarian" approaches to social problem-solving. Liberal-humanitarians define certain problems in terms of their humanitarian mores (sense of justice, etc.). But Waller says that really to solve social problems a change in the more fundamental "organizational" mores would have to be effected—that is a change in the values (e.g., the reverence for private property) which are the foundation of the American social order. Humanitarians, in spite of their adherence to humanitarian mores, balk at such basic change; they want the organizational mores to be left intact, even if this means not solving the problems which they seem so concerned about from the perspective of their humanitarian mores. See G. Myrdal: *An American Dilemma*, New York: Harper and Row, 1962, on how such value conflicts affect the social situation.

[43] L. Killian and C. Grigg, *op. cit.*, p. 133.

[44] B. Rustin, *op. cit.*

"the simple people on the streets" denotes a lack of rapport with his less privileged fellow Negroes' own perception of their plight. As Horton says: [45] "[The liberal sociologist] probably speaks least of all for the Negro. The liberal sociologist will have some difficulty describing the world from the view-point of Negro 'rioters' in Los Angeles and other cities.[46] In any case, he will not agree with anyone who believes (in fact or in ideology) that the Negro may have a separate and self-determining identity." Similarly, as Carmichael and Hamilton put it: ". . . The white liberal must view the racial scene through a drastically different lens from the black man's." [47] As an example of this, Silberman quotes an East Harlem Negro adolescent's attitude towards the social workers who attempt to implement the liberal's point of view: "They're all around the neighbourhood, and most of them are rat fink types. They act like they think we're not human. They think they've got all there is, and all they've got to do is convert us to think and do whatever they think and do." If the Negroes or lower-class people do not endorse the liberal's view of their dilemma, it follows that there is little probability of their long-term cooperation with white liberal policies. "Because of the middle-class orientation of the integration movement, and because of its subconscious racism, and because of its non-violent approach, it has never been able to involve the black proletariat," says Stokely Carmichael, in a recent lecture on Black Power.[48]

According to Carmichael and Hamilton,[49] "The goal of black self-determination and black self-identity—Black Power—is full participation in the decision-making processes affecting the lives of black people . . ." They maintain that existing liberal organizations, both black and white, compromise this goal.

The passivity and dependency of subordinate groups has been fostered by a variety of factors. The bureaucratic implementation of liberal policies has meant that already powerless members of subordinate groups are confronted by a monolithic structure of associated administrative bodies with unified interests. And, as Silberman points out,[50] the whole history and nature of American social welfare has been one of social workers doing things for, by, to and because of, but never *with* their clients.

Indeed, one of the characteristics of bureaucratic organization is that officials tend to develop interests of their own, including the perpetuation of the organization's existence. By their focus on individual "maladjustment" officials avoid dealing with the basic structural preconditions of problems and

[45] See J. Horton, *op. cit.*, p. 712.
[46] See J. Cohen and W. Murphy: *"Burn, Baby, Burn": The Los Angeles Race Riots, August 1965*, London: Gollancz, 1967, for a similar argument (our note)
[47] See S. Carmichael and C. V. Hamilton: *"Black Power": The Politics of Liberation in America*, New York: Vintage, 1967, p. 61.
[48] Carmichael's lecture is transcribed in D. Cooper: *The Dialectics of Liberation*, London: Pelican, 1968, pp. 150–74 (quotation from p. 162).
[49] S. Carmichael and C. V. Hamilton, *op. cit.*, p. 47.
[50] See C. E. Silberman, *op. cit.*, p. 313.

thus continue to produce the "clients" who are the *raison d'être* of their welfare organization. A frequent liberal rationalisation for the non-participation of the "clientèle" is that there are barriers to communication. Better communication, however, would only reveal the previously latent conflicts. One cannot assume that a general consensus already exists which improved communication would make manifest. The liberals' "community consensus" may not exist if the clientèle are admitted as being part of the community.

The changes brought about by administrative bodies or legal measures may be even less significant than even the liberals hope for. The liberal Samuel Lubell has unwittingly made the point for us: [51] "Individuals may continue to fear, hate or shun the Negro, but that should be their own private affair and not be enforced or institutionalized by law. A barber's wife in Greenboro expressed the distinction to be drawn when she said, 'I don't believe in intermarriage but I can teach my children to avoid that. We don't have to keep abusing the coloured people to avoid that.'" In Weberian terms, discrimination may remain institutionalised by virtue of convention instead of law.[52]

SOCIOLOGICAL ORIENTATIONS FOR PRACTICE [53]

To prescribe or devise specific educational techniques would be both sociologically elliptical and space-consuming. Therefore, we shall limit our comments to (a) recommending a few immediate, short-term measures for redressing some of the present inadequacies and (b) suggesting some sociological foundations upon which a more "universalistic" practice may be built.

a) First, from a general point of view, knowledge regarding how educational processes affect large categories of children must be disseminated; theoretically at least, the mass media contain much potential in this area. Existing knowledge on educational disadvantage simply never reaches subordinate group members. However, in approaching the mass media, one obviously comes up against barriers of ideology, as well as financial and other vested interests. Mass media in nations where the ideology of democratic equality of opportunity is supported at the institutional level have a political vested interest in ignoring educational equality. There is a need for the creation of greater consciousness among subordinate group members of their own collective position, in order to intensify critical pressure upon the establishment. On the other hand the media for fostering such consciousness reflect the interests and perspectives of the establishment themselves. From a practical point of view, one can only say that the dilemma and fate of the education of subordinate groups is but one aspect of a wider power struggle. This means that our suggested orientations for practice within education will

[51] See S. Lubell, *op. cit.*, p. 191.
[52] We are indebted to Mr. M. A. Atkinson for this point.
[53] For an outline (though lacking in rigour) which at some points parallels our proposals, see Fantini, *op. cit.*, p. 13.

have little effect unless wider structural reorientations, which our suggestions imply, are effected. Related to the role of the mass media is the gap between educational theory and practice, between researchers and teachers.[54] Researchers in education (especially sociologists) have for some time been aware of certain aspects of the dominant group orientation of formal education, but most teachers have been unable to avail themselves of the full significance of these findings.

As short-term measures, one might suggest such things as staff-student critical seminars (with students in a numerical majority, as they are in the classroom) on improving the education of both parties, plus compulsory[55] and subsidized refresher courses held in colleges and universities at regular intervals for practising teachers. These courses would be explicitly geared to apprising teachers of the dominant group orientation of formal education, how this orientation comes about, and to the presentation of research on how teachers inculcate this orientation. More extensive libraries for teachers should be made available in each school, with budget provision for the on-going addition of relevant research reports, manuals, and other volumes.

Moreover, parent-teacher associations and other links with parents might be extended, but on the parents' terms, not the teachers'. This is also of crucial importance in achieving a more permanent solution, as we will see below. Parent-teacher associations have usually been heavily oriented (in terms of key personnel, etc.) to the teachers, and their views, perspectives and plans. PTA's in the past have all too easily been the mere mouthpiece of the local "teaching establishment";[56] they have been perceived as such by minority group members, and have done little to elicit genuine feedback from a representative cross-section of the parents. It is also notable that most PTA's have excluded the one group who can provide true experiential links between parents and teachers—the students themselves. Much softening of long-hardened bureaucratic and procedural arteries seems called for, as well as a very substantial redistribution of power and the authority to make decisions.

b) However, all such recommendations are of a short-term, makeshift character. To begin truly to redress the problem of dominant-group bias in formal education, one must embark upon fundamental structural reorganiza-

---

[54] It has often been noted that the (hopefully) research-based principles which are taught to student teachers never come to be used by the practising teacher, nor are they by any means always used even by the education lecturer. B. Bernstein, in his paper "A Critique of the Concept of Compensatory Education" to be published in F. Williams (ed.): *Language and Poverty: Perspectives on a Theme,* Chicago: Markham, in press, has said that the simple principle "Work with What the Child Can Offer" has never been fully implemented in practice.

[55] Or, if one shies from compulsory courses, one might compromise to the point of providing strong incentives for teachers to attend such courses—e.g. gearing graduation from such courses to salary increments, or paying above-average salary for course attendance.

[56] Those parents who did participate with any kind of influence were usually middle-class. Fantini, *op. cit.,* points out the "public relations" role of PTA's as well.

tion while possibly using the above measures and principles as an initial lever. In a recent paper, Bernstein [57] has provided some insights into possible means of making such changes fully effective. He advocates basic social reforms to encourage ways in which subordinate-group parents can relate their spheres of competence to the child's educational experiences. This means orienting these experiences to the local subcultural community, not only in order to render formal education consistent with and relevant to the child's total life-situation, but also so that parents, through their competences, can become more fully involved in educating their children.

For teachers, not only does this involve accepting the experiences of the local community members as valid and worthwhile, but above all, it means that teachers should *know* the culture and social structure of their communities, and should be involved in them in ways other than simply performing their present job within the school. Teachers must cease to view the local community simply as the source of all educational deficits and seek to accept and relate to the skill orders, moral symbols, cultural meanings and sensitivities of the local community. In the past, only lipservice has been paid to this principle, partly because to go beyond lipservice involves not only basic changes in the organization of the school and its relation to the local setting, but also assumes fundamental changes in teachers' professional commitments and ideology.

Fantini [58] puts the question this way: "How can an educational process be developed that can deal effectively with diversity?" An important step is the recognition that children are motivated within their own experiential framework as conditioned by their immediate social context as a whole. In relation to IQ testing, Havighurst [59] has claimed that

> . . . middle-class and lower-class children bring to the intelligence-test situation widely disparate cultural experiences by virtue of their social class experience, and that middle-class children get more out of themselves in the ordinary school test situation than do lower-class children. An intelligence test which is to get at the "real" problem-solving ability of children must draw its problems entirely from experiences which are common to all or nearly all the children to be tested; at the same time, such a test must be given under conditions which motivate lower-class children to do their best and which teach them to expect that they will be rewarded for doing their best.

It may very well be that such "culture-fair" IQ tests are an impossibility and that any IQ test is bound to compare groups in terms of a set of standards not equally espoused by all groups. The orientation of IQ tests toward *individual* performance may well in itself imply a positive valuation of individualism which some groups clearly espouse more than others.

---

[57] B. Bernstein: "A Critique . . . ," *op. cit.*
[58] M. Fantini, *op. cit.*
[59] See K. Eells, *et al., op. cit.,* p. 21.

The fundamental reorientation of the structure of the school (both internally and in relation to its wider social context), whilst involving basic changes, is not impossible. We shall deal first with the teacher-pupil relationship. According to Bernstein,[60] most working-class children do possess in their *passive* vocabulary the vocabulary used by middle-class children. The use of what Bernstein calls a "restricted (linguistic) code" does not mean that most working-class children do not use or implicitly grasp the basic linguistic rule system as such. Nor, for that matter, does anything in the structure of dialects prevent children from learning to use universalistic meanings (i.e. meanings which are relatively freed from implicit reference to the specific context referred to).

However, the existence of a restricted code does mean that, owing to differences in working-class as opposed to middle-class values and socialization experiences, the social conditions under which a working-class child will linguistically realize universalistic meanings will differ from those presently expected by a middle-class teacher. Moreover the nature of the context referred to also helps dictate whether the working-class child will linguistically realize relatively universalistic and elaborated meanings, compared to his realization of more particularistic, more context-bound meanings in other contexts.[61]

Bernstein and Henderson's research on induction of children into the moral (person) orders and skill (object) orders helps specify the conditions and contexts in which children of varying class background will orient themselves to the elaborated explication of meanings.[62] Teachers must make the effort to grasp these contexts, and to establish their specific manifestations in their community, using data related to the specific community setting in which the teacher is working; Bernstein's researches provide an invaluable framework for interpreting such data.

This is where the parents come in, in all sorts of ways. They can teach the teacher many things about their children and their experiences. Once the teacher appreciates the relevance of such knowledge, he can then begin to use it—hopefully, by more adequately relating his teaching to the child's experiences—to build upon the child's tacit understanding of the linguistic rule system in order that the child learns to realize orders of relevance and relation, universalistic meanings, and public modes of thought in *new* conditions and contexts. The task of "context-creation" does not in itself make working-class children into middle-class children. Any teaching relationship, formal or informal, uses techniques of context-creation. It is simply that teachers must create teaching contexts which are relevant to the experiences of working-class children. This is not "compensatory education"; it is simply "education." Working-class children need not be segregated temporally or spatially for this to be achieved.

---

[60] B. Bernstein: "A Critique . . . ," *op. cit.*
[61] Bernstein and Henderson, *op. cit.*
[62] *Ibid.*

But it does require basic changes in the existing school setting, since at present the conditions and contexts used as starting-points for the educative process are far more consonant with the socialization and out-of-school experiences of middle-class children and are therefore less effective in triggering working-class children's imaginations and capacities. To counteract this bias requires the fullest appreciation of varying social backgrounds and contexts, and their relation to the child's experiences. It involves the teacher learning to build experiential bridges on the basis of this appreciation. As Bernstein says: "We should start knowing that the social experience the child already possesses is valid and significant, and this social experience should be reflected back to him as valid and significant. It can only be reflected back to him if it is part of the texture of learning experience we create." [63]

Bernstein also makes the point that such "context-creation," if it is to be effective, cannot be of the "piecemeal" kind, but must be a continuous, consistent and systematic process. As research has shown, any possible advantage gained in a special pre-school compensatory education programme for the three-to-five age range will almost certainly be lost if the educational contexts of the child after age five show no consonance with his previous experiences. Bernstein implies that the primary stage of education should be seen as an irreducible unit based on systematic, co-ordinated sequencing of learning. From this point of view, the traditional administrative infant-junior division in Britain, and the growing middle-school division in the USA not only reflect the piecemeal bureaucratic approach to social problem-solving but actually work against the aims of educators who show concern for children from subordinate groups.

To dissolve the present administrative divisions requires a basic restructuring, not only of the present school system but also of teacher education which at present is based upon the tacit assumption that these administrative divisions are clearly recognizable and valid in terms of child development and educational methods. A reorientation would, in fact, necessarily force those teachers who consider themselves to be experts on (for example) "the primary stage" to consider the educative process in a wider and, from an educational point of view, more fruitful developmental context. Redistribution of power, in a direction favouring the parents and students, would also serve to guide teachers into such a reorientation.

In a broad sociological frame of reference, then, it is crucial that both research and action recognize that subordinate group members live, function, and are motivated within the experiential framework which is appropriate to their immediate social context. This of course, will often include exposure to the stigma of discrimination as well as other components of subordinate-group status.[64]

[63] B. Bernstein: "A Critique . . . ," op. cit.

[64] The stress on the participants' own terms, the terms of their own values and life-experiences, rather than those of the dominant groups are, in part, what differ-

We contend that failure to take this diversity of life experiences and values into account, is in all probability a major factor underlying the failure of many antipoverty and other welfare programmes (including those of compensatory education), in spite of rapidly increasing expenditure on these programmes during the middle 1960's.

The Political Functions of the Educational System*

HARMON ZEIGLER AND WAYNE PEAK

V. O. Key, Jr. (1963:316) observed that "all national educational systems indoctrinate the oncoming generation with the basic outlooks and values of the political order." The conservative implications of this statement (and of others similar to it) are obvious to all who take time to reflect upon it. However, one cannot neglect the possibility that the conservative role of education in the socialization process partially is a consequence of the state of the development of the society in which it occurs. In "developing" countries, for instance, Coleman (1965:3) suggested that the educational system is viewed as the key to rapid, if orderly, social change: "Once regarded as an essentially conservative, culture-preserving, culture-transmitting institution, the educational system now tends to be viewed as the master determinant of all aspects of change."

We suspect that Coleman's statement will be modified substantially when empirical research establishes what is expected of educational systems in developing nations. For instance, the goals of teachers in developing countries do not appear to be radically different from the goals of teachers in stable, industrial democracies. In both cases, the objectives are the conveying (or creation) of consensus values. Indeed, the *overt* instillation of consensus values probably is more characteristic of developing than established countries. In Kenya, Tanzania, and Uganda, the primary objective of the educational system is the teaching of good citizenship. In these areas, schools have the responsibility of establishing patterns of integration to replace the previously existing intra-societal tensions and cleavages (Dawson and Prewitt,

---

entiates the "left-wing" ideological stance from liberal stances stressing "maximum feasible participation." If one stays within the dominant group notions in liberal policies espoused by community agencies and administrations, maximum "feasible" participation is, in fact, very low indeed, as Silberman points out (*op. cit.*, chapter X).

* Revised version of a paper presented at the Western Political Science Association Meetings, Honolulu, Hawaii, April 1969. The authors wish to acknowledge the support of the Center for the Advanced Study of Educational Administration, University of Oregon, during a portion of the time that they devoted to the preparation of this paper. CASEA is a national research and development center which was established under the Cooperative Research Program of the U.S. Office of Education.

FROM *Sociology of Education*, Vol. 43, No. 2 (Spring 1970), pp. 115–42. Reprinted with permission.

1968:162). Therefore, one would suspect that the extent to which schools deliberately propagandize consensus values depends to some degree upon the extent to which societal integration has been achieved. Russia's relatively youthful regime undertakes overt indoctrination to a far greater extent than is true in the United States. English schools are less concerned than American ones with the inculcation of patriotism.

It is our intention to examine the extent to which the American educational system propagates consensus values in its citizens and to assess the degree of conservative bias thus injected into the political system. Such an undertaking necessarily must be concerned with the content of the values thus transmitted and with their compatibility with the fundamental precepts of the American political order. Therefore, before taking a closer look at education in the United States, we must present a brief analysis of consensus values and change within the context of political theory.

CONFLICT, VALUES, AND SOCIAL CHANGE

E. E. Schattschneider (1960:13) has suggested that "government in a democracy is a great engine for expanding the scale of conflict." Implicit in this assertion is the assumption that men are in constant competition over a limited supply of values. Such competition, or conflict, is ubiquitous and exists on as many dimensions as there are objects of men's desires. It is precisely because conflict is endemic to social existence that the need for a political system arises, for it is through the political system that conflict is taken out of the private sector (where few if any checks exist on the virulence with which it is conducted) and placed in the public domain. The function of the political system is *not* that of stifling or smothering social conflict but rather that of providing an arena wherein it can be conducted within prescribed limits. In fact, it has been argued that societies which suppress conflict are inherently unstable.

Lewis Coser (1956), in expanding on earlier work by the German sociologist, Georg Simmel, has analyzed the social functions of conflict. His central thesis is that the expression of some minimal degree of conflict is necessary for any social group to survive. He discusses a number of major propositions relating to this thesis. For present purposes, however, these propositions can be grouped into two general categories, each of which pertains to a socially desirable function of conflict. In the first place, Coser indicates several ways in which conflict creates or strengthens social bonds:

1. It creates and modifies common norms necessary for the readjustment of the [antagonistic] relationship.
2. It leads each party to the conflict, given a certain equality of strength, to prefer that the other match the structure of his own organization so that fighting techniques are equalized.
3. It makes possible a reassessment of relative power and thus serves as a

balancing mechanism which helps to maintain and consolidate societies. And:

Multiple group affiliations of individuals make for a multiplicity of conflicts criss-crossing society. Such segmental participation, then, can result in a kind of balancing mechanism, preventing deep cleavages along one axis. The interdependence of conflicting groups and the multiplicity of noncumulative conflicts provide one, though not, of course, the only check against basic consensual breakdown in an open society (Coser, 1956:79, 137).

With regard to this last point, Schattschneider (1960) has presented an illuminating analysis of what he calls "the socialization of conflict" within the American political arena. He recognizes the inevitability of competing interests, and like Coser, he points out the fact that widespread involvement in multiple conflicts reduces the likelihood that a society will become polarized along any given battle line.

We should make it abundantly clear that the positive effects of increased conflict discussed by Coser and Schattschneider and implied by traditional theorists evolve from increases in the *scope* of conflict and not from increases in its *intensity*. The scope of conflict refers to the breadth of participation—the number of individuals party to it; intensity of conflict refers to the virulence with which it is conducted. It is precisely the recognition of such negative effects that underlies Coser's second category of the social functions of conflict.

After accepting the universality of conflicting values, Coser argues that societies which allow the relatively free expression of competition for values have less pent up hostilities and, therefore, lower levels of conflict intensity than societies which inhibit such expression. Thus,

Realistic conflicts arise when men clash in the pursuit of claims based on frustration of demands and expectancies of gains.
Nonrealistic conflicts arise from deprivations and frustrations stemming from the socialization process and from later adult role obligations, or they result . . . from a conversion of originally realistic antagonism which was disallowed expression . . . [T]he second type [of conflict] consists of a release of tension in aggressive action directed against shifting objects . . . satisfaction is derived from the aggressive act itself (Coser, 1956: 54–55).

An additional societal level function performed by conflict has to do with ease with which social and, more specifically, political change is achieved. If one assumes that the environment within which a social system exists is in a state of constant flux (and we believe that it is safe to make such an assumption), then the relationship of social conflict to political change is straightforward. Individual values are developed partly in response to environmental conditions; thus, as changes in the latter are perceived, so are the individual value demands made upon the political system.

The survival of the political system is determined by the level of support which it receives, and support—particularly support in democratic polities—is a function of demand satisfaction and socialization (see Easton, 1957, 1965). Therefore, it follows that democratic political systems must respond to changes in value demands resulting from environmental change or suffer the consequences of decreased popular support. A political system which is open and admits the entry of new value demands is said to be in a state of dynamic equilibrium, or stable. The more unresponsive and rigid the political system is, the more it must rely on socialization to generate at least the minimal level of support necessary for its continued legitimation and, consequently, for its very existence.

Of course, coercion is an alternative source of support; however, any democratic political system which must rely principally upon negative outputs for its requisite support forfeits its claim to democracy and degenerates into totalitarianism.[1] But since socialization can never be totally effective, the fact remains that a rigid democratic political system has little or no chance of surviving. Moreover, when socialization is held constant, we can expect the level of support to vary directly with the amount of value satisfaction emanating in the form of policy outputs. Such outputs initially are dependent upon the free articulation of competing demands; consequently conflict is related directly to political change and, therefore, to the stability and health of the political system.

One undeniable fact emerges from our examination of conflict: regardless of the perspective from which it is approached, widespread social conflict is imperative for the vitality of democratic political systems. It is a necessary condition for the maximization of individual values, for the maximization of support for the political regime, and for the maximization of social cohesion; it facilitates equilibrating political change; and it reduces the intensity with which inevitable social and political competition is conducted.

It is not our intention to imply that every petty quarrel should be injected into the political system, for surely no system could cope with the fantastic volume of demands thus transmitted to it (see Easton, 1965:57–69; 85–89). To guard against system overload developing from such a situation, some criteria must be established to screen conflicting value demands. However, our point is that the criteria so established must admit all demands which are so basic or widespread that failure to allow them expression would result in socially disruptive nonrealistic conflict outside of the political arena or the demise of the political system itself.

The importance of the screening function cannot be overemphasized nor

---

[1] Concerning the use of coercion to generate support for a political system, Easton (1957:396) has stated that where policy outputs are negative: ". . . they threaten the members of the system with various kinds of sanctions ranging from a small monetary fine to physical detention, ostracism, or loss of life, as in our own system with regard to the case of legally defined treason. In every system support stems in part from fear of sanctions or compulsion; in autocratic systems the proportion of coerced support is at a maximum."

can the delicacy and difficulty involved in the establishment of screening criteria, for to err in the direction of leniency is to run the risk of overload, and to err in the opposite direction is to endanger the very existence of the political system. In one sense, the establishment of screening criteria can be considered a more important political act than the making of policy.

The delicacy to which we have alluded may become somewhat more apparent if we distinguish between two aspects of the problem. On the one hand there is the quantitative factor of the *volume* of demands which enter the system. With respect to considerations of volume, systemic requirements dictate the need for screening agents in order to avoid overload.

On the other hand, however, there are qualitative considerations of the *range* of demands. This aspect pertains to the extent of deviance from consensual norms that is tolerated. The more rigid and intolerant the screening agents, the greater is the likelihood that realistic demands will be disallowed entry to the political system. The dangers inherent in such a situation are apparent. The ideal balance to be struck is one which restricts the *volume* of demands while permitting entry of the full *range* of realistic demands.

The difficulty in arriving at such an ideal is complicated further by the fact that the realism of demands is a function of environmental characteristics, which are ever-changing. Thus, constant vigilance over screening criteria is required if they are to keep pace with environmental change. A rigid, "frozen" set of screening criteria can be expected to exclude more and more realistic demands the longer it remains unchanged. Coser's above-cited warning that "nonrealistic conflicts arise . . . from a conversion of originally realistic antagonism that was disallowed expression" points out the undesirability of overly restricting the range of legitimate demands.

Limits on the range of acceptable demands largely are derived from the value consensus which obtains throughout society. In other words, tolerance of nonconformity is itself a social norm; the degree of tolerance directly affects the extent to which society will permit the expression of demands which depart from the existing consensus. Thus, to control the socialization process by which social norms are transmitted is also to control the screening criteria used to evaluate the acceptability of demands to the political system. Since the educational system is an important agent of socialization, it bears much responsibility for the establishment of tolerance, which makes realistic conflict and social change possible.

THE EDUCATIONAL EXPERIENCE

Students of socialization have made a strategic error in concerning themselves primarily with the manifest content of social studies programs. In advanced industrial societies, especially stable democracies, the important thing about socialization is not the explicit content of political education programs; *implicit* assumptions are more important. We need to address ourselves to the question of what is *not* told to American children as well as to what is told to them. At the outset, one could assert that the differences beween the political education programs of developing and advanced societies are superficial at best.

In American schools, the emphasis clearly is upon orthodoxy. Hess and Torney, noting the repetitive emphasis upon symbolic indications of loyalty, such as singing patriotic songs and saluting the flag, are disturbed by what they view to be the excessive emphasis upon compliance with laws and authority and the underemphasis upon citizen rights. "The school stresses the ideal norms and ignores the tougher, less pleasant facts of political life in the United States" (Hess and Torney, 1967:218). While Hess and Torney are concerned with elementary education, research by the senior author into high school teaching leads to the conclusion that there is less difference than we normally assume (Zeigler, 1967:116–119). What, then, is the difference between Tanzania, Russia, and the United States? The only appreciable difference is the extent to which indoctrination is explicit. Actually, the explicitness of the indoctrination might work to reduce its effectiveness, since the most persuasive communications usually are those with the least deliberately persuasive content. American schools actually might be doing a better job than Russia of grinding out loyal, compliant citizens.

What we are suggesting is that studies of socialization in the schools may be going about the problem in the wrong way. It is the manifest content of such programs which attracts most attention from political scientists, even though there probably is less of this content in American schools than in other educational systems. What is needed is a careful assessment of the latent consequences of the educational experience. While the effect of education upon political values and orientations has been examined, the extent to which values are shaped without any conscious attempt to do so has not been studied with any degree of care. There is, then, the process of "schooling" whereby the older generation attempts to instruct the young through a set of institutions explicitly designed for that purpose, but there also is the process of *education* which may have more immediate effect than deliberate indoctrination. In directing our attention to this latter, less direct influence, we shall pay attention to two aspects of the education process: (1) aspects of political life not included in typical social studies courses, and (2) techniques of instruction.

Non-instruction

Concerning the first topic, the task is somewhat difficult and is not unlike the current dispute between the neo-elitists and pluralists in the study of community power. Pluralists have taken a hard-headed approach in insisting that the only legitimate datum is the *decision*. Neo-elitists have argued that the process of non-decision-making is more significant for the understanding of community power. Bachrach and Baratz have become the leading spokesmen for the neo-elitist position, and their remarks seem directly applicable to the argument herein advanced. By focusing entirely upon the process whereby highly contested decisions are reached, pluralists ignore both the more numerous routine decisions and the more mysterious "non-decisions" which, Bachrach and Baratz (1962, 1963) assert, are of more impact upon the overall political style of a community than the more spectacular and tangible decisions. The process of non-decision-making allows only the relative minor disputes—those well within the limits imposed by the consensus of the community—to become the subject of community conflict. The "mobilization of bias"—by which Bachrach and Baratz mean the perpetuation of values tending to favor the maintenance of the *status quo*—sets the margins within which conflict can take place.

We are well aware of the ghostly quality of this type of argument, and are bothered almost as much as Merelman (1968) by the conspiratorial "they" who can *overtly* set the margins of debate. We find it difficult to imagine a sort of community council of "they" who decide what can and cannot be subject to dispute. However, there are some merits in this type of argument. Rather than talking about the overt mobilization of bias by individuals, we are in better empirical shape if we inquire into the social institutions which might serve the *covert* function of the mobilization of bias. We suggest that this is the real function of schools.

Consensus has substantial value for political elites. If their positions of dominance and power are not challenged by opposing value demands, elites are relatively free to conduct the affairs of state with a minimum of difficulty. Dissensus clearly makes this task of elites more difficult. In spite of what social scientists assert about the functions of social conflict, most practicing politicians do not appreciate its role. Social conflict tends to weaken the independence of elites by forcing them to resolve disputes not of their choosing.

Schattschneider (1960:4) correctly has observed that a question with importance at least equal to "who gets what, when, and how" is the question, "What shall we argue about?" When a social system erupts into conflict, it may indicate that a portion of the masses normally excluded from routine political behavior has become dissatisfied. If the conflict continues and increases in intensity, something will have to be done about a problem which did not originate from within the elite. Even though the elite has to solve the problem, it is not a problem which they would have chosen to solve had they enjoyed the freedom of action which normally is theirs.

Conflict—which indicates the increasing imperfection of the consensus—generates a more intense mobilization of bias. The mobilization may shift from covert to overt. Pressures to cling to accepted interpretations of reality increase, even though these interpretations of reality appear to the more intense participants in the conflict to be faulty. The educational system, under such conditions, assumes part of the responsibility for the repudiation of fundamental criticism—a task for which it is admirably suited, partially because of the professional values which have achieved a high degree of stability within the educational establishment. As conflict reaches the level of challenge to the basic assumptions of a society, the reaction of the educational system matches the challenge. Etzioni (1968:117) speaks of a "community of assumptions" which characterize any social unit. In advanced societies, a community of assumptions, once established, can be maintained for long periods of time without challenge. Individuals assume that the world really is as they see it; therefore, dissent is tolerated only within the margins set out in the community of assumptions. When dissent extends beyond these margins, the society has institutions to remove legitimacy from dissent and the screening agents of the political system deny entrance to demands thus branded as illegitimate. Thus, such "margin-defending" institutions operate to limit the range of acceptable policy alternatives.

It might be argued that the extent to which margin-defending institutions —such as educational systems—engage in overt indoctrination is a function not of the degree of development of the political system, but rather of the extent of illegitimate conflict excluded from that system. In America of the 1960s, there is as much need to strengthen societal identifications as there is in Tanzania. If this assumption is correct, schools (which formerly avoided hard-line indoctrination) will begin to bear down upon those challenging the community of assumptions.

With regard to the performance of various societal institutions, it seems more helpful to avoid thinking about development as a linear process and to think of institutional reactions as cyclical. We are, then, currently going through a period in which the community of assumptions is being challenged and defended. Ours has been a fundamentally conservative society with popular opinion exercising a coercive and cohesive influence. Defensive institutions have enjoyed a more secure role within the society, and the education system is sensitive to the potentially dangerous consequences of the mistreatment of "sacred objects" (children). Long before the advent of surveys, and indeed long before the industrialization and political development of America, de Toqueville (1835:263) observed the basic conservatism and coercive power of the American mass opinion. He concluded that only the "presence of the black race on the soil of the United States" was capable of destroying the fundamental tranquility of the American policy. De Toqueville's insightful comment suffers only because of its failure to offer predictions of what sort of responses might be expected in the event that the "presence of the black race" created tensions sufficient to shatter the consensus.

Whether one takes an alarmist position or not, the 1960s have produced a pattern of political behavior not characteristic of the American political process. We are not speaking so much of the urban violence—the United States has always been a violent nation—but rather we are referring to the existence of a relatively large body of opinion willing to challenge a basic tenet of the community of assumptions. The protests about Vietnam should be understood against the coercive power of mass opinion to which de Toqueville referred. Even the crudest indicators of public opinion suggest that the masses have no patience with the Vietnam protestors, yet, the opposition increases in intensity. One can conclude that the agents of socialization charged with defensive operations have failed.

This assertion—that the socialization process is imperfect because we are undergoing fundamental criticism—does not resemble in any way the "normal" interpretation of the educational function. Education is "supposed" to make "good citizens" of us all. Therefore, if some of us have become critical thinkers, the educational process should take credit. Many studies, of which the Almond-Verba (1963) study is merely the most recent, stress the role of formal education in the creation of efficacious, contented citizens: the more one is educated (at least in America) the more politically competent one becomes.

The main thrust of this type of argument is that education and commitment to the "system" are linked closely. Without considering the implications of this finding, many political scientists became elitists. They argued that, since the educated minorities were those who really understood and appreciated the ongoing political process, extensive participation by the masses was dangerous. However, no distinction was made between secondary and higher education. Actually, if one examines the association between education and a variety of attitudes normally attributed to the political elite, it can be discovered that commitment to democratic decision-making becomes apparent only after substantial exposure to higher (as distinguished from secondary) education. At least through high school, learning how to be a good citizen does not include respect for the rights of minorities.

Making the usual assumption that racial progress and education were highly related in the South, Matthews and Prothro were surprised to learn that there was a substantial negative correlation between median school years completed by whites and Negro voting registration. As the average education of whites in a county increases, Negro voter registration decreases. Puzzled by this contradiction to one of the "laws" of political behavior, Matthews and Prothro performed the usual controlling operations and found that the correlation withstood any assault. The authors clearly did not expect to find out that education was unrelated (indeed negatively related) to a worthwhile goal: "These findings . . . are completely contrary to what we would have expected from earlier studies and 'common sense' interpretation" (Matthews and Prothro, 1966:129).

However, their explanation fits quite closely with the theory we are outlining for a social function of the secondary school. While it is true that the proportion of whites who are strict segregationists decreases with each increase in formal education, the combined number of moderates and integrationists does not exceed the number of segregationists within any educational level below college. Education decreases segregationist attitudes, but it takes extremely high doses of education to make much of an impact. For instance (Matthews and Prothro, 1966:343) the percentage of strict segregationists among high school graduates is 66 per cent, an improvement of 4 per cent when compared to those who did not complete high school.

One might suspect that schools—even if they had overtly confronted the biases of Southerners—would have failed to improve the racial climate in the South. However, the fact of the matter is that Southern schools were, with few exceptions, segregationist to the core. The administration and faculty of Southern schools was as much involved in encouraging resistance to the *Brown* decision as were the Klan and white Citizens Councils. Further, the minimum effect of education upon racial attitudes can be observed in non-Southern contexts. Campbell and Schuman's analysis (1968:35) of racial attitudes in 15 cities reaches the conclusion that:

> The schools appear to have accepted without question the prevailing culture of race relations. Since World War II, those white students who have gone to college have evidently been exposed to influences which have moved their attitudes away from the traditional pattern. . . . We cannot say whether this resulted from specific instruction regarding questions of race or from a general atmosphere of opinion in the college community, but it is clear that a sizeable proportion of these postwar college students were affected. In contrast, the high schools which our respondents attended during the postwar years seem to have been little more involved in the nation's racial problems than they were in the prewar period. Or, to be more precise, their involvement has been so peripheral that it has had relatively little influence on the racial attitudes of their graduates.

The rather dismal conclusions reached by these scholars about the effects of high school education should come as no surprise to those familiar with the attitudes of professional educators and with the content of texts in high school civics courses. While one hardly can assert that the civics curriculum is directly and solely responsible for the unrealistic attitudes about race relations characteristic of American whites, it is clear that there is a missed opportunity for schools to inject some realism into the situation. The numerous studies of racial attitudes which have appeared since 1964 have been consistent in indicating that whites view America as a land of equal opportunity. To take one illustration, the Gallup Political Index of July, 1968 reported that a substantial majority believe that Negroes are treated the same as whites and only a minority agrees with the conclusions of the President's Commission on Civil Disorders that our nation is moving toward two societies. In Table 1, we can see that the only appreciable impact of education upon attitudes occurs after high school. . The relationship between education and realism is not necessarily positive; indeed, the high school experience, in many cases, seems to contribute to *less* realism.

Thus, the basic argument is that high school education is unrealistic; not because of what is said, but more because of what is *not* said. Among

TABLE 1

Attitudes of Various Educational Groups Toward Racial Problems
(Percentages)

	GRADE SCHOOL	HIGH SCHOOL	COLLEGE
Agree with Kerner Commission	33	35	40
Believe Negroes are treated the same as whites	71	75	71
Believe Negroes are more to blame for present conditions than whites	56	58	42
Believe that businesses discriminate against Negroes in hiring	17	19	30
Believe that labor unions discriminate against Negroes in membership practices	13	18	30
Believe that looters should be shot on sight	54	55	46

SOURCE: Gallup Political Index (July, 1968):15–22.

high school students who have taken courses in civics, the results are conflicting and inconclusive. In general, Langton and Jennings (1968) found there to be no association between being instructed formally in civics and any attitude (e.g., tolerance) which might be expected to result from such instruction. We can conclude that, with few exceptions, the formal education of youths makes no difference in regard to their image of the political world. Such courses are redundant; they are largely symbolic reinforcements of the "democratic creed"—a liturgy heard by most students so many times that sheer boredom probably would allow for, at the most, slight increments in loyalty, patriotism, and other virtues presumed to be the goal of such courses.

An interesting exception is Langton and Jennings' (1968) discovery that the civics curriculum has a more impressive impact upon Negro children. Of particular interest is the effect of the civics curriculum upon the "good citizen" role of Negroes and whites; 70 per cent of the whites and 63 per cent of the Negroes defined the "good citizen" role either in terms of loyalty or participation. Among Negroes, the emphasis is upon loyalty while the opposite is true for whites. When the effect of civics courses is examined, we find that there is a very modest increase in participation emphasis and a decrease in loyalty emphasis among whites. However, among Negroes the opposite is true. The more courses taken, the greater becomes the emphasis upon loyalty, while the emphasis upon participation declines. The authors (Langton and Jennings, 1968:864) conclude that civics courses ". . . inculcate in Negroes the role expectation that a good citizen is above all a loyal citizen rather than an active one." Presumably, loyalty and participation are emphasized in about the same degree. It is not likely that civics instructors overtly would discourage Negroes from seeking an active role in political society. However, Negroes (especially those with relatively high status) may be aware of the realities of discrimination and select from the curriculum those role characteristics which are congruent with their notions of their chances in life.

If we want to get an idea of the limitations of the civics curriculum, the best data would appear to be the responses of Negro youths. Since their prior exposure to the norms typically conveyed in such courses is significantly less than that of their white counterparts, their potential for absorbing them would appear to be uniformly greater. Thus, the selection of any particular norm for disproportionate acceptance by Negroes implies that a corresponding emphasis has been placed upon it in the classroom. It seems, then, that loyalty is the goal of the civics curriculum. Loyalty, perhaps admirable in the abstract, has become the catchword behind which a variety of parochial attitudes are hidden.

Given the natural clannishness of teenagers, it is not surprising that the experience of schooling does not decrease the ethnocentristic and chauvinistic propensities of this group. The early work by Remmers and Radler (1957) may have been unduly alarmist. The general conclusion of their work was that teenagers are an intensely patriotic group with little inclination to tolerate what they perceive to be disloyal conduct. For instance, a majority agreed that "in these days, patriotism and loyalty to established American ways are the *most* important requirements of a good citizen," and that "the average citizen does not show enough respect for the U.S. flag" (Horton, 1963:40). As students work their way through the curriculum, there is little evidence that their chauvinism changes. Seniors appear to be about the same as freshmen; those who have had civics courses are, if anything, worse—Remmers and Radler (1957:195) say they are "more totalitarian."

However, one gets the impression that the generation of teenagers studied by Remmers and Radler was characterized by a deterioration of once-held beliefs (in spite of the high correlation between the values of parents and children). Actually, we know that the attitudes reported by Remmers and Radler are not unique to any age group. Further, recent research by Jennings and Niemi (1968) indicates that high school students of the 1960s are somewhat more tolerant of diversity and less chauvinistic than those of the 1950s. On the other hand, in neither case was there much evidence of an unusually strong commitment to tolerance. On the slightly encouraging side, Jennings and Niemi found a *very slight* tendency for the pre-adults to take a more libertarian stance than their parents; however, the increments are not sufficiently impressive to justify a conclusion that "things are getting better all of the time."

Even if we assume that the educational process is primarily responsible for conveying a mythology to each generation and, therefore, do not expect that student values necessarily will change, we should not neglect the fact that some aspects of the mythology are organized more cogently than others. For instance, Pock (1967:134) found little comprehension of, or support for, "several of the most fundamental tenets embodied in our heritage and expressed in the Bill of Rights." Pock, rather than relying upon the use of items scales, presented high school seniors with a series of 18 cases, each raising a separate constitutional question. Most of the cases were based upon actual legal conflicts. Respondents were asked to agree or disagree with the specific action or decision involved in the case. He concluded (1967:134): "Confronted by descriptions of situations in which both explicit and implicit civil rights has been violated, a preponderance of students responded approvingly to the use of improperly gathered evidence, secret trials, search without probable cause, setting of excessive bail, and to the use of anonymous witnesses."

Here again we have evidence that the most significant aspect of civic education in American society is not the manifest content of the instructional program. It is very likely that students are presented with little more than the appropriate slogans, e.g., "America is a land of freedom," without much effort to operationalize the concepts implicit in a slogan. It is possible that the same students who proved so discouraging to Pock would appear quite tolerant on an abstract scale. Agreement with abstract ideals while disagreeing with application of these ideals to concrete situations is characteristic of the adult population; presumably, such a characteristic is typical of high school seniors also.

Techniques of Instruction

The inferences we can make about the nature of civic education should be corroborated by direct observation of the classroom situation. Failing this, we can learn something more about civic education from examining the attitudes of social studies teachers and the content of textbooks. In general, teachers are not inclined toward using the classroom as a medium for the discussion of controversial issues. While there are considerable variations in approach to the classroom, teachers find their lives much less complicated if they avoid controversy. We are referring here not only to the potential for trouble within the community, but also to the potential for trouble within the classroom. Classes are easier to manage if the authority structure is not challenged. Engaging in controversy presents a challenge to the authority structure and, therefore, is avoided.

Avoidance of controversy is reinforced by the content of texts which, for better or worse, establish the nature of the content of a course of instruction. A brief survey of the quality of public school texts in history, government, or civics indicates the Victorian attitude toward politics which is typical of American education. The main object of most texts apparently is to protect rather than to inform the minds of youths.

In 1943, Hunt and Metcalf (1943:230) listed six closed areas in social studies texts. They were:

1. Economics. Students and teachers could find little about possible shortcomings in the free enterprise system. They could certainly

find nothing about the extent to which we actually have a free enterprise system.

2. Race and minority relations. There are virtually no realistic discussions of this problem.
3. Social class. In spite of obvious facts about the significance of social
   class in political behavior, the prevailing theme is that "there are no
   social classes in America."
4. Sex, courtship, and marriage. It should come as no surprise that this
   subject is treated in a wholly unreal fashion.
5. Religion and morality. Texts tactfully advised teachers to avoid this
   subject entirely.
6. Nationalism and patriotism. Nationalism as a destructive force is not
   mentioned. Patriotism is unquestionably accepted as an over-arching
   goal, but the specific behaviors which are presumed to be patriotic
   are not discussed. Hence, saluting the flag is an unquestioned ritual.

From the available evidence, we conclude that Hunt and Metcalf's
description is just about as valid today as it was in 1943. We cannot
check each of the six closed areas as carefully as we should like, nor can
we be assured that our survey is truly representative of the available
texts. However, a few quotations from some widely used texts might prove
helpful. Take, for example, the following statement about the American
economic system:

> One needs only to look at the great achievements and the standard of
> living of the American people to see the advantages of our economic
> system. . . . We believe that a well regulated capitalism—a free choice,
> individual incentives, private enterprise system—is the best guarantee
> of the better life for all mankind (McClenoghan, 1966:20 cited in Mas-
> sialas, 1967:179).

There is no discussion of any alternatives to this economic system, not
even in the "some say—others say" style that characterizes some efforts
to consider alternatives. Further, as Massialas (1967) notes, a picture accompanying this discussion shows people waiting in line in the rain to
be treated in the English National Health Service.[2]

Race relations is regarded as a "controversial social issue" and is treated
with extreme caution. While there are some texts which are more realistic
than others, the following quotation is typical:

> In 1954, the United States Supreme Court made a decision stating that
> separate schools for Negro children were unconstitutional. This deci-
> sion caused much controversy, but there has been general agreement,
> however, that some system must be developed to provide equal educa-

[2] Much of our analysis of texts is based upon material contained in this volume.
Massialas' excellent article has been particularly useful, and citations from it have been of
great help in the present undertaking.

tional opportunity for all children—regardless of race, nationality, religion, or whether they live in cities or rural areas (cited in Krug, 1967:202).

Of course, this statement is patently false; but it also could allow support for the separate but equal doctrine. There is no discussion of the vigor with which Southern states resisted the order. Presumably, the students were given no explanation for the fact that race relations remain America's most divisive dilemma.

Concerning social class, sex, and religion, little can be said because the treatment of these topics is so sparse. Consider, for example, the following treatment of class (Cole and Montgomery, 1963:365 cited in Girault, 1967:227): ". . . classes in society are more or less inevitable . . . it is important to keep the social classes open." Warner, Hollingshead, the Lynds, and, in fact, most American sociologists might never have written if this text is to be taken as evidence of their impact below the college level. Sex usually is discussed in psychology texts. Students are exposed to the arguments for and against going steady. One of the most obvious advantages, an advantage seized by the majority of those who "go steady," is, needless to say, ignored. In an age in which open cohabitation is becoming an alternative to marriage, such discussions are absurd. The treatment of religion, which occurs occasionally in sociology texts, appears to be as far removed from the sociology of religion as the treatment of sex is from the concerns of youth. Many texts assert that reason alone cannot sustain man; faith is necessary. Usually faith and Christianity are equated (Girault, 1967).

Patriotism, which is characteristic of the study of American government in the public schools, may be less jingoistic than it once was. However, texts carefully intersperse discussion of government structure (considered in purely legalistic terms) with appropriate exhortations such as: "No other country has more nearly approached the goals of true democracy as has our United States. . . . No doubt many of the early settlers were inspired men . . ." (Cole and Montgomery, 1963:341–342 cited in Girault, 1967:227); and, "Because the nations of the world have not yet learned to live permanently at peace, the United States today must maintain large defensive forces" (Ludlum, et al., 1965 cited in Massialas, 1967:180).

The treatment of the American political process is totally unreal. A single example selected from the abundance that exists should serve to make the point. One text (Ludlum, et al., 1965) devotes an entire chapter to the electoral process but fails to mention such standard sources as *The American Voter*. As Massialas (1967:182) observed: "The five main ideas of the chapter on voting are: (1) 'voting is a process that makes possible peaceful change,' (2) 'voting promotes citizen participation in government,' (3) 'voting helps to promote equality,' (4) 'voting promotes obedience to government,' and (5) 'voting promotes the self-respect of every individual.'"

The manner in which texts treat communism is even more astonishing. In both the "challenge of communism" courses which have become quite popular recently and in the general civics courses, communism is pictured as a total evil. Most state departments of education primarily are concerned with demonstrating the fallacies of communism rather than encouraging objective comparison. An unswerving, ruthless conspiracy dominated by the Soviet Union (texts have not yet discovered the shift toward China as the source of all evil) is the image which is presented, almost without exception. Texts warn students that they will be "badly fooled" if they "take the Russians at their word"; the "errors" of Marx are listed (no communist sources are cited); and the contrast of good versus evil is made quite explicit. In the remote event that the student fails to get the message, end of chapter assignments, maps, and other visual aids are equally biased (Brown and Pelthier, 1964:20–21, cited in Massialas, 1967:183). For instance, four projects accompanying one text are: (1) Write a short paper on agreements with other nations broken by the Soviet Union; (2) Draw a chart contrasting the way of life in a democracy and in totalitarian government; (3) Organize a panel to discuss United States Policy toward Cuba (preceded by the statement, "The presence of a communist dictatorship in Cuba poses a threat to the peace of the Western Hemisphere"); (4) Compile a list of Marx's errors.

To provide a sense of geographical continuity, maps frequently are included in social studies texts. One such map divides the world into four camps: The United States, the communist bloc, the uncommitted nations, and the Free World—including Spain, Portugal, Formosa, and Haiti. (Presumably, "free" is a synonym for degree of friendliness with the United States rather than a description of the internal politics of a country.) If, given the boredom which might be expected to accompany class discussions of such simplistic notions, the class still has not figured out how to get a good grade, the final assignment should reduce any remaining ambiguities: "List as many criticisms of communism as you can" (McClenoghan, 1966, cited in Massialas, 1967:184).

Since most social studies teachers are not trained to distinguish facts from values and, in any case, probably find most of the anti-communism and ethnocentrism of the texts quite compatible with their own values, little contrary information filters into the classroom. Furthermore, since such unreal descriptions are reinforced by other souces of information (mass media and family), it is possible that our attention should be directed away from attitude change and toward attitude organization.

The notion of attitude organization, as developed by Jules Henry (1957), consists of grouping and focusing poorly articulated attitudes. Given the goals of the educational system, its success might be better measured in terms of providing order to attitudes and directing them toward larger social goals, such as the maintenance of positive attitudes toward national symbols. We suspect, however, that the crude indoctrination typical of texts is less effective in achieving organization than are the more subtle learning experiences manifested by means of teacher-student interaction and the norms of school organization. Furthermore, the consequences of the social studies curriculum might operate, in the long run, to increase cynicism rather than trust. Jennings and Niemi (1968:178) argue that the social studies curriculum—in postponing an encounter with the realities of political life—makes an increase in cynicism a natural consequence of the departure from high school. They find a "rather sharp rise in the level of cynicism as high school seniors move ahead in a few years into the adult world."

There is also the possibility that cynicism is latent in the high school population and, therefore, is released from constraint when adulthood is reached. Teachers, in keeping with the general norms of public education, are overly concerned with authority. The style of teaching, emphasizing the authority of the teacher, may seem to some students to be in contrast with the democratic norms which comprise the official ideology. The available evidence, such as that presented in Table 2, strongly suggests that

TABLE 2

Attitudes of Teachers Toward Authority

ITEM	PER CENT AGREE	PER CENT DISAGREE
Children should be given greater freedom in expressing their natural impulses and desires, even if these impulses are frowned upon by people.	42	58
Schools should return to the practice of administering a good spanking when other methods fail.	59	41
A good teacher never lets students address him or her except as Mr., Miss, or Mrs.	75	25
What youth needs most is strict discipline, rugged determination, and the will to work and fight for family and country.	69	31
The main purpose of social studies courses is to teach students to be good citizens.	88	12
Obedience and respect for authority are the most important virtues children should learn.	60	40
Students today don't respect their teachers enough.	57	43

teachers are not capable of conducting an interaction with a student on an equal basis. Some of the data collected by Jennings and Zeigler is suggestive of the atmosphere of the class.

In Table 2, a few items which have yet to be analyzed systematically give some evidence of the concerns of teachers. While we do not know much about the actual behavior of teachers, we might assume that such attitudes provide a strong propensity for creating a rigid classroom situation. Furthermore, in spite of the shibboleths of texts, to which teachers undoubtedly pay lip service, teachers appear to be as unclear about the application of democratic ideals to concrete situations as is the general population. A minority believe that police should not have the power to censor books and movies; a majority do not wish to provide First Amendment freedom to social or political nonconformists (Weiser and Hayes, 1966:477–478).

Since teachers are part of the educational grouping generally presumed to be the staunchest supporters of civil liberties, their attitudes are in conflict with what we have learned about the role of education in contributing to the open mind. However, teachers are part of an authoritarian system and develop appropriate occupational values (Jennings and Zeigler, 1969:77–79). This comment leads directly into our final section, but first there is the need to note the apparent contradiction between what we are saying and the evidence presented by Almond and Verba (1963:332–334). Forty per cent of their American adult respondents remembered participating in class discussions and debating political issues in school, in contrast with only 16 per cent of the British respondents and slightly fewer of the respondents in other countries. Two comments seem to be in order. First, a majority of adults do *not* recall participation, a fact which should be placed against the context of America's cultural emphases (as contrasted with those of England). Second, if the nature of the discussion resembled the study guides as set forth in texts, such discussions simply served to provide peer group reinforcement of prevailing ideologies.

The Controllers of Education

Why is the situation as it has been described? Three possible explanations come most readily to mind. First, and certainly the most popular, is the "pressure group" argument. Schools are described as the victims of unrelenting pressure from extremist groups who keep a sharp lookout for deviations from the majoritarian ideology. Second, there is the assumption that schools mirror the dominant values of the society they serve and, therefore, can be expected to be replicas of the value structure of the society. Third, there is the argument that schools, because of the structure under which they are governed and because of patterns of occupational recruitment and socialization, are of necessity institutions that function to set limits to the legitimacy of policy alternatives. While each argument has some truth in it, we find the third more in keeping with the facts as we see them.

Pressure Groups

The pressure group argument collects information about cases in which teachers have become the focus of community controversy because of the manner in which they conduct their classes. However, a review of this literature does not tell one about the relative frequency of such attacks.

When attacks occur, they are indeed spectacular. However, relative to the total amount of interaction between teachers, students, and the community, the activity of pressure groups seems to be relatively minor. This is not to suggest that pressure, when it is exerted, is not effective. One well publicized case may be enough to constrain many more teachers than those personally involved in the dispute. Nevertheless, there is virtually no evidence concerning the extent to which the demands of interest groups are communicated to administrators and teachers, and the extent to which demands can be linked to decisions regarding the values of the interest groups.

The principal author's own evidence indicates that teachers are not especially aware of—nor concerned about—the activities of interest groups (Zeigler, 1967:128–130). Administrators, on the other hand, are more sensitive to group demands. Therefore, it is possible that administrators, who have more immediate access to the weapons of sanction and who are viewed by teachers as a more potent threat, serve as transmission belts between interest groups and teachers. Such a possibility is given some credence because of the tendency of administrators to avoid conflict whenever possible. Thus they are likely to try to satisfy a group demand (by sanctioning the teacher) before it becomes public and places the school system within the context of a community conflict. Furthermore, both administrators and teachers might anticipate adverse response and, hence, modify their behavior before a demand is made explicit.

Parents, perhaps, are a more potent source of external pressure. The potential for conflict between parent and teacher is substantial because of incompatible claims of each for authority over the child. Parents are likely to be hostile toward an educational system which threatens to socialize their children away from the values dominant within the family. The majority of a sample of Oregon residents voiced this concern. Corroborating the Oregon findings, Jennings (1966:18) reported that the substance of parental complaints lies in the domain of religion and politics. He suggests that, "Instruction in the school—no matter how oblique—which threatens to undermine these orientations may be viewed very dimly by parents jealous of this prerogative. Even teaching about presumably objective facts, to say nothing of calling for tolerance of nonconformity or outright pitches for a point of view, may be enough to elicit a grievance. . . ." On the other hand, there was no clear direction to the complaints; parents about as frequently felt the content of a course was too conservative as too liberal.

Thus, parental pressure cannot be used to explain the status quo orientation of the social studies curriculum. Furthermore, many of the parents who were disturbed did nothing about it. Only 19 per cent of those parents who were upset by what a child was taught contacted the school in order to seek a redress of grievances. Again, one genuine hell-raising parent can have an influence beyond what is indicated by this percentage. The point is that in the normal, day-to-day operation of the schools, external demands are a less important source of contraint than are internal (especially administrative) expectations. Even when action against the school is initiated, it is rare that the strategy of influence will be an organizational effort. Organizational participation, probably signifying that a particular grievance has surfaced into a public issue, occurs in about 10 per cent of the cases of attempted influence that Jennings discovered.

Schools As Mirror Images

The idea of the school as the mirror image of the society certainly is compatible with the argument of this paper. Lacking values in conflict with those dominant in the community, schools hardly can be expected to act as agents of change. Yet the evidence for this conclusion is less than satisfying. Some sparse evidence, such as the work of Litt (1963) and Pock (1967), suggests that the values typical of a school's personnel seem to be comparable to values presumed to be typical of a particular type of community; for example, schools in upper income areas have teachers and students with more liberal values and offer more realistic social studies curricula than schools in other areas.

The basic problem with this argument is that no explanation has been offered for the fact that the personnel within a school do not necessarily have social class characteristics similar to those dominant in the community. Moreover, such arguments assume that social classes have clearly discernible values which are more or less automatically translated into an educational philosophy. The fact that most of the early work in school-community relations was done by sociologists probably contributed to the conclusion that classes and values could be roughly equated. However, this line of research neglected the role of occupational socialization in the organization of attitudes. While it certainly is true that teachers and administrators are "middle class," they are products of a unique recruitment process which makes it likely that they will exaggerate, rather than merely reflect, a stereotypic middle class set of values. The role of the community, however this role is made manifest, is to set margins within which the educational task is to be performed. It is only upon the relatively rare occasions when the margins are breached that conflict between the school and community erupts. As Charters (1953:282) notes:

> It is possible that something which we shall call a "margin of tolerance" describes the school-community relationship. Citizens of each community may delegate to school personnel the freedom to educate youth according to their professional consciences—but freedom within a certain well defined (or ill-defined) bounds. The boundary is composed of values dear to the particular community. If school personnel over-step the boundary, crisis ensues and community values enter the determination of school affairs.

Internal Structure

According to the above interpretation, we should look more closely at the internal structure of the school system to find out why it operates in defense of the status quo. If, as we can probably assume, administrators would prefer to keep community values out of the determination of school affairs, they must make certain that the margin of tolerance is not approached. In order to do this, they need to recruit teachers whose conduct is likely to cause little trouble. In short, the key to understanding why education is so admirably suited for its task is the recruitment process. The recruitment process in public education should be understood within the context of the educational "establishment." The word "establishment," which has been ridiculed when applied to the general political system, seems quite apt when considering the educational subsystem. Teacher training programs, through which teachers must pass in order to be certified, provide the manpower. Schools of education are more closely coordinated than are most academic departments. They have become part of a stable pattern of interactions with accrediting associations, state departments of education, professional associations of teachers, and administrative associations. Certainly the most powerful force within the establishment is the school of education; but this power is reinforced by the support of the other components of the establishment. The crucial determinant of the existence, or lack thereof, of an establishment is a value consensus. Without having the evidence which would make such an assertion beyond question, it seems to us that there is substantial agreement among professional educators concerning the appropriate role of controversy in the classroom and the expected behavior of teachers. The point may be disputed, but the low level of tolerance within the establishment seems to operate in the direction of driving out the dissenters.

Schools of education are very poor. Academically, the faculty of education schools ranks near the bottom. Attitudinally, the faculty of education schools appears more conservative and authoritarian than the faculties of other academic disciplines. Consequently, students attracted to education generally are the least capable on the college campus; they tend to be somewhat more conservative than the norm. Given the quality of education and the type of student recruited, it is not surprising that the products of schools of education do not view the classroom as an opportunity to develop creative thinking on the part of students. For instance, Jennings and Zeigler (1970), using an index of expressivism, found that 19 per cent of the social studies teachers with education majors in college as compared with 55 per cent of those with majors in social sciences were highly expressive.

Occupational socialization operates to reinforce the biases introduced in teacher training (Guba, et al., 1959:274–275). The longer one teaches, the less likely the possibility of engaging in risk taking behavior; the longer one teaches, the more custodial becomes one's approach to the classroom.

The goals of education gradually become dominated by concern with control of behavior, creation of respect for authority, and establishment of orderly behavior. Recently we have seen, in the current determination of schools to establish dress regulations for students, the extent to which such concerns are significant. Teachers, in insisting upon their authority over students, readily acquiesce to administrators' power over them. Corwin, for instance, noted that teachers accept the legitimacy of administrative decision-making even in the area of classroom performance. In the authority system of the schools there is a place for everybody; in order to succeed it is merely necessary that one avoid trying to move up. Thus Jennings and Zeigler (1969) found a strong association between administrator's approval and acquiescent teacher behavior.

The recent disturbances in public education—teacher strikes and student unrest—can be understood as attempts to move up in the structure of authority. Consequently, administrators resist teacher demands and teachers resist student demands. In neither case has the making of demands escalated to the point of seriously threatening the established order. In both cases the responses to demands for restructuring have been repressive (see Rosenthal, 1969:96–109).

If we accept the argument that a conservative establishment is the major influence upon educational decision-making, then the participation of competitive units in the decision-making process becomes crucial. Generally, as we have argued, the school and the community interact only in cases of margin violation. In the normal decision-making process, the school board has a greater opportunity to compete with the administration for the control of educational policy. Generally it has been assumed that because school board members are recruited from the dominant class within a community, this body operates to reinforce commitment to the status quo. This assumption, however, is not supported by the available evidence.

Since all political bodies are dominated by those with the time and money to engage in politics, why should the school board—merely because it is typical of the political recruitment process—operate to maintain the status quo any more than other political institutions? Actually, the classes from which school board membership is drawn tend to be among the more liberal and tolerant within the community. Further, school board members have not endured the crippling *professional* socialization of the educational establishment.

Therefore, it is possible that school boards—to the extent that they can resist the strong pressure of cooptation from the administration—can serve as agents of change within the educational system. Such an assertion is supported by the recent research of Crain (1968). He found that school superintendents were likely to resist demands for desegregation but that, when the power to make decisions was taken from the superintendent by the school board, progress toward desegregation was more likely to occur. Likewise, Rosenthal (1969:143–153) reported that school boards in the cities he studied (with but one exception) tended to take the lead in establishing policies relating to integration.

The initiative that school boards have exhibited with respect to integration policies well may prove to be an issue-specific phenomenon rather than an indicator of a general trend. It may be the case that changes in school integration policies are inevitable and that board-inspired innovation merely is an example of short run marginal adjustment. Or, it may be that the nature of the integration issue is such that the school board—inasmuch as it is a lay institution which is roughly representative of non-professional values—is the only agent of the educational system which is competent to deal with it. Integration has much broader ramifications and attracts much wider attention than other issues confronting education. Perhaps it is "too hot" or too political an issue for professional administrators (whose expertise and resources do not extend to such matters) to handle.

Wherever the truth of the matter lies, the fact remains that in this one issue area, lay boards *have* exerted themselves, and they *have* established policy independent of the more conservative and "professional" organs of the educational establishment. It remains to be seen whether the momentum thus generated will lead them into other areas of involvement in which professional resources are more apparent and, if so, whether they will be able to withstand the pressures imposed by their respective administrations. These pressures—to resist intrusion into technical matters—might be less irresistible if the scope of conflict is enlarged. In conditions of expanded conflict, the resources of non-professionals are potentially greater. Viewed from this perspective, the characteristic style of the educational establishment (the minimization of conflict) is rational because there is a higher value placed upon technical resources. We would argue, however, that at this particular juncture in the development of the nation, the social consequences of technical expertise are too costly.

REFERENCES

Almond, Gabriel, and Sidney Verba. 1963. The Civic Culture. Princeton: Princeton University Press.

Bachrach, Peter, and Morton S. Baratz. 1962. "The two faces of power." American Political Science Review 56(December): 947–952. 1963. "Decisions and non-decisions: an analytical framework." American Political Science Review 57(September): 632–642.

Brown, Stuart Garry, and Charles L. Pelthier. 1964. Government in Our Republic (revised edition). New York: Macmillan Publishing Co., Inc.

Campbell, Angus, and Howard Schuman. 1968. "Racial attitudes in fifteen American cities." Pp. 1–215 in Supplemental Studies for the National Advisory Committee on Civil Disorders. Washington, D.C.: Government Printing Office.

Charters, W. W., Jr. 1953. "Social class and the control of public education." Harvard Educational Review 23(Fall):268–283.

Cole, William E., and Charles S. Montgomery. 1963. High School Sociology. Boston: Allyn and Bacon.

Coleman, James S. (ed.). 1965. Education and Political Development. Princeton: Princeton University Press.

Coser, Lewis. 1956. The Functions of Social Conflict. New York: The Free Press.

Crain, Robert L. 1968. The Politics of School Desegregation. Chicago: Aldine.

Dawson, Richard E., and Kenneth Prewitt. 1968. Political Socialization. Boston: Little, Brown and Company.

Easton, David. 1957. "An approach to the analysis of political systems." World Politics 9(April):383–400. 1965. A Systems Analysis of Political Life. New York: John Wiley and Sons.

Etzioni, Amitai. 1968. The Active Society. New York: The Free Press.

Girault, Emily S. 1967. "Psychology and sociology." Pp. 218–237 in C. Benjamin Cox and Byron G. Massialas (eds.), Social Studies in the United States. New York: Harcourt, Brace and World.

Guba, Egon G., Philip W. Jackson, and Charles E. Bidwell. 1959. "Occupational choice and the teaching career." Educational Research Bulletin 38:1–12. Reprinted in W. W. Charters and N. L. Gage (eds.), Readings in the Social Psychology of Education. Boston: Allyn and Bacon (1963).

Henry, Jules. 1957. "Attitude organization in elementary school classrooms." American Journal of Orthopsychiatry 27:117–133.

Hess, Robert D., and Judith V. Torney. 1967. The Development of Political Attitudes in Children. Chicago: Aldine.

Horton, Roy E. 1963. "American freedom and the values of youth." Pp. 18–60 in H. H. Remmers (ed.), Anti-Democratic Attitudes in American Schools. Evanston: Northwestern University Press.

Hunt, Maurice P., and Lawrence E. Metcalf. 1943. Teaching High School Social Studies: Problems in Reflective Thinking and Social Understanding. New York: Harper and Row.

Jennings, M. Kent. 1966. "Parental grievances and school politics." Paper presented at the CASEA Conference on Politics and Education, University of Oregon, Eugene, Oregon.

Jennings, M. Kent, and Richard G. Niemi. 1968. "The transmission of political values from parent to child." American Political Science Review 62(March): 169–184.

Jennings, M. Kent, and L. Harmon Zeigler. 1969. "The politics of teacher-administrator relations." Education and Social Science 1:73–82. 1970. "Political expressivism among high school teachers." In Roberta Siegel (ed.), Learning About Politics. New York: Random House (forthcoming).

Key, V. O., Jr. 1963. Public Opinion and American Democracy. New York: Alfred A. Knopf.

Krug, Mark N. 1967. History and the Social Sciences. Waltham, Massachusetts: Blaisdell.

Langton, Kenneth P., and M. Kent Jennings. 1968. "Political socialization and the high school civics curriculum." American Political Science Review 62(September):852–867.

Litt, Edgar. 1963. "Civic education, community norms, and political indoctrination." American Sociological Review 28(February):69–75.

Ludlum, Robert P., et al. 1965. American Government. Boston: Houghton Mifflin.

Massialas, Byron G. 1967. "American government: we are the greatest!" Pp. 167–195 in C. Benjamin Cox and Byron G. Massialas (eds.), Social Studies in the United States. New York: Harcourt, Brace and World.

Matthews, Donald R., and James W. Prothro. 1966. Negroes and the New Southern Politics. New York: Harcourt, Brace and World.

McClenoghan, William A. 1966. Magruder's American Government. Boston: Allyn and Bacon.

Merelman, Richard M. 1968. "On the neo-elitist critique of community power." American Political Science Review 62(June):451–460.

Pock, John C. 1967. Attitudes Toward Civil Liberties Among High School Seniors. Washington, D.C.: U.S. Department of Health, Education, and Welfare. Cooperative Research Project No. 5–8167.

Remmers, H. H., and D. H. Radler. 1957. The American Teenager. New York: Charter Books.

Rosenthal, Alan. 1969. Pedagogues and Power: Teacher Groups in School Politics. Syracuse: Syracuse University Press.

Schattschneider, E. E. 1960. The Semi-Sovereign People. New York: Holt, Rinehart, and Winston.

Tocqueville, Alexis de. 1835. Democracy in America. Richard D. Heffner (ed.). New York: The New American Library (1956).

Weiser, John C., and James E. Hayes. 1966. "Democratic attitudes of teachers and prospective teachers." Phi Delta Kappan 47(May):476–481.

Zeigler, L. Harmon. 1967. The Political Life of American Teachers. Englewood Cliffs, N.J.: Prentice-Hall.

B. Systemic Controls on Education

School Desegregation and School Decision Making

Robert L. Crain and David Street

In many ways the school desegregation issue is an ideal context in which to examine the general question of how school systems make policy decisions. First, it is an issue of some importance, so that the decision-making process uncovered can be assumed to be a nontrivial one. Second,

from *Urban Affairs Quarterly*, Vol. 2, No. 1 (September 1966), pp. 64–82.

it is a relatively new issue, so that the system can make decisions without much reference to traditional decision-making rules; this means that the social scientist need not be greatly concerned with the impact of prior historical accidents. Finally, the issue has arisen in nearly every large city with only minor differences among cities in the way in which it has been raised and with such idiosyncratic factors as the taxing power of the system being of minor importance. This means that the setting is almost ideal for comparative analysis.

This paper principally discusses some of the conclusions of a comparative study of integration in eight northern large city school systems carried out by the National Opinion Research Center in 1965.[1] Data were gathered by teams of graduate students who spent ten man-days in each city interviewing school administrators, school board members, civil rights leaders, political leaders, members of the civic elite, and other informants. The cities were selected by a modified random sampling design from the cities having a population between 250,000 and 1,000,000 of which at least 10 percent was Negro. The findings are supplemented by observations made in the course of research on the social organization of the large city school system carried out principally in the Chicago schools.[2]

The Issue

Very little research has been devoted to the school desegregation issue as a problem in policy-making. Consequently, almost everyone, including most social scientists, has been dependent upon the popular media for information about the issue. This has produced a widespread acceptance of some important misconceptions. Perhaps the most common is the view that intense conflict over school desegregation is unavoidable because civil rights leaders want major concessions which the white voters are too prejudiced to give. This statement contains, we believe, three errors: First, our findings indicate that in some circumstances intense conflict is avoidable. In the eight cities studied, three (Newark, Baltimore, and St. Louis) have at least temporarily resolved their conflict with the civil rights movement. In three other cities (Pittsburgh, San Francisco, and Buffalo), the controversy has cooled down and shows promise of being resolved. In the two remaining cities the controversy is still raging. Second, our data indicate that most civil rights leaders will be satisfied (or at least call off their attacks) if they receive even minimal concessions. Third, survey data have

[1] This research is reported in Robert L. Crain, Morton Inger, Gerald A. McWorter, and James J. Vanecko, *School Desegregation in the North: Eight Comparative Case Studies of Community Structure and Policy Making*, Chicago: National Opinion Research Center, Report #110A. The research was sponsored by the U.S. Office of Education.

[2] This research was supported by the Russell Sage Foundation. Major findings will be reported in David Street, *The Public Schools and Metropolitan Change*, forthcoming publication.

indicated relatively little opposition to school desegregation in national samples of white voters.[3]

In short, the school system has some freedom to establish a policy which will prevent conflict. This is not the same as saying that the school system has the power to develop a policy which will actually alter the basic nature of the schools' treatment of Negro students; indeed, we doubt that any big city school system can do this. Thus, it will be necessary to divide our discussion into two sections: first, viewing school desegregation as an issue of symbolic politics, and then looking at the actual outputs of the school system—the extent of school integration and the extent to which educational opportunities can in fact be equalized.

SYMBOLIC POLITICS: THE DEMANDS OF THE CIVIL RIGHTS MOVEMENT

Traditional civil rights groups have pressed for school integration in all eight cities studied in the NORC research. To these groups the integration issue means two things: (1) the prevention of discrimination in allocating students to schools; and (2) the acceptance on the part of the school system of the principle that integration is desirable. Beyond these rather minimal goals, the civil rights leaders would prefer, of course, a maximum amount of actual integration, but most of them view true integration as a nearly unattainable goal.[4] If the school system can be persuaded to make racial integration one of its major goals, the civil rights groups will have achieved an important victory, for this commitment exerts normative pressure on the total community to accept the principle of racial equality and to define the efforts to segregate Negroes as illegitimate. Thus, for the traditional civil rights movements, the written policies and pronouncements of the school system are important regardless of their impact. (Of course, if the system took no efforts to implement the policy, the civil rights leaders would raise the cry of hypocrisy.) The civil rights groups would probably endorse the definition of integration given by the Pittsburgh Urban League: "We regard a community as integrated when opportunities for the achievement of respect and the distribution of material welfare are not limited by race."

One is tempted to draw parallels between the school desegregation issue and labor–management negotiations. The major difference is that the corporation is required by law to negotiate with a labor union, while the school board is not. The school board is in the position of the corporation of

---

[3] For a general review of this and other survey data, see Paul B. Sheatsley, "White Attitudes Toward the Negro," *Daedalus*, 95 (Winter, 1966), 217–238; and Harriet B. Erskine, "The Polls: Race Relations," *Public Opinion Quarterly*, 26 (1962), 137–148.

[4] It is for this reason that we have chosen to use "desegregation" rather than "integration" in the title of this paper.

four decades ago, when management had to decide whether it was wise or morally proper to negotiate with labor unions. The Northern school board is not required to recognize the civil rights movement as legitimate, and indeed many whites who appear otherwise unprejudiced do not consider it so. But another problem is that even when the school system decides that negotiation is proper, the question remains of whom to recognize as the true spokesmen for the civil rights movement. For these two reasons, actual back-room negotiations with the civil rights movement are not common. In our eight cities only two school systems have been able to maintain this sort of communication with the civil rights groups. This means that we will have to analyze the school systems' policy-making as taking place with only limited private face-to-face communications between the "negotiators."

THE FIRST STAGE OF THE DESEGREGATION DECISION: THE SCHOOL SUPERINTENDENT AS DECISION-MAKER

We shall see that the policy decision on desegregation is made by the school board, not the superintendent. However, in each case the board attempted to avoid making a decision for as long as possible. The typical school board seems to operate in a highly pragmatic, fire-fighting fashion. It has limited time, resources, and information with which to make policies, and the result is that it seems not to have a clear policy perspective but primarily makes *ad hoc* decisions as issues become "hot." [5] In the case of desegregation, none of the eight school boards took action when the issue was first raised, and this placed the burden of decision-making on the superintendent. Of ten superintendents who served in the eight cities during the racial controversy, seven can be said to have acted autonomously without board direction to reject demands made by the civil rights movement, while three urged the board to take a liberal position. This comes as no surprise. It is now fashionable to accuse superintendents as a group of being narrow-minded and arrogant in their dealings with civil rights leaders. As our data indicate, superintendents do not uniformly reject civil rights demands, but enough do to require us to discuss this point.

The statements of school superintendents frequently stress three themes. The first is that the appropriate stance should be "color blindness"—the refusal to pay any attention to race. This sometimes leads to statements that racial census of school children is illegal or at least immoral. Coupled with this concern with color blindness is the stress placed on a narrow definition of the function of the school as "educational" rather than "social." The third theme which recurs (although with somewhat less frequency) is an extreme defensiveness and an intolerance for "lay" criticism.

---

[5] Support for this hypothesis is provided by L. L. Cunningham, "Decision-making Behavior of School Boards," *American School Board Journal* (February, 1962).

Lay persons are dismissed as unqualified to make recommendations, and their criticisms are frequently answered with flat disagreement or with vague, overly detailed, and off-the-point replies.

Of course, these reactions are common to all organizations which must meet criticism, but the educators go further than most public officials in reacting defensively to political demands. Educational administrators are insistent on defining themselves as professionals and have an entrenched ideology that grants lay control but stresses the importance of the teaching certificate and "educational experience" as the boundary between the expert and the layman. In part, the response to the demands for integration is only another instance of the professionals' tendency—developed through generations of conflict over political interference, progressive education, charges of communism in the schools, and other issues—to perceive any criticism as an "attack upon education."

Further, civil rights demands also strike deeply at one of the most firmly held tenets of the ideology of the large city superintendent: universalism. In the development of the large city schools, insistence on equality of programs for all populations in the city marked a dramatic accomplishment as it gave the schools protection from the pleas for special treatment from various political and ethnic groups. Without this universalism, Northern schools would be more segregated than they are; even after World War I, biracial high schools still discriminated against their Negro students in extracurricular activity participation.[6] Yet, demands by the civil rights movement give the lie to the assumption of universalism, thereby provoking a defensiveness around a highly salient theme and, often, the administrators' counterattack that civil rights demands are themselves a case of special pleading. The defensive response may also be increased by the superintendent's knowledge that even if he were wholly committed to making integration a prime value of the schools, many of his personnel are too traditionalist, too prejudiced, or too recalcitrant to make the needed adjustments without great resistance.

Thus, we can understand the superintendents' initial defensive response. But in most cases, the school board has little difficulty taking control of the decision from the superintendent. Why is this? The answer seems to lie in what areas the superintendents can make believable claims to expertise. On many issues—for example, curriculum construction, textbook selection, or design of facilities—the superintendents' judgments generally go unchallenged, not only because they usually fall into areas of indifference but also because the superintendents' accumulation of detailed information, his technical background, and his appeals to standard or good practice argue well for honoring his professional claims. On such issues, the superintendent

[6] J. H. Tipton points out that in the late 1940s Negro students were not allowed to use the swimming pool in one high school in Gary, Indiana. See his *Community in Crisis*, New York: Columbia Teachers College, 1953.

in effect runs the schools. Any criticism in these areas may cause the superintendent to accuse the board of interference with his administrative role.

But it is only in the extreme case of Benjamin C. Willis in Chicago that a superintendent has been willing to take the stand that he must have autonomy or he will resign over a racial issue.[7] This is understandable, for there is not truly marketable expertise on racial integration anywhere, and there is certainly little claim possible in this area from within the education profession. Therefore, the superintendent, after his initial negative response, often finds his upstaging by the board to be the least awkward exit.

In addition, the origins and backgrounds of the large city superintendents generally do not provide them with a sensitivity to urban social change and problems and to the current revolution of rising racial expectations in the large cities which would lead these men to play a leadership role in the absence of professional claims. Evidence bearing on this point comes from the biographies of the eleven big city superintendents contained in Who's Who. Of the ten whose birth date was given, the mean age was fifty-seven. Nine of the eleven began as teachers, and only one finished graduate school before beginning his career. Six of the ten American-born superintendents were from very small cities or farms, and none of the eleven attended a first-rank undergraduate college. Seven of the eleven began their teaching in small towns, and much of the administrative experience of all but four had been outside the large cities.

While many of these men had been administrators in smaller, suburban, and often vanguard or experimental school systems, their experiences in the large cities have not stimulated their desire to be experimental. The financial problems of the large city systems, the sheer administrative problems of size, scale, and change, and the often inert middle-level personnel and principals (who frequently are political appointees left over from an earlier era) tend to move these superintendents toward an emphasis upon a traditionalistic philosophy of education that stresses the three R's, the standard neighborhood school, and "sound programs." When racial and other social changes place new demands on the schools, these superintendents generally are unable to articulate a leadership ideology dealing with integration and broadened welfare goals.

The Second Stage of the Controversy: The School Board Takes Over

In the typical city studied, the civil rights movement first approaches the board cautiously over a period of a year or two, making statements and

---

[7] Willis' temporary resignation was apparently triggered by a taxpayer's suit charging that he had arbitrarily changed a voluntary transfer plan designed by the board to further integration. The incident is described in Joseph Pois, The School Board Crisis, Chicago: Aldine Press, 1964, pp. 109–114.

testifying at hearings. In general, the school system does not respond to this; the issue is still below the level of saliency. The integrationists then step up their campaign, and their demands are rejected by the school superintendent at this point. When the movement replies to this with demonstrations or threats of demonstrations, the school board begins to take the issue seriously and responds in a variety of ways. At this point, the second stage of the controversy has begun. The board has taken over racial policymaking. In six of the eight cities it is possible to find a point at which the superintendent's recommendations were ignored or a point when he was instructed to alter his policy. In the other two cases, the system changed superintendents without changing its policy, so that we must assume that the board supplied policy continuity to the system.

The first response made by the school system during this second phase we call the "key response," because it sets the tone for the remainder of the conflict. This key response by the board seems to be made with almost complete autonomy. One might expect the community political and civic elites to exert great influence, but we have only one clear case where this was done successfully. In two cases, the school board seemed to ignore the recommendations of the mayor; in another case, the community's most prominent industrialist was flatly rebuffed. It is not possible to describe all the actions taken by various actors in this short paper, but in general it seems clear that there is less direct influence exerted on the board than one would expect and that attempts to influence the board usually are not very successful.

The most complex question is: To what extent can the civil rights movement control the outcomes of the school desegregation decision by their use of power? The evidence seems to indicate that they have surprisingly little influence. The civil rights movement can force the school system to deal with the issue, of course; few if any of these systems would have done anything about civil rights if they had not been pressured by the movement. Generally, the movement is successful in part—that is, the system will usually desegregate schools to some limited extent, and all of the eight cities have adopted a policy statement advocating integration. But concessions may be minimal and may come so late and be given so grudgingly as to be nearly meaningless.

Apparently, there is little that the civil rights leadership in a typical city can do to prevent this. Once the key response of the board is taken, the process is "locked in." If the key response is conciliatory, continued low-keyed civil rights activity will extract additional concessions; if the key response is negative, the civil rights movement will retaliate with demonstrations, but this usually leads to an escalation of the conflict and the school board's subsequently becoming more reluctant to negotiate or make additional concessions. The only way in which the movement can control the outcome is by introducing a new authority—for example, the state government may step in to order desegregation, and this is sometimes very effective.

Altogether, the findings mean that the school board usually is nearly autonomous in its policy-making on racial issues. It generally is not effectively influenced by political or civic leadership, by its superintendent, or even by the behavior of the civil rights movement, despite the fact that the decision on race is probably the issue of greatest immediate importance to the largest number of actors.

In order to demonstrate this conclusion, the research staff of the eight-city study ranked the cities on four variables: the level of civil rights activity prior to the key response, the level of civil rights activity after the key response, the degree to which the key response indicated a willingness to acquiesce to the civil rights demands, and the final level of acquiescence of the board to the demands made. Acquiescence is based on the number of demands met and the general public tone taken by the schools with respect to the civil rights movement. Put another way, the research staff attempted to rank the cities according to the degree to which a typical civil rights leader would feel satisfied with the response of the school system. The eight cities varied greatly in their acquiescence. In Pittsburgh, for example, the school board reacted very early to civil rights demands with a transfer plan which integrated two previously all-white schools. When demands for integration reappeared later, the school board committed itself, in a long and candid statement, to integration; adopted some short-range integration programs; and began planning for large scale educational parks as the long run answer to the integration question. In Baltimore, a demand for the elimination of overcrowding in Negro schools led to a summer of negotiation between civil rights leaders and the school board, resulting in a decision to transport 4,000 Negro students and eliminate all double-shift schooling in the system, effective only six months after the issue was first raised. These two school systems are scored at the top of the acquiescence scale. At the opposite extreme, two school boards have refused to meet any of the demands for integration made, despite repeated demonstrations and pressure from other governmental officials. These two systems are located at the bottom of the scale.

Figure 1 diagrams the rank-order correlations between the initial level of civil rights activity, the acquiescence of the key response, the level of civil rights activity following the key response, and the total level of acquiescence of the school system. The correlations indicate that the key response is not dependent upon the level of civil rights activity directed at the board, and also that the key response predicts quite accurately the final amount of acquiescence of the school system. If the rank correlations are accurate, they indicate that the civil rights movement principally responds to the behavior of the school system rather than being a cause of the character of the school system's behavior.

This is only indirect evidence that the boards can be quite autonomous in their decision. We also have some direct evidence of this. In Figure 2, the eight boards have been ranked by a combination of two closely correlated

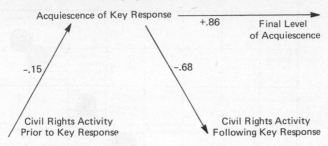

FIGURE 1.   Rank–Order Correlations Between Civil Rights Activity and Acquiescence of School Boards to Civil Rights Demands.

variables: the percentage of the board members having high socioeconomic status (men from large businesses, corporation lawyers, or professionals) as against the percentage who are professional politicians or related in other ways to the political parties in their city. (High-status men are, of course, generally independent of the parties.) This single variable predicts quite well the final level of acquiescence of the school system. Since the variable is clearly independent of the actual decision situation, this seems to be strong evidence.

The autonomy of the nonpolitical board is not so surprising. However, the five boards which are partly or wholly made up of political appointments are also largely autonomous. Two of these boards are elected boards in cities where political power is quite decentralized. In a third city, the mayor's recommendations seem to have been largely ignored. In another, the mayor's appointments have disagreed strongly with each other and have involved the city in a lengthy controversy. In the fifth city, the mayor seems to have maintained control over the school system, and here the board has been persuaded twice to change its position on a racial issue.

It is usually assumed that political leaders wish to maximize their power and, therefore, detachment from school politics may seem surprising; but the mayor who tries to run the schools would be taking a great risk for a very small reward.

Before considering the implications of these findings, we also should consider why it is that the civic board is more acquiescent than the political board. The answer is a simple but empirical one: On our measures, the civil board members are more liberal on racial issues and the political board members are more conservative. This is not a trivial statement, because it is certainly not necessary that there be a high correlation between the personal attitude of government officials and their public actions. In fact, a similar study of Southern school boards indicates that there is at best a weak correlation between racial attitudes and behavior regarding school desegregation.[8] The presence of this high correlation in the North indicates the extent

[8] See Robert L. Crain, Morton Inger and Gerald A. McWorter, "School Desegregation in New Orleans: A Comparative Study in the Failure of Social Control," Chicago: National Opinion Research Center, Report #110B.

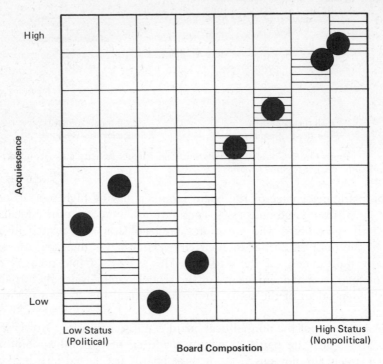

High

Acquiescence

Low

Low Status
(Political)

High Status
(Nonpolitical)

Board Composition

(Note: The two boards in the upper right are tied on both rankings.)

FIGURE 2. Status and Political Activity of School Board Members and Acquiescence to Civil Rights Demands.

to which the school desegregation issue is unstructured. In the absence of clear legal guidelines for action, of efficient communication between the contesting parties, and of a coherent educational ideology to draw upon, the school board members are "on their own" in deciding what to do. Board members are very conscious of this; more than one has publicly appealed for a decision by a local or Federal court to clarify the situation. Buffalo, New York, furnishes a striking example of what this kind of clarification by an authority can do. The state commissioner of education, James E. Allen, demanded that the board desegregate the schools, and immediately the board became a cohesive decision-making body even though it had been torn by internal conflict for well over a year prior to his intervention.

The lack of structure and clarity in the civil rights arena is, we think, also reflected in the fact that heterogeneous school boards and boards with a history of internal conflict have the greatest difficulty in meeting civil rights demands. Only two of the eight boards have contested elections for membership (five are appointed while another is *de facto* appointed by a slating committee); these two boards were the least acquiescent, probably because of their heterogeneity and the pressures on the boards to make their disagreements public. The board with internal conflict cannot acquiesce to the demands made on it for two reasons: First, it cannot agree on what is being asked of it, and what strategies are available to it; second, it cannot prevent public controversy which polarizes the community and further limits the alternatives available to it.

The great debate over community power structure hinges about the amount of autonomy which governmental officials have and the extent to which the civic elite are able to influence policy. The findings of this research suggest that it is possible for government officials to have great autonomy and at the same time for the civic elite to have great influence. In the case of the schools, the nature of the local civic elite is a principal factor in determining the conposition of the school board, and thus the elite indirectly controls policy, even though it makes little or no effort to influence any single decision (and probably could not do so if it tried). The three most acquiescent cities all have high-status school boards, and the civic elite in all three cases plays an important role in locating school board members. These three cities have elites which are highly active across a wide range of local policy issues. In the other five cities, the elites are weaker, and the result is that school board members are selected either from the ranks of the political parties, or from the leadership of voluntary organizations or in order to represent various ethnic groups.

Even the degree of heterogeneity and internal conflict in the school board has its roots in the structure of the political parties and the nature of the elite. The conflict-ridden boards which resist desegregation appear in cities with weak political parties, for example. Thus, the school board is autonomous in its decision-making procedure, yet the degree of acquiescence of the school system is determined by the overall political structure of the city.

SYMBOLIC POLITICS AND REAL OUTPUTS

To this point we have not discussed the real outputs of the school system's racial policy—the actual changes in quality of education or the actual increase in the number of students in integrated schools. It is not difficult for a school system to adopt a racial policy which will partially satisfy civil rights leaders without actually making a large impact on the operation of the schools. (These symbolic victories may have a considerable impact on the attitudes and behavior of individual Negro students, but this is outside the range of the two studies.) Conversely, it is also possible for the school system to have in operation policies which increase school integration without satisfying the civil rights groups. In two cities, Negro students were routinely bussed into white schools, but the school adamantly refused to state that such integration was desirable, and the board in each case was subject to a great deal of attack.

The actual amount of integration is, of course, small. Among the eight cities, the greatest acquiescence, as judged by the research staff, was in Pittsburgh, Baltimore, and St. Louis. In Pittsburgh, the school system has succeeded in remaining on cordial terms with the civil rights leaders and has committed itself wholeheartedly to integration; but to date, Pittsburgh has done little to increase integration. St. Louis and Baltimore have adopted bussing programs which have successfully relieved overcrowded Negro schools, but less than 5 percent of the Negro students are directly involved. In the eight cities, the proportion of Negro elementary school children attending schools which are at least 90 percent Negro varies from a low of 30 percent in San Francisco to a high of 86 percent in St. Louis; the median for the eight cities is 68 percent. If the largest cities—Chicago, Detroit, Cleveland, Philadelphia, Washington, and New York City—had been included in the study, the picture would look even bleaker.

The school board may commit itself to a policy of integration but find its efforts to implement this policy restricted by a number of factors outside of its control. The superintendent may undermine the design and implementation of the policy through his role in developing technical details of the plan. Voluntary plans for pupil-transfer may have a minimal effect because of a lack of interest among Negro parents, or may even further segregation by allowing whites to transfer out of integrated schools. (This is another example of universalism; transfer plans explicitly based on the race of the pupils involved are quite *avant-garde*.) Or track systems or practices of homogeneous grouping, discriminatory or not, may segregate pupils rigidly within the "integrated" school. And in cities where racial tensions are especially high, such as in Chicago and Cleveland, Negro students attending white schools have been assaulted, and it is often a community prophecy (and in a part a self-fulfilling one) that integrated schools will become all Negro.[9]

More important, the school system cannot control its own personnel. The heart of successful integration is the classroom teacher, and many big city teachers do not feel comfortable teaching Negro students or handling an integrated class. Further, it is a big city tradition that the integrated school is a "changing" school, where teachers transfer out, morale drops, and high-level programs are phased out as no longer appropriate to the clientele.

The difficulties encountered by the school systems in implementing effective integration go beyond the particular personality problems of the individual actors. They are tied to basic inadequacies in the organizational capacities of the large city school systems for adapting to social change. Briefly, these inadequacies include the following:

1. A bureaucratic rigidity flowing from the statutory and quasi-legal restrictions placed on the school systems by states and accrediting associa-

[9] Each of these problems is potentially subject to remediation as shown, for example, in St. Louis's ability to bus approximately 2,600 Negro students into white schools in 1965–1966. The bussing program seems to have an informal "quota"; none of the integrated schools is over 40 percent Negro. After the initial shock, there has been virtually no opposition in this border city, and bussing of Negro students is now taken for granted.

tions. These restrictions limit the scheduling of the school year, prescribe certain courses and curricula, bureaucratize teacher recruitment, etc. This rigidity is related to the great emphasis upon universalism, a stress which in large part is a heritage of many cycles of reform. The result is administration by numbers: an attempt at innovation becomes merely an elaborate formula for assigning X numbers of specialists to Y numbers of schools. Another example is the procedure of allowing teachers to pick whatever schools they want on the basis of seniority, a practice which usually undermines the "difficult" school. And a crucial result is the highly standardized curriculum, which exists despite obvious differences in the needs of different schools.

2. The fact that teachers are basically solo practitioners. Unlike most professions, teaching offers relatively little opportunity for collegial contact which could provide the opportunity not only for respite but for communication of new practices and the development of new attitudes. In-service training tends to be restricted to short-term workshops which are likely to have a minimal impact on teacher attitudes relevant to racial change. Yet, intensive resocialization procedures are apparently essential because of the conventional perspectives with which persons enter teaching.[10] Further, rewards for the teachers are largely ascriptive, based on seniority and on graduate work which in most schools of education is not oriented to the problems of urban education. As solo practitioners, the teachers frequently are reluctant to have anyone enter their classrooms, including subprofessionals or volunteers who could play a significant role. Principals and middle-level administrators face similar problems of poor lateral and vertical communication except on purely administrative matters.

3. Given these patterns, the large city school systems have very primitive mechanisms of control, which limit them severely in producing change. These systems are overcentralized in the sense that standardized curricula and administration by formula do not provide enough fiscal and administrative autonomy to permit "decentralized" administrators to vary their programs to local needs with any real facility. Yet they are undercentralized in the sense that it is very difficult for decisions made at the top of the organization to alter the traditional operating procedures. This is particularly the case in cities where principals or other

[10] The tendency for even city-bred teacher trainees to have quite negative orientations toward the challenges of "problem schools" in the inner city is described in Bryan Roberts, "The Effects of College Experience and Social Background on Professional Orientations of Prospective Teachers," unpublished dissertation, University of Chicago, 1964. Findings of an experiment conducted by Bruno Bettelheim in cooperation with the Russell Sage project indicate that teachers' difficulties in dealing with Negro children who present behavior problems flow not principally from racial prejudice but from social class views in which the teacher assumes that the children are unlikely to learn. The Bettelheim work also seems to demonstrate that really intensive in-service training can produce a reduction in these stereotypic views.

personnel have become highly entrenched in their positions; the man who has been principal of the same school for twenty years is not responsive to supervision. Commitment to the status quo is often heightened by inbreeding and by the associations of principals and other personnel which act as mutual protective associations.[11]

4. Also limiting the school system in producing innovations in racial practices and programs for the deprived is their general weakness in research and development. The large systems have numerous special projects for dealing with Negro pupils, and many have generated a sense of success and excitement. But evaluation research is usually poor, and attempts to expand the program to other schools are so haphazardly administered that few survive to become incorporated into standard operating procedure.

Cumulatively, these characteristics of the large city school system imply that more adequate integration of the large city schools will require not only higher levels of leadership in broadening and pursuing educational goals, but also substantial transformations in the organizational format.

Conclusion

It has often been said that in a large and complex organization the leadership does not have control over the operation of the system. These data indicate that there is considerable truth in this. Control over the classroom teacher is limited by the fact that she cannot be supervised directly and by the nature of her contract and the character of her professional organization. Control over individual principals is limited because supervision must be from a distance and by a strict universalism in administration. The board cannot supervise a school superintendent unless he supplies information to them, presents the full range of policy alternatives, and permits the board to believe that it knows something about how to run a school system. Similarly, the men who select the school-board members must defer to them as "experts" once the selection has been made.

On the other hand, we do see a clear line of influence which runs from the top of the system to the bottom. When members of the mayor's staff or members of the civil elite choose school-board members (and in most cities they do choose them), they have in mind an operational image when they say they want a "good man" for the job. It is hardly a surprise that they get the kind of man they want most of the time. These men then control the school's "image" on racial matters and to a limited extent this style can filter down to the classroom. The board selects the superintendent, and some boards have definite criteria in mind; if he does not meet them, he may

---

[11] For a discussion of the power of this sort of clique, see W. S. Sayre and H. Kaufman, *Governing New York City*, New York: W. W. Norton & Company, Inc., 1965, 279–280.

then be subject to what one board member called a "learning experience." And the superintendent, through his choice of subordinate administrators and his use of policy directives and public relations, can project a "style" into the school system. Granted there is no close isomorphism between this "style" and the actual day-to-day operations of the schools, but at least there is some order in the system.

An Analysis of Curriculum Policy Making
MICHAEL W. KIRST AND DECKER F. WALKER

Any organization or institution with purposes of its own develops policies— "a body of principles to guide action [Lerner & Lasswell, 1951, p. ix]"—for dealing with recurring or crucial matters. Schools normally formulate policies on a variety of matters including promotion of students, grading, grouping of students for instruction, and dress for students. Schools also implement policies formulated by other bodies, most notably policies of the district administration, the state and local board of education, and the U.S. Congress. The policies executed by schools include specifically educational policies as well as others which, while they may have educational aspects, are not unique to schools or even characteristic of them. Among the most important of the specifically educational policies of schools are those pertaining to what children study in school. Children in school are normally required to study certain subjects and forbidden to study others, encouraged to pursue some topics and discouraged from pursuing others, provided with opportunities to study some phenomena but not provided with the means of studying others. When these requirements and pressures are uniformly and consistently operative they amount to policy, whether we intended so or not. We shall call such explicit or implicit "guides to action" *curriculum policy* and the process of arriving at such policy we shall call curriculum *policy making*.

Our purpose in this paper is to explore what is known about curriculum policy making in the public schools of the United States, relying whenever possible on the demonstrable conclusions of formal studies, but resorting when necessary to conventional wisdom, common sense, personal experiences, and outright speculation. We do not intend to give an historical account of the development of either the policy making process or the policies produced by it. Rather we are primarily interested in the present status of the policy making process. For this reason we direct our attention exclusively to works published since 1950. Even though we are aware of many interesting and informative earlier treatments of parts of this topic (e.g., Lippmann, 1928; Counts, 1928; Nelson & Roberts, 1963; Krug, 1964), limi-

KIRST, Michael W., and Walker, Decker F., "An Analysis of Curriculum Policy Making," *Review of Educational Research*, Vol. 41, No. 5, pp. 479–509. Copyright by American Educational Research Association, Washington, D.C.

tations of time, space, and energy forbid a more historical approach. The reader should also keep in mind that treating such'a broad topic in a paper of this size means that we have to deal in national-scale generalizations without mentioning the numerous exceptions that can be found in the country's diverse regions, states, and 19,300 school districts. We hope that the perspective for future research directions such an approach provides on the problems of curriculum policy making will compensate for the exception cases that, despite our best efforts, we overlooked.

In this country school policy, including curriculum policy, is determined at many levels. State legislatures require the study of some subjects. State and local boards of education commission and endorse courses of study, specifying the content to be included in these courses. The professional employees of the school districts, from the superintendent to the teacher's aide, have varying degrees of influence in the determination of courses of study, textbooks, supplies, allotments of time, etc. which embody curriculum policy. Given a complex system of public policy making, an unfamiliar observer might expect curriculum policy-making to be the scene of conflict and uneasy accommodation, as are most political issues in our democracy. And, indeed, we do find signs of powerful influences of political and social events on curriculum policy making. For example, in a survey of professional discourse in the field of curriculum—the periodic policy statements of the Educational Policies Commission, the yearbooks of the National Society for the Study of Education, the publications of professional scholars, and their influential publications in the curriculum field—Pilder (1968) found that this literature reflected most of the major national political tensions in the period he studied (1918–1967). When immigration was a national issue, Americanization was a curriculum issue. When totalitarianism posed a threat to democracy, education for democratic life was a concern in curricular discourse. When World War II created a shortage of trained workers, manpower training became an important theme in writings on curriculum. When Sputnik shocked the nation, the softness of existing curricula was cited as a major contributing factor in our national decline. The school curriculum was entangled in these national political issues even though the federal government was formally and in theory not a party to educational questions, especially curriculum questions.

Such evidence as this indicates that the determination of the public school curriculum is not just influenced by political events; it is a political process in important ways. By "political" here and elsewhere in this article we refer not merely to the processes by which we are governed or govern ourselves. Throughout curriculum policy making, political conflict is generated by the existence of competing values concerning the proper basis for deciding what to teach. The local school system and the other public agencies responsible for these decisions must allocate these competing values in some way, even though this means that some factions or interests win and others lose on any given curriculum issue. The inevitability of conflicting demands, wants, and needs is responsible for the necessarily political character of curriculum policy making, a character which cannot be avoided even by the adoption of some mathematical decision-procedure. Some legitimate authority must decide (and perhaps bargain and compromise) among the conflicting policy viewpoints.

Yet when professional educators write about or study the curriculum, they rarely conceive of their subject in political terms. The words "policy," "politics," and "political" do not even appear in the indices of any of the major textbooks in the field (Tyler, 1949; Smith, Stanley, & Shores, 1950; Gwynn, 1960; Taba, 1962; Saylor & Alexander, 1966). These authors treated conflict always as conflict among ideas, never as conflict among individuals, interest groups, or factions within school system bureaucracies. One finds consistent acknowledgement of the existence of political influence on curriculum, but no mention of policy or policy making, nor any attempts to compare or contrast curriculum policy making with other types of public or private policy making. Instead, terms such as "decision making," "planning," "development," and "management" were used. National, state, and local political figures, as well as parents, taxpayers, and other interested parties and the organizations that represent their interests were treated as "influences" on curriculum "decision making." These terms and the ideas that accompany them embody an image of curriculum determination that plays down—if it does not altogether ignore—the conflict and accommodation characteristic of policy making in all but the most monolithic institutions. Consistently followed, this image leads the investigator to search for some sort of mechanism for deciding "scientifically" what children should study in school. More important for present purposes, this ideal sidesteps the political questions of who should have a say in determining curriculum at what stages in which ways with what impact. Instead, it holds out the promise of resolving competing claims at the level of principle. Here is one clear statement of this position.

> If curriculum development is to be a rational and a scientific rather than a rule-of-thumb procedure, the decisions about these elements [of the curriculum] need to be made on the basis of some valid criteria. These criteria may come from various sources—from tradition, from social pressures, from established habits. The differences between a curriculum decision-making which follows a scientific method and develops a rational design and one which does not is that in the former the criteria for decisions are derived from a study of the factors constituting a reasonable basis for the curriculum. In our society, at least, these factors are the learner, the learning process, the cultural demands, and the content of the disciplines. Therefore, scientific curriculum development needs to draw upon analyses of society and culture, studies of the learner and the learning process, and analyses of the nature of knowledge in order to determine the purposes of the school and the nature of its curriculum [Taba, 1962, p. 10].

Once such an ideal has been adopted, it is difficult to avoid disapproval of political resolutions of curriculum questions. And, once political solutions to curriculum questions are seen as deficient or inferior, the tendency is to lump all the complex and varied means by which personal and group interests are defended and advanced in curriculum issues under the vague and somewhat sinister term "influences" and to treat them as aberrations rather than as normal and necessary, if not altogether desirable, aspects of public policy-making.

In this review we treat the determination of the public school curriculum as a process of public policy making which is necessarily political in character. We choose not to concentrate on the interaction of strictly political (in the narrow sense of political) and educational institutions. Our concern is with the whole range of processes which eventuate in the curriculum of the local public schools. Since local districts have ultimate authority and responsibility for carrying out curriculum policy, and much authority for determining it, we focus our attention on the curriculum decisions of local schools and the activities of individuals and groups in local school systems as they engage in these collective decisions. Inevitably this focus draws us into a consideration of the state, regional, and national factors—governmental and private—that condition and constrain local decision-makers. In light of these aims this paper is perhaps most accurately described as an exploratory review of the literature—exploratory not because the topic is new, but because it has not been treated in this way before.

Value Bases

For most of their recorded history, schools have regarded their curricula as fixed quantities, not variables to be adjusted in the interest of achieving some goal. The Latin root for the word "curriculum" means "race course" and the virtue of a race course is that it is fixed and standard. For centuries the European curriculum was fixed, bounded by the study of the trivium and the quadrivium. Moreover, for most of the last three hundred years the curriculum in Western schools has changed slowly, consisting of literacy training in the vernacular and in arithmetic, supplemented with Bible study for most of those who got any education, and study of the "disciplines"— higher mathematics, history, the national literature, languages, philosophy, and, increasingly, the natural sciences—for the intellectual elite. So long as the curriculum changed only slowly there were few occasions for conflict and little use for political processes.

But the image of the race course has not really been an accurate one for the curricula of the schools in Western civilization since the 17th Century. The race itself would be a more accurate symbol of the increasingly agitated jockeying for position in the curriculum that has characterized the last three hundred years. First the vernacular languages, then the physical sciences, then the biological sciences, the applied sciences, engineering, and, most recently, the social sciences successively fought their way into the curriculum at the upper levels of the educational system, from whence they have exerted pressure for entry into the curricula of the lower schools. In the lower schools other pressures to include more immediately useful material in the curriculum, dating from at least the 1850's (Spencer's *Education: Intellectual, Moral and Physical* (1870) is an early landmark), eventually produced such curricular offerings as home economics, the agricultural and industrial arts, physical education, driver training, and sex education.

These developments have reached their logical (and absurd) conclusion in the present situation of the elementary schools where teachers may be expected to teach and children to learn reading, writing, several varieties of arithmetic, geography, spelling, science, economics, music, art, foreign languages, and history at the same time that the children are supposedly helped to develop physically, morally, and intellectually, and are molded into good citizens. Furthermore, if the school is to take advantage of the millions of dollars invested in national curriculum development, each of these matters must be addressed independently with specially developed and packaged materials in the hands of specially trained teachers. Things are hardly less chaotic in secondary schools.

All this confusion has provoked continued conflict over the proper bases for deciding what to teach. Should schools teach those things that are likely to be immediately useful in life outside the school or should they teach those things that are most fundamental to an understanding of organized knowledge? Should they emphasize the development of individuality or the transmission of the cultural heritage? What are schools *for*, anyway? So long as there is disagreement on the proper bases for assessing the worth of the curriculum, there are bound to be conflicting views concerning its composition. The authoritative allocation of these value conflicts is the essence of what we mean by the political process in curriculum decision-making. We would identify as salient over the last several decades four broad bases for assigning value to curriculum elements—tradition, community, science, and individual judgment. These value bases are positions around which people's preferences tend to congregate. They are neither mutually exclusive nor exhaustive, but they do represent major streams of thought and feeling among individuals and groups concerned with the school curriculum.

The appeal to tradition, exemplified in recent times by the Great Books program and the Council for Basic Education, rests on the assumption that those subjects of study that have survived the test of time are in the long view most beneficial and therefore should receive the highest priority in the curricula. The appeal to science, the newest and probably the fastest growing basis for curriculum decision-making, has received strong support from many influential groups including the U.S. Office of Education. This appeal rests on the assumption that educational and psychological research will reveal those capabilities that are essential to the performance of the activities which the school is responsible for cultivating. In this view the school curriculum should give first priority to the development of these scientifically identified capabilities. The appeal to community presupposes that every school is part of a community of association and interest in which resides the ultimate criterion of usefulness, relevance, and beneficiality of any curriculum element. Therefore, those matters which deserve first priority in the curriculum are to be determined by the community, either directly or via its representatives or by studies of the community. The appeal to individual judgment amounts to a skeptical denial of any rational value basis for curriculum-making beyond the student's own values, needs, and desires as these are manifested in his own considered judgments. Adherents of this position argue that any basis for curriculum that purports to provide general, impersonal answers to Spencer's (1870) question "What knowledge is of most worth?" is doomed to failure.

Each value basis has its supporters and detractors who use political techniques to bolster their position. There are schools that stand primarily and reasonably consistently on only one basis. The curriculum of St. Johns University in Annapolis is based largely on the appeal to tradition as are the curricula of a number of private "Latin" schools; several medical schools have reorganized their curricula along predominantly scientific lines (Henderson, 1969), and experimental programs with a scientific basis are widespread, most visibly in preschool and primary school programs (Pine, 1968; Bereiter & Engelman, 1966); many so-called free schools and free universities across the country as well as "progressive" or "radical" schools base their programs on a particular community or on the free choices of individual students (Stretch, 1970). But by and large public school programs seem to be a heterogeneous mixture of these different bases reflecting political compromises among the heterogeneous values in any state or local district. A study of the value bases for various elements in the school curriculum and the groups who advance and defend each basis would add considerably to our understanding of curriculum policy-making.

The Use of Decision Tools: Disjointed Incrementalism

The acceptance of any definite value basis, when this is possible, simplifies the determination of the curriculum considerably by providing a limited and well-defined set of criteria for narrowing the bewildering array of curricular choices. But adopting a single clear and consistent basis of value does not entirely resolve the political conflict in curriculum policy-making. Those who agree that the truths honored in our tradition should be the primary curriculum elements may still disagree over whether certain classics should be taught in English translations, Latin translations, or the original Greek. They may argue whether to include Vergil together with Tacitus and Julius Caesar in a fixed time of study. They may differ over the amount of time to be allotted to the Bible and other more strictly oriental texts. The resolution of such problems requires a decision procedure in addition to a value basis.

The oldest and simplest solution to this problem is to endow an individual or small group with the authority to make these decisions by exercising professional and presumably expert judgment. This decision-making body can be related to the community that gives it power as a government is related to its constituency (traditional school boards), as the management of a firm is related to its customers (coucher systems), or in any of a number of other ways ranging from tight control of decision-makers by the community to virtual independence.

But this only pushes our search one step further. What sort of decision procedures do these groups follow? They adopt what Lindblom and Braybrooke (1963) called a strategy of disjointed incrementalism. Disjointed incrementalism is a name for a collection of "relatively simple, crude, almost wholly conscious, and public" strategies for decision making which "taken together as a mutually reinforcing set . . . constitute a systematic and defensible strategy [Lindblom & Braybrooke, 1963, p. 82]." The major features of disjointed incrementalism are (a) acceptance of the broad outlines of the existing situation with only marginal changes contemplated, (b) consideration of a restricted variety of policy alternatives excluding those entailing radical change, (c) consideration of a restricted number of consequences for any given policy, (d) adjustment of objectives to policies as well as policies to objectives, (e) willingness to formulate the problem as data become available, and (f) serial analysis and piecemeal alterations rather than a single comprehensive attack. In short, curriculum decision makers use informal methods of decision making.

This is no surprise considering the history of the field, the state of the art of formal decision-making methods, the complexity of the school as a phenomenon, and the paucity of reliable data about the events taking place within the classroom and their effects on children. This absence of formal decision-making procedures complicates the task of comprehending the political processes involved in decision making since informal methods are more complex, diffuse, and irregular. There are indications that modern decision-making tools may eventually be used to decide what to teach however, and before looking more carefully at the existing decision processes it is interesting to glance at three of the most promising of the developing formal procedures.

The first sort of formal procedure to be employed still does not have a name, although several of the operations that make it up are named. For convenience let us call it behavioral analysis. This method, an educational application of techniques developed in the time-and-motion studies of the early 1900's (see Taylor, 1911; Gilbreth, 1914), begins with the activities students are being trained to engage in. It consists of analyzing these activities into a hierarchy of prerequisite capabilities, i.e., performances such that success at a higher-level performance implies the ability to succeed at all the lower-level performances which together constitute the prerequisites of the higher-level performance. After this "task analysis" has been completed, instructional sequences are designed which lead students step-by-step up the hierarchy to more and more complex performances. For examples of behavioral analysis see Gagne' (1965), Lewis and Pask (1965), and Miller (1962).

Like behavioral analysis, which was developed by psychologists engaged in military and industrial training, the next cluster of related techniques have been taken from military and industrial contexts and applied to educational problems. These techniques go under various names, e.g., Program Planning and Budgeting Systems (PPBS), cost-effectivenesses analysis, and systems analysis. We need not describe these widely known methods, but their educational applications may not be familiar and therefore merit a few words. The first step in all these methods is to specify either the complete set of achievements desired of students or a representative sub-set of these. Measures are then constructed of these educational outputs. Measures are also taken of the costs of the inputs used in teaching students to succeed in achieving these goals. Then the relative costs and benefits of different educational programs are compared quantitatively. For examples of these methods applied to education see Levin (1970), Ribich (1968), Kaufman (1967), and Joint Economic Committee (1969).

The third method of formal curriculum decision making might be called empirically-derived computer-based decision making. It consists of identifying a large number of content units, each containing a large number of specific desired competencies. Students and teachers are asked to complete questionnaires, and these, together with aptitude and achievement information on each student, are stored in a computer. The machine uses this information to make initial content decisions for each student. Achievement test information and student and teacher reactions are fed into the machine and it, in theory, at least, automatically changes its decision-rules to optimize achievement subject to constraints of interest and involvement. No such system is in full operation now, to our knowledge, but simpler versions are (Harnack, 1969), and there is no reason to doubt that fully operational systems will be available presently.

These are tentative first steps toward more formal procedures for designing curricula. Whether further significant steps will follow quickly or at all is a moot question. The methods outlined above are relatively simple applications of simple ideas, almost certain to prove less than fully adequate. Curriculum decision making presents a severe test for any formal decision making tool. There is no clear and simple criterion of success such as profit or number of enemy dead. Each of the methods sketched above relies on behavioral objectives as criteria of value. That is, the users of each method assume they have been supplied with a complete list of the "behaviors" desired by the school and that all the school's real objectives can be expressed in the form of these behaviors. This point is vigorously disputed in the professional literature. For examples, see Atkin (1963), Eisner (1967), Eisner (1969), Jackson and Belford (1965), and Moffett (1970). Some individuals and groups strongly oppose even the attempt to define such criteria on the grounds that they would necessarily leave out the more evanescent benefits of education. Indeed, we are hard-pressed to specify the educational benefits of, for example, play for children even though most of us believe that play can and does have educational value.

Even if we could get wide agreement on operational goals, however, the most significant goals are likely to take a long time to achieve and the assessment of the beneficial effects of a complex treatment on a distant objective is a presently insoluble technical problem. An even more elementary problem is to find satisfactory measures of the subtle effects we want, such as the ability to apply what is learned to unfamiliar situations, the ability to learn new things quickly and surely, and the ability to decide what knowledge is appropriate to a given problem. It will be interesting to see how far we are able to get toward a solution of these difficulties in the last third of the twentieth century.

And finally, these formal decision-making procedures leave open the political questions of who will determine the goals and the decision-rules and in whose interest. It seems reasonable to suppose that if the staff of the school —teachers and administrators—make the determinations the results would reflect their value bases. Are their bases substantially different from those of the public at large? Even assuming they are not, is it not possible that they would become different in the future? And is it not virtually certain that the goals and decision-rules adapted will differ markedly from the preferences of some substantial groups or interests in the larger society? How will the conflicts generated in these situations be resolved?

In summary, curriculum decisions are not based on quantitative decision techniques or even on a great deal of objective data. This leaves a great deal of latitude for deliberation and for complicated political processes to resolve conflicts of values among various groups and individuals. As we will see, these value conflicts are resolved through low profile politics, but, even so, there is a considerable amount of overt political interaction.

MAJOR INFLUENCES ON CURRICULUM POLICY

At this point we would like to turn our attention to the structure and process of political influence in the making of local school district curriculum policy. By influence we mean the ability to get others to act, think, or feel as one intends (Banfield, 1961). A school superintendent who persuades his board to install the "new math" is exercising political influence on a curriculum issue. A related concept is what Gergen (Bauer & Gergen, 1968) called points of leverage—individuals or institutions that have the capacity to effect a substantial influence on the curriculum output of a school system. An individual or group that has leverage is one that can make a big difference in the outcome of conflicts over curriculum policy. Our focus here is on the content of curriculum policy rather than the priority curriculum receives in budget allocations, etc. Our perspective is that of the local school system and our focus is on the decisions of what to teach to children.

A mapping of the leverage points for curriculum policy making in local schools would be exceedingly complex. It would involve three levels of government, and numerous private organizations including foundations, accrediting associations, national testing agencies, textbook-software companies, and interest groups (such as the NAACP or the John Birch Society). Moreover, there would be a configuration of leverage points within a particular local school system including teachers, department heads, the assistant superintendent for instruction, the superintendent, and the school board. Cutting across all levels of government would be the pervasive influence of various celebrities, commentors, interest groups, and the journalists who use the mass media to disseminate their views on curriculum. It would be very useful if we were able to quantify the amount of influence of each of these groups or individuals and show input-output interactions for just one school system. Unfortunately, this is considerably beyond the state of the art, and we must settle for a less precise discussion. (For a critique of such concepts as political influence for constructing empirical political theory see James G. March, "The Power of Power," in Easton (1969).)

We distinguish three ways in which national or regional agencies affect state and local curriculum policy making: by establishing minimum standards, by generating curricular alternatives, and by demanding curriculum change. We treat these three types of effect on policy making separately, even though some groups affect policy making in more than one of these ways.

Groups That Establish Minimum Curriculum Standards

From the vantage point of a local public school system, flexibility in determining curriculum content is constrained greatly by several outside groups. The political culture of this country has emphasized "local control" and played down the role of the national government. The curriculum area has been singled out as one where a uniform national standard and substance should be avoided. Federal aid to education was stalled for years, in large part because of a fear that the federal dollar would lead to a uniform national curriculum (Sundquist, 1969). Visitors from abroad, however, are usually surprised by the coast to coast similarity of the curriculum in American public schools. In effect, we have granted political influence over curriculum to national *non government* agencies that demand a minimum national curriculum standard below which few public schools dare to fall.

A good example of this is the leverage on curriculum that private accrediting associations display. State governments also accredit but it is the private regional accrediting organizations that really concern the local school officials. These accrediting agencies define specific curriculum standards and criteria required for their stamp of approval. The largest of the regionals, the North Central Association, used written reports for their judgments, but others employ site visitors. The accrediting agencies' curriculum standards are highly detailed. For instance, a sample recommendation included in the *Visiting Committee Handbook* of the Western Association of Schools and Colleges (1965) provides "that written criteria be set up for the evaluation and selection of textbooks [p. 20]," "that continuing study be given to offering four years of language [p. 22]," and "that broader use of the audio-lingual approach be explored [p. 21]."

The political influence of the accrediting agency is based on the faith other people have in the accreditation. Since loss of accreditation is dreaded by every schoolman, these accrediting agencies can bring almost irresistible pressure on the curriculum offerings of a local school. The accrediting agencies often are a force for supporting the traditional curriculum and resisting radical changes (Koerner, 1968). In effect, accrediting agencies make value judgments about what should be taught while their credo stresses professional judgments.

Testing agencies in the United States are also largely in private hands and exert a "standardizing" influence on curriculum. Educational Testing Service, for instance, has an income of about $20,000,000 a year from its tests. Over one million students take the College Boards and seven hundred institutions require it. Consequently, local schools do not have a choice as to whether or not they offer the dozen subjects covered by the achievement exams of the College Boards. These tests do not entirely determine the detailed content of the curriculum but they do limit what teachers can spend their time doing. Moreover, national standardized reading or math tests given in the pre-high school grades may determine a great deal of the specific content of the reading or math curriculum. Local schools want to look good on these nationally normed tests.

While the testing agencies and their panels of expert advisers largely determine the content of the standard tests used in elementary and junior high schools, in high schools the tests tend to be dictated largely by the colleges and universities. The tests follow guidelines presented by colleges as part of their entrance requirements. For those students who take a college-preparatory course, the high school curriculum is determined almost entirely by college entrance requirements. And the prestige accorded to the subjects required for entrance by colleges undoubtedly influences many non-college-bound students (probably via their parents) to take these courses. The tyranny of college entrance requirements over the secondary school curriculum has been a persistent complaint of high schools. In the late thirties the Progressive Education Association sponsored a study, called the Eight Year Study (Aikin, 1942), of the secondary school curriculum in which they asked for and received permission to waive entrance requirements for the students in the experimental schools. Students from these schools were not required to have so many units of English, history, etc. in order to be admitted to college; only a recommendation from their principal was needed. An evaluation of the performance of these students in college showed them to be equal to students in similar schools in every respect and superior in many (Chamberlin, 1942). The design of this study has been criticized (see Travers & Wallen, 1963, pp. 472–493), but no one has attempted to replicate it, and entrance requirements remain.

State Departments of Education and State Boards of Education have also had a traditional role in setting and enforcing minimum curriculum standards. This role has varied enormously depending on whether the political culture of the state supported what Elazar (1965) called a centrist or localist policy. In New England, the local schools enjoy an autonomy from state controls that goes back to the hatred of the English royal governor, while some Southern states often mandate textbooks and courses of instruction. Most states do not mandate the school curriculum to any great extent. A 1966 survey (Conant, 1967) revealed that the great majority of states mandated courses in the dangers of alcohol and narcotics, only half required work in U.S. History and physical education, and less than half (ranging from 46% to 2% of the states) required instruction in other specific subjects. Although California and Iowa had over 30 curriculum prescriptions, over half the states had fewer than ten. Enforcement of state board curriculum mandates was very spotty, and local districts with strong views were able to circumvent the weak enforcement machinery.

It is often the newer subject areas (vocational education, driver training) that have used state law to gain a secure place in the curriculum. These subjects were introduced into the curriculum after 1920, amid great controversy, whereas mathematics and English never had to use political power to justify their existence in the school curriculum. Consequently, the "standard" subjects are less frequently mandated by state law.

Associations of teachers of special subjects can be very influential at the state level and use their power base for preserving state curriculum requirements. Vocational education, physical education, and home economics teachers use their NEA state affiliate to ensure that their specialities are stressed in the local schools. They are also supported by the manufacturers of sports equipment and home applicances. The driver education teachers are a new state lobby, but so effective that almost all states mandate driver education.

Ironically, teachers of academic subjects are usually poorly organized and not united at the state level. Nobody consults them and their minimal influence is indicated by the national trend to require less professional training for teaching licenses in physics, math, or history than for home economics or industrial arts (Conant, 1967). The impact on curriculum policy of these organizations that set minimum standards that tend to support the status quo was summarized by Koerner:

Suppose a local board, aware of the obsolescence and flaccidity of much that passes for vocational training . . . decides to reduce its program in these areas. In theory this is one of its sovereign rights. In practice several things occur to change its mind. First, the vocational education lobby goes to work on other members of local government and on the state legislature or state department of education to protect the extensive interests of vocational education teachers. Second, the regional accrediting association comes to the aid of the status quo and makes threatening noises, suggesting and then perhaps demanding, on pain of disaccreditation . . . that the board rescind its decision. Third, the NEA state affiliate "investigates" and through its considerable power "persuades" the board to a different view [1968, pp. 126–127].

Alternative Generators

Operating in the political environment of the local school are several organizations and individuals who provide alternatives with respect to curriculum. The range and nature of the curriculum alternatives proposed by these organizations is restricted by the minimum standards and requirements discussed in the prior section.

Most curriculum decisions are made at the local level; outside agencies can only provide alternatives to choose from. School boards, superintendent, directors of curriculum, principals, department chairmen, and teachers must take the final steps in deciding what to teach. As we have seen, state officials and the state legislature usually prescribe certain rather broad limits. The power of local officials to select is also bounded, however, perhaps more severely than by state laws, by the decision-alternatives available to them. If, 10 years ago, a school had wanted to teach a history of America that gave the black man a place in it, the teachers would have had to write the textbook themselves. Some schools attempt such things, but most do not. Teachers do not feel able to do the job, and the board has little money for released time or research assistants. So, until recently, most schools could not opt for an integrated history even if they were so inclined. It is only now becoming possible for schools to teach a reasonably balanced account of the wresting of this continent from its aboriginal inhabitants. Until 1960 it was not possible for a school to teach modern physics unless it was blessed with a truly outstanding teacher.

The bald fact is that most teaching in our schools is and must be from a textbook or other curriculum package. We do not trust teachers to write their own materials, we do not give them the time or money, and we insist on standardization. So long as this is true, the suppliers of teaching materials will have a potentially powerful effect on the curriculum.

Who supplies decision-alternatives to local schools? Until 10 years ago the unequivocal answer to this question would have been "textbook publishers." But a lot has happened in the interim. Textbook publishing has become part of an enlarged education industry which produces all sorts of printed, electronic, and mechanical devices for classroom use. Also, the federal government, private foundations, and various nonprofit organizations of scholars, teachers, and laymen have taken a more active role in producing curriculum materials. Nevertheless, the textbook is undoubtedly still the most widely used piece of educational technology and textbook publishers are still powerful influences on the curriculum. It was estimated in Texas that 75% of a child's classroom time and 90% of his homework time is spent using textbooks (Governor's Committee on Public Education, 1969). Thus the publisher's control of the content of the textbook is virtual control over the curriculum.

But the power of the textbook publishers is a brittle sort of power that cannot stand up against serious opposition from any large segment of the population. Some publishers still put the unit on evolution in the center of the biology textbook so that the books destined for Southern and Western schools can readily be bound without those pages. Sections on "Negro history" were once added in the same way. Publishers cannot (or will not, which amounts to the same thing) stand against the demands of their customers. Nor can publishers spend millions of dollars developing materials for one course in the way the National Science Foundation has supported projects in the sciences and mathematics. Apparently, in spite of their potential power, publishers have not been able to operate as independent agents. Instead, they reflect the conflicting desires of their customers, i.e. the local schools and in some areas the state authorities. Black (1967) offered an account of this process, but more careful and systematic studies of the influences (in this context the term is useful and accurate) on textbook content are needed.

Research is also needed on the relative efficacy in determining what is actually taught in classrooms of textbooks and various other factors such as teachers guides, courses of study, and the teachers' own views. Most studies of the curriculum assume that what appears in the textbook or course of study is what is taught. But a few observational studies of science teaching (Gallagher, 1967; Smith, 1969; Kaiser, 1969) seem to show that teachers do not simply reflect the views of the curriculum writers. The teachers in these studies projected a conception of their subject and of teaching that was different in important ways from the conception embedded in the phalanx of curriculum materials they were using. We should exercise extreme caution in interpreting the results of studies of curriculum policy-making which assume that policies formulated outside the classroom make their way undistorted to the pupil. Studies which describe the kinds of change which policies tend to undergo in filtering through the school staff to pupils would be extremely valuable.

Where there is state adoption, the State Department of Education seems to exercise considerable leverage. In Texas the State Commissioner nominates members to serve on the State Textbook Committee and must approve books recommended by the Committee. Texas State Department specialists draw up the detailed criteria for the publishers' bids including the topics to be covered. The selected books are distributed at state expense to every school room, but the same textbook must stay in service for six years. Districts who want to "stay on top of things" must do so at their own expense (Governor's Committee, 1969).

The U.S. Government has become a very powerful influence on the curriculum in the past 10 years. Because of the fragmented federal budgeting of monies for curriculum development it is not possible to determine exactly how much the government, mainly through the National Science Foundation and the Office of Education, has spent on curriculum development over the past 10 years. This figure is very large, however, and dwarfs all previous curriculum development efforts by states, regions, localities, and private enterprise. As an index of the impact of government-sponsored courses, it was estimated that over 50% of our schools use the new physics and chemistry programs while 65% use the new biology (Koerner, 1968).

Federal agencies have not sponsored the development of controversial curricula. The National Science Foundation, in particular, perceives its role as one of "course improvement," not the creation of new courses (Campbell & Bunnell, 1963). Therefore, almost all of the money allocated to curriculum development by the federal government has gone to up-date and improve the existing curriculum. Thus we have new math, new physics, new biology, new social studies, and new English, but not psychology, sociology, economics, philosophy, problems of modern living, interpersonal relationships, sex education, or film-making and viewing. But federal agencies have decided which proposed "improvements" to finance and they have exerted certain pressures on the staffs of projects they finance, including pressure to state objectives and to conduct evaluations using these objectives. See Grobman (1969) and Marsh (1963) for accounts of the interactions between project staffs and federal agencies. Will these federal agencies continue this pattern, will they expand their efforts to genuinely new courses, or alternatively, will they cut back on their funds for curriculum development in disillusionment over the failure of test results to show definite superiority of the new curricula?

No one can foresee the path federal curriculum policy will take in even the next few years. Agencies of the federal government jumped from virtually no influence to a place of preeminence at one stroke when the National Defense Education Act was signed into law. President Nixon proposed the creation of a National Institute of Education. He also inaugurated a "right to read" campaign to encourage emphasis on reading in elementary and junior high schools. "Sesame Street," a nationally televised preschool program, has been produced under the auspices of the U.S. Office of Education. Until now, the federal government's influence has been a conservative one, educationally speaking; but the government's role has been an important one, and when the right circumstances arise we have every reason to believe that federal agencies will seize the initiative in curriculum matters.

Another set of powerful agents in curriculum making are the foundations. Over the past 10 years they have generally seen their role as one of supplementing and balancing the efforts of the federal government. When the federal government was financing only projects in mathematics, science and foreign languages, the foundations were financing projects in the arts and social sciences. The foundations have also been bolder in funding efforts in nonstandard courses including psychology, economics, and photography, among many others. All that is known of the policies of the foundations that have supported curriculum development over the past decade —chiefly the Ford, Rockefeller, Carnegie and Kettering foundations—are their declarations. We have not been able to locate a single study or evaluation of the foundations' effects on curriculum. We can understand the difficulty of studying this problem, but in view of its importance one might expect at least a case study. The foundations, like the federal government, are relatively new to curriculum development, and also must rely on local or state education authorities to accept the new materials or on interest groups to present political demands for change to such authorities.

Although the two major sources of funds for curriculum planning in this country are relatively new and therefore not fully dependable, there are steadier, if less copious, sources. Professional associations of scientists, engineers, and business and professional men have supported curriculum development efforts related to their professional interests. They will no doubt continue to do so as long as they can be convinced of the need for new curricula in their special field. Local school districts provide a modest amount of money for updating their schools' curriculum. We have no dependable estimates of the amount of money spent by individual school districts on curriculum but the figure must surely be quite small for individual districts. Occasionally regional or statewide curriculum development projects have been funded well enough and long enough to permit thorough substantial efforts. The state of New York through its Board of Regents has been outstanding in this respect. And, of course, private businesses (chiefly textbook publishers in the past, but increasingly amalgams of publishing and electronic firms) spend nobody knows how much for curriculum development. Curriculum development will likely be forced to rely chiefly on these traditional sources of money in the next decade, since the pressing problems of foreign involvement and noneducational domestic issues such as race relations, the environment, and poverty will leave at best a moderate priority for educational concerns unrelated to such issues.

But sources of money are not the only factors influencing the alternatives placed before the local decision-maker. Sources of ideas and expertise are also crucial. The major source of ideas for curriculum change has always been the college or university. The last 20 years have seen an intensified reliance on college and university professors in the form of national curriculum commissions and university-based projects. In most cases the participation of professors has been as subject-matter experts, e.g., scientists, mathematicians, or historians. But a few psychologists have been employed to advise projects on methods. Education faculty have not been heavily involved in projects.

University professors do not, of course, constitute anything like a unitary block of opinion on curriculum questions. In fact, they have been a major source of much-needed diversity in the once seemingly stagnant curriculum of the American school. Nevertheless, university professors tend to regard education as an entirely intellectual affair, whereas long tradition in this country and, indeed, the Western world, emphasizes moral, physical, and aesthetic concerns. Many of the scholars who became involved in the public school curriculum through the federal-government-supported national curriculum projects shared MIT physicist Jerrold Zacharias' view that "our real problem as a nation was creeping anti-intellectualism from which came many of our educational deficiencies" [Koerner, 1968, p. 62]. This value orientation differs significantly from that of the general public which, if it chose, could reassert the claims of less intellectual matters for attention in the curriculum.

If university faculty do not represent any organized body of opinion, their professional associations sometimes do, and when they do they can be extremely influential. The role of the American Association for the Advancement of Science and the American Institute for Biological Sciences in getting evolution into biology books over the strong objections of fundamentalist Christians (Grobman, 1969; Black, 1967) shows that these associations can be influential when they are united and determined. The American Mathematical Society sponsored the School Mathematics Study Group (SMSG) until the Sputnik-induced National Defense Education Act authorized the National Science Foundation to finance SMSG as an independent enterprise. As Turner (1964) described its activities, the American Council of Learned Societies was extremely influential in recent revisions of social studies curricula. This organization urged its constituent societies to see what they could do about revising the curriculum in their disciplines; it commissioned nine scholars in various social sciences to investigate the relations between the social sciences and the social studies (National Council for the Social Studies, 1962); it conducted a survey to determine what the constituent societies were doing about curriculum questions; it sponsored a conference of scholars and educators to formulate a K-12 design in the humanities and social sciences; and, finally, it commissioned a study of the present state of the social studies curriculum. How effective were these actions? We cannot say without further research.

In addition to universities and professional associations, private firms harbor vital curriculum expertise. Publishers use their sales organizations to ferret out the likes and dislikes of the schoolmen who buy their books and they "edit" the books with one eye on this information (Black, 1967). Strangely enough, this network of salesmen is the only reasonably dependable comprehensive mechanism for compiling the preferences and prejudices of local schools on curriculum matters. This part of the curriculum policy-making process badly needs careful study.

Twenty years ago the contributions of private firms to curriculum decisions was restricted to textbooks. But not anymore. IBM has bought SRA, Xerox has bought American Educational Publications, GE and Time have formed General Learning, RCA has bought Random House, and CBS has bought Holt, Rinehart and Winston. These firms can produce curriculum alternatives in the form of text materials, programmed sequences, films, software and hardware for use in computer-assisted instruction, and similar devices which have potentially powerful effects on the school curriculum, and which few other agencies have the resources or expertise to produce. The new notions of performance contracts and vouchers are supported by both federal agencies and private firms, but the corporations will formulate the specific curriculum packages and contract with local districts who have federal money.

Finally, we cannot conclude this discussion of groups that generate curricular alternatives without considering professional educators themselves. Teachers, former teachers, supervisors, and administrators write textbooks and devise curriculum materials. Their ideas, published in professional journals and school district publications, constitute a constantly renewing pool of alternatives from which they and their colleagues can draw in making curriculum decisions. Frequently, however, teachers' contributions are specific practices rather than general principles. But teachers often produce the teachers' guides and courses of study that embody the details of district curriculum policy. Furthermore, teachers served on the staffs of the major curriculum development projects which have powerfully affected the public school curriculum in recent years. The published accounts of these projects (Marsh, 1963; Merrill & Ridgway, 1969; Wooten, 1965; Grobman, 1969) raise some doubts about the importance of teachers in the decision-making that took place in these projects. For the most part it seems that teachers were assigned the role of commenting on the "teach-ability" of the ideas generated by university scholars. It is a measure of the depth of our ignorance that we cannot cite any reasonably hard evidence pertaining to the kind and degree of power teachers have in curriculum policy-making at any level.

Groups Demanding Curriculum Change

Most of the groups generating curricular alternatives are also important sources of demands for curriculum change. Foundations are concerned mainly with inducing certain kinds of changes in schools. They supply money to finance individuals willing to generate alternatives that show promise of encouraging these changes. The U.S. Office of Education has in recent years taken a more active stance in dispensing funds for research, development, demonstration, and dissemination. They stated that "the goal of these efforts is to generate alternatives to current educational practices that schools may adopt in whole or part as they see fit [United States Office of Education, 1969, p. i]." But they seem more and more to see their role as one of producing change, rather than simply making change possible. Some organizations demand curriculum changes but do not concern themselves with creating additional options. Rather, such groups support one of a number of existing competing alternatives. An example of this sort of organization is the Council for Basic Education (CBE). The CBE has lobbied consistently for greater emphasis on the fundamental intellectual disciplines.

CBE's credo is the following:

> That school administrators are encouraged and supported in resisting pressures to divert school time to activities of minor educational significance, to curricula overemphasizing social adjustment at the expense of intellectual discipline, and to programs that call upon the school to assume responsibilities properly belonging to the home, to the religious bodies, and to other agencies (Descriptive Leaflet, "Council for Basic Education," p. 4).

CBE attempts to influence curriculum policy makers through publication, conferences, and other uses of the media. It does not produce curriculum materials but it lobbies for existing materials consistent with its views. The organization does not have local chapters. It is an example of an interest group operating entirely through journalism and popular writing to influence board members, PTA's, and voters to demand curriculum change in their locality.

Most large national organizations, e.g., the Chamber of Commerce, the National Association of Manufacturers, the John Birch Society, and the AFL-CIO, have attempted at one time or another to influence curriculum policy on particular nationwide issues. In fact, such a variety of powerful national interest groups can enter the arena on any given disputed question that it is probably desirable to think of two separate policy-making processes —normal policy-making and crisis policy-making. These not specifically educational interest groups would probably be relatively weak forces in normal policy-making, but extremely powerful in crisis policy-making. The relevant literature on crisis policy-making is much too large to review here. It includes many, if not most, of the references cited already. Crises occur at such short intervals in the history of American education—immigration, the great Red scare, war depression, war again, Sputnik, racial violence, war again—that crisis policy-making is normal and normal policy-making exceptional. What seems to be needed in this area is theory which would distill some useful generalizations from the details presented in the numerous case studies and historical and journalistic accounts.

In summary, when a school district faces the problem of putting together a course they have only three basic choices. The whole problem can be left to individual teachers; groups of teachers can make the plans and devise teaching materials for the whole school; or materials can be purchased. American public schools increasingly favor the last approach. Therefore the sources of these materials are, and will probably remain, important determinants of the curriculum. The sources we have identified are the projects financed by the federal government and private foundations, college and university faculties, professional associations, private business, and organizations of laymen. But the fact of the matter is that any group with sufficient talent and resources can prepare curriculum materials and possibly start a trend that will sweep these other sources either aside or along.

The Local Community and Curriculum Policy

Pellegrin surveyed the whole field of innovation in education and concluded:

> the greatest stimuli to changes in education originate in sources external to the field. What I have shown is that the sources of innovation lie largely outside the local community, and in most instances outside the education profession [Pellegrin, 1966, p. 15].

This statement would appear to apply to curriculum and to refer to the organizations and individuals (discussed in the previous sections) which provide most of the ideas, alternatives, and value orientations adopted by school officials. Today we see a good example of this in the teamwork of corporations and the federal government to implement performance contracts. The role of the local lay community in curriculum change, however, appears minimal. In the local community, it is primarily actors within the school system that decide whether a break is to be made with the traditional curriculum. The mayor and city council have no influence.

The minimal political leverage of the community was demonstrated by a nationwide Gallup poll (Gallup, 1969) which showed that the public knew almost nothing about the substance of education and was not involved with broad curriculum issues. Gallup reported that most of the information that the public received about schools concerned "happenings" —the hard news—reported in the newspapers or other media. Gallup concluded, "knowledge about education is very limited, at least the kind of knowledge that has to do with curriculum and goals of education." When asked to tell on what they would judge a good school, the public replied, first, qualified teachers (vaguely defined by most respondents), second, discipline, and third, physical equipment. Discipline was considered the "biggest" problem of the public schools (26%) while only 4% saw curriculum as the biggest problem. Gallup observed that this lack of information did not stem from a lack of public interest:

When asked specifically what kind of information they [the public] would like to have, the answers deal to a large extent with the courses taught —the curriculum—innovations being introduced and why—college-requirements—and the like. Significantly there is great interest in the very areas that most school publicity presently neglects—the content of courses and the educational process versus school operations [Gallup, 1969, p. 9].

This limited public role undoubtedly stems in large part from the point made at the outset of this paper, i.e., curriculum is considered an issue to be properly settled by professional educators trained in these matters. Of course, the community does get involved in curriculum issues on occasion. Martin (1962) surveyed a large sample of surburban citizens, mayors, presidents of Leagues of Women Voters, and officials of local Chambers of Commerce and concluded:

> These areas (curriculum, textbooks, subversive activities, personalities, athletics, race relations) provide a reservoir for what we have called episodic issues—issues which emerge under usual or special conditions and shortly subside. Thus, it is not textbooks which cause concern, but a particular textbook under a special set of circumstances [Martin, 1962, p. 55].

Martin and other writers conclude that community influence seemed most often to be a negative action such as the defeat of a bond issue, tax increase, school board member, or the termination of controversial curriculum offerings like sex education. On the other hand, Gittell et al. (1967) in a study of six cities concluded:

> innovation can only be achieved as a result of strong community participation with power to compel both new programs and expenditure increases necessary to finance them. The brief experience in Philadelphia under Dilworth suggests that substantial community involvement provides both the pressure for change and a community atmosphere favorable for obtaining the necessary financing [Gittell, 1967, p. 212].

Gittell et al. were referring to innovations of all types and it is not clear to what extent their findings are relevant to curriculum. All the studies demonstrate, however, that the historic separation between education and general government has left minimal influence to the mayor and the city council in curriculum (Salisbury, 1967; Gittell et al., 1967; Martin, 1961; Rosenthal, 1969; Saxe, 1969). Saxe (1969) in his survey of 50 mayors noted a traditional "separation of functions" between schoolmen and city officials epitomized in one mayor's comment that "I do not intend, however, to become involved in school issues such as curricula, busing of students, and matters of that type, since this is clearly the responsibility of another agency [p. 249]"; however, Saxe noted that "a majority of the mayors cooperating in this survey (20 out of 32 . . .) . . . [were] reconsider[ing] their 'hands off' attitude [p. 250]."

At the local level, then, curriculum decisions have been very much an internal issue to be decided by school professionals. Indeed we have some evidence that decisions on curriculum in middle-sized and large systems are often made within the school bureaucracy beneath the superintendent. The formal institutional description of powers and prerogatives would lead one to believe that the school board plays a more decisive role in curriculum policy-making than it seems to play. Indeed, research has shattered the myth of lay control of schools, at least in the area of curriculum.

The School Board

The limited influence of the school board deserves further examination. Curriculum decisions require an analysis of the philosophy and substance of education. Lay school boards usually have no expert or even part-time staff independent of the school bureaucracy. Board members are also part-time officials who meet at night once or twice a week after a full day in a responsible position. These busy laymen are usually not presented with performance criteria or test data upon which to question the curriculum judgments of the superintendent and his staff. Curriculum proposals are rarely related to measurable objectives nor do they undergo systematic analysis, as we saw in the first section. The use of disjointed incrementalism for curriculum decisions does not assist a lay board in playing a crucial decision-making role.

The method of school board elections also limits the board's perspective on curriculum matters. The Gallup poll indicates that curriculum issues are usually not presented to the voters as election mandates. Moreover, as Salisbury (1967) pointed out, traditionally the board has the same viewpoint as the superintendent as far as representation of wards or ethnic groups is concerned: "regardless of ethnic, racial, religious, economic, or political differences in other areas of urban life, education should not legitimize those differences. Education is a process that must not be differentiated according to section or class, and the city is a *unity* for purposes of the school program [Salisbury, 1967, pp. 408-424]." Consequently, school boards and superintendents have historically resisted a differentiated curriculum for Italians, Irish, blacks, chicanos and other ethnic, racial, or religious groups.

The Superintendent

To date, very few studies have differentiated political influence and leverage within the school bureaucracy. There has been a tendency to treat the superintendent and his bureaucracy as one actor and to compare their role to that of school boards, city officials, community interest groups, etc. Those studies of large school systems that examined the bureaucracy found that it wields substantial influence.

Superintendents have guarded curriculum decisions as an area of their professional competence, and have been viewed by many researchers as the key figures in the innovation process (see Carlson, 1965; Mackenzie, 1964). As Martin (1962) concluded:

> he (the superintendent) is as much a policy maker as he is a manager in the narrow sense; for he enjoys an expertise, a professional reputation, and a community position which combine to give him an almost irresistible voice in school affairs [p. 61].

In his study of Allegheny County, Pennsylvania and the state of West Virginia, Carlson (1965) found that superintendents were the "agricultural extension agent" as well as the "experimental station" for the new math. The superintendents who adopted new curricula interacted frequently with a peer group of other superintendents who were also innovators. In short, a group of professional friends spread the new math to each of the members of the group. There were certain key superintendents in these counties who were viewed by other superintendents as good advisors and opinion leaders on curriculum. In West Virginia, however, the State Department's advice was often sought. Looking at Carlson's data from another vantage point, superintendents who did *not* adopt curriculum reform programs (a) had less formal education, (b) received fewer friendship choices among local superintendents, (c) knew well fewer of their peers, (d) participated in fewer professional meetings, (e) held less prestigious superintendencies, (f) perceived less support from their school boards, and (g) relied more on local sources for advice and information [Carlson, 1965, p. 64]. It is worth noting that the innovations Carlson explored were developed by the federal government and foundations. In effect, the superintendent mediates between outside demands for change and the local population.

Since Carlson's study, a new group of federally supported regional educational laboratories have sprung up and very little is yet known about their role. But a recent study in the San Francisco Bay area (Hamrin, 1970) found that ideas for curriculum change were derived generally from the literature and from awareness of changes occurring in other schools.

The School Bureaucracy

While a superintendent can, if he chooses, block most internal demands for changes in official district-wide curriculum policy (other than "episodic issues" like sex education), it is not clear, especially in large cities, whether he is closely involved in many important curriculum decisions. The key bureaucratic officers appear to be Assistant Superintendents for Instruction and Department Chairmen (Hamrin, 1970; Carlson, 1965) who work in committees with groups of teachers. These committees of curriculum administrators and teachers employ a decision procedure of disjointed incrementalism and mutual adjustment. In effect, many curriculum policies are made on a piece-meal basis—academic department by department—and they may not be reviewed or changed for many years through any formal decision by the superintendent or anyone else. We know very little about this bureaucratic bargaining and conflict.

We are more certain that the influence of the principal seems small because, as Pellegrin (1966) noted, "he is burdened with such a multitude of managerial activities that it is extremely difficult for him to devote the time and effort required for innovation on a substantial scale (p. 9)." In effect, the principal is too bogged down in day-to-day management to be more than a middle man between the teacher and the central office for the implementation of curriculum. This is despite the stress the formal job description of the principal puts on curriculum leadership.

Teachers

It may seem somewhat odd to leave detailed consideration of the teacher until so near the end of a paper on curriculum policy making, but we have been concerned with curriculum policy that affects several teachers (e.g., the entire English department). Teachers have autonomy with regard to the mode of presentation of material within their own classroom. The teacher regulates her own schedule and methods of instruction. But studies dealing with curriculum innovation at the classroom level find "teachers seldom suggest distinctly new types of working patterns for themselves [Brickell, 1964, p. 528]." Another study put it this way:

> It is a unique school indeed in which teachers discuss their classroom problems, techniques, and progress with one another and with their principal. In most schools teachers practice their own methods—rarely hearing, or even caring, if one of their colleagues is experimenting with some new teaching device or technique [Chesler et al., 1963, p. 76].

Teachers are increasing their control of salary, promotions, and working conditions through collective bargaining. But surveys reveal that the political energies of teachers at this time are focused on "bread and butter" issues, such as pay, class size, and relief from noninstructional duties. To date, their influence or bargaining rarely extends to curriculum. James (1966) found that demands from teacher organizations in 14 cities related to staff benefits and not to curriculum. It is quite possible, however, that curriculum will become a concern of future teacher negotiations. Curriculum issues are beginning to appear among the contract demands of teacher organizations but as yet these have not been central issues, issues over which a strike might occur. Perhaps as differentiated staffing arrangements bring teachers together over curriculum concerns, curriculum issues will receive more attention from teacher organizations. The accountability movement may result in curriculum performance standards in teacher contracts.

Students

Students have no influence in any formal sense over what they learn. This is so obvious a fact that research to establish it would be superfluous. Of course, decision makers sometimes take students' views into account, but not usually. Even surveys to assess student opinion are rare. But students, to the distress of parents and school officials, vote with their feet on major curriculum questions. Enrollments in high school physics are declining even faster since the new physics began to be taught. It is only speculation, but perhaps the increased interest among students in "free schools" is a reaction to a curriculum over which they have little control and which they see as overly rigid and intellectualized. This is a matter that needs further study.

What we have described as the actors and organizations that influence curriculum policy making are presented in Table 1.

TABLE 1
Influences on Curriculum Policy Making

	NATIONAL	STATE	LOCAL
General legislative	Congress	State legislature	(City Councils have no influence)
Educational legislative	House Committee on Education and Labor	State school board	Local school board
Executive	President	Governor	(Mayor has no influence)
Administrative	HEW-USOE	State Department	School superintendent
Bureaucratic	OE (Bureau of Research), National Science Foundation (Division of Curriculum Improvement)	State Department (Division of Vocational Education)	Department chairmen, Teachers
Professional association	National testing agencies	Accrediting associations, NEA State Subject Matter Affiliates	County Association of Superintendents
Other private interests	Foundations and business corporations	Council for Basic Education	John Birch Society NAACP

DISTINCTION FEATURES OF CURRICULUM POLICY MAKING

It might be useful as a summarizing device to compare curriculum policy making with other types of policy making. For several reasons economic policy provides a fairly close analogy to educational policy. In our economic system everyone's decisions to buy and sell ultimately shape the economy. In our educational system the decisions of thousands of local boards shape educational policy. Economic questions are usually considered too complex to permit direct voting. For this reason some economic decision makers are insulated from the electorate and those who are not insulated usually confine their economic campaign positions to being against inflation and recession, although they will take stands on particular "hot" issues such as the oil-depletion allowance or wage-price controls. Similarly, although to a lesser degree, parents are not expected to understand or to vote on the new math or the new social studies. Nor do candidates for election to local school boards normally take campaign stands on curriculum issues, except on particular "hot" issues such as sensitivity training and sex education.

But the analogy between economic policy and curriculum policy cannot be carried very far. Curriculum policy is primarily and traditionally the concern of the states and localities, even though the federal government's role is rapidly expanding. And when curriculum policy is determined it is still a long way from being implemented. Supposing that a policy decision survives emasculation by the administrative hierarchies of federal agencies and state and local officials, it still faces a pocket-veto by 2,000,000 classroom teachers. So long as teachers consider themselves professional agents with some autonomy in curriculum questions by virtue of their professional expertise, policy implementation will be a matter of persuasion rather than direction. Of course it is possible that teachers will be replaced by mechanical and electronic devices. Or they may be so cowed as to make them dependable implementers of administrative policy. But the increasing unionization of teachers indicates that they will at least have a say in the determination of the policies they are asked to carry out.

Not only classroom teachers stand between policy-makers and their goals, however. Numerous other agencies such as the College Entrance Examination Board, the national accreditation committees, scholarly, scientific, and professional organizations, as well as specifically educational pressure groups, vie for a voice in curriculum policy making. It seems highly unlikely that any one agency, even the federal government, could wrest policy-making autonomy from so many hands. But the example of Sputnik has shown that if national emergency is frightening enough, centuries-old traditions can be swept aside in one session of the Congress; the possibility of national educational planning for the U.S. should not be ruled out.

Even assuming that curriculum policy could be successfully formulated and consistently carried out, several barriers to the attainment of policy objectives remain that are inherent in the educational enterprise. One of these is the necessary long-range nature of educational goals. A significant and stable change in the reading level of junior high school cannot be obtained in less than a year and will probably take three or four years to appear, assuming we know how to get it. Learning anything important takes time and therefore results are delayed. When results appear it is difficult to counter the argument that other forces than the policy change account for the results. For example, Tuddenham (1948) found evidence of a striking increase (a full standard deviation) in the mean absolute score of the Army Alpha intelligence test between World Wars I and II. Schaie and Strother (1969) reported a similar finding in a study comparing the differences in the tested mental ability among cohorts (generations) with the changes in score due to aging. He concluded that "a major proportion of the variance attributed to age difference (i.e. to aging) [on tests of basic mental abilities] must properly be assigned to differences in abilities between successive generations [p. 679]." Both investigators speculated that improved education of later generations was largely responsible for the apparent increase of scores on tests of mental ability. No propensity to assign this effect to the efforts of the public schools has yet appeared in or out of educational circles, but might they not be responsible? But then the result could be due to TV or to the training programs of industry or to the armed forces efforts. The question seems academic in any event. How could one determine the extent to which this increase in scores was due to the continually shifting practices of public schools over a quarter century?

Another difficulty of making, executing, and evaluating curriculum policy is the necessary ambiguity and generality of educational goals. Some educational goals are unnecessarily ambiguous. Such blatant examples as "appreciation" and "understanding" are notorious among students of education. But when these gratuitous sources of ambiguity have been eliminated, considerable additional ambiguity remains. This is necessarily so for at least two reasons. First, because of the necessarily long interval between teaching and the adult use of the thing taught, together with the rapid rate of change in society generally, we must prepare students for a world whose outlines can be seen dimly at best. The age group with the largest responsibility for running the world today is, let us say, about 50 years old. They began school in 1926 and graduated from high school in 1938. Could we reasonably expect the educational planners of that period to have anticipated the specific knowledge, skills, and attitudes that would have begun to prepare these people for their lives today—for urban decay, television, atomic power, cold war, guerilla war, computers, pollution, future shock, and the knowledge explosion? If we make curriculum policy we must either make it concretely and in detail, with virtual certainty that much of the plans will be rendered useless by unexpected change, or make it somewhat general and loose in the expectation that in this way our students will be prepared for a greater variety of possible futures. It is somewhat like the difference between training an athlete for the decathlon and training him for a single event. If you don't know what events will appear in the games you can either train for one event and hope it appears or train for the decathlon and hope your athletes can bone up on their best event when they find out which events are scheduled.

A second barrier to precise, detailed curriculum policy-making is our meager knowledge of the phenomena of schooling. An elaborate argument to substantiate our ignorance is out of place here. Suffice it to say that trying to construct a complete school curriculum according to the currently accepted principles of behavioral science would appear to be roughly equivalent to trying to create a living plant with the principles of the 17th century alchemy.

In spite of the difficulties of systematic curriculum policy-making, efforts in this direction are virtually certain to increase. The steadily increasing role of federal and state governments, the increasing willingness of elected officials to speak out on educational questions, the increasing willingness of mass media to publish achievement test scores of local schools, National Assessment (which will provide detailed information on the educational attainment of American youth), and demands for community control are portents of an increasingly political approach to curriculum questions on the part of the general public. As one observer noted: "It seems to me that, at least in the giant cities, it is academic to debate closer educational-political cooperation. Whether we like it or not, the events of the day will not permit a fragmented approach to education in the city (Saxe, 1969, p. 251)." This development, whether one anticipates it with eagerness or dread, merits careful attention from educational scholars and researchers.

REFERENCES

Aikin, W. The story of the eight-year study. New York: Harper, 1942.

Atkin, J. Some evaluation problems in a course treatment project. Journal of Research in Science Teaching, 1963, Vol. 1, p. 1.

Banfield, E. Political influence. New York: Free Press, 1961.

Bauer, R., & Gergen, K. The study of policy formation. New York: Free Press, 1968.

Bereiter, C., & Englemann, S. Teaching disadvantaged children in the preschool. Englewood Cliffs, N.J.: Prentice-Hall, 1966.

Black, H. The American schoolbook. New York: Morrow, 1967.

Brickell, H. M. State organization for educational change. In Miles (Ed.), Innovation in education. New York: Teachers College Press, 1964.

Campbell, F., & Bunnell, R. A. Nationalizing influences on secondary education. Chicago: Midwest Administration Center, 1963.

Carlson, R. A. Adoption of educational innovations. Eugene: University of Oregon, 1965.

Chamberlin, C. D. Did they succeed in college? New York: Harper, 1942.

Chesler, M., et al. The principal's role in facilitating innovation. Theory Into Practice, 1963, Vol. 1, p. 2.

Conant, J. B. The comprehensive high school: A second report to interested citizens. New York: McGraw-Hill, 1967.

Counts, G. *School and society in Chicago*. New York: Harcourt, Brace, 1928.

Easton, D. (Ed.). *Varieties of political theory*. Englewood Cliffs, N.J.: Prentice-Hall, 1969.

Eisner, E. W. Educational objectives: Help or hindrance? *School Review*, 1967, Vol. 73, p. 3.

Eisner, E. W. Instructional and expressive educational objectives: Their formulation and use in curriculum. In American Educational Research Association, *Instructional objectives*. Chicago: Rand McNally, 1969.

Elazar, D. *American federalism*. New York: Crowell, 1965.

Gagné, R. M. The analysis of instructional objectives for the design of instruction. In R. Glaser (Ed.), *Teaching machines and programmed learning II: Data and directions*. Washington: National Education Association, 1965.

Gallagher, J. J. Teacher variation in concept presentation in BSCS curriculum program. *BSCS Newsletter*, 1967, No. 30.

Gallup, G. *How the nation views the public schools*. Princeton, N.J.: Gallup International, 1969.

Gilbreth, F. B. *Primer of scientific management*. New York: D. Van Nostrand, 1914.

Gittell, M., et al. Investigation of fiscally independent and dependent school districts. Cooperative Research Project No. 3237, 1967. Office of Education, Washington, D.C.

Governor's Committee on Public Education. *Public education in Texas*. Austin: Texas Education Agency, 1969.

Grobman. A. *The changing classroom*. (BSCS Bulletin No. 4) Garden City, N.Y.: Doubleday, 1969.

Gwynn, O. M. *Curriculum principles & social trends*. (3rd ed.) New York: Macmillan Publishing Co., Inc., 1960.

Hamrin, G. An analysis of factors influencing educational change. Unpublished doctoral dissertation, Stanford University, 1970.

Harnack, R. S., et al. *Computer-based resource units in school situations*. Buffalo: State University of New York, 1969.

Henderson, A. D. Innovations in medical education. *Journal of Higher Education*, 1969, Vol. 40, p. 7.

Jackson, P., & Belford, E. Educational objectives and the joys of teaching. *School Review*, 1965, Vol. 73, p. 3.

James, H. T., et al. *Determinants of educational expenditures in large cities in the United States*. Stanford, California: School of Education, 1966.

Joint Economic Committee. The analysis and evaluation of public expenditures: The PPB system. 91st Congress of the United States, 1969.

Kaiser, B. Development of a teacher observation instrument consistent with the chemical education material study. Unpublished doctoral dissertation, Stanford University, 1969.

Kaufman, J. An analysis of the comparative costs and benefits of vocational versus academic education in secondary school. Contract OEG-1-6-00512-0817, 1967, U.S. Office of Education.

Koerner, J. *Who controls American education?* Boston: Beacon Press, 1968.

Krug, E. *The shaping of the American high school.* New York: Harper and Row, 1964.

Lerner, D., & Lasswell, H. D. (Eds.). *The policy sciences: Recent developments in scope and method.* Stanford: Stanford University Press, 1951.

Levin, H. M. A cost effectiveness analysis of teacher selection. *Journal of Human Resources,* 1970, Vol. 5, p. 1.

Lewis, B. N., & Pask, G. The theory and practice of adaptive teaching systems. In R. Glaser (Ed.), *Teaching machines and programmed learning II: Data and directions.* Washington: National Education Association, 1965.

Lindblom, C., & Braybrooke, D. *A strategy of decision.* New York: Free Press, 1963.

Lippman, W. *American inquisitors.* New York: Macmillan Publishing Co., Inc., 1928.

Mackenzie, G. N. Curricular change: Participants, power, and process. In Miles (Ed.), *Innovation in education.* New York: Teachers College Press, 1964.

Marsh, P. The Physical Science Study Committee: A case history of nationwide curriculum development. Unpublished doctoral dissertation, Harvard University, Graduate School of Education, 1963.

Martin, R. *Government and the suburban school.* Syracuse, N.Y.: Syracuse University Press, 1962.

Merrill, R. J., & Ridgway, D. W. *The CHEM study story: A successful curriculum improvement project.* San Francisco: W. H. Freeman, 1969.

Miller, R. B. Analysis and specification of behavior for training. In R. Glaser (Ed.), *Training research and education.* Pittsburgh, Penn.: University of Pittsburgh Press, 1962.

Moffett, J. Misbehaviorist English: A position paper. In Maxwell & Tovatt (Eds.), *On writing behavioral objectives for English.* Champaign, Ill.: National Council of Teachers of English, 1970.

National Council for the Social Studies. *The social studies and the social sciences.* New York: Harcourt, Brace and World, 1962.

Nelson, J., & Roberts, G. *The censors and the schools.* Boston: Little, Brown, 1963.

Pellegrin, R. J. An analysis of sources and processes of innovation in education. Eugene, Ore.: Center for the Advanced Study of Educational Administration, 1966.

Pilder, W. The concept of utility in curriculum discourse: 1918–1967, Ph.D. dissertation, Ohio State University, 1968.

Pine, P. Where education begins. *American Education,* 1968, Vol. 4, p. 14.

Ribich, T. I. *Education and poverty.* Washington: Brookings Institution, 1968.

Rosenthal, A. Pedagogues and power. Syracuse, N.Y.: Syracuse University Press, 1969.

Salisbury, R. H. Schools and politics in the big city. *Harvard Educational Review,* 1967, Vol. 37, p. 3.

Saxe, R. W. Mayors and schools. *Urban Education,* 1969, Vol. 4, p. 3.

Saylor, J. G., & Alexander, W. M. *Curriculum planning for modern schools.* New York: Holt, Rinehart and Winston, 1966.

Schaie, K. W., & Strother, C. R. A cross-sequential study of age changes in cognitive behavior. *Psychological Bulletin,* 1969, Vol. 70, p. 6.

Smith, B. O., Stanley, W. O., & Shores, J. H. *Fundamentals of curriculum development.* New York: World Book, 1950.

Smith, J. The development of a classroom observation instrument relevant to the Earth Science Curriculum Project. Unpublished doctoral dissertation. Stanford University, 1969.

Spencer, H. Education: Intellectual, moral, and physical. New York: D. Appleton, 1870.

Stretch, B. B. The rise of the "free school." *Saturday Review,* June 20, 1970.

Sundquist, J. *Politics and power.* Washington: Brookings Institution, 1969.

Taba, H. *Curriculum development: Theory and practice.* New York: Harcourt, Brace and World, 1962.

Taylor, F. W. *Principles of scientific management.* New York: Harper, 1911.

Travers, R. M. W., & Wallen, N. E. Analysis and investigation of teaching methods. In N. L. Gage, *Handbook of Research on Teaching.* Chicago: Rand McNally, 1963.

Tuddenham, R. D. Soldier intelligence in world wars I and II. *American Psychologist,* 1948, Vol. 3, p. 2.

Turner, G. B. The American Council of Learned Societies and Curriculum Revision. In Heath (Ed.), *New curricula.* New York: Harper and Row, 1964.

Tyler, R. *Basic principles of curriculum and instruction.* Chicago: The University of Chicago Press, 1949.

United States Office of Education, Bureau of Research. Support for research and related activities, April 1969.

Werle, H. D. Lay participation in curriculum improvement programs. *Dissertation Abstracts,* 1964, Vol. 25, p. 5081.

Western Association of Schools and Colleges. *Visiting Committee Handbook,* Upland, California, 1965.

Wooten, W. *SMSG: The making of a curriculum.* New Haven, Conn.: Yale University Press, 1965.

C. Control and Communication Systems in Schools

Students and Schools: Some Observations on Client Trust in Client-Serving Organizations

CHARLES E. BIDWELL

This chapter centers on a question neglected by most sociologists of education: the conditions under which students enter schools and the consequences of these conditions for students and for schools. Students become members of the schools they enter, so that schools are shaped as much by the characteristics, aggregate and structural, of the student body as the students are by their exposure to the school. The incorporation of students as full-fledged members of schools imposes distinctive problems of organizational control, while breaking down the barriers of distance and privacy that are imposed, say, between a commercial enterprise and its customers. How teachers conduct their work and how students respond to instruction cannot be understood apart from their relations to one another as two orders in the membership of schools.

In the following pages, I shall outline a few key variables that define the membership status of students and some of the consequences of these variables for the ways schooling is conducted and organized. I shall assume that students as the direct recipients of education are the prime clientele of schools, although schools have major responsibilities to parents and various publics.[1] Nonetheless, the relation of students and schools in several ways differs from the classic bond between professionals and clients. Three of these ways especially merit our attention as they set the terms on which students become client-members of schools.

The classic professional-client relation is voluntary, dyadic, and centered on the exchange of service and fees.[2] The relation of student and teacher,

---

[1] In colleges and universities, to be sure, the issue of the clientele is complicated by the multi-functional character of these "higher" schools. Nonetheless, instruction appears to be the ultimate justification of their existence. To abandon teaching is to transform the organizational character: from school to research institute or consultant agency.

[2] Fee-payment is less critical to the professional-client relation than voluntarism and the dyadic exchange. Fees at times are paid by friends, family, or public agencies without disrupting the relation. Nonetheless, when client and professional directly exchange fees for service, the bond between them is strengthened. This discussion leaves aside the problem of clients who are minors and therefore usually neither voluntary clients nor fee-payers. I shall return to this problem in the specific discussion of schools. Teaching is the only profession in which adult clients are the exception.

FROM W. R. Rosengren and Mark Lifton (Eds.), *Organizations and Clients* (Columbus, Ohio: Charles E. Merrill Publishing Co., 1970). Reprinted by permission.

in the usual case, is involuntary—the result of the official status of students and teachers in school organizations, and collective—one teacher, but many students. Moreover, while students may reward teachers with esteem or responsiveness (as may the clients of any professional), they seldom pay fees. Since education in modern societies is a welfare good, payment (except for unusual forms of schooling) is a generalized public burden. These differences, I shall argue, affect the conduct and organization of schooling as they constrain the formation of student-teacher trust. To make these effects clear, I shall first review the ideal-typical professional-client relation and then examine the divergence from this pattern, generally in client-serving organizations and more specifically in schools.

Professional and Client: The Ideal Type

In the ideal case, because the client is more or less ignorant of the professional's esoteric knowledge and inept in his specialist skills, the client must trust the professional. He places himself openly and freely in the professional's hands, confident that skilled and effective help will be forthcoming. At the beginning of the relationship, the client is ready to trust the professional on the basis generally of his professional role and more specifically his reputation (his record of past success, insofar as it is known to the lay public). Prospective client trust thus rests on the assumption that the professional will act responsibly (that is, that there is effective social control of the profession, by the state and the professional guild) and on the availability of information about the reputations of individual professional workers.

Once the professional goes to work, he must maintain the client's trust, not only by virtue of the technical quality of his performance (of which the client is not a competent judge), but in part because of his ability to inspire confidence—in the absence of concrete evidence of quality—and in part because of periodic signs that the client is being helped (e.g., he feels better, or no worse, or finally recovers; his case in law is going well or at least better than it might, or finally is won).

As Freidson reminds us, the free professional need not always, in the absence of technical evidence, persuade his client that he is trustworthy. The authority of his position may suffice.[3] That is to say, confidence is inspired as much by the professional's status as by his personality. The general principle follows that the more eminent the profession, the fewer the failures of client trust for any reason (from malpractice to trivial anomalies of the professional's appearance or behavioral style). But in contrast to the professional employee of a client-serving organization (e.g., the social worker or teacher), his authority does *not* inhere formally in an office.

[3] Eliot Freidson, "The Impurity of Professional Authority," Howard S. Becker *et al.* (eds.), *Institutions and the Person* (Chicago, Aldine Publishing Co., 1968), pp. 25–34.

Thus the relation between professional and client is a moral relation and an asymmetrical one—the client submits to the authority of the professional not because he is coerced or paid to do so but in the expectation, however inchoate, of responsible and effective performance. Having once submitted to this authority, he has little control over events. If they go badly, he thinks, he may become recalcitrant; but foot-dragging only impedes the performance of a competent and ethical professional, although it may protect the client from an incompetent or unethical one. Ultimately, if the client does not like what he is getting, he can go elsewhere.

For the professional, trust, as the sole basis of his moral authority, is essential for effective performance. Unless he enjoys his client's confidence, he may be denied access to the client's person, or to the full range of necessary but often covert information about the client while the client may not follow the professional's directives or counsel. Hence the professional cannot fulfill his responsibilities to the client or to his peers for the client's welfare, unless the client trusts him. Thus the responsible professional must reject the client who will not trust him.

But in actual professional service, even that provided by the old-fashioned free professional, trust is a relative matter. Although at times the professional might prefer absolute trust, feeling harassed by a querulous or suspicious clientele, absolute trust is neither functional nor desirable for the client or the society. As I have suggested, it is the tentative quality of trust—its ultimate grounding in the controls of a responsible profession and its more immediate dependence on earned reputation and on performance (however imperfectly demonstrated)—that is at once the client's means of safeguarding his own well-being and in the aggregate a major bulwark of collective professional self-control.

Although the level of client trust seems basically to rest upon the popular prestige of the profession, the professional's public reputation, and his subsequent ability to inspire his client's confidence, two additional factors also induce important variation in the level of client trust. These factors are the client's technical familiarity with the professional service (his access to purportedly esoteric knowledge and ability to assess the skillfulness of performance) and the client's need for professional service (how critical his situation and keen his sense of helplessness).

The less knowledgeable the client, the more absolute must be his trust. The teacher and lawyer, more often than not, are less able than the minister or physician to command an immediate, full grant of moral authority from clients.[4] If, with time, clienteles become more knowledgeable, and more confident of their knowledge, professional authority may tend toward a rational, technique-centered base and away from the moral mystique of the secret. Perhaps, then, the relation of professional and client

---

[4] On knowledge and control in modern societies, see Robert Lane, "The Decline of Politics and Ideology in a Knowledgeable Society," *American Sociological Review*, 31 (1966), 649–66.

will become more an instrumental collaboration between equals—a matter of the convenience of a specialist division of labor among members of a knowledgeable community—and less that of trusting subordination to the esoteric.

As a general rule, it would appear that the more the client thinks he needs professional assistance, the greater his willingness to give up control over his own fate and turn to any reasonable source of assistance, not hesitating over fine distinctions of competence, ability, or personal charm. The client's trust then will be more absolute, and his control over the professional correspondingly weaker. To the extent that the prestige of a profession directly affects the tendency of prospective clients to define their needs for professional service as personal crisis, this effect will be reinforced.

The level of trust is one major problem that clients must solve; another is what shall be taken in trust.[5] In the ideal-typical relation of client and free professional, what is to be taken by the client in trust is a function of the professional mandate. The relationship is segmental and specialized; the professional can demand of the client only those items of information or action that will further their joint aim of setting right some specific disorder in the client's life or of preventing potential disorder or loss. The doctor, repairing a fracture, may require his patient to wear a cast but not divorce his wife; the lawyer, writing a will, may ask about his client's investments and property, but not about his sexual habits.

Nonetheless, the boundaries of the purportedly specific professional task are almost always uncertain. Some aspects of a professional's demands on his clients are fixed by tradition or are obviously intrinsic to the professional technique; for example, the items of a medical history or a client's appearance at the sessions of his trial. Others, however, may become matters of contention between the professional and his client, subject to their differing conceptions of the scope of the professional mandate, or the necessity for certain information to be given, orders to be followed, or advice to be taken for effective professional help. The physician, having decided, say, that a skin rash is of psychosomatic origin, may probe into the patient's relations with his wife, or boss, while the patient, seeking only physical treatment for physical symptoms, may regard his doctor as a meddling busybody and seek another who will prescribe a salve and stay out of personal affairs that are "none of his business."

More often we think of the client as on the defensive in these disagreements, but the professional may also find it necessary to deflect client demands that are, according to his own conception of his mandate, embarrassing, irrelevant, or beyond his competence. These efforts most often center on boundary definitions of the professional specialties, but not always. The physician who treats only physical ailments may send a neurotic patient to a psychiatrist, but, to reverse our earlier example, may tell a patient

---

[5] Cf. Georg Simmel, *The Sociology of Georg Simmel*, K. Wolff (trans.) (Glencoe, Illinois: The Free Press, 1950), pp. 317–29, 361–76.

with a rash, who begins to pour out marital woes, to confine himself to the details of the presenting symptoms.

I have suggested that the problem of the scope of trust—what is and is not to be entrusted to the professional—is mainly a matter of variant professional and client conceptions of the professional mandate. These jurisdictional definitions in turn arise from ideas about both the relevance of items in the technical repertoire of the profession to solution of the client's problem (e.g., that following a low-fat diet will in fact lessen the danger of heart attack) and the scope of the professional's moral authority (e.g., that, though diet has little apparent connection with heart trouble, the doctor "knows best").

In general, it would appear that client willingness to honor a broad professional mandate is a function of the same variables that govern the level of client trust. Reputation of the professional, the prestige of his profession, the severity of the client's need, and the client's sophistication, all affect not only the degree but also the scope of trust. The more the client stands in awe of the professional, the greater his tendency to accede to any demand made upon him for revelations or compliance to professional direction. The more he needs help, the more likely he is not only to comply willingly with the professional's requests or orders, but also to do anything that he is told to do. And the sophisticated client, while more likely than the ignorant or naïve to do whatever is demanded once he has decided the demand is legitimate, is at the same time also more likely to reserve the right to make this decision. Thus a sophisticated client is especially likely to differ with a professional on the issue of what is to be taken in trust—educated laymen indeed may be in advance of the professions in their conceptions of professional help, demanding of the internist attention to emotional problems, of the clergyman social relevance, or of the lawyer a conscience.

CLIENT-SERVING ORGANIZATIONS AND CLIENT-MEMBERSHIP

Professional service, of course, need not be offered in the classical manner of the free professions. In fact, in modern societies free professional service is undergoing bureaucratization, as the individual practitioner yields before the client-serving organization.

Client-serving organizations are of two principal kinds. One admits its clients to organizational membership, the other does not. The former, among which hospitals and schools are the clearest cases, provide sustained professional services—services that require the constant presence of the client within the immediate purview of the organization's staff. These services involve more or less continuous staff intervention, corrected by equally continuous monitoring of the client's progress. The latter, of which law firms, medical clinics, and social service agencies are examples, provide episodic professional services—each episode requires only a brief encounter of the client with one of the professional staff, although these episodes may stretch out in a long series. A few minutes in the office or the client's home, or a few hours in court, are all that an episode requires.

If we take as the defining attribute of organizational membership generalized subordination to the authority structure *of the organization* (in contrast to subordination to one or more of the organization's staff, individually), then the clients of the first variety of client-serving organization are client-members. The decision to accept the organization's services involves payment to the organization, not to the professionals whom it employs (the payment, however, may be made either by or for the client), immersion of the self into a client-member "mass," and a commitment to accept, within the scope of the organization's service jurisdiction, direction from any of the professional staff.

There are, of course, further jurisdictional definitions within the organization that govern staff prerogatives to serve and control categories of client-members—in the school, the classroom; in the hospital, the service. But allocation of client-members among these jurisdictions is ultimately not a matter of client-member judgment, although organizations with responsible and sophisticated client-memberships may permit some freedom of client-member choice (e.g., graduate students who select their dissertation advisers, courses, and specialized fields of study). And once assigned to a jurisdiction, the client-member must defer to any of its professional staff (e.g., the house physicians on the hospital service of one's own doctor, the faculty of one's own university department).

The fact that client-members and professionals share, in these organizations, a common (though stratified) membership radically changes the conditions under which professionals help clients and client trust is nurtured. But this fact does not diminish the importance of trust.

If client-membership is voluntary, it is entered chiefly according to the generalized prestige of the service organization, its more specific reputation for providing some particular kind of service (e.g., the prospective graduate student who chooses a mediocre over a first-rate university because it has nonetheless an outstanding offering in his own field), and some information, more or less flawed, about the organization's facilities and staff.

The reputations of certain of the professional staff may be of great importance in choosing the organization (e.g., one's choice of a physician may fix one's choice of hospital, and, as I have suggested, the eminent department or even one outstanding professor may determine graduate school selection). The more eminent the organization, the more likely it is that any of the staff will be taken on faith by the client-members and the more apparently trustworthy (and often the better known) will be individuals on its professional staff. Nonetheless, having entered the organization, the client-member encounters an array of professional staff about whom he knows nothing but to whom he is subordinated because they, along with (at times, instead of) their better-known colleagues, are responsible for the client-member's welfare.

Moreover, many client-membership organizations are better known than any of their staff or are chosen by clients *faute de mieux*. The question of level of trust, therefore, is complicated by the necessity of repeated client-member decisions about whom to trust at all, let alone how much.

Confronted by unknown professional staff whom the client-member must trust for the simple reason that they have official jurisdictions over him, the first question that he must answer is whether to submit or resist. Here we have the familiar example of the hospital patient surprised to find himself prodded and poked by a stranger identified as a doctor only by his white coat and authoritative manner. In contrast to the ideal-typical professional-client relation, in which prospective client trust is earned indirectly through the professional's reputation, the client-membership organization is not an automatic guarantee that any of the staff is worthy of trust.

Thus the fact of client-membership makes client trust markedly more problematic and indeterminate than it is in the ideal-typical professional-client dyad. There the question of how much to trust is resolved minimally when the client selects the professional. The upper bound of trust may remain to be determined, but the relation itself is severed whenever the client refuses to trust at all. Instead, in client-member organizations, specific client-member staff relations are subject to organizational determination. They are a matter of official jurisdictions; hospital services, university departments and subject specialists, and the like. Although both client-members and staff may be given some latitude for choice (as in elective systems or the right of professors to select students whose theses they will direct), this freedom is usually constrained by formal rules or by conventions that safeguard staff reputations and work loads. Failures of trust more often are to be endured, and perhaps remedied by the staff and client-members involved, than escaped.

The question of what to take in trust also is complicated by client-membership, for it brings the clientele into the organization as total personalities and as a client collectivity—whether for a substantial series of client "work days" as in the day school or commuter college or around the clock as in the hospital or residential school. In either case, the broad scope of the client-member role makes it more difficult to maintain a functionally specific client-serving relation than in episodic professional service. In the latter, whether provided by a free professional or client-serving organization, clients are seen seriatim as individuals and in situations narrowly defined by the information-collecting or treatment-giving requirements of the professional technique.

For one thing, the simple exigencies of administering a client-membership require rules and procedures that are only indirectly related to the organization's professional task. Patients and boarding students must be fed and housed, their movement from place to place regulated, and use of scarce staff time and facilities scheduled, so as to be present in sufficient amounts and kinds where clients happen to be in time and space. Since none of these logistical necessities can, without chaos, be left to a free market of client-member choice, the client-members find themselves hemmed in by organizational constraints on what they may regard as their private lives—what they can eat and when, what and how many visitors they may receive and at what hours, whether they can enter and leave the premises and at what times, the location and conditions of residence, and so on.

Moreover, the fact that a client-membership is a collectivity means that organizational requirements for order extend into relations among the client-membership. Some of these regulations prevent client-members from getting in each other's way (e.g., hours at which radios are to be played), while others may be more central to the professional task. In schools and therapeutic communities, for example, service is given to groups of clients. If the client-member group is simply an aggregation of client-members brought together for economical staff use, as in college lecture courses, these rules will define the conditions of order necessary for staff interventions or client-member use of organizational facilities. In schools such regulations would be those governing classroom behavior or library circulation.

If social bonds among client-members are themselves to be tools of professional service, these rules may constrain the formation of such bonds. Examples of such limitations are the assignment of client-members to a "work group," team, or residential unit; or the differential assignment of responsibilities for client-member leadership according to some criterion of "progress" or seniority (of which the perfect system in the English Public Schools is a well-known instance). Finally, client-members tend to form client societies that may center on resistance to organizational demands, whether peripheral or central to the service function. Because these societies may organize collective distrust of the organization or its staff, arrangements are necessary to coopt client-member leaders and siphon off client-member unrest. The elaborate arrangements typical of high schools and colleges for "student government," "due process" hearings on disciplinary cases, and student representation to the school's administration (all of which antedate, in however ineffective a form, current student activism) are mechanisms of this kind.

Some or all of these regulations may be rejected by client-members as unwarranted (i.e., professionally irrelevant) intrusions. When this is true, the less willing or certain was entry into client membership, the less eminent is the organization or trustworthy its staff, and the less critical is the client-member's need for the organization's services. When client-members decide that the organization's motives in these matters are not to be trusted (viewed, perhaps, as prurient, "bureaucratic," or imperialist), the organization may find it hard to maintain order or coordinate central activities, as the client-members oppose "intrusive" organizational claims. This opposition will be especially disruptive if it emerges as collective client-member resistance—in which case the organization's mechanisms for the controlled release of client-member hostility are likely to be chief among the objects of scorn.

The staff of client-membership organizations, aware that such resistance is always possible, may seize upon the rhetoric of responsibility to justify to the client-members the apparatus of client-member control. This rhetoric may appeal to external legal requirements (e.g., fire laws), to external constituencies (e.g., *in loco parentis* arrangements or observance of community moral standards), or directly to the client-member's own welfare (e.g., balanced meals or, in the case of college parietals, the defense of female chastity). Generally, however, this rhetoric is more effective if professional responsibility can be invoked, so that the regulation exemplifies legitimate professional concern for client-member welfare.

Apart from rhetorical considerations, the broad scope of the client-member role is an inducement to the staff to use the resources thereby provided to surround the client-member with salutory environments, whether of their fellows, of physical amenities, or of encompassing forms of staff-given treatment (e.g., the dormitory that becomes the Oxbridge-style "college," provisions for bed rest, or intensive nursing care). And, of course, many client-member organizations are founded with the idea of the total professional relevance of the client-member role originally in view.

This thrust toward a professionally inclusive setting may help to justify organizational intrusiveness and broaden client-member trust in organizational policies restricting client-members' self-determination, and therefore in all sorts of staff interventions. If these policies have been associated traditionally with the organization's service, wide-ranging client-member trust will be easier to attain than otherwise, while the same factors that promote high levels of trust also tend to broaden its scope: client-member need, organizational eminence, and a convincing or charismatic staff.

But the absence of one or more of these factors, or a change in the social status of the population elements from which the client-membership is drawn that strengthens their claims to autonomy, will tend to narrow client-member trust, at the same time making any form of trust more tenuous. As a result, unless the client-membership can find immediate justification in the organization's professional technology for restriction of the right to do as they please, trust will come to be focused on specific service activities of a direct instrumental value to the client-members and, in the more extreme case, trust will be weak or absent even there. In the latter instance one may find not only client-member disorder and confrontations with the staff, centered on the regulations immediately at issue, but more pervasive client-member disaffection. This disaffection may occur at several levels of intensity from general distrust of the motives or competence of the staff demonstrated through resistance to staff direction of all kinds, to efforts to elevate the organizational position of the client-membership by gaining the right to affect or set "peripheral" regulations, or even influence central professional policies.

Thus the current wave of American college and university student protest has accompanied both increased latitude for sub-cultural and behavioral independence on the part of adolescents, and, for more and more males, labor market entry deferred for advanced training. At the same time, to the extent that it has focused on conditions in the colleges and universities, this protest has tended to generalize from student claims for viable self-government—of residence, student discipline, and political involvement—into demands for student participation in making curricular policy and faculty appointments. This tendency suggests that the rights claimed by colleges and universities for more or less "total" control of the conditions of student life—never very secure in the United States—have come increasingly into question with changes in the age composition of their student bodies and the social definition of adolescence. As a result student trust in these schools and the faculties and administrators has declined generally.

Hospitals provide an only apparently far-fetched contrast. The traditional right of the hospital to regulate closely the lives of the sick, the more apparent linkages between diet, rest, nursing, and medical treatment, the critical needs of the sick, and the authoritative position of the physician as a guardian of esoteric therapeutic techniques all safeguard the hospital from patient uprisings. "Patient activism" is not likely soon to be a pressing social problem, although physicians may find patient trust eroding on other grounds: rising levels of lay sophistication about medicine and, perhaps, a consequent tendency for laymen to take a more instrumental stance toward medical help. The recurrent restiveness of mental hospital patients, where the technical base of treatment procedures and arrangements for patient life are less apparent and less secure, the status of hospital personnel less exalted, and the patient's frequent uncertainties or recalcitrance about commitment and subsequent treatment, also should be noted.[6]

SCHOOLS AND STUDENTS

Schools share with other client-membership organizations these problems of winning and keeping client-member trust. But trust is especially tenuous in schools—the result of a typically involuntary clientele, of the batch processing of students, and of the affectivity-based techniques and limited reputations of teachers. The remainder of this chapter considers how these quantities of schools bear upon student trust and the relations between schools and teachers and their students. Since schools, especially by level, vary in the degree of student voluntarism, "batching," and faculty eminence, differing effects of these factors for student trust at the several levels of the educational system also will be examined. I shall discuss first trust in teachers as individuals, centering on the question of the level of trust. Then I shall turn to aspects of student trust in schools as organizations, a topic which involves questions of both level and scope of trust.

a) Faculty reputation and technique. Although a few college and university teachers have national and international reputations as teachers, and

[6] See for example William Caudill, *The Psychiatric Hospital As a Small Society* (Cambridge, Mass.: Harvard University Press, 1958).

others local reputations soon discovered by freshmen, most are simply un-known as to their teaching styles or competence until the student enters their classrooms. This is even more likely in lower schools, though certain teachers again may have very potent local reputations. More often teachers' reputa-tions, favorable or unfavorable, have little to do with teaching skill, especially in the universities and better colleges, where the fusion of instruc-tive, scholarly, and service functions in a single faculty means that a professor may be a well-publicized adviser to governments or a Nobel prize-winner, but still an unknown in the classroom.

But even when a teacher's reputation as a teacher is negative, students more often than not can do little to avoid him. In lower schools, students are assigned to teachers. In colleges or universities, assignment of students to teachers is less common; even so he may be the only man offering a course that is needed or required. All the student can do is prepare for the worst, his motivation declining the more precipitously the less the intrinsic or instrumental value he places on the subject matter. And once the course is under way, the student typically is stuck with the man who proves a poor teacher—only in the college or university is there escape by the dropped course (if one's program permits this) or infrequent attendance. Otherwise students escape by inattention or more active resistance—devices that pre-sumably lower teaching effectiveness.

In short, schools at times on grounds of rationality—staff utilization, equitable teaching loads, or the need to spread or balance faculty competence, for example—at other times on grounds of tradition—tend to be indifferent to student preferences among teachers thus making students exceedingly cautious about whom and how much to trust. As a result teachers find them-selves living down reputations or, at the least, preoccupied with the problem how to earn the trust of each new crop of students. They are as constrained by school policy as are their students. Typically, neither can reject the other, and failures of trust must be lived with, whatever their impact on what and how much is learned. So, while the responsible free-earning doctor rejects the patient who will not trust him, the responsible teacher redoubles his efforts to "reach" the recalcitrant. (Or, he may choose professional irresponsi-bility, only keeping order in a custodial classroom.) To put the point some-what differently, school policy constraints on teachers' and students' freedom to choose or reject one another, coupled with widespread anticipatory student ignorance of the qualities of their teachers, remove from all but a few schools the self-selective mechanisms, found in the relations of clients and free professionals, by which prospective trust is maximized and failures of trust dealt with, ultimately, by withdrawal by either client or professional.

At the same time, teachers' use of the authority of office—insistence on student compliance with directives without regard for trust—generates little in the way of learning. Whether the teacher seeks to modify students' beliefs, understanding, or motor skills, what is learned is expected to persist beyond the classroom—to carry over into situations in which teacher sanctions are no longer present. Consequently student trust in teachers is of the greatest importance in teaching as it generates those affective bonds between teachers and students—whether between the "mothering" teacher and her brood in the elementary school classroom or between the respected scholar and his disciples in the university laboratory or professor's study—that generate in students motivation to learn (whatever the content to be learned) independently of teacher demands for compliance. That teachers redouble their efforts with reluctant or indifferent students is, therefore, a joint function of the necessity to raise student motives and of the assignment of students to teachers.

It should be clearer now why the less responsible teacher tends to become a custodian—or in higher institutions, a time-server. The teacher's responsibility is three-fold. He is accountable to his employing school, to his colleagues (given the relatively undeveloped quality of teaching as an organized profession at any of the levels of the educational system, this is for the most part the immediate colleague group of the school), and to a set of publics, some of which may have fairly clear expectations about the outcomes of schooling (especially parents and future employers of the student "product"), others of which have only relatively unformed notions of what the schools should do (e.g., general public stress on the "importance of good schools").

But the specific mechanisms through which the teacher is held accountable tend to insulate the teacher, and to only a lesser extent the school or school system, from external control, unless local constituencies in the still exceptional case are mobilized for political action on school issues. As a result, in the day-to-day operation of schools (I am not considering constraints on the long range formation of school policies or forces affecting change in forms of school organization), students, to whom teachers are not directly accountable but whose trust they must win, are a major controlling force. What, then, accounts for the short-run autonomy of the school and school class? How do teachers' attempts at building student trust differ in various sorts of schools, and to what effect?

In modern societies, education is a welfare good, entailing mandatory, universal school attendance up to some specified school-leaving age. Education, moreover, becomes increasingly a public enterprise—through direct government operation, or some form of government subvention or inspection of privately-run schools. Although in the latter, parental wishes are of direct concern to the school and its staff, because the parents pay the fees, in the former the most direct form of teacher accountability is bureaucratic—as a state official he serves students and, most immediately among the school's publics, a parent clientele who can bring their wishes to bear primarily through organizational channels and whose range of choice among schools is severely limited. Other of the school's publics tend to have little interest in its daily work, with a greater interest in employable graduates, low taxes or the appearance of conventionally acceptable facilities, curricula, and teachers.

Although schools are, in fact, constrained by parental wishes—more so in decentralized systems like those of the United States than in ministry-dominated systems like those of France—both the reality and the rhetoric of uniform school policies and curricula severely limit the impact of parental demands on what teachers do in class. And although more knowledgeable and well-fixed parents may make effective indirect choices for their children among public schools as they decide where to live, nonetheless, in comparison with the services of free professionals, the supply of qualitatively different forms of public schooling is restricted and freedom of client (i.e., parent) choice limited by the costs of residential mobility.

The public school system, of the various school types in the United States, is the most clearly insulated from parental preference. Thus responsibility for effective teaching and for student welfare has become principally a matter of internal, organizational accountability. For the teacher, for the individual school, and for school systems, it is a question of political accountability through formal governmental channels. Given the internal structure of public school systems—the virtual isolation of the teacher in her classroom, the thinness of teacher collegiality, the weakness of colleague controls, and the fitful quality of inter-school coordination in school systems—how this responsibility is exercised becomes largely a matter of individual teacher judgment, as Durkheim noted some years ago.[7] Perhaps its exercise is constrained by the general framework of a required curriculum or course of study (in the American case usually not very detailed and not very closely enforced) and occasional "controls by results" (e.g., standards achievement tests, to which relatively little systematic attention is given by the teacher's superiors).

The teacher's relative isolation, physical and social, in the company of his students, may lead to the excesses of autocracy that Durkheim feared, but may also result in a partial cooptation of the teacher by his pupils.[8] This outcome is made even more probable if one considers that teachers, even in the secondary grades, look more to their students than to colleagues, superiors, parents, or the intrinsic content of the curriculum, for the rewards of teaching.[9]

The teachers' stance toward his students obviously varies with school and grade level, that is, with the age-grades and consequent normative orientations and peer affiliations (in school and out) of the school's student body. In the early elementary grades, where peer affiliations and norms are rudimentary, the teacher's position is relatively powerful, and her own preferences with respect to the conduct of the class are especially decisive. Here the isola-

[7] Emile Durkheim, *Moral Education*, E. K. Wilson and H. Schnurer (trans.) (New York: The Free Press, 1961).

[8] Cf. C. Wayne Gordon, *The Social System of the High School* (Glencoe, Illinois: The Free Press, 1957).

[9] Dan C. Lortie, "Authority and Control in Teaching," Amitai Etzioni (ed.), *The Semi-Professions* (forthcoming).

tion of the teacher in the classroom is especially marked, while her pupils, although not yet having learned to be students or to evaluate teacher competence, are moved primarily by what Robert Dreeben calls "goodwill." [10] Goodwill is not contingent on given items of student performance, but comprises "those forms of gratuitous pleasure not tied to specific acts in a relationship of exchange"—an analog to the affective climate of the family.[11]

In these classrooms, the teacher may terrorize or brow-beat her students, and Jules Henry has given us rather frightening descriptions of the irresponsible use by elementary school teachers of their diffuse, affective power.[12] But such cases are probably not common, a tribute less to a responsible professional community of teachers than to the benevolent impulses of the larger number of elementary school teachers and to the durability and force of the conventional wisdom that informs so much of the teacher's work. In classrooms of this kind, controls on the teacher's actions are in fact essentially those of personal commitments.

In the upper elementary and high school grades, students will have developed more or less solidarity peer societies within their schools and classrooms. These provide students with the collective organization for standing off or partially coopting teachers, while past experience of classroom life has equipped them with shared understandings about what good teaching is and what the limits of legitimate teacher authority are. Depending on the social origins of the students, their abilities and emergent interests, and the nature of their earlier experience with school, these understandings will dispose students more or less favorably toward a new teacher and toward high levels of academic effort and competitiveness. That is, by the time students have been in schools awhile, trust becomes a group concern, determined by collective student solutions to the problems of studentship (e.g., how hard to work, what to learn and to ignore, how far to push the teacher's patience).[13] At the same time, the student group, like the teacher, remains constrained by legal and administrative requirements. No matter how frequent or how blatant the teacher's violations of group-defined student trust, students cannot escape the teacher's classroom unless a parent decides to move or the students become so unruly that the principal must intervene. They can, however, fail to perform and can seduce the teacher into accepting student definitions of performance standards in exchange for classroom order and, perhaps, willing effort.

The teacher's situation in a private school is rather different. First, the student body is more or less selected, although selection on parental ability to foot the bill may confront the teacher with a very recalcitrant student

[10] Robert Dreeben, *On What Is Learned in School* (Reading, Mass.: Addison Wesley Press, 1963), pp. 33–37.

[11] *Ibid.*, p. 37.

[12] Jules Henry, "Attitude Organization in Elementary School Classrooms," *American Journal of Orthopsychiatry*, 27 (1957), 117–133.

[13] Cf. Howard S. Becker, *et al.*, *Making the Grade* (New York: John Wiley and Sons, 1968).

group. When ability also is an admissions criterion, the private school teacher is more favored, although as the result of school policy and position in the student market, not of a mutually voluntary student-teacher bond.

More important, parents are a visible surrogate clientele. But their power to influence the teacher's actions differs with the school's reputation. When, for every student admitted, several of equal promise are turned away, the parent-clients may serve for the school and its teachers as a buffer against failures of student trust. By choosing the school, one's parents have chosen what it stands for—in academic program, religious training, or social standing—and the faculty, by doing what it thinks is best for its students, also does what the parents presumably want. The student whose failures of trust lead to unsatisfactory performance can be expelled safely. Control over the work of these schools comes from the colleges to which they send their graduates, from tradition, from the background and training of their faculties, and from a sense of what the market will bear (what will maintain the substance and appearance of eminence), rather than from either student resistance or parental demand.

On the other hand, as the eminence of the school declines, and the competition for students correspondingly grows, the parent clientele may be enormously powerful—through direct intervention and faculty anticipation of what parents will demand. This may reinforce the influence of students over teachers—as when parents wish simply to be rid of their children—or of teachers over students—as when the parents demand a specific form of moral or religious upbringing. But whatever the balance of power, we find that both members of the student-teacher pair are constrained as in public schools; the student being unable to bring legitimate controls to bear on the teacher, the teacher being unable to reject untrusting students.

In higher institutions, the nature of the teacher-student relation is not much changed. Although a college student may enjoy somewhat greater latitude than before for teacher choice in the first year or two of college, by the junior and senior years, the range of choice narrows as the specialist requirements of his "major" involve him in more or less set sequence of courses for each of which there is but one instructor. If the college class presents less evidence of student-teacher strain than high-school classrooms, it is mainly because the student population is self-selected and, in the more eminent colleges, screened upon admission. Indeed, there is some evidence that "open-door" colleges are, in this as in other respects, not very different from high schools.[14]

College teachers may feel less compelled to "reach" or "motivate" all of their students, perhaps selecting proto-disciples from the classroom group, teaching to the "top of the class," or lecturing in take-it-or-leave-it fashion, but undergraduates are not their only clients and teaching them not their only tasks. Even the anonymous instructor, teaching in the most parochial

[14] Burton Clark, *The Open-Door College* (New York: McGraw-Hill, 1960).

college, can turn to his books and away from his students, under the guise of "scholarship." Only in graduate school, and then only when the thesis is being written, does a student attain many of the same rights as those enjoyed by the client *vis-à-vis* the free professional.

b) School goals and client aims. To this point, I have argued that the involuntary assignment of students to teachers combines with the affective quality of teaching and the opaque reputations of teachers, as teachers, to produce in most schools recurrent problems of student trust. Each new teacher that the student encounters is potentially untrustworthy, while during the involuntary association the teacher tries over and over to "reach" even the least trusting. Moreover, after the early grades, the teacher confronts a student society with a shared perspective on the trustworthy teacher that must be satisfied before trust is forthcoming.

I have discussed these factors as they bear on the relations between teaching in these grades, the "good-will" of young children, and the students' decisions about whom to trust among a school's faculty. Of course, these relations also vary in scope, as for example, between a narrowly task centered academic classroom and the more diffuse bonds that may link an athletic coach and the members of his team. These variations are largely a function of differences in the organizational structure of schools, and there are in addition, important differences in the scope of the student role itself that require broader or narrower grants of student trust, as between residential and day schools. In the primary grades, as I have already suggested, the questions of the intensity and scope of student trust are one, given the heavy affective loading of teaching in these grades, the "good-will" of young children, and the classroom-centered quality of pupils' lives. Beyond these grades, however, decisions about whom to trust and what to take in trust are more distinct, and the latter becomes an issue especially of those factors that may lead students to commit themselves to their schools. Most important among these factors are the school's goals (i.e., the kind of education it seeks to provide) and students', or parents', aims for schooling.

Clearly the constraints on the willingness of students to commit themselves to their schools center on the involuntary status of most student bodies. If, at the outset, a school cannot select its students, it must accept them without clear evidence of their willingness to grant the legitimacy of the school's authority, that is, the authority of its administrators and teachers. The procedures used to cope with this problem appear to depend especially upon the school's power relative to parties whom it more or less directly serves— parents, the state, and the students themselves. Where its power is relatively great, it may establish a probationary period, during which students may be induced to commit themselves to the legitimacy of staff authority, after which they are either fully admitted as students or sent away.

The power of private schools *vis-a-vis* parents and students nearly always permits this, unless the flow of new students is insufficient. Moreover, they can screen student applicants, although the less eminent may be forced to take almost everyone who applies. But *vis-a-vis* the state, the public school has less power to expel, and none at all if the schooling is compulsory. In this situation, a school that does not by virtue of its locale draw already committed students may either tend toward a custodial function or mount long-range efforts at inducing student trust, granting full client-membership without clearcut probation and in the face of uneven results.

Above the school-leaving age, public schools vary markedly in their ability to screen or later reject student recruits, a variation that occurs primarily according to their eminence and the availability to students of alternatives for schooling or jobs. Thus, the great state universities freely reject students, both before and after matriculation, while many junior colleges "cool-out" the recalcitrant, as well as the over-ambitious, into other forms of post-high school training or into the labor force.

It is difficult for selective schools, in their admissions procedures, to make a detailed assessment of student commitment, since students often do not know precisely what they want, or are being sent to school at their parents' behest. The screening effort consequently is limited to evidence of general favorability to the school and of some minimal desire for the kinds of education the school provides. If the prospective students are fairly sophisticated, complex statements of purpose may be required, or plans concerning specific programs of study. These items of information provide at least indirect evidence that the student is taken sufficiently with the reputation of the school or, better, of its faculty and sufficiently eager for its particular brand of teaching to respond, if not whole-heartedly at least without complaint, to the guidance or direction of his teachers and to the necessities of the school's curricular or residential arrangements. That is, initial commitment is taken by the school as a reasonable sign of readiness to trust any of the school's staff and to take in trust whatever school policies may require.

Probation involves a search for early evidence of a student's trust at once firm and broad enough to span the student role as the school defines it—for example, compliance to school rules, "citizenship" (which may include the beginnings of an extra-curricular career), and the level of initial academic performance (on the assumption that admission to the school indicates the ability to perform adequately). Similarly, efforts at socializing students to the student role typically stress generalized loyalty to the school (i.e., grants of trust of generous amount and scope), through assemblies, athletics, and other collective rituals. With older and more sophisticated student bodies, these efforts may also stress the distinctive educational mission of the school or eminence of its faculty (undoubtedly, for example, one of the chief purposes of the college freshman "orientation week").

The position of the student's parents in the choice of school also must be considered. Where the student himself has chosen, parental wishes are of no more than secondary importance, as they support or contradict, and thus may strengthen or weaken, the student's own aims. At times, parental wishes may be unknown or no longer relevant, as in the various forms of adult education.

If the parent has chosen, his conception of desired schooling is of paramount importance. It affects the kind of school to which the child will be sent, which may or may not coincide with the child's wishes. Also, according to the child's openness to parental influence, the parents support or confound the school's efforts to socialize the child to the student role and maintain his trust. Here one must consider not only direct parental influence, but also indirect influence resulting from wider kinship circles and the normative quality of the family's neighborhood and other circles of affiliation.

If neither the student nor his parents has acted on preference and the child appears at school simply by virtue of attendance laws, parental attitudes toward education may be as indeterminate as those of the student and may be forecast and subsequently used, ignored, or hopefully altered so that the school will have parental support. The school may try to establish a bond of trust with the parents, while it attempts to socialize the student. Parental sentiments more often are ignored and prime reliance placed on capturing the student's good wishes because negative parental attitudes place parents at some social distance from the school. The traditional apartness of schools —their lack of community involvement and cooperation with other government and voluntary agencies—compounds the problem.

In our earlier discussion, we suggested four characteristics of client-serving organizations as variables that affect the intensity and scope of client-member trust:

1. The prestige of the organization.
2. Its reputation.
3. The level of client-member sophistication.
4. The degree to which the client-members perceive their needs for help as critical.

With respect to schools, as other client-serving organizations, the effects of organizational prestige and reputation are straightforward: the more prestigious the school and the more favorably regarded its educational services, the more ready student trust will be across the full range of school activities. Reputation and prestige are likely to have greater effects on student trust if the student body is knowledgeable concerning the aims and techniques of their education, but the child culture of almost every neighborhood creates a reputation for the local school. I have noted that the same propositions hold for individual teachers, so that the quality of a school and of its faculty, which are usually related positively, have mutually reinforcing effects on both the scope and intensity of student trust.

For individuals, the need for education never becomes as critical as may the need for medical or legal help. Instead, the student, or his parents, will think that he "needs" schooling to the extent that his own aims for education and those of some available school coincide. The effects of school goals and student and parent aims, like those of school prestige and reputation, differ with the level of the student's prior exposure to schools and teachers and thus varies directly with age. Students' cumulative school experience and acquired conventional student wisdom are major determinants of their identification with the school, their compliance to school or classroom rules, and their vulnerability to teacher, peer, and parental influence.

Student age is also related to variation in two of the important organizational conditions of school life: the agent to whom the school is most immediately responsible—the state, parents, the student himself—and the social structure of the school grades—from the relatively undifferentiated classroom society of the primary grades to the highly differentiated complex of relations to teachers and peers in multiple academic and residential settings during college and university. Because these differences define for the student the organizational world of the school, they profoundly condition the formation of trust in school and teacher.

In the first years of schooling, the classroom is, in effect, all that school means to the child. Students venture infrequently beyond the boundaries of the classroom and almost never for instructional purposes. Even on the playground, they are rigidly segregated by age and often by classroom group. Thus school authority is the teacher's authority, and the peer society is very largely a segment or extension of the play relationships of the neighborhood. In contrast to the more socially heterogeneous and structurally complex student societies in high schools and colleges, the classroom group in the primary grades is cohesive and undifferentiated, its members unselfconscious of their collective identity as students (in part because all their age-mates undergo the same experience of school). In these classrooms, teachers can foster a family-like classroom culture especially conducive to the growth of broad and intense student trust. As I have noted, the child's trust in school is formed among students upon his first encounter with school essentially as the establishment of trust in his own teacher. The teacher *is* the school.

The organizational character of higher schools is very different. Here the collective quality of schools becomes more real to students; they are engaged from the outset with the school as a corporate unit. If one must apply, he applies to the school, not to a person, and is accepted or rejected by the school. Upon matriculation, he enters not a classroom but the school itself and within its walls forms multiple affiliations. In the high school, for example, he is involved with several teachers and class groups, with extracurricular activities, with a distinctive friendship circle, and perhaps a specific track or course of study. His work is judged by standards that to some extent override the judgments of individual teachers, while his progress toward graduation is governed by some form of corporate decision.

As he enters the school (assuming some consistency in sophistication among the student entrants to any given school), his initial commitment to the student role and willingness to submit to school authority are determined, as I have suggested, largely by the school's prestige and reputation (its facilities and evidence in the form of his impression of the character of its total faculty and student body) and by his conception of what he wants and what the school has to offer. As he continues his studies, he can compare teachers, courses, and curricula, establish his identity as student by reference to a student sub-culture more or less engaged with the work of the school, and compare his experiences with those of his fellows, both within and outside his own peer circle.

From these considerations, two conclusions can be drawn about student trust at post-primary levels of education. First, in the general case, both the formation and maintenance of trust, in intensity and scope, will respond more to the collective character of schools as organizations and student societies than to relation of students and individual teachers. This is not to gainsay the recurrently problematic question of trust in individual teachers, discussed earlier, or to deny that particularly skillful, attractive teachers may have powerful effects on certain students. But as a student participates in his school, his differential perceptions and evaluation of teachers and peers and of his own experiences compared with those of his fellows are of especial importance to trust. Second, trust is a collective attribute of student bodies, as well as an individual trait of students. As student bodies are more or less trustful of their schools, or as peer circles differ in levels of trust, individual students, according to their peer affiliations, are induced to trust or suspect the school and its teachers. Now we can return to the problem of variation in school goals and in student and parent aims, especially as these variations affect student readiness to make broad grants of trust to their schools.

Variation in School Goals

Particularly relevant to the present argument is the relative stress given by a school to expressive or instrumental socialization. By instrumental socialization I mean the acquisition of motor or intellective skills or items of information that will be used as tools in enacting specified social roles. A curriculum with a strong instrumental emphasis consists primarily of subject areas differentiated both in content and instructional technique.

At higher levels of schooling, the instrumental curriculum usually prepares for social roles (Weber's "specialist" form of education[15]). This curriculum is most clear-cut in graduate and professional education. In high schools and colleges, it is reflected in the differentiation of faculties and courses according to subject matters. In elementary schools, these divisions are less clear, although still present in the form of "subjects" or "units" that divide the school day. But the relevance of these subjects to adult destinations is nonetheless pervasive; for example, preparing for multiple adult settings (e.g., arithmetic for work and family) or for more

[15] Max Weber, *From Max Weber*, Hans Gerth and C. W. Mills (eds.), (New York: Oxford University Press, 1946), p. 243.

generalized adult destinations (e.g., citizenship). By high school or late in elementary school, differing instrumental curricula are linked to social class differences and are ranked as are the classes (e.g., in high school, vocational and collegiate tracks, among colleges the differential prestige ranks of four-year and junior colleges).

By expressive socialization, I refer to the development of beliefs and various forms of sensibility. A curriculum that stresses expressive social-ization may be more or less differentiated with respect to styles of life, affected especially by the level of schooling and degree of social selec-tion in the student body. Thus one finds, for example, an emphasis on "character building" in the early grades, on commitment to political re-sponsibility in high school, and on preparation for responsible leadership or the pursuit of gentlemanly leisure in the "elite" colleges.

It is important to note that the instrumental and expressive forms of socialization are not strictly dichotomous. While instrumental content can be taught without much reference to belief or sensibility, expressive teaching almost always accompanies instrumental content and is con-cerned at least in part with the formation of certain evaluative or ap-preciative orientations to the content of the instrumental curriculum.

The two kinds of socialization involve distinctive incentives for stu-dent performance. Instrumental socialization can rely heavily on sanc-tions that are extrinsic to the content taught—grades, prizes, and the like. Among older students, already somewhat knowledgeable and so-phisticated, trust centers especially on the teacher's competence, as it legitimates his award of extrinsic sanctions. Because such teaching involves mainly didactic instruction or coaching, the relation of teacher and stu-dent is specific to the instructional act and need not involve diffuse accep-tance by the student of the teacher as an attractive or admirable person (although such acceptance may foster an acceptance of teachers' judg-ments, whatever their intellectual or pedagogical skills). The requirements for student trust are correspondingly narrow, centered on the specific in-structional task and the student's willingness (whether because of his own aims or the teacher's competence) to do the work that it requires.

In the lower grades, the incentive system is mainly expressive, reflecting the instrumental-expressive mix in the curriculum. In these schools the growth of trust centers on the establishment of a family-like climate that capitalizes on students' earlier affective experiences. The teacher is in a diffuse relation to her students. Trust requires acceptance of her as a per-son, in response not to her competence but her friendliness and nurturant qualities. In fact, for young children, what to take in trust from the teacher and how much to trust her are not really questions—as a mothering adult the teacher is extremely powerful.

Expressive socialization at whatever level of schooling, because the teacher functions as an agent of persuasion or as a moral exemplar, rests on a generalized acceptance of the teacher's moral authority—whether as a maternal surrogate in elementary schools, or as an eminent scholar or charismatic lecturer in universities.[16]

Expressive socialization requires not only strong affective bonds between teacher and students but an intensity and scope of involvement of students with one another greater than that required for instrumental purposes. Expressive outcomes are generated not so much by the teacher's indoctrination of students as by their participation in the school as a prototype of the moral order for which they are being prepared.[17] Here the teacher is only one among a number of role models, although a preeminent one, and sentiments and perspectives are learned largely as they are experienced in daily life of the school.

The school, to be a powerful model of an adult moral order, requires not only students' identification with teachers, but also a more general acceptance of the legitimacy of its immediate normative structure. As I have noted, after the early grades the presence of numbers of students uncommitted or antagonistic to the school's expressive aims fosters a moral order that will socialize students to sentiments quite different from those sought by the school, both within alien student sub-cultures and through the medium of latent hostility or open warfare between students and teachers.

Clearly then the demands on student trust are more absolute and more pervasive in scope in expressive-oriented classrooms or schools than in those centered on instrumental training. The whole round of life in school is potentially the means of instruction, where the effectiveness of moral teaching is a function of the scope as much as of the strength of student-trust. I have already noted how favorable primary classrooms are for moral teaching because of their child client-membership. At higher school levels, the scope and intensity of student trust that moral teaching requires suggests that its effectiveness will depend on the selection of the student body with respect to initial levels of commitment (e.g., self-selection by students or their parents into denominational schools, or indirect self-selection according to the life style of the school community) and on the degree to which the school staff and, collectively, the student body live up to the moral sentiments they seek to teach.

The two forms of education, instrumental and expressive, are tied to different aspects of the stratification system: expressive to styles of life, instrumental to occupations. Hence, the mobility goals of students or their parents have quite different effects on student trust—as education is conceived by student or parent as fostering mainly occupational or "cultural" modes of mobility or status maintenance. One would expect, as a result,

[16] Durkheim noted that a teacher's effectiveness as an agent of expressive socialization rests mainly on his own evident and exemplary commitment to the moral order. At the higher levels of education, where expressive teaching centers more than in the lower grades on specific belief systems or life styles, the teacher's commitment must be equally firm, though more narrowly focused. Cf. Emile Durkheim, *op. cit.*

[17] Durkheim, *ibid.*

students of lower social origins to have greater trust in instrumentally-centered schools, those from families of higher rank to have greater trust in schools with expressive goals. Stress on sensibility, the humanistic ideal, and student involvement in, say art or music beyond the classroom, may seem irrelevant or alien to the student-vocationalist. These effects, however, will be more marked in the post-primary years of schooling.

These two forms of education also appear to be linked to sex-typing; to the sex roles that parents expect their children to assume and to the students' own emergent sexual identities. These linkages are intertwined with the effects of social class and students' and parents' educational aims. But in general it would appear that boys, after learning early to be indifferent to schooling, become vocationalist and centered on instrumental forms of education. Girls, at first compliant and academically competitive, tend to lose their competitive drive and to withdraw into the more explicitly expressive fields of study. I shall consider these points in greater detail in the next section.

EDUCATIONAL AIMS OF STUDENTS AND PARENTS

Children, I have said, enter elementary school with a diffuse expressive orientation. Young children are prone therefore to trust schools and teachers from the outset, providing adequate ground for expressive socialization and for developing responsiveness to such extrinsic incentives as grades. But parental aims are more varied and are linked to social class. Moreover, they are salient because young children are not supposed to know what is good for them and in any case have no legal right to choose. Although parents can select elementary schools by residential mobility or by paying tuition, these options are closed to families of scant means and restricted information. At the same time there is increasing evidence that working class parents tend to stress instrumental aims for schooling (e.g., the 3 R's, acquisition of specific information) and are likely to be antagonistic to efforts at "character-building or individualized instruction." [18] These parents are least likely to participate in PTA's, while the public schools' traditional aloofness from other community agencies restricts their channels for influencing or persuading such parents.[19] Students in these circumstances may learn at home not to trust their schools or teachers.

Middle-class parents, on the other hand, are less concerned with instrumental and more with expressive factors, such as attention to aesthetic sensibilities and social skills. And as Litwak has noted, the problem these parents pose for schools is to keep their interest in their children's educa-

---

[18] Sam Sieber and David Wilder, "Teaching Styles: Parental Preferences and Professional Role Definitions," *Sociology of Education*, 40 (1967), 302–315.

[19] Eugene Litwak and Henry Meyer, "Administration Styles and Community Linkages to Public Schools," A. J. Reiss, Jr. (ed.), *Schools in a Changing Society* (New York: The Free Press, 1965), pp. 49–98.

tion within manageable proportions.[20] On these grounds alone, one would expect parental tolerance, or enthusiasm, for more encompassing forms of schooling (whether at the extremes boarding vs. day schools, or between varieties of moral socialization or more narrow "academic" or subject-centered instruction) to be a direct function of social class—whatever the additional effects, for example, of family income.

In upper elementary grades and particularly in high schools, I suspect that there is a decline in expressive orientations on the part of both pupils and parents and a rise in instrumental aims centered on preparation for either work or college. This parallels the increased achievement emphasis and subject-specialization at these levels, and in this sense facilitates student trust based on teacher competence, while at the same time narrowing the limits within which trust is given.[21]

But in less selective junior or senior high schools, the narrower scope of the student role does not insure adequate levels of student trust. For students in these schools, whether any trust will be forthcoming is problematic, let alone how broad a grant will be made. One problem of trust in these schools involves the content of students' instrumental aims. Students with relatively unfavorable life chances may reject the more humane subjects and college-centered curricula that still dominate most high schools and find the extra-curricula irrelevant, while at the same time they resent the low prestige and meager resources of vocational or "basic" tracks or schools. These attitudes are likely to be mirrored in parental sentiments. Another problem results from the failure of a certain proportion of students to become responsive to extrinsic school sanctions. The more instrumental curriculum of the high school is likely to produce in these students low levels of interest and effort, while the seeming irrelevance of the curriculum to probable adult destinations makes it difficult for the high school to re-socialize them to the student role.[22] And of course, the now-ascendent peer society will reinforce these tendencies, where there are sufficient numbers of uncommitted or hostile students for contra-cultures to emerge.

High schools faced with such failures of trust, in fact, must reconstitute the moral order of the school in directions that support student discipline and effort and recast its instruction to be more immediately related to students' life chances.[23] But public high schools typically are constrained

[20] Sieber and Wilder, op. cit.

[21] Teacher competence, however, has a somewhat imprecise link to the growth or maintenance of trust. First, above the early grades teachers inherit students already socialized, albeit imperfectly, to the student role and responsive to such extrinsic sanctions as grades, however poor or indifferent the teacher may be. Second, the intellectual or motor performance involved in learning instrumental content may be rewarding in itself, so that the student works independently of the teacher's incentives.

[22] Arthur Stinchcombe, Rebellion in a High School (Chicago: Quadrangle Books, 1965).

[23] Cf. Morris Janowitz, "Institution Building in Urban Education," Working Paper, Center for Social Organization Studies, University of Chicago, 1968.

from doing so, given the persistent heritage of the academy, the subject centered training of the large majority of high school teachers and administrators, and their responsibility to a public that is itself often traditional in outlook and suspicious of apparent efforts to "water down" high school programs.

Among American colleges, one finds at least as great a diversity of student aims as of organizational goals, reflecting the multiple occupational and status destinations to which colleges lead, students' more and differentiated interests, and their greater freedom of choice. Although there is a very imperfect fit between what students want and what their own colleges provide, there is nonetheless a noticeable strain to consistency when student aims and college goals are ordered on the instrumental-expressive continuum. This fit is a complex function of such variables as college selectivity; the constraints of information, money, and sophistication of college choice; and parental preferences and influence.

In any event, among colleges that can exert some control over admissions, relative to high schools, aggregate levels of initial student commitment by students to colleges should be high, especially when instrumental purposes have governed college choice. Such choices are based largely on students' anticipatory commitments to their specialist role destinations and their more or less informed judgments about the quality of facilities and faculty competence in one or another academic subject matter. When colleges are selected on expressive grounds, students evince a more generalized form of trust, centered less on the specific competence of teachers or school quality, more on the college's presumed linkages to status groups or on diffuse "styles," "climates" or "tones" presumed to inhere in the school. Such forms of trust are problematic, for conceptions of expressive education are less clear-cut than ideas about technical preparation, and are likely to be at variance with those of the faculty. These disagreements may have to do with both the tentativeness and scope of trust. The faculty expects "commitment"; the students wait to see whether the school will live up to its promise and whether the expressive content of the curriculum in fact will be personally satisfying. They also may try to reserve a domain of privacy against the moral imperialism of a faculty seeking a "total" educative environment.[24]

When expressive socialization is at issue, then, whether in first grade or college, student trust is more emergent than explicit. At the college level, however, its explicitness varies with the clarity of the adult life style or status destination in view. In societies, for example, where col-

---

[24] Probably more destructive of student trust has been the assumed necessity for college administrators to safeguard the morals of students, a task abandoned by the faculties, in deference to presumptive parental, or community, standards. Not clearly related to the college's academic programs (signified especially by faculty unconcern), these efforts have been challenged increasingly by students no longer deferent to *any* parental demand and unwilling to trust colleges in areas not clearly related to instruction.

lege education prepares for or validates claims to a well-defined gentlemanly status, students are likely to have quite firm commitments to expressive forms of education. The decline of the gentleman, however, may be accompanied by declining student commitment to liberal aims, a greater tendency to be seduced by instrumental-vocational goals, and a struggle, even in select colleges, to preserve a humane tradition and re-socialize students to the gentlemanly ideal.

These matters are complicated by the sex composition of student bodies, but differently at the several school levels. These differences arise as students learn what peers and parents expect of them as boys and girls or men and women. Little clear-cut evidence exists on the effects of sex-typing for schools. There is some reason to believe, however, that in the elementary grades (beyond the earliest years when sex roles are quite diffuse), boys tend generally to reject teacher demands for competitive academic performance and to resist involvement in the more explicitly expressive aspects of the school curriculum—art, music, and the like.[25] Both parents and peers reinforce this boyish masculinity, which weakens and narrows boys' trust in schools and teachers. Girls, on the other hand, as they learn to be docile and compliant, tend to be broadly trusting in school and to excel academically.

By high school, these tendencies are accentuated, partly because the male student society becomes more tightly integrated (around athletics, for example), while girls, involved in the "rating and dating complex" can afford, or may be forced, to be academic competitors.[26] This competitiveness, however, may be less among girls from working class families, whose parents are likely to find home more than school the appropriate arena for learning womanly responsibilities.[27] At the same time, a cleavage may appear among male students between those for whom the instrumental aspects of schooling are a sensible preparation for jobs or college and those for whom school is a senseless barrier to full-fledged adulthood.[28] In general, then, the effect of sex typing among middle-class high school students is to reinforce among boys the tendency toward instrumentally-centered narrow grants of trust, while encouraging trust of greater scope among girls. Among working class students of either sex, it may cause generalized failures of trust in school.

By college and university, the effects of sex typing have changed. Women appear to withdraw from the rigors of academic competition, especially in the more "masculine" instrumental subjects, and in coeducational schools. On the average, they do less well in these settings than men

[25] Eleanor Maccoby, *Development of Sex Differences* (Stanford, California: Stanford University Press, 1966).

[26] Gordon, *op. cit.*, J. S. Coleman, *The Adolescent Society* (New York: The Free Press, 1961).

[27] Cf. Herbert Gans, *The Urban Villagers* (New York: The Free Press, 1962).

[28] Stinchcombe, *op. cit.*

of equal ability.[29] They are found in disproportionate numbers in the more expressive fields—not only education, but, for example, the humanities and more humane social sciences.[30] These fields are defined as less "masculine" and also seem to give freer rein to the "creative," "artistic," and nurturant impulses suitable to the female role.[31] Men now begin to excel in the "tougher," and more instrumental areas of the curriculum, as the competitive rigors of the higher occupations make themselves felt both in the curriculum and in sex-typed performance.[32]

About the effects of these phenomena on college student trust, one can only speculate. But, recalling that college student boｕｉes are more or less self-selected (on grounds of social class, motivation, ability, and the like), the effect of sex identities appears to be less on the level than the scope of trust, as women are drawn into the more diffuse, expressive fields and there find greater stimulus to academic performance than in the more specific, instrumental areas in which men come to excel. If this is so, it should be more difficult to maintain a viable "total" educational environment in a college the greater the proportion of men it enrolls. For this assertion I have no real evidence. It is interesting, though, that men's colleges in America have not had notable success as peaceful or human student communities, while the women's colleges purportedly have been more successful at capturing and manipulating the loyalties of their students. Current student demands from the women's colleges for coeducation may be only a new statement of the expressive orientation, with the resistance of the alumni and faculty of these colleges as the sign of a persistent sense of community.*

[29] Maccoby, op. cit.

[30] Ibid., also James A. Davis, Undergraduate Career Decisions (Chicago: Aldine Press, 1965).

[31] Jesse Bernard, Academic Women (University Park, Pennsylvania: State University Press, 1964).

[32] Maccoby, op. cit.

* I am grateful especially to Eliot Freidson for his helpful comments on an earlier draft of this chapter.

Institutional Paternalism in High School [†]

BUFORD RHEA

Prominent in the literature of contemporary educational criticism is the charge that schools stifle learning, that they are basically self-defeating. This criticism takes several forms, e.g., that the school extinguishes vital adoles-

[†] Reference notes are grouped at the end of this article, pages 287–88. They are coded a, b, c, etc.—Ed.

FROM The Urban Review, Vol. 2, No. 4 (February 1968), pp. 13–15. The Urban Review is a publication of the Center for Urban Education in New York City.

cence,[a] that it perpetuates student inadequacies,[b] that it destroys creativity and the desire to learn,[c] or that it positively brutalizes: [d] but a common theme is that the "system" itself, the bureaucratic system, is largely at fault.

This is no new criticism, nor is it indigenous to education; in most respects it is merely the traditional complaint against bureaucracy in general applied to the school in particular. There, however, it acquires a special urgency. When a Harvey Swados (or an Adam Smith) [e] suggests that factory workers are lessened by their work, we are inclined to feel sorry for the worker, but, after all, a factory is intended to produce automobiles, or pins, not happy workers. Yet when a Paul Goodman (or a Robert Owen) [f] makes the same charge about the school, we are inclined to be indignant: schools *are* supposed to improve their student members, that is their reason for existing in the first place.

Is it really true, though, that the bureaucratic structure of the school subverts education? In spite of the obvious importance of the question, and in spite of a great deal of discussion, the fact of the matter is that we simply do not know, and one of the reasons we do not know is that we do not have enough information about how students react to their schools. In early 1965, therefore, my colleagues and I began to gather information about just how this educational version of the organization-individual encounter is actually experienced by students. The present paper is a first report of some of our findings.

ARE STUDENTS ALIENATED?

Most of the undesirable human consequences of bureaucratization are summarized by the term "alienation," [1] and certainly the condition of the American high school student seems to exhibit most of the organizational features which are said to alienate: they are virtually powerless, their work seldom has relevance to their immediate concerns, they are segregated from the larger community, etc.[2] So our research question was: Does the bureaucratic organization of the school alienate students?

[1] The term is an ancient one, taken from Roman law, and thus has a number of accredited meanings; that is why so many social and psychological events can be designated by it. Karl Marx is usually credited with first presenting the term as a researchable variable, though there is great confusion about just what he meant by it, and its most orthodox employment still seems to be to describe the psychological consequences of routinized work. That at any rate is the sense in which it is used in this paper, though the final report of our project ("Measures of Child Involvement and Alienation from the School Program," U. S. Office of Education, 1966) discusses other meanings. A good overview of contemporary studies in alienation is provided by Eric and Mary Josephson, eds., *Man Alone* (New York: Dell, 1962); for industrial applications see Robert Blauner, *Alienation and Freedom* (Chicago: University of Chicago Press, 1964); and for the Marxist tradition see Milorad M. Drachkovitch, ed., *Marxist Ideology in the Contemporary World* (New York: Praeger, 1966), especially the essays by Sidney Hook and Lewis S. Feuer.

[2] The most influential discussion of alienation for purposes of empirical research in

To explore this topic we gave questionnaires to the entire student bodies of two leading high schools in the Boston area, one ("West High") a public school, the other ("Parochial High") a Roman Catholic school. The questionnaires were supplemented by verbatim transcripts of interviews with 46 students at "East High," another leading public school.[g] Selecting only superior schools made optimum such otherwise influential factors as quality of staff, administration, facilities, and student background, thus allowing us to concentrate on the purely organizational aspects of the schools. Similarly, interview topics and questionnaire items emphasized organizational matters, and many of the questions were taken directly from studies of alienation in other settings.[h]

If bureaucratic structure alone alienates, then students in these schools might be expected to speak poorly of them, and to take no pride in being members of them, despite the adequacy of the components. This, however, was emphatically not the case: large majorities agreed that "Compared to other schools, this school provides a first-rate education" (55 out of 2,329 disagreed), and all but one hundred agreed that "I'm proud to be a student here" (another 144 were neutral).

An "aggrandizement effect"[3] is doubtless operative here, but it apparently only magnifies the genuine satisfaction felt by these students. When, for example, we asked about specifics, our respondents also expressed satisfaction with the teachers, the curriculum, the marking system, and indeed *every* organizational feature of the school that was mentioned. In sum, and to make a long story short, the great majority of our students simply did not exhibit the usual symptoms of alienation, so these highly bureaucratized schools cannot be said to alienate their student bodies.

On the other hand, we quickly discovered that the students, though involved, were involved in relatively uninspiring things:

---

sociology is Melvin Seeman, "On the Meaning of Alienation," *American Sociological Review* 24 (December, 1959), pp. 849–52. Seeman concludes from a survey of the literature that alienation is used in five ways: to describe feelings of powerlessness, meaninglessness, anomie, isolation, and self-estrangement. With the exception of the latter, all of these terms refer to some environmental characteristic, to situations in which the individual has no power, where purpose is not apparent, where means are ambiguous, or where the individual is isolated from the larger community—these presumably lead to alienation. The classic description of student powerlessness is still Willard Waller, *The Sociology of Teaching* (New York: John Wiley, 1965), first published in 1932. For meaninglessness and anomie in school, see David Mallery, *High School Students Speak Out* (New York: Harper, 1962). The segregation of the school from the rest of society is a common theme whose surrealism is nicely captured by *Up the Down Staircase.* For a more methodical listing of relevant organizational characteristics, see Arthur N. Turner and Paul R. Lawrence, *Industrial Jobs and the Worker* (Boston: Division of Research, Harvard University Graduate School of Business Administration, 1965), and for additional discussion of the school as a bureaucracy, see Ronald G. Corwin, *A Sociology of Education* (New York: Appleton-Century-Crofts, 1965).

   [3] ". . . an upward distortion of an organization's prestige by its own members," Theodore Caplow, *Principles of Organization* (New York: Harcourt, Brace and World, 1964), p. 213.

Have your courses been helpful? Just to get into college. I need them to get into college. I do like History, though, and English.

My main purpose is to get the diploma. College is a help, but if you don't get that diploma, well, that's pretty bad. It's getting pretty tough to get a good job, you know. The main purpose for me and to other students who are not going on to further education is to get that diploma.

I think in high school the goal you are trying to reach is college, and in college the goal you are trying to reach is knowledge and social maturity as well as intellectual maturity.

There are some things of intrinsic worth in high school, but the experience is generally viewed as an instrumental one, as a means to college admission or to a better job. Among the most unequivocal responses to our questionnaire was a 91 percent agreement with the statement: "What we do in high school is essentially preparation for what will come later; the payoff will be in college or on the job."

And our respondents were utterly realistic about what was required: A good record.

Well, in East High you work for good grades so you can go to college. It's just—you know—everybody is obsessed with the fact, and I know even I [am].

Your parents don't know what you know, and people don't know what you know, and the colleges don't know what you know, so if you're going to try for anything you're going for the grade. I mean the payoff. I mean, you may have the knowledge, but it's not going to do you any good. If you want to go someplace and you want to go to college or anyplace, you have to have the grades, anyway at least to graduate from high school.

In high school kids go out for clubs and athletics and things of that nature to build up their all-aroundness so that they can get into college. *Extra-curricular activities help you get into college?* Yes, they are very important. Colleges like students of varied interests. *What if you just like to sit and think?* Well, I suppose you could put this down on your application.

I think if you're popular in this school you've got half the battle licked, because so many kids go home and, I think, they worry just because they're not known, and that cats away at them so much that their grades go down. . . .

Everything, it would seem, from class work to extra-curricular activities to social life, comes to be related to the maximization of the record, to the building of a favorable "paper shadow" in the files of the front office.[4]

[4] On paper shadows, see Erving Goffman, *Asylums* (Garden City, New York: Doubleday Anchor Books, 1961), p. 75. The paper image is so important because it is an "actionable entity" (*loc. cit.*), and the actions taken on the basis of it, as our students fully recognized, have a major effect on one's life.

With "looking good" thus defined as the matter of highest priority, it is not surprising that some 40 percent of our students would rather cheat than flunk, and that most would hypocritically give the teacher a wrong answer if the teacher thought it to be a right one.[5] Over-emphasis on this sort of success breeds concentration on what Argyris calls the "skin-surface" performance aspects of work,[1] and this too is reflected in various student responses: most felt that "personality, pull, and bluff" get students through many courses, that performance is more important than character, and that ability to express oneself is more important than knowledge.

Our students are involved, then, but they are clearly involved in the *task* of getting through school, or maximizing the record, not in the *experiences* which educators postulate as the essence of curriculum.[6] The resulting student attitudes may be disturbing to the educator, but they should come as no surprise to the sociologist: given the prime fact of task-orientation, the students' attitudes could be predicted from the literature of industrial sociology.

But there is still a problem here. Organizational theory indicates that trivial work alienates, and that a condition of powerlessness alienates. Our students recognize that "making out" in high school is not true education, but they are also proud of making out; they take a sort of pride of workmanship in accumulating good marks and looking good. Our students also recognize their virtual powerlessness, but this too does not lead to feelings of alienation.

[5] Parochial High differs somewhat from West High on this, for although Parochial High students begin as freshmen by generally denying that they would cheat or give a hypocritical Right Answer, by the time they are seniors a majority would do both. Proportions saying that they would rather cheat than flunk, for instance, are: Freshmen (33.7 per cent), Sophomores (34.7), Juniors (48.0), Seniors (59.2). West High responses do not change appreciably over time, though interview respondents noted that they had become "savvy" in junior high, i.e., earlier than the relatively unsophisticated Catholic students. Incidentally, these figures should not be interpreted as reflecting moral decay caused by attending Parochial High; rather they seem to measure the greater pressure to succeed found there.

[6] The distinction between performing and experiencing has been central to educational theory since Rousseau's *Emile*. A child, or a horse, can be trained to *do* almost anything; all that is needed is a big stick and proper supervision. But education in the best sense is a process whereby the child comes to *be* something better than he was, and this requires that he experience educational events in a personal way. Cf. John Dewey, *Experience and Education* (New York: Collier Books, 1963). Of course one experiences the doing of a task, but the experience need not be an educational one: factory workers, for example, frequently experience nothing but boredom. Similarly, when students are forced to act as if they are educated, the act of looking good need not itself be educational. See John Holt, *How Children Fail* (New York: Pitman, 1964). There is in fact some reason to believe that performing a task and becoming educated involve *opposite* processes: cf. Talcott Parsons, Robert F. Bales, and Edward A. Shils, *Working Papers in the Theory of Action* (Glencoe, Ill.: The Free Press, 1953), esp. Chap. 5, and later works of Parsons and his associates contrasting task-performance sequences and socialization or re-socialization. One of the most seminal articles in the recent educational literature makes a similar point: Chandler Washburne, "Conflicts Between Educational Theory and Structure," *Educational Theory* VIII (April, 1958), pp. 87–94.

If students can most profitably be viewed as task-oriented workers, and this seems to be the case, how is involvement in trivial work possible? And how does near-total powerlessness fail to result in alienation? These are the questions to be discussed in the remainder of this paper. It will be our general contention that a special set of definitions, which we call "the myth of institutional paternalism," intervenes between the perceived situation and the student's reaction to it, converting the situation from one conducive to alienation into one characterized by a high level of involvement.

MEANING IN SCHOOL

One of the most popular sociological explanations for poor performance in school—often referred to as the "articulation hypothesis"—argues that the academic curriculum is meaningless to students who do not expect to go to college.[j] This is a plausible hypothesis, but our research indicates that it needs more consideration.

First, as we have seen, there is little or no intrinsic motivation exhibited by students in our elite high schools: Grades, not substantive achievement, are the important thing. Presumably these students would be just as workmanlike in the performance of *any* task, regardless of its content, so long as it resulted in an entry for the dossier. The importance of class work for college-bound students, therefore, stems primarily from the importance of *marks*, not from any supposed relationship between high school and college subject matter.

In point of fact, and this is our second observation, student goals are very poorly defined by students:

> You know, ever since I came up here they've been testing me and one of the tests was in mathematics and another in business stuff. I guess business is just what I'm headed for.

> I didn't know what I wanted to do until maybe a couple of weeks ago, and I don't think any of the other kids do either (laughs); and, I don't know if that's what I'll be, so these are just general courses that you've got to take to fill the quota.

Most of our respondents intended to go to college, but just what going to college means is another question. Of course students recognize that going to college is the best way to become successful, but it is also interesting to note that college is an alternative to making the sort of *commitment* that would give meaning to present activities:

> I'd rather go to college than work. Like going to college for four years I can also gain learning that will help me and also postpone my having to go to work.

> I'm not sure what I'm going to do and I don't want to limit myself. I don't want to sit back and say I'm going into business. I'm afraid I

wouldn't be happy at this point if I decided to go into a four year business school like (School). I'd come out and, O.K., I could go into business; but if I said I wanted to do anything else, I wouldn't be able to. I want to go to a liberal arts school.

This hesitancy about making a commitment ran through all of our interviews, and it appears in our questionnaire returns as a willingness to let others, i.e., the school staff, make the major decisions for the student.[7]

Of course students *are* young, and this means that they cannot be sure of their "real" desires. Our interview respondents frequently pointed this out to us, and it would in fact be unrealistic to expect them to have clear-cut notions about adult roles; they have never been adults.

In such a situation, students behave quite rationally, i.e., they pursue a policy of noncommitment, delaying it for as long as possible. Commitment means abandoning alternatives, and premature commitment can mean abandoning opportunities which might later prove more desirable.[k] But noncommitment also means not having criteria to assess the meaning of current experiences.

High school work is thus viewed as a generalized preparation, a "making ready" (*praeparae*) for future commitments. And so, paradoxically, the very absence of specific purpose allows the student to impute a sort of generalized worth, or "preparation value," to all of his school activities. Conversely, to know one's specific goal in life might reveal many of these activities to be irrelevant.

To elaborate on the articulation hypothesis, then, we might first suggest that it is the critical relevance of marks, not the academic nature of the typical high school curriculum, that makes college-bound students work harder than others. Second we would suggest that plans for further education do not necessarily reveal the long-range significance of high school studies; rather such plans allow the student to avoid or postpone the entire issue of relevance, and thus allow him to impute a vague preparation-value to his current activities. Students not destined for college and the white-collar world may accurately perceive the lack of articulation between school work and adult role, but this need not mean that college-bound students perceive a congruence; they do see the relevance of good marks, though, and that is sufficient to account for their dedication to the task of accumulating them.

POWERLESSNESS AND PATERNALISM

The most common cause of (or synonym for) alienation mentioned in the research literature is powerlessness, and high school students are among the

[7] For example, 61 per cent of our students disagree with the statement: "Students have too little responsibility for their own education here," with another 10 per cent having no opinion, while 66 per cent agree that: "Students should be sufficiently supervised so that their mistakes have no serious consequences." Students in fact have very little authority, but that is apparently not "too little."

most powerless members of our society. By and large, though, our respondents said that they had *enough* power, and our interviews indicate why:

> I think the student has freedom to take more or less what he wants. [This is wrong] because a kid can take very easy courses the rest of the year and maybe, maybe he's got the potential to do something with himself instead of being lazy. I don't know how they could fix it or pre-arrange it, but I think the student is given too much freedom to choose what he wants.

> *Do you think students have enough say about who runs this place and the policy of the school?* Yes, I think if it wasn't run by the administrative part of the school system then things would get out of hand. I think there has to be somebody to lay down the law and say it's going to be this way. . . . I don't think students at this age know everything, and I think they need somebody to guide them and tell them what's right. They might think something is right now, but twenty years from now it might not be, in their opinion.

These students do not *want* power, in part because, as implied, they would not know what to do with it even if they had it. Their educations are too important to be left in inexperienced hands, and they are quite realistic about their own inexperience.

Satisfaction with powerlessness, though, must reflect satisfaction with the way power is wielded by those who possess it, and indeed our students thought highly of their superiors, especially their teachers.[8] They liked their teachers because they thought them competent, but what they think teachers are competent *at* is not entirely clear. It seems that teachers make school work more pleasant, by being entertaining, informed, clear, in control of the classroom, enthusiastic about the subject, and fair. In addition, teachers are apparently expected to make the student want to do the work; teachers motivate. In any event, the teacher is seen as the major determiner of the educational process, he rather literally "makes" education happen.

The student, on the other hand, sees himself as relatively passive: he learns, to be sure, but it is the teacher who causes the learning to occur. Accordingly, teachers are often evaluated by the critical standards of an audience, as actors are, with performance being judged by the relatively nonvolitional responses of the student-critics. A better analogy would be the doctor-patient relationship: The patient is expected to follow orders, and to that extent he participates in his own cure, but the prime responsibility for a successful outcome rests with the physician. It is the student's job to do what the teacher tells him to do; it is the teacher's job to know what to tell the student to do, and it is therefore the teacher's responsibility to know *why* the student should do it.

As in the doctor-patient relationship, so in the teacher-pupil one, confidence in the professional is a necessary ingredient. This is not only confi-

---

[8] Students were asked to "grade" (A, B, C, D, F) various aspects of the school. Teachers wound up second—and a close second—to peers as a source of satisfaction.

dence in technical ability, it also includes the belief that the professional is working for the client's benefit. From the student's point of view, then, the teacher is both competent and benevolent, and the relationship is a professional one, or, as we have phrased it (in order to avoid unnecessary implications), a *paternalistic* one.

But competence and benevolence are not personal qualities of teachers, they are attributes of the teaching role. Thus students do not express gratitude for adequate teaching services, though they may be warm in their critical applause for an exceptional performance, and they tend to be morally indignant about uninspiring teaching: teachers are *supposed* to be capable and concerned, that is the nature of their job. We have therefore referred to this set of attitudes as faith in "institutional" paternalism.

It should be emphasized that these are student beliefs, not necessarily school policy or actuality; but if students define the situation to be paternalistic, then for them it is. So institutional paternalism may be thought of as a "useful myth," a myth because its reality-content has little to do with its efficacy, and useful because it intervenes between the potentially alienating conditions of student powerlessness and curricular meaninglessness to produce a *faith* that one is in good hands and that there is meaning in what one does. Indeed, belief in institutional paternalism may appear precisely because there is a *need* for a faith of this sort, a need for some sort of redefinition of what might otherwise be an intolerable situation.

Our evidence is only impressionistic on this point, but many interview respondents described how they "willed" a good opinion of their teachers. To think poorly of a teacher means to do poorly in the course, so in order to make a good mark (and to enjoy, or at least make tolerable, the work) these students go into new classes with a determination to like them, i.e., to think the teacher able and the subject somehow worthy of serious effort. Need therefore seems to precede experience, and it is not at all hard to see why students need to believe in institutional paternalism: to be at the mercy of unconcerned incompetents, in school or in surgery or wherever, is hardly a pleasant prospect, and to be forced to spend the first part of one's life doing pointless exercises would be no better. Unable to withdraw or rebel (this route leads to failure), these ambitious students seem eager to detect, and perhaps even to fantasy, competence and concern among the staff. Whether faith in institutional paternalism stems from the genuine ability of the personnel of these privileged schools, though, or from the ambition and single-mindedness of these middle-class students, or from some combination of the two, remains an open question.

Conclusions

Our initial research question was, "Does the formal organization of the school alienate students?" and we may now answer, "No, not necessarily," at least not if the myth of institutional paternalism intervenes. On the other hand, bureaucratization does apparently lead to a massive and near-total conversion of organizational means into proximate student goals, so that what the student is involved *in* is something much less than what either educators or students think of as true education. Students give meaning to these activities by defining them as preparation for the real education that will come later, in college, or as contributions to some distant good known to teachers and other adults. In the meantime they may take pride in their skill at obtaining marks and building a presentable dossier.

During the course of our research we had occasion to amend some educational sociology, e.g., the "articulation hypothesis" was seen to be incomplete, and we raised questions about current formulations of the concept of alienation, e.g., it is obvious that powerlessness *per se* does not cause alienation, nor can it be equated with it. There are also numerous practical implications that might be drawn from this study. For example, if the present findings are correct, it is obvious that a good deal of our national effort to erase class and ethnic differentials in educational achievement may be misguided: to succeed in school and to become truly educated are quite separable goals, and the means to one need not at all be suitable for the other.[1]

But there is a more important question which has not been dealt with here, a question which probably cannot even be answered yet, but one whose eventual answer will determine the larger significance of what we have discussed: Although the myth of institutional paternalism allows students to become involved in their work, *is that what we want?* If involvement in work shapes character, and if the work of the student is as shallow as the task-performance model suggests, then might we not be guilty of shaping trivial personalities in our schools? This is the *moral* charge behind the alienation issue, and our present findings lend themselves more to its support than to its refutation.

If the charge is correct, and it may or may not be, then alienation is vastly preferable to involvement, for under these conditions alienation is a positive response of the healthy personality insulating itself against the effects of an unhealthy situation. The myth of institutional paternalism, that is to say, may not be so useful after all.

[REFERENCE NOTES]

[a] Edgar Z. Friedenberg, *The Vanishing Adolescent* (Boston: Beacon Press, 1959).

[b] Frank Riessman, *The Culturally Deprived Child* (New York: Harper and Row, 1962).

[c] Jules Henry, *Culture Against Man* (New York: Random House, 1963), Chapter 8.

[d] Jonathan Kozol, *Death at an Early Age* (Boston: Houghton Mifflin, 1967).

[e] Cp. Harvey Swados, *On the Line* (New York: Bantam Books, 1957); Adam Smith, *An Inquiry into the Nature and Causes of the Wealth of Nations* (New York: Modern Library, 1937; from the fifth edition of 1789), Book I, Chapter II.

[f] Cp. Paul Goodman, *Compulsory Mid-education* (New York: Horizon Press, 1964); Robert Owen, *A New View of Society* (Glencoe, Ill.: The Free Press, m.d.; facsimile reproduction of the third edition of 1817), esp. those comments on the Bell-Lancaster system, an early form of bureaucratized education.

[g] East and West Highs are almost identical, and are neighbors, so interview materials

from the former can be applied with some assurance to the latter. West and Parochial Highs differed primarily in the reactions of their students to authority, but the differences were not great.

ʰ In addition to the works by Blauner and by Mallery cited above, the most useful sources were: Arthur Stinchombe, *Rebellion in a High School* (Chicago: Quadrangle Books, 1964); John P. Clark, "Measuring Alienation Within a Social System," *American Sociological Review* 24 (December, 1959), pp. 849–52; Dwight G. Dean, "Alienation: Its Meaning and Measurement," *American Sociological Review* 26 (October, 1961), pp. 753–58; Rose Laub Coser, "Alienation and the Social Structure," *The Hospital in Modern Society*, ed. Eliot Freidson (New York: Free Press, 1963), pp. 231–65; Leonard I. Pearlin, "Alienation from Work: A Study of Nursing Personnel," *American Sociological Review* 27 (June, 1962)., pp. 314–26; Leonard I. Pearlin and Morris Rosenberg, "Nurse-Patient Social Distance and the Structural Context of a Mental Hospital," *American Sociological Review* 27 (February, 1962); and Russell Middleton, "Alienation, Race, and Education," *American Sociological Review* 28 (December, 1963), pp. 973–77.

ⁱ Chris Argyris, *Personality and Organization* (New York: Harper, 1957), pp. 59–60, *et passim.*

ʲ For a good discussion of this hypothesis see Stinchombe, *op. cit.*

ᵏ *Cf.* Howard S. Becker, "Notes on the Concept of Commitment," *American Journal of Sociology* 66 (July, 1960), pp. 32–40.

ˡ Buford Rhea, "School Organization and Differential Achievement in Education," paper read at the 1967 meeting of the Missouri Society for Sociology and Anthropology.

Variations on the Theme of Primary Groups: Forms of Social Control Within School Staffs*

Donald I. Warren

Since Becker's (1952) descriptive work on the horizontal processes of teacher career patterns was published, inquiry concerning colleague and school system effects on teachers has been neglected. School climate as it relates to pupil socialization has been discussed, but *teacher* socialization has not.[1] The present report pursues this area of inquiry by suggesting some theoretical views of social groups and social control phenomena and testing some of these views with survey data from a large metropolitan school system.

Essentially we ask two questions: (1) What qualitative differences in the structure of colleague relations exist between school staffs? (2) What

* I wish to acknowledge the valuable assistance of Mrs. V. Louise Everett in the preparation of this manuscript.
[1] Brookover (1955, 1964) mentions informal faculty relationships in connection with clique formation, and indirectly alludes to veteran versus novice socialization bases. Brim (1958:29–35) discusses personnel recruitment and selection pattern limited to occupational choice and personality attributes and refers to colleague relations and the neglect of research on this issue. The present author's work in this area includes Meyer et al. (1968); Warren (1964 and 1966).

FROM *Sociology of Education*, Vol. 43, No. 3 (Summer 1970).

mechanisms of social control within school staffs are most effective under the conditions set by these differences?

To answer the first question we will present a typology of peer groups that is based on the elements of the primary group as defined by Cooley (1909:23–31; 1933:55–60 and 208–215). To answer the second question we will consider four familiar ways that group members exercise influence over their peers, relating these to the group types to discover which control mechanisms may be effective in given school staffs. We shall not consider *external* administrative controls on teaching staffs. Effects of external controls are considered elsewhere (Warren, 1969).

The framework is clearly sociological. As Freidson (1964) pointed out, the analysis of the professions tends to point to individual deficiencies or improper training as causal factors in the failure of a professional to perform well—that is, according to the highest standards of the profession—when after more careful analysis the work environment or setting is frequently seen to have important effects on individual professional behavior. Quite aside from the gross physical features of a school building, the *social* setting of a school staff can differ from that of another school that is otherwise comparable within a community and a school system.

Elements of Primary Group Structure in Work Groups

In his classic definition of primary groups Cooley (Cooley et al., 1933:208–215) identified several essential properties: (a) face-to-face interaction, (b) diffuse and unspecialized interaction, (c) relative permanence, (d) "sympathy and mutual identification for which 'we' is the natural expression," and (e) small size. (The last, size, is not considered here.) Cooley's definition is an ideal type, the elements of which contrast in most respects with properties of secondary or "formal" groups. Cooley's definition of primary groups was not originally meant to be divisible in the sense that given elements may be present or absent. These elements, however, can be considered as independently varying attributes and can be measured. An association of individuals in a work setting who share a common formal status, such as teachers in an elementary school, forms a distinct kind of primary group according to the values taken by each of the four elements. By measuring the degree to which each element is present in a work group we can discover the differences between groups. Thus it is useful to recognize the heuristic function of Cooley's formulation.[2]

Figure 1 illustrates our conception of three types of peer groups: Consensual, Diffuse, and Job-specific. The figure also includes the ideal-typical primary and secondary groups for conceptual comparison. Each type is

---

[2] A task analogous to that undertaken in this paper is presented for Weberian ideal types by Stanley H. Udy (1959).

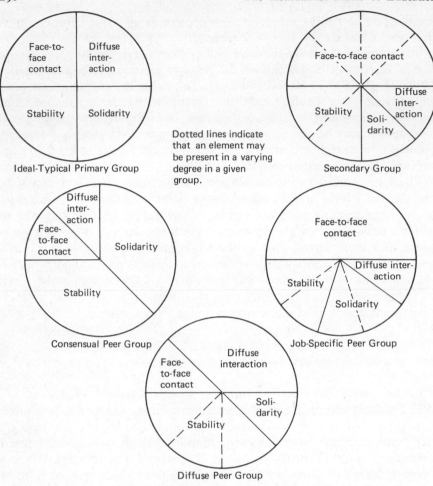

FIGURE 1. Elements of Primary Groups.

defined by the degree to which each of four elements—face-to-face contact, diffuse interaction, solidarity, and membership stability—is present. *Our purpose is to suggest, from particular combinations of the elements, three types of peer social groups whose elements facilitate or hamper the use of given mechanisms of social control.*

Each of the four elements may be present or absent, maximal or minimal among work peers in a given social setting. Together these elements retain the essence of Cooley's primary-group concept, but separately they offer the means of empirically assessing peer relationships. Treating them separately serves two functions. (1) It points out that the arbitrary dichotomizing of "primary group" versus "secondary group" (or "formal" versus "informal" organization) is oversimplification; it should be replaced by a conceptual scheme that recognizes several group attributes. (2) Each element of

Cooley's definition has particular consequences for group functioning; therefore at the points at which empirical situations differ in a given element, the group's strength or weakness should be specifically definable.

Face-to-face contact here denotes peer surveillance in role performance, subtle or intended. Persons working in the same place, such as teachers in the same building, observe and communicate with one another if the job requires it. This aspect of face-to-face contact has been treated extensively in work-group studies of the 1930s and later. It is predominant in the Job-specific peer group (see Figure 1), which is typified primarily by interaction within the job context alone. Although face-to-face contact is often a key element of primary-group relationships, it is not related either to high group cohesiveness or to strong identification with the group.[3] In the "typical" primary group, the family, this is apparent: even frequent interaction does not necessarily promote value-sharing, especially in times of rapid social change (a "generation gap" can occur). But face-to-face contact does aid all group members in understanding both the similarities and the differences between individual normative orientations—that is, in being aware of, if not in agreement with, the values held by other group members.

When authority is delegated to one's peers, as is the case with teachers or other professionals when direct surveillance by superiors is traditionally limited, the Job-specific peer group may come to resemble the secondary group. The coercive power of punishment for rule violation or the use of legitimate authority serves effectively as a control when values and attitudes are not internalized.[4]

Diffuse interaction denotes the informal contacts that sometimes develop when work peers perform in a shared setting. Such leisure-time interaction can stimulate discussion and influence values and attitudes toward work. A crucial difference between diffuse interaction and face-to-face contact is that social relations off the job are voluntary and selective; face-to-face contact occurs within the job context in the process of handling tasks and is neither voluntary nor selective. The predominance of diffuse interaction in the Diffuse peer group, as conceptualized in Figure 1, occurs when social acceptance among work peers is established as a central value. Once an individual has won social acceptance and participates fully in the interaction of his peer group, he begins to internalize the group values to which his earlier

---

[3] As Broom and Selznick (1963:142) note: "The primary group is to be contrasted . . . not with the group whose members are separated in space, but with the group whose members are related to each other only in formal, impersonal, and institutionalized ways. . . . Not all face-to-face groups are primary groups. It is essential to the primary group that a certain kind of relation exist among its members, a relation that is personal, spontaneous, emotional. Such primary relations may exist without face-to-face contact, and they may be absent even where there is face-to-face contact."

[4] Face-to-face interaction is one form of visibility. The relationship between visibility and conformity is an area for further research. For an attempt to explore this question see Warren (1968).

conformity may have been simply utilitarian.[5] Thus socialization of members to group values is characteristic of Diffuse peer groups.

Diffuse interaction is particularly effective in converting new members and does not rely on an initial selection of peers by experience, homogeneity of background, or personal values (selective recruitment). At least part of the positive incentive for conformity to group norms comes from a feedback of supporting communication that breaks down the individual's earlier insulation between personal values and work requirements. This is quite similar to the interaction processes described by Homans (1950).

Group solidarity refers to intense identification, similar to Cooley's description of "we-feeling." It is clearly akin to the reference-group concept and is an important element in the Consensual peer group (see Figure 1). The awareness of consensus, mutual attractiveness among peers, and shared values is strongly salient.

When "we-feeling" is isolated from the other elements of the primary group, the emphasis is on homogeneity of interests. Here cohesiveness becomes a product of the initial composition of the group. Similarity of background creates a highly subjective sense of unity and solidarity; neither frequent contact nor an elaborate socialization process is required.[6] Consensus develops as a "natural" response from common values and orientations to any problem that members may take to the group. Consensus is a direct outgrowth of perceived common bonds. Cohesion results from prior selection of group members, intended or unintended. Homogeneity provides a basis for social control of "significant others" in the group and maximizes internalization of social norms because of a shared frame of reference. For these reasons and because the group tends to define itself on the basis of them, face-to-face contact and diffuse interaction are low in the consensual peer group; they are unnecessary.

Membership stability is perhaps the most easily defined of the elements described by Cooley. Groups are primary, he wrote, "in the sense that they do not change in the same degree as more elaborate relations" (Cooley,

[5] In his study of social work settings, Blau (1960) notes that earlier findings support the view of conformity as associated with social acceptance, and social acceptance as a basis for *deviation* from group norms. We would suggest that where sociability is a primary attribute of a group—that is, high diffuse interaction—conformity may begin as a rather superficial or expedient response involving overt compliance with certain group norms. Once this is established, the individual member may be relatively free to violate these norms, particularly if the group members as a whole are themselves relatively uncommitted to these norms. In any event, the need to examine types of conformity—behavioral or attitudinal—would seem pertinent to the anomalous findings noted by Blau (1960).

[6] The distinction between so-called "free-forming" and "functional" groups is pertinent. In the former, friendship cliques and similar groups seem to form on the basis of similarity in background interests and social origins; the latter may comprise a heterogeneous membership. Often in the social-psychological literature the concept of "attractiveness" to groups is used to refer both to cohesiveness based on developed "we-feeling" through intense interaction or "we-feeling" existing on a selectivity basis. Propositions about group cohesion do not unravel the causal sequence. This is true of Homans' (1950:120–122) hypotheses concerning sentiments and group cohesion.

1909:27). A low turnover of group members can be an operational measure of Cooley's concept of stability. The development of a deep-seated identification, such as occurs in the ideal-typical family group, may be dependent on membership stability. In the absence of a high rate of interaction, the cumulative impact of even the most formal modes of social contact may take on qualities otherwise associated with intense and intimate contacts as long as the roles that individuals occupy are constant.

While it is possible to imagine stable groups without face-to-face member contacts maintaining a primary-group relationship because of the strengthening effect of membership stability on "we-feeling," it is difficult to expect such solidarity to develop if membership turnover is high. For this reason we view membership stability as an important element in Consensual peer groups and as important but not crucial in Diffuse peer groups. Membership turnover is likely to be high in the Job-specific group in which members have little feeling of solidarity or fellowship; in Job-specific peer groups the roles are formalized and can be occupied by others without detriment.

To summarize, in the Consensual group, solidarity ("we-feeling") and membership stability are of the essence; in the Diffuse group, off-the-job socializing predominates; and in the Job-specific group the inevitable daily interaction with peers of equal status in the work context is most typical.

Social structures are not static. The proportional relationships of the elements of primary groups can vary over time (e.g., school staffs experience changes in personnel that can alter group structure). A group [that] is clearly Job-specific (or Diffuse or Consensual) at a given point in time may undergo changes in the values of certain of the four elements relative to one another and thus move into a new category. For example, in a new school building membership stability is low among the staff of "new" teachers, and face-to-face contact will tend to be high as teachers "learn the ropes" and adjust to their new environment. The teachers are too new to each other for diffuse, off-the-job interaction; and membership homogeneity, even if present, is not likely to be accompanied initially by a sense of solidarity among the staff. Thus we find a typical Job-specific peer group.

In time, membership will stabilize and face-to-face contact diminish as work becomes routine. Other characteristics of the teaching staff, perhaps similarities of training or social background, or an increasing rate of off-the-job interaction, then will tend to shape emergent group properties toward the Consensual or Diffuse types. To some degree the proportions of the four elements in a group can be manipulated either by a peer group member or by an outside authority, but they must first be recognized and their effects on group functioning realized.

FOUR SOCIAL CONTROL MECHANISMS
USED IN PEER GROUPS

What mechanisms of social control are most effective in each of the three peer group types?

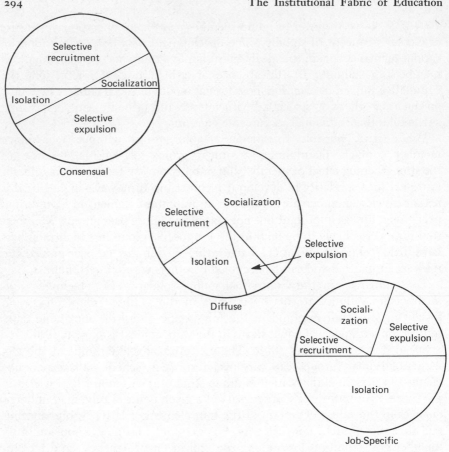

FIGURE 2. Control Mechanisms Related to Three Conceptual Types of Primary Groups by Degree of Use.

Figure 2 illustrates a hypothetical relationship between four mechanisms of social control and the three types. These relationships are meant to be comparative, neither absolute nor mutually exclusive. All mechanisms of control may be found to occur together, as might peer-group elements, although *certain elements of peer groups tend to facilitate or undermine the operation of one or more of those mechanisms.*

The relationships illustrated in Figure 2 exclude any external acts of social control directed to the group or its members. This is not to say that a given peer-group type is uniquely insulated from external authority, but only to suggest the distinction between internal peer and external administrative control. An attempt to exert a certain kind of external control when peers already exercise it may be superfluous. Conversely, a social control mechanism that is not operant may have to come from an outside source if it is needed.

Selective recruitment insures that new members will come to the peer group with similar values, attitudes, or work habits. In a school system, apart from the administrative application of appointment standards, selective re-

cruitment can operate through an informal grapevine that leads individuals
to avoid or seek appointment to a given school.

Socialization defines the role of individual work settings as they mold or
reshape the attitudes and values of members. It may be a general occupational socialization or a more local process among peers. Novice teachers, for
example, can be "clued in" by veteran teachers.

Selective expulsion is simply the departure of deviants. It may be an expression of the unresolved pressures of adjustment to the work setting. High
turnover of membership in itself does not measure the selective expulsion
mechanism, but it may be symptomatic of it.

Isolation is the use of ostracism by peers. An individual is excluded from, or
excludes himself from, a high rate of involvement with peers, especially when
(1) interaction is voluntary, (2) it reflects group solidarity, and (3) it offers
a way to reward social acceptability. Isolation can function to delay full
acceptance of newcomers or to punish a long-term group member who resists
group pressures.

A peer group that maintains consensus via the value-sharing of its members
—a Consensual peer group—is more likely than any other type of group to
employ the mechanism of selective recruitment (see Figure 2). Selective
expulsion is equally important in Consensual peer groups because this type
of group depends on the implicit identity of interests and values of its members; an individual who does not "belong" is expelled. Expulsion is seldom a
formal or clear-cut procedure in small groups, but even without the trappings
of ceremony or official reprimand it is effective. The socialization mechanism
is ineffective in the Consensual peer group because there is a relatively low
rate of interaction in this group type. Isolation also requires a high rate of
interaction and face-to-face contact in order to communicate to the deviant
his lack of acceptance and is therefore used infrequently in Consensual
groups as a means of control.

Socialization is the most significant means of control in Diffuse peer groups
because of the high rate of interaction in this type of group and because the
frequent informal contacts among members redefine values and attitudes.
The deviant can be converted and the newly-arrived member shaped by the
socialization mechanism. At the same time the isolation mechanism is used
to limit a newcomer's participation until he has proved himself and to
ostracize the deviant long-term member.

Selective expulsion is least useful in the Diffuse type. Deviance can serve
positive functions in a group by reinforcing the behavior of the non-deviants
and by creating a boundary around the normative system of the group.
(Views on the functional consequences of deviance are given by Dentler and
Erikson, 1959; Erikson, 1962; Coser, 1962.) Since membership in Diffuse
peer groups does not rely on value-sharing, a functional differentiation of
roles can emerge and the Diffuse peer group will embrace the deviant where
the Consensual peer group could not. Selective recruitment is also of only
moderate importance in the Diffuse peer group as compared to Consensual;

socialization compensates for it. Initial differences between members matter little (and may even be welcome) to members of Diffuse peer groups.

Isolation is most useful in Job-specific peer groups because of the high degree of face-to-face, work-defined interaction coupled with relatively little off-the-job contact. Without a means of creating internalized commitments to group norms, the Job-specific peer group must use overt means to achieve conformity; punishment for deviation is isolation. In most teaching situations, in which peer surveillance is somewhat limited as compared with some other occupations, isolation is less effective than it is in industrial work groups in which peers are constantly visible to one another. Thus isolation may be found in combination with selective expulsion, since ostracism may be a first step in a dual-control procedure.

Socialization occurs to some extent in the Job-specific peer group, but with low levels of shared values and off-the-job interaction, the opportunities to socialize a member are limited. As for selective recruitment, this is essentially external to the Job-specific peer group. When it does occur as a result of group member activity, the motive for selective recruiting is not grounded in commitment to the group. A staff vacancy may exist, for example, and one teacher informs another of it. A Job-specific peer group is not likely to have any special interest or role in the recruitment procedure.

A TEST OF THE THEORY

The Sample

To test the relationship between peer-group types and social-control mechanisms, data about a sample of Detroit schools were subjected to a secondary analysis. This sample of schools had been drawn for an evaluation study of an on-going program of school improvement in low-income areas of Detroit.[7] As part of a specially-funded demonstration project, four elementary schools in the Detroit system had been given extra resources and personnel with the explicit purpose of developing close school-community relations.[8] These four schools were in the city's poorest economic areas.

Each project school had been matched with two other schools according to racial composition of students and median income of students' families. Although it was not possible to have totally matching schools, the "control" schools were in geographical proximity to the project schools and differed little from them on such attributes as physical plant, size of faculty, and administrative control structure. This procedure yielded twelve inner-city working-class schools.

[7] This research was conducted under U.S. Office of Education Project No. 1796.
[8] Project schools differed from the other elementary schools in that about a ten per cent increase in funds was made available to each school and additional "resource" teachers were allocated. Furthermore, intensive programs of innovative teaching methods and certain school-community relations programs were promoted. Workshops in human relations for teachers were another adjunct of the program of school improvement.

Then six schools in the outer middle-class areas of the city were included to permit further comparisons. The characteristics of the eighteen elementary schools is not a random selection from Detroit schools; however, it does include schools that differed in student social class and ecological characteristics.

It is important to note that these schools were not selected on the basis of any of the variables of immediate concern in the present study. Neither teacher relationships, selection patterns, or teacher norms were defined *a priori* in the school sampling procedure.

During a two-week period in 1963 the staffs of the eighteen schools were given detailed questionnaires to complete. These were administered during a faculty meeting held between school terms. By mail and telephone contacts with teachers, the study obtained nearly perfect response; all but six of the 534 teachers in the eighteen schools completed the questionnaires, a 98.9 per cent completion rate.

Certain characteristics of the teacher peer groups analyzed should be noted.

TABLE 1

Characteristics of Sample Schools

SCHOOL	NUMBER OF TEACHERS	NUMBER OF STUDENTS	MEDIAN INCOME OF FAMILIES	% NON-WHITE STUDENTS
O[a]	27	717	$3,000–3,999	25
K	30	1,062	4,000–4,999	50
A	23	877	4,000–4,999	21
D[a]	36	980	2,000–2,999	96
J	43[b]	1,536	4,000–4,999	98
F	24	804	2,000–2,999	100
Q[a]	56[b]	1,516	3,000–3,999	25
R	25	870	3,000–3,999	47
I	32	1,092	4,000–4,999	22
E[a]	26	941	3,000–3,999	96
C	28	994	4,000–4,999	94
M	27	918	4,000–4,999	91
P	28	874	7,000–7,999	0
II	27	807	6,000–6,999	0
L	18	616	7,000–7,999	0
N	27	872	8,000–8,999	0
B	28	883	9,000–9,999	0
G	23	712	7,000–7,999	0
Total	528			

[a] Project schools.
[b] K-8th, not K-6th.

(1) We dealt with groups larger than those usually considered to be "primary groups." School staffs averaged twenty-seven members, excluding the larger staffs in two schools that included the seventh and eighth grades. (2) Observability (face-to-face contact in job performance) by peers was limited as compared to industrial work groups. (3) We analyzed attitudes, not behavior, in defining and analyzing staff norms. (4) We used the aggregate responses of each staff as a basis for measuring colleague norms. (5) There are processes of selection and socialization in the teaching profession not explicitly taken into account here. These include the general occupational socialization of teachers, selective processes based on professional training and experience, and the market conditions of teaching. (6) The urban schools used in this study do not represent a wide variety of school settings in their administration or organization, but were under one school board. Thus some innovative techniques such as team teaching and non-subject-oriented curricula were not employed in any of the sample schools.

Identifying Peer Groups

On the basis of the teachers' questionnaire responses, each school staff was classified with respect to our three theoretically-defined peer group types. Several questions on perceived unity or lack of internal dissension were formed into a Consensual index that was used to define Consensual peer groups. The operationalization of this measure included a set of seven questionnaire items. All but one of the components is drawn from responses to the question: "Which of the following, if any, tend to produce lack of unity in the teaching staff of your particular school?" A check could be placed by each of the sources of disunity. A seventh item was included by weighting responses to a question regarding "differences that seem to be important in the teaching staff of your building." A score of 5 was assigned to the alternative of "no differences within the teaching staff"; a score of 4 to the response "a high degree of unity, but a few who differ"; a score of 3 to the answer "a majority group, with a conflicting minority group"; and a score of 1 to the response "several differing groups." Each staff was then ranked according to the mean score of this index item. In a similar fashion the other components were used to rank each staff, employing the per cent of teachers who checked the listed source of disunity. The final index was then computed using the average of the seven ranks which a given staff obtained. In turn, schools were divided into "high" or "low" using the median rank of all staffs. Eight schools fell into the former category, 10 into the latter.

Except in the case of the proportion of teachers saying "no differences within teaching staff" and the proportion saying "there is no lack of unity at all" $(R_s=.04)$ modest to high positive correlation occurred between all items in the index. This suggests that the overall index of perceived staff solidarity and homogeneity is basically a single scale.

The Diffuse peer group index was based on two questionnaire items.

In order to exclude clique structure from the measure, these questions were used to rank schools by the proportion of staff giving particular responses, not merely the mean response score for the school. The questionnaire asked, "In general what would you say was the tendency in your particular building with respect to relationships between teachers . . . ? Do they tend to be informal or business-like and formal?" Responses were treated in two ways. First the proportion of teachers in each school who indicated either "very informal" or "quite informal" on a six-point scale were computed. Then a weighted average was computed using a simple scoring base of one to six starting on the "very informal" side of the scale.

The second component of the Diffuse peer group index consisted of the responses to the question, "How many staff social gatherings . . . have you attended this semester?" The proportion of teachers indicating no attendance at staff gatherings was computed for each school. Items of the Diffuse peer group index were positively correlated except when paired. Mean number of staff gatherings and mean staff informality correlate .53, while proportion of staff attending no gatherings and proportion of staff "very" or "quite" informal correlate .66. Mean staff gatherings and proportion of "very" or "quite" informal correlate .11, as do proportion of staff attending no meetings and mean informality. The reliability coefficient for the items in the index is .88.

Each staff was given a rank based on each of the four data items comprising the Diffuse peer group index. Then the average of these four ranks was employed to define the designation on the index. Schools whose average of ranks was above the median of ranks were classified as "high," those below as "low." In this manner a total of nine schools was assigned to each category.

Job-specific peer groups were identified by ranking schools on (1) the extent to which teacher committees had important responsibilities in policy-making, and (2) whether or not faculty meetings were held for the purpose of policy-making by teachers. Both items fit a setting in which the interaction between teachers is formalized by the work role and yet is face-to-face. Teachers were asked, "In this building how much responsibility do committees of teachers have in making decisions about tasks that have to be done?" A mean score, on the basis of which the schools were ranked, was established for each school by weighting responses of "a great deal," "some," "little," and "very little" from 4 to 1.

The proportion of teachers saying committees had "a great deal" of responsibility next was calculated. Teachers had been asked to indicate the purpose of faculty meetings. Among the possible purposes (more than one could be checked) was "so faculty can make major policy decisions for the building." Teachers were asked also to indicate how often faculty meetings were held for this purpose (or the ones they indicated). The choices were "generally the purpose," "sometimes the purpose," "seldom the purpose," and "never the purpose." Again both a weighted mean and the proportion of teachers making a given response were used to rank schools on the Job-specific index. Inter-item reliability of the index was .97.

As in the case of the other indices, schools were ranked separately on each of the index components, and the final average of these ranks formed the basis of the overall index. In this manner 7 of the 18 staffs had an average of means which was above the median rank of all schools, while 11 fell below this cutting point.

Table 2 shows the schools that received "high" ratings on each of the peer group types. Since our measures were independent, school staffs could rate "high" or "low" on one, two, or three of the peer group measures. Three school staffs displayed each of the three peer group types, four staffs two types, and seven displayed one type only. Four staffs received no "high" ratings on any of the three types.[9]

Defining Peer Group Norms

To identify the social control mechanisms at work in each school setting, we needed first to measure the norms endorsed by the majority of teachers in each school. The measures of group norms were based on two sets of data: (1) responses of teachers to ten Likert-scale social attitude questions [10] and (2) teachers' responses to seven items in the questionnaire concerning their job situation. Dichotomous "high" or "low" ratings for each Likert item were assigned to each teacher, using median item scores as cutting points. Six of the job attitude items required dichotomous responses; responses to the seventh were collapsed from four to two categories.

[9] Even when measurement procedures for identifying peer group types become refined there is no reason to expect the peer group types a future study might reveal to be "pure" cases. The elements of peer groups as Cooley defined them are not mutually exclusive. Given that size is an arbitrary factor in primary groups, these other four elements are seen to vary in value across groups. It is precisely this inconstancy of proportions of the primary-group elements that reveals any small group as discrete. The working assumption is that the idea-type construct is both empirically and theoretically useful, and that the independent variable in a consideration of peer social control—our prime concern here—is the predominance of a given element, *not* its exclusive monopoly in a group. Thus the operationalization of the theory reported here, though crude, does not undermine the reliability of the assumptions and information accumulated to date on the structure and functions of small groups. Rather, it underlines the need for further multivariate analysis.

[10] Henry J. Meyer developed an attitude scale which was first used to assess the values of social workers. The ten items are: "Public aid vs. private effort," "personal freedom vs. societal controls," "personal goals vs. maintenance of group," "social causation vs. individual autonomy," "pluralism vs. homogeneity," "secularism vs. religiosity," "self-determination vs. fatalism," "positive satisfaction vs. struggle-denial," "social protection vs. social retribution," and "innovation-change vs. traditionalism." These dimensions were based on four item statements with Likert responses from "Strongly Agree" to "Strongly Disagree." All scales were defined in terms of a "liberal" vs. "conservative" direction. See McLeod and Meyer (1961) and Meyer et al. (1968). Meyer's attitude scale was modified somewhat for our study. Total scores for each dimension were tabulated for individual teachers and the median score for the population of teachers on each item dichotomized responses into "high" and "low."

TABLE 2
Distribution of Ratings on Three Peer Group Indexes

| | I | II | III |
SCHOOL	CONSENSUAL	DIFFUSE	JOB-SPECIFIC
A	High	High	High
B	High	High	High
C	High	High	High
D	Low	High	High
E	Low	High	High
F	High	High	Low
G	High	High	Low
H	Low	High	Low
I	Low	High	Low
J	Low	Low	High
K	Low	Low	High
L	High	Low	Low
M	High	Low	Low
N	High	Low	Low
O	Low	Low	Low
P	Low	Low	Low
Q	Low	Low	Low
R	Low	Low	Low

The job situation questions sought teachers' views about introducing an experimental program into the school, the taking of additional courses to qualify for pay increments, and detrimental factors within the school structure. The question on the experimental program was, "Suppose there were a discussion about introducing an experimental program in your school. It would require some important changes in your teaching pattern, although the teaching day would still be the same. Which of the following best reflects what you would prefer to do?" In analysis answers were divided between alternatives 1 and 2, "would not wish to participate," "would be willing to participate only after others had found that it increased teaching effectiveness," and alternatives 3 and 4, "would be willing to participate at the beginning if I knew it wouldn't disrupt the children," "would be willing to participate at the beginning if I like it regardless of possible problems."

The pay increments question was, "Do you think that teachers should be required to take extra courses in order to obtain pay increments after they have been teaching ten years?" (Yes, No). Teacher views of detrimental factors were determined from responses to the general query, "Please check as many of the following as you think might make it harder in your building for teachers to teach as well as they have been trained to teach." The possible choices included, (a) too much clerical work and extraneous duties, (b) classes too large, (c) school's philosophy of education, (d) inadequate physical facilities, and (e) quality of students. Each of these five items was either checked or not checked and was thus dichotomous.

Combining the responses to social value questions and the job situation items yields a total of 17 responses for each teacher. The normative climate of a school was defined by the majority percentage for each dichotomized item provided that 60 per cent of the "oldtimers" (staff members for two years or more) appeared in that majority. The result of combining these majority percentages produces an "average level of consensus"—an index of a relatively stable normative climate operative in a given school.

Measuring Social Control Mechanisms

Social control mechanisms are employed by a peer group to bring each member into conformity with the norms of the group. Their use can be determined from our data by comparing for each school the per cent of responses of newcomers and oldtimers to a given item. The normative climate is based on the attitudes of the oldtimer group, and in comparison with this base-line it is possible to determine whether newcomers are more, equally, or less likely to share such attitudes.

The use of the socialization mechanism in a given school is indicated when the difference between the conformity of newcomers in that staff to the group norms and the conformity of oldtimers in the staff is substantially above the mean difference for all schools. Table 3 presents the newcomer and oldtimer conformity scores for each school, and the differences. Although some socialization of newcomers appears to occur in all but one school setting, the differences between newcomer and oldtimer conformity scores in ten of the eighteen schools were significantly above the mean differences for all schools of +7.8, and thus were rated "high" on the use of the socialization mechanism.

When a school's newcomer conformity score is significantly above the newcomer conformity score mean for all schools, the use of the *selective recruitment* mechanism is apparent. The mean of newcomer conformity scores in all schools is 67.1 per cent, as shown in Table 3. On this basis, seven of the eighteen schools were rated "high" on the use of the selective recruitment mechanism. Moreover, these seven schools are among the eight rated "low" on the socialization mechanism, suggesting that a negative relationship obtains between the use of the socialization and selective recruitment mechanisms.

The argument can be made that our measures of socialization and selective recruitment have created the inverse relationship observed in Table 3, school Q being the only exception. However, the mean of conformity scores for oldtimer teachers in the ten "high socialization" schools is 74.8 per cent while the corresponding mean of oldtimer scores for the eight schools rated "low" on socialization is 75.0 per cent. The difference is only 0.2 per cent. This same difference computed for newcomers is

TABLE 3
Conformity to Group Norms: Socialization and Selective Recruitment Patterns
(By Percentage Ranking)

SCHOOL	STAFF NEWCOMER CONFORMITY SCORES (A)	STAFF OLDTIMER CONFORMITY SCORES (B)	DIFFERENCE: (B)—(A)
G	60.2[a]	77.7[a]	+17.5 H[b]
H	61.0	78.2	+17.2 H
A	62.5	78.1	+15.6 H
M	62.5	75.9	+13.4 H
K	65.1	75.0	+ 9.9 H
B	63.1	72.6	+ 9.5 H
O	61.7	70.8	+ 9.1 H
E	65.0	73.4	+ 8.4 H
I	63.2	71.3	+ 8.1 H
D	66.7	74.7	+ 8.0 H
P	73.6 H[c]	80.5	+ 6.9
R	68.8 H	75.7	+ 6.9
Q	63.9	70.3	+ 6.4
F	72.2 H	76.4	+ 4.2
L	76.9 H	77.5	+ 0.6
C	70.0 H	70.6	+ 0.6
J	74.0 H	74.3	+ 0.3
N	76.5 H	75.0	− 1.5
	x = 67.1%	x = 74.9%	x = + 7.8%

a The base for the percentages is neither the number of teachers nor the number of responses but the multiple of the two. The Ns include teachers who entered the computation more than once when a peer norm qualifies in a given school more than once. Since teachers are included more than once, independence is violated. However, the fact that teachers *across* schools are compared does not appear to undermine the validity of the assumptions common to statistical tests.

b High rating on Socialization.

c High rating on Selective Recruitment.

8.9 per cent.[11] Thus the variation in newcomer scores is what differentiates schools. Had the oldtimer scores varied as much, this apparently inverse relationship would not have obtained.

Our data did not contain a direct measure of attrition from which the use of the *selective expulsion* mechanism might have been measured. However, if oldtimer staff members express dissatisfaction with their jobs and

[11] Mean of newcomer conformity scores in the ten "high socialization" schools is 63.1 per cent. Mean of newcomer conformity scores in the eight "low socialization" schools is 72.0 per cent. Mean of newcomer conformity scores in the seven "high selective recruitment" schools is 73.1 per cent. Mean of newcomer conformity scores in the eleven "low selective recruitment" schools is 63.2 per cent. Thus the difference of means of newcomer conformity scores in "high" versus "low" selective recruitment schools is 9.9 per cent.

also deviate from the group norms, we can presume that they are more likely to leave than are satisfied teachers. Deviation from group norms, determined from a comparison of individual teacher conformity scores with the school staff conformity score, does not in itself suggest dissatisfaction; our data revealed no over-all correlation between dissatisfaction and deviance.

Each of the eighteen school staffs was ranked on the potential turnover of staff using two indicators: (1) satisfaction with present job and (2) plans about future jobs. Teachers were asked: "How satisfied are you with your assignment to this building?" A large majority of teachers indicated they were "very satisfied." Where other responses were selected a classification as "dissatisfied" was established. Each school then had a given proportion of teachers in each grouping. A second division involved comparing in each school whether newcomers were more likely to be in the "satisfied" category than oldtimers.

In a similar manner a question concerning "what you expect to be doing five years from now" permitted an assessment of potential for staff turnover. Where the choice of "teaching in another elementary school" was given, this response was used to measure discontent with the present school setting, since other alternatives reflected upward mobility, retirement, or remaining at the present job.

If the selective expulsion mechanism is in use, dissatisfaction must be coupled with deviance. Therefore, we should find oldtimers to be both more likely to share prevailing values and also more satisfied with their job if this social control mechanism is effective. Selective expulsion was high for a school where oldtimers were substantially more satisfied than newcomers (using the average level for all schools as a cutting-point) and where the oldtimers who were *dissatisfied* conformed less than those who were *satisfied* with their job (using the average difference for all schools). Both conditions had to be present. Using these criteria 8 of the 18 schools ranked "high" as staffs in which selective expulsion appeared likely to be employed.

The use of *isolation* was determined from the conformity scores coupled with teacher responses to the question on the frequency of attendance at staff social gatherings. Teachers who attended no such gatherings were classified as isolates. The failure of newcomers to attend social gatherings would not be a reliable measure, as it could be a function of their brief time in the school. Thus schools were compared on the differences between the conformity scores of the isolated oldtimers and of the non-isolated oldtimers. For example, if 70 per cent of the non-isolated oldtimers conform to the group norms, but only 50 per cent of the isolated oldtimers conform to the group norms, the difference is +20 per cent. Such a difference is substantially above the mean difference for all schools of +3.1 per cent. A negative difference would suggest that since more of the isolated teachers conform to group norms than do the non-isolated, the mechanism of isolation is *not* in use to bring members into conformity with the group norms. This was the case in four schools, rated "low" on use of the isolation mechanism, and in six schools the difference was negligible. In eight schools the difference was positive and also significantly above the mean difference for all schools. These eight schools were rated "high" on the use of the isolation mechanism.

USE OF SOCIAL CONTROL MECHANISMS AND PEER GROUP TYPES

Table 4 is a summary of the findings regarding the extent of use of the four social control mechanisms we have measured. This table indicates with

TABLE 4

Use of Social Control Mechanisms by School Peer Group Type

PEER GROUP TYPE	SCHOOL	SELECTIVE RECRUITMENT	SOCIALIZATION	SELECTIVE EXPULSION	ISOLATION
I, II, III	A	Low[a]	High	High	High
	B	Low[a]	High	High	High
	C	High	Low[a]	High	High
II, III	D	Low	High	Low	High
	E	Low	High	Low	High
I, III	F	High	Low[a]	Low[a]	Low
	G	Low[a]	High	Low[a]	Low
II	H	Low	High	High[a]	High[a]
	I	Low	High	Low	Low
III	J	High[a]	Low	High[a]	Low
	K	Low	High	Low	High
I	L	High	Low	High	Low
	M	Low[a]	High[a]	Low[a]	Low
	N	High	Low	High	High[a]
	O	Low	High[a]	Low	Low
	P	High[a]	Low	High[a]	Low
	Q	Low	Low	Low	Low
	R	High[a]	Low	Low	Low

[a] Error from hypothesis. The errors are not absolute; e.g., high utilization of any of the social control mechanisms by the last four schools (O, P, Q, and R) is not inconsistent with the hypothesis; these schools did not receive high ratings on any of the three peer group forms; therefore, which mechanisms these groups may or may not utilize cannot be predicted. In cases in which the hypotheses predicted low-to-moderate use of a social control mechanism, and the data revealed extensive use of that mechanism (e.g., school H, a Diffuse peer group, and use of selective expulsion), we have identified this as an error, although it is an error only in degree, or extent, of utilization.

   I = Consensual.
  II = Diffuse.
 III = Job-specific.

small a's the cases in which the use of a given mechanism varied from our expectation. For example, school A obtained "high" ratings on all three peer group indexes and would thus be most likely to show the use of all four mechanisms, yet it is rated "low" on use of selective recruitment. More of the errors from hypothesis occur in the selective recruitment summary than for any other control mechanism, suggesting that our method of measuring selective recruitment could be improved.[12]

Among the seventy-two cells in Table 4, nineteen are errors from the hypothesis. This is less than half the number of errors that would occur using a random designation of highs and lows on the mechanisms.

Table 4 suggests that none of the schools, even those ranked "high" on all three peer group indexes, makes extensive use of all four mechanisms of social control. Even more interesting is the finding that, although most school staffs show the use of more than one, there are some notably incompatible mechanisms and others that occur frequently together. Selective recruitment and socialization appear to be incompatible. A group that preselects its members does so, presumably, in order to avoid the necessity of socializing them, or has no need to do so. A group that is cohesive by virtue of its gregarious members who enjoy diffuse interaction is able to socialize its members effectively and has no need to preselect them.

Mechanisms found often together are socialization and isolation (six schools); selective recruitment and selective expulsion (five schools); and selective expulsion and isolation (five schools). We have discussed theoretically the likelihood that these pairs of mechanisms would be compatible.[13]

Schools that ranked high on all three peer group indexes used multiple control mechanisms to a greater extent than other schools, according to Table 4. The opposite also is evident: the four schools low on all three measures of peer group structure (O, P, Q, and R) show the lowest rate of over-all use of social control. This finding supports the view that peer social controls tend to operate apart from effects of external controls. It is at the level of the given school building that occupational and school-system effects are filtered. Both in terms of defining the values of the fledgling teacher and reinforcing or altering those of the teaching veteran, staff climate and its mode of influence is the crucible for testing these larger forces.

The relationships between peer group type and mechanism use are shown

[12] The similarity of conformity of newcomers and oldtimers to group norms is one measure of selective recruitment, but it does not take into account other social processes that draw into a peer group a teacher who is known to share the values and attitudes of its present members. Thus this error and other errors from hypothesized relationships of Figure 2 (notably those in selective expulsion use) may be attributable to the fact that the data did not include patterns of teacher mobility across time. Improved methods would include serial data, asking teachers their reasons for choosing their present school or for leaving it and uncovering patterns of administrative selection policies.

[13] Selective recruitment and isolation occur together in only two schools, C and N; socialization and selective expulsion in three: A, B, and H.

in Table 5 as ratios, giving a clearer picture of the findings. The ratios are proportions of the total number of schools scoring high or low on a given peer group index that ranked high on use of one of the four social control mechanisms. In general, the mechanisms appear to have been used frequently in the work groups that were predicted to make extensive use of them: notably, socialization in schools scoring high on the Diffuse peer group index (7/9) and isolation in those scoring high on the Job-specific (6/7) peer group index. Selective recruitment and selective expulsion also occur with high scores on the Consensual peer group index (as predicted), but no more so than the other two that were expected to be used infrequently in staffs with high scores on this index.

The patterns of use of social control mechanisms by teacher peer groups revealed in this study are consistent, generally, with our theoretical perspective. But neither theory nor data should be construed as evidence that maximum consensus and conformity are achieved *only* by the dynamics of peer groups. The data reveal only which of the mechanisms (as we measured them) were operative in the eighteen sample schools and relations between use of these mechanisms and the degree to which a school's faculty resembled the ideal-typical Consensual, Diffuse, or Job-specific peer group.

TABLE 5

Frequencies of Use of Each of the Four Social Control Mechanisms, As Ratios to Number of High- or Low-Scoring Schools on Each Peer Group Index

| | PEER GROUP TYPE | | | | | | |
| | I CONSENSUAL | | II DIFFUSE | | III JOB-SPECIFIC | | |
MECHANISM USED	HIGH	LOW	HIGH	LOW	HIGH	LOW	NOT CLASSIFIED
Selective Recruitment	4/8[a]	3/10	2/9	5/9	2/7	5/11	2/4
Socialization	4/8	6/10	7/9[b]	3/9[b]	5/7	5/11	1/4
Selective Expulsion	5/8	3/10[c]	4/9	4/9	4/7	4/11	1/4
Isolation	4/8	4/10	6/9	2/9[e]	6/7	2/11[d]	0/4

[a] With correction for continuity and direction predicted, the chi-square value is significant at the .20 level between High and Low schools.
[b] Significant at the .05 level.
[c] Significant at the .10 level.
[d] Significant at the .01 level.
[e] Significant at the .05 level.

Our findings suggest the co-variation of structures of colleague relations and colleague social controls in elementary schools. The need to refine a peer group typology and appy it to data from a greater variety of other work group settings is indicated.

REFERENCES

Becker, Howard S. 1952. "The career of the Chicago public school teacher." American Journal of Sociology 57(March):470–477.

Blau, Peter. 1960. "Patterns of deviation in work groups." Sociometry 23(3): 245–261.

Brim, Orville G., Jr. 1958. Sociology and the Field of Education. New York: Russell Sage Foundation.

Brookover, Wilbur B. 1964. A Sociology of Education. New York: American Book Company.

Broom, Leonard, and Philip H. Selznick. 1963. Sociology. New York: Harper and Row. (Third Edition.)

Cooley, Charles. 1909. Social Organization. New York: Scribners.

Cooley, Charles Horton, R. C. Angell, and L. J. Carr. 1933. Introductory Sociology. New York: Scribners.

Coser, Lewis A. 1962. "Some functions of deviant behavior and normative flexibility." American Journal of Sociology 68(September):172–181.

Dentler, Robert A., and Kai T. Erikson. 1959. "The functions of deviance in groups." Social Problems 7(Fall):98–107.

Erikson, Kai T. 1962. "Notes on the sociology of deviance." Social Problems 9(Spring):307–314.

Freidson, Eliot. 1964. "The organization of professional behavior." Paper read at the Annual Meeting of the American Sociological Association, Montreal.

Homans, George C. 1950. The Human Group. New York: Harcourt, Brace.

McLeod, D. B., and Henry J. Meyer. 1961. "A study of the values of social workers." Manuscript: University of Michigan School of Social Work.

Meyer, Henry J., Eugene Litwak, and Donald I. Warren. 1968. "Occupational and class differences in social values: a comparison of teachers and social workers." Sociology of Education 41(Summer):263–281.

Udy, Stanley H., Jr. 1959. " 'Bureaucracy' and 'rationality' in Weber's organization theory: an empirical study." American Sociological Review 24(December):791–795.

Warren, Donald I. 1964. "Modes of conformity and the character of formal and informal organization structure: a comparative study of public schools." Unpublished Doctoral Dissertation, University of Michigan. Microfilm. 1966. "Social relations of peers in a formal organization setting." Administrative Science Quarterly 11(December):440–478. 1968. "Power, visibility, and conformity in formal organizations." American Sociological Review 33(December):951–970. 1969. "The effects of power bases and peer groups on conformity in formal organizations." Administrative Science Quarterly 14(December):544–556.

D. Managing Differences and Conflict

Culture Conflict and Mexican-American Achievement

NEAL JUSTIN

It appears that the least-educated citizens in the U.S. are the Mexican-Americans. Nearly 1,000,000 Spanish-speaking children in the Southwest never will go beyond the eighth grade.[1] In some areas, up to 90% of the Mexican-Americans fail to complete high school.[2]

What are some of the causes of deprivation and failure among the Mexican-Americans? Four closely related areas are of concern: language, discrimination, lower socioeconomic status, and culture.

The most obvious identifying characteristic of the Mexican-Americans is their language. The Tucson Survey of the Teaching of Spanish to the Spanish-Speaking by the National Education Association placed great emphasis on the influence of the Spanish language and its use as related to academic achievement.[3] In fact, the language barrier currently is given more attention than any other factor affecting Mexican-American achievement.

The use of the Spanish language by the Mexican-Americans has played a definite role in the isolation and discrimination of these people by the Anglos. The preservation of the Spanish language has been interpreted by the dominant group as "a persistent symbol and instrument of isolation."[4] While the Anglo tends to consider the use of Spanish as an indication of foreignness, the Mexican-Americans consider it a symbol of their unity and loyalty to La Raza.[5]

In his discussion on barriers to Mexican integration, Officer stated that "the greatest hindrance to complete cultural assimilation of Tucson's Mexicans is the language problem."[6] Apparently, this opinion has been shared

---

[1] Department of Rural Education, National Education Association, *The Invisible Minority*, Report of the National Education Association-Tucson Survey on the Teaching of Spanish to the Spanish-Speaking (Washington: National Education Association, 1966), p. 6.

[2] John H. Chilcott, "Some Perspectives for Teaching First Generation Mexican-Americans," in John H. Chilcott, et al., eds., *Readings in the Socio-Cultural Foundations of Education* (Belmont, Calif.: Wadsworth, 1968), p. 359.

[3] *The Invisible Minority*, ibid.

[4] Leonard Broom and Eshref Shevsky, "Mexicans in the United States . . . A Problem in Social Differentiation," *Sociology and Social Research*, 36: 153, January-February, 1952.

[5] William Madsen, *The Mexicans of South Texas* (New York: Holt, Rinehart, and Winston, 1965), p. 106.

[6] James Officer, "Barriers to Mexican Integration in Tucson," *The Kiva*, 17: 7, May, 1951.

REPRINTED from *School & Society*, January 1970, by permission of the author and the publisher.

widely by educators, if we can judge from the adjustments made for Mexican-Americans in curricula.

There is evidence that the language barrier, although important, may be overrated. Available research shows that language need not be an insurmountable barrier to the academic and intellectual achievement of youngsters who come from foreign language-speaking homes.[7] Henderson points out that "the current mania for structural linguistics as a panacea for educational problems of Mexican-American children is another example of a language centered curriculum emphasis."[8] Moreover, he shows that the Mexican-American pupils who spoke the most Spanish also could speak the most English.[9] Nevertheless, most educators consider the language barrier as the major obstacle to the Mexican-American's success and achievement in school.

There is substantial evidence, however, that the greater emphasis should be placed on the socio-cultural problems of the Mexican-American. The ugly factors of discrimination and prejudice have played and continue to play an important role in keeping the Mexican-Americans in a subservient position. The Mexican coming to the U.S. is confronted with a double problem of prejudice. In Mexico, class discrimination is commonplace, but discrimination against color is unusual. Here, unfortunately, discrimination and prejudice commonly are based on both class and color.

Prejudice against the Mexicans and Mexican-Americans in the Southwest generally follows this pattern: lack of job opportunities, lack of educational opportunities, segregation in housing, lack of equality before the law, and various kinds of social discrimination.[10] Among the major reasons for this situation are a strong history of lower socioeconomic status, darker skin color, language, conflicting cultural traits and customs, and religion.

For the most part, discrimination against the Mexican-Americans is subtle in nature. While the Mexican-American enjoys all the legal rights of citizenship, he is the victim of extralegal discrimination. It is this special type of discrimination which led Tuck to call her book *Not with the Fist*. In it, she comments: "Rather than having the job of battering down a wall, the Mexican-American finds himself entangled in a spider web, whose outlines are difficult to see but whose clean, silken strands hold tight."[11]

The inferior socioeconomic status of the Mexican-Americans may be greater than most Americans would like to admit. Although Mexican-Americans are found in all walks of life, an examination of the 1960 U.S. Census

[7] Leona Elizabeth Tyler, *The Psychology of Human Differences* (New York: Appleton-Century-Crofts, 1956), p. 305.

[8] Ronald W. Henderson, *Environmental Stimulation and Intellectual Development of Mexican-American Children: An Exploratory Study* (Unpublished Ph.D. dissertation, University of Arizona, 1966), p. 142.

[9] Ibid., p. 144.

[10] John H. Burma, *Spanish-Speaking Groups in the United States* (Durham, N.C.: Duke University Press, 1954), p. 107.

[11] Ruth Tuck, *Not with the Fist* (New York: Harcourt, Brace, 1946), p. 198.

data shows that they occupy an overwhelmingly large position in the lower-ranking occupations. Almost 75% of the Mexican-Americans are employed as manual workers. This concentration in the unskilled occupations has had a severe effect upon their incomes. The 1960 Census data indicate that the Mexican-Americans in the Southwest earned between $1,000 and $2,000 less per year than did the Anglo unskilled workers. In all of the five Southwestern states, the average incomes of Mexican-Americans are far below that of the population in general.

The greatest barrier to the acculturation, assimilation, and achievement of the Mexican-Americans probably is culture conflict. Other immigrant groups to the U.S. have felt the blow of discrimination.[12] The Chinese, Jews, Italians, Irish, Polish, etc., are common examples. However, the faster the immigrant group moves toward adopting the customs and language of the dominant culture, the less discrimination they seem to experience.[13] Madsen believes that any ethnic group that fails to show a maximum faith in America, science, and progress will be subject to discrimination. It would be additionally difficult for the members of this group to assimilate if they are physically distinguishable, if they use a foreign language, and if they hold to cultural ways that are not compatible with the dominant culture.[14]

Unlike other immigrant groups, the Mexican-Americans have preferred to hold to their Mexican cultural ways and Spanish language. This may be attributed to their close proximity to Mexico.

The question then arises: Which of the Mexican-American cultural ways is in greatest conflict with the dominant Anglo culture? Extensive and careful review of numerous studies by Angell, Chilcott, Kluckhohn, Madsen, Simmons, Strodtbeck, Zintz, and others indicates that there are two Mexican cultural characteristics that are the mirror image of the Anglo culture. These are concerned with feelings of personal control (fatalism) and delay of gratification (future orientation). Could it be that even third- or fourth-generation Mexican-American students are actually more fatalistic and present-time oriented than their Anglo peers? What might this mean in terms of curriculums and cultural conflict?

To answer these questions, the writer set up an exploratory study at the College of Education, University of Arizona.[15] A total of 168 male, Mexican-American seniors and 209 male, Anglo seniors were selected randomly for testing at four urban Tucson high schools. A special questionnaire, adapted from a similar instrument developed by the Institute of Behavioral Science, University of Colorado, was revised, judged for content validity, tested for reliability, and then administered to the sample population.

[12] Raymond W. Mack, *Race, Class and Power* (New York: American Book Co., 1963), p. 118.

[13] Ibid., p. 118.

[14] Madsen, op. cit., p. 1.

[15] Neal Justin, *The Relationships of Certain Socio-Cultural Factors to the Academic Achievement of Male, Mexican-American, High School Seniors* (unpublished Ed.D. dissertation, University of Arizona, 1969).

The statistical analysis of the data pertaining to the two cultural character-istics of delayed gratification (future orientation) and feelings of personal control (fatalism) provided a number of significant differences when the means of the two sample populations were subjected to independent tests.

The Mexican-Americans showed a mean of 6.90 on the measurement of their feelings of personal control, while their Anglo peers had a mean of 8.51. Measurement of the tendency to delay gratification provided a mean of 3.99 for the Mexican-Americans and 4.63 for the Anglos. In each case, the differ-ences between these means were significant at the .05 level.

Marked contrast, therefore, is seen between the Mexican-Americans and the Anglos. The Mexican-Americans are significantly lacking in feelings of personal control and concern with delayed gratification when compared to their Anglo peers. These findings indicate that, whatever culture change has taken place among the second-, third-, and fourth-generation Mexican-Amer-icans, it has not been great with reference to these two characteristics. It also should be considered that the students selected for this study were second-semester seniors and were, therefore, a select group of achievers in relation to their many peers who already have dropped out of school. One may have good cause to wonder how great these differences would have been if the study had been done with junior high students. Even with these very con-servative results, the Mexican-Americans are seen to be significantly different from their Anglo peers.

Assuming that most of our school curricula are constructed by Anglos who apparently have significantly different orientations to life, then what over-all effect does this have upon the Mexican-American youngsters? What conflicts may be built into the curriculum that could permeate the whole subculture of education. Kneller provides a word to the wise when he asserts that, before we can attain our educational goals, we must be aware of the internalized antagonisms of the culture that may thwart the efforts of teach-ers.[16] Could it be that our Anglo-dominated curricula inadvertently thwart the efforts of both the Mexican-American students and their teachers? There may be a good reason to consider the findings of this study. Perhaps, we should examine the appropriateness of our curricula as they apply to the Mexican-American student in particular.

[16] George F. Kneller, *Educational Anthropology: An Introduction* (New York: Wiley, 1965), p. 14.

The Present Failure to Educate
the American Indian

ROBERT B. KAPLAN

The anomie exemplified in the following poem, which was written by Daveen Graybeal, a 12th-grade Indian boy from Rapid City, S. Dak., is typical of the central psychological problem of the American Indian today, caught as he is between two worlds.

LISTEN TO THE DRUMS

i sit here all alone trying to
find myself.
from the distant hills i hear the
drums of my people.
they are calling out to me, i hear
them but i can't answer.
i am a half-breed, part of me belongs to my tribe but . . .
the other part does not. do i have
the right to answer,
to claim the heritage i have in my
blood?
do i have the right to answer the
call of the drums?
i have been raised away from the
drums.
by color, i am white, in my heart
i am both.
can i expect my people to honor my
blood when i have never honored it.
only now has it become real . . . and
a part of me.
i only know how to be white, never
before have i been red.
i hear the drums, they're louder.
i want to answer them,
to go to the holy men of the tribe,
they are wise.
i know they can help me, if they only
would . . .
i want to learn the old ways and
teach my people the new

FROM Brickman and Lehrer (Eds.), *Education and the Many Faces of the Disadvantaged* (New York: John Wiley & Sons, Inc., 1972), pp. 153–63. Reprinted by permission of John Wiley & Sons, Inc.

but i am not sure they can be patient
with me till the knowledge comes.
the drums are dying now.
they have set me wondering of new
problems,
and knowing the goal i must fight
to obtain,
the answer to the call of the
drums, the drums of my people.
i sit here all alone trying to
find myself.
it is silent.
i no longer hear the drums.

The situation, the state of mind, of this young boy may be demonstrated in its implications by a look at some cold, hard facts. Bruce Gaarder, chief, Modern Foreign Language Section, U.S. Office of Education, speaking before the Senate Special Subcommittee on Indian Education in the 90th Congress, December, 1967, cited the following "Salient Facts": Total population of all ages (Bureau of Indian Affairs, 1960), 553,000; total age 6–18 (Bureau of Indian Affairs, 1966), 152,114; enrolled in public schools, 86,827; enrolled in federal schools, 46,154; enrolled in Mission and other schools, 8,713; not in school, 7,757; not located, 2,663.[1] Senator Paul J. Fannin, testifying before the same Senate subcommittee, stated that, ". . . of the 142,000 Indian children in school, 50% drop out before the 12th grade. In 1966 it was determined that at least 16,000 school age Indian children did not attend school at all. . . . Among the Navaho, our largest tribe, it is estimated that 40,000 are illiterate and cannot speak English. . . . 50% [of all Indians] are unemployed, housing is 90% substandard, average life span is 42 years (compared to national average of 62.3 years), infant mortality is five times the national average, one in five deaths result from infectious diseases, incidence of tuberculosis is seven times the national average, the birthrate . . . is more than double the national average. . . ."[2]

Estelle Fuchs reports: "In 1900 when most children in this country had at least an elementary education, only one out of every ten Navaho children was in school and then for only a year or two. In 1949, one out of every four Navahos was attending school. By 1950, there were schools available for only half of the eligible Navaho children. . . . By 1964 there were 38,117 Navaho children in school, an increase of 23,000 [since] 1953. Symptomatic of the

[1] *Indian Education:* Hearings before the Special Subcommittee on Indian Education of the Committee on Labor and Public Welfare (Washington: U.S. Government Printing Office, 1969), Vol. I, p. 67.

[2] *Indian Education:* Hearings before the Special Subcommittee on Indian Education of the Committee on Labor and Public Welfare (Washington: U.S. Government Printing Office, 1969), Vol. I, p. 9.

deficiency is the fact that among Navahos twenty-five years or older, the average length of schooling has been two years. . . ." [3]

Senator Fannin testifies that "the median number of school years completed by the adult Cherokee population as a whole is only 5.5." [4] He points out that 40% of all adult Cherokee are functiónally illiterate in English and that only 39% have had an eighth grade education. In 1963, the median annual income per person among the Cherokee people was less than $550.

Ronnie Lupe, chairman, White Mountain Apache Tribe, testifies that the unemployment rate among the 5,300 White Mountain Apaches is 50%, that the infant mortality rate is 99.2 per 1,000, and that the average life expectancy is between 40 and 46. [5] According to Henry Montague, president, Quechon Tribal Council, the Pima Community ". . . more and more has a need for college trained individuals but has not had a college graduate in over 30 years." [6]

These facts are, indeed, almost incredible. That one of the most technically developed nations in the world, a nation capable of sending men to the moon, of helping to feed the hungry all over the world, of maintaining an enormous military establishment, could ignore so completely more than half a million of its own citizens seems somehow unreal. Quite aside from any collective guilt feelings relating to the dispossession of the Indian from his ancestral lands, simple humanity cries out against an "oversight" of such magnitude.

Yet, the situation has improved. The schools at Rough Rock and at Many Farms, Arizona, are doing some remarkable things. Many of the agencies involved in Indian education have developed more realistic attitudes toward the Indians in general. There are hardly any instances of strict prohibition of the use of the tribal language; there are only isolated instances of corporal punishment of Indian children for minor infractions, and there is a growing tendency to recognize the validity of the Indian cultures and languages.

These forward steps have been many years in coming. Like the young militants among the black communities and among the Mexican-American communities, the younger Indians are rapidly growing impatient. The pressures they have exerted and will continue to exert will, as they have in other minority communities, tend to produce hasty and half-baked efforts to expedite the process. Panaceas are being proposed which have the expected efficacy—nothing.

[3] Estelle Fuchs, "Innovation at Rough Rock: Learning to Be Navaho-Americans," *Saturday Review*, 82–84, September 16, 1967.

[4] *Indian Education:* Hearings before the Special Subcommittee on Indian Education of the Committee on Labor and Public Welfare (Washington: U.S. Government Printing Office, 1969), Vol. II, p. 540.

[5] *Indian Education:* Hearings before the Special Subcommittee on Indian Education of the Committee on Labor and Public Welfare (Washington: U.S. Government Printing Office, 1969), Vol. III, p. 1007.

[6] Ibid., p. 1013.

We need massive, but carefully planned activities that will attack the root of the problem instead of leveling out a few surface blemishes. Language is a basic problem and, since language and culture are inseparable, culture is a problem.

In 1962, Wallace Chafe said that nearly 300 different recognizable American Indian languages were in use in the United States and Alaska. (That means that there were also nearly 300 different tribal groups.) However, only about 40% of these are spoken by more than 100 persons.[7] In about half of these language-tribal groups, the only remaining speakers are of advanced age. Thus, within a generation, some 160 of these languages may perish, may become extinct, may never again be heard by men. Chafe also found that about 45 of the languages are presently spoken by more than 1,000 people.[8] An estimate made in 1964 indicates that some 60% of school age (6–18) children in states with special Indian schools and 20% in states which put Indian children in public schools retain some use of their native languages.[9] These estimates may be low since individual tribal groups may have retained the language in as much as 91% of the population. Hard data are almost impossible to get because individuals may, for a variety of reasons, conceal information.

Of the 45 languages spoken by more than 1,000 persons, only seven have adequate reading and considerable literacy among the speakers; two do not even have written forms, 29 have no reading materials and no literacy among native speakers. The remainder have some materials and some literacy. Thus, some 85,000 Indian people, speaking 29 separate major languages, have nothing to read in their native languages and would be unable to read it if they had it.[10] And there are some 250 languages for which information is not available.

Tests administered to Indian children show that, in both verbal and nonverbal skills, they, like average pupils from other minority groups, score significantly lower than average Caucasian pupils at every grade level and that the gap is significantly greater in the twelfth grade than it is in the first. Thus, Indian children fall farther behind their Caucasian peers each year they remain in school. It is not surprising that the Navaho have produced only one professional with advanced academic degrees. It is not surprising that only one percent of Indian children in elementary school have Indian teachers and only one percent have Indian principals (in secondary school two percent have Indian teachers and none have Indian principals).

[7] "Estimates Regarding the Present Speakers of North American Indian Languages." *International Journal of American Linguistics*, 27: 3, January, 1962.

[8] "Estimates Regarding the Present Speakers of North American Indian Languages." *International Journal of American Linguistics*, 31: 4, January, 1965.

[9] Cited by Bruce Gaarder in *Indian Education*, 1969, loc. cit.

[10] "Extent of Literacy Materials for 45 Indian Languages Spoken by 1,000 or More Persons of All Ages in the United States," in *Indian Education* (Hearings of February 9, 1968), Vol. II, p. 541.

Indian children consistently characterize themselves as "below average" and "poorly prepared." Their self-image has consistently been beaten down by repeated failure and by the attitudes of Caucasian teachers and administrators. Some 25% of all teachers dealing with Indian children report that they would prefer not to teach them (they would prefer to teach Caucasian children). As a result, the Cherokee, for example, show a level of educational achievement two full school years lower than the black population. They are, in the words of Senator Fannin, ". . . the least educated group of people in the State [Oklahoma]. . . . Others of the Five Civilized Tribes —Creek, Choctaw, Chickasaw, Seminole—have roughly the same educational levels as do Cherokees." [11]

As noted above, massive efforts are needed in the area of language and culture. Some efforts are now being made. A number of schools offer courses in English as a second language (ESL), but that alone, on the basis on which it frequently is offered, is not nearly enough. Most commonly, English as a second language is offered as a remedial course, meeting three to five hours per week for as many terms as appear necessary to provide the student with enough English ability so that he can move into the main stream of the curriculum. Most commonly the approach employed is the oral/aural approach. This concept appears inadequate on three counts.

English as a second language is not in any sense remedial. It is often assumed that any student who is not prepared to read at grade level needs some sort of remediation. That assumption is commonly in error, but it is especially so in the second-language situation. French or Spanish language instruction is not considered remedial for native English-speaking students. English is, on the same basis, not remedial for native speakers of Spanish, or Navaho, or Swahili. The attachment of the stigma of remediation to ESL courses tends to dispel the motivation of the student, to degrade the content of the course, and to malign the teacher.

A course which provides 48 hours of instruction over a period of four months (16 weeks, three hours per week) hardly can be considered successful. John Carroll has pointed out that somewhere between 400 and 800 continuous contact-hours of instruction are necessary to implement any significant change in language behavior. Furthermore, it has been shown that, if the 400–800 hours is administered too slowly, the rate of learning drops below the rate of forgetting; and that, if the instruction is administered too quickly, the psychological pressure may become so great as to produce anomie, identity crisis, or other serious problems. Depending on the age and motivation of the learner, somewhere between 20 and 30 hours per week appears optimal if the instructional period can be extended to 20 or 30 continuous weeks. Obviously, during this period of intensive instruction in language, the student will be unable to study other subjects and may drop behind his peer group. But, although the

[11] Ibid.

danger is admitted, it would appear to be far less a danger than allowing a student to fall behind in smaller increments over a period of twelve years so that by grade 12 or earlier he is literally forced to become a drop-out.

The oral/aural approach, at least as it is currently practiced by most teachers, contains one or more factors which assure failure. The technique, as practiced, calls for the instructor to drill the student in oral structures of the language until the student internalizes the patterns. Properly used in just proportion with other approaches, this technique will produce adequate results. But used as it presently is, the approach succeeds only in making the learner into a parrot capable only of repeating the patterns generated by the instructor or by the textbook. Thus, the technique can produce relatively good performance but it is unlikely to produce competence in the language. Competence may be defined as the ability to use all aspects of the language with near-native skill to produce and to receive completely original and unique utterances expressive of the intellect and personality of the speaker.

It is exactly in relation to this third problem that the massive effort is necessary. The oral/aural approach contains the implicit assumption that language consists only of a phonology, a morphology, and a set of grammatical rules, of finite number, capable of being reduced to formuli and learned as formuli in a short time. That assumption, while it is in part valid, ignores vast areas in the communication process. It ignores all the concepts of nonverbal communication which act in any given situation to furnish the communicants with clues as to the relationship between them, the level of formality, the reaction of one to the other, and so on. In short, the oral/aural technique, as it is practiced, seems to ignore the fact that communication occurs between real people in real situations.

In real situations, among real people, the following areas (and many others) become real concerns. First, the physical distance between speakers. In each culture there exists, for the bulk of the individuals within that culture, a sense of the appropriate distances for specified kinds of communication. Thus, in the Anglo-culture, businessmen separate themselves by the physical barrier of the desk or the conference table; casual conversations occur at handshaking distance, and intimate conversations at hand-holding distance. But in other cultures other rules apply. Unacculturated Indians are made uncomfortable, for example, by the desk barrier.

Second, touch taboos. Anglo teachers who wish to express their affection for a child do so by patting the child or by an affectionate hug. Indian children do not expect such signs and may be embarrassed by them. People from the Middle East accept public hand-holding as a sign of affection among men; Anglos do not. It is perfectly acceptable for one football player to pat another on the posterior as a gesture of congratulation for a good play, but U.S. Senators do not use such contact on the floor of the Senate to congratulate each other for good speeches.

Third, eye contact. Anglo teachers expect to maintain eye contact with students. But students from other cultures, including some Indian cultures, have been taught to look down as a sign of respect for adults.

Fourth, linguistic matters. Often, a message is conveyed not so much by lexical content, by words in the message, as by the suprasegmental characteristics of the message—the tone of voice, the inflection, the pitch. When English speakers greet each other in passing with some phrase as "Hi, How are you?" they characteristically raise pitch, increase rate, and slur. The vocal features carry the message, and other words can easily be substituted—even vulgar ones—so long as the vocal characteristics are maintained. But this same set of vocal characteristics may carry other messages in other languages. In some linguistic systems the same set of vocal features may indicate anger or irritation. The English speaker may thus appear to be hypocritical since his physical manner is not in accord with his vocal signals.

Indian children may lack the linguistic frames for certain types of polite utterances. The frame "Would you please . . ." does not exist in Navaho, for example. A Navaho child may say "Give me water," instead of "Would you please give me a drink of water." He is not trying to be rude; rather he is using English words in a frame familiar to him in his own language.

Fifth, control of units beyond the sentence. Once the student has learned to control individual syntactic units—that is, to write individual sentences containing proper word order, agreement, and modification—he still must learn to control larger structures. He must relate material in terms of subordination and coordination—in terms of logical relationship—in such a way that the logical expectations of native readers are not violated. Speakers of certain languages, for example, rely much more heavily on structures of coordination while native English speakers rely more heavily on structures of subordination. In part, this is a manifestation of grammar, since English contains many more syntactic devices for subordination than it does for coordination while other languages may have different distributions of the syntactic capabilities.[12]

Sixth, world view. Each language permits its speakers to view the phenomenological world in certain ways and only in those ways. Speakers of Eskimo have a far larger inventory of lexical items for the phenomenon English speakers designate with the one word "snow." That does not imply that Eskimo eyes are physiologically different from Caucasian eyes; rather it means that speakers of Eskimo are conditioned by the interaction of language and environment to view this "real" phenomenon in the phenomenological world quite differently than speakers of other languages. Speakers of English employ active voice statements to indicate that they view themselves as active operant entities in a universe in which they can initiate actions in terms of their own wills and in which the actions which they initiate can affect other beings, both animate and inanimate. But many speakers of Indian languages live in a world in which they function as passive recipients of action, in which

[12] Robert B. Kaplan, "Cultural Thought Patterns in Inter-Cultural Education," *Language Learning*, 16: 1–20, 1966.

their individual wills play no role (perhaps do not even exist), and in which they have no direct power to influence other beings. Thus, speakers of English can posit the meaningful utterance "I see you." But speakers of some Indian languages can neither generate the utterance in terms of the linguistic capabilities of their language nor understand it as meaningful when it is generated by another speaker. They can approximate the idea only by some such statement as "you appear to me." [13]

Seventh, conflicting views of the role of education. The way in which students and teacher view each other linguistically determines to a large extent the potential success of the educational process. Students (and parents) often view the teacher as an antagonistic force. This view may be related to economic or social origins in cultures of poverty in which labor provided by the child is an important factor in survival and in which the economic level of the teacher may be viewed as unattainable and therefore alien. But the problem is also likely to have a linguistic base. The Navaho, for example, have a world view which divides all human beings into two polarized sets—Navaho and others. The Navaho word which designates all non-Navahos, while it often is interpreted to mean "others," really means "enemies." It is easy for an Anglo teacher to regard any cultural group that has no written language, that lives at the level of subsistence economy, and that prefers to live in virtual isolation in an inhospitable climate and terrain, as primitive and, hence, childlike. The teacher is likely to view the learning of English as a maturation process leading to adulthood. Thus, the Eskimo or Indian who speaks English inadequately may be viewed as an adult by his own people but as a child by the Anglo teacher. The Eskimo child is treated in a more adult fashion at an earlier age in his own culture than Anglo children are. Indeed, the Eskimo family has far more real regard for individual differences than has the Anglo family. The child's thoughts and opinions are sacred. When the Eskimo child is placed in the situation of learning English from a teacher who regards him as a child, indeed who regards his parents as children, he associates the role of child with language. The Eskimo learns and uses English in a condition of dependency; it is a code used with authority figures—teachers, government figures, missionaries, job foremen. These authority figures frequently adopt parental roles. Thus, the teacher forces the child to regard language as role criteria.[14]

Many Indian cultural groups have no written language. Anglo children, of course, tend to come out of basically literate environments. Anglo children tend to respect literacy as a value in itself. Indeed, some of the more militant leaders in Indian communities are pressing for strong cultural identity among their people. Cultural identity is often related to values transmitted

[13] Leo Spitzer, "Language—The Basis of Science, Philosophy, and Poetry," in George Boas, et al., eds., *Studies in Intellectual History* (Baltimore: Johns Hopkins Press, 1953), pp. 83–84.

[14] Lee H. Salisbury, "Role Conflict in Native Communication," *Teachers of English to Speakers of Other Languages Quarterly*, 2: 187–192, April, 1969.

in the literary tradition. Even among those Indian languages which have been reduced to written form, no real written literary tradition exists; the tradition is oral. Thus, there is no special respect for or motivation toward learning a written form. An Indian child is educated, outside the school, by example. He receives a cooperative orientation toward life in his society. He learns from watching adults, from listening to stories in the oral tradition (stories which are often allegorical), from observation of members of his society in inter-action with each other and with the environment. He is never consciously taught. His learning style is completely alien to the formal school situation.

Quite aside from learning style, these same factors militate against compe-tition in the sense in which it is often fostered in the Anglo classroom. In a tribal society operating on the tightly knit group at the subsistence level of existence, communal activity is essential. The worst punishment possible is ostracism, ritual murder by the group when it ceases to recognize the existence of one of its members. A child so oriented cannot compete by being "better" or "cleverer" than the other members of his social group because he cannot risk the price.[15]

Eighth, problems in cognition. Both the nature of particular languages and the nature of poverty tend to affect cognitive processes. The Indian cuts up the spectrum in quite a different way than the native English speaker does. It is therefore not enough to tell a young Indian child that the apple in his picture book is "red." Anglo children are taught color and space concepts in kindergarten. The Indian child must be taught two sets of such concepts—his own and those appropriate to English. In cultures of poverty, individuals are likely to own only one of any particular kind of item. Under these circum-stances the child may lack entirely, or be severely limited in, the conceptual ability to compare and contrast. He may even lack the lexical items "bigger" and "smaller." [16] On the same basis, the child from a culture of poverty may be unfamiliar with the concept "set" since his family probably does not possess a "set of dishes," or a "set of silver," or a "set of books." Modern mathematics is based on the concept of "set." If the child lacks the concept, he may be inhibited in learning in other areas which seem only vaguely related to language.

These are a few of the problems directly related to language learning which are presently ignored in language teaching.[17] But these problems are the

[15] Anita Pfeiffer, in a personal conversation, Rough Rock Demonstration School, Ari-zona, May 28, 1969.

[16] Newton Metfessel, in an unpublished report presented at the Second Annual Con-ference on Language Testing, Idyllwild, Calif., November, 1968.

[17] Pertinent additional reading: Jerome Bruner, "On Going Beyond the Information Given," in Robert J. C. Harper, et al., eds., Cognitive Processes: Readings (Englewood Cliffs, N.J.: Prentice-Hall, 1964); Francis Christensen, Notes Toward a New Rhetoric: Six Essays for Teachers (New York: Harper & Row, 1967); Mikel Dufrenne, Language and Philosophy, Henry B. Veatch, trans. (Bloomington: Indiana University Press, 1963); Alfred S. Hayes, "New Directions in Foreign Language Teaching," Modern Language Journal, 49: 281–293, May 1965; Robert B. Kaplan, "Contrastive Grammar: Teaching Composition to the Chinese Student," Journal of English as a Second Language, 3: 1–14,

proper and immediate concern of language teachers. It should be obvious that no single methodology can possibly cope with such a broad spectrum of problems. As has been pointed out several times, what is urgently needed is a massive approach. Single methodologies, even intelligently applied, can only eliminate single aspects of the broad problem; in a way, partial solutions may be more dangerous than no solutions because they hold out to the deprived the promise of a relief which is illusory. A nation capable of sending men to the moon should be capable of learning to teach little children who only wish to aspire to what their Anglo peers have had long enough to take for granted. The cost of one average week's material losses in Vietnam would provide the teacher training and research necessary to implement the kind of massive approach required. This essay [18] is neither a pacifist plea nor a militant response. The references to political and military events in the real world outside of education are only points of reference from which to consider the value of 600,000 people in urgent need as opposed to developments in other sectors of society. The massive effort necessary to meet the problem is well within the capability of the government and the academic community.

The following steps could be undertaken in the immediate future: Research designed to preserve those languages which are on the verge of extinction; research in the linguistico-cultural structure of those larger language groups whose languages have not been adequately studied; development of pedagogical materials in both language and culture designed to meet the specific needs of particular language communities; training of teachers to use the new materials; training of teachers to understand the problems of the communities in which they are going to teach; training of Indian specialists to staff all of the preceding categories; training of Indian specialists to supervise all of the preceding activities; and training of Indian specialists to develop whatever steps are necessary beyond this point.

While there is a building pressure to institute immediate action programs, the panic for action must not be allowed to supercede the need for intelligent and organized action. Massive effort is necessary, but massive effort is time-consuming. Perhaps what is most necessary now is the courage to abjure

---

1968; "491391625162541253661," *Journal of English as a Second Language*, 4: 7–18, Spring, 1969; "Contrastive Rhetoric and the Teaching of Composition," *Teachers of English to Speakers of Other Languages Quarterly*, 1: 10–16, December 1967; "On a Note of Protest . . . ," *College English*, 30: 386–389, February 1969; Paul Lorenzen, *Logik und Grammatik* (Mannheim: Bibliographisches Institut, 1965); William Ritchie, "Implications of Generative Grammar," *Language Learning*, 17: 45–69, July 1967, and 1: 111–131, December 1967; Edward Sapir, *Culture, Language, and Personality* (Los Angeles: University of California Press, 1964); Valter Tauli, ed., *Proceedings of the Ninth International Congress of Linguistics* (The Hague: Mouton, 1964); U.S. Department of the Interior, Bureau of Indian Affairs, Division of Education, *Fiscal Year 1968 Statistics Concerning Indian Education* (1968); Albert Valdman, *Trends in Language Teaching* (New York: McGraw-Hill, 1966); Benjamin Lee Whorf, *Language, Thought, and Reality* (Cambridge: MIT Press, 1956).
[18] The author would like to acknowledge the assistance of Mrs. Mary K. Ludwig in the preparation of the manuscript and some of the initial research.

seeming panaceas and to start toward ultimate solutions. The problem concerns all of us and demands the best efforts and talents our society can muster.

Sexism in the Elementary School
CAROL JACOBS AND CYNTHIA EATON

"We are willing to share our thoughts with mankind. However, you happen to be a girl."

"Women's advice is not worth two pennies. Yours isn't even worth a penny."

"Look at her mother. She is just like a girl. She gives up."

"We don't want to play with girls," Jeff said. "They'd be too easy to beat."

"He didn't want anyone to talk about feeling sorry for him. He felt so sad he was afraid he might cry."

These quotes from widely used school readers are concrete examples of the narrow sex-role stereotyping of children that is taking place in classrooms everywhere.

The following quote comes from a teacher recruitment brochure in a school district with a reputation for being progressive. "Are you a female elementary school teacher searching for more effective ways to reach children? Join us as we experiment with team teaching and ungraded classes. Are you a male elementary school teacher with career goals in administration? Join us as we seek to develop education leadership for the future." The brochure is being rewritten, but the attitude behind it may take longer to change.

The subject of sexism in schools is becoming a major concern of people interested in child development. There is growing awareness of the damage done to individual growth by channeling people into narrow roles according to sex. School is only one facet of a child's world which contributes to stereotyping. However, because a large portion of a young person's life is spent in the classroom (10,000 hours by the time he or she graduates from high school), the messages transmitted to the child in school carry much weight.

What messages are children getting in school? A task force of the National Organization for Women in Princeton, New Jersey, initiated a two-year study of sex-role stereotyping in children's readers. The purpose of the study was to find a reading series which portrayed males and females in a nonstereotyped manner. Despite the fact that task force members read 134 books from 12 different publishers and carefully documented 2,760 stories, no such series was found.

The ratio of boy-centered stories to girl-centered stories was 5 to 2; the

FROM *Today's Education*, Vol. 61, No. 9 (December 1972), pp. 20–22.

ratio of stories with an adult male character to an adult female character was 3 to 1; the ratio of male biographies to female biographies was 6 to 1. Boys in the stories built and created things and used their wits. Girls rarely appeared in these roles. Clever girls appeared 33 times, clever boys 131. Boys showed initiative and were strong and brave; girls were rarely depicted as having these characteristics. When a girl mastered a grown-up skill, it was usually a domestic one. Boys were competitive, girls were not. Girls did not act independently; they were smaller and more fearful than boys.

The books showed adult males as jobholders and fathers, while adult females were jobholders *or* mothers. Mothers in the stories were colorless, mindless creatures, never shown as having any interests of their own. Fathers, on the other hand, were pictured as well-rounded, vibrant adults. It is father who does things with the children, helps them build things, takes them on outings, and solves their problems. Father is the person with whom children have fun.

Clearly, this is not a fair or balanced picture. As products of a sexist culture, teachers carry with them biases about what boys should be and what girls should be which may no longer be useful. The world into which our children will emerge is different from the conventional stereotype (mother, father, two children, dog and cat, white frame house). We must begin to face this and prepare children for life as it really is.

The key to dealing with sexism in the classroom is teacher awareness. Start with yourself. Do you have different expectations for boys than for girls? Do you expect girls to be more verbal and boys to be more mathematical and scientific? Do you expect boys to be more aggressive and active? Do you ever say to girls, "It isn't ladylike to talk like that!"

Teachers need to sort out their ideas and rethink many of the things they do. For example, do boys carry the books and operate the projectors in your class while girls dust the furniture and water the plants? If something is too heavy for a girl to carry, perhaps it's too heavy for any child that age to carry. Then again, maybe a girl could carry it. Female strength isn't understood; women are strong enough to carry bags of groceries or a child on each arm.

One of the best ways to increase one's sensitivity to how role conditioning is perpetuated is to analyze the books you use in your classroom. Why not do so, following the checklist in the box on page [325].

As your awareness increases, you will become much more sensitive to sexism. For example, you may see two girls on the playground watching some boys playing baseball. Do they really want to watch or would they like to play? You may see a tomboy having a wonderful time. When will she start to realize that she has to quiet down and start acting like a lady? And what about the boy who got hit in the head but is bravely holding back his tears? Isn't it wonderful that he's not a sissy! Or, would it be better if he expressed his emotions?

How can you break the vicious circle and change the pattern that children

EVALUATING SEXISM IN READERS

	MALE	FEMALE
1. Number of stories where main character is:	_____	_____
2. Number of illustrations of:	_____	_____
3. Number of times children are shown:	_____	_____
(a) in active play	_____	_____
(b) using initiative	_____	_____
(c) displaying independence	_____	_____
(d) solving problems	_____	_____
(e) earning money	_____	_____
(f) receiving recognition	_____	_____
(g) being inventive	_____	_____
(h) involving in sports	_____	_____
(i) fearful or helpless	_____	_____
(j) receiving help	_____	_____
4. Number of times adults are shown:		
(a) in different occupations	_____	_____
(b) playing with children	_____	_____
(c) taking children on outings	_____	_____
(d) teaching skills	_____	_____
(e) giving tenderness	_____	_____
(f) scolding children	_____	_____
(g) biographically	_____	_____

5. In addition, ask yourself these questions: Are boys allowed to show their emotions? Are girls rewarded for intelligence rather than for beauty? Are there any derogatory comments directed at girls in general? Is mother shown working outside the home? If so, in what kind of job? Are there any stories about one-parent families? Families without children? Are baby-sitters shown? Are minority and ethnic groups treated naturally?

accept so readily? Again, the main thrust is awareness—this time the children's. You can help them see the difference between what they really want to be and what they think they can be.

Take a poll. What do your students want to be when they grow up? Repeat the poll a month later—after you have encouraged them to evaluate their roles critically. See if more children step out of the stereotyped roles they had set for themselves. Do some girls now aspire to be doctors instead of nurses? Do any boys consider being librarians?

Ideally, teachers should stock their classrooms with books that present men and women in nonstereotyped roles, but even if you have the money to purchase them, such books are hard to find. (See a list of sources on page 29 of this special feature in *Today's Education*.)

Most of the time you will use books in which females are either forgotten or shown only in a nurturing role and where males are usually the heroes (often presenting a model impossible to copy).

It is important to deal with issues as they occur. For example, there is the story of a mother who can't get her young son down from a tree. She runs to get father to help, who comes out with a ladder.

This presents a good opportunity to ask the children: Could mother have gotten the ladder herself? What happens in their homes when there is a catastrophe and their fathers are at work? Now, ask the children: Have you noticed that mothers and young girls are usually portrayed as helpless in books? The children could then go back over the stories they've read to find instances where the mother is pictured as a helpless person. Can anyone find a story in which the mother is a problem solver?

Take a quick poll in your class. How many mothers work? (Only two instances of working mothers were found in 134 different readers.) What else do mothers do with their time besides cooking and cleaning? Your class may come up with a very long list of things mothers do. Then, ask the children to go through their readers. How many different things do mothers do in these stories? Is mother ever seen doing something for her own personal enjoyment?

As children become aware of sexism in books, they can explore other communication media. They might look through magazines and note the advertisements. How many products are sold because the ads contain the picture of a pretty girl? How many times are women shown as unable to do a simple task without the help of a man? ("This is so easy even a woman can do it.")

The children can also talk about TV programs. How are women depicted? What are they doing? Are they ever shown as intelligent, self-reliant individuals or are they usually irrational, dependent persons?

On game and quiz shows, is the master of ceremonies usually a male? Does a female contestant describe herself as being married to a lawyer and the mother of two lovely children—thus describing herself in terms of the other people in her life? Children can watch certain shows and then talk about the roles the characters play. The insight this will give them about their own lives may be far-reaching.

Children arrive in kindergarten armed with many attitudes about what boys and girls should do. Until recently, schools merely reinforced these ideas. But society is changing rapidly. Single parent families, situations where mother works and father stays at some, and extended families are already joining the traditional family pattern as acceptable life-styles.

Should the job of education be to prepare children to meet change? Should each child be offered as many alternatives as possible? Should the role of education be to stretch people's minds and make them more aware of the options? The answer to these questions is undoubtedly "Yes!"

E. The Nonschool Socializing System

The Generation Gap

EDGAR Z. FRIEDENBERG

The idea that what separates us from the young is something so passive that it may justly be called a "generation gap" is, I believe, itself a misleading article of middle-aged liberal ideology, serving to allay anxiety rather than to clarify the bases of intergenerational conflict. It is true, to be sure, that the phrase is strong enough to describe the barrier that separates many young people from their elders, for a majority still accept our society as providing a viable pattern of life and expectations for the future. Liberalism dies hard, and most young people, like some Negroes even today, are still willing to attribute their difficulties with their elders and society to mutual misunderstanding.

I believe, however, that this is a false position. Though most adults maintain a benevolent posture in expressing their public attitudes toward youth and—though, I think steadily fewer—young people still accept this as what their elders intend in principle, both young and old seem trapped in a false view of what is actually a profound conflict of interest in our society. What appears to be a consequence of mere cultural lag in responding to a new social and political maturity in the young, with distressing but unintended repressive consequences, is rather the expression of what has become genuine class-conflict between a dominant and exploitive older generation and youth who are slowly becoming more aware of what is happening to them as demands on them are, in the language of the time, escalated.[1]

DISCONTINUITY IN AN OPEN SOCIETY

In all societies, so far as I know, young people enter the social system in subordinate roles while older people run things. This is true even in technically primitive cultures where the crude physical strength of youth is still of real productive advantage. Is there always a generational conflict? And, if so, does it always reflect as profound a division, and as severe a conflict of interest, as generational conflict in America today?

[1] I am indebted to John and Margaret Rowntree, of York University and the University of Toronto, respectively, for demonstrating, in their paper "The Political Economy of Youth in the United States," the class-dynamics of generational conflict. This document, prepared for presentation at the First Annual Meeting of the Committee on Socialist Studies in Calgary, Alberta, in June 1968, was published in the Montreal quarterly journal *Our Generation*, Vol. 6, No. 1, 1968. Their radical analysis simplifies many apparent paradoxes in the relationship between the generations.

REPRINTED from "The Generation Gap" by Edgar Z. Friedenberg in *The Annals* of The American Academy of Political and Social Science, Protest in the Sixties, Book Department: New Literature in the Field of the Social Sciences, Philadelphia, March 1969, Vol. 382, pp. 32–42.

There is, I believe, indeed an inherent basis for such a conflict in the fact that the old dominate the young and the young wish to replace them, but it is not as severe in most societies as in ours. Here, it has become different in kind, as the brightest and most articulate of the young declare that they will not even accept, when their turn comes, the kinds of roles—in the kind of society—which their parents have held. As Bruno Bettelheim [2] pointed out in a classic paper some years ago, factors that have traditionally mitigated generational conflict have become feeble or inoperative even in this country. The family, for example, which is the context within which the strongest—albeit ambivalent—affectual ties between the generations are formed, plays a decreasing role in the lives of its members and, certainly, in the socialization of the young. It has less effect on their life-chances than it once had. If the Victorian father or the head of a traditional rural household was often a tyrant, and more or less accepted as such by his neighbors and his children, he was also a man who felt that he could transmit his wealth, his trade, and his position in the community, by inheritance. His relationship to his sons was not purely competitive but complementary as well: it was they who would have to carry on his work as his own powers failed, and on whom he was therefore ultimately dependent if his accomplishment in life was to lead to anything permanent. The proper attitude of father to son—both the authority and the underlying tenderness—took account of this mutual though unequal dependency. And while excessive and inconsiderate longevity in a father might make his son's position grotesque, as that of mad old George III did to the Prince Regent's position, the problems of succession were usually made less abrasive by the recognition of mutual need.

Moreover, so long as society changed slowly, elders really knew more that was useful than the young did; they were wiser; their authority was based on real superiority in the subtle techniques of living. This was never a very strong bond between the generations in America, where the sons of immigrants have always been as likely to find their greenhorn parents a source of embarrassment as of enlightenment; and generational conflict has probably always been more severe here than in more stable cultures—or would have been had there not also been a continent to escape into and develop.

But today, the older generation has become not merely an embarrassment, but often an obstructive irrelevance to the young. We cannot even defend our former functions with respect to youth; for the ethos of modern liberalism condemns as inequitable, and a violation of equal opportunity, the arrangements on which continuity between the generations has been based. Bourgeois emphasis on private property and the rights of inheritance gave to the family the function of providing this continuity, which, under feudal conditions, would have been shared among several institutions—apprenticeship, for example. But the development of an open, bureaucratic society has weakened

2 Bruno Bettelheim, "The Problem of Generations," *Daedalus*, Vol. 91, No. 1 (Winter 1962), pp. 68–96.

the influence of the family, and has transferred the task of distributing status among claimants primarily to the schools, which profess to judge them, so far as possible, without regard to their antecedents.

Today, college admissions officers agree that the sons of alumni should not be favored over more gifted applicants who seek admission solely on the basis of their academic record and recommendations. But this amounts to redefining merit to mean the kind of performance and personality that high school teachers and, increasingly, counselors like. Counselors now virtually control many a high school student's future chances, by their decision whether to assign him to a college-preparatory course, and by monitoring his applications for admission. Whether this whole process makes the contest more open, or merely changes the criteria for preferment, is hard to say.[3]

The effect of the high school, and especially of the counselor, on continuity of status between the generations, and hence on the bond between the generations, is the subject of a fascinating study—still little known after five years—by Aaron V. Cicourel and John I. Kitsuse.[4] While the entire work bears on this issue, one particular interview excerpt is worth quoting here because of the clarity with which it shows a high school student from an upper-status suburban home being punished for his lack of humility in school by restriction of his future chances. This young man had already been classed by his counselor as an "underachiever." Here are some of the counselors' comments to Cicourel and Kitsuse's interview:

COUNSELOR: His mother says he's a pleasant outgoing boy. His teachers will say he's either a pleasant boy or that he's a pest. I think he's arrogant. He thinks he's handsome. He's nice-looking, but not handsome. He thinks he owns Lakeshore. He talks to his teachers as if they were stupid. He's a good student. He's in biology and algebra honors.
INTERVIEWER: Is he going to college?
COUNSELOR: He plans college. I think he said he plans to go East like MIT, Harvard, etc. He won't make it. He's a candidate for a midwestern school.[5]

This excerpt, of course, illustrates certain very positive reasons for conflict between youth and older people: the constraint imposed by the school and its basic disrespect for its young captive. But I have introduced it here specifically to call attention to the fact that the school is here destroying the basis for continuity in the home by making it a condition—for higher- as well as for lower-status students—that the student *unlearn* what the home has taught him about himself if he wishes to retain access to his family's present socioeconomic status. In this way, older middle- and upper-class life-

---

[3] Christopher Jencks and David Riesman, in *The Academic Revolution* (Garden City, N.Y.: Doubleday, 1968), pp. 146–154, provide a thoughtful, if rather gingerly, discussion of this issue.

[4] Aaron V. Cicourel and John I. Kitsuse, *The Educational Decision-Makers* (Indianapolis: Bobbs-Merrill, 1963).

[5] *Ibid.*, p. 72.

patterns are made positively dysfunctional for the young, just as lower-class life-patterns are, in the equalizing process of the school. Unless the tendency of the home is toward docile acceptance of the common-man pattern of life and expectation, the school will run counter to its influence.

The influence of the school itself is, in a matter of this complexity, difficult to isolate and appraise. But it is clear—and, I think, significant—that dis-affection in the young is heavily concentrated among both the bright middle-class and upper-middle-class youth, on the one hand, and the lower-class, especially Negro, youth, on the other. The working class, young and old, is, in contrast, much more likely to be hostile to dissent, and especially to demonstrations, and to regard the school as the pathway to opportunity; its children are more willing to put on a clean shirt and tie and await the pleasure of the draft board or the interviewer from industry. For them, the school and family have worked together, and adult role-models retain their quite possible fatal appeal.

YOUTH AS A DISCRIMINATED-AGAINST CLASS

I have already asserted that conflict between the generations is less a consequence of the ways in which old and young perceive, or misperceive, each other than of structurally created, genuine conflicts of interest. In this, as in other relationships, ideology follows self-interest: we impute to other people and social groups characteristics that justify the use we plan to make of them and the control over them that use requires. The subordinate group, in turn, often develops these very characteristics in response to the conditions that were imposed on them. Slaves, slum-dwellers, "teen-agers," and enlisted men do, indeed, often display a defensive stupidity and irresponsibility, which quickly abates in situations which they feel to be free of officious inter-ference, with which they can deal, by means of their own institutions, in their own way.

For American youth, these occasions are few, and have grown relatively fewer with the escalation of the war in Vietnam. The Dominican inter-vention, the scale and permanence of our military investment in Southeast Asia, and the hunch that our economic system requires the engagement of its youth at low pay, or none, in a vast military-academic complex, in order to avoid disastrously widespread unemployment—even under present circum-stances far greater among youth than among older persons—suggest to thoughtful young people that their bondage may be fundamental to the American political system and incapable of solution within its terms.

That bondage is remarkably complete—and so gross, in comparison to the way in which other members of the society are treated, that I find it difficult to accept the good faith of most adults who declare their sympathy with "the problems of youth" while remaining content to operate within the limits of the coercive system that deals with them, in any official capacity. To search for explanations of the problems of youth in America in primarily psychological terms while suggesting ways of easing the tension between them and the rest of society is rather like approaching the problem of "the American turkey in late autumn" with the same benign attitude. Turkeys would have no problem, except for the use we make of them, though I can imagine clearly enough the arguments that a cadre of specialists in poultry-relations might advance in defense of Thanksgiving, all of them true enough as far as they went: that wild turkeys could not support themselves under the demanding conditions of modern life; that there are now more turkeys than ever before and their general health and nutritional status, if not their life-expectancy, is much more favorable than in the past; that a turkey ought to have a chance to fulfill its obligations and realize the meaning of its life as a responsible member of society; that, despite the sentimental outcries of reformers, most turkeys seem contented with their lot—those that are not content being best treated by individual clinical means and, if necessary, an accelerated program; and that the discontented are not the fattest, anyway, only the brightest.

Young men in America, like most Negroes, are excluded from any opportunity to hold the kind of job or to earn the kind of money without which members of this society committed to affluence are treated with gross contempt. In a sense, the plight of youth is more oppressive, for the means by which they are constrained are held to be lawful, while discrimination against Negroes is now proscribed by law and what remains, though very serious indeed, is the massive toxic residue of past practice rather than current public policy.

Students are not paid for attending school; they are held to be investing in their future—though if, in fact, they invested as capital the difference between the normal wage of an employed adult high school graduate for four to seven years and what little they may have received as stipends during their academic careers for the same length of time, the return accrued to them might easily exceed the increment a degree will bring. But, of course, they have not got it to invest, and are not permitted to get it to live on. The draft siphons off working-class youth, while middle-class youth are constrained to remain in college to avoid it. If there were no draft, their impact on the economy would probably be ruinous. Trade-union restrictions and child-labor laws, in any case, prevent their gaining the kind of experience, prior to the age of eighteen—even as part of a high school program—that would qualify them for employment as adults by the time they reach their legal majority, though young workers could be protected by laws relating to working conditions, hours, and wage-rates, if this protection were indeed the intent of restrictive legislation, without eliminating his opportunity for employment.

Even the concept of a legal majority is itself a social artifact, defining the time at which the social structure is ready to concede a measure of equality to those of its members whom youthfulness has kept powerless, without reference to their real qualifications which, where relevant, could be directly tested. Nature knows no such sharp break in competence associated with maturation, except in the sexual sphere; and comparatively little of our economic and political behavior is overtly sexual. Perhaps if more were, we would be more forthright and less spiteful. Nor is there any general maturational factor, gradual but portentous in its cumulative effect, which is relevant to society's demands.

Neither wisdom nor emotional stability is particularly characteristic of American adults, as compared to the young; and where, in this country, would the electoral process become less rational if children were permitted to vote: southern California? Washington, D.C.? If there should be any age limitation on voting, it ought to apply, surely, to those so old that they may reasonably expect to escape the consequences of their political decisions, rather than to those who will be burdened and perhaps destroyed by them. Certainly, the disfranchisement of youth is impossible to square, morally, with the Selective Service Act—though politically, there is no inconsistency: the second implies the first. But the draft is pure exploitation in a classical Marxian sense. The question of the need for an army is not the issue. A volunteer army could be raised, according to the conservative economist Milton Friedman,[6] for from four to twenty billion dollars per year; and to argue that even the larger sum is more than the nation can afford is merely to insist that draftees support the nation by paying, in kind, a tax-rate several times greater than the average paid by civilian tax-payers in money, instead of being compensated for their loss in liberty and added risk. To argue that military service is a duty owed to one's country seems quite beside the point: it is not owed more by a young man than by the old or the middle-aged. And, at a time when a large proportion of enlisted military assignments are in clerical and technical specialties indentical with those for which civilians are highly paid, the draft seems merely a form of involuntary servitude.

Without a doubt, the Selective Service Act has done more than any other factor not only to exacerbate the conflict between generations, but to make it clear that it is a real conflict of interest. The draft makes those subject to it formally second-class citizens in a way to which no race is subjected any longer. The arrogance and inaccessibility of Selective Service officials, who are neither elected nor appointed for fixed terms subject to review; the fact that it has been necessary to take court action even to make public the names of draft-board members in some communities; the fact that registrants are specifically denied representation by counsel during their dealings with the Selective Service System and can only appeal to the courts after risking prosecution for the felony of refusing induction—all this is without parallel in the American legal process.

But the laws of the land are, after all, what define youth as a discriminated-against class. In fact, it is their discrimination that gives the term "youth"

[6] Quoted in Newsweek, December 19, 1966, p. 100.

the only operational meaning it has: that of a person who, by reason of age, becomes subject to special constraint and penalties visited upon no other member of the commonwealth—for whom, by reason of age, certain conduct, otherwise lawful, is defined as criminal and to whom special administrative procedures, applicable to no other member of the commonwealth, are applied. The special characteristics of "youth culture" are derived from these disabilities rather than from any inherent age-graded characteristics. "Youth culture" is composed of individuals whose time is pre-empted by compulsory school attendance or the threat of induction into the Armed Service, who, regardless of their skills, cannot get and hold jobs that will pay enough to permit them to marry and build homes, and who are subject to surveillance at home or in school dormitories if they are detected in any form of sexual activity whatever. Youth and prisoners are the only people in America for whom *all* forms of sexual behavior are defined as illicit. It is absurd to scrutinize people who are forced to live under such extraordinary disabilities for psychological explanations of their resistance or bizarre conduct, except insofar as their state of mind can be related to their real situation.[7]

LAW ENFORCEMENT AND LEGAL PROCESS APPLIED TO YOUTH

In their relationship to the legal structure, youth operate under peculiar disabilities. The educational codes of the several states provide for considerably more restraint even than the compulsory attendance provisions provide—and that provision would be regarded as confiscatory, and hence doubtless unconstitutional, if applied to any member of the commonwealth old enough to be respected as having the right to dispose of his own time. Soldiers are at least paid *something*. But the code does more than pre-empt the students' time. It is usually interpreted by school authorities as giving them power to set standards of dress and grooming—some of which, like those pertaining to hair length, of a kind that cannot be set aside while the student is not in school. It becomes the basis for indoctrination with the values of a petty, clerical social subclass. Regulations on dress, speech, and conduct in school are justified by this subclass as being necessary because school is supposed to be businesslike; it is where you learn to behave like a businessman. This leaves the young with the alternative of becoming little-

---

[7] To be sure, as we become more sophisticated in our conception of mental illness, this becomes more and more clearly true of all forms of mental illness. All states of mind have their psychodynamics; but, regardless of the school of psychodynamic thought to which one adheres, the most basic possible definition of mental illness seems to be "a chronic or recurring mental or emotional state which disturbs other people more powerful than the victim." Sometimes, of course, as in the case of certain kinds of paranoid schizophrenics, with good reason.

As a corollary to this, it seems to follow that the head of a modern, centralized, national state—unlike his poor, royal predecessors—can never go officially mad until his government is overthrown.

league businessmen to juvenile delinquents, for refusal to obey school regulations leads to charges of delinquency—which seems a rather narrow choice among the possibilities of youthful life.

But I have written so much more elsewhere [8] about education as a social sanction that it seems inappropriate to devote more space to the functioning of the school as such. I have introduced the topic here simply to point out that the educational code, from the viewpoint of those subject to it, constitutes the most pervasive *legal* constraint on the movements and behavior of youth. It is not, however, from the viewpoint of legal theory, the most fundamental. The juvenile code and the juvenile court system provide even more direct contradictions to the standard of due process afforded adults in American courts.

For the juvenile court is, ostensibly, not a criminal court. It is technically a court of chancery before which a respondent is brought as a presumptive ward—not as an adversary, but as a dependent. It is assumed—the language is preserved in the legal documentation used in preparing juvenile court cases—that the authorities intervene *on behalf of the minor,* and with the purpose of setting up, where necessary, a regime designed to correct his wayward tendencies. The court may restrict; it may, as a condition of probation, insist that a respondent submit to a public spanking; it may detain and incarcerate in a reformatory indistinguishable from a prison for a period of years—but it may not punish. It is authorized only to correct.

Because action in juvenile court is not, therefore, regarded as an adversary proceeding, the juvenile courts provide few of the legal safeguards of a criminal court. There is considerable public misunderstanding about this, because the effect of recent Supreme Court decisions on the juvenile court process has been widely exaggerated, both by people who endorse and by people who deplore what the Court has done. What it *has* done, in effect, is to require the juvenile court to provide the usual safeguards if its actions are ever to become part of an adversary proceeding in a regular criminal court. Since the state may at its discretion, try as adults rather than as juveniles youngsters over a certain minimum age who are accused of actions that violate the criminal code, and since the more serious offenses are usually committed by older adolescents, it may choose to provide these accused with the safeguards granted adults from the time of arrest rather than impair its chances for subsequent successful prosecution. It is, therefore, becoming usual, for example, to provide counsel for juveniles in serious cases; to exclude, in the event of a subsequent criminal prosecution, statements taken by probation officers or youth-squad members in a legally improper manner; and to permit juvenile respondents to summon and cross-examine witnesses —procedures which have not been part of juvenile court practice in the past.

These are improvements, but they leave untouched the much vaster poten-

[8] See the books listed in my biography on p. 32 of this article. [This reference is to the original Journal article.—Ed.]

tial for intergenerational conflict afforded by the summary treatment of casual offenders, and, particularly, of those youngsters of whose behavior the law could take no cognizance if they were older; for example, truants, loiterers, runaways, curfew-violators, and twenty-year-olds who buy beer in a tavern. For such as these, there is no question of compromising future prosecution in a formal court, and their treatment has been affected very little, if at all, by high-court decisions. The law still presumes that its intervention in their lives is beneficial *per se*, and they have few enforceable civil rights with respect to it. If young people are "troublemakers," they are punished for it—this is all. Step out of line, and the police "take you away," as the Buffalo Springfield described it—on the occasion of a Los Angeles police roundup of the youngsters strolling on the Sunset Strip in the autumn of 1968—in the song, "For What It's Worth," that gained them a national reputation among teen-agers.

It is quite clear that one's moral judgment of the legal position of youth in American society depends very largely on the degree to which one shares the fundamental assumption on which juvenile proceedings are based: that they are designed to help; that the adults who carry them out will, by and large, have the wisdom and the resources, and the intent to help rather than to punish. Legal authorities have caviled at this assumption for some time. Thus, Paul W. Alexander writes in a paper on "Constitutional Rights in Juvenile Court":

> In the area of the child's constitutional rights the last decade has seen a minor but interesting revolt on the part of some highly distinguished judges. So repellent were some of the juvenile court practices that the judges were removed to repudiate the widely held majority rule that a delinquency hearing in a juvenile court is a civil, not a criminal action. . . . This doctrine appeared so distasteful to a California appellate court that the following language appeared in the opinion: "While the juvenile court law provides that adjudication of a minor to be a ward of the court should not be deemed to be a conviction of crime, nevertheless, for all practical purposes, this is a legal fiction, presenting a challenge to credulity and doing violence to reason." [9]

YOUTH TODAY HAVE NO RESPECT FOR THE LAW

The kind of legal structure which youth face would appear to be, of itself, sufficient to explain why young people are often inclined to be skeptical rather than enthusiastic about law and order—and about those of their number who are enthusiasts for law, as student leaders and prominent athletes tend to be. Yet, the hostile relations that develop between youth and law-enforcement agencies are, even so, probably more attributable to the way in which police generally respond to young people than to the oppressive

[9] Included in Margaret K. Rosenheim (ed.), *Justice for the Child* (New York: Free Press of Glencoe, 1962), p. 83.

character of the legal system itself—though the two factors are, of course, causally related, because the fact that youth have few rights and many liabilities before the law also makes it possible for law-enforcement agencies to behave more oppressively.

With respect to youth, law-enforcement agencies assume the role of enforcers of morals and proper social attitudes, as well as of the law, and—having few rights—there is not much the young can do about it. Police forces, moreover, provide a manpower-pool by "moonlighting," while off duty, as members of private enforcement squads hired to keep young people from getting out of hand, a task which they often try to perform by making themselves as conspicuous as possible in order to keep the young people from starting anything—exactly what police would *not* do in monitoring a group of orderly adults in a public place.

My own observations at folk-rock concerts and dances, for example, which are among the best places for learning how young people express themselves and communicate with one another, confirm that surveillance on these occasions is characteristically officious and oppressive. It often expresses a real contempt for the customs of the youngsters, even when these are appropriate to the occasion. Police, clubs in hand, will rush onstage or into the pit at any sign that the performers are about to mingle with the dancers or audience—if a soloist jumps down from the stage, say, or if members of the audience attempt to mount it; or they will have the lights turned up to interrupt a jam session or freakout that has gone on too long, or with too great intensity, for their taste; or insist on ruining a carefully designed and well-equipped light-show by requiring that the house-lights be kept bright. All this is done smirkingly, as if the youngsters at the concert knew that they were "getting out of line" in behaving differently from a philharmonic audience. It should be borne in mind, considering the fiscal basis for rights in our culture, that tickets for the Beach Boys or Jefferson Airplane are now likely to cost more than tickets for a symphony concert, and the youngsters are poorer than symphony subscribers, but they rarely enjoy the same right to listen to their music in their own way, unmolested.

The music itself provides some of the best evidence of the response of the "further-out" youngsters to police action, which, indeed, sometimes inflicts on them more serious damage than the annoyance of having a concert ruined. In Watts, San Francisco, and Memphis, the civil disorders associated with each city in recent years were triggered by the slaying of a Negro youth by a police officer. "Pot busts" are directed primarily against young people, among whom the use of marijuana has become something of a moral principle evoked by the destructive hostility of the legal means used to suppress it: thirty students at the State University of New York at Stony Brook, for example, were handcuffed and herded from their dormitories before dawn last winter, before the lenses of television cameras manned by news agencies which the Suffolk County police had thoughtfully notified of the impending raid.[10] Rock artists, speaking to, and to some degree for, youth, respond to the social climate which such incidents, often repeated, have established. I have already cited the Buffalo Springfield's song "For What It's Worth." The Mothers of Invention are even more direct in their new album, *We're Only in It for the Money*, where they represent the typical parent as believing that police brutality is justified toward teen-agers who look "too weird" and make "some noise." [11]

BRINGING IT ALL BACK HOME

Finally, exacerbating the confrontations between youth and adults is the fact that the control of youth has largely been entrusted to lower-status elements of the society. Custodial and control functions usually are so entrusted, for those in subjection have even lower status themselves, and do not command the services of higher grades of personnel that their society affords. Having low status, moreover, prevents their being taken seriously as moral human beings. Society tends to assume that the moral demands made on the criminal, the mad, and the young by their respective wardens are for their own good and to reinforce those demands while limiting the subjects' opportunities for redress to those situations in which the grossest violations of the most fundamental human rights have occurred. The reader's moral evaluation of the conflict that I have described will, therefore, depend very largely, I believe, on the degree to which he shares society's assumption.

As has surely been obvious, I do not share it. The process by which youth is brought into line in American society is almost wholly destructive of the dignity and creative potential of the young, and the condition of the middle-aged and the old in America seems to me, on the whole, to make this proposition quite plausible. Nevertheless, the violation of the young in the process of socialization fulfills an essential function in making our society cohesive. And curiously—and rather perversely—this function depends on the fact that custody and indoctrination—education is not, after all, a very precise term for it—are lower-status functions.

American democracy depends, I believe, on the systematic humiliation of potential elites to keep it going. There is, perhaps, no other way in which an increasingly educated middle class, whose technical services cannot be spared, can be induced to acquiesce in the political demands of a deracinated and invidious populace, reluctant to accept any measure of social improvement, however generally advantageous, which might bring any segment of the society slightly more benefits than would accrue to it. Teachers, police, and parents in America are jointly in the business of rearing the

10 *The New York Times*, January 18, 1968.

11 Copyright by Frank Zappa Music Company, Inc., a subsidiary of Third Story Music, Inc. (BMI).

young to be frightened of the vast majority who have been too scared and embittered by the losses and compromises which they have endured in the process of becoming respectable to be treated in a way that would enrage them. Anything generous—or perhaps merely civil, like welcoming a Negro family into a previously white community, or letting your neighbor "blow a little grass" in peace—does enrage them, and so severely as to threaten the fabric of society. A conference of recent American leaders associated with a greater measure of generosity toward the deprived—John and Robert Kennedy, Martin Luther King, Jr., and Malcolm X, for a start—might, perhaps, agree, if it could be convened.

Many of today's middle-class youth, however—having been spared, by the prevailing affluence, the deprivations that make intimidation more effective in later life—are talking back; and some are even finding support, rather than betrayal, in their elders—the spectacle of older folks helping their radical sons to adjust their identifying armbands during the spring protests at Columbia University is said to have been both moving and fairly common. The protest, in any case, continues and mounts. So does the rage against the young. If the confrontation between the generations does pose, as many portentous civic leaders and upper-case "Educators" fear, a lethal threat to the integrity of the American social system, that threat may perhaps be accepted with graceful irony. Is there, after all, so much to lose? The American social system has never been noted for its integrity. In fact, it would be rather like depriving the Swiss of their surfing.

The Socialization Community

Ronald Lippitt

Introductory Perspectives

This paper attempts to develop a conceptual framework as a guide for research analysis and the designing of experimental interventions aimed at the improvement of the socialization process. Most of the work on socialization has focused on processes of interaction between socialization agents and children, particularly young children. Anthropologists, sociologists, and "social commentators" have also focused on the characteristics and functioning of the total society as it influences personality formation. Most have neglected to look at the linkage between the characteristics of a national society and the goals and techniques of individual parents and teachers. Our focus on what we call the "socialization community" attempts to examine the structure and process of such linkage.

CENTER for Research on the Utilization of Scientific Knowledge, The Institute for Social Research, The University of Michigan, Ann Arbor, Michigan, 1969. Mimeographed. Reprinted by the permission of the author.

Defining the Socialization Community

"Every society has a critical vested interest in the procedures and processes by which the young are socialized into the functioning of the society." (Alex Inkeles, "Society, Social Structure, and Child Socialization," Chapter 3 of *Socialization and Society*, Little Brown and Co., 1968.) Inkeles, in his discussion of the analyses by Levy and others of the needs of society in relation to the process of socialization, emphasizes that every society needs to have its young members learn some of the general values, knowledges, and skills needed for functioning as a committed and contributing member of the society. This means learning the goals and means which provide effective self control of disruptive forms of behavior and a readiness to respond to the sanctions of others "if one gets out of line" as a member of the society. Also, the society is interested in having every member acquire commitments and competencies to social and occupational roles that will maintain the functioning and development of the society. In a rapidly changing society it is crucial that the young be socialized into the attitudes, knowledges, and skills relevant to flexibility or changeability because they must be prepared to prevent the obsolescence and deterioration of the society and contribute to its survival and development. The key elements in this total process of "raising the young" are the institutions and individuals who frequently interact with the young. These individuals and agencies are the links between the interests and needs of society and the actual learning activities of the young. We have called this cluster of influences the "socialization community."

Most typically we think of community in other terms. We think of its economic functions which might be designated as the economic community, or we think of it as a physical community located in a given physical ecology of buildings, transportation, communications, etc. But it is just as valid to think of the educational or socialization functions of the community and to think in terms of a socialization community. In our analyses we have identified a number of clusters of personnel that have a delegated interest and responsibility of influencing the development of the values, knowledges, and behaviors of the young. Each of the following clusters of institutions, agencies, and personnel has some type of program of socialization, more or less planned, and publicly articulated as a program to influence the socialization of the young members of the community. These clusters are:

1. *The formal education agencies, public and private.* This includes the education programs from the pre-school through the community colleges and other institutions of higher education. Some specialize in general education programs and others in more technical and specialized programs. All of them provide curricula, many compulsory,

for the formal education of the children and youth of the community.
2. *The churches.* Almost all churches have religious education programs
   for the young, with a special emphasis on values education. Many of
   the churches also provide other types of activity programs emphasizing
   opportunities for significant educational dialogue between adults
   and the young. A few have become involved in political socialization.
3. *The leisure time (non-school) child and youth serving agencies.*
   This large cluster of socialization agencies specializes in recreational,
   cultural, and "character education" programs. Many of them attempt
   to provide an orientation into citizen roles and family life functions.
   Although many of the socialization agents are volunteers rather
   than professionals they all have delegated socialization responsibilities
   and some type of training to do their volunteer jobs of working with
   the young.
4. *The legal enforcement and protection agencies.* This includes the
   police juvenile bureaus, juvenile courts, traffic-safety agents, and school
   truant officers. All of these agencies and agents have responsibility for
   defining deviancy in terms of legal codes and exerting sanctions to
   prevent or correct deviant behavior and to protect the community
   from the disruptions and destructions of deviant behaviors.
5. *The therapeutic, rehabilitative, and resocialization services.* This varied
   cluster of professional helpers includes the counselors and therapists
   who work with various types of deviants, the remedial specialists who
   work with those who have fallen behind in various types of learning
   activity, and those working with the deprived and the handicapped
   who require more intense and specialized socialization and educational
   opportunities.
6. *Employers and work supervisors of the young.* There are several types
   of personnel who have the responsibility for linking the young into
   the economic system of the community. Some of them act as trainers
   for occupational roles, others provide placement and referral services,
   recruit and make employment decisions, or act as work supervisors.
   All of these functions are related to the socialization of the young into
   the economic community.
7. *The political socializers.* In the American community there is very
   little responsibility delegated for the political socialization of the
   young. In recent years some of the adult leaders involved in social
   protest and civil rights activities have taken some responsibility for
   socialization of the young into political roles. There has been very
   little interest or responsibility shown by the regular political system.

In addition to these seven clusters of personnel, paid and volunteer, which
have delegated responsibility and articulated programs of socialization in
varying degrees, there are two additional and very significant populations of
socialization agents:

8. *The parents*. The parents certainly have a delegated responsibility for the socialization of the young. Our interviews with a sample of professional socialization agents reveal that they perceive the parents as the most influential, at least in the early years, and the most responsible for deviancy. On the other hand, the parents are neither paid nor trained to take responsibility for particular socialization functions. They have a very crucial but anomalous position in the socialization community.

9. *Older and like-age peers*. The social system of peers is another major source of influence which has no delegated responsibility and no training, except in very rare cases, to take the role of socialization agents in relation to other young ones. Even in such familiar patterns as babysitting, no socialization functions are typically defined or expected.

In addition to these nine populations of socialization agents who interact in a face-to-face way with the young, there is a tenth population present in most communities that performs a significant socialization function.

10. *The mass media agents*. This is the population of agents who control and distribute the socialization interventions addressed to the young through the channels of the mass media—TV and radio programs, newspapers, and other newstand materials. Many of these agents address only a small amount of their attention to the youth population as targets. However, many of the messages specifically addressed to adults are consumed and utilized by the young.

These ten clusters of personnel we will call the segments of the socialization community.

THE STRUCTURE OF THE SOCIALIZATION COMMUNITY

There are several different ways in which we can look at the organization or structure of the socialization community.

1. *Functional clusters*. We have described the socialization community in terms of ten different functional clusters of socialization agents and agencies. We can inquire into whether there is a high homogeneity of purpose within the clusters or between clusters. We can explore whether there is more communication and co-ordination of efforts within clusters as compared to between clusters. We can inquire into whether the workers within the different clusters compete with each other over the same socialization targets, and whether there is competition between clusters for the mind and ear of the socializee.

2. *Vertical systems of programmatic effort*. Another way of looking at the structure of the socialization community is in terms of the way in which the programmatic efforts of each socialization agency are organized and conducted. Typically there is a top policy-making

structure of laymen, such as the school board or agency board, which defines the allocation of the budget, selects the top professional personnel, and makes general decisions about programming policy and possible content. Under the policy-making group in the vertical structure is the administrative and program staff of professionals such as the school principal and superintendent and curriculum co-ordinators or the agency executive and program director or the directors of the juvenile board of the police or mental health clinic, or the personnel director, etc. Under the administrative and program supervisors there are the direct workers with the young, the socializees. These direct workers may be professionals or volunteers, for example school teachers, scout leaders, club leaders, juvenile officers, work supervisors, counselors, Big Brothers, Sunday school teachers, etc. And in the vertical structure under the direct workers are the young people themselves, who are the targets of the socialization efforts of the agency.

3. *Horizontal communication and collaboration.* One of the most interesting questions about the socialization community is the question of the degree to which the various levels of the vertical structures have communication and collaboration horizontally. For example, to what degree do the policy makers in the various socialization agencies have communication with each other and co-ordination of effort? To what degree do the Council of Social Agencies or the Council of Churches or any of the other co-ordinating mechanisms provide for collaboration within any of the ten segments of the socialization community? To what degree is there any communication between policy makers across the various segments? Is there more communication at the level of administrators and program people than there is at the level of the policy makers? Do the direct workers, school teachers, scout leaders, juvenile officers, etc. have any direct communication and co-operation in the sharing of information or techniques of socialization?

4. *Professionals, para-professionals, and volunteers.* Another way of looking at the socialization community is in terms of the types of personnel who are involved in socialization functions. In some of the sectors most of the direct socialization work and interaction with the socializees is carried out by full-time professionals such as classroom teachers, police officers and probation officers, counselors and remedial workers. In other sectors almost all of the direct socialization work is carried out by volunteers, Sunday school teachers, Big Brothers, club leaders, political leaders, parents, and older peers. In many agencies there is an increasing population of para-professionals and part-time aides who are taking on important roles of direct socialization.

5. *Formal and informal socialization efforts.* Another way of looking at the socialization community is in terms of the extent to which some of the socialization inputs represent formal planned programs of effort

to influence the growth and development of the young as compared to the degree to which other patterns of influence are unplanned and informal. This includes much of the efforts of parents and certainly of older peers and charismatic peer leaders. Also, we can probably differentiate between those socialization agents who are acting as linkers with delegated responsibility for certain types of socialization content and methods and those who have no sense of responsibility for representing the values and ideas of others.

We will want to look at the functioning of the socialization community in terms of all of these dimensions of structure.

THE LIFE SPACE OF THE SOCIALIZEE: PATTERNS OF INPUT AND COPING

If we turn our focus of attention to the recipient of all this effort, the child or youth, other questions are generated about the functioning of the socialization community. Are there some populations of the young who are overloaded with the attention and inputs of the medley of socialization efforts in terms of time, energy, and readiness? Are there other populations of the young who are neglected, avoided, or rejected by most of the socialization agencies? Are some agencies in direct conflict with each other for the time and values and behaviors of the young, such as older peer leaders who are in conflict with the "establishment" for the loyalties and energies of the young? Do some agencies provide important alternative paths for the young to pursue the development of their skills, and interests, and values? To what extent is there a division of labor among the agencies in their focus on certain socialization priorities and population targets? Is there a collusive neglect of certain target populations by most of the agencies? Do some agencies support and complement the functions of parents while others attempt to function as substitutes for and competitors with the parents? Do some agencies have a very articulate program of direct indoctrination of values and behaviors as contrasted with agencies that have an emphasis on supporting the development and experimentation of the young in the development of their own values and decisions?

All of these questions point to the importance of learning about the patterning of inputs into the life space of individual children which flow from the autonomous or collaborative efforts of the various socialization agents and agencies.

A closely related way of looking at the life space of the individual socializee is to inquire into the patterns of response which socializees show in coping with and learning from the inputs of the socialization community. Do some socializees develop a pattern of avoiding or ignoring all input? Do some develop patterns of being exposed to or hearing only what they choose to hear, and see as models? Are some conformity-oriented utilizers of all socialization efforts struggling to meet expectations and adopt the values of all of the agents impinging on them? Are others active initiators for whom the process of growing up is primarily a process of self socialization, using the resources of socialization agencies as opportunities but not imperatives? In just what ways do the socializees of different age levels, different positions in the community, and different types of identity development utilize the input patterns of the socialization community?

This then is our orientation to the concept of the socialization community and to some of the exciting questions about its structure and the way it operates to exert influence in linking the socialization demands of society to the lives of the young as they develop into more or less committed and more or less productive members of the society.

PROBLEMS AND ISSUES IN THE OPERATION OF THE SOCIALIZATION COMMUNITY

Inkeles (p. 96) states the basic issue very well when he says "getting society's mandates expressed in a systematic way and consistent way so the different spokesmen will speak with one voice and in the proper sequence, is a great challenge to any social system. But the problem may seem more formidable to us in the United States precisely because of the size and complexity of our system, and, perhaps most important, because as an open society we often shy away [from] specifying too public, official and explicit a doctrine of individual behavior." We certainly do fail, in a variety of ways, to meet our obligations to our young and their needs for our help. "Shying away" is manifest in many ways and for many reasons. Let's explore some of these manifestations and reasons.

Unclarity About Goals

Interviews with Socialization Agents, at all levels, policy makers, administrators, programmers, direct workers, reveal their difficulty in articulating clear goals for their socialization efforts. On the whole they lack the clarity needed to formulate specific statements of desired behavioral outcomes and value and attitudinal outcomes of their interactions with young children and older youths. They can often talk quite easily about teaching techniques or desirable learning activities but are quite unclear as to whether the desired end product of their efforts is a certain state of information in the child, or a certain attitude towards adults—skills of learning, or certain resultant values and behaviors. It turns out to be a very puzzling task to ask most socialization agents, professional or volunteer, to write down concrete descriptions of what the values and attitudes and behaviors of the children or young people would be like if they, as adult helpers, had achieved their mission with the young ones. There are certainly several good reasons for this unclarity about goals.

First, the recommendations and proposals and expectations received from sources of authority and expertness are quite ambiguous and often con-flicting.

Second, the parent or teacher or other agent has his or her own ideals and needs to draw from. These sources of goal ideas derive from one's own growing up experience and from models observed and what is arrived at as one's own philosophy of educational objectives. Very few adults have had the necessary confrontations and help with which to explore reflectively sources of their own experience and to integrate them into a meaningful orientation toward their objectives as developers of the next generation.

A third issue that prevents goal clarification is that of non-communication between adults about goals. Our interviews reveal a sense of guilt about un-certainty, a perception that "others are more adequate and clearer than I am," and that "I'll look bad or inadequate if I share my dilemmas with others in this area." Therefore, socialization agents deprive themselves of the dialogues they critically need about ideals and goals and desired outcome.

There is also the ever-pervasive fact that children are different from one another and that these different characteristics of children must somehow be taken into account in the socialization process and must in-fluence the nature and style and degree to which particular social impera-tives are promoted by the socialization agent.

These are some of the reasons there is a serious lack of clarity about socialization goals, and a serious lack of effort to achieve clarification.

EXPLORATION ABOUT CONSENSUS

Interviews with populations of socialization leaders reveal a fair con-sensus agreeing that the least liked behavioral outcome in socializees is the lack of respect shown by the young for authority and adults, and that the most liked outcomes have to do with getting along well with each other and with adults, and showing active commitment to work and achievement. Beyond this there is much difference of opinion about priority objectives and much difference in weights given to the priorities of con-forming citizenship, self-fulfillment, moral values, problem-solving skills, capacity for enjoyment, etc. Two patterns of interaction seem to main-tain the process of non-exploration about consensus. Some interviewees maintain that they perceive the goals of others as similar to their own and therefore have no sense of need to enter a dialogue. Others perceive great difference and either want to avoid conflict or rationalize that a pluralism of goals is a natural state of affairs and that there is no need for them to expose themselves to influence toward change. "The American dilemma" of avoidance of compromise is a serious restraint to confronta-tion and creative dialogue of the kind which is needed to help clarify differences and to support the emergence of collaboration and consistency. It is interesting that many of the youths who were interviewed indicated a desire to keep parents and teachers apart because if they began to work together there would be more collusive strength against the needs of the youths themselves. It is our guess that the explorations of consensus among social agents would have the opposite effect of developing more sensitivity and concreteness about the needs, interests, and welfare of the young.

THE CHOICE OF APPROPRIATE MEANS

If someone is unclear about their child-rearing objectives and desired outcomes, they lack the criteria for selecting the most appropriate means of helping the young ones develop. A second problem is that there is an even more confusing medley of voices from the experts about the best means and then about goals. Brim has pointed out (Brim, O. G., Jr., *Education for Child Rearing*, New York, Russell Sage Foundation, 1959) that there is remarkably little research or derivations from research, to help a parent or other socializing agent select the correct socialization procedures to attain the socially preferred objectives. It is our impression that there is much more consensus among the experts than would be apparent if they had the opportunity to confront each other, to explore differences in populations studied and concepts and language used in interpretations.

But perhaps the most serious problem is that most socialization agents have little opportunity to develop a repertoire of interaction techniques to use with the young at different times, under different conditions, with different ages and types of children, and with different objectives. Most of the needed and appropriate techniques for helping the young have been invented by some particular agent or group of agents but there has been no communication of this resource. The lack of dissemination about means of socialization is acutely serious and is particularly difficult in a social system of our size and complexity.

There is another serious problem which limits the choice of appropriate socialization means. This is the existence of misleading assumptions about causation which limit intelligence and flexibility in the choice of behaviors toward children and youth. For example, there is a commonly held misleading assumption that "clamping down" on and isolation of our young is a necessary and beneficial disciplinary procedure. The techniques of repressions and isolation no doubt help the adult agents to cope with their fears and anxieties but there is no evidence that these techniques result in either the development of internal self-control or the resocialization of deviancy. Another typical misleading assumption is that there is a single or major cause of any behavioral outcome and therefore that a single course of action is needed and sufficient to cause certain growth outcomes, such as "providing them with a father," "giving them more intellectual stimulation," "teaching them to know what's right and what's wrong." A third frequently misleading assumption is that "youth are not old enough to know what is good for them, not mature enough to participate in the planning and operation of their own development and education." Holding this assumption greatly limits the flexibility in choice of socialization means because so many of the most effective socialization techniques require various types of involvement and collaboration of the young in their own socialization.

Problems and Issues for the Socializee

Although the major concern of this paper is with the functioning and structure of the socialization community we must keep our perspective on the central task, i.e., creating effective and appropriate learning experiences for children and youth. One of the most important generalizations about social learning is that the learner will be open to listen and ready to be influenced in proportion to his perceptions that his teachers are ready to listen to and be influenced by him and his needs. One of the critical issues, which many of the young ones cannot articulate, is that the young are not basically a part of the socialization community. They are targets or objects rather than participants or members. They are *talked to* rather than *with*. They are planned *for* rather than planned *with*. The adult socialization agents put a great deal of thought and planning and energy into observing and diagnosing the needs of the young and their reactions to various educational efforts, but rarely are the young asked directly to give their reactions to these efforts and even more rarely are the young given feedback from the adults about how the reactions of the young have been listened to and used to influence and guide the adults in their efforts to do a better job of collaborating with the young in their growing up process.

The young are constantly busy with their own initiatives of self-socialization. If the efforts of the elders are to be influential it must be because the young are initiating postures of reaction and utilization of the inputs from the elders. The fact that the elders can teach but it is the young that choose to learn is a frightening conception for many elders and a source of strength for many of the young. Many elders are threatened, just as many are challenged, by the understanding that they must also be learners in this process to work efficiently and productively.

It may appear at first though that the concept of self-socialization and initiative of the socializee is a more relevant dynamic for the older young ones than it is for the pre-schoolers and elementary school agers. It is certainly true that resistance and confrontation are less manifest in the earlier years but it has become very clear that even in the pre-school years the young organism is developing a definite policy about his postures toward and participation in the learning opportunities provided and initiated by adults.

And, as we have seen above, the adults present the young with a variety of problems to cope with in trying to learn from what the adults are offering. The messages are often so confusing, inconsistent, competing, and discontinuous. And even more critically, there is often a serious lack of positive support for the efforts to learn and to actually apply these learnings in behavior. The messages of reinforcement which come from the adults are predominantly critical. They are messages which create feelings of low self worth and incompetence and result in both discouragement and a need to protectively withdraw from interaction with adults. Fortunately there is another source of support and self-esteem which becomes very important for the majority of the young ones quite early. This is the resource of one's own peers. With them there is a better chance to be influential, and during the school years to develop coalitions and collusions which provide the strength to take initiative and to resist the power field of the adults. The age-grading practices used by the adult socialization agents, i.e., the practice of separating the young for most activities into separate age groups, inhibits many of the natural opportunities for nurturance and support between older and younger peers and introduces much discontinuity into the socialization process as a result. Many of the things they need to learn could be learned most efficiently and easily from the older peers. This is prevented both by the policies of separation and the resultant attitudes of competition, status difference, and exploitation which follow as a consequence.

What are some of the postures of initiative the young develop in coping with the pluralism of inputs from the adult socialization agents who try to influence them each week? In coping with the complexity they try to simplify their task in several ways. Here are some of their patterns:

1. Particularly with many of the older ones the sense of irritation and confusion which results from being exposed to inconsistent and competing demands and expectations is being reacted to by a psychological response which in effect says "if you can't agree then there are no authoritative standards and I am free to do what seems most attractive to me." This resolution receives support from the young one's need for autonomy and the attractiveness of the pleasure-seeking impulse which is one of the inner voices helping determine initiative in most decision situations. So the young one feels legitimized in "doing his own thing" as a simplification and defense against the competing medley of voices from the socialization community.

2. Another tempting and frequently used way to avoid the stress of conflicting demands and loyalty pressures is to avoid the confrontation, to deny that there is an issue of conflict. Some children and youth are remarkably successful in keeping their relations with adult socialization agents separated. When they are with their parents, then their teachers and other adults do not exist. And likewise when they are with their teachers, their parents have no psychological existence. This type of situational and relationship opportunism can be carried to remarkable lengths to avoid internal confrontation and conflict. But one conse-

quence is a delay in the development of personal identity which emerges from personal decision making, and from confrontation, and internalization of the many disparate socialization influences.

3. Another way to simplify these complexities is to make one of the sources of influence the psychologically dominant one providing guidance in all situations. By making loyalty to the mother or a best peer friend the dominant loyalty, it is possible to avoid a great deal of discomfort in decision making. One can think of the other voices as irrelevant and thus stop paying attention to them, or quickly and easily reject the competing messages as incorrect or misleading. One of the consequences of selecting a dominant external voice among the multiple voices of the socialization community is that the child tends to inhibit the development and use of his own internal voice as a legitimate guide.

4. Many young ones try anxiously and conscientiously to listen to all the voices from the socialization community and arrive at some kind of compromise which will somehow please everybody. More frequently than not this attempt to balance all the voices in the situation results in the dissatisfaction of pleasing no one, including the self. But if this other directed posture of problem-solving is at least partially successful it prevents the development of a posture of self-initiative, self-worth, and self-potency in the young person.

5. Many children are helped by adults, or help themselves, to develop more creative and self-integrating postures of using the input of the socialization community as a resource for growth. These young ones have learned that decisions and actions genuinely belong to them but that there is responsibility and opportunity to listen to, to seek out, and to use the ideas of others for the *self*. A second thing they have learned is that they are not just targets of influence and pressure from others but are in a reciprocal relation with others with the right and responsibility to attempt to influence adults with their ideas and feelings. This more active posture of participation in the socialization process is not one of dependence, as contrasted to independence, but is rather a posture of active inter-dependence which is far more potent and self-enhancing than efforts at autonomy and separateness.

In some ways then, the biggest problem the young ones have to cope with in regard to their role in the socialization process is the challenge of how to more effectively influence the functioning of the socialization community so that they can be a better resource themselves in meeting their needs to grow and develop.

DERIVATIONS FOR DIRECTION OF CHANGE IN THE SOCIALIZATION COMMUNITY

From the foregoing analysis of the issues of the socialization process, and the problems of the functioning of the socialization community, and the needs of the young we have arrived at a number of derivations about needed developments in the socialization community and directions for research on the macro-processes of socialization. Several of our major derivations are summarized in this section. Clearly they need further conceptualization, and testing through experimentation.

COMMUNICATION BETWEEN THE SEGMENTS OF THE SOCIALIZATION COMMUNITY

We visualize further development of the model begun in the Flint youth study. Through a nomination survey the major policy and administrative power figures in seven or eight sectors of the socialization community have been identified. Information has been collected from them about their priorities in regard to the values outcomes and behavioral outcomes of their socialization efforts, and their patterns of communication, collaboration, and competition with the other socialization leaders. These data were the start-up of a continuing inter-agency seminar for key community leadership. Differences in policy, program priorities, target populations, and approaches to co-operation and competition have been confronted and a series of adult task forces are working on some of the major issues of collaboration.

This seminar has activated a process of sharing practices between direct workers in the different agencies who are working directly with children and youth. In these "sharing of practice institutes" the scoutmaster has much to learn from the classroom teacher, the classroom teacher has much to learn from religious education workers, religious education workers have much to learn from Big Brothers and school counselors, the counselors have much to learn from the probation officers and juvenile officers, and so on. The sharing institutes are using techniques of identifying and documenting innovative practices so there can be effective reviewing, evaluating, and distributing of the most significant socialization techniques in working with the young in all sectors of the socialization community.

The direct workers have become very sensitive to the need for help from the young in evaluating practices and collaborating on program development. This resulted in an inter-generation weekend laboratory with a focus on helping the adults, the children, and the youth to listen to each other and to explore consensus in defining major directions for improvement of the socialization and educational process. As a result of this initial and continuing work on communication between the agencies and agents of the socialization community a number of changes have developed within many of the agencies, as indicated below.

TEAM-BUILDING WITH THE SOCIALIZATION AGENCIES

One of the weaknesses discovered in the problem-solving efforts described above was the lack of communication between policy, administrative, direct worker, and youth levels within the various agencies. As a result several agencies have initiated vertical team-building activities such as weekend team building laboratories, and agency councils. Several school buildings, for example, are experimenting with supplementing the student council, administrative council, and parents' council by a building council, which includes representation from the administration, the teachers, the parents, and the students. Many issues have been brought to the surface for creative work, and much energy has been released by this structure of legitimizing communication and problem solving between the levels of the socialization system. Many task forces and committees have been created which are intergenerational in composition.

THE DEVELOPMENT AND CO-ORDINATION OF COLLABORATION BETWEEN PROFESSIONAL AND VOLUNTEER RESOURCES

One of the strongest feedbacks from listening to the young has been the need for much more in the way of individualization of opportunities for learning and for intimate sympathetic relationships with adults. This has emphasized dramatically the impossibility of doing the job of socialization primarily through the direct efforts of professional personnel, or the growing cadre of para-professionals. This realization has led, in several agencies, to the development of the concept of functional teams of professionals, para-professionals, and volunteers all related to a group or sub-population of children or youth. This has been a very difficult job of team building because of the problems of defensiveness about standards on the part of the professionals, problems of commitment and mobility needs on the part of the para-professionals and issues of marginality and lack of rewarding personal development for the volunteers. But the team-building efforts have been very rewarding for all three groups and many professionals have now come to see themselves as the leaders and orchestrators of educational teams where they get their satisfaction out of the role of consultant and trainer rather than from the direct rewards of being the central figures in interaction with the young ones.

One interesting development in several schools and agencies has been experimentation with the concept of the "life space conference" where all the adults who have significant contact with a particular child or children explore their differences of approach, of expectations, of assumptions about causality, and begin to understand ways in which they can provide a more meaningful and consistent input into the life of those youths.

Several of the youth-serving agencies, including elementary and secondary schools, have responded to the research evidence that in many situations young children are most responsive to help and influence from peers several years older than themselves, and the evidence shows that being asked to help teach is probably one of the most effective techniques for stimulating learning. Asking children and youths to help take responsibility for teaching the youngsters is one of the most effective and successful ways of helping the olders develop their own knowledge, skills, and values about responsibility and the use of adults as resources. So in several of the agencies and schools, groups of older children and teenagers have volunteered to work with the young in programs of recreation, character education, and classroom learning. All of these older volunteers participate in regular training seminars and have opportunities to develop and discuss their own learnings as they work with the young ones. This mobilization of cross-age helping motivations within the peer culture has represented the greatest expansion of socialization man-power, and has the greatest impact on opening up the readiness of the young to learn from the olders. In many ways the older helpers act as linkers between the generations.

The Youth Participation Co-ordinating Council

From the ferment of activities described above have emerged three new key structural elements of the socialization community.

From the many inter-generational discussions has emerged a Youth Participation Co-ordinating Council which has had as its major purpose the development of initiative and collaboration of the youth sector in relation to many socialization activities. The Council involves representation from two age sectors of the youth community, the thirteen to seventeen age sector, and the eighteen to twenty-one age sector. Half the members of the Council are elected representatives from those agencies and organizations in the community who have a youth clientele or constituency (e.g., school system, youth-serving agencies, the churches, labor-sponsored groups). The other half are selected by a community-wide nomination and election pro-cedure organized separately for the two age sectors. Special efforts have been made in the nomination procedure to identify influential children and youth who are not part of the "establishment" of adult organized programs. The Council itself has continuing responsibility for identifying organizations in the community which have the right to elect youth to the Council. It has been actively involved in developing active relationships with the City Council, the City Planning Commission, and the City Human Relations Commission. It has been successful in getting representation on the Chamber of Commerce, the council of social agencies, and in stimulating the selection of youth as members of many policy-making boards in the community. They are becoming involved in discussions with the Board of Education about appropriate representation. A sub-committee of the Council has the re-sponsibility for continually working with all types of employment opportuni-ties with special emphasis on gradients of opportunities for occupational exploration for younger youths as well as part-time apprenticeships and full-time jobs for older youths. In collaboration with the school system the Council has organized a training program for child care services. The program certifies trainees as being prepared for various types of paid and volunteer services in relation to young children. The funding of youth council programs and office functions is derived from several sources. At the local community level the annual budget, as well as special project requests, are presented to the City Council. In addition, the Council solicits and receives contributions from the private sectors—agencies, businesses, and individuals. One local foundation is also very actively involved. The council has been involved in securing some funds from state level resources and is exploring the availability of some types of federal funds.[1] The important fact is that young people from all sectors of the child and youth community are actively represented and the confrontations about activism, about impatience with the establishment and the testing of the conservatism of the adult community can be carried on within a legitimized structure of organization and procedures and can exert significant and satisfying influence on the larger community.

The Family Development Co-ordinating Council

In spite of the general agreement of all socialization leaders about the crucial importance of competent parental behavior, there is a conspicuous lack of both pre-service and in-service parent training within the socialization community. Of all the socialization agents, parents receive the most blame for inadequate performance, but the least training and supplementary support for their activities. A co-ordinating council for family life development has been formed in which the agencies in the socialization community have pooled manpower resources to provide a professional staff for an extensive program to recruit volunteer pairs (often a husband and wife team) to conduct a carefully designed series of parent and family development sessions. These volunteer pairs are recruited from all segments of the community and play an active role in the outreach efforts to attract parents to the training programs sponsored by all types of organizations and agencies. A very significant public service recognition procedure has been developed to reward and give visibility to the effort of the volunteer teams in this area of community service. The local papers and other mass media have collaborated in giving public recognition and information about the significant "inventions" which have been identified and documented as part of the family life development program. Every effort is being made to recognize and reward parenthood as one of the most important social practice roles which contribute to the strengthening of the community and the society.

This family development program includes activities for teenagers and young people before marriage and has also been experimenting with family development laboratories for total family units focused on applying the con-

---

[1] This description of the youth council is an adaptation of a model developed by Task Force VI of the Joint Commission on Mental Health of Children for presentation to Congress.

cepts of team development to the family unit. Another important part of the educational program has been the training of parents to be active and effective collaborators with teachers and other adults working together on the challenges of sex education, drug use, work orientation, destructive behavior, and other current issues requiring dialogue and action with the young and the old working together.

THE SOCIALIZATION COMMUNITY COUNCIL

Even though the many responsibilities and efforts to nurture and socialize the young will continue to be a varied pluralistic activity in every community, it is crucial that some openness of communication and confrontation and some co-ordination of planning and collaborative action be developed if we are to cope adequately with the challenges of social change and of inter-generational confrontation which are a major context of our life today.

It seems quite reasonable and feasible that the various vested interests of the socialization community should create some type of co-ordinating council in the interests of improving and guiding the socialization processes of the community. This council would have representation of all sectors and levels of the socialization community, and all levels of the structures, which certainly include the unorganized sectors, i.e., the parents and the youth themselves.

This co-ordinating council would have responsibility for giving leadership to long-range planning activities and to the continual retrieval of knowledge about socialization and new developments in social practice in other communities.

The co-ordinating council would have a major duty to link with the functions of the local community, i.e., the economic, political, and physical development functions, etc. One of the purposes would be to develop a widespread consensus within the community about priority, of focusing planning and resources on the socialization function, and on the development of the younger generation as the major priority of community life.

The co-ordinating council would have the responsibility for continuous stimulation of research and development activities in the various collaborating agencies, sanctioning of experimental demonstrations, and the continuous linkage to the use of scientific professional resources of local institutions of higher education.

Perhaps their most important function would be that of having the responsibility for the development and maintenance of community-wide programs, of recruiting and training volunteers, and of giving leadership to the development of opportunities for continuous in-service professional development for the staffs of all socialization agencies. It is possible to organize much more effective training programs, with much more high level training resources, if the professional training programs provide for interaction between the para-professionals and professionals of all the agencies.

One of the most exciting innovations in the area of training has been that socializees, the young themselves, are in need of training in the basic skills of "learning to learn," of taking active initiative in using the opportunities and resources of the adult socialization community effectively, selectively, and with discrimination. Within the school curriculum, and within several agency programs there has been the development of very crucial continuities of teaching children and youth the values, skills, and initiatives of being active and selective participants in the total education and socialization process. One of the interesting outcomes of this activity has been the development, with sponsorship with the youth participation co-ordination council, of a series of teams of young people who are giving leadership to parent and teacher education sessions organized and sponsored by the young. These have been called "bridging the generation" sessions in which, with the use of role-playing episodes, there is presentation of critical issues of communication and collaboration between teachers, parents, and youths, and opportunity for diagnostic observation and discussion of the episodes, and thorough analysis of approaches to the improvement of effective working relationships between the generations.

One other significant activity of the socialization community council is the maintenance of a computerized resource directory of volunteer and professional manpower resources in the socialization community, with information about areas of competence and availability for use.

Essentially what the socialization community co-ordinating council has provided is leadership for the development of an effective problem-solving and self-renewing operation. . . . As each problem is solved the community increases its competence at problem solving and also contributes new resources of knowledge and skilled manpower to the community and also to the larger society.

Such a socialization community is prepared to identify and cope with its current issues, whether they be drug use, illegitimate pregnancies, educational drop-outs, or riots in the high school. These symptomatic problems will tend to diminish and disappear as a healthy socialization system is developed where the young have their opportunities for participation and their responsibilities for helping maintain and develop the operation of the community.

THE STRATEGY OF ENTRY AND START-UP

If we review the efforts to accumulate basic knowledge about the macroprocesses of socialization (i.e., at the level of the functioning of the socialization community and the socialization agencies) we find very little in the way of efforts to make derivations from descriptive or diagnostic knowledge to intervention theory and plans. One reason for this is there has been very little research and theorizing focused on the issues of entry into the system for purposes of inducing experimental change. Converting descriptive research about the social system into diagnostic ideas about readiness to change, resistance to change, and directions of change is one important and challenging task of conceptualization. But converting these images of potential and desirable directions of change into specific action strategies for initiating a change process is an additional discipline often neglected, with the consequence of much resultant frustration, disillusionment, or avoidance of the use of knowledge as a basis for action. Action tends to remain rule of thumb, intuitive, and ad hoc rather than systematic and based on hard-headed derivations from basic analysis.

DEVELOPMENT OF A "TEMPORARY" SYSTEM TEAM

Much of the recent work on successful planned change efforts in social systems indicates that a temporary change agent composed of insiders and outsiders has several crucial advantages in gaining access, getting acceptance, and linking the leverage of outside expertness to inside sensitivity. The concept is that this is a small additional "temporary system" with cohesion and loyalty to an intervention task, merging the objectivity and resources of outsiders and the internal commitment and knowledge of insiders into an intervention mechanism will have no intention of becoming a permanent new sub-system. It will go out of business as a team as the new processes and structures which are needed for the initiation and maintenance of change are internalized by the system.

DEVELOPMENT OF INTERNAL DATA COLLECTION: MANPOWER AND PROCEDURES

Usually the start-up of an intervention process involves the need to collect data on such questions as degree of consensus about goals, difficulty with communication between sub-systems, desire for change, locus of conflicts, distribution of leadership, and degree of satisfaction with the present state of affairs. The most effective and economical access to the various parts of the system to get such information involves the recruiting and training of individuals in the system who are appropriately located and ready to become temporary objective data collectors. The evidence is that there are individuals in a community system who are ready and eager to take on the challenge of being trained as members of a scientific team. The evidence is that with appropriate intensive training they can do a high quality job of data collection and get access where outsiders find it difficult or impossible and, certainly, far more expensive. Perhaps a more important aspect, from the point of view of intervention strategy, is that training and participation in the "objectivity role" of data collector tremendously lowers defenses and creates a readiness for involvement in change effort.

REVIEWS AND DERIVATIONS FROM EXTERNAL RESOURCES

Very often one of the most effective initial entry points is a knowledge review and derivation conference with key leaders of the system in which research generalizations relevant to local problems are retrieved and summarized from the research literature. Such a derivation conference extending from two or three hours to a day or two starts with work on the implications of the first generalizations for understanding the local situation, and implications and possible directions of change. The problem-solving design continues with brainstorming of action alternatives, developing a criteria for selecting the most feasible and appropriate alternatives, and moves to planning for action and evaluation of initial experimental efforts. We have observed that focusing on "what they have discovered about other situations like ours" often provides the necessary "safe" start-up for beginning to look objectively at internal issues and problems.

MICRO-EXPERIENCES FOR LEADERS AND SANCTIONERS OF CHANGE EFFORT

One of the most frequent bases for resistance to the initial risk taking of considering the need for change and designing directions for action commitments is the apprehension and mystery of "what it would be like if we got involved in this." Also "is what they're proposing anything new and different from what we've tried before?" One of the most effective ways to cope with this problem is to provide an opportunity for those whose sanction is needed, or whose leadership is desirable, to actually participate in capsule form in some of the perspectives and activities of an intervention program. For example, one school board in a two-hour session went through the experience in small groups by brainstorming a day in the life of an elementary school child and secondary-level student, getting them out of bed in the morning and carrying them on a half hour basis throughout the day, all the contacts they had with adults, what the adults expected and wanted from them and what the reactions of the young ones probably were to these contacts. The school board members became very tied up about the need for planning a more consistent and meaningful educational experience for the young and sanctioned and funded a start-up project. Another group of leaders from black and white segments of an educational community spent an hour first projecting from their imaginations observations of dialogue and interaction between black and white students two years in the future which made them pleased with the way things had progressed in terms of their values. From this initial experience they spent the rest of the hour identifying the various kinds of movement in the direction of their images of a desirable future state of affairs. This provided the motivation and understanding of what the proposed action program was all about and its relevance to their needs. Such micro-experiences are frequently the first step in getting sanction for initiation of an intervention process.

Temporary Commitment to a Try-out Period

Very frequently the committed intervention team wants too much too fast. Usually it is feasible and desirable to define an initial period of try-out and evaluation which represents a more acceptable level of risk with regard to the responsibilities of leadership and control felt by the leadership of the system. Obviously the try-out period must be long enough and provide an opportunity for the intervention to be felt and for there to be some opportunity for observation of the consequences.

Commitment to Supportive Follow-through

One of the frequent, and justified, apprehensions of the inside leadership is that the outside experts have only a temporary interest in them and their problems and they fear the experts will disappear about the time the going gets rough and additional help is needed. The outsiders must be prepared to clarify their commitment to continuity of support beyond the start-up period if their help is needed and desired by the community or agencies.

These represent some of the core issues and dimensions of design and commitment as part of the strategy of initiating experimental intervention in a socialization community or any part of it. These kinds of start-up problems must be dealt with in moving toward any of the innovations described in a previous section of this paper.

Strategic Issues of Research and Dissemination in Work with the Socialization Community

Let's review now some of the issues and challenges involved in building the accumulation of basic knowledge and effective dissemination of knowledge into the total process of working with the socialization community.

Balancing Action and Research Orientations and Skills

One of the most critical issues in the launching and conducting of significant intervention experiments is the recruiting and building of an intervention team that includes well-trained scientific personnel with an acceptance and understanding of the action process and skilled action personnel who accept commitment to and responsibility for research goals. A large proportion of field experimentation has failed to make significant contribution to science, and even to other practice systems, because the researchers were trained in and committed to a "purist tradition" of controlled laboratory work, or became so involved in the action process that they retreated from vigorously representing research values. And, on the other hand, the action members of the team have lacked the background to understand and feel commitment to the knowledge production potentialities of the project, or have abrogated responsibility for representing the complexities of high quality action intervention through their efforts to identify with higher status research functions. A volume on interdisciplinary teamwork in mental health research by Margaret Luski analyzes in detail some of the major problems, challenges, and possibilities of building integrated action and research teams.

Building an Internal Scientific Apparatus

We mentioned previously involving members of the target system in research activities as a part of the start-up intervention process. We want to emphasize here the great potential scientific value of having persons distributed through the system who are functioning as part of a research apparatus, therefore able to get access to critical phenomena of a change process on a continuing longitudinal basis. The participant observer has been a very important methodological tool of the anthropologist. Our own experience indicates that one can go even further in recruiting and training of strategically located indigenous personnel as committed and objective collectors of data through observations and interviewing.

Systematic Description of Process Flow

One of the great inadequacies of most field research is that measurement tends to be "a beginning and end" procedure. These efforts to assess change between two widely spaced time periods fail to yield very much basic information about the causes of change, the dynamics of resistance to change, the sequential phases of change process, and the specific effects of particular intervention efforts. The designs most needed to make basic contributions to knowledge about social system change are those which provide for continuity of measurement guided by conceptual models of the change process and the expected effects of the designed interventions.

A Cluster of Micro-designs

Instead of thinking of the total change efforts as one research design it is usually more productive and feasible to think of the total change effort as made up of a series of intervention efforts with hypotheses or predictions about intended consequences. In this way it is possible to be continuously involved in "little experiments" and to continuously be challenged to conceptualize what one "has learned so far" as a basis for designing new inquiry questions and data collection efforts.

The Continuity of Outcomes

There usually is no place in an intervention program where it is possible to say this is the time and place to measure outcomes to see whether purposes of intervention have been achieved. The process of cause and effect is a continuous flow in which resistance to change at one point seems to wipe out all effects observed at previous points, or a slow accumulation of small effects seems to suddenly snowball into major changes in the system. Scanning for evidences of change, sequences of change, and rates of change are crucial challenges for the measurement operation in such change efforts as are interests in developing the functioning of a socialization community.

Documentation and Dissemination

In order to report the effects of any social intervention it is necessary to provide a systematic and detailed description of the interventions. And if one of the responsibilities of social experimentation is to disseminate discoveries about successful models of social practice then the communication of the model and details of its operation are a crucial part of making adoption and adaptation by others a possibility. For both these reasons the documentation procedures used in field experimentation are crucially important. This is not a secretarial function of writing down what happens. The responsibility requires a high level of skill and careful planning of the dimensions of description and procedures for description. One of the typical problems of many conscientious efforts is "the file full of tapes" which prove far too expensive and difficult to convert into effective and functional communication. Economical and conceptually sophisticated documentation is one of the most confronting challenges of significant field research.

Converting documentation into the packages of communication materials needed and relevant for dissemination is an additional discipline which typically requires some integration of audio, visual, and written materials designed specifically for this purpose. The effective dissemination of experiences and learning from a change experiment require more than clear-cut communications. Essentially, communications must be designed as a training experience which helps the potential adopters and adapters to confront their own values and defenses as part of the working through of the implications and potentialities of the social experimentation which is being communicated to them.

CONCLUDING COMMENT

We have attempted to deal with several conceptual challenges in this paper.

First, we have attempted to present and clarify the notions of a socialization community and its role as one of the major functions of community life in our society.

Second, we have attempted to identify the elements of the structure and operation of this community function.

Third, we have attempted to point out some of the ways in which the activities of the socialization community can be identified as patterns of input into the life space of the children and youth of the community.

Fourth, we have attempted to identify some of the issues of dysfunction and lack of development in the structure and operation of the socialization community.

Fifth, we have made a series of derivations as to what the socialization community might look like in operation if it were functioning more effectively and structured more rationally to meet the requirement of the socialization task.

Sixth, we have attempted to identify some of the strategic issues involved in initiating processes of change in the directions indicated by our "images of potentiality."

And finally, we have reflected on the challenge and responsibility of designing intervention efforts to have activities which have a research mission and a commitment to responsibility to dissemination of social discoveries.

It is our conclusion that the directions for change we have presented are a critical social necessity and will become increasingly more so as the issues of inter-generational relationships continue to move towards new areas and level of tension and alienation. We believe the approaches to change which we have conceptualized are feasible and that the approaches to inquiry we have suggested represent a scientific as well as a social priority.

Part III

Programs and
Problems
of Change

There are several reasons why any book
focusing upon American society and
education ought to include a section on
changes in these systems. *First,* observing
an institution in the throes of change is a
good way to learn about its nature—not
just its rhetoric and carefully polished public
image, but what really goes on and what's
really important. Many important and
buried outlines of our schools become
sharply visible during times of stress and
modification. *Second,* the press for change,
and responses thereto, reflects the major
controversies about public education in the
United States and, indeed, about the nature

of the society itself. Thus, many of the debates cited throughout this book are publicly exposed and joined in the encounter between advocates and resistors of any specific set of changes. *Third,* change is an inexorable process, and we need to understand it as well as we understand stability, nonchange, or any other characteristic of social or educational institutions. *Fourth,* our readings make it clear that even the most generous observers of American schools acknowledge that there are serious instances of failure, injustice, and inequity in their operations. It is as important to employ our intelligence resources to altering these states of affairs as it is to study them. Further it is the business of scholars who understand their roles as valuing beings to act on those values in the pursuit of change in existing social and educational structures.

Of course this is our own perspective on the study of schools, and it is not shared by all other writers, editors, or scholars in the field. In fact, most texts in the area of sociology and education do not include major sections explicitly devoted to change, preferring to bury change-oriented articles in one or another of the categories otherwise established.

Change efforts must start from the "what is," and so they are reliant on a diagnostic understanding of current states of affairs. But change inevitably proceeds in the direction of the "what ought to be," and this involves judgments and evaluations of the present and value preferences for and vision about the future. So it should be clear that change is a value-centered enterprise and that whether it is attempted from the top or the bottom, it proceeds according to value preferences and ideological commitments. No matter what the rhetoric—whether of increased technical efficiency, better citizens, higher priorities placed on basic skills, more humanistic people, different control patterns, or nicer facilities—educational and community values are at stake!

Of course, this means we must know on whose behalf any change effort is proceeding. To the extent that school managers finance and arrange for consultants to help bring about change, we must assume that the managers' priorities will be most nearly met. Whether or not they are shared by others is a moot question. To the extent that indigenous community or student leadership (or staff leadership, for that matter) directs a change effort, we must assume it will most nearly meet the values of that partisan subgroup.

In this section we try to illuminate several different strategies of change. In so doing, we have selected from among the variety of targets or goals of change a few outstanding arenas. We stress here those targets of change already stressed throughout this volume: pluralism of power and culture, professional roles and controls, adult power and influence with students, and the roles of educators and parents or community members in interaction with one another.

One major strategy for approaching change in these arenas is *retraining*. The focus of this strategy is usually key individuals—teachers, administrators, students, or parents and community members. The retraining might be in levels of information, skill, attitudes, and values.

A second major strategy is *organizational innovation or modification*. The focus of this strategy is the structure of the roles, relations, or programs that delineate the organization. Rather than individuals themselves, the relations among individuals are seen as the manipulatable aspect of school life. These may include norms and instructional technologies as well as interpersonal structures.

A third major strategy we discuss is *client or community development*. In this approach the focus is upon organizing new forms of influence among people served by the educational system, whether the service be as direct as with students or as indirect as with the parents, community members, taxpayers, and so on. Forces outside the institutional structure are here being mobilized in order to bring collective concern to bear on the school itself. Problems of representation, evaluation of service, and accountability, as well as ultimate control—all are relevant targets here.

A fourth major strategy is the *manipulation of social policy*, alteration of the formal and legal guidelines upon which schools operate. The modification of laws and policies may be brought about through the legislative agencies, the executive offices, or the judicial channels of major societal decision-making, but all of these filter down to and affect the school.

A fifth, and final, strategy we review is the *establishment of institutional alternatives*. In this approach, there is not a direct attempt to alter traditional institutions; rather the effort is made to develop new institutions that substitute for old ones. Sometimes the newer models may exist within established patterns; at other times they may be built partially or completely outside.

RETRAINING PERSONNEL—ATTITUDES AND ROLE BEHAVIOR

Education is a process involving interpersonal transactions and transformations. Sooner or later, it involves individuals' relating to one another directly. Thus one of the most popular strategies of educational reform has been to try to alter the personal attributes of those in command of the schooling system. Individuals' attitudes, skills, and styles of behavior all affect the way they behave with others, that is, more specifically, the ways they teach or otherwise partake in the teaching-learning process. There is little point in the development of a new curriculum, or new educational structures, if the individuals using or staffing those innovations are not also helped to alter their behavior.

The focus upon individual behavior does not mean that this strategy excludes consideration of the social context of teaching. In fact, it has become typical recently for groups of teachers to be trained or retrained together. It is hoped that as a result these teachers can support each other in their new ways of behaving. Similarly, it is not unusual to find students, administrators, and community members also undergoing training, with the assumption that all parties to the educational enterprise require new ways of dealing with one another and their common efforts.

One primary target of retraining strategies is the level of information educators have about the students or the character of the community. It is assumed that teachers who "know their students" or "know their backgrounds" will be better able to deal with students on their own terms and meet their needs more directly. Whether or not the correlation is quite so direct, a number of preservice and in-service programs have been devised on this assumption. Thus teachers may be provided with information about the community and about typical youngsters from the community. Teachers may also be provided with access to records or to diagnostic instruments that they may use to gather local information directly from their students.

A second major target of retraining strategies is the personal feelings educators may themselves have about their jobs, their students, their own lives, and so on. Greater clarification of one's own feelings of anger, fear, and joy is assumed to help in dealing with others. This kind of knowledge is especially potent given the deeply personal and interpersonal nature of educational transactions. Because so much of what goes on between students and staffs is a matter of emotional identification and reaction, sweeping away debris in this arena can be nothing but helpful.

A third set of targets includes the teacher's typical behaviors and relationships with others in the school—students, other teachers, administrators, and the like. In this context it is clear the educational staff works as some sort of a team, consciously or not, well or poorly; they do have a cumulative effect on student life. To the extent that persons in these roles can operate together, they will be better able to attain their goals. Of course, for administrators it is also important that they consider their relations with subordinates, the ways they play out their supervisory roles with the teaching staff.

A fourth set of targets in retraining efforts is the practical skills or the technology of instruction. There is a considerable gap between intention and practice, between rhetoric and reality, and many educators simply do not know how to innovate in their classroom or school—they do not know how to act upon cherished principles. For instance, principals newly committed to democratic staff meetings may not know how to help a teaching staff take the initiative in solving school problems. A teacher committed to autonomous student group work may not know how to proceed: on what basis to form groups, how much latitude to permit, how to deal with neighbors' complaints about noise, how to help students improve their group operations, and so on. By the same token, parents wishing to change the schools may not know how to organize: whom to approach and whom not to, how to call a meeting, how to plan an exciting meeting, whom to form coalitions with, and so on.

In the selection by Richard A. Schmuck, "Helping Teachers Improve Classroom Group Processes," attention is directed to three action research interventions designed to assist teachers in improving group processes in their classrooms. Observation, role playing, and classroom practice may be essential elements in a training program devoted to the understanding and the employment of new managerial or instructional technologies.

A final target of retraining efforts is the various images of the future that any member of a school or a school system may have. As we have indicated, change is based upon some conception of alternative futures and some effort to avoid an unpleasant or unsatisfactory present. To the extent that more informed futures can be examined, or more hopeful futures imagined, changes can be directed to even more cherished goals. But for those of us who live in a hassled present, there often is not enough time to conceptualize the future, and special training events may permit us that necessary luxury.

The discussion of futures brings us once again to a major concern in all retraining efforts. All too often retraining programs are developed with a focus upon skills or techniques, with little attention to the ends of education or to the goals that teachers and administrators elect to pursue. From our own point of view, matters of control, of racism, and of respect for the rights of youth ought to be a part of any retraining effort. Whether these issues are dealt with at the level of information, attitudinal and emotional exploration, skills in implementation, and so on is a matter of local design. But no training effort can be free of these educational and social issues, and the problems of ends are as vital as matters of technique and social relations. "Better-qualified teachers" means to us not just teachers skilled in classroom processes or peer conversation. It means teachers knowingly and skillfully committed to antiracist education and youth's freedom from constraining rules and regulations.

Finally, retraining techniques may be misused as devices to take the pressure off other change necessities. The handy solution to all educational ills is often pictured as a better-trained staff, and thus staff retraining is a popular strategy. But it may also be a distraction, a way of drawing energy and concern away from fundamental organizational failures, from basic normative oppression, from serious school-community cleavage, and the like. As one example, our national concern with racism and economic injustice has never taken the form, until lately, of dealing with community accountability and control of schools. Rather, we have dealt with the "problems of the disadvantaged" by training teachers to know them better and to relate to such youngsters better. But this approach did little except to delay a more wholesale and structural approach to our basic conception of education in a pluralistic society and to pluralistic educational organizations. Problems that are organizational in character cannot be effectively dealt with via altering the mental states or behavioral patterns of individual educators or educational consumers.

ORGANIZATIONAL CHANGE

Among the major targets of organizational change in schools is the structure of goals and norms that reflect ideological or value commitments of school members or the surrounding community. All schools state their goals in vague and attractive terms; there seldom is debate over the general goals. Goals are visible in programs and governing norms that outline expected and appropriate behavior. When goals are tied to workable objectives, we can begin debates. And when goals and priorities are institutionalized in a set of norms that guide the behavior of students and adults, we are more likely to see both conformity and resistance. *The selection by Irwin Katz, "Desegregation or Integration in Public Schools? The Policy Implications of Research," provides a striking example of this problem.* The continuing debate over the issue of desegregation in the face of mounting social science evidence is linked to the possible implications that the findings may have for goal implementation at the local level.

Goals and norms also direct the structure of rewards and reward allocations among adult and student members of the school. The criteria for rewards reflect the system's priorities, and the teacher who is rewarded for having a quiet classroom well understands the major norms of the profession. Likewise, students who are rewarded for obedient and studious behavior are adapting well to the main outlines of mass education. Innovative and creative students and teachers, to the extent that they violate expected and normal behavior, cannot expect to receive high rewards. Thus any attempt to alter the behavior of school members must include an attempt to alter the current criteria for allocating rewards—whether these rewards are merit increases, collegial respect, good grades, outstanding recommendations, peer approval, and so on.

The content of the educational enterprise, the curriculum, is a representation of major goals and values in practice. It also is another element of the technological structure of the organization. Many recent efforts have been made to increase the curriculum's relevance and appeal to third-world groups, to contemporary youth, and so on. Parallel efforts oriented toward the processes of instruction, common teaching techniques, begin to overlap with the retraining focus on individual skills. But whereas one strategy focuses upon changing individuals' skills and styles, the other focuses upon the systems of norms and rewards that surround, constrain, and help guide individual behavior.

The patterns of social interactions among persons represent another feature of all social organizations. In schools we often find sharp divisions in communication patterns between teachers and students. Each group may engage in substantial communication and interaction internally but may communicate very little with the other group. The norms of professionalism mitigate against intimacy between educators and students; these norms suggest that distance and impersonality are prime requisites for the ability to make impersonal and fair judgments. Of course this very impersonal style often denies to both students and teachers some of the joys of close social interaction. Students, then, develop similar intragroup norms, with appropriate peer penalties and jibes for spending too much time in interaction with adults.

Lines of influence are marked even more clearly. The staff exerts influence on students in a variety of formal and casual ways, in the classroom and outside it. Students are limited to the exercise of informal influence, and usually the withholding of respect or diligent attention represents the major tactic involved. The net effect, of course, is that teachers do not feel that students willingly accept their influence. For their part, students often feel impotent to affect major portions of their daily activities in school. The barriers to mutual influence and communication take their toll in decreasing the informal channels of interaction that are necessary to provide the glue for most organizations. As a result, there is little informal processing of grievances in school, and concerns for injustice or change seethe throughout the system until they explode in some formal appeal or public outburst. Efforts to alter these patterns of interaction, in terms of either communication or influence, could conceivably permit the establishment of informal networks that would support the formal structure. *The redistribution of power, Mark A. Chesler and John E. Lohman argue in their article, "Changing Schools Through Student Advocacy," should be a central priority in altering the influence structures of schools.* These authors suggest that in many ways students are in more strategic positions to transform schools; hence they should have a more formal voice in the decision-making process.

Another target of change efforts is the relatively formal decision-making system in the school. In a multischool system the power to make policy and most program decisions is located in the board of education and the office of the superintendent. Some local autonomy is provided for building principals, and some further degree of autonomy for classroom instructors. But by and large most teachers feel that they have little influence upon most important school decisions. Students, of course, share these feelings because they have no formal involvement in school policy-making. The community elects the board but clearly is isolated from ongoing decisions. Many recent change efforts focus their concerns on the alteration of these decisional structures. To the extent that new represel. ational structures are built, new kinds of people and interests may be located at or near major decisions.

The final characteristic of organizations that is a target of change efforts is the boundary-maintaining system—the system of relations that moderates input–output from the community to the school and the reverse. Who comes in, that is, how students and teachers are selected, is but one example. Who goes out, that is, how students are dropped or graduated—criteria, mechanisms and so on—and how teachers are terminated, is another example. To the extent that the school exists to serve the community, efforts to change these prime interfaces consume considerable attention. *In "People-*

Changing Institutions: The Transformed Schools," Morris Janowitz *argues that the absence of a comprehensive, conceptual model has been a major barrier to change and increased effectiveness in public school systems.* Schools, Janowitz maintains, must become "people-changing institutions" if they are ever going to be responsive to societal demands.

The tactics used to bring about change vary considerably. From our point of view, two major variables help order the various strategies: the attempt to gain parity of power across organizational subgroups, or the acceptance of existing power imparities; and the attempt to work on recognized conflicts in values or goals among subgroups, or the continued acceptance of an apparent consensus. For instance, efforts to change organizational structures or to create innovative organizational forms often begin with some of the following tactics: opening up communication systems, increasing inter-personal trust and interaction among members, broadening the base of involvement in system policy issues, establishing cross-status problem-solving groups that will work on organizational problems, and having lower-level members advise the managerial elite on their problems and needs. All of these tactics deal with organizational characteristics; in that they differ markedly from the tactics of manpower retraining. However, they can be used only at the convenience of people with power, and none of them alter the existing power structure significantly. Moreover, none of them speak to the possibility of dramatically different goals or more plural criteria for organizational operations.

We can highlight these two key variables further by noting some other tactics that deal differently with the two underlying variables: negotiations among groups that have different positions on issues, massive noncompliance with policy directives, spontaneous protest or confrontation, alteration of the reward structure via the establishment of new norms, and alteration of the power structure itself. Not all but some of these tactics clearly suggest that new norms and new bases of power have been developed and are being served up: negotiation does not occur unless the ruling group cannot rule unilaterally and must bargain; negotiation among groups that differ clearly reflects divergent values. Massive noncompliance must grow out of divergent values that have reached the breaking point; for noncompliance to be massive, rather than individually deviant, must mean that a counterorganizational effort has been going on. And, of course, direct alterations of the reward or power structures are definitions of changes in value and power.

CLIENT OR COMMUNITY DEVELOPMENT

The goals of educational systems are tightly enmeshed in the major norms and values of the community. Some have argued that community values direct the schools; others believe the reverse. More cautious scholars argue that these systems are codeterminate and often exist in constant negotiation with one another. Except for these informal transmissions of values and norms, community members are involved directly in the school only through the election of boards of education, except in those communities where the mayor or the council appoints the educational rulers. We have already indicated the biases inherent in this process, the overloading of school managers with members of white and elite groups.

Students have even less direct influence upon the school than do parents and members of the community. Of course to the extent that interaction culminates in influence, students do engage others in the school every day. But they seldom exert formal influence or power over school policy and program.

These states of affairs have led to a new emphasis upon a strategy for school change that stresses the organization and the expression of need and power on the part of the clients of the educational system—students and members of the local community. Of course, "the community" always has influenced the school—the community as represented by political or economic elites. We are talking about new forms of community influence; and that means "new communities" and "new clients" as the previously unrepresented speak to their own concerns for the educational system and the changes they advocate.

The concern for new client or community power may take two principal forms: (1) working on the talents and representation of governing elites; and (2) working on organizing and articulating the needs and demands of oppressed groups. The former focus involves retraining operations and the development of new systems of accountability so that elites can get in touch with their constituencies. It may also require structures that select or rotate elites from groups of oppressed peoples directly. The latter focus involves organizing people into working groups, into groups that can present themselves effectively and powerfully on key issues.

Targets developed through this strategy focus upon the establishment of new forms of control and accountability in educational systems. This process may take the form of greater citizen and student involvement in school decision-making; or it may become established in more formal mechanisms of accountability, wherein the school and its staff are periodically judged by the community. Accountability systems are often difficult to employ because of teacher probationary regulations and tenure laws. *The selection by Ellen Lurie, "Firing the Staff: How to Get Rid of Incompetent Teachers, Principals and Supervisors," discusses this problem and reviews procedures governing the dismissal of incompetent staff members.*

Of course such accountability systems would have to use community or student criteria for performance, not merely another battery of verbally oriented achievement tests. Beyond formal accountability, it is clear that many student organizing efforts, and those in the community as well, are geared toward fuller control of the educational system by its clients.

The tactics of community or client organization must begin with the recognition of indigenous leadership or the importation of skilled outside help in the organizing effort. For the outsider, entry into the social system is the key; for the insider mobility within the system is vital. In both cases this leadership must be legitimized and accepted by the client/constituency system at hand. Trust is vital. Without trust in the leadership that is undertaking the organizing effort, no client system is likely to have later trust in itself. And the process of trust making cannot be rushed; it must proceed from the myriad interpersonal linkages that are the building blocks of new social systems. As people relate to new leadership, and vice versa, and as new leadership encourages persons to relate to one another in new peer arrangements, new social networks are being born. Of course the process of leadership development is continuous. In the case of the outsider, for instance, he or she must quickly move out of that role to help others in the local community develop their own potential and exercise initiative in organizing others. Only in this way can initial leadership avoid the dependency and the ultimate political stagnation of a youth movement or a community activity.

Another tactical perspective is that of advocacy and partisanship. One can not assume that everyone else is seeking the same objective. If they were, debates about change would be unnecessary. A new client movement, especially, must be concerned first and foremost about the protection and advancement of its own values and goals. (It is safe to say that established community elites will look after their own interests.) It must be assumed that any social change effort necessarily has friends or allies and enemies or opponents. In an organizing effort it is crucial to avoid fighting with one's friends in public. It is dangerous to share one's plans in front of one's opponents and just as dangerous to give them information about internal disagreement and priority making. This is also the surest way to destroy growing public confidence in a new movement. So priorities and tactical guides should be established among allies, and these lines should be maintained in public. As a corollary, one should assume the need to meet and plan in private and to exclude opponents or potential enemies from these planning sessions. This procedure should not be taken to mean the development of hatred or rejection of one's opponents but simply a recognition of the need to have separate strategy and tactical sessions. By all means, the focus of further organizing efforts should be on the masses of uncommitted persons. It simply doesn't pay to try to convince enemies; rather work should progress on those who are unconvinced and who are not yet in either camp.

Sometimes protest or confrontation tactics may be necessary to engage the attention of those in power. Such activities should be carefully planned, because all persons will be looking for ways to discredit new political movements on the basis of their extreme tactics and "lack of good sense." Carefully organized protests can be very helpful in raising issues, solidifying a nascent client organization, recruiting members, and requiring ruling elites to discuss issues with new organizations of clients. *The selection by John*

Birmingham, "Mobilization: Gettin' the Students Together," describes a series of strategies and mobilizing efforts by students to change the New York City schools. He concludes that organized radicalism must employ more effective means to achieve desired goals, particularly the use of "arts" such as diplomacy.

In this context, the tactics of negotiation become vital. Of course, negotiations are not likely to occur unless the people formerly holding power see that it is in their interest to compromise and discuss changes with those previously out of power. In this sense, negotiations are an admission of alterations in the power structure; people have to be approximately equal, or at least mutually vulnerable, to negotiate. Knowing when and how to negotiate, or to escalate protests and confrontations, requires highly developed skills in community organizing and change.

Finally, any organizing effort must seek reforms that can be put into practice and that support new ways of doing things. Organizing represents a constant activity, an ongoing process. However, its products must be realizable and visible in new ways of doing business in schools that recognize the legitimate rights of clients to share in the control of an educational system that is ultimately accountable to them. In fact, some scholars have maintained that community participation in educational decision-making represents the most plausible approach to institutional reform. *In "Participation, Decentralization, Community Control, and Quality Education," Mario D. Fantini attempts to relate what he terms the "emerging participatory movement" to quality education in urban schools and educational development, suggesting that such a movement might be viewed as the avant-garde of the second progressive period of education.*

Social Policy Restructuring

Part of the context of schooling and educational systems lies beyond the local community; it can be located in the nature of the political structure of life in the total society. A major change strategy oriented toward this larger system focuses on the direct manipulation of social policy and program. Changes in national values and commitments clearly are reflected in the organization and conduct of our schools, and sometimes changes in these national priorities occur fairly rapidly.

There are three major targets for a strategy based upon the manipulation of social policy. One target is the legislative system itself and the making of laws governing the public conduct or the content of schooling. A second target is the judiciary and its role in conducting hearings or deciding cases relevant to educational lore and practice. And the third target is executive action and the many activities of federal and state agencies that provide support and leadership for regular and special educational programs.

Some examples of the operation of legislative efforts as an avenue of educational change may be provided by our experience with Congressional action on new funds for education. Special passage of funds for innovative projects, for aid to disadvantaged youngsters, and for assistance to school systems trying to desegregate their schools are illustrative. Further, efforts are currently underway to influence state legislatures to pass an equal rights amendment for women that would affect women's rights in schools as well as in other areas. Another example is the recent action in city councils and state houses on efforts to legalize or reduce the penalties for smoking or selling marijuana.

Examples of efforts to bring about changes in schools by working through the judiciary include a number of fairly recent and potent examples. The process of school desegregation, that minor but relevant assault on social and educational racism, is largely the fruit of changes sought in the judicial arena. Certainly this is clear today in the spate of cases involving district consolidation and cross-district bussing for desegregationist reasons. A 1971 court decision affecting one of the largest school systems in the nation serves as an example of efforts to bring about school change via the judiciary. *In "The Detroit School Decision," U. S. District Judge Stephen J. Roth's ruling that the Detroit school system is racially segregated has received national attention, prompting a number of large urban systems seriously to reconsider their own status regarding illegal bussing, the shaping of school attendance zones, and racial segregation practices in the schools.*

Still another example of change within the judicial arena is seen in the courts' activities toward altering the patterns of school financing and the attack on local property taxes as the sole and inequitous base for school funds. *John E. Coons, Stephen D. Sugarman, and William H. Clune III, discuss judicial intervention in public school financing in the selection "Reslicing the School Pie."*

The rights of youth have been tested in the courts over the past five years, and many school administrators have had to revise their managerial styles and practices as a result. Judicial appeals have energized efforts to protect the civil rights and liberties of students as a class deserving of the same rights of due process, privacy, and freedom of speech and assembly as other Americans. *Ironically, as Ira Glasser so dramatically points out in his article, "Schools for Scandal—The Bill of Rights and Public Education," the military and public schools comprise the only two public institutions in the United States that continually deny that the Bill of Rights is applicable to them.* Procedural rights, First Amendment rights, and personal rights—all are seen by Glasser as a part of a pattern of total denial of student rights for which judicial intervention is needed and desired.

The changes brought about through the executive branches may be even more widespread and visible, as is appropriate in an age of highly active and far-reaching executive and centralized power. Presidential and gubernatorial commissions and hearing bodies have examined national issues relevant to education and have come up with findings and recommendations often translated into new policies and programs. The Kerner Commission on violence and the presidential pornography commission, to mention only two have been quite relevant for school issues and designs. The actions of the Office of Economic Opportunity in setting guidelines and policies for disadvantaged youngsters, communities, and schools have affected ghetto and barrio education in particular.

Certainly the actions of the U.S. Office of Education, through the Department of Health, Education, and Welfare, have created a number of programs that have been implemented on local levels. These programs range from school lunches to aid in retraining teachers, from support for voucher programs and educational alternatives to the development of new classroom curricula. Child-care programs and new vocational and career education programs are only a few of the more recent thrusts of these executive agencies at the federal level. In any particular state department of education, one can find similar examples.

The tactics for promoting changes in social policy and program are in many ways used similarly at the legislative, the judicial, and the executive levels. In all cases changes at these levels take time; they cannot be hurried and any particular grievance or injustice may get buried or bypassed by the time an agency can respond. There also is many a gap between policy and action, and change at this level does not automatically mean that new things will happen in the local community. At the same time, changes that occur at these levels have a good chance of becoming firmly institutionalized and of being maintained over time. They carry the weight of new public norms and lawful order. Although they may be resisted, the "moral" shoe is now on the other foot.

There is a variety of formal and informal tactics that can be used in the political arena. One obvious set of tactics would be to present a formal appeal through proper judicial channels or through one's appropriate legislative representative. Appeals that are buttressed with accounts of how these changes will fit the needs of prevailing elites clearly make it easier for policy structures managed by elites to respond. On the other hand, when emerging movements of a nonelite character are seen to have substantial power, particularly in a single legislative district, they may also command rapid and dutiful attention.

Long-standing relationships may also help gain attention and action. It is in this context that so many ex-executive personnel seek and find leadership positions in local school and community groups—they are seen as having "an in with the people in power" and an appropriate set of skills.

ALTERNATIVE EDUCATIONAL PATTERNS

An increasingly popular current strategy for change in schools involves leaving them more or less as is and setting up alternative models on the outside. The thrust of this strategy is to go beyond the political and institutional constraints of existing systems and to imagine, invent, and try to operate from new myths, norms, structures, and assumptions about learning and teaching. Sometimes these systems are ends in themselves in that they represent new environs for students to learn in. At other times their ends are realized in the traditional system's efforts to renew itself by adopting some aspects of the alternative models.

The current alternative systems appear to focus largely upon learning structures that release students from a high degree of adult, professional control. Thus some alternatives emphasize student autonomy and peer-directed learning as antidotes to adult-directed activities. Others have been set up by students themselves and are run by them, including their own hiring of any adult staff that they feel they need. Attempts to escape the racism prevalent within traditional schools has led to the development of black- or brown-controlled experiments in some major cities, experiments with schools that may be public or private but that represent major alterations in the structure of the learning activity and the cultural content of the curriculum. The generation of a new curriculum, one more in tune with youths' own desires for learning, seems to be another main target in alternative schooling patterns. And some innovators have promoted alternative schooling systems as a way to avoid and counter the traditional stress upon schooling as a credential-producing apparatus, a channel for the class-stagnating system of economic discrimination in the society at large.

One of the major tactics used in the alternative movement is the generation of an innovative subsystem within the traditional school system. The Parkway Program in Philadelphia, special academic programs in many large city systems, and the pluralistic range present in the Berkeley schools are examples of this tactic. The view of the proponents of such programs is that the public system must be maintained and that the creation of a demonstration alternative may be the way to encourage change in the larger institution. Of course, although this is a popular and an often feasible tactic, minor pilot programs that do not immediately spread to the larger system are notoriously short-lived. They tend to get swallowed up, to be themselves the target of change and reinclusion rather than the reverse.

A second major tactical approach has been to leave the traditional public system and to create new schools outside of it. These "free schools" may have special arrangements with the accrediting system, or they may be completely on their own. To the extent that they last, and draw more than a few deviant students, they usually link up with some mainstream institution in order to serve as an effective accrediting ground for later college attendance or reentry into the regular school system. Sometimes these alternatives are established by students; in other cases teachers or parents have been the initiators or co-initiators in a community experiment. To the extent that these alternatives attract some of the school's "best" students they represent a substantial threat to the traditional apparatus. However, to the extent that they draw students primarily from the upper middle classes and from white stock, they help perpetuate a separatist, elitist, and racist vision of education and educational experimentation.

Two selections illustrate this second tactical approach—creating "new" schools external to the "old" institutions. *The first, "Alternative Systems of Education" by Jessie E. Wray, describes the development of the Community School concept in Milwaukee—originated, supported, and controlled by parents. The second, "Mississippi's Freedom Schools: The Politics of Education" by Florence Howe, illustrates the basic idea of the Freedom School—its political objectives, curricular content, and fundamental alteration of the conventional teacher role.* In both selections, the basic strategy incorporates the establishment of an alternative school or school system, operating outside the channels of the public school and supported by the community.

The selection, *"Open Education: Its Philosophy, Historical Perspectives, and Implications,"* by Ewald B. Nyquist traces some of the philosophical and historical bases that account for the current level of interest in Open Education, and discusses the difficulties of implementing the concept in America's public schools. The author draws heavily from the British experience.

A third tactical position is that schooling as we know it and can imagine it operating within major institutional settings is obsolete and should be abolished.

The selection, "After Deschooling, What?" by Ivan Illich, assumes the inevitable indefensibility and, hence, disestablishment of public schools. It links this inevitability to political and cultural crises in the larger society and probes the implications of deschooling and its attendant radical demands. Here the call is not for substitutes of a more humane character but for no formal schooling. According to this plan young people would move around the society in a variety of internship experiences that would benefit them more than the experiences they currently have in schools. The focus of concern here is as much on societal credentializing as upon the state of affairs within given institutions. For those ready to reject major aspects of the American society this is an attractive alternative, a way into seriously countercultural styles of life. For those who feel they still need to live within the society, perhaps those without the resources to sustain a survival level of existence outside the main society, credential-granting institutions would remain more or less essential.

A. Retraining Personnel–Attitudes and Role Behavior

Helping Teachers Improve Classroom Group Processes [1]

RICHARD A. SCHMUCK

Classroom groups, like other groups, have both formal and informal aspects. The formal aspects have to do with ways in which various members work toward carrying out the official or specified goals of the group. In the classroom, for instance, one formal feature is the way in which any child performs the role of academic student, as it is defined by the teacher, school system, and adult community at large.

The informal aspects of a group involve the manner in which each member relates to other members as persons. In the classroom, an informal aspect is the way affection, or students' friendship for one another, is distributed. These informal features often have an important bearing on the formal aspects. Many of them, such as the amount of liking members have for one another or their willingness to help and support one another, may be thought of as positive and enhancing classroom group processes.

Informal classroom group processes, in the form of peer relations and norms as well as students' perceived group statuses, can have consequences for the students' self-esteem, attitudes toward schoolwork, and academic achievement. In previous studies (Schmuck, 1962, 1963, 1966), we showed that classroom groups with diffuse patterns of friendship and influence, compared with those with more hierarchical patterns, had greater cohesiveness and more supportive norms for learning. Most students in these diffuse groups perceived themselves as having high group status, while in the hierarchical groups only students who actually had high status perceived themselves as having it. Students who perceived themselves as having high peer status tended to have higher self-esteem, more positive attitudes toward

[1] This paper summarizes over three years of action research on improving classroom group processes in schools in the metropolitan areas of Detroit, Michigan, Philadelphia, Pennsylvania, and Portland, Oregon. Acknowledgments of organizational assistance are extended to the Cooperative Research Branch of the United States Office of Education and the Center for Research on the Utilization of Scientific Knowledge of The University of Michigan for Project 1; to The Mental Health Association of Southeastern Pennsylvania and the Group Dynamics Center of Temple University for Project 2; and to the Oregon Compact and the Center for the Advanced Study of Educational Administration of the University of Oregon for Project 3. Many persons from these organizations contributed to the studies reported here. Special thanks are given to Denis Carville and Mark Chesler who worked on Project 1; to Anne Edelmann and Steven Saturen, co-workers in Project 2; and to Philip Runkel who collaborated in Project 3.

schoolwork, and were applying their intellectual abilities better than other students. Students' academic performances were shown to be conditioned by affective contents associated with their self-concepts as peers and students and these self-concepts were influenced, in part, by the students' friendship and influence relations with their classmates.

Other studies have shown that teachers can influence classroom group processes. Flanders and Havumaki (1960) showed that teachers' support and constructive praise were likely to increase students' sociometric position among their classmates. In contrived classroom settings teachers interacted with and praised only students seated in odd-numbered seats, while in comparison groups all students were encouraged to speak and the teachers' praise was directed to the whole class. Students in the odd-numbered seats, in the former situation, later received more sociometric choices than students in the even-numbered seats. In the comparison classrooms, the difference between sociometric choices of students in the odd- and even-numbered seats was insignificant: The peer choices were spread around more evenly, indicating greater general acceptance.

In another study (Schmuck & Van Egmond, 1965), the results of a multi-stage analysis indicated that when the variables—familial social class, perceived parental attitudes toward school, perceived peer status, and satisfaction with the teacher—were compared for their relative relationship to academic performance, pupils' satisfactions with the teacher and performance were associated when the effects of the other three variables were held constant. The results indicated that the teacher, especially as a social-emotional leader, had an effect on the academic performances of both boys and girls which was independent, to a significant degree, of the effects of parents and peers.

Further research indicated that teachers of more cohesive classroom groups, compared with other teachers, attended to and talked with a larger variety of students per hour (Schmuck, 1966). Many teachers with less positive classroom group processes tended to call on fewer students for participation and seemed especially to neglect the slower, less involved students. Teachers with more supportive peer groups tended to reward students for helpful behaviors with specific statements and to control behavioral disturbances with general, group-oriented statements. Teachers with less positive climates tended to reward individuals less often and to publicly reprimand them more often for breaking classroom rules. All of these results indicated that teachers can and do influence classroom group processes. The three action research interventions described below illuminate how teachers might be helped to create more psychologically supportive classroom group processes.

PROJECT 1: TEACHER DEVELOPMENT LABORATORY

In Project 1 we assumed that for classroom changes to be effective and viable, teachers need to learn more than theories, research facts, and specific innovative practices or techniques. Teachers must integrate theories, facts,

and techniques into their value systems, emotional styles, and role conceptions. Sensitivity training and role-playing experiences accompanied by a
scientific problem-solving orientation were hypothesized to facilitate such a
reeducation process. These experiences aim to encourage a teacher to search
for alternative ways of teaching, stimulate him to try out new ideas, and
press him to collect feedback from colleagues and students on the new
practices.

Seven core training activities were carried out: (1) sensitivity training and
related human relations laboratory experiences, (2) didactic discussions on
basic research about classroom group processes, (3) problem-solving techniques for improving group processes, (4) analyses of diagnostic data from
the teachers' own classrooms, (5) discussions about useful classroom practices
developed by other teachers, (6) role-play tryouts of new classroom practices,
and (7) follow-up discussions during the school year.

Twenty teachers participated in all of these activities and formed Laboratory Group A. Twenty other teachers participated in all the activities except
sensitivity training, related human relations laboratory experiences, and role-
play tryouts, and formed Seminar Group B. Ten teachers rounded out the
design, received no special treatment, and formed Control Group C.

This project began in the spring of 1965 when a brochure announcing a
four-week summer laboratory for upper elementary teachers went to 12
school systems in Metropolitan Detroit. The selection of school systems was
accomplished by sampling broadly across social classes and racial and ethnic
groups. Chief school officers in all systems agreed to inform their upper
elementary teachers of the program. Over 75 teachers applied, and 20 teachers
were placed in Laboratory Group A and were matched with 20 others who
constituted Seminar Group B. The 10 teachers in Control Group C were
selected later from other schools in the same school systems. The final selection of the entire sample was based on principles of demographic heterogeneity of students within the experimental categories and demographic
similarity among the categories. All three categories of teachers, then, had
students with a full range of social characteristics, but were quite similar to
one another in their constellations.

The training period lasted six months for Laboratory Group A, starting in
July and ending in December 1965. Seminar Group B met from September
to December. There was no training for Control Group C. The program for
Group A began with a six-hour daily intensive laboratory during the four
weeks of July, and was followed up with feedback discussions with individual
teachers and bimonthly discussion sessions from September to December.
The program for Group B constituted weekly seminar meetings and individual conferences.

Laboratory for Group A

The first week of the four-week laboratory consisted almost entirely of
general human relations training; the T Group, focusing on personal sensi-

tivity, was the core of this program (Bradford, Benne, & Gibb, 1964). Twenty teachers were divided randomly into two T Groups that met separately for two-hour periods twice daily. While a skilled trainer was present in each group to maximize learning, the teachers created a group with their own concepts and in their own ways. Through this semistructured process, some of the teachers became more aware of how groups are formed, some, of the significant events in group development and of the kinds of functions they personally perform in groups. Many participants gained the insight that their manner of speaking and relating to others could be just as important as the content of their communication.

Theory presentations, discussions, and skill exercises supplemented these T Groups. Theoretical lecturettes and discussions dealt with topics such as "Roles persons play in groups," "Communication and feedback," and "Personal styles in groups." Often skill exercises were based on these theory sessions. For instance, the discussion on communication and feedback was followed by a skill exercise in which the teachers gave feedback to one another in small groups and, at the same time, were required to indicate that they were "hearing" by paraphrasing what another had just said. In another combination session of theory and skill training, the teachers privately completed the *Edwards Personal Preference Inventory*, received their own scores on ten psychological needs, were informed of what the scores meant conceptually, and then role-played how such need patterns would be expressed behaviorally in the classroom.

During the second week T Groups continued to meet but only once each day, as the laboratory's discussions centered on the classroom as a human relations setting. Three categories of information were presented during the second week:

1. Some basic research on classroom group processes was presented to the teachers.
2. A problem-solving scheme was presented and included these stages:
   a. identifying classroom group problems
   b. diagnosing the classroom problems
   c. developing a plan of action
   d. trying out the plan, and
   e. getting feedback and making an evaluation (Schmuck, Chesler, & Lippitt, 1966).
3. Classroom diagnosis, the second stage of the problem-solving scheme, was explored in depth and included the following topics:
   a. assessing the classroom learning climate
   b. social relations in the classroom
   c. peer group norms
   d. student-teacher interaction
   e. outside influences on students' learning
   f. parental influences on school adjustment

      g. the student's self-concept, and

      h. students' attitudes toward school and teachers (Fox, Luszki, &
          Schmuck, 1966).

Pairs or trios of teachers took one of these diagnostic topics and were responsible for teaching the entire workshop group how to use questionnaires and other measurement procedures on that topic. The trio working on teacher-student interaction received special instructions in Flanders' Interaction Analysis and used this procedure for collecting data on the teachers' instructional styles as the others taught about the various diagnostic techniques. After all of the other teachers had completed their instruction, this group reported on interaction analysis by giving feedback to all of the instructional teams on how they behaved according to the observation categories. Discussions on diagnosis were completed by the end of the second week.

Next, the teachers were assigned to skim through a booklet containing other teachers' practices and to decide tentatively on some practices they would like to try to improve classroom group processes or, more specifically, to solve classroom peer relations problems (Kaufman, Schmuck, & Lippitt, 1963). The teachers' techniques, devices, and special procedures included in this booklet were examined for their soundness by skilled teachers, educational administrators, and social psychologists. A few examples drawn from the booklet are:

Development of a classroom group government to assist in social relations management. Early in the year the class votes for a Rules Committee which sets up a Bill of Rights for all students and presents it to the rest of the group for discussion and approval. A Judiciary Committee is constituted to enforce the rules and serves for four weeks. Every day a member of the Judiciary Committee puts a schedule of the day's activities on the board, including the name of the committee member who will be responsible for supervision of behavior during each period. The Judiciary Committee and the class officers meet to arrange the class seating plans and rearrange them as necessary. Every month four students who have not been on the Judiciary Committee are elected to serve, and this method is followed until all students have taken part.

Formation and clarification of peer group behavior standards. The teacher divides the class into small subgroups for discussion of behavioral standards. The groups initially are led by sociometrically high students who are given some leadership training before commencing with the groups. Each subgroup reports its findings orally to the class, the whole class identifies the standards they like best, and these become classroom rules. These subgroups meet once every week, and each student receives some leadership training and a chance to lead a group.

Role playing for helping to teach a better understanding of group behavior. The teacher asks the class to create a play and the class discusses what the content of the play should be. The class is advised to choose a plot that would be familiar to all and that includes at least one group relations problem. The play is written, actors are chosen, and the play is enacted. Discussion takes place on applications of the play to life together in this classroom. Human relations in the classroom peer group in general are discussed.

Teaching human relations skills. Short class meetings are held three times each week concerning human relations topics. Some of these discussions are taped so that they can be played back later and evaluated by the students. The students also are encouraged to express their opinions by answering questions such as "What did you like about today?" and "What do you like (or not like) about our school?" When problems are identified, role-playing situations are set up and enacted. The students suggest alternative ways of behaving during the role-plays and discuss the meaning of role-plays for their classroom group relations.

On Monday and Tuesday of the third week the T Groups discussed the teachers' perceptions of the classroom practices presented in the booklet. Each teacher was asked to develop at least one practice that he wished to try out as a way of improving classroom group processes. On those same days, several two-hour sessions were held on the rationale for, and some ways of using, role playing (Chesler & Fox, 1966). Also one session was given on collecting feedback from students. From Wednesday of the third week to Wednesday of the fourth and final week, each teacher spent one hour simulating part of his chosen practice in a role-play enactment using the other teachers in roles as students or as outside observers.

During the last two days of the laboratory the teachers made specific plans for how they would implement these new classroom procedures during the school year. Lewin's field of forces analysis was presented so that each teacher could estimate the restraining forces that would deter him from following through with the plan (Coch & French, 1948). After considerable thought was given to implementing the plan, each teacher conferred with a staff member about his plan. This conference took the place of a final examination and was tape recorded. A schedule was formed for playing the tape early in the fall at a similar conference as a reminder and motivational device for supporting tryouts of the plan.

From September until December of 1965, the teachers continued to be involved in the program. Early in September, data were collected on the quality of group processes in all classrooms. Some data were immediately presented to the teachers. Next, the teachers listened to their tape recordings with a person from our staff and made more realistic plans based on the new data and their summer plans. Group discussions were held bimonthly during which the teachers discussed the strong and weak points of their teaching experiences. Attempts were made to support the teachers' efforts to follow through on their plans and to help the teachers to engage continuously in the problem-solving process. The program of training for Laboratory Group A was ended with an informal gathering one week before winter vacation.

Seminar for Group B

Group B met weekly from September to December, 1965. They were initially presented the same problem-solving sequence used by Group A. They learned about the uses of diagnostic tools and received group processes data from their classrooms for analysis. Basic research findings about classroom group processes also were presented to them, and they read about the classroom practices of other teachers and discussed ones they would like to try. The principal activities omitted from the Seminar for Group B were sensitivity training and role playing.

Results of Project 1

Early in the fall, during the school year, and again late in the spring, students completed self-report questionnaires on classroom group processes and their attitudes toward peers, school, self, and teacher. Teachers in Groups A and B kept diaries concerned with their planned attempts at improving group processes. Every teacher was also observed for an hour's duration three or four times during the school year. Data were collected on teachers in Group C only during the spring. The assumption made was that Group C classes, in which no interventions were tried, would more nearly reflect the fall than the spring patterns of classes in Groups A and B.

An overview of the results indicates that the Laboratory Group A teachers and students made more positive changes in their group processes than those in Seminar Group B and that both Groups A and B were more improved at the end of the school year than Control Group C.

Perhaps the most obvious difference between teachers in Groups A and B was their group cohesiveness. The *esprit de corps* in Group A was extremely positive, while almost none existed in Group B. Group A teachers telephoned one another 25 times about professional matters, while only two such calls were reported by Group B teachers. Fifteen of the 20 teachers in Group A visited socially during the school year; only three from Group B met informally. Numerous instances of sharing classroom teaching ideas occurred in Group A, while the teachers in Group B talked about their practices only during seminar time. Group A teachers talked more about their classrooms before and after class and during coffee breaks. Group A initiated a party at the end of the laboratory, and many members indicated strong desires to continue or at least to keep in touch. Group B teachers showed more interest in receiving college credit than in one another.

These differences would not be very significant in themselves if they were not accompanied by changes in classroom practices. Evidence from diaries and observations indicated that the Group A teachers were much more innovative than the Group B teachers. Teachers in Group A produced more elaborate plans of action and attempted more practices for improving group processes than the Group B teachers. Group B teachers typically tried one or two practices during the year to improve group processes, while teachers in Group A tried from five to 17 different procedures with their students. Indeed, the enthusiasm of two teachers was discussed by several students critically when they wrote on their questionnaires that they wished their teacher would keep one grouping procedure for at least two weeks instead of the usual one week. Even though some similar criticisms were aimed at other Group A teachers by their students, these represented a minor percentage of the students.

The most emphasized goal of the practices tried by Group A teachers was increasing openness in classroom communication among peers and between students and teacher. Communication was encouraged by using activities such as summarizing data from student questionnaires and discussing their meanings, role playing difficult classroom situations, discussing critical statement placed in a suggestion box, discussing thoughts about what makes for a "good" or "bad" day in class, and reviewing how the class had been proceeding by holding a once-weekly evaluation and review-discussion. Group B teachers used a few of these practices but tried fewer per teacher and continued using them for shorter durations.

The most widespread interest, manifested by 15 out of the 20 Group A teachers, was in raising students' participation levels in deciding upon classroom regulations and procedures. In seven Group A classrooms, student governments were formed and functioned successfully throughout most of the year. Teachers with such governments attempted to increase the diffusion of influence in the peer group by encouraging all students to take part at some point in the classroom government.

We also collected before and after self-report questionnaires from the students in Group A and B classrooms in the fall and spring of the school year. Students in Group C completed questionnaires only in the spring. Averages from the fall measure taken on students in Groups A and B were used as estimates of the before data in Group C.

In general, the questions centered on the students' perceptions of their influence and friendship statuses in the classroom group and the extent to which they supported one another and felt a part of the group. Students were asked to estimate whether they saw themselves in the highest part (quarter) of the class, the second highest part, in the third part, or in the lowest part on these two questions: (1) Influence—"Compared with others in the class, how often can you get others to do what you want them to do?" and (2) Friendship—"Where would you place yourself on the basis of how much the others in the class like you?" Improved group relations would be indicated by the students' feeling that they were more influential and had more friends in the spring as compared with the fall.

Furthermore, we asked students to describe, through a symbolic drawing, the friendship structure of the classroom group as they saw it. Students were presented the five rectangles as shown in Figure 1. Each rectangle represents a different group pattern. Students selected the rectangle that best represented their view of the peer group, or drew their own version

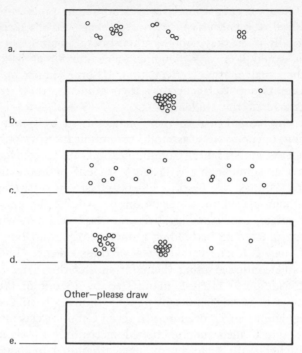

FIGURE 1.   The Classroom Group (A Method for Measuring Friendship Structure).

If you were to think about this class as a group, which one of these drawings would most nearly resemble your class? Pretend that each circle stands for a person in the class. Circles that are close together stand for people who are friends. (Check the one most like your class.) Place an "X" within the circle that stands for your position in the group.

in the blank rectangle. About 40 per cent of the students drew their own picture of the group. Each student also was asked to place an "X" within one circle that would stand for his own position in the group.

We defined a friendship group as more than two circles in a cluster and compared the average number of these perceived to exist in the class early and late in the school year. We also categorized the place a student perceived his own position to be in the group during fall and spring by using these four categories: (1) at the center of a larger group, defined as more than four circles; (2) at the periphery of a large group; (3) in a smaller group, defined as four or fewer circles; and (4) alone or isolated. Finally, as a means of getting some idea of the supportive nature of the group, especially with regard to academic matters, we asked a series of questions about the frequency of supportive behaviors in the classroom. The one presented here differentiated thus: The students in this class help one another with their schoolwork (a) almost always, (b) usually, (c) seldom, or (d) almost never.

The data on perceived influence clearly supported the hypothesis that the Laboratory for Group A would result in greater benefits than the Seminar for Group B, and that both would show gains over the Control Group C. The data on friendship were not so clear but did suggest the same pattern. Results shown in Table 1, on the perceived influence status

TABLE 1

Student Perceptions of Influence Status in Their Classroom Groups, Early and Late

	LABORATORY GROUP A				SEMINAR GROUP B				CONTROL GROUP C			
									ESTIMATED			
	FALL		SPRING		FALL		SPRING		FALL		SPRING	
PERCEIVED INFLUENCE STATUSES	NO.	PER CENT	NO.	PER CENT	NO.	PER CENT	NO.	PER CENT	NO.	PER CENT	NO.	PER CENT
Highest part	55	10	28	5	45	9	44	9	31	10	29	9
High												
Second part	236	43	309	56	168	35	154	32	126	39	113	35
Third part	206	37	155	28	187	39	202	42	124	38	120	37
Low												
Lowest part	55	10	60	11	80	17	80	17	42	13	61	19

chi-square = 48.90   chi-square = 2.39   chi-square = 10.16
$df = 3$ $df = 3$ $df = 3$
$p < .005$ $p = NS$ $p < .025$

of each student early and late in the school year, indicated the positive significance of the laboratory experience for the Group A classrooms. The students with Group A teachers, who perceived themselves as high (above the median) in peer group influence, increased significantly from 53 per cent to 61 per cent during the school year. Students in Group B, on the other hand, showed no significant change from fall to spring on perceived influence. In the Control Group C classes, the results were that the students became significantly more negative in their perceptions of influence. While 49 per cent viewed themselves as high in influence during the fall, only 44 per cent perceived that they were high in the spring.

Results in Table 2 indicated that positive gains in perceived friendship status were made in all three categories of classrooms during the school year. Comparisons of the chi-square totals as well as the percentages indicated that the positive gains made in Laboratory Group A were greater than those made in either Seminar Group B or Control Group C. Fifty-seven per cent of the students in Group A classrooms viewed themselves as highly liked early in the year. This number increased to 77 per cent in the spring, an increase of 20 per cent. Percentage increases in Groups B and C were significantly positive also, but were only half as great as the increase in Group A. We conclude that in most classrooms students tended to perceive that they were liked by more people in the spring than in

TABLE 2

Student Perceptions of Friendship Status in Their Classroom Groups,
Early and Late

	LABORATORY GROUP A				SEMINAR GROUP B				CONTROL GROUP C			
									ESTIMATED			
	FALL		SPRING		FALL		SPRING		FALL		SPRING	
PERCEIVED FRIENDSHIP STATUSES	NO.	PER CENT	NO.	PER CENT	NO.	PER CENT	NO.	PER CENT	NO.	PER CENT	NO.	PER CENT
Highest part	79	14	99	18	101	21	91	19	56	17	58	18
High												
Second part	237	43	326	59	221	46	278	58	143	44	171	53
Third part	171	31	105	19	106	22	72	15	87	27	55	17
Low												
Lowest part	65	12	22	4	52	11	39	8	37	12	39	12

chi-square = 92.39	chi-square = 29.84	chi-square = 17.37
$df = 3$	$df = 3$	$df = 3$
$p < .005$	$p < .005$	$p < .005$

the fall, but the laboratory teachers appear to have increased this positive trend even more than the others.

Additional data indicating changes in classroom friendship patterns are summarized in Tables 3 and 4. In general, these data also supported our

TABLE 3

Student Perceptions of Number of Classroom Friendship Groups,
Early and Late

	LABORATORY GROUP A				SEMINAR GROUP B				CONTROL GROUP C			
									ESTIMATED			
	FALL		SPRING		FALL		SPRING		FALL		SPRING	
NUMBER OF FRIENDSHIP GROUPS	NO.	PER CENT	NO.	PER CENT	NO.	PER CENT	NO.	PER CENT	NO.	PER CENT	NO.	PER CENT
0 or 1	157	30	89	17	143	31	83	18	97	31	70	22
2	100	19	68	13	78	17	83	18	57	18	73	23
3	22	4	37	7	41	9	37	8	20	6	16	5
4 or more	245	47	330	63	199	43	258	56	143	45	158	50

chi-square = 69.17	chi-square = 43.37	chi-square = 14.38
$df = 3$	$df = 3$	$df = 3$
$p < .005$	$p < .005$	$p < .005$

expectation that the laboratory would have positive benefit for Group A classroom groups. Results in Table 3 showed that positive gains in the number of friendship groups perceived by the students to exist in the class were made in all three categories. As in Table 2, comparisons of the chi-square totals as well as the percentages in Table 3 indicated that

TABLE 4

Student Perceptions of Own Position in a Classroom Friendship Group,
Early and Late

OWN POSITION IN FRIENDSHIP GROUP	LABORATORY GROUP A				SEMINAR GROUP B				CONTROL GROUP C			
	FALL		SPRING		FALL		SPRING		ESTIMATED FALL		SPRING	
	NO.	PER CENT	NO.	PER CENT	NO.	PER CENT	NO.	PER CENT	NO.	PER CENT	NO.	PER CENT
At center of large group	96	20	120	25	48	16	51	17	55	18	81	27
At periphery of large group	120	25	97	20	72	24	66	22	74	25	66	22
In a small group	158	33	245	51	151	50	155	51	119	40	117	39
Alone	106	22	18	4	31	10	30	10	52	17	36	12

chi-square = 131.35   chi-square = 0.81   chi-square = 18.10
$df = 3$ $df = 3$ $df = 3$
$p < .005$ $p = NS$ $p < .005$

the positive gains were greatest for teachers in Laboratory Group A. Whereas 51 per cent of the students in Group A classes saw three, four, or more friendship groups during the fall, 70 per cent perceived that same number during the spring. Comparable increases in Group B, 52 per cent to 64 per cent, and in Group C, 51 per cent to 55 per cent, though statistically significant, were not so great.

Results in Table 4 emphasized the success of the laboratory even more than those in Table 3. Here significant changes occurred in the extent to which students viewed themselves as being an integral part of either large (four or more persons) or small (three or fewer persons) friendship groups in the class. Fifty-three per cent of the Group A students saw themselves at the center of a large or small group during the fall. This increased to 76 per cent by the spring. The comparable increase in Control Group C classes was from 58 per cent to 66 per cent, representing a minor increment compared with the laboratory classes. No significant change was made during the year in the Seminar Group B classroom groups on perception of friendship group position.

Finally, the data in Table 5 indicated that the students in both the Group A and Group B classrooms increased during the school year in the degree to which they were helpful to one another with their schoolwork. A comparison between Groups A and B indicated that Group A classes made greater gains in helpfulness. For instance, in the fall 45 per cent of Group A students reported "almost always" or "usually" helping one another, while in the spring, 58 per cent reported similarly, representing a gain of 13 per cent. Group B, on the other hand, increased from 49 per cent to 57 per cent, an increase of only 8 per cent. Students in the

Group C classroom groups showed no difference from fall to spring in helpfulness.

TABLE 5

Student Perceptions of How Often They Help One Another with Schoolwork, Early and Late

HOW OFTEN THEY HELP ONE ANOTHER	LABORATORY GROUP A				SEMINAR GROUP B				CONTROL GROUP C ESTIMATED			
	FALL		SPRING		FALL		SPRING		FALL		SPRING	
	NO.	PER CENT	NO.	PER CENT	NO.	PER CENT	NO.	PER CENT	NO.	PER CENT	NO.	PER CENT
Almost always	56	11	86	17	71	15	71	15	42	13	48	15
Usually	172	34	206	41	162	34	200	42	110	34	107	33
Seldom	187	37	171	34	157	33	162	34	113	35	120	37
Almost never	92	18	44	8	85	18	42	9	58	18	48	15

chi-square $= 49.19$ chi-square $= 30.81$ chi-square $= 3.09$
$df = 3$ $df = 3$ $df = 3$
$p < .005$ $p < .005$ $p =$ NS

PROJECT 2: CLASSROOM MENTAL
HEALTH CONSULTATION

In Project 2 skilled psychological consultants attempted to enhance teachers' capabilities for coping with group processes in the classroom. Our hypothesis was that through problem-oriented discussions with mental health specialists teachers would develop a better understanding of and be more skilled in working with the social-emotional aspects of classroom groups (Edelmann & Schmuck, 1967). Consultation sessions centered on the relationships of consultant to teachers, teachers to teachers, and of teachers to the children they taught. Since the project was carried out in Metropolitan Philadelphia, some attention was given to increasing teachers' facilities for working with groups of students from disadvantaged families.

Six highly trained consultants, two psychiatrists, two clinical psychologists, and two social workers were employed for the project. The bias of the consultants was psychodynamic and interdisciplinary. Only the social workers, however, had had professional experience in public schools. The consultants were assigned one to a school for half a day each week for 15 weeks. Three consultants worked in schools with mostly middle class children, while the others worked in schools with culturally disadvantaged youngsters. Forty upper elementary teachers received consultation. Three consultants worked with groups of six teachers each; the other consultants worked with five, eight, and nine teachers, respectively. Two additional schools, one middle class and one lower class, were included for comparison purposes. The 20 upper elementary teachers in these two schools received no consultation.

The consultants received special training prior to and concurrent with their work with the teachers in the schools. Drs. Eli Bower (Hollister & Bower, 1967) and Ruth Newman (Newman, 1967) were responsible for much of this training. They discussed their respective approaches to school consultation and guided the six specialists through problematic situations that would arise during the consultations.

This project began during the fall of 1966 when pre-data were collected; consultation took place during the fall and winter months, and final data were collected in May 1967, three months after the consultations were completed. The consultants spent two hours each week in group discussions with the teachers. They also visited classrooms to make observations which would often culminate in individual conferences. The project plans called for both the group discussions and the individual conferences to center on teachers' own reactions to the classroom groups, especially to problem incidents involving several students. The consultants were to emphasize the development of trust in the group and to open up new pathways of behavior and new understandings of desired changes only after some trust had developed. Finally, they were to explore in depth how teachers might interact with students with interpersonal relations problems, low self-esteem, marked disinterest in learning, or recurrent daydreams and inattention.

Consultation Sessions

The consultants wrote historical accounts of every meeting with teachers, whether in group discussions or individual conferences. Along with these detailed descriptions of each encounter with teachers, the consultants were asked to jot down at the close of each session any problems they were having in establishing themselves as helpful and to specify any changes they saw in the schools, especially changes in the teachers with whom they were consulting.

Analyses of the consultants' reports indicated that certain recurrent themes appeared during the 15 weeks. During the first several sessions, classroom group problems were viewed as resulting from forces outside the control of the teachers. The teachers primarily ventilated their antagonistic feelings toward the "impersonal and unhelpful central office," the "authoritarian principal," the "incompetent counselor," the "uninterested parents," or the "intransigent students." These parties were seen as limiting the level of effectiveness that could be expected of the teachers. Some teachers felt that membership in the consultation group was involuntary, feeling that a school counselor, parental group, or the principal had really organized the group. Others needed reassurance that the principal or central office personnel would not be involved directly in the consultation groups.

After the teachers had a chance to voice these feelings in a supportive atmosphere, without being sanctioned by the consultants, they were more likely to discuss problems present in their classrooms and to see themselves and their students as jointly involved in them. As classroom group or individual problems were brought up for discussion, the teachers looked to the consultants for the solutions. They expected the consultants to recommend concrete actions that could be taken to solve the problem. At times, they expected the consultant to direct the principal or central office administrators that certain students perceived as mentally unhealthy should be removed formally from the regular classroom and placed in special education classes. The consultants generally assumed the point of view that they could only help teachers find their own answers, that these answers would most likely involve the teachers' changing their own classroom behavior, and that they did not have the authority to remove youngsters from classes.

Toward the end of the 15-week period, the teachers talked more about their own insecurities, doubts, and lack of knowledge and skills. During this phase the teachers turned more to one another for sharing ideas on handling classroom group problems. They offered to meet with one another at other times during the week to share teaching practices. The consultants' role became less prominent as the teachers conversed more freely and openly about their own classroom problems.

Results of Project 2

The consultants generally agreed that significant and positive changes occurred in many teachers as a consequence of the consultations. Perhaps the most striking change was in teachers' asking one another for help. Early in the year, many teachers reported that they were ashamed to ask for one another's assistance. The teachers were generally discouraged or indifferent about staff relations. But after the consultations many teachers had formed a strong group feeling, had a new sense of challenge and interest, and were using one another outside the sessions to talk over problems, trade materials, and respond to new ideas. Some teachers who had decided during the fall to give up teaching changed their minds as they noted how much support they felt from their colleagues.

Another general direction of change in the teachers was toward a more differentiated examination of their standards and attitudes, with somewhat greater leeway for accepting a variety of student behaviors. One consultant noted that his teachers showed more interest and ability to deal with individual differences. Another commented that a number of students had been perceived by their teachers as being disturbed, but that during the course of consultations this was changed to perceiving the students as more energetic, restless, and child-like than disturbed. According to one consultant, because the teachers' behaviors toward these children changed, some classroom problems seemed to disappear.

Some teachers were seen as reaching a stage in which they could examine their own behavior as a factor in creating undesirable behavior in their students. Other teachers spoke less judgmentally of students and parents at the end of the consultation and instead were more likely to explore their own relationships to their students. Some began to sort out their own needs from those of the students, while others noted publicly that "problem students" often ceased being problems when a teacher extended special help, affection, and arranged for some success.

Early during the fall and again late in the spring, four self-report questionnaires were collected from the total group of 60 teachers. Three teachers' questionnaires focused on perceptual variables, measuring conceptions about self as teacher, ways of categorizing students, and conceptions of positive mental health in the classroom. Two skilled raters who had no contact with the consultants scored the results of these three questionnaires without knowing whether the teachers being rated were in the consultation or comparison groups. Their initial ratings were in high agreement, generally above 90 per cent, but they continued to score items about which they disagreed until they achieved 100 per cent agreement.

The fourth questionnaire queried teachers on how they might handle a variety of problematic situations in the classroom. Each consultant scored all of these protocols. The consultants did not know what teacher or school they were scoring, nor did they know whether they were scoring the fall or the spring data. Scores of plus, zero, minus, or question mark were given. A plus meant that the situation was handled effectively. A score of minus meant that the consultant viewed the teacher's response as ineffective. A zero meant that the consultant was unable to make a judgment because the verbal content required a certain kind of nonverbal response or context. A question mark meant that the response was unclear and therefore could not be coded. In the analysis of these data, we required that four or more of the consultants agree before giving the response a plus, minus, or zero score. When only three or fewer consultants agreed, we scored the item with a question mark. The consultants did not see any results of the four questionnaires until after the consultations were completed.

In measuring the teachers' self-concepts, they were asked to write down ten phrases which described themselves as teachers. Then they were asked to go back to each phrase and to place a double plus sign if they considered that characteristic very positive, a single plus sign if they considered it somewhat positive, and a negative sign if they thought of it as somewhat negative, or a double negative sign if they considered it to be very negative.

We anticipated that the consultations would lead to a more balanced view of oneself as a teacher. We thought that those teachers who viewed themselves in the fall as quite negative and insecure would gain a greater sense of competence and self-esteem from the consultation. On the other hand, we considered that those who saw themselves as solely positive and effective in the fall would begin to uncover some areas within themselves that required some improvement. Thus the raters judged as more positive those self-concept patterns which became more balanced, containing both positive and negative attributes, or which changed from more negative to more positive, and judged as more negative those patterns which remained predominantly negative or defensively positive.

In the questionnaire on categorizing the students, teachers were given a set of cards with the names of all students, one to a card, and the following instructions:

> In your mind, there are probably many ways in which the students can be seen as similar to and different from one another. Place these cards in piles in as many different ways as might occur in your thinking. Each time you place the cards into piles, you should have some main idea in mind and a descriptive title for each pile.
>
> For instance, in your mind, you might divide the class into boys and girls. Then you would sort the cards into two piles, the main idea is "sex difference" and the descriptive titles of the piles are "boys" and "girls." Another division which might occur could be color of hair. Then "color of hair" would be the main idea, and "blondes," "brunettes," and "redheads" could be the descriptive titles.

We expected the teachers to develop in several ways as a consequence of the consultation. For one thing, we considered that teachers with consultation would use more main ideas having to do with emotional factors, attitudes, motivations, and interpersonal relations at the end of the school year. We expected more categories on topics such as anxiety, security, self-esteem, attitudes toward school, and peer relations. Further, we expected that the teachers who received consultation would increase the number of differentiations that they made under the main categories. We felt that the consultation would facilitate a more sophisticated and differentiated view of the students. We expected that the teachers might see their students more in terms of feelings but also as being increasingly different from one another.

The third questionnaire was aimed at measuring teachers' cognitive structures concerning "mental health" in the classroom. Each teacher wrote about his ideas of good mental health practices and conditions in the classroom by placing one idea each on a maximum of 25 small index cards. The teachers received the following directions:

> Let us suppose that the following situation occurs. A visiting teacher from a foreign country engages you in conversation about school practices in this country. Assume that your visitor knows very little about American teaching practices. He wants to know what you consider to be good mental health practices and conditions in the classroom. What sorts of things would you include in a list which he could refer to as he tries to learn about classroom mental health?
>
> Using these cards which have been provided, write one word, phrase, or sentence on each card which describes good classroom mental health

practices or conditions. Use as few or as many cards as you need. A total of 25 cards is supplied.

In order to ensure that the foreign visitor has understood you, try to organize the items you listed on the cards. Do this in the following way: Lay out in front of you all the cards you used in listing mental health practices and conditions. Look them over to see whether they fall into some broad, natural groupings. If they do, arrange them into such groups. Now look at your groups to see whether these can be broken into subgroups. If they can, separate the cards accordingly. It is also possible that these subgroups can be broken down still further.

The range of groupings generally included physical properties of the room and school, physical properties of teachers or students, intellectual skills, personality characteristics including attitudes and motives, interpersonal relations, and group social relations, climate, and cohesiveness. We expected that after the consultation the teachers would emphasize students' attitudes, feelings, and motives, as well as classroom interpersonal relations and group climate. Although physical characteristics might be included, we viewed these as less central to effective classroom group processes. We further considered that the mental health categories would have more detailed subgroupings and that the teachers would relate these more directly to the students in their class.

The fourth questionnaire, titled "Classroom Situations," was made up of 44 situations which were taken from actual classrooms and presented in the form of dialogues. The teachers received these directions:

Pretend you are the teacher in each situation (even if you have not met such a situation or would not have allowed it to develop). When the dialogue closes, write the exact words or nonverbal responses you would use at that point.

Data collected from the teachers generally indicated positive and significant changes during the school year in their perceptions of self as teacher, their cognitions of mental health categories, and their views on how to work with problematic classroom situations. The data on categorizing students did not change greatly during the year. These data are summarized in Table 6. Fisher's Exact Test, applied because of the very small sample, requires a two-by-two contingency table, and thus for purposes of this statistical analysis the data labeled "more negative" were dropped. In each case, except for the data on categorizing students, results of Fisher's Exact Test showed probabilities less than .01 (Hays, 1963). We can assume that these data indicate significant changes and therefore that the consultations altered many teachers' cognitions related to successful teaching.

The students also were asked to complete four questionnaires in the fall and spring. One questionnaire measured students' perceptions concerning the informal group processes in the class. Each student answered 12 questions on how he saw others in the class behaving, with one of four answers: almost always, usually, seldom, or almost never. Some of the items were:

TABLE 6

Summary of Teachers' Perceptions of Self, Students, and Classroom Processes by Group, Fall and Spring

EVALUATION IN SPRING COMPARED WITH FALL	SELF-CONCEPT				CATEGORIZING STUDENTS				MENTAL HEALTH CATEGORIES				CLASSROOM SITUATIONS			
	CONSULTATION GROUP		COMPARISON GROUP		CONSULTATION GROUP		COMPARISON GROUP		CONSULTATION GROUP		COMPARISON GROUP		CONSULTATION GROUP		COMPARISON GROUP	
	NO.	PER CENT	NO.	PER CENT	NO.	PER CENT	NO.	PER CENT	NO.	PER CENT	NO.	PER CENT	NO.	PER CENT	NO.	PER CENT
More positive	14	35	2	10	5	12	0	0	15	38	0	0	19	48	3	15
No change	24	60	16	80	35	88	20	100	24	60	20	100	14	35	13	65
More negative	2	5	2	10	0	0	0	0	1	2	0	0	7	17	4	20
Probabilities from Fisher's Exact Tests	$p < .01$				$p = NS$				$p < .01$				$p < .01$			

"Help one another with their schoolwork," "Laugh when someone mis-
behaves," and "Work well with one another." The second questionnaire
measured attitudes toward school and self-esteem with incomplete sentence
stems. Examples of items used to measure the former were: "Studying is
————," "Homework is ————," "Learning out of books is ————." Self-
esteem was measured with stems such as "When I look at other boys and
girls and then look at myself, I feel ————," "When I look in the mirror,
I ————," and "My teacher thinks I am ————." The third questionnaire
presented sociometric questions on friendship and helping relations, asking
students to choose the four other students in the class whom they liked
the most and the four who were most helpful to other students. They also
estimated their own status in the group on being liked and helpful. The
fourth questionnaire dealt with students' attitudes about academic work
and school in general. The students were asked about such things as how
hard they saw themselves working, whether the teacher really understood
them, and whether the students helped one another.

An overview of the results indicated that positive and significant changes
did *not* occur in the consultation classes. The students' attitudes toward
school and self did not improve in either the consultation or the comparison
groups. The informal group processes appear to have remained about the
same throughout the year, except for some evidence that helpfulness increased in the consultation groups.

The overall results do, however, obscure some positive changes that occurred in a few classrooms. Out of the 40 consultation classes, six showed
distinct improvement and these, interestingly, were all within two schools.
In these six classes, the friendship and helpfulness patterns became more
diffuse over the course of the year. Moreover, significant changes occurred
in the positive self-esteem of many of these students. In contrast with this,
no changes whatsoever occurred in the students' attitudes toward school.

It appears that the cognitive and attitudinal changes which occurred
in the teachers were *not* also accompanied by behavioral changes that
made a difference in their classrooms. The teachers grew in their intellectual
awarenesses about interpersonal relations in the classroom and in their
willingness to explore new ways of handling them, but they did not in fact
make major shifts in their classroom behavior. Any behavior changes that
did occur, as reported by the consultants, were probably short-term and
motivated out of desires to please the consultants. The group processes in
the classrooms, by and large, remained unaffected by the consultations.

PROJECT 3: ORGANIZATIONAL DEVELOPMENT
LABORATORY

In Project 3, we did not attempt to influence directly teachers' capabilities
for working more effectively with classroom group processes. Rather we
assumed that the social relations of a school set the stage for classroom inno-

vation and that more effective organizational processes support teacher innovativeness and performance in the classroom (Lippitt, Barakat, Chesler, Dennerell, Flanders, Worden, & Schmuck, 1966). Some aspects of effective school processes that we assumed to be related to classroom innovativeness and productivity were the interpersonal relations and feelings, communication patterns, and group norms of the staff.

This project was aimed at improving school organizational processes in the short run so that classroom innovations might be made more easily in the long run. It employed an organizational training program to help a junior high school faculty to become more aware, open, analytic, and skillful about its interpersonal relationships, communication patterns, behavior norms, decision-making processes, and group problem-solving skills.

A six-day laboratory was held before the beginning of school, 1967, and involved the entire faculty—except for two with illnesses in their families—including the head custodian, head cook, and administrative secretary, making a total group of 54 participants. The laboratory staff was composed of five trainers. The laboratory was designed to help the staff discuss its interpersonal relations, identify and explore its communicative problems, and move toward tentative working solutions through group problem solving. Several follow-up training sessions were also scheduled during the 1967–68 school year. Some early developments warrant inclusion here because of the light they shed on helping teachers improve classroom group processes. A report is currently being written (Schmuck & Runkel, in press).

Laboratory for the Faculty

During the first two days of the laboratory the design called for a series of structured group exercises which were to lead the faculty into discussions about its own organizational processes. For instance, a "NASA Trip to the Moon" exercise was employed in which five groups of 10 or 11 persons formed to decide on those items that would be most important to carry on a fictitious 200-mile trip across the moon's surface. The underlying theme of this exercise concerned the efficient uses of individual resources in making group decisions. After the exercise was completed, discussions were initiated by the trainers with such questions as: "What were your reactions to the exercise?" "How did you feel?" "What were you thinking?" "How similar or different were your behaviors here from the way they usually are in school?" and "What implications does this exercise have for your staff?" These discussions were followed by a general assembly of the entire faculty in which staff members gave their reactions to what they learned during the exercise. Each group chose its own way to report back on what it had experienced. Some elected a spokesman, while others held a group discussion in front of the general assembly. These group processes also were discussed as they took place. The trainers attempted to support openness and the giving and receiving of helpful feedback during these sessions.

Subsequent sessions during the first two days were similar in form. They began with a structured activity, were followed by discussion in small groups about the activity, and ended with some sharing of various insights on organizational processes within the entire faculty. Some of the structured activities involved nonverbal cooperation, preparation of murals depicting psychological views of the school, planning and executing a complex puzzle requiring coordination, and a communication and feedback exercise in which staff members gave feedback to one another in variously sized groups and were required to indicate that they were "hearing" by paraphrasing what the other had just said. In all of these activities the faculty members regrouped each time using the criterion of seeking out persons with whom they had communicated very little.

The remainder of the laboratory was spent in working through a six-stage problem-solving process. The staff was asked to choose "real" issues that were bothersome to the organizational functioning of the school. Three problems were identified as being the most significant: (1) a lack of role clarification, (2) low degrees of staff involvement in meetings, and (3) the nonuse of staff resources. While proceeding through the initial problem identification stage, several group formations and processes were employed that would be useful forms for the staff's operations during the school year.

After the three problems were identified, staff members volunteered to work jointly on one of them and proceeded through the problem-solving processes that involved five more steps: (1) further problem refinement and operationalization, (2) force field diagnostic exercises, (3) brainstorming action alternatives to reduce restraining forces, (4) designing concrete plans of action, and (5) trying out the plan with a training activity involving the rest of the staff.

The three training activities designed by the problem-solving groups represented high points of the laboratory. The group who worked on role clarification felt that a lack of trust among the staff was one important restraining force keeping staff members from clarifying their roles. They carried out a variety of nonverbal exercises to explore feelings of trust in the total staff. Each of these was followed by discussion on its meanings for the organizational functioning of the faculty. The second group, on staff involvement, organized several small discussion groups and acted as outside observers. During these discussions, persons who had been talking a great deal during the last five-minute interval were asked by the observers to move back from the group and to stop talking. Others still in the group were told that those who had moved back were not to answer any questions asked of them. When only two persons were left, discussions were held in each group on "feelings toward involvement during staff meetings." The third group, involved with using staff resources, set up several small groups, each of which was a simulated mini-staff of a junior high school. A crisis was pictured in which no texts or materials were available, but youngsters were coming to school the next day. Each staff person was told to specialize in an area other than his own subject matter and to seek help from others in his group. The fictitious staffs were to construct a curriculum by using one another's resources. The whole faculty assembled at the end to discuss implications for their organizational functioning.

The laboratory ended with a "strength exercise" that was designed to raise members' self-esteem and contribute to group cohesiveness. The staff divided into small groups of seven or eight. Each staff member spent a few minutes reflecting alone on his own strengths as a staff member and the unique strengths of others in his group. The time spent alone was followed by a sharing of these "strength perceptions." No admissions or observations of weaknesses were allowed. Every group included each of its members in its discussion and then the entire faculty discussed meanings of the exercise.

Results of Project 3

Faculty members were asked to complete several self-report questionnaires just prior to or during the laboratory. These were designed to measure the schools' organizational climate, reactions to staff meetings, staff communication patterns, and perceptions of the principal. The research evaluation also called for some interviews and observations to be collected during the school year, as well as these same self-report questionnaires again in the spring. All the measures, whether they were questionnaires, interviews, or observations, were designed originally to center only on organizational processes. They did not include questions about classroom innovations.

We learned only inadvertently about the teachers' making use of experiences from the laboratory in their classrooms. The first signs came immediately after the laboratory when a one-page questionnaire was filled out by all faculty members on their reactions to the laboratory. Even though no question about classroom applications of the workshop was asked, seven teachers mentioned plans to make use of some laboratory experiences in their classrooms.

A second indication came in some of the essays about the laboratory written by 21 teachers. All workshop participants had the opportunity of receiving two hours of university credit for active participation. Twenty-one teachers desired three credit hours and were required to prepare an essay on their laboratory experiences. Their assignment was to write about any changes, positive or negative, in the school's operation which they considered attributable to the laboratory. They were asked to complete the essay no later than six weeks after the end of the laboratory. Most papers came in about one month after it closed. We expected to receive analyses of the school's organizational functioning primarily. Many of the faculty members, however, wrote extended reviews of how the laboratory had positively influenced their classroom performances. Some were quite specific about having used, with their students, some of the group formations, techniques, or processes employed during the laboratory.

Finally, a third sign of classroom application came about six weeks after the laboratory closed when we visited the school to interview staff members about the faculty's organizational processes. Again, even though no question was asked formally in the interview about classroom innovations, 15 teachers mentioned using new group processes in their classrooms. With these unanticipated data, we added one question to the interview schedule for the next round of interviews. The question was, "Has the laboratory experience influenced your classroom teaching in any ways? If yes, in what ways?" Of the 20 teachers who were interviewed on the second round, 19 answered yes to the question.

The teachers' comments on "in what ways" the laboratory influenced their teaching divided into three categories. Some teachers mentioned only very general outcomes such as "a change in my general approach to students," "a better atmosphere in my classroom," or "more attention to the feelings of the students." Another small group of teachers commented on specific attitude changes such as "I am more comfortable this year," "I am sensitive to students' feedback," or "I am more relaxed in letting the students discuss things." Eleven of the 19 teachers fitted into the third category. They mentioned specific group procedures that they actually were using in their classrooms such as "using small groups for projects," "using nonverbal exercises to depict feelings about the subject matter being studied," "using 'theatre in the round' or 'fishbowl' formations for having students observe one another," "using a paraphrasing exercise to point out how poor classroom communications are," "using the problem-solving sequence and techniques in social studies classes to learn more about social problems," and "using small groups for giving and receiving feedback about how the class is going." As far as we know, none of these practices was used by these teachers before the organizational development laboratory.

DISCUSSION AND CONCLUSIONS

The three interventions discussed above helped teachers, directly or indirectly, to work toward improving classroom group processes.

The organizational development laboratory for a school staff, described in Project 3, set the stage unexpectedly for staff members' attention to classroom group processes by encouraging them to experiment with innovative group procedures in the school organization. Training activities carried out during the laboratory presented group forms, techniques, and procedures that could be used just as appropriately in the classroom as at staff meetings. The laboratory was a living example of McLuhan's dictum that "the medium is the message" (McLuhan, 1964). A majority of the teachers tried new group processes in their classrooms that were directly patterned after their organizational laboratory experiences.

In Project 2, regular discussions about classroom group processes with psychological consultants helped improve teachers' perceptions of self as teachers, their cognitions of mental health categories, and their views on how to work with problematic classroom situations. However, these cognitive and attitudinal changes were not accompanied by behavioral changes in the classroom. This is not surprising since verbal learning is quite different from skill learning. Persons do not learn to play baseball, to dance, or to give speeches by reading books or through discussions. Nor should a teacher be expected to improve the complex skills of classroom instruction through mere discussions. Discussions on classroom group problems, students' psycho-dynamics, and different approaches to teaching can be expected to assist a teacher to think, talk, or write more intelligently about the issues, but actual behavioral tryouts and experiences are necessary before new skills are used easily in the classroom.

A teacher development laboratory which included problem-solving techniques, sensitivity training, and role-play tryouts did lead to behavioral changes in the classroom. The sensitivity training and related human relations activities seemed to challenge teachers' cognitions of interpersonal relations, to lead teachers to introspect on their effects on others, to encourage teachers to explore their values about teaching, and to develop colleague norms of support and helpfulness. The problem-solving procedures helped teachers think more systematically about new patterns of classroom behavior, and the role-play tryouts helped build psychological connections among new cognitions, attitudes, and behaviors.

Taken together, these interventions can fit well into integrated action programs that might be employed by school systems for improving classroom group processes. Two integrated programs of different durations can be mentioned here.

One would take place over an 18-month period. It would commence with an organizational development laboratory during the latter part of August, just prior to the beginning of the school year. Following this, teachers would be asked to volunteer for a program of consultation and training in classroom group processes. A psychological consultant, skilled in interpersonal relations theory and classroom processes, would work with them two hours each week for the entire academic year. Then, during the following summer, a teacher development laboratory would take place. Follow-up discussions could occur during the fall semester to help the teachers follow through on trying out new procedures and to reinforce continuously any insights or new skills developed during the previous year.

Another, shorter program, lasting for only about six months, would be launched with an organizational development laboratory just two weeks before school begins. Since many school systems now grant some days prior to the school's opening for inservice training, it would be possible to extend those days into a week and to spend that week in a teacher development laboratory. This two-week, back-to-back laboratory program would facilitate the translation of group processes found to be useful during the organizational laboratory into classroom innovations during the teacher development laboratory. Then, during the fall semester, follow-up discussions could be led by psychological consultants who would emphasize the problem-solving process and give support to teachers trying to implement their plans.

Many other action designs might be developed using these three basic interventions as the elements. We hope that behavioral scientists and educators will collaborate in trying some of them.

References

Bradford, L., Gibb, J., & Benne, K. *T-group theory and laboratory method.* New York: Wiley, 1964.

Chesler, M., & Fox, R. *Role-playing methods in the classroom.* Chicago: Science Research Associates, 1966.

Coch, L., & French, J. R. P., Jr. Overcoming resistance to change. *Human Relations*, 1948, 1, 512–532.

Edelmann, A., & Schmuck, R. Pilot study in exploring the use of mental health consultants to teachers of socially maladjusted pupils in regular classes. Unpublished final report. Philadelphia, Pa.: Mental Health Association of Southeastern Pennsylvania, 1967.

Flanders, N., & Havumaki, S. The effect of teacher-pupil contacts involving praise on the sociometric choices of students. *J. educ. Psychol.*, 1960, 51, 65–68.

Fox, R., Luszki, Margaret, & Schmuck, R. *Diagnosing classroom learning environments.* Chicago: Science Research Associates, 1966.

Hays, W. *Statistics for psychologists.* New York: Holt, Rinehart & Winston, 1963. Pp. 598–601.

Hollister, W., & Bower, E. (Eds.). *Behavioral science frontiers in education.* New York: Wiley, 1967.

Kaufman, M., Schmuck, R., & Lippitt, R. *Creative practices developed by teachers for improving classroom atmospheres.* Document No. 14, Inter-Center Program on Children, Youth, and Family Life. Ann Arbor, Mich.: Institute for Social Research, 1963.

Lippitt, R., Barakat, H., Chesler, M., Dennerell, D., Flanders, Mary, Worden, O., & Schmuck, R. The teacher as innovator, seeker and sharer of new practices. In R. Miller (Ed.), *Perspectives on educational change.* New York: Appleton-Century-Crofts, 1967. Pp. 307–324.

McLuhan, M. *Understanding media.* New York: McGraw-Hill, 1964.

Newman, Ruth. *Psychological consultation in the schools.* New York: Basic Books, 1967.

Schmuck, R. Sociometric status and utilization of academic abilities. *Merrill-Palmer Quart.*, 1962, 8, 165–172.

Schmuck, R. Some relationships of peer liking patterns in the classroom to pupil attitudes and achievement. *School Rev.*, 1963, 71, 337–358.

Schmuck, R. Some aspects of classroom social climate. *Psychol. in the Schools*, 1966, 3(1), 59–65.

Schmuck, R., Chesler, M., & Lippitt, R. *Problem solving to improve classroom learning.* Chicago: Science Research Associates, 1966.

Schmuck, R., & Runkel, P. Organizational training for a school faculty. Eugene, Ore.: Center for the Advanced Study of Educational Administration, in press.

Schmuck, R., & Van Egmond, E. Sex differences in the relationships of interpersonal perceptions to academic performances. *Psychol. in the Schools,* 1965, 2(1), 32–40.

B.   Organizational Change

Changing Schools Through Student Advocacy *

MARK A. CHESLER AND JOHN E. LOHMAN

American high schools typically do not involve students in the legitimate exercise of influence or control over their school life; the major educational decisions are made by trained professionals. Young people are expected to obey such adult decisions and to believe that their best interests are being served thereby. In more and more schools across the country, students are expressing their alienation and anger at this situation. They are advocating their own definitions of "what's good for them," and are demanding new and more responsive forms of school governance. In this article, we review some of the problems and potentials of greatly increased student power in the conduct of school matters, and some relevant training programs and organizational renewal strategies.

CURRENT POLITICAL ISSUES IN SCHOOLS

Contemporary events in secondary schools reflect a breakdown in the traditional operation of professionals and professional systems. Haug and Sussman (1969) detail the generic phenomenon: "Students, the poor and the black community no longer accept uncritically the service offerings of the establishment . . . this is the revolt of the client."

Bases for Client-Professional Conflict

There are three general bases for the current conflict between professionals and clients. First, many students and parents have argued recently that educa-

---

* The authors have drawn many of the ideas and examples discussed here from the thinking and work of their colleagues in the Educational Change Team of the School of Education, University of Michigan. This chapter is a product of their combined efforts.

REPRINTED from *Organization Development in Schools* by R. A. Schmuck and M. Miles (Eds.) by permission of National Press Books.

tors are not automatically competent and may in fact lack the technical skill to make and implement decisions in the interest of other people's welfare.

In a second and more value-laden context, it is clear that some clients do not define their interests in the same way that professionals define the clients' interest. Since professionals and clients sometimes come from different backgrounds and cultures, they may have different perspectives and goals. For example, a secondary curriculum drawn from a certain historical context may be in conflict with many youngsters' preferences and needs. When the professional defends and implements the historical plan he may run counter to his clients' notions of their self-interest. As Bennis (1970) points out:

> Questions of legitimacy arise whenever "expert power" becomes ineffective. Thus black militants, drug users, draft resisters, student protesters and liberated women all deny the legitimacy of those authorities who are not black, drug-experienced, pacifists, students or women.
>
> Moreover, the very roles of professional and client may provide another basis for value conflict—as witnessed by student and teacher conflicts over the definitions of such things as dress, grooming, and order and discipline during class. To the extent that professionals retain the power to make decisions for others, they are vulnerable to the challenge of conflict over moral choice.
>
> A third base of contention derives from experience with professionals' gradual accretion of privilege, which now must be defended against violation or intrusion. The economic and political self-interests of a class of professionals establish new bases for interest-group conflicts. For instance, teachers who have gained power over clients are now unwilling to relinquish that aspect of their role. The professional tradition of accountability to peers protects the educator from client evaluation and interference. This protection may or may not be in the client's best interest, but it surely adds to the comfort and power of the profession.

Consequences of Client-Professional Conflict

Clients recognize that professionals have interests that may be in conflict with their own and they naturally experience a loss of trust in the ability of professionals to act in the best interest of clients. The following statement from a student we worked with may exemplify this loss of trust.

> What's very important is that you need trust. It's got to the point where nobody don't trust nobody, and that's all the student body got to look up to. If you've got a problem you're supposed to take it to the administration—if you feel that your teacher or counselor can't handle it—you go to the administration. When you can't do that because you don't trust them, what can you do with your problems?

Deterioration of trust in schools is not, in our view, to be conceived primarily as a problem in interpersonal relations. Individual predispositions and expectations surely play a part, but the erosion of trust noted here is essentially *systemic*. It is established and maintained by organizational assumptions, priorities and role structures. For example, educators insulate themselves from students both through lack of contact and elaborate control devices (passes, locked toilets, etc.). Similarly, students employ defenses of distance as a protection against the distrust they feel. But distance will not do as a solution; since school does matter to most youngsters they must somehow insure its relevance for them. Without trust in the system to meet their needs in their own terms, these clients must take the management of their interests into their own hands. In order for them to do so, power entrusted to professionals must accrue to clients.

Lack of interpersonal trust and organizational role reciprocity between students and educators, and stress upon adults' control of youthful clients, make it clear to students that they are without authority. Thus the lines of distinction between the "rulers" and the "ruled" are overt, visible, and liable to attack. A greater potential for highly escalated conflict exists where such role characteristics constantly remind students of their lower status and influence.

Kvaraceus (1965) points out that a heavy stress upon external and adult controls "tends to deepen the misunderstanding and resentment that exist between youth and adult," and notes further that when strong bureaucratic controls in the school are successful they create "a reluctant and recalcitrant conformist living close to the letter of the law." On the other hand, if unsuccessful, they create "the overt aggressive delinquent who is a member of an 'outlaw gang.' " Neither of these alternatives is an attractive educational outcome, although only the latter presents a challenge to good order and harmonious relations in school.

When large numbers of students resent and distrust the control mechanisms employed by educational professionals, the effect is to undermine the collective and legitimate authority of the school. Continued belief by clients that those in authority are abusing their prerogatives sooner or later leads to a denial of the legitimacy of that authority. And students no longer believe that school personnel will act in their immediate behalf, or even in their long-run best interest; thus they are more likely to rely on coercive influence attempts. This proposition is further explicated in Gamson (1968). For students, who have few legitimate channels for the exercise of influence or control over school life, coercion usually means the use of disruptive power. The traditional distrust and powerlessness of clients in the educational system thus sets the stage for the unmodulated and disruptive exercise of power.

When previously impotent groups finally do attain the right and opportunity to influence policy, they are often treated by prior influentials as unwelcome. They may also lack experience and skill in the judgment of issues that do require some professional expertise. Educators faced with such new definitions of the relations between professional and client, and with clients' use of power to redress past relations, often feel severely threatened and generally resist both a redefinition of the role of expert and a reallocation of power within the organization. The cultural clash between the revolutionary demands of many young people and the reformist or essentially traditional change goals of those in power makes this conflict even greater.

RATIONALES FOR CHANGE IN POWER RELATIONS

Regardless of their social, ethnic, or racial backgrounds, or their level in the status hierarchy of the school, many students are engaged in a common quest—the search for some control over their lives in school. The disparity between students' actual influence and the educational rhetoric of democracy, community, national solidarity, etc., is particularly acute when youngsters attempt to change something. One urban teen-ager we know asserted that:

. . . administration's always saying they wanted student participation . . . it seems to me that all they wanted us to say, lookit, there's kids that are participating, there's kids that want to do something . . . but they don't really want us to get what we're asking . . . they just said why don't you wait until next week, and why don't you wait until next month? Talk to some more people. Pretty soon everybody [in the group] quit. Got tired out.

Some of the issues in the student search for power are evident in the following quotes from other students:

The administration invited us to this meeting, and said how they wanted us to make a new dress code and how it would be real nice . . . and then they said that the only problem is that the Board of Education won't permit the different schools to have different dress codes—that's not true. There's high schools all over—two in one district—that have different dress codes. I don't know why they said that. Guess they really don't want us to have a new dress code.

The principal was supposed to bring it to the Board meeting and he didn't bring it up. He just talked to them a couple seconds before the meeting. And they said, "Well don't bring it up now, we've got too much to do." And then later he told the student council advisor that students shouldn't come to the Board meeting any more because they might mess something up.

Last time all the kids went to the Board meeting for something all they did was kick 'em out of school.

These comments indicate a confusion or lack of clarity on the part of students about their appropriate participatory roles. Administrative evasion and false rhetoric serve to muddy these dangerous waters further. Students have a geat deal of pluralistic ignorance about a political system in which the real mechanics are invisible to them. The power structure is more visible to teachers who do participate in some decisions, or at least are acquainted with the vagaries and nuances of school decision-making. Likewise, students who hold office and go to meetings have greater sophistication (and often cynicism) about what is happening there. But many others, uninvolved and ignorant about influence processes, are confused when asked about their influence. They are certainly not informed rebels or followers, but *non-citizens* of the most potent political organization in their lives so far.

Chesler (1969) suggests that students' desires to control their own lives and to influence the behavior of others in order to make their demands heard and implemented are at the root of many protests and school disruptions. Although these issues may be surfaced most dramatically in protests, Duggal (1968) argues that the level of student participation is low for our schools regardless of their "unrest."

On what grounds can such proposals for change be made? We believe there are three important bases for the claim that increased student power is desirable: educational, moral, and political.

The Educational Rationale

Youth are clearly justified in feeling that their power is a key variable in determining the quality of life in school. The degree to which influence is shared among the various parts or levels of institutions affects members' feelings of involvement and commitment.[1] When an organizational structure does not permit student participation in decision-making, the results may thus be political alienation, rebellion, and efforts to exert coercive influence or control.

Wittes's (1970) study of crisis-torn high schools indicates that students' perceptions of their ability to influence school policy have important implications for their desire to achieve academic success. When students feel they have influence, and when they are in a peer group that has access to school power, they more often believe that they can control their own educational fate. Participation in influencing school policy, then, may be meaningful for educational outcomes and purposes in one's personal life.

In a similar vein, Polk (1968) found that students who attended a high school with modular scheduling (emphasizing the students' responsibility for their own learning progress) were more likely to score higher on Rotter's scale of internal control than were comparable students who attended traditional high schools. Coleman's (1966) nationwide survey of schools found that the feeling of being able to control one's own environment was related more highly to the academic achievement of students than all other characteristics of a student's background put together, or than all other school characteristics put together. Thus there is clear evidence that school political structures are not trivial, but are associated with student attitudes and perceptions that are important for successful academic performance.

---

[1] Several theorists of organization development (Likert, 1961; McGregor, 1960; Argyris, 1964) also have postulated interdependent relationships among the formal structure of an organization, the perceptions and norms of the organization's members, and the individual's performance. Currently we know far less about the way such factors interact in schools than we would like; few studies have been carried out. Three major difficulties discourage research on such factors in schools: (1) difficulty in specifying the criterial measures; (2) long delays in school feedback loops (knowledge of results); (3) the hesitancy of researchers and administrators to deal with "political" variables.

Educationally speaking, changes in the allocation of decision-making power may also be supported on the basis of the added perspective and expertise that students may bring to organizational management and administration and to the conduct and supervision of learning experiences. Only students, of course, can truly represent their own unique interests, views, and preferences in school life. Organizations that do permit representation and utilize the skills of all their component groups are more likely to fulfill most members' needs.

The Moral Rationale

The reasons for increasing student power lie only partly in research indications that people are more likely to increase their learning in and commitment to organizations in which they are involved and for which they make important decisions. Among the other stimuli for change are more philosophic considerations of the justice and appropriateness of institutions' being governed by those people who live in and are affected by the decisions of those institutions.

More democratic forms of management and instruction may also be important models for students' personal and intellectual learning about the nature of and opportunity for democratic political influence in American society. This is not to suggest that such learning is the only issue; but the absence of democratic procedures in any of our social institutions obviously weakens the entire society.

The Political Rationale

Some very pragmatic political considerations also make reallocation of power imperative. Changes which meet the demands of protesting student groups may help cool the crisis in American secondary schools. But more importantly, they may also permit students legitimate power to alter the other things that make school life untenable. Since most school management is reactive rather than pro-active or creative in character, increased student power does provide very real promise that needed educational reforms will come about.

Meaningful student involvement may very well *not* "cool the crisis" but may increase conflict, since students—like other role groups—have unique goals and priorities which compete with others' goals and priorities. Obviously, political accommodation is in itself an insufficient rationale for student power; such accommodation only has viability when implemented for reasons or in ways that complement other more positive philosophical and educational rationales.

THE EXERCISE OF STUDENT POWER

If student power is to become real, not just a hoax or a cynical token to protesters, it will be expressed in procedures and structures that not only deviate from but even threaten current major institutional traditions and ways of life in school. It is crucial, therefore, to distinguish between programs which alter basic power arrangements and those activities which are limited to opening communication channels and encouraging informal influence or advice. The increase of communication and advice is a worthwhile activity, but it does not constitute sharing power; essentially power remains located in the same places while efforts are made to engender a psychological sense of participation.

Domains of Student Power

Some features of what we mean by the exercise of student power should help make the above distinction clear. It is our view that students should exert significant control over major portions of the formal activities and events of the school, including budgetary and fiscal policy; hiring, salary, and tenure of teachers; development and approval of curriculum and course offerings; development, approval, and enforcement of regulations governing conduct on school property; local graduation requirements; the school's role in the community; and development and implementation of procedures during crises.

Students, along with persons from other role groups in the district, must have adequate and timely access to information about the internal functioning of the school and its external transactions with the environment. If they are to have real power, students must have the opportunity and freedom to make mistakes. Along with other participants in the decision-making process, their roles must be legitimized by the school district, and their behavior made accountable to those who are affected by their decisions. The entire purpose of increased power of students is to expand the process of adult accountability to their clients. Some of these areas of decision-making deserve more comment.

Curriculum. One of the areas of school life where students can exercise power most immediately is the determination and implementation of the curriculum. The content of the curriculum, organization of classes, choice of classroom method, paths of curriculum sequencing, and criteria for success and fulfillment of a high school education all can be subject to review, guidance, and management by students. At the present time, many students who feel strongly about such matters vote individually by dropping out, sleeping in class, avoiding certain courses, and the like. Others rebel and organize protests to seek redress and change. Still other students obediently move through the system, having learned that power is not shared and, for them, is not worth arguing about. Yet they chafe at the lessons of impotence and exclusion and feel the alienation and distance between students' needs or goals and the organized content of instruction.

Finance. Students also need to play a role in the administration of school finances and in the allocation of moneys among various portions of the budget. Since innovative school activities and programs often founder on inadequate, unwise, or controversial allocations of funds, control over such areas may be required before anything else productive can happen. To shield students from making decisions on fiscal matters is to remove them from confrontation with some of the harshest realities (and most closely guarded preserves) of the school.

Personnel Matters. Student participation in decision-making also means that the qualifications of teachers as they are recruited, evaluated, considered for merit pay and promoted or transferred must be open for student review. Student voice in making decisions about the professional staff may also extend to the selection and evaluation of the high school principal. A great deal of arbitrary behavior by educators could be curtailed by using personnel procedures that reflect accountability of this sort. The development of criteria for teacher behavior, of observational or attitudinal instruments, and of methods for providing performance feedback would be helpful supports for such decision-making activities. Students' exercise of this responsibility is not merely self-serving; many teachers could benefit from knowing how their students experience the classroom and what suggestions or preferences they have. There is no reason why such a help or growth focus could not be built into student decision-making. Greater acrimony and distance between students and educators is not inevitable.

In these examples, we have gone beyond suggesting that students can be advisors to adult policy-making groups, or that the acme of student power is for students to have autonomy over their own social and athletic facilities and activities. Clearly, open channels of informal influence and autonomy in extracurricular activities are important innovations, but they represent only the beginning of strategic reform.

Of course, unilateral student control over clubs, dances, and other school-associated social or athletic events may be helpful in developing certain student skills and can lead to involvement in more sophisticated and serious efforts. For student decision-making to have the educational effects noted above, however, students must have real power, real authority, and hence *responsibility* for educational decisions and administrative governance of the school.

Suggestions that actualize these perspectives clearly threaten current legal and professional definitions of administrative power, union or association standards and agreements regarding teacher security and tenure, criteria for high school graduation, and customary notions of students' appropriate roles in school. (The professional reader who doubts this should pause at this point to envision what his role and his school would be like were student power to increase substantially—and to experience his feelings as he does so.)

A final aspect of involving students in decision-making should not be overlooked. It is best described in terms of the pluralism of interests among students on many issues. It is as overly simplistic to describe *the* student viewpoint on any educational issue as it is to assign a single viewpoint to *the* community of which the school is a part. Although there are some basic and pervasive issues on which a large proportion of students may be in agreement, adequate structures for student involvement in decision-making must acknowledge, legitimate, and be responsive to legitimate differences among students' values, goals, and life styles.

A New Model of Student Advocacy in School Change

Bold new approaches to fundamental educational change are needed. In the remainder of this chapter we shall describe one approach to educational change that is emerging out of our work with secondary schools facing severe conflict and crisis throughout the country. This approach might best be described as a *power-conflict model*.

While the foregoing analysis documents the systemic nature of educational problems, and our approach to educational change involves multiple role groups in school districts, we shall focus primarily upon the part student advocacy plays in our approach. This bias is justified, we believe, partly because it serves to highlight unique aspects of our work in schools and partly because in secondary schools today this is "where the action is." Student advocacy strategies are in use in many relatively spontaneous movements for school change. The development of a student Bill of Rights in New York City (Reeves, 1970), the Freedom Annex School in Washington, and free schools throughout the country represent such programs. The crucial question is whether professionals in organization development and training can (or will) adopt and use some of these strategies.[2]

Some Underlying Assumptions

It may be helpful at this point to clarify some of the distinctions between the power-conflict model of change proposed here and other approaches to organization development. Three premises or assumptions are present in our previous diagnosis of schools which most other OD models do not discuss explicitly. The first premise is that schools as social organizations are strain- and conflict-producing systems; that is, legitimate but competing and sometimes incompatible interests are endemic in the current structure of the school organization. Recognizing the need for legitimacy of pluralism, with the inevitable conflict that attends it, necessitates OD strategies which use conflict in an overt and constructive manner.

The second assumption in our model is that the members of a school district—students, teachers, and administrators—occupy roles and structures and operate with professional and organizational norms and procedures which keep them separate, and work against formal (and even informal) interaction and the development of cross-cutting ties of common interest, values, or feeling.

---

[2] Some of the issues relevant to the difficulties of advocacy for professional educational consultants are discussed in Chesler and Arnstein (1970) and Guskin and Ross (in press).

The third assumption is that all of the legitimate power, authority, and expertise in schools (and much of the informal power) presently resides entirely in the hands of boards, administrators, and some teachers in the school. A sizeable proportion of the total school district therefore has no formal access and (because of the communication and role barriers discussed previously) little informal access to power, influence, and control. The power-conflict model overtly addresses the distribution of power in the system by helping participants become aware of the nature of power inequities, and the feelings and behavior which such inequities engender in people. It focuses directly on strategies for power equalization.

Crucial Variables in Organizational Change

Katz and Kahn (1966) and Buchanan (1967 and 1969) review several approaches to OD and change. As they point out, few of these approaches attempt to change such major variables as the distribution of power or the priorities placed on the organization's goals. Thus they do not deal centrally with structural characteristics of the organization but focus on attidunal and interpersonal modifications. The most frequently documented models of OD in schools focus on opening communication channels and improving communication skills, increasing skills in "consensus" decision-making, or developing sophisticated data-gathering procedures through which "problems" can be detected and remedied by supervisory and administrative elites. The power-conflict model differs from other OD strategies in the emphasis which it gives to certain organizational dimensions and variables.

Conflict. The power-conflict model explicitly recognizes and legitimizes pluralistic or multiple goals and the goal and value conflicts which follow. As Leavitt (1965) suggests, most approaches to OD do not deal explicitly with this dimension, or make naive, idealized, and questionable assumptions (e.g., that organization goals and values are widely shared). Other strategies, assuming falsely a general commonality of interests, are vague about goal-setting or use only such criteria as expertise and a general organizational perspective in dealing with the issue.

An assumption common to many OD approaches is that decision-making by consensus is possible and desirable; this often ignores the possibility of incompatible differences. Such an approach may in fact be highly coercive: it results in action taken on the assumption of consensus where none may exist and moves decisions out of the public domain because of fears of "destructive and unmanageable" conflict.

The power-conflict model, on the other hand, assumes that differences are inevitable and that processes (such as voting or coercion) which include dialogue and negotiation and which enable decisions to be made in the face of strong opposition are at times necessary. The acknowledgment of such goal differences reinforces the moral or philosophical position that all relevant parties need to be actively involved in goal-setting.

Yet this perspective on the normality (and even virtue) of conflict is rare in educational circles. Campbell (1968) points out, for instance, that literature on the government and administration of education would lead one to suspect that there is high consensus within schools and little evidence of conflict. Such a public presentation is perhaps predictable: the literature is created by, written for, and consumed by educational professionals and members of community elites. No manager wants to hear that his operation is in conflict, and few who serve managers get around to saying it openly.

Yet "harmony" of this sort is quite atypical of schools. The assertion of harmony is especially preposterous in heterogeneous communities where there is high conflict and rapid change in the social, economic, and moral character of school life.

Social theorists and researchers have suggested certain organizational conditions most likely to make positive use of conflict and to avoid crisis. Social systems (such as schools) that do not recognize the existence of internal differences in values and interests and do not respond to or organize in terms of such divergence have no buffer against highly escalated conflict.

Yet conflict need not lead to the crisis or chaos which many educators fear and experience directly. For instance, Coser (1956) argues that conflict is most likely to be functional when groups are not completely polarized but when there are some possibilities of individuals' having membership in several groups at once. Smelser's (1963) concept that system stability is dependent on multiple internal cleavages is essentially the same.

In most schools, however, sharp divisions between people of different status and race do not permit overlapping or multiple memberships. Teachers who try to "fraternize" with students are rebuffed by students and viewed askance by peers. The reverse occurs as well; students cannot gain membership in the school faculty.

Power. A second principle is that groups in conflict may be able to negotiate and adjudicate differing interests when they have relatively equal amounts of power in an organization. However, it is quite clear that such parity does not exist in schools; there is not even the appearance of legitimate power-sharing among adult educators and their students. Largely for this reason, protesters seek the use of illegitimate and highly coercive power to force the school to respond to their interests. Temporary power balances can of course be brought into being through the use of disruption, but the issue is more one of developing new legitimate power structures. Laue (1968) argues similarly in reviewing the use of direct action techniques in community desegregation efforts. He notes that through the use of their bodies, blacks "developed a new source of power" as a substitute for participation in normal political channels. Excluded as they were from normal democratic means, they invented new procedures for influencing policy.

Power, including not only formal and legitimate organizational authority, but informal influence, is a crucial concept in our model. While many OD strategies focus on developing procedures and interpersonal skills for gaining access to influencing key decision-makers in organizations, we are also concerned with more formal and permanent structural changes, including the introduction of multiple roles in legitimate authority positions and decision-making groups. We do not necessarily assume, as others apparently do, that such power will be shared benevolently by those in authority. Power may have to be taken, as well as given up, in part because those newly in positions of authority need to test the limits of their power, and in part because those already in authority, despite noble intentions, are likely to see their self-interest (and probably the interests of the organization) threatened by any new power distribution.

Trust. A key variable in many of the person-oriented OD models is trust. Such strategies focus on opening up channels of communication about feelings, and require the development of an atmosphere of openness, support, and trust. The trust that develops is essentially personal or interpersonal in form: one trusts in the benevolence and common interests of other persons.

Trust is a key variable in the power-conflict approach as well, but it may take a different form. Trust that others will behave with your best interest in mind is less prevalent. Instead, one develops trust that others will adhere to certain norms or procedures: the "rules of the game" by which all parties have agreed to abide—rules for handling conflict, making decisions, upholding bargains, and so forth. Dahl (1967) has pointed out, for example, that conflict is most likely to be productive amidst organizational agreement about the fairness of the rules and the legitimacy of different parties' interests. Thus, in our model, *procedural* trust and *functional* trust—confidence that each will perform his organizational duties and responsibilities effectively—replace *interpersonal* trust as the basis for organizational integration to bind and hold the structure together.

We must point out, however, that such procedural consensus on the morality of protesting interests and issues does not typically exist in schools. Educators often do not believe that students have real grievances or, indeed, the *right* to be aggrieved, and students often do not trust educators to deal fairly with their concerns. In high-conflict situations, whatever trust students have in administrators' sense of fair play may evaporate quickly. The schools' organizational failure to maintain trust is only partly an issue in personal or interpersonal integrity. It also stems from students' exclusion from the decision-making arena, and their suspicion about the processes that go on in it.

Communication. As indicated above, other OD strategies tend to emphasize the opening of communication channels and the removal of barriers to the honest sharing of information.

Communication may also be dealt with differently in the power-conflict model. The political nature of communication is explicitly recognized, and restricted access to certain information across status and role groups is legitimized. Such an emphasis is particularly important under conditions of unequal power, when authorities are less vulnerable than others to the abuse and misuse of such information. We are not advocating deception and chicanery, but pointing out that naive assumptions regarding common interest and collaborative decision-making do not take into consideration the constraints on communication which usually are considered management's prerogative. These restrictions on "openness" are typically encountered not only in "regular" organizational functioning but also in efforts to innovate in and change any system.

Structure. One final aspect of the power-conflict model, already alluded to, is the importance of relatively long-term structural changes in the organization of the school. Our approach recognizes the need to restructure schools to provide students and teachers with formal access to authority and decision-making procedures and with the necessary organizational support structures, such as active constituency and interest groups. At the same time, we also believe (like other OD practitioners) that it is necessary to provide training to help participants develop the necessary personal and organizational skills to operate effectively in new structures.

NEW MODELS FOR ORGANIZATIONAL GOVERNANCE

New organizational forms to deal with concerns such as those expressed above will require more than retraining personnel or transferring them to different organizational slots; we are advocating far more than the replacement of a principal or a ruling faculty administrative body by several students. An exchange of persons to fulfill already established roles or positions is a personnel move which does not constitute organizational change. Substituting one set of persons for another will accomplish little unless the intervening structure of representative politics and governance is changed. The replacement of a principal by six students does not automatically decrease the distance, or increase the dialogue, between the mass of students or faculty members and the decision-makers.

Some Examples of New Models

Several elaborate models of innovative organizational governance have been proposed by educators pursuing such issues (Robinson and Schoenfeld, 1970). One set of proposals deals with *representative bicameral systems*. Students and teaching faculty each elect representatives from among their numbers to compose two legislative or policy-making bodies. An executive or administrative committee implements policies and handles routine day-to-day matters. Babbidge (1969) suggests that such a model for higher education also include a final judicial authority residing with the board of trustees. John Adams High School, a public school in Portland, Oregon, is currently operating with a bicameral governance system.

Unicameral systems represent another basic model to broaden representa-

tion in school decision-making. These approaches invest the formal responsibilities of the principal and his staff in a single body composed of
representatives from student, teacher, and administrative groups. In order to
facilitate decision-making, this group is kept relatively small, or an executive
committee is formed to handle details. Ramapo High School in Spring
Valley, New York, is currently using this approach to governance (Sugarman,
1970).

"*Town meetings*" and similar face-to-face decision-making groups in which
all members of the school subunit may participate (Mann, 1965; Raskin,
1968) represent a third, less formalized approach. The movement toward the
decentralization of schools by unitizing, house plans, schools within schools,
and educational parks tends to reduce the size of the learning unit and provide opportunity for town meeting participation. Although there is as yet no
history of experience to evaluate these models, each attempts to deal with
some of the generic issues raised earlier. Each broadens the representation of
different interests within the school. Each model also encourages the surfac-
ing of hidden conflicts in the formal decision-making mechanism. Although
specific designs and models may vary, new structures should recognize and
legitimize the endemic nature of differing interests, should provide appropriate organizational procedures for utilizing group differences and conflicts,
and should be manned by individuals skilled in coping constructively with
conflict and the need for change.

Some Problems with Participatory Structures

Research evidence bearing upon the "participation hypothesis" (Verba,
1961) is relevant to understanding the problems involved in new and more
participatory forms of school governance. We generally assume that involvement in decision-making leads to decreased alienation from the organization
and to increased satisfaction with both the process and the outcome of
decisions. However, such consequences are more or less likely under varying
circumstances and with varying organizational structures. We describe some
attenuating conditions below to illustrate some of the complexities with
which the advocates of increased student involvement must deal.

The first few problems in making participatory structures successful stem
from potential dissatisfaction with the *outcome* of decisions made.

1. The *costs* involved in participating in the decision-making process can
   be too great and are not worth the actual benefits. For example, members of a fact-finding committee on student dress regulations may come
   to feel that the long weekly meetings of the group require more time
   than they expected, that the goal of establishing new policy is not being
   achieved, and that the testimony obtained is not worth the energy
   invested.
2. The *quality of the decision* can be impaired by increased participation.
   Decisions can be impaired because (a) the necessary resources are

absent or scarce, (b) resources are *too* plentiful to be used efficiently, or
(c) some are scarce while others are too plentiful.

3. Participation can bring to the surface *latent conflicts* that are relevant to
the group but which cannot be utilized or handled constructively, and
therefore immobilize the decision-making process.

The remaining conditions reflect some dissatisfaction with the *process* itself.

4. The *scope of participation may not match expectations*. For example,
the principal who discusses with his teachers ways of implementing a
new curriculum may find them angry that they were not involved in
deciding the shape of the new curriculum in the first place.

5. Participants find they *lack the skills or values* for effective participation
or have difficulty making decisions. This results in frustration, feelings
of inadequacy, and decreased self-esteem.

6. Finally, an individual may find that participation does not meet his
own *personal and interpersonal needs*.

New governance structures will require major elements of time, energy,
and training to work effectively. One solution is to set aside an hour a day,
and several additional hours a week, for students or faculty to meet in small
cell groups or assemblies. At these times they can consider the political
and educational decisions that must be (or have been) made for the school
that week, and provide support and commitments for policy suggestions.
Moreover, representatives can then transmit their feelings, findings, and
decisions to their constituents, and receive feedback, suggestions and pressure from them. This time should be scheduled during the school day and
not in stolen hours at night or on weekends. Only with continuing, legitimate,
planned opportunities for political conversation and activity will new structures succeed despite lack of time, low energy, other priorities, traditional
professional role definitions, political opposition, and the like. These problems are typical of the stumbling blocks in the movement from traditional
to innovative forms of school power and governance. Effective training programs and strategies for organization development may help ease this
process. We now turn to this topic.

Strategies for OD Through Student Retraining

The best of recent innovative OD projects in schools (Miles and Lake,
1967; COPED, 1967; Schmuck, Runkel and Langmeyer, 1969; and Schaible
and Piotrowsky, 1970) do use interventions that change organizational
structures and improve organizational skills of participation. New communication structures, rather than communication skills alone, are the focus
of this recent work. Some of these efforts have also dealt with the problem
of power, although it is approached cautiously and with assumption of ra-

tional benevolence at the top of the hierarchy. Benevolence, like trust, is an important component of authority, but it cannot be *assumed* out of the context of the self-interest of an authority regarding goals, control, and stability.

None of these recent efforts, however, deals with students, student interests, and student power in more than minimal terms. Change efforts have focused almost entirely on adult administrators and teachers; any effort to train students in these areas is relatively new. Both because they are clients, and are seen as an immature and oppressed group, students generally have not been treated as part of the resources available to a system. Thus, we find few OD examples in which students are trained in new ways of relating to or altering the social system of the school.

Perhaps the key questions to be raised in the training of students cut across all of the particular skills or functions discussed above. One vital question is whether students should be trained primarily for *collaboration* with other parties in the school or for *advocacy* of their own interests. This issue cuts to the heart of one's diagnosis of the nature and ills of the educational bureaucracy. On the one hand, students may be envisioned as one of several collaborating parties in the school. In this context there would be a high priority on creating trust and positive forms of interaction among students, teachers, and administrators. This is in fact the primary choice made in most OD strategies.

An alternate perspective is to argue that collaboration is extremely difficult, if not impossible; the very structure of relations between adults and students in schools makes them natural opponents. The kinds of trust required for reciprocal pay-off simply may not exist at present, even if they may have at some point in history. In this context, it would be most important for the previously impotent majority to advance its own cause, and to let those in power figure out how to accommodate students' interests as well as advancing their own. This approach places the major burden of accommodation and system integration on those who have legitimate power and the historic obligation to seek integration, rather than on those out of power who seek redress and change in their roles. The extent to which these perspectives (collaboration and advocacy) may or may not be in conflict is simply not clear to us at present.

A second vital question is whether students seeking redress and change in the school should organize advocate groups solely among other *students* or among sympathetic and committed *non-students* as well. On the one hand, the argument can be made that only students can be straightforward and reliable with one another, and that role group interests are so unique that they ought not to be contaminated. On the other hand, it is argued that various categories of oppressed people—students, faculty, and community—have enough in common to form intense coalitions. Advocate groups formed on the basis of common values rather than roles may cut across role group lines, making future system integration easier. Practical data on the relative ease of organizing efforts and the tested depth of commitment may be the only means for resolving this strategic dilemma.

These two questions each focus attention on the dilemma of system integration and subgroup interests. In brief, the conflicts attendant on and generated by subgroup interests must co-exist with efforts to integrate the system.[3] We are not urging interest group advocacy at the price of disintegration and chaos. However, neither are we encouraging (in the manner of much educational literature) system integration at the price of mere superficial consensus and the repression of subgroup interests. The tension between these issues is the central theoretical dilemma in the discussion of the change strategies that follow.

The retraining strategies discussed below have typically not been followed through to the actual implementation of new governance structures. It is our view, however, that they hold considerable promise for such implementation, and more real promise than most traditional organizational renewal strategies.

Training for Understanding and Collaboration

A prime focus of some efforts to train students for new roles in schools is *preparation for collaborative problem-solving* with other role-takers in the school district. This focus generally assumes that an overarching consensus of interests does (or can) exist among the various parties in schools and that areas of dissensus can be given lower priority or made subordinate to areas of consensus. Further, it assumes that building on areas of agreement is a useful way to integrate an organization. In this context an emphasis is placed on understanding of others as a prerequisite for work and collaboration in the conduct of school life.

The concept of collaboration seems to have several other implications as it is generally practiced. In our view, collaboration does not occur merely among people with like views; we use the term explicitly for situations in which people work together even though they have quite differing views. If people who did differ now come to total agreement, we will not call this collaboration either. The basis for meaningful collaboration must be built from assumptions and experiences of difference, as well as explorations of commonness. Respect for and maintenance of differences is clearly vital. This requires, in some cases, resistance to premature collaboration which denies or overwhelms differences or conflicts among subgroups.

Illustration 1: Training for Cross-Status Problem-Solving. One effort to train students for collaborative roles occurred in a summer program in an Illinois high school. Thirty-five students and faculty members were self-selected to constitute several cross-status problem-solving teams. In order

---

[3] Coser (1967) makes this point well in criticizing both establishment-oriented consensus theories and conceptual trends toward societal anarchy.

to develop cross-status groupings that could work efficiently, all participants had to learn to work together as a cohesive and collaborative unit. They began their summer activities with a two-day workship focusing on inter-personal sensitivity and group dynamics. In small group meetings, students and faculty discussed their relationships with one another and their gen-eral concerns about interpersonal and group relations in school. Several other sessions were held in which participants were stimulated to identify and to resolve conflicts between different school groups. Sometimes the group of thirty-five persons was divided into student groups and adult groups, and sometimes they met in cross-status learning units.

Illustration 2: Training for Cross-Status Problem-Solving. Guskin and Guskin (1970) describe a similar effort in a Southwestern high school; forty students, twelve teachers, and the principal met together every day for three weeks during the summer. The focus of this program was also on developing a cadre of students skilled in group problem-solving procedures. The report indicates that consultants to the school tried

> . . . to build a feeling of concern, and to create the necessary interpersonal relationships among workshop members that could support the later de-velopment of specific tactics for change. Attention was given to the develop-ment of skills in group organizations, discussion leadership and political management.

Sessions of this sort may be effective mechanisms whereby persons learn how to cross status lines and develop cooperation and collaboration across previously impermeable boundaries separating persons from one another. At times, however, it has become important to recognize and deal with the natural desire for *separateness* with which persons come to such groups. Occasional separation of members into homogeneous role groupings or status groupings has proven effective in helping to create the articulation and un-derstanding of differences so necessary for intergroup collaboration.

Illustration 3: Training for Cross-Status Perception Clarification. In a New Jersey high school workshop, student and teacher groups were separated. Each group was asked to develop a list of the ways in which they perceived members of the other group. The lists so created follow:

How Students Perceive Teachers

Unaware, think they are correct because they are older, putting on a big show, some making honest effort, think they are more mature because they are older, less outspoken, passive when the principal is there, take things personally, don't really listen, are prejudiced, some willing to listen even when they don't agree, curious about students' views.

How Teachers Perceive Students

Cherish individuality, hopelessness, confusion, self-confidence, frustration, sensitivity, eagerness, resistance to seeing both sides of the question, clannish, irresponsible, candid, bored, angry at inequities, powerless, flexible, racially polarized.

After the separate groups of students and adults shared their perceptions of one another, they attempted to explain the meaning of these perceptions to the other group. This design stressed the non-rational perceptions and stereotypes which people of differing status had of one another. The examination and clarification of mutual misperceptions is a necessary precursor of serious and honest collaboration.

These training programs appeared to be quite successful at the time. Cadres of students and teachers did learn to work together and developed provocative plans for school change. During the course of the year, however, the groups fell apart, and teachers and students ceased collaborating. The pressures to separate overcame the interpersonal bonds created in the training sessions. It appeared that the OD consultants had underestimated the time and energy it would take to maintain the openness of collaboration under normal school pressures.

In the development of such collaboration, it is crucial to stress the need for honesty and reciprocity across status groupings. All too often, dishonest collaboration develops: it involves one group's "dancing to another's tune" (e.g., students adjusting to administrators' priorities). Of course, such manipulation, conscious or otherwise, will not succeed for long. Students quickly reassert those differences or cite evidence of pseudo-collaboration which they have experienced. One junior high school student expressed her frustration to us in the following terms:

> We set up and approved this new constitution for the student government and it doesn't include an administration veto over our activities. But our advisor, who was mainly responsible in setting it up, only wants us to talk about certain things that won't rock the boat. We all know that he really controls it. So what good was the whole business?

One of the prime hazards of training for collaboration is that it may co-opt students into ignoring their needs and doing the bidding of the school administration. Students who are duped or seduced into collaboration and trust, and who find the trust unwarranted, will create far greater havoc and destruction for the school than if such "collaboration" had never occurred. An antidote to this danger may be provided by use of the following approaches to student training.

Training for Self-interest Advocacy

A second major focus of training for students involves *preparing them to identify, develop, organize, and prosecute their own special interests.* If students are not able to look after their own interests, who then will protect or advance them? One traditional assumption is that trained educational professionals will act in their clients' best interests. But, as we have seen, this is a forlorn hope. Professionals now constitute a separate class in our society and schools; as such they have their own vested interests to protect and cannot be depended on to protect anyone who comes into conflict with them.

Rational conflict between students and adults having different goals and status is quite natural. Such conflict requires that each group seek the adjudication and prosecution of its own interests. The prosecution of one's self-interest does not necessarily exclude collaboration with other or opposing groups, but, it does suggest the necessity for careful consideration of the time and place for collaboration. The critical issue here is to treat both advocacy and collaboration as means to an end such as quality education, improved schooling, or greater learning. The collaborative stance described above comes close to urging collaboration as an end—as a desired style regardless of other organizational consequences. But for students, the outcome of the educational process is crucial, and preferred organizational and interpersonal styles must be judged by whether they lead to maximum learning, the basic purpose of school.

Needed Outcomes. The development of advocacy-oriented programs requires the separate training of students for different purposes in different ways with potentially different ends—in comparison to what might be needed for other members of the educational system. Students must be trained to identify their common interests, to organize peers around those interests, and to understand their opponents' positions and likely responses. They will also need to learn how to establish conditions for collaboration, to set terms and limits for negotiation and compromise, to decide when and whom to press in confrontation situations, to distinguish between "good" and "bad" principals, and to begin the establishment of institutional agreements for continued student participation in decision-making and curriculum reform.

As students learn more about the strange and often invisible workings of the school district and its personnel they will be able to reduce the non-rational, or stereotypic and ignorant, components of their conflicts with the school. Rather, rational conflicts around different structures of interest, privilege, and reward can receive fuller attention. With these ideas and skills, students will be able to develop action strategies that advance their unique interests.

Students are already learning informally, on their own, how to organize in their own self-interest and in support of their definitions of quality education. Our basic concern here is whether organizational change programs can help them do this in more disciplined and effective ways.[4]

---

[4] In implementing this approach, we have found that highly trained student consultants have to be responsible for conducting the actual interventions with student groups. Adult professional consultants seldom "put their bodies on the line" and lack credibility in the actual politics of school life. However, opportunities to work with and learn from adult consultants, removed from their local school setting, can give high school students and recent graduates a chance to develop the techniques and strategies needed to train fellow students in advocacy and change.

One of the major results of such a training program should be the students' increased understanding of *how to influence other persons* in the school district. When students' interests have become clearly identified, and when students have become organized as a potent political force in their own right, they are more likely to be heard and others are more likely to respond to their concerns. As they understand the system better, students can exert leverage more judiciously and effectively. Sometimes rational discussion brings about rapid and effective adult responses; at other times a meaningful response can be secured only by dynamic political confrontation.

There is no implication here that students need to develop hatred or antagonism toward people with different interests—people we call opponents. Opponents do not have to be conceived of as enemies in a hostile interpersonal sense. In fact, we are concerned that people exercise compassion and respect for their role opponents, but that does not mean they should take those opponents as benevolent partners in a complex and partisan political enterprise. In American society, separateness and conflict seem to be feared greatly; it is understandable how opposition may become hostility or be interpreted as such. Particularly when individuals have been taught to fear such authorities as parents and teachers, they may have a personal need to escalate emotions in order to overcome fears and confront the authority figure at hand. Responses by authorities to these perceived attacks often further escalate the interaction. As part of the training program all parties must be helped to *avoid irrational attacks and defenses*. Probably the greatest help should be available to those whose historic interests and privileges are most threatened by student initiative and organization for change.

Another outcome of advocacy-oriented student groups should be more honest and effective forms of *collaboration* and *negotiation for change*. Students and adult educators generally have not dealt with one another in the context of equal power to affect outcomes, or equal vulnerability to each other's influence. One purpose of developing students' self-interest and political strength may be to equalize (at least temporarily) the balance of power so that true collaboration and negotiation can begin. Otherwise, negotiation among members of unequal power remains negotiation by dint of the superior group's altruism and sufferance, not because of functional necessity or the necessity for system survival. The *recognition of students as a legitimate and necessary political force* and the treatment of their demands as legitimate political and educational priorities are also key outcomes of any program preparing students for their role in school change.

Illustration 1: Training for Conflict Utilization. In one school in the West it became clear that school administrators were rejecting student-initiated conversations and suggestions for change. As a result, students were at the point of rioting and leaving school. A team of external consultants received administrative permission to work with the students in the midst of impending disorder. The consultants' entry into this highly politicized situation required the establishment of a relationship with the mistrustful and aggressive student groups. As the consultants presented their ideological and political credentials, they also presented to students some alternative images of influence and protest.

After several such entry and testing sessions, student leaders agreed to attend a series of training events. The training staff included two adults but was composed mainly of specially prepared older students from other school districts. Training in the outcomes discussed above was conducted solely for students and dealt with the district from their point of view, with their goals and needs in mind. A prime instructional procedure was the use of role-playing or simulation exercises in which students tested their skills and strategies in mock situations.

Skill training in negotiation and compromise, as well as confrontation and escalation with educators, was necessary. So, too, was practice in organizing a disciplined group of supporters. In the context of these sessions, student leaders considered anew their goals and their relations to larger groups of their peers.

As one result, large groups of students were organized in a disciplined, highly focused class boycott and potential school shutdown. Student leaders were then asked to join district administrators in direct negotiations, and large groups of students waited on the results of these sessions. Changes that met student demands came about through students' patient and non-violent, but militant and hard-headed, advocacy of their own interests. A student organization was developed which proved to last over a period of time. Throughout the school year, students continued to mobilize strength and unity when it was required. The disciplined and non-violent nature of their subsequent protests prevented over-reactions from local administrators, police officers, and parents. This school now faces the challenge of institutionalizing this organizational revolution in a new governance form, one like the models of innovative governance discussed in the prior section.

Illustration 2: Training for Student-Administrator Confrontation. In another advocacy-oriented project, students from several high schools were trained to be consultants to a group of administrators concerned with problems of disruption, desegregation, and decentralization. The students identified their interests and concerns in these areas, with considerable anger about the ways they were treated in school. In planning their consultation with the group of administrators, the students initially discussed strategies of confrontation that included revenge and punishment. As they discussed the probable reaction of administrators to such approaches, they were able to put some additional perspective into their planning.

Even so, at the meeting itself, they threatened and distanced many administrators present. Their articulate analyses and unique perspectives on school problems were not heard and could not be used until each group was able to work through some of its feelings about the new role and power relationships being exemplified. While several consultants worked directly with the students, another tried to help the administrators. In this instance, part of the consultants' advocacy strategy involved opening up adults to the students' positions. The adult who worked with administrators was a partisan link: not a representative of students or a promoter of collaboration, but an advocate seeking to "soften up" the targets of change. He aided them in understanding students' positions, in examining and minimizing their defenses, and in beginning to make relevant responses. Since student militancy generally is likely to threaten educators, linkage to them in an organizational change program may help reduce some of the non-rational components of escalation.

Comments. Students who take leadership in organizing and representing their role group's interests must be carefully prepared so they will not be co-opted as tools of adult interests, just because they are negotiators or act in liaison with the adult establishment. Similarly, adults who wish to negotiate with students in good faith must take care not to put students in the co-opted position, a position that renders them impotent to themselves, their constituencies, *and* their opponents. Preparation of both students and adults for such negotiation and collaboration is undoubtedly a necessary part of the development of advocates.

It should be emphasized that a student advocacy approach can be practiced in its "pure" form only if students are considered the clients of the OD consultants. If administrators or "the district" is seen as the client, compromises will constantly be made to serve this end; there is no initial guarantee that "system" interests, especially as defined by administrators, are the same as or represent student interests. (Later, when student needs are articulated and integrated into a systemic picture, "system" and student interests are likely to be closer.) If, on the other hand, students request, pay for, or convince consultants to volunteer their services, they are the only group to whom the consultants are responsible. Students are more likely to be real clients as the sophistication of consultants, student groups, and community groups grows, and as the understanding grows that all parties to a conflict need expert help.

Training for Value-Homogeneous Groups

Up to this point, we have been considering change strategies that primarily involve working with separate or partially separate student groups on the basis of their role in school. This rests on the sound assumption, given our present educational structure, that there are significant common interests within role groups and significant difference between them.

Another strategy of organizational renewal may require the grouping of individuals from various parts of the district who share a common set of values or goals. This cross-role cadre then can be trained to operate as value advocates, much as the "role advocates" were trained in the previous section. It should be recognized that it is not easy to identify specific and common value positions in American education. The rhetoric of educational values and goals is so encompassing that it makes asserting and clarifying specific issues quite difficult. Therefore, organization and proselytization on this basis is harder than on the visible basis of role groupings.

Illustration: Training for a Value-Homogeneous Group. In a Northwestern high school a training program was initiated at the request of several students and a few teachers deeply committed to the concept of "shared power." They did not know exactly what this term meant to them, but they did want to provide students, especially, and teachers with more potent influence and authority in school affairs. Very careful screening of participants was undertaken to insure value-commonality about desired changes in power relations. Each member of an initial informal discussion group of eight spoke to three or four trusted colleagues, and the target population was gradually built to around seventy (thirty-five students, twenty-five teachers, two administrators, and eight parents).

This group met together for several retreats and working sessions with outside OD consultants. The initial training task focused on clarification of both role-related and "value-centric" issues. This was done by generating discussion around value issues in groups separated by role. Some examples of issues raised include

Students have significant skill and expertise to add to school decisions.

Shared power should mean student, administrative, and community involvement in decisions about teacher recruiting, hiring, evaluation, and firing.

People in different groups should talk with one another honestly and openly.

It was discovered quickly that there were value and strategy differences within the role groups, but within much narrower limits than would have occurred in a randomly selected group. In the student group, particularly, the hope of potent outcomes caused other barriers to be crossed. As white and black students started to disagree about some racial issues, one black student, a Black Panther member, said, "Let's stop bickering about this; if we can get together on the other issues that's good enough."

Discussions in cross-role groups followed. In these groups, it became essential for persons to be sure about the positions of others, especially those others occupying different roles. Teachers inquired in depth in order to understand students' feelings about unfair and arbitrary discipline and bad teaching; then they were called on to share views about their own vulnerability to student evaluation of instruction. One of the most important events was an open discussion of others in similar roles who were not in attendance. For instance, students truly began to trust teachers' commitments when teachers talked openly about other teachers and their positions on issues, and likely ways of influencing or subverting them.

Such honesty was evidence of willingness to break with one's role group and to place greater loyalty in the cross-role value group than in the professional role group.

This value-homogeneous group continued to meet throughout a year (sometimes with the blessings of the school administration) in order to develop plans for change and strategies to implement their plans.

One immediate outcome was the establishment of a student and faculty group that reviewed all key issues in the school and the principal's decisions, and advised him on policy matters. The student-faculty cadre was committed to the right to veto the principal's decisions but decided to build toward that end rather than raise it as a condition of their existence. Clear commitments were made by the administration to work toward that end.

A second outcome was establishment of a special class, for members of the cadre and a slowly increasing interest group, on educational issues and school decision-making. This official class was taught by the student and teacher members, with occasional visitors from outside groups and agencies.

A third outcome was the development of plans to organize a constitutional convention, with documents spelling out a new governance structure to be approved school-wide and city-wide. A position was taken by student and faculty members of the cadre and a negotiated agreement was finally made with key local administrators. The basic element of the negotiated agreement was as follows:

> It is proposed that the secondary schools accept a *shared power concept* for decision-making to enhance the teaching-learning process at the building level. Power shall be shared by the students, community members, teachers and administrators in their respective schools as they participate in policy-making decisions pertaining to *any* aspect of the school. Representation of constituent groups shall be proportional to the population of the respective constituent groups, with the exception of the community, whose members will be decided by the constitutional committee. Implementation in each building shall be carried out by a constitutional committee elected by constituent groups of each school. The constitutional committee is to be selected in each school building, with the object to create, ratify, and present to the Board a constitution.
>
> The principal's veto power in all areas will be relinquished as the shared power group becomes the recognized and accountable decision-making body of the school.

This statement reflects the slowly developing agreement to establish a local veto power as procedures become clearer and more implementable. In working toward all these outcomes the cadre met often and was instrumental in obtaining local and federal funds to sponsor planning sessions, workshops, and consultancies.

Comments. It is especially important in value-homogeneous groups for members from different role groups to recognize and deal with their own differences and goals. Given the tendency of such cadres to be organized against the larger "system," to mobilize around common conceptions of system injustices and brutality, internal differences are often initially masked or ignored in the pursuit of common goals. The focus of all energy outward is heightened by the magnitude of the task such cadres undertake, and the fear of consequences if they are not successful. However, the same intergenerational and cross-role issues mentioned in the earlier strategies apply here. Respect, honesty, and reciprocity must characterize relationships within the cadre. Given the threat of outside forces on the cadre, it is even more likely that student members of such cadres will be co-opted by outsiders if attention to internal processes is neglected.

The ability of such a cadre to resist splintering or inappropriate fraction, while at the same time respecting tolerable differences within, is a crucial issue. Similarly, it is vital to sustain internal integrity while not alienating non-cadre collaborators or targets of change. In many schools where cadres have worked well internally they have done so at the cost of productive links to the outside. Although one excellent defense against outside pressure is to wall it off, internal secretiveness and "in-groupness" often alienate persons not in the group. To the extent that this reaction is based on real differences in values, it is quite appropriate, but it may be a strategic "red herring" and a tactical error if resistance is the reaction of outsiders.

People who decide to work together toward a specific end must know where each other stands, be able to count on one another, and be able to stand up together under pressure. There will be efforts made to break apart a cohesive team that threatens others' interests: adult educators may be tantalized by offers to be advisors to the superintendent or to be district specialists on community affairs; and students may be offered select seats on faculty committees. Such efforts to co-opt leading individuals with unique rewards and privileges must be placed in proper context. If the overriding issue is the attainment of collective power by new groups, then positions on a committee or new roles for radical advocates are mere tokens. Individuals recruited into an effective cadre must be prepared for the seductions of personal influence and gain.

The value-homogeneous group strategy differs from the collaboration model of OD in that there is no assumption that the cadre should necessarily include the legitimate or formal authority figures in the district. A simple collaborative model usually requires such involvement of top influentials.

Also, this strategy clearly assumes that the group so formed will reflect a much narrower range of value positions on the control and distribution of resources than is present in the larger school system. During different stages of the change process, the value-homogeneous model of change may utilize aspects of both the collaborative and advocacy orientations described earlier in its dealings with other groups in the school district.

In general, the major advantage of the collaborative approach is that it links students and student needs immediately to other parts of the district. Its major disadvantage lies in encouraging premature collaboration that obviates differences and conflict. This is especially true given the presence of skilled traditional practitioners of such collaboration.

The major advantage of role advocacy is precisely its mobilization of students' unique interests and their organization into a potent and disciplined subgroup. Its major disadvantages are potential escalation into chaos and difficulty in reintegration.

The value-homogeneous approach has the advantage of linking students and committed members of other groups in an enterprise with philosophic overtones. Its disadvantages lie in the difficulty of identifying and maintaining real collaboration via a value framework.

Some Risks and Benefits in Advocating Changed Decision-Making Structures

The strategies of change discussed here can bring many advantages to the school. Governance, the instructional process, and political participation should all be affected positively in ways described earlier. But advocates of these processes also run some risks; we speak in detail of these here to give a realistic view of school resistance to such strategies and thus to protect advocates and schools from naive notions of immediate reform.

Some Typical Risks. Regardless of the strategy or approach used, attempts to suggest change in educators' norms regarding professional sanctity and security, principals' legal responsibilities, and student roles are likely to create considerable public and professional resistance. Persons advocating such restructuring will be asked, induced, and sometimes coerced to change their behavior and conform to prior standards. Colleagues may snicker, jeer openly, or otherwise try to dissuade individuals involved in change processes. In some schools, teachers who have advocated such changes have suffered disciplinary action or have had their contracts terminated. Students have discovered notations about political conduct on their records, faced suspension, or found their own peers deriding the "non-coolness" of trying to change things. Some of these responses may be especially painful for students requiring a good record for college or for the immediate job market. School officials may also encourage students' parents to act as a pressure to prevent efforts at serious change.

Beyond interpersonal pressures and the invocation of traditional norms, there are also potential legal constraints which can be used against cadres attempting meaningful change in non-traditional ways. A small group of people may be seen as a "conspiracy" with the intent to create disruption. They may be charged with contention or disturbing the peace. The adults may be seen as contributing to the delinquency of minors. Some federal research and scholarship agencies have already agreed that funds may not be used for persons convicted for participation in some form of educational disorder or disruption.

Administrators typically are reluctant to have people they see as agitators organize students. The natural tendency of administrators is to avoid risk and reduce any tension in the school, not only because of their personal predilections, but also because of the pressure exerted on them by the superintendent's office, the school board, and the community. In crisis situations particularly, the options that principals feel are available to them are extremely limited: "tunnel vision" sets in.

Finally, the immediate effect of the approaches to change which we have described may be to intensify and polarize conflict, because of the increased coherence and articulation of the student groups. Furthermore, advocacy for this or any other segment of the school community may seriously antagonize other elements in the school and increase the scope and intensity of the conflict. However, the self-interests of various groups do exist, whether expressed openly or covertly; this approach can help to bring hidden tensions and conflicts into the open.

Each of the members of an advocate group or cadre faces somewhat different pressures. However, all can expect to be pressured not to hang together, not to truly focus on the dramatic changes we have described, and not to take the personal risks discussed here. One of the things group members may do to help each other is to examine and share the pressures that each member faces. Time must be found to allow for the sharing and potential resolution of such feelings; otherwise, dysfunctional anxieties or righteous indignation may result. Internal support also can be provided by assiduous attention to the dynamics of group and interpersonal processes.

Benefits. There are a number of benefits that may accrue to people committed to change processes like those we describe. First, their schools may avoid the risk of continuing school crisis and disorder. Student requests and demands for involvement and power in school decision-making, and educators' resistance and reluctance to meet those demands form a central focus of contention in schools across the nation. In numerous cases this has led to escalated confrontation and crisis. Crisis and confrontation are in themselves neither good nor bad; the question is whether they lead to improvement of the quality of life, in school and out. We believe that strategies using the power-conflict model of OD can do so.

If students are able to create and participate in new governance structures which represent their interests—and the competing interests of other school groups—our belief, supported by much practical experience, is that the living and learning processes in such schools will be more humane, more creative, and closer to national educational goals. It is not simply that the students' sense of control over their fate, so closely allied to other educational outcomes, increases. It is that the educational activities which ensue are better ones.

A final benefit may sound apocalyptic. Though it is clear, as we have said, that change agents and advocates face risks in trying to improve the quality of life in schools, it is even clearer that *not* to risk improvement attempts will lead to even greater risks and perhaps to disaster. The absence of imaginative and just change may very well result in more numerous and extreme short-term crises and the eventual collapse of our public educational system as we now know it. The renovation and restructuring of systems of power will not totally rejuvenate our schools nor guarantee correction of a series of other injustices. But it is one reform that holds large promise for a more adequate future in our schools.

Concluding Comments

Can important changes in schools be generated and implemented without some alteration in the allocation and distribution of power? Our conclusion is: No. In particular, the redistribution of power to people now impotent in role, style, and training will be required for meaningful response to student initiatives and organization. The creation of new internal decision-making structures which reflect and take advantage of new forms of power and newly trained individuals within the school promises higher quality in schools. We believe that long-range designs for change or organizational restructuring that do not stress such participation in school decision-making are bound to fail.

It is important to recognize that people entrusted with the management of schools have become a separate class (with special interests of their own) which may not always act in the best interest of the clients of the educational process. Regardless of their race, age, status, or skill, clients must be provided with the training requisite for full participation in society at large.

Programs to train students for self-governance or for active roles in school renewal must generate skills both in self-advocacy and collaboraton with others. Traditional training activities have focused too much on collaborative styles, to the point where collaboration is viewed as an end rather than a means. The endemic nature of role-related and value-centric conflicts in schools requires that each group, and especially students, develop a means of articulating and presenting its own views.

Advocacy and collaboration are not exclusive; rather, they are each essential components of political change, of change in decision-making structures. Collaboration as a *sine qua non* neglects the interests of impotent groups; advocacy alone fails to provide for systemic integration. Advocacy that leads to collaboration and negotiation among differing but respected opponents is most likely to rejuvenate our schools in directions more satisfying to the people who live, work, and learn in them.

References

Argyris, C. 1964. *Integrating the individual and the organization.* New York: Wiley.

Babbidge, H. D., Jr. 1969. *Eighth annual faculty convocation.* Storrs, Connecticut: University of Connecticut.

Bennis, W. 1970. A funny thing happened on the way to the future. *American Psychologist* 25:595–608.

Buchanan, P. 1967. Crucial issues in organization development. In *Change in school systems*, ed. G. Watson. Washington, D.C.: National Training Laboratories.

———. 1969. Laboratory training and organizational development. *Administrative Science Quarterly* 14:466–80.

Campbell, A. 1968. Who governs the schools? *Saturday Review*, December 21, 1968, pp. 50–52, 63–65.

Chesler, M. A. 1969. Student and administrative crisis. *Educational Leadership* 27:34–42.

———, and Arnstein, F. 1970. The school consultant: change agent or defender of the status quo? *Integrated Education* 8:19–25.

Coleman, J., et al. 1966. *Equality of educational opportunity*. Washington, D.C.: United States Government Printing Office.

Cooperative Project for Educational Development (COPED). 1970. Final Report, USOE Contract OEG 3-8-080069-0043 (010) Project # 8-0069. Washington, D.C.: U.S. Office of Education.

Coser, L. 1956. *The functions of social conflict*. Glencoe, Illinois: Free Press.

———. 1967. *Continuities in the study of social conflict*. New York: Free Press.

Dahl, R. 1967. *Pluralist democracy in "the US"; conflict and consent*. Chicago: Rand McNally.

Duggal, S. 1969. *Relationship between school unrest, student participation in school management, and dogmatism and pupil control ideology of staff in high schools*. Unpublished dissertation, University of Michigan.

Fantini, M. D., and Young, M. A. 1970. *Designing education for tomorrow's cities*. New York: Holt, Rinehart and Winston.

Gamson, W. 1968. *Power and discontent*. Homewood, Illinois: Dorsey.

Guskin, A., and Guskin, S. 1970. *A social psychology of education*. Reading, Massachusetts: Addison-Wesley.

———, and Ross, R. In press. Advocacy and democracy: the long view. *Journal of American Orthopsychiatric Association*.

Haug, M., and Sussman, M. 1969. Professional autonomy and the revolt of the client. *Social Problems* 17:153–61.

Janowitz, M. 1969. *Institution building in urban education*. New York: Russell Sage Foundation.

Katz, D., and Kahn, R. 1966. *The social psychology of organizations*. New York: Wiley.

Kvaraceus, W. 1965. Negro youth and school adaptation. In *Negro self-concept*, ed. W. Kvaraceus, et al. New York: McGraw-Hill.

Laue, J. 1968. Power, conflict and social change. In *Riots and rebellion; civil violence in the urban community*, eds. Masotti and Bower. Beverly Hills: Sage Publications. Pp. 85–96.

Leavitt, H. J. 1965. Applied organizational change in industry: structural, technological, and humanistic approaches. In *Handbook of organizations*, ed. J. G. March. Chicago: Rand McNally. Pp. 1144–1170.

Likert, R. 1961. *New patterns of management.* New York: McGraw-Hill.

Mann, E. 1965. A new school for the ghetto. *Our generation* 5:67–73.

McGregor, D. 1960. *The human side of enterprise.* New York: McGraw-Hill.

Miles, M., and Lake, D. 1967. Self-renewal in school systems, a strategy for planned change. In *Concepts for social change*, ed. G. Watson. Washington, D.C.: National Training Laboratories.

Perlmutter, H. V. 1965. *On the theory and practice of social architecture.* London: Tavistock Publications.

Polk, B. 1968. *Sense of internal control in a non-alienative environment: a flexible-modular school.* Unpublished dissertation, University of Michigan.

Raskin, M. 1968. Political socialization in the schools. *Harvard Educational Review* 38:550–53.

Reeves, Donald. 1970. A student voice on policy, a short history of the student bill of rights. New York City. Mimeographed (2 pp.)

Robinson, L., and Schoenfeld, J. 1970. *Student participation in academic governance.* Washington, D.C.: ERIC Clearinghouse on Higher Education. Pp. 1–3.

Schaible, L., and Piotrowsky, L. 1970. Ann Arbor public school project. Terminal Report, USOE Contract Grant OEG-0-9-324128-2008(725). Ann Arbor, Michigan: University of Michigan.

Schmuck, R., Runkel, P., and Langmeyer, D. 1969. Improving organizational problem-solving in a school faculty. *Journal of Applied Behavioral Science* 5:455–82.

Smelser, N. 1963. *Theory of collective behavior.* New York: Free Press.

Sugarman, A. 1970. Students take over at Ramapo Senior High. *Inside Education*, February, p. 9.

Verba, S. 1961. *Small groups and political behavior.* Princeton, New Jersey: Princeton University Press.

Wittes, S. 1970. *Power and people: high schools in crisis.* Ann Arbor, Michigan: Institute for Social Research.

People-Changing Institutions:
The Transformed Schools

MORRIS JANOWITZ

By any measure, the amount of progress in inner city schools during the past twenty years of social ferment is not impressive. Innovation has been highly fragmentary. A decade of vigorous intellectual criticism from 1955 to 1965,

FROM *Teachers College Record*, Vol. 72, No. 2, pp. 249–55.

plus extensive professional and experimental efforts, did not produce educational developments in the inner city that satisfied the demands of public pressure. There has been considerable inventive thinking about the pacing of the classroom curriculum, namely in development of various schemes of nongrading, multigrading, or continuous education. Vast efforts have been undertaken in developing administrative schemes for achieving racial integration both of teachers and of pupils. There have been various formulations of new roles in public education ranging from the master teacher to the school-community agent. But all of these efforts must be considered to be partial models of transformation, none of which significantly changed the school.

One crucial barrier to strategic change and increased effectiveness of public school systems is the absence of a comprehensive, conceptual model—an holistic and integrated one at that—that offers a goal for professionals and policy makers. Mental hospitals and custodial institutions have a better recent record of change than schools because their administrators no longer have a limited "custodial" concern, but are involved with the more meaningful goals of treatment and rehabilitation. They are "people-changing institutions," and this is what the schools must become if they are to meet societal demands. The school has been assigned the task of socializing or resocializing the motives and values of its pupils, in a manner comparable to the mental hospital or the correctional institution. Ideally, the school in the lower-class community should supply a link by which youngsters are able to enter the mainstream of American society.

By 1968, most school systems of the United States had had some experience with conscious efforts to improve the quality of their educational programs. Efforts ranged from such limited programs as new libraries to "saturation" programs in selected schools. These experiences in educational innovation seem to underline the conclusion that the infusion of new funds into existing or only partially modified structures does not produce higher levels of performance. The basic response has been to continue the same procedures but on a more intensive basis. In Chicago, Federal funds were actually used to increase the length of the school day. The educational procedures that produced a 40 percent dropout and massive academic retardation by third grade were extended, with only minor modifications, for another hour. The per pupil costs of education in New York City are the highest in the United States, but there is no evidence that the level of performance is discernibly higher. Moreover, Federal funds that have not been absorbed by higher teaching costs have been allocated for segmental change mainly in the form of demonstration projects rather than planning for fundamental institution building. Yet the life history of most demonstration programs seems to be self-limiting. They have tended to be small scale and short lived, with a high turnover of personnel so that the consequences of a particular demonstration face gradual extinction. The most critical argument is that after the decision to spread the demonstration project throughout the system, it faces death by diffuse and partial incorporation.

Mental Health Model

At the same time, because of professional concern with the slum school, it was inevitable that there would be efforts to impose the strategy of the mental health movement directly on the school system, to develop an organizational model that fundamentally parallels the therapeutic setting. This approach assumes that the resources of the family in the slum are so limited or its values so at variance with the goals of the school that the school must seek to become responsible for the total social space of the child. The teacher becomes a teacher-counselor, and the ratio of teacher to pupil is drastically reduced to about one to fifteen or even one to ten. The teacher sets the pace and guides the formal educational program, but only in the light of the interpersonal need and social reality of the child. The basic thrust is to establish stable and gratifying interpersonal relations. Critics, however, feel that the impact of such intense relations with teachers produces an adjustment to the school, and not to the large society. Moreover, given the mobility and disruption of the social life in the slum, only a small portion of youngsters are likely to develop relatively enduring relations with a teacher-counselor. A second and more pointed criticism concerns the problem of translating the model into an organizational system. An organization cannot function on the basis of the sheer energy of its constituent elements, but requires a division of labor and a system of effective supports. Any conventional administrative apparatus would by its very nature tend to thwart many positive elements of this approach.

Early Education Model

At best, the early education movement can be considered another partial strategy. At worst, it was a basic error in priorities. A partial strategy of change which allocates highest priority to the preschool youngster is a reflection of a concern for the management of the individual rather than with the management of the slum community. The counter-strategy of intervention with the oldest school-age groups seems more plausible. The fourteen- to eighteen-year-old males are opinion leaders in the slum youth culture and the effective bearers of the culture of the slum from one generation to the next. If these youngsters develop a sense of frustration and a group life in opposition to the goals of the school, as they generally do, they are able to frustrate innovation. The case can be made that this group represents the highest priority, not the youngest group, if comprehensive change is to be effected.

Institution Building

While recognizing the attractiveness of the mental health and early education approaches, we nonetheless need more powerful conceptual models if the public system is to become a more effective social institution. The first phase in "inner city" experimentation has ended. This first phase, roughly designated from 1960 to 1967, emphasized piecemeal change, the demonstration project, and the process of change from the bottom up or by lateral diffusion. It is not to be concluded that no progress was made. There has been a great deal of social learning, but of course, this whole first phase might well have been avoided or more readily terminated by more rational analysis and more forthright leadership. The emerging second phase is that of strategic innovation, or institutional building, which focuses on the system as a whole. It involves a strategy from the top down, it is more comprehensive in scope, and it is concerned with the realities of authority and decision making. What is needed from our social scientists is a conceptual framework, as comprehensive as the schemes that have been developed for other "people-changing" institutions.

The purpose of this analysis is to present two alternative models of organizational change in educational institutions: the *specialization model* and the *aggregation model*. I prefer the latter, but both of these models see the school as a social institution. Both supply criteria for judging and evaluating specific research findings and particular innovations, and both focus on the classroom teacher.

SPECIALIZATION MODEL

The specialization model is in effect an expression of the major trends over the last decade of innovation programs. It encompasses a variety of the current segmental and administrative changes and appears to be an *ad hoc* adaptation by introducing, on a piecemeal basis, new techniques, new programs, new specialists, and even new specific administrative procedures.

Under the specialization model, the traditional activity of the teacher is modified as the teaching process is broken up into more and more specialized roles. There is an increased use of specialized personnel and specific teaching techniques. This model has as its goal the elaboration of cognitive processes and the enhancement of academic achievement mainly brought about by reconstructing the contents of the curriculum according to the principles of cognitive development. The consequence of this perspective—even though it may be an unanticipated consequence—is to create a group of specialists whose impact is felt through a restructuring of the curriculum, without adequate regard for the full institutional milieu. The curriculum specialist is typically concerned with subject-matter issues rather than with fundamental issues of student instruction in academic and vocational programs. The impact of the curriculum specialist has been, in general, to weaken further the authority and self-respect of classroom teachers rather than to serve as an effective resource for them.

The end result of the curriculum development movement, based on the theory of cognition, has been an additional pressure toward educational rigidity with a commitment to a spiral curriculum and its mechanical emphasis on earlier and earlier exposure to more intellectually complicated material.

AGGREGATION MODEL

The aggregation model, put most simply, is a notion of potentialities. Specific programs and specific techniques are of secondary concern, as compared with organizational climate, institutional milieu, or operational doctrine. In contrast to the specialization model, the aggregation model emphasizes the necessity for maintaining and strengthening the teacher's role as the central manager of the classroom in which he creates the conditions for teaching and learning. The teacher makes use of specialists and resource personnel, but manages their introduction into the classroom. Teacher aides, volunteers, and personnel supplied by VISTA and the National Teacher Corps become members of a team under the teacher-manager and are able to develop an effective sense of cohesion and enhance the position of the teacher. Under such an arrangement curriculum specialists are not part of an external hierarchy, but resources that can be utilized at the request of the teacher. The teacher-manager becomes a focal resource for in-service training that is designed to assist new personnel entering the slum school. The principal finds himself not directing a group of relatively isolated teachers, but rather supporting and coordinating the work of an aggregation of teacher teams. He is the principal-teacher, the doctor among the doctors, engaged in teaching and available to parents and students as well as outside community leaders.

Under the aggregation model the principles of curriculum construction depend not only on cognitive (rational) processes but, equally, on affective (emotional) considerations. Structuring of materials is of less importance than the sheer question of mobilizing interest in the subject matter. A central question is a set of rewards and pattern of motivation which lead youngsters to undertake the necessary "intellectual" struggle and effort. These rewards are most effective if they are immediate, mediated through personal relations, and are strengthened if they are unconditional. Strong emphasis is placed on making available to the youngster tutorial assistance offered by one person. Recommendations stress intensive human effort rather than elaborate but impersonal technology—labor intensive methods versus the capital intensive methods of the specialization model.

Youngsters with high academic motivation or with clearcut vocational goals can make the most effective use of complex and capital intensive technology. Within limits, their school behavior corresponds to the psychologists' theories of cognition. But this is not the case for students—from inner city schools or suburban schools—whose attitudes are diffuse and whose commitments to learning are not clearcut; for them the school must cope with the fusion of academic and socialization goals. For them, labor intensive techniques—the volunteer, the teacher aide, and team teaching—are essential elements. The investment of a significant amount of human resources makes possible developing positive and stable interpersonal relations which must precede effective learning. School behavior under such circumstances is best understood as an aspect of the social process and organizational behavior.

Under the aggregation model, the teacher seeks out those aspects of technology which will serve his purpose. The mimeograph machine will make possible personalized and immediately relevant material more important than the elaborate teaching material. Paperback books—no prepackaged closed circuit TV programs—are relevant items. To the limited extent possible, materials prepared by the students are reproduced and included in the teaching technology.

The aggregation model does not emphasize classroom size per se, nor the introduction of an independent hierarchy of curriculum specialists. Instead, the aggregation model is concerned with improvement in the overall management of the classroom and in increasing the professional authority and professional autonomy of the teacher. The teacher accepts responsibility for managing all that goes on in the classroom and for coordinating the relations between the classroom and the family as well as other community contacts. The teacher-manager seeks to prevent the classroom from becoming detached and isolated from the rest of the school and the larger community.

Emphasis is on organizational flexibility and away from fixed standards of classroom size. The goals are toward organizing a series of daily and weekly educational experiences in which the ratio of instructional personnel (and their qualifications) vary from one educational task to another. The teaching of history and geography can proceed in normal size classes, while there can be no effective reading program in a slum school without small group activities, augmented by individual tutorial instruction. These practices have existed informally under superior teachers in a single classroom; the objective is to institutionalize them and make them part of the total school program.

The teaching team seeks explicitly to face the grim realities of the disorganized slum and its negativism toward education. Instead of semiannual grading, a continuous development format is more appropriate to deal with the high degree of residential mobility found in the slum community. Basically, the youngster is permitted to proceed through the curriculum at a speed compatible with his intellectual capacity. The curriculum is organized into much smaller segments, and grading and evaluation is done each month or each six weeks. The child is not permitted to pass on to a new level until some effort is made to help him master his present level. Research results indicate that the continuous educational program not only produces short-term overall improvements in performance, but also that the teacher knows more about the children and the attitudes of the students toward the teacher and the school are improved.

The notion of the aggregation model was formulated because of the dilemmas of the slum school. But it has relevance for the entire social structure. In suburban areas, the "crisis" in public education presents an equivalent tension between academic and socialization goals. The growth of hostility toward educational authority and the patterns of personal disorganization derive from overemphasis in high school on narrower and narrower criteria of test achievement, as well as from a separation of the life experiences of the school from the community. In particular, the aggregation model should serve to produce a more varied educational experience and should help to blend school with nonschool experience through community service and work experience.

Finally, the aggregation model has to face the tremendous problems of large-scale organization in American education and the issues of Federal aid to education. Slogans of decentralization are not sufficient since the present structure of American education is more fractured than overcentralized. There is great need for decentralization at the operating level; effective principals and effective teachers under the aggregation model will require greater latitude in the use of their resources. Yet there is equally a need for national standards and greater equality of resources which cannot be achieved by decentralized operating procedures. In short, we must think of a more unified and more national system. In short, there are policy-making functions, and even specific administrative tasks, which require more centralization. Federal aid, if guided by appropriate standards, could be a powerful instrument for achieving such minimum and equal standards. In the American scene compromises are likely to emerge between Federal standards and local implementation which will be fully compatible with the aggregation model.

Desegregation or Integration in Public Schools? The Policy Implications of Research

IRWIN KATZ

The author's research reported in this article was performed under contract with the Office of Naval Research.

The dominant fact that emerges from the recent research endeavors of the U.S. Office of Education and the U.S. Commission on Civil Rights is that educational opportunity is greater in racially balanced than in racially isolated schools. These historic studies show beyond any reasonable doubt that the academic attainments of both white and Negro pupils are significantly higher in majority-white classrooms than in majority-Negro classrooms.

There is continuing debate over what causal factors underlie this unequivocal finding. (Some writers even have maintained that racial composition of enrollments *per se* is not an important determinant of the obtained

FROM Irwin Katz, "Desegregation or Integration in Public Schools? The Policy Implications of Research," *Integrated Education* 30 (September–October 1967), pp. 15–27.

school differences in pupils' achievement.) Much of the discussion arises from the inability of the two Federal documents (reports of large-scale survey data) to provide detailed information about the psychological processes that mediate superior learning in racially balanced environments. Such information can best be obtained from relatively small and intensive studies of children's reactions, in carefully controlled achievement situations.

The purpose of this paper is to bring relevant knowledge from such psychological research to bear on the issue of desegregation and its scholastic effects. It will be seen that *racially balanced classrooms can generate both favorable and detrimental influences on the performance of minority-group students:* the conditions promoting one or the other define the difference between mere physical desegregation and true racial integration.

THE COLEMAN AND COMMISSION REPORTS

I will begin by reviewing briefly the findings of the two Federal reports on the scholastic effects of racial balance and isolation. The survey of the U.S. Office of Education, executed by James Coleman and others in 1965, involved administration of questionnaires and objective tests to a fairly representative sample of about 650,000 pupils in over 4,000 public elementary and high schools throughout the Nation.[1] All teachers, principals, and district superintendents in these schools also participated. The report indicates that the achievement of both Negro and white pupils, when their family background characteristics are controlled statistically, is more closely related to the social class backgrounds of their classmates than to all objective school characteristics together (curriculum, expenditure per pupil, physical facilities, size of classes, and so on) and to all teacher characteristics together (type of education, experience, verbal ability, attitudes, and the like). In the upper grades the apparent influence of student body characteristics on individual achievement was two to three times greater for Negro pupils than for white pupils.

Given the close relationship between socio-economic status and race it is not surprising that as the proportion white in a school increased, Negro achievement rose, and that the effect was cumulative. The seeming impact of desegregation can be illustrated by comparing scores on reading comprehension for Negro high school students in the metropolitan North who never had a white classmate with scores of metropolitan northern Negroes with similar family backgrounds who attended racially mixed schools from the early grades. When figures from Table 3.3.2 of the Coleman report are consolidated, it is revealed that Negro ninth-graders in predominantly white classes whose first interracial experience occurred in the primary grades had an average score of 48.2. This is about five points below the white norm for the same region, but less than two points below the national norm of 50. In contrast, Negro ninth-graders who had never had white classmates averaged 43.8—almost 10 points below the white regional norm. Thus it seems as though desegregation reduced the racial achievement gap by almost half.

The results based on Negro twelfth-graders are similar to the foregoing findings for ninth-graders. In addition, the data reveal considerably more variability in the test scores of Negroes in majority-white classrooms than of Negro children in classrooms with a smaller proportion of whites.

Due to the time pressures under which it was prepared, the Coleman report devoted relatively little attention to the effects of desegregation. Therefore, the U.S. Commission on Civil Rights undertook to analyze more thoroughly portions of the Coleman data bearing upon this question and to carry out new investigations as well.[2] The Commission was particularly interested in establishing whether the apparently favorable effects of desegregation on Negro scholastic achievement could be attributed at least in part to racial composition *per se*. Hence the following factors were controlled by means of cross-tabulations: (a) quality of educational services available; (b) academic ability and social-class background of classmates; and (c) academic ability and home backgrounds of the Negro students. Even with the influence of these three sets of factors neutralized to a large extent, the Commission found a consistent relationship between racial composition of the classroom and Negro test scores. The apparent benefits of desegregation were not linear; that is, Negroes in predominantly white classrooms scored higher on the average, but those in classrooms where Negroes constituted a majority did no better than pupils in all-Negro situations. As in the Coleman report, the beneficial effect of desegregated experiences appeared to be greatest for Negro children whose biracial contacts began in the early grades. As regards white children, the achievement test scores of those in classes with some, but less than a majority of, Negroes, were just as high as the scores of children in all-white classes.

To sum up, the Federal data strongly suggest that (a) on average, children of both races, of all levels of ability, and from high and low social-class backgrounds learn best in schools with majority-white enrollments; and (b) racial contact in and of itself contributes importantly to the effect. Those who prepared the Civil Rights Commission's report were fully aware of the ideological implications of these findings. Elsewhere, Thomas Pettigrew, Chief Consultant of the Commission's study, has pointed out that Negroes can rightfully reject the implication that "white is right," that predominantly Negro schools cannot be "good schools."[3] Pettigrew referred to a statement by Commissioner Frankie Freeman of the Civil Rights Commission in which she addressed herself specifically to this issue:

> The question is not whether in theory or in the abstract Negro schools can be as good as white schools. In a society free from prejudice in which Negroes were full and equal participants, the answer would clearly be "Yes." But we are forced, rather, to ask the harder question, whether in our present society, where Negroes are a minority which has been discriminated against, Negro children can prepare themselves to participate effectively in society if they grow up and go to school in isolation from the majority group. We must also ask whether we can cure the disease

of prejudice and prepare all children for life in a multiracial world if white children grow up and go to school in isolation from Negroes.[4]

Why does satisfactory progress in school on the part of Negro children demand day-to-day contact with majority-group peers and adults? To answer the question, one must analyze the psychological dynamics of racially mixed and isolated learning environments. While the Coleman Commission reports suggest that the conditions generally prevailing in northern desegregated classrooms are, on balance, favorable to Negro performance, it is important to recognize that these biracial situations can possess academically detrimental features as well. As mentioned earlier, the Coleman survey revealed considerably more variability of performance among Negroes in classrooms where Negro pupils were a majority. In its reanalysis of these Coleman data the Civil Rights Commission was able to relate between-school differences in Negro achievement and attitudes to the *quality* of interracial contacts, as measured by teachers' reports of interracial tension. In desegregated schools where most teachers reported no tension, Negro students were more proficient, college-oriented, and optimistic about being rewarded for their efforts.

PSYCHOLOGICAL ANALYSIS OF BIRACIAL LEARNING ENVIRONMENTS

In order to clarify the behavioral effects of various types of biracial achievement situations I and some colleagues embarked several years ago on a program of experimental research that is still in progress.[5] Though most of the research has been done on college students, the main findings have implications for younger age groups as well.

Our first discovery was that biracial situations can have notably detrimental effects upon the intellectual performance of Negro youths. In two early studies conducted at a northern urban university, various mental and physical tasks were assigned to male groups composed of two Negro students and two white students, all of whom initially were total strangers. In general, Negroes displayed marked social inhibition and subordination to white partners. When teams were engaged in cooperative problem solving, Negro subjects made fewer proposals than did whites, and tended to accept the latter's contributions uncritically. On all tasks combined, Negroes made fewer remarks than did whites, and spoke more to whites, proportionately, than to one another. White men, on the other hand, spoke more to one another, proportionately, than to the Negroes. These behaviors occurred even when group members could expect a monetary bonus for good teamwork, and were informed that their abilities were higher than those of subjects in other groups.

In the second experiment we made special efforts to increase the self-confidence of Negro subjects. Negro and white team mates were matched on intelligence by means of individual pretesting, and were then told that they were matched. In addition, they were made to display apparently equal ability on certain mental tasks that were administered in the group situation, through secret experimental manipulation of the tasks. Despite these procedures the Negro subjects later revealed feelings of inferiority and anxiety. On a post-experimental questionnaire they ranked the whites higher on ability on the very tasks that had been rigged, and expressed relatively low satisfaction with the group experience.

That this type of face-to-face biracial situation produced genuine impairment of intellectual functioning in the Negro students, rather than just an inhibition of outward behavior, is apparent from another study that was conducted at the same northern college. Racially mixed pairs of subjects were given a series of mental problems to solve cooperatively. But before discussing each problem the men had to record privately their individual solutions. *Negroes made more errors than they had made on the same problems at a prior, individual testing session.* White subjects, on the other hand, made *fewer* private errors than they had made previously.

Similarly, in a study conducted in the South, individual Negro students from a predominantly Negro college were told that they would receive a painful stimulus (electric shock) while working on a digit-symbol task. The performance of those who worked in the presence of a white peer and a white tester was more adversely affected by the shock instructions than was the performance of subjects in a Negro peer–Negro tester situation. Thus, we see that feelings of insecurity at being alone in a strange white environment made the Negro highly vulnerable to additional stress.

These experiments suggest three factors that may detrimentally affect Negro students in face-to-face confrontations with whites. First, it can be assumed that novel types of contact with white strangers possess a *social threat* component for members of a subordinated minority group. Negroes may be fearful of arousing white hostility by being assertive or displaying intellectual competence. The degree of social threat should be a direct function of (a) the amount of evidence of white hostility (or the extent to which evidence of white friendliness is lacking) and (b) the amount of power possessed by whites in the contact situation, as shown by their numerical predominance, control of authority positions, and so on. Note that in all of the experiments described, except the one that used electric shock instructions, white subjects tended to ignore their Negro partners, the institutional setting was a predominantly white college, and the experimenters were white faculty members.

It seems likely that Negro children would be under some degree of social threat in a newly integrated classroom. Cold indifference on the part of white peers could frustrate their needs for companionship and approval, resulting in lowered self-esteem and a desire to escape from an unpleasant environment. The Negro child would thereby be distracted from the task at hand, to the detriment of performance. An example of how the presence of white adult strangers can seriously disrupt verbal learning in Negro children of grade school age is provided by an experiment we recently carried out in a Negro section of a large northern city. Negro boys of average age 8 were tested individually by either Negro or white adult males. They were required to learn a list of paired words. Irrespective of actual progress on the task, half of them periodically received approval from the adults and the other half just as often received disapproval. The results were clear-cut: for each type of examiner, approval was more effective than disapproval, but regardless of type of feedback, children learned better with Negro testers than with white testers. The poorest learners were boys with a high need for approval, as measured by a personality test, who experienced disapproval from white testers. In short, the white adults' expressions of approval were relatively ineffectual, while their disapproval was sometimes highly disruptive. Apparently, Negro pupils in northern segregated schools react anxiously to white strangers in authority roles. However, it is entirely possible that a relatively brief period of friendly acquaintance would dispel the Negro child's apprehensions. Our experiment did not explore that possibility. It is also noteworthy that the adults in the experiment were male. When we conducted a similar experiment using female examiners, there were no differences in learning due to the race of the adults. That white males had a detrimental influence, but not white females, can perhaps best be explained in terms of relative strangeness—children whom we tested had had one or more white female teachers but no white male teachers.

Another factor that could detrimentally affect Negro students' performance in biracial situations is *low expectancy of success* in competition with white standards. Our northern Negro undergraduates may have lacked motivation to engage in the experimental tasks for this reason. The experiments indicate that the Negro's low expectancy of success may result from feelings of inferiority that have no basis in reality, but likely reflect an emotional accommodation to the demeaning role in American society that has been imposed upon his racial group by the dominant white majority. However, because of the lower achievement standards and inferior educational services that often mark the predominantly Negro school, low expectations of success on the part of newly desegregated minority group pupils will often be quite realistic. When the Negro transferee enters a school that has substantially higher standards than he knew previously he may become discouraged and not try to succeed.

As a third type of detrimental influence, the Negro college students in our northern experiments may have anxiously anticipated disapproval, disparagement or rejection by their white partners and the white experimenter as a consequence of poor performance. This factor can be called *failure threat*. A high expectation of failure at a task does not by itself constitute failure threat—it is necessary also that the failure have a *socially punitive meaning*. For the elementary and high school pupil, academic failure often entails strong disapproval by parents, as well as by teachers and perhaps classmates.

To diminish the adverse influence of the three factors that have been mentioned—social threat, low expectation of success, and failure threat—the Negro child should begin his desegregated experience as early as possible. Recall that this principle is well supported by the Federal data. There is also objective evidence to suggest that as social threat diminishes in biracial situations—that is, as white acceptance increases—Negro academic attainment benefits. An investigation of southern Negro scholarship winners who attended predominantly white colleges in the North revealed that those who participated in extracurricular activities and had a satisfactory number of friends got better marks than those who did not.[6] Similarly, the Civil Rights Commission found that in predominantly white classrooms, Negro pupils who said they had one or more close white friends tended to have higher achievement scores and college aspirations.

Returning to our experiments with college students, it follows logically from the foregoing analysis that if Negro subjects could be made to perceive intellectual competition with whites as neither socially threatening nor hopelessly difficult their performance would improve markedly. To test this proposition, northern Negro undergraduates were placed in a secretly controlled problem-solving situation. They were given instructions which, in effect, *forced them to disagree openly* with a white partner while displaying competence equal to that of the partner. As a result of this experience, the Negroes were able to function more effectively and autonomously when they later worked on another, unrigged task with the same white person. This study demonstrated that in biracial situations, Negro *inhibition* could be removed quite readily through an appropriate type of training.

More important, in a later phase of our research program we were able to establish that under certain conditions biracial environments actually have a *facilitating* effect upon Negro intellectual achievement. We discovered that *with anxiety-arousing factors minimized by various experimental procedures, Negro youths performed better when anticipating comparison with white peers, or evaluation by white authorities, than they performed in all-Negro settings.* While our evidence at present is limited to Negro male college students, there is no reason to doubt that further research can extend the finding to younger age groups.

Four types of experiment have thus far been done. The first type consisted of studies in which the anxiety of Negro subjects was diminished by presenting a task (digit-symbol) with instructions that emphasized its lack of evaluative or competitive significance. Two such experiments were carried out at a private, predominantly Negro college in the Upper South, that is known for its high academic quality. The first used instructions which stated: "This is not a test of any kind. Your scores will not be shown to anyone at your college, and you will not be compared . . . [with other students]." Subjects worked at the task in two racial settings. One featured a Negro confederate who posed as a second subject, and a Negro experimenter who introduced himself as a psychologist. In the other condition the confederate and experimenter were both white. The white environment, we found, occasioned higher achievement scores.

The second study was similar to the one just described, except that subjects worked individually with no confederate present. Again digit-symbol scores were higher with a white tester than with a Negro tester.

To account for the *social facilitation* effect of the white adult, it was assumed that he was perceived by Negro subjects as a more powerful and prestigious figure than the Negro examiner. (Whites, after all are the economic gate-keepers in American society.) Therefore, the prospect of white approval had *high positive incentive value*, while the prospect of white disapproval had *high negative incentive value*. Since the task was explicitly defined as non-evaluative subjects were not unduly fearful of doing poorly, and could strive to make a favorable impression on the white authority figure. That Negro students view white experimenters as more powerful evaluators than Negro experimenters was confirmed in a subsequent study at another Negro college, where subjects rated the former as being more "competent" and "important."

In another type of experiment, such tasks as digit-symbol, arithmetic and scrambled words were presented to students at predominantly Negro colleges as tests of intelligence. Instructions typically read: "This test is part of a new scholastic aptitude examination that all students will take. It will be used to evaluate your intellectual ability. Your score will be used in advising you about your academic and professional potentialities . . ." In addition, subjects were informed either that their scores would be compared with norms for students at their own, predominantly Negro college (Negro comparison), or with norms for all college students throughout the state (white comparison). Finally, to allay anxiety the tester was always a Negro.

Five experiments of this type were done, involving four colleges. Two of these were in the Deep South and at the time of testing had relatively low admission standards. Subjects at these colleges achieved higher scores when they expected to be compared with other Negroes. The other three experiments used one of the same Deep South colleges after a new, selective admissions policy had been introduced, as well as two non-selective, state-supported institutions in the Upper South and North. Better performance was obtained in the white comparison condition. In sum, when tested by a Negro, and not placed in face-to-face confrontation with white peers, students in Negro colleges of moderate academic quality were favorably motivated by the challenge of white-norm comparison, while students in Deep South institutions of relatively low quality worked better in competition with Negro norms.

Our interpretation of these results is that, except in the most depressed types of segregated learning environment (Deep South non-selective colleges) the opportunity for biracial comparison is highly stimulating because it provides more useful information for self-evaluation than does comparison with other Negroes. This is so because, in general, white standards of intellectual ability and achievement are more relevant to future career prospects. *Thus biracial peer comparisons are socially facilitating because of their informational value.* By using only Negro testers in these experiments the biracial facilitation effect was not offset by subjects' fear of eliciting white disapproval if they failed to meet what was for them a difficult standard.

The outcome of the peer-norm comparison experiments is all the more remarkable when one notes that most of the subjects had never sat in a biracial classroom throughout more than twelve years of schooling. The facilitation effect of cross-racial comparison should, if anything, be even greater for younger Negro pupils, who likely are well aware of the significance of white achievement standards, but who have had less time to fall behind them in segregated schools. This generalization is consistent with what we know about the superior performance of Negro children who entered desegregated classrooms at an early age. Moreover, as Pettigrew points out, Negro pupils in predominantly white schools who have white friends, and therefore are apt to be particularly aware of the importance of white standards, are higher achievers than Negroes in the same schools who do not have white friends.[7]

Consider a third type of experimental demonstration of biracial facilitation of the achievement of Negro college students. Again, simple mental tasks requiring speed and accuracy were used in conjunction with intelligence-test instructions. But now, the race of the tester was varied, while the race of ostensible peer norms was either varied or held constant by means of suitable instructions. To maximize the social effect of the experimenter, the subjects—all freshmen—were told that immediately after completion of the testing the experimenter would see each of them privately, score his work, and explain what the score meant with regard to prospects of future academic and vocational success.

We found, as our theory predicted, that the white examiner occasioned better performance than the Negro examiner when Negro norms (that is, a relatively easy standard) were employed, while the Negro examiner was more favorable for achievement than the white person when white-peer norms (that is, a relatively hard standard) were used. *The poorest experimental condition was the combination of Negro tester and Negro norms.*

To review the principles upheld by the results, when there was no anxious anticipation of possible face-to-face devaluation by a white authority figure, the riskier but also more informative white-peer standard was preferred by the Negro subjects. On the other hand, when white evaluation *was* expected, the less informative but also less risky Negro-peer standard was preferred.

It would of course be fallacious to make a literal application of these findings to the desegregated classroom—that is, to conclude that Negro pupils should not have both white teachers and predominantly white classmates at the same time. On the contrary, what our study suggests is that even when performance is endowed with strong evaluative significance both cross-racial comparisons and cross-racial evaluations can improve Negro motivation, *provided ego-threatening features of the situation are kept at a minimum.* Here emotional supportiveness on the part of teachers would be of critical importance, both in its direct significance to Negro children, and in its influence upon the social reactions of their classmates.

Of considerable import are the findings of another experiment of the type just described. It differed from its predecessor in two ways: it was conducted at a Negro college with relatively high standards of admission, and all subjects were told they would be evaluated against white-peer norms. Now, even though only the cross-racial comparison was used, higher test scores were attained with a white examiner than with a Negro examiner. Apparently, for the able Negro students who had been accepted into this college, meeting a white standard of competence did not seem so difficult as to dampen their desire for evaluation by a white authority figure.

Finally, I come to a fourth type of research on the factors that produce optimal achievement in biracial environments. Its special feature is the experimental manipulation of subjects' expectations of success on an ability test, accomplished by giving them different types of information, ostensibly based upon their scores from a prior administration of the same test. Subjects at a non-selective State college in the Upper South were told that they had either little chance, a moderately good chance, or a very good chance of equaling the norms for their age groups. The most relevant finding has to do with the impact of expectancies under white-norm instructions. In this condition low expectancy of success was highly detrimental to performance, while in a Negro-norms condition the low-probability feedback did not impair motivation. Both groups had sharply higher test scores when expectancy of success was moderately high, and then declined somewhat as it became very high. The results suggest that in cross-racial competition, Negro students may be readily discouraged by unfavorable feedback, but also highly responsive to reasonable chances of success.

To recapitulate, research on minority group youths and children is on the whole consistent with a five-factor model of Negro achievement in biracial educational settings. On the negative side of the ledger are the following:

Social threat—given the prestige and power of the white majority group, rejection of Negro students by white classmates or teachers should tend to elicit emotional responses (fear, anger and humiliation) that are detrimental to intellectual functioning.

Low probability of success—where there is marked discrepancy in the educational standards of Negro and white schools, or where feelings of inferiority are acquired by Negro children outside the school, minority-group newcomers in integrated classrooms are likely to have a low expectancy of academic success; consequently their achievement motivation should be low.

Failure threat—when academic failure entails disapproval by significant others (parents, teachers, and perhaps also classmates), low expectancy of success should elicit emotional responses that are detrimental to performance.

On the positive side are these factors:

In an atmosphere of social acceptance Negro pupils will desire to meet the high academic standards of white classmates because of their *high informational value* for self-evaluation, and the *high incentive value* of favorable evaluation by white adults and peers.

Our experiments indicate that when the strength of negative factors is kept low, biracial environments facilitate high Negro achievement.

DESEGREGATION AND THE LOW-ACHIEVING NEGRO PUPIL

One might too hastily conclude from the evidence presented in the preceding section that desegregation benefits only the more capable Negro. But according to the analysis of the Civil Rights Commission the apparent gain in achievement test scores associated with racially balanced schooling is roughly as large for Negroes of low ability as for those of medium and high ability. Why is it that the low ability children give no indication of being demoralized by the large achievement gap between themselves and their white classmates? I do not know the answer, but should like to suggest where it may lie. Research recently conducted by myself and associates in an all-Negro elementary school in the North revealed that boys of mediocre ability (and this included most of the boys in the school) tended to be harshly self-critical of their work, even when they were not being observed by teachers. In contrast, the superior students were more readily satisfied by their private efforts. The low-achieving students were also highly anxious about their school work in general, and felt inadequate with their parents. It was as though these overly self-critical, segregated children had accepted a grossly exaggerated conception of their inferiority as Negroes.

The Commission's data on achievement suggest that an opportunity to compare themselves with white peers would have a corrective influence on the self-evaluations of these Negro children, thereby improving their will to learn. The Federal reports provide little additional information pertinent to this line of reasoning. The Coleman questionnaire included items on self-concept regarding school ability, but it is difficult to interpret the meaning of Negro responses, which were not different from whites' and were not closely related to school achievement. However, another attitude was closely related to school achievement. This was the child's belief in the responsiveness of the environment to his achievement efforts (that is, his sense of fate control). Negroes had less sense of fate control than whites. But the Commission's analysis shows that attending majority-white classes increased the sense of control of Negro children from homes of both high and low educational attainment. The gain occurred whether the desegregated schools had student bodies from homes of similar or dissimilar educational attainment. Since scholastic ability is closely related to the education quality of the home, these data suggest two things: that desegregation increases the Negro child's sense of competence in that he feels more adequately rewarded for his efforts, and that the attitudinal gain is as great for children of low ability as for those of high ability.

The Influence of Teachers

For reasons already mentioned, the behavior of teachers in desegregated classrooms is of far greater importance to Negro children than to whites. Anxiety about one's social worth and intellectual adequacy is bound to be more prevalent among the minority newcomers. Hence the research of Seymour Sarason and his associates on school anxiety is particularly relevant for this discussion.[8] From their observations in classrooms, the Sarason group have concluded that teachers vary greatly in the degree to which they provide direction and support to children who approach academic tasks apprehensively. They write:

> In some classrooms failure or lack of progress by a child is responded to by the teacher in a way that increases the child's feeling of inadequacy. In other classrooms such a child is responded to in a way that, while it recognizes the child's failure or rate of progress, does not make him feel that the teacher is rejecting or derogating him, i.e., the teacher likes and accepts him despite his inadequacy or failure. It is too frequently forgotten by parents (and also by teachers) how important a figure the teacher is in the life of the child. From the standpoint of the child, what he thinks is the teacher's attitude toward him is of great moment to him, *particularly if he likes the teacher and wants to be liked by her.* . . . It is when the child is disposed to like and respect the teacher that the ways in which the teacher responds to an adequate performance of the child are of great significance. This would be especially true for the anxious child, who, as described previously by us, is dependent on the positive attitudes of others toward him for a sense of security (p. 272).

Two related points can be made about the Sarason group's emphasis upon the emotional impact on children of the teacher's behavior. First, their own research shows that the relationship between anxiety and scholastic progress is quite substantial. In their most recent study, grouping children on the basis of test anxiety and defensiveness scores revealed mean differences in test performance as large as two years in reading achievement. Controlling for differences in IQ showed that the gap between high-anxious and low-anxious children in average grade assigned by teachers was about as large as differences between children in the highest and lowest of four IQ levels. A second point has to do with the long-term changes that occur in anxiety scores. Hill and Sarason report moderate test-retest correlations over two-year intervals, but little relationship between scores over a four-year interval. Moreover, changes in anxiety scores were associated with changes in academic attainment. It stands to reason the changes are in large measure a reflection of different types of experience in the classroom and in the total school culture.

Also pertinent to the situation of the desegregated Negro child is the ingenious and widely publicized experiment of Rosenthal and Jacobson on the effect of teachers' expectations upon the intellectual growth of their pupils. Elementary school teachers were told at the beginning of the year that certain children were likely on the basis of fictitious test scores, to "spurt ahead" intellectually during the ensuing year. At the lower grades the randomly designated "intellectual bloomers" showed larger IQ gains at the end of the year than their classmates. The effect was due entirely to the expectation that had been implanted in the minds of the teachers.

Unfortunately, there is reason to suspect that some teachers are inclined to react negatively to minority group pupils. For example, Davidson and Lang found that *regardless of their scholastic* standing, elementary school pupils from blue-collar homes tended to perceive their teachers as rejectant.[9] In two small-sample studies the race of teachers seemed to make a difference in how they viewed Negro students, with white teachers being more critical of their motivation and ability.[10]

ABILITY GROUPING

It has often been remarked that when ability grouping is practiced, teachers' attitudes and expectations tend to get frozen into rigid patterns that are particularly disadvantageous to minority group children. Yet the placing of pupils at the beginning of each year in so-called "homogeneous" ability groups is a widely accepted policy throughout America. All too often, the effect is to create racially isolated classes in schools that are nominally desegregated.

The arguments in favor of ability grouping are usually taken for granted. As Joseph Justman observes, "If one were to ask an elementary school supervisor why he uses ability grouping . . . he would probably cite a number of reasons—pupil achievement is better, teachers find it easier to teach classes showing a narrow range of ability, the slower children do not become a hindrance to those who learn more readily, etc." [11] But Justman notes that when the research in the field is examined, the findings are generally inconclusive. One of the problems has been the ambiguity of the terms "homogeneous" and "heterogeneous." A so-called "heterogeneous" class drawn from a population with a narrow ability range may actually show less variation in ability than a so-called "homogeneous" class drawn from a broad-range population.

Both my comments about the influence of teachers' attitudes and expectations, and my earlier discussion of the benefits of being exposed to white achievement standards, clearly imply that ability grouping as usually practiced cannot be helpful to Negro pupils, and indeed may be detrimental. In this connection, a recent study by Justman in New York City is illuminating. Justman's is perhaps the most comprehensive and adequately executed evaluation yet done on the academic effects of ability grouping. Parallel forms of the Metropolitan Reading Test were administered to third-grade and fourth-grade pupils in two successive years. Scores for a total of almost 5,000 pupils in 181 classes drawn from 42 schools were available for analysis. The standard deviations of class scores at the initial testing were used to divide them into high, medium, and low homogeneity categories. These categories were then cross-tabulated with the average achievement levels of classes, also divided into three categories of high, medium and low. The results show that on the Word Knowledge and Reading subtests the effects of various degrees of homogeneity were not consistent for different levels of class ability. However, for all ability groups combined, average and low homogeneity groups were more effective than high homogeneity. Low-homogeneous classes showed the highest mean growth in reading ability.

Justman concludes that ability grouping is of little value unless definite programs, specifically, designed for the several ability levels into which classes are grouped, are developed.

Concluding Remarks: Some Implications for Educational Policy

The psychological evidence that I have presented is consistent with a definition of racial integration which emphasizes the beneficial effects to Negro pupils of attending racially balanced classes, *when an atmosphere of genuine respect and acceptance prevails.*

Integration must be seen as the end-goal of all long-range educational planning. Where full integration is not immediately feasible for technical reasons, educational standards of Negro schools should be raised to the level of white schools, so that when minority group children eventually enter desegregated classes they will have a good chance of succeeding academically. This means, among other things, that the quality of training received by Negro teachers and the criteria used in selecting them for jobs must be raised to white levels, where they are not already at those levels, and racial integration of school faculties must be carried out.

Programs must be instituted for contacting parents and helping them to understand what they can do to prepare children for schooling, and to foster achievement once children are in school.

There should be in-service training of teachers and other personnel in newly desegregated schools to develop awareness of the emotional needs of children in biracial situations. The training should include the imparting of techniques for helping children get acquainted with one another.

The widely accepted practice of assigning children to homogeneous ability groups should either be abandoned entirely or modified to afford maximum opportunity for periodic re-evaluation of potentiality. Ability grouping tends inevitably to freeze teachers' expectations as well as children's own self-images, hence it is particularly dangerous to intellectual development in the early grades.

[1] Coleman, J. S., et al. Equality of Educational Opportunity. United States Department of Health, Education, and Welfare, Washington, D.C.: United States Government Printing Office, 1966.

[2] Racial Isolation in the Public Schools, a Report of the U.S. Commission on Civil Rights. Washington, D.C.: U.S. Government Printing Office, 1967.

[3] Pettigrew, T. F. The Negro and Education: Problems and Proposals. Paper read at Conference on Research in Race Relations, University of Michigan, April, 1967.

[4] U.S. Commission on Civil Rights, op. cit., p. 214.

[5] Much of the research is reviewed in the following article by this author: "Review of evidence relating to effects of desegregation on the intellectual performance of Negroes," American Psychologist, Vol. 19, June, 1964, pp. 381–399.

[6] National Scholarship Service and Funds for Negro Students. Annual Report 1959–1960. New York: NSSFNS, 1960.

[7] Pettigrew, op. cit.

[8] Sarason, S. B., Davidson, K. S., Lighthall, F. F., Waite, R. R. and Ruebush, B. K. Anxiety in Elementary School Children. New York: Wiley and Sons, 1960. Hill, K. T. and Sarason, S. B. The relation of test anxiety and defensiveness to test and school performance over the elementary school years: a further longitudinal study. Monogr. Society for Res. Child Development, 1966, 31 (Whole No. 2).

[9] Davidson, Helen H., and Lang, G. Children's perceptions of their teachers' feeling toward them related to self-perception, school achievement and behavior. J. exp. Educ., 1960, 29, 107–118.

[10] Clark, K. B. Dark Ghetto. New York: Harper and Row, 1965. Gottlieb, D. Teaching and students: the views of Negro students and teachers. In Webster, S. W. (Ed.), The Disadvantaged Learner. San Francisco: Chandler, 1966.

[11] Justman, J. Ability grouping—what good is it? The Urban Review, Feb. 1967, Vol. 2, No. 1, 2–3.

C. Client or Community Development

Participation, Decentralization, Community Control, and Quality Education

Mario D. Fantini

Those who, like myself, view emerging community participation patterns with more hope than despair hypothesize that school governance—the

FROM Teachers College Record, Vol. 71, No. 1 (September 1969), pp. 93–107.

politics of urban education—is instrumentally related to the form, shape and direction of educational institutions and, therefore, to their quality and relevance. Participation by the clients of the city public schools—students, parents, community residents—represents the emergence of important publics wielding an enormous amount of energy. These publics can combine their energies with those of the professionals to bring about fundamental reforms, or they can level their energies against the officials of city schools. A collision course can only be avoided if basic changes are made in urban schooling, changes which—ironically—are not likely without these publics' support. The schools do not now have the capacity to respond to the multiple new demands being made upon them. Rooted in 19th century concepts, the educational system simply cannot be expected to solve 20th and 21st century problems; and the consequences are loss of confidence, frustration, disconnection, alienation, and retaliation by the new publics.

The problem is not, therefore, with any particular group. It is with the form and shape of the institution in which administrators, teachers, supervisors, students, parents, communities, *et al.* function, with the institutional environment and its effects on the parties concerned. In brief, the problem is with the "system," not the people. The parties of interest all want to see the schools updated and made relevant; but they have been tragically sidetracked into conflict. This is a fantastic waste of energy which can be mobilized to generate the power necessary for school reform. It will be my purpose, therefore, to provide a rationale in defense of the emerging participatory movements and relate them to educational development.

Justifying Community Participation

There are at least three levels of justification for the community-centered participatory approaches now being advanced as alternatives for urban educational reform. The first is the *conceptual* level, i.e., the *theoretical* assumptions on which the community participation plans are based. The second is at the educational *input* level; the third, the *output* level. Before moving into these three levels of analysis, which will hopefully provide an overall framework for reviewing the school participation movement, let me provide a few direct answers to the questions most often posed by the critics.

Is there any evidence that neighborhood control of urban schools improves student achievement? The answer is that, if there is no evidence, it is because there are really no community-controlled urban public schools. There are several experiments underway in New York City, Washington, D.C., and Chicago, for example; but these have been in existence only for a couple of years—years mainly consumed by community struggles to wrest some element of control from a usually unsympathetic centralized structure. Moreover, these communities inherit a failing situation. *We do have ample evidence of the massive failure that the standard (centrally controlled) urban school has produced*. It is ironic, therefore, that those in control of a failing system should demand results of people who are offering constructive, democratically oriented alternatives before they have had a chance to implement them.

The second objection usually pooh-poohs community participation as a political gimmick without relation to quality education: Transferring control isn't the real answer; more money to urban schools is. There is logic to this. For, if all that occurs through participation and decentralization is merely a shift of authority, if all that happens is a transfer of control as an *end* itself and not as a *means* to reform, the cycle of educational decline will not likely be reversed. The problem is still with the outdatedness of the educational system, regardless of who is in control. However, parents, community residents and students who are seeking an increased voice in decision making have moved to this stage of activity as a result of the failure of the existing educational system. In a sense, their involvement platform has been to change the present system, not to accept it through control.

The answer continues, more money for what? In New York City, for example, the school system doubled its budget in the last decade from $508,-622,151 in 1959 to $1,251,153,235 in 1968. The per pupil expenditures rose to the $1000 per pupil level above most other cities and even some suburban school districts. Medium elementary school class size was reduced by 8 per cent and classroom teaching staff increased by 37.6 per cent—with no results. Special compensatory programs which increase per pupil expenditure also fail to show increase in student performance. The point is that more of the same approach has limited payoff, and most of the money being requested is for more of the same.

Outdated Models

There are also some real questions concerning universally accepted "inputs" said to be central to quality education. For example, many argue that class size is crucial to quality, then point to the lowering of pupil-teacher ratios as a prime indicator of quality. There is little evidence, however, to suggest any actual relationship between lowered class size from 35 to 30 or from 30 to 25 and student performance. Moreover, the cost of lowering class size in urban school systems is staggering. A reduction of class size for a teacher in a self-contained classroom, age-graded, egg-crated school with irrelevant curricula, etc., will have a minimal effect because the total institution is dysfunctional. If the educational system is outdated so is its conception of education. Hence trying to improve one "piece" of the system, e.g., class size, is like trying to improve an old car by putting a new carburetor in it. Instead of pouring money into an outdated model of education, we need to build a new model. A key question becomes: What is the process by which a major social institution like the schools is reformed in an open society? In our society, building a new model of education requires direct *participation* by parents, students and other citizens. Basic educational reform is not exclusively a professional undertaking; it cannot or should not be in an open society.

The other dominant question concerns desegregation: Don't these types of local efforts hinder desegregation? The responses vary but they usually start with the observation that since 1954 there has actually been more segregation rather than less. Moreover, there is a distinction between desegregation and integration. Desegregation refers to the physical mixing of black and white students; integration refers to humans connecting as *equals*. Agreeing on the goal of integration, one could argue that it is necessary for black and other minority groups to have a sense of cohesion and identity. This can in part be achieved through the control of their own institutions. Once blacks attain a status of potency, they will be in a better position to connect up with white society as equals rather than as "junior" members. Therefore, such participatory efforts as decentralization and community control can be viewed as necessary steps toward a further stage of integration.

Under the *present concept* of desegregation, blacks are moved to white areas and a kind of dependency relationship develops in which improvement is dependent on the presence of a majority of whites. For many, this is another indication of a superior-inferior relationship, communicating once again, albeit subtly, another form of discrimination. Nevertheless, most argue that the goal of desegregation stimulated by the civil rights movement is quality education. That goal remains, as does the option of school desegregation, having been opened to many who had been denied this path to equality. Yet, desegregation moved slowly at best; other options to greater education were needed. Enter the greater local control alternative.

This participation made a great deal of sense, given the present reality. If the schools are still largely segregated and an inferior quality of education is continued, the natural approach seems to be for the community to take a hand in reshaping the institution toward quality education. Many of those favoring greater local control claim that those who are now talking about desegregation and integration are using this as an excuse for not allowing communities to pursue the option of community participation and increased involvement in decision making.

The clients of our city schools are demanding a voice in updating and thereby raising certain philosophical and theoretical arguments which take us to the conceptual level of justification.

Accountability and Control

The first concept concerns public *accountability* and *control* of education. In our society, public schools belong to the public. It is the *public* that decides on *policies* and *objectives* for the school; it is the public that *delegates* to the *professional* the role of *implementor* and reserves for itself the role of *accountant*. The people are the trustees of the schools. They have a right to ask why Johnny can't read. Moreover, if 85 per cent of the Johnnies can't read, as is the case in most of our so-called inner city schools, then the public has the right and responsibility, as trustee, to supervise or monitor the needed changes—changes aimed at reducing the discrepancy between policy and implementation.

This process has in essence been in effect; black parents and community residents have been asking why so many black children are failing. The usual answer is that the children are "culturally deprived" or "disadvantaged," that they are failing because there is something wrong with *them.* This verdict has increasingly been rejected, and in the absence of improvement in the performance of the children, the public—in the form of certain communities—has begun to exercise its role as both accountant and trustee. Those in the forefront of this urban movement poignantly ask: What would happen in Scarsdale or Grosse Pointe if 85 per cent of the children in these schools were academically retarded and if 1 per cent went to college? What would be the reaction of the parents and the community?

Many black parents who had patiently waited for improvement through such efforts as compensatory education and desegregation have begun to turn away from these efforts. Increasingly, communities are rendering the diagnosis that the problem is not with the learner: the problem is with the system, with the institution. The cry now is: "We need a new system, one that is responsive to our kids and to us. It is up to us to build this new and relevant system."

Sincere schoolmen have been aware of the crises for some time, but they have been victimized by the constraints of an outdated system. Often the professionals have become defensive in the belief that the public expects the school and the schoolmen to solve all the ills of society. Many have attempted to respond with programs of remediation on the one hand and token desegregation on the other. Both approaches, although stimulated by federal legislation, have been less than successful. Some educators attribute the failures to the underlying assumption that the problem was with the *learner* and not with the *institution.* Certainly it is difficult, if not impossible, for those trying to keep the present system running to serve also as the major agents of institutional change. Other legitimate parties are needed. And surely the parents and students constitute legitimate parties of the public school.

But even if school people were able, by themselves, to bring about radical institutional changes, they would thereby be denying opportunities for parents and students to learn and grow through the process of involvement and participation. Through involvement, parents and students can learn more about the complexities of teaching and learning and relate this learning to their own roles of parents as teachers or students as teachers. Through involvement, parents and students can be more attuned to the role of the schoolman as an individual in a setting which places severe constraints on him; have a better view of program options; be more cognizant of the need for increased funds for education. Even more important, perhaps, is the realization that if the professional tries to go it alone, this could lead to a professional monopoly.

THE IMPORTANCE OF PROCESS

The second major principle emerging from the new participatory movement concerns the importance of *process*. Communities no longer accept the process of something being done *for* or *to* them—even if the product is desirable. Increasingly, the acceptance process is *with* or *by* the community, and this includes students as well. This principle is intrinsically tied to the broader self-determination movement embraced by many blacks and other minority groupings. The reasons for this shift are not difficult to understand. Generally, they are a reaction to the bitter realization that whites cannot solve black problems. Accompanying this are the distrust and alienation that come from the feeling of powerlessness.

By emphasizing the process of participation in decision making, communities are employing the basic tools of democracy itself—tools which increase people's sense of potency. Professionals, including researchers, are increasingly referring to the drive for self-determination as the "fate control" variable. The preliminary findings indicate that fate control fundamentally affects human motivation essential to achievement in all areas.

It is during this process that student participants, for example, can begin to translate their concern for relevance into policy. Students can begin to legitimize educational objectives that deal with individual and group identity, potency and disconnection, in short, with humanistic concerns. They are concerned with legitimizing *affective* educational objectives, in order to restore a needed balance with the present *cognitively*-oriented school. They can contribute to making the educational process more experiential and reality-oriented with instrumental links to the major societal roles, e.g., worker, citizen, parent, and community residents can add support for more diversity in school staffing. Talents can be tapped from various sources, including the immediate community. This would lead to the valuing of *performance* over *credentials* as the major personnel criterion. Included in performance is how human (sensitive, authentic, emphatic, trustworthy) the person is.

EXPECTANCY AND SOCIALIZATION

Two other key principles have their roots in social-psychological theories. The first has to do with *expectancy*. The concept that it is the system, rather than the child, that has failed is a hopeful concept for black parents and communities. The transition from blaming the client to doing something about institutional renewal is illustrated by perceptions of schoolmen—largely white—who possess attitudes which brand black children as inferior. "After all," say black parents, "they call our kids 'culturally deprived' and disadvantaged,' don't they?" The argument continues: "The white professionals *expect* black children to fail, and so do Negro professionals who have been taught the ways of the system. These attitudes are, at best, colonial behaviors that have a negative effect on the motivation and learning for black children. Our children *can* learn and indeed they *will* learn!"

Attempting to reverse the psychology of institutional expectations is difficult indeed; but it is crucial. We are all familiar with the self-fulfilling prophecy—the apparent relationship between expectation and performance. We all seem to agree that a school is better when positive instead of negative self-fulfilling prophecies are made. When parents, students, and communities participate in reform, we can assume that the chances for developing a climate of high rather than low expectations will be significantly increased. Parents have an intrinsic interest in the maximum growth and development of the children. Couple this intrinsic tie with the choice to break the shackles of inferiority, and the opportunities of generating a new climate of "making it" are enhanced considerably.

The other theoretical principle deals with *socialization*, that is, the broader processes of growth, development, and cultural transmission. We have known for some time now that the major agents of socialization for the young child are his *family*, his *peer group*, and his *school*. We seem to know, also, that growth and development are significantly affected, positively or negatively, depending on the relationship that exists among these major socializing agents. When there exist disconnection and discontinuity between or among them, the child's potential can be affected adversely.

Such is the case now in most urban schools; the family is disconnected from the school. Moreover, the culture of the family is often different from the culture of the school, and frequently the child is asked to make a choice between them. The result is deep internal conflict. Add to this the fact that the peer group is at odds with both the family and the schools, and we get a picture of a disjointed socialization process. Achieving continuity in socialization seems to depend on the ability of these three agents to become joined. This connection can emerge through the process of participation and involvement. When parents, students, and professionals join together in the common pursuit of reform, the process itself serves to cement new relationships among them. Too, each has a stake in what has developed jointly.

PRESERVING DIVERSITY

Another principle emanating from the community participation movement has to do with respect for the preservation of *diversity*. When black communities participate in the process of educational decision making, they will most likely favor programs that emphasize black culture: language, dress, food, music, art, history, and so on. The basic point is that to be black is to belong to a rich cultural identity—an identity largely dissipated and relinquished as blacks attempted to adjust to the demands of white cultural social institutions of which the school is the most prominent. In this adjustment process, blacks were—and still are—made to feel that their own values and culture are nonexistent or at best inferior to the acceptable cultural standard. This left many blacks with an "identity" problem, a problem induced by the dilemma of accepting the culture of white society—a culture which has discriminated against them and is, by its own admission, racist. To adjust, therefore, is to accept the very environment that they were struggling to change.

Other cultural groups were beginning to come to this same conclusion. Spanish-speaking populations, for example, are beginning to demand bilingual programs—programs which would maintain the legitimacy of Spanish, the language of the home and the culture. The issue raised by this emphasis on cultural differences is quite fundamental: diversity is not just a reality to be tolerated; it is a value to be nurtured. Cultural diversity is important to the individual cultural group; it is equally important to the vitality and renewal of society itself. To be assimilated or homogenized into some colossal mainstream culture has a stultifying effect on both the individual and society. Growth and development of individuals and society feed on a diet of pluralism. Diversity is essential to human and social renewal.

INSTITUTIONAL CHANGE

Another concept deals with the *institutional change*. Fundamental change leading to a new and more relevant educational institution cannot really happen unless three major pillars of the present educational system are altered.

A. Governance—The realignment of the parties involved in the process of educational decision making. A shift toward giving parents, community residents and students an increased voice in policy. The *politics* of education.

B. Substance—The objectives to be achieved and the content to be learned. The search for relevance toward a more humanistically oriented curricula dealing with individual and group problems, e.g., identity, disconnection, powerlessness—a more functional emphasis— e.g., preparation for major societal roles—e.g., worker, citizen, parent.

C. Personnel—The people who will be responsible for implementation. Opening the educational system to a far broader base of talent than the conventionally prepared career educator; training through the reality of community needs and expressions.

These are the pillars which are being altered at the several community-oriented experiments in New York, Washington, D.C. and Boston. The experiments in increased participation have first altered the governance pattern, which in turn has triggered change in the other basic pillars. The direction of the change appears to be as follows: [1]

[1] Taken from papers prepared for Brookings Conference (December 12, 1968) on Community Schools and to appear in an edited collection of conference papers.

	TRADITIONAL	REFORMED
Center of control	Professional dominance	The public, the community as partners
Role of parent organizations	To interpret the school to the community, for public relations	To participate as active agents in matters substantive to the educational process
Bureaucracy	Centralized authority, limiting flexibility and initiative to the professional at the individual school level	Decentralized decision making allowing for maximum local lay and professional initiative and flexibility, with central authority concentrating on technical assistance, long-range planning and system-wide coordination
Educational objectives	Emphasis on grade level performance, basic skills, cognitive (intellectual) achievement	Emphasis on both *cognitive* and *affective* (feeling) development. Humanistically oriented objectives, e.g., identity, connectedness, powerlessness
Tests of professional efficiency and promotion	Emphasis on credentials and systematized advancement through the system	Emphasis on performance with students and with parent-community participants
Instructional philosophy	Negative self-fulfilling prophecy, student failure blamed on learner and his background	Positive self-fulfilling prophecy —no student failures, only program failures—accountable to learner and community
Basic learning unit	Classroom, credentialized teacher, school building	The community, various agents as teachers, including other students and paraprofessionals

Participatory Vehicles

The final set of concepts deals with the participatory vehicles for implementation. It is necessary to examine the different patterns and schemes that are intended to search out improved education. The vehicles are all manifestations of a basic participation movement. The differences among them are largely the result of *how much* of a voice in school governance is sought.

The first of the patterns is *decentralization*. Participation under this form comes through, in part, as shared decision making: The clients—in this case, the parents and community residents—have anywhere from an advisory to an equal voice with those who are operating the existing educational system. The difference between *administrative* decentralization, which is established practice in many large school districts, and *political* decentralization (governance) is that the latter creates a new public relationship between communities and their public schools—a relationship in which there is a basic redistribution of authority and responsibility. Under political decentralization in big city systems, for example, parents and community residents *share* certain decisions and not others with a central school board. The same is true with the superintendent of schools, teachers and/or supervisors' association, and so on.

An illustration may be helpful. If, under decentralization, a local school board elected by the community demands the right to select a district superintendent, various shared decision-making plans can be advanced. The superintendent may indicate that the local board can submit to him the names of three candidates from which *he* would make the final selection. The supervisors' association may demand that the three names submitted be from the top three on a qualified list. The central board would then approve or reject the final candidate. Another procedure could be that the superintendent present the names of three candidates whom he has checked with the supervisory group. The local board then makes its choice for district superintendent and submits it to the central board for final approval.

If the local board wished to select candidates from outside the established city-wide personnel policies, it could have serious problems attempting to do so. The local board would have to initiate a new personnel policy with the other parties. If agreement were not reached, the local board could appeal to the state department of education, but this would begin to lead to controversy and conflict unless the appeal to the state were done with the cooperation and support of all the parties in question.

Decentralization is a *federation of local school boards,* each with limited authority over a portion of the total school system. Under this scheme, there would be a city-wide school system with a central school authority which may have final veto power over most decisions which local boards could make, or which can impose sanctions on local districts through appeals to the state. Procedures governing recruitment, selection, transfer, and tenure of personnel; budget; maintenance; and curriculum must be worked out together. Usually each group must compromise to achieve a consensus. These consensus procedures become the new ground rules for making decentralization work.

Community control, in its purest form, shifts to a local school board the bulk of the authority necessary for governing schools. Under maximum community control, a locality does not share decision making with a central school board; the local board is *independent* of the central board and assumes the same status as *any other school district in the state.* Since education is a state function, the local district shares authority with the state and is subjected to state regulation. There is, therefore, no absolute total control as such. However, under community control, sections of city schools—usually in the heart of the city—*secede* from the larger school system to become an *independent school district.* As an independent district the community is free to recruit, hire, transfer and release personnel—the same as, for example, a Scarsdale or a Newton. Harlem CORE has developed a plan for an Independent Harlem School District which it hopes will be considered by the New York State Legislature.

Communities which reach an advanced stage of frustration and concern over the failure to supply quality education for their children tend to assume an increasingly stronger stance of reform, sometimes called "militancy." They begin to demand that basic and fundamental changes be made. They are demanding a relevant educational system: one that works, one that has pay-off for the children. In other words, the community is sanctioning change.

INPUT QUALITY

The second level of justification concerns the quality of the *inputs* in the community-oriented school experiments; inputs of the programs developed to achieve educational objectives. Since standard school programs are not working, there is a need for innovation measures. There is a problem of determining the general worth of any innovation. Usually educators legitimize innovations through the medium of professional journals. A review of the professional literature would indicate that the following innovations are among those most frequently mentioned as holding considerable promise:

    Individualized learning
    Continuous progress
    Upgraded schools
    Cooperative teaching
    On-the-job staff development
    Pre-school education
    Community involvement
    Paraprofessional development
    Bilingual teaching

These are the very programs being utilized in community-oriented sub-districts. For example, in the Ocean Hill-Brownsville demonstration district in New York City, there are two quite different early childhood programs in operation—Montessori and Bereiter-Englemann, with still a third model—Leicestershire integrated infant school—being introduced. Moreover, in the Ocean Hill community-centered district, an individualized, nongraded elementary school utilizing programmed reading curricula is in operation. In the same district (at P.S. 155) a bilingual program is attempting to reach Spanish-speaking children in their native language during the early phases of schooling. Of course, bilingual programs are not uncommon but there is a qualitative dimension which sometimes is captured by the clinical judgment of experts such as Professors Vera John and Vivian Horner who surveyed existing bilingual programs in the United States:

> The work at P.S. 155 is unique. To begin with, it is the first program in a major U.S. city in which the members of the Spanish-speaking community have been given an opportunity *de facto* to cooperate actively in an innovative program. One might describe the program as refreshingly audacious . . . bilingual program is not a copy of anything—it is a truly innovative approach and has drawn attention to itself among bilingual educators at the national level. . . .

In the Ocean Hill district each school has a full-time teacher-trainer. The trainer is responsible for developing an on-the-job staff development program. Working with teachers individually and in groups, the teacher-trainer tries to deal with the developmental instructional problems in each school.

The Adams-Morgan Community School in Washington, D.C., utilizes a nongraded cooperative teaching format. Under this arrangement, teams of teachers and paraprofessional community interns (four teachers, two community interns) work with a family of children (approximately 100). Each of the team teachers selects one area of specialization in order to maximize individual talents and interests.

Personnel utilization and staffing patterns are also important "input" areas. The staffs of the community-centered schools vary along a wide horizontal spectrum from the professional to the lay, the latter including parents, community residents and students, themselves. They vary vertically as well to include not only professional educators with administrative and supervisory credentials but specialists from other fields and disciplines.

The chief education officer in the I.S. 201 experimental district in New York City, for example, is foremost a public administrator. The administrator of the Adams-Morgan Community School in Washington, D.C., is a social worker. Community districts such as Ocean Hill have made wide use of lawyers, engineers, and others outside professional education. The recruiting pattern of regular teachers has broken with tradition in the New York City experiment by fanning out beyond the city limits for personnel. Further, the sub-districts have a high proportion of new teachers who are graduates from top-ranking liberal arts colleges and former Peace Corpsmen and VISTA Volunteers.[2] The principals appointed in the Ocean Hill demonstration also depart from convention. The first male black principal of a secondary school, the first Puerto Rican principal and the first Chinese-American principal in the history of New York City are found there.

IMPROVED OUTPUTS

The third level of justification concerns *outputs*, i.e., the results, especially on student achievement. Because all of the community-controlled experiments have been in existence for only a short period (no more than two years), reporting at this level is limited. However, despite both the developmental problems confronted by each experiment, together with their short existence span, there are more signs of hope than despair.[3]

Most of these signs come from observations, judgments and testimony of various visitors to and workers in these community schools, but more objective data are being reported. They range from a report on improved school climate to reading gains reported from standardized tests. For example, a

---

[2] See, for example, "Teachers Who Give a Damn"—October 4, 1968 ed. of *Time* Education Section; and "With Love . . .," *Newsweek*, October 7, 1968.

[3] See, for example, *New York Times*, Sunday, March 16, 1969.

teacher who has worked in one of the Ocean Hill schools for three years was quoted as saying:

> You get a really positive feeling when you go into the school. The children give those teachers a tremendous amount of respect. There have always been discipline problems, but now there aren't as many as before.

Another teacher in I.S. 201 describes what it means for her to teach in a community-controlled school:

> Being a teacher at I.S. 201 is a way of life. It makes teaching more than a job. Teaching is a career at 201. If you ever come to visit 201, and just about every one does eventually, in the principal's office there is a slogan that sums up the goals and ambitions of the professional staff:
> Parent Power + Teacher Power = Powerful Children.

Other results are more invisible as one of the Ocean Hill principals reported. He explained that the custom before the community experiment was for the staff to leave shortly after the 3:00 P.M. dismissal so that by 3:15 P.M. the chains were fastened on the school gates. The custom began to change when members of his staff began to be locked in for staying until 5:00 P.M.

NEW EDUCATIONAL PROCESSES

However, skeptics will also call for "hard data." For example, are the students reading at grade level? There are several points to be made here. First, the experiments in community participation, in addition to consuming most of their energies in a struggle for survival, in addition to starting from a position with the schools which they have inherited, are also in the *process of developing* a new educational process. What is therefore being evaluated is the *process of development* and not the results of a developed program.

Secondly, the experiments are attempting to implement new pedagogic concepts and are after new educational objectives. These new arrangements do not lend themselves to "objectives measures" especially if those measures are ones associated with conventional education. The newer educational objectives are more *process*-oriented objectives dealing with rather intangible forces: quality of "human interaction," empathy, feelings, awareness, style and the like.

Nonetheless, more *objective* indices are being reported. In the Adams-Morgan experiment, for example:

1. *Suspensions*
   There were *no* suspensions or expulsions of students since the project's inception (1967)—an obvious improvement from the pre-experiment period.
2. *Vandalism*
   The superintendent of schools in Washington, D.C. reported a 70 per cent decrease in vandalism since the experiment.

3. *Reading*

During the 1967–68 school year, of the 176 elementary schools in Washington, D.C., Adams-Morgan was among only six schools in which reading scores had improved. Standardized tests now being analyzed (STEP) are expected to show similar gains for the 1968–69 school year.

At the Ocean Hill Demonstration District in New York City, Mr. Rhody McCoy, Unit Administrator, reported the following: [4]

1. *Suspensions*

During the period since the beginning of the community experiment (less than two years) there were fewer than 30 suspensions for the eight-school complex. In a similar period immediately prior to the experiment 628 suspensions were reported for the same eight schools.

2. *Vandalism*

Acts of vandalism were practically non-existent in the district in the past year—two cases for the year. In the year prior to the establishment of the district at least two per week reported for the year.

3. *Attendance*

The average pupil attendance for the elementary schools in the district is now 90%. The average pupil attendance before was between 70 and 75%.

4. *Daily Teacher Absences*

The daily absence rate among teachers prior to the experiment was 15%. The present rate is closer to 2%.

5. *Teacher Turnover*

Teacher turnover before Ocean Hill was between 20 and 25%. Presently the rate of turnover is 3%.

6. *Teacher Vacancies*

At the time of the formation of the Ocean Hill District there were 78 vacancies and no waiting list. Presently there are no vacancies and a waiting list of 130 persons.

7. *Community Participation*

Each school has parent associations which reported "handful" attendance prior to the experiment. During the past year the attendance averaged closer to 100 per meeting. At every open meeting of the Ocean Hill Governing Board there was an average attendance of 250 persons. In over half of these meetings the attendance was reported to be closer to 500.

8. *Reading*

Utilizing standardized tests (Metropolitan Reading Test) nearly 98% of the children in the seven elementary schools in the district showed growth in reading with an average gain of 1½ years.

---

[4] Reported by Mr. McCoy in a testimony before the California Senate Education Committee, May 26, 1969.

Also one might be tempted to add the numerous testimony from thousands of visitors from all parts of the United States and the world who visit these community schools.

In conclusion it is important to emphasize that to achieve quality education for urban schools we will need to develop an entirely new conception of education housed in an updated educational institution. Today, certain communities—especially black and other minority—are deciding on a new, more human education system. In one way, the new lay participatory movement appears to be ushering in the second progressive period of education. The first, a short-lived attempt by a key group of professionals, faltered earlier in this century and ended with the second world war. Hence the new participatory movement seems to be exactly what professional reformers have been waiting for these many years. The participants carry with them the seeds to a new humanistically oriented educational process which they themselves legitimize. Lest we forget, when professionals attempted to impose a type of progressive education onto a community which was not receptive, the results were a defeat for both the professional and the concept of education.[5] The professional has to provide the public with educational options that maximize growth for students. These options must be presented in as vivid a manner as possible, but in the last analysis, it is the public which must decide. The future of our civilization may well rest on how well this is achieved.

[5] The Pasadena Story.

Firing the Staff: How to Get Rid of Incompetent Teachers, Principals and Supervisors
ELLEN LURIE

It is slightly less difficult to dismiss a probationary exployee than it is to get rid of one who is tenured. The word "fire" is never used by professionals. "Discontinue the services," "remove," "discharge," "dismiss," all are considered nicer terms.

CURRENT PROCEDURE FOR DISCHARGING PROBATIONARY STAFF MEMBERS [1]

Local school boards are authorized to discontinue the services of any probationary employee on recommendation of the district superintendent with the approval of the city chancellor.

[1] State Education Law, Sections 2573 (c–1), 3019 (a), 2590 (j–7); Board of Education Bylaws, Section 105 (a); UFT Contract, Article IV, F–15.

—The principal files a report with the district superintendent on any probationary teacher he wants to dismiss.

—In some districts the local school boards have also invited parent associations and community organizations to submit their recommendations.

—Before any action can be taken, the employee is entitled to a fair hearing. This is often called due process. The district superintendent may hold the hearing himself, or he may appoint a committee to conduct the hearing for him. (Traditionally he asks other principals or district superintendents to do this but this is not required by law.)

—At the hearing the employee is entitled to bring an attorney or union representative with him. He may call witnesses or cross-examine anyone who testifies. He may buy a copy of the minutes (transcript) of the hearing.

—The district superintendent may accept, reject or modify the findings of the committee which held the hearing. He makes his recommendation to the local school board.

—The local school board, by a majority vote of the whole, then decides whether or not to dismiss the employee. If they decide to dismiss him, they must give written notice of at least thirty days in advance of the effective date of termination of service.

Before any of the steps outlined above may be taken, the city chancellor must be notified. No probationary employee may be dismissed, even after all these steps are taken, without the approval of the chancellor.

This procedure applies to teachers, principals, assistant principals, district superintendents and school secretaries. Paraprofessionals and other part-time employees do not go through probationary or tenured periods, so it does not apply to them. If your local school board does not make public a list of who is and is not on probation in your district, you can obtain the information from the Bureau of Teacher Record, Office of Personnel.

Current Procedure for Discharging Tenured Staff Members [2]

The New York State Education Law specifies that "persons who have served the full probationary period *shall hold their positions during good behavior and satisfactory service and shall not be removable except for cause* . . ." Local school boards are now authorized to hold hearings when specific charges are brought against a tenured employee, and under specific conditions and procedures, they may discontinue his services.

—The district superintendent may bring charges against any employee on any of the following grounds: unauthorized absence or excessive late-

[2] State Education Law, Sections 2573 (6) and 2590 (j–7); Board of Education Bylaws, Sections 100 (8 and 105); UFT Contract, Article IV, F–15, and Article XX.

ness; neglect of duty; conduct unbecoming his position; incompetent or inefficient service; violation of any bylaws of the city or community board; or any substantial cause that renders the employee unfit to perform his duties properly.

—No charge may be brought against an employee more than six months after the alleged misconduct occurred.

—Although principals may recommend that charges be brought (and perhaps parents may also recommend this, although no such possibility has ever been admitted), only the district superintendent may actually file formal charges. Before he can do this, however, he must notify the employee, the local school board and the city chancellor of his intentions, and the employee is immediately entitled to a preliminary hearing with counsel and full due-process procedures. (He may cross-examine witnesses, etc.)

—After the preliminary hearing, if the district superintendent decides to continue and bring formal charges against the employee, he must notify the city chancellor, who will decide whether or not the employee will be temporarily suspended from active duty, with full pay, until the hearing takes place. In any event, no employee may be suspended in such a procedure for more than ninety days.

—The local school board officially receives the charges, and appoints a trial examiner from a panel of examiners which has been drawn up by the city chancellor and approved by the UFT.

—At the hearing, the employee has the right to be represented by an attorney, to cross-examine witnesses, to call his own witnesses and to get a copy of the minutes.

—After the trial examiner gives his decision, the local school board may reject, confirm or modify it by a vote of the majority of the entire local board membership.

—The local board may then decide on the penalty. It may reprimand the employee, fine him, temporarily suspend him without pay, transfer him within the district or dismiss him.

—The employee may then appeal any of these decisions to the city Board of Education.

—The city Board of Education may review the case itself, or must submit it to arbitration if so specified in the UFT contract.

—After the decision of the city board or arbitration panel, the employee may still appeal an unfavorable decision to the State Education Commissioner.

—If the decision of the State Education Commissioner does not satisfy the employee, he still has the right of appeal through the courts.

What Is Wrong with the Procedure

Before the fight over local control, supervisors often complained that they were unable to fire incompetent employees. The procedures for documenting charges against tenured personnel were so complicated and cumbersome that it wasn't "worth the trouble." When a particular staff member could no longer be tolerated by a principal or parent group, he was quietly transferred. According to the *New York Times*, between 1962 and 1967, out of a citywide staff of over 55,000, only 170 regular and 82 substitute teachers were marked unsatisfactory. *During the entire five-year period, only twelve tenured teachers were dismissed!* There is no reason to believe the pattern since then has changed. This practice has to produce a sizable number of unskilled and incompetent teachers and principals who are permitted to remain in daily, unproductive, sometimes destructive contact with our children.

Several years ago I was shown a copy of an actual file of documents and statements that had been collected by a district superintendent in preparation for a disciplinary hearing involving a tenured teacher. The teacher was charged with corporal punishment—hitting kids. However, before the school system could fire him, a total of twenty-seven separate incidents were witnessed and recorded by various staff members in two different schools! Here are some sample entries in the file which was presented to the trial examiner:

Oct. 21

Letter from junior high principal to district superintendent:

I am reporting Mr. B. for repeated use of corporal punishment. Yesterday for the fourth time this term he was involved in striking a child. I informed him in writing that if he used corporal punishment once more I would report him to you as violating the law . . .

Nov. 18

Letter from the junior high principal to the district superintendent:

This is to inform you that Mr. B. once again struck a child. Towards the end of period 7 he punched Eleanor U——— of Class 6–4 in the stomach and pulled her arm. She went to the guidance counselor who informed me that the child was doubled over in pain when he saw her . . . I hereby request that Mr. B. be immediately removed from his duties at this school because I consider him a danger to the safety and welfare of the children entrusted to his care.

Dec. 21

Letter from an elementary school assistant principal to the district superintendent (The teacher had been transferred from the first school to this this one):

When I went into Class 2–3 at about 10:15 this morning I noticed one of the boys holding his face and crying. When I asked him what was troubling him, he and several other children answered, "The teacher hit me." The boy David M——— had left his seat to talk with another child. When he returned to his place, the teacher struck him on the back with the wooden room pass and then grabbed him by the back of his neck pushing his head down so that his face struck the desk . . .

On January 5 the teacher in question was transferred to the district office with pay until the disciplinary hearing could take place in February. I was not able to find out what happened as a result of that hearing.

Now that some measure of "decentralization" has been legislated, the procedure for disciplining or dismissing a New York City teacher has been made even more difficult. What was formerly almost impossible for professionals to accomplish is now absolutely impossible for community boards or parents!

Everywhere in New York State a tenured teacher is protected by the State Education Law, and properly so, or no teacher would have any protection if he spoke out on a controversial issue. In fact, that was the original purpose for most tenure legislation—to protect a teacher's freedom of speech. However, in New York City we now have a double layer of additional "security." Elsewhere in the state the education law stipulates that a tenured teacher is entitled to a fair hearing before either the local Board of Education *or* its trial examiner before any disciplinary action may be taken. In either event, final authority for action is left to the local board, but the teacher has the right to appeal any decision to the State Education Commissioner and then to the courts. In New York City the following procedures have been added:

—Our local boards must obtain prior approval from the city chancellor before they may institute a hearing.

—Our local boards may not hold the hearing themselves; they *must* appoint a trial examiner, but they are not even permitted to make their own choice. They must select an examiner from a list which has been approved by the city chancellor and the UFT!

—After the local board makes its decision, the teacher may appeal to the city board—and then he may appeal again to the State Commissioner and the courts.

Unlike the rest of the state, local school boards in New York City are not permitted the right to temporarily suspend the teacher, with pay, pending the hearing. Instead, our district boards must request the chancellor to approve a temporary suspension. At P.S. 39 in East Harlem, where the district superintendent had filed charges against nine teachers, the local school board petitioned the city board for permission to temporarily suspend (or reassign) the teachers, with full pay, until the hearing took place. The city board denied their request. While the UFT delayed the hearing's implementation, eighteen policemen were required to protect the presence of the nine teachers reporting to school each day, against the wishes of the school board and the parents—but with the approval of the city board and the UFT.

The city board has further aggravated this impossible situation because it keeps changing its mind, and adds or takes away powers from the local boards almost monthly. At first, for example, it told the I.S. 201 Governing

Board that it could suspend its teachers pending a hearing, but after union pressure mounted, the city board rescinded its decision. How can a local board play the game if the ground rules keep changing?

Even if local boards are given unambiguous authority to discipline their staff members, a "fair hearing" can be useless if the charges which the parents substantiate are considered illegitimate by the teachers' union. When the local board and unit administrator in Ocean Hill-Brownsville brought charges against several teachers in that district, the Board of Education appointed a trial examiner. As far as I can find out, this was the first time the decision of such a hearing officer was ever made public. Studying his findings, it is easy to despair.

Several witnesses testified that a particular teacher had "failed to maintain control of his class." The students were found throwing paint at each other in the teacher's presence, and he had done nothing to stop them. The trial examiner found that since the teacher had performed no better and no worse than the average teacher under similar circumstances, he could not be dismissed, transferred or disciplined! Now, suppose you take over a business that had gone bankrupt under the old management. As you see it, your first job is to shape up the employees who had become terribly lazy and unproductive under the careless supervision of their former boss. You can't very well fire them all, so you decide to take one or two of the worst offenders and make examples of them in order to set new standards of performance for the rest of your workers, to show them that you are not going to stand for any more nonsense. Well, under the rules followed by the trial examiner you cannot do this, because if the teacher you want to discipline is not doing his job properly but if everyone else is not doing theirs either, then he is performing up to "average standards"—never mind if "standards" means "god-awful."

The Decentralization Law permits a local superintendent to bring charges against an employee for "excessive lateness" for class. What is excessive? In Ocean Hill-Brownsville the unit administrator brought charges against a teacher who had been late twenty-two times in seven months but the trial examiner ruled that no evidence had been offered that these latenesses "were more than those suffered by a teacher of a similar status under similar circumstances" and he dismissed the case.

The Board of Education and the union have rather restricted notions regarding "qualified witnesses." For example, in the Ocean Hill-Brownsville hearing, after a principal testified that a particular teacher had failed to perform his job properly, the trial examiner took great care to point out that this principal lacked authority because he had not been appointed through regular channels and that his predecessors, who had been "duly qualified" by the Board of Examiners, had given the teacher "satisfactory" ratings the four previous years—therefore his transfer was not justified.

The Decentralization Law stipulates that charges may be preferred against a teacher whose "conduct is unbecoming his position." In Ocean Hill, when the unit administrator brought one such teacher up for discipline, the main witness against her was a respected community resident who was an educational assistant in that teacher's classroom. She testified to having heard the teacher use profane language to the children on a number of occasions; in actuality the community was seething because of the strong names that teacher had been calling the kids. The unit administrator asked that she be suspended or transferred "in order to maintain a safe atmosphere in the school." The parents were ready to tear the building down if the teacher remained. The hearing officer stated that the parent-witness "holds no license from the Board of Education" and that "I find that testimony incredible and hence give it no weight in this instance." The unlicensed teacher kept her license to teach—and curse—the children.

Recently the head of the city supervisory association charged that 47 school supervisors and teachers had been forced to leave their positions because of harassment. Under the unworkable and unfair "fair hearing" procedures set forth by the State Education Law *and* the Decentralization Law *and* Board of Education bylaws *and* the UFT contract, the system will be lucky if it can "properly" discipline or discharge *any* staff members. Is it any wonder that parents, compelled to send their children to public school, find themselves equally compelled to do everything in their power to get rid of the really terrible teachers and supervisors?

Mobilization: Gettin' the Students Together

John Birmingham

"High school students are gettin' together" is a statement that is found in many high school underground papers and in almost every issue of the *New York High School Free Press*. The slogan is not original; a version of it has been used in the black-power movement. However, it does express an important part of the high school movement. If high school students do not get themselves together, they have no movement.

The press is the most effective tool that the high school underground has to mobilize students. The papers themselves serve as advertisements for the movement. The ideas they express and the opinions they hold both tell the students something about the movement. When the papers tell the students that they are niggers or cattle, the underground is trying to make students aware of the need to get together. This is the first step. After that, the press can unite the students by showing them concrete programs that will change things. The program can consist of an attack on part of the present educational system that the students want to be abolished. Dress codes, censorship, and disciplinary measures are three examples. Or

FROM John Birmingham, *Our Time Is Now: Notes from the High School Underground* (New York: Praeger Publishers, 1970), pp. 95–101, 110–15, 138–50.

the program can be centered around an outside-of-school program that students can learn from and enjoy. The activity can be a film festival or even a student-run course. What it *is* isn't as important as what it is *like*. The activity must be exciting, educational, and worthwhile because it is fun. If the students don't really want to take part in the activity, it has no reasons for being.

Since *Smuff* was started near the end of the year, we didn't have time to concentrate on instituting this kind of program to mobilize students. This year, however, some such programs are being initiated. This year's staff intends to hold a film festival at the local Y.M.H.A. They hope to rent some films from Newsreel, an organization that rents radical films. Also starting this year will be an entirely student-run independent study course. So I will have to look to the future to see how well these activities mobilize Hackensack students.

The mobilizing methods that revolve around programs are usually meant to muster support from the general student body. They are not expected to be very successful in recruiting students to *work* for the underground movement, helping put out a newspaper or organizing future activities. The best way to get students to actually work together is to actually get them started putting out the underground paper.

Naturally, we had to do this to get out *Smuff*. We got people to work on *Smuff* by simply making them aware of it. We put out a first issue. The first issue was not too ambitious, but it was enough to get some other students interested in working with us. We put the first issue out with little help and with few contributors. But by the time we were finishing our work on the second issue, we had help from several more students and we had many more contributors.

Then we came against a new problem—keeping the *Smuff* spirit alive over the summer. Teachers speculated that *Smuff* would die out after Bob Cohen and I graduated. And we expected that we would have a difficult time disproving them without putting out *Smuff* ourselves again the following year. We had successfully organized students in 1969. Would this organization survive through 1970? Well, it did. The first issue of the 1969–70 school year came out with new ideas and new programs for the new year. Bob and I did not have too tough a time, because Edd Luwish and several other students thought it was well worth reviving after the summer.

Maintaining support for the underground movement is a job that is tackled differently by different papers. A way of mustering support that is used in many underground papers is a form of advertising. For example, *Think*, a "Youth for Peace, Freedom, and Justice Newsletter," from Royal Oak, Michigan, ran an ad that said, "Girls: do you worry about the color of your hair? the style of your clothes? . . . Do you suffer from bad breath? Just remember: *struggle makes you gorgeous!*" This ad was as much for entertainment purposes as for advertising. It is a humorous approach that is taken by many underground papers. The ads do not result in the deeper support that comes from getting involved in the underground press or in a program for students, but they do catch the attention of the reader.

Weakly Reader also ran a general ad for revolution:

IT'S AS AMERICAN AS . . . "MOM"

Stuyvesant!! The perfect school! The epitome of AMERICAN know-how! Why, where else could you find:

—a knowledge-tight assembly line that moves the product from junior high school to college with a minimum of contamination by education

—2500 well oiled walking talking eating wetting moving parts—guaranteed to jump at the boss's command

—a sellout union in full (almost) control of its faculty

—spot-checks, speed-ups, lock-outs, grade slavery, suspension of Constitutional rights fobbed off under the guise of "liberal education" and benevolent paternalism always so profitably employed by Big Capital.

And its 99 44/100 per cent PURE (LILY-WHITE).

Well, Brother, that doesn't sound so great to us. We're sick of slavery, this contract to spend four years of our lives training to throw away the rest. We're obedient little niggers that Massa whips with grades, darkies who jump when the Man says Jump! We're sick of it—students, workers, blacks and oppressed people everywhere: We're going to claim our birthright—dig that Manifest Destiny—we're going to be Americans and what's more American than REVOLUTION?

We're getting together—pulling together for our human rights and needs —and it's time that you are either WITH us or AGAINST us!

We demand:

—Open Admissions to Colleges

—No Suspensions or Expulsions

—Freedom of Speech, Freedom of the Press

—Establishment of Black, Puerto Rican, and Radical Studies Courses

—End to the Tracking System

—Cops, Nacos, and Security Guards OUT of the Schools!

WE'RE MAKING A REVOLUTION—JOIN US!

Stuyvesant Radical Coalition

Weakly Reader, No. 13, New York

The *Weakly Reader* "ad" for revolution is general, but it ends with seven specific demands. By listing a seven- (or ten- or twelve-) point program, the high school underground unites the students with common goals. These demands from the *Weakly Reader* outline the program for the Stuyvesant Radical Coalition.

Stating demands can be an effective method of organizing students, but it also tends to hurt communication between the students and the administration. One mistake that is often made by students is to refuse to compromise on demands. Because of this, administrations call the demands and the students unreasonable. Another problem is that these demands are called demands and not requests. The word "demand" backs the administration into a corner.

The students who most often use the word "demand" are also the ones who use words like "struggle" when they refer to the underground movement. They see the administration as the enemy, an enemy that they don't mind backing into a corner.

Although making demands does hurt communication, the students who make demands can easily be defended. Often they have tried making requests and working through the student council, and they have discovered that "playing by the administration's rules" doesn't work.

The following letter explains a little further why students resort to making demands:

Dear LINKS,

A few students of D.C. Everest High School, Schofield, Wis., came to some rather controversial conclusions this fall—controversial simply because they happened to disagree with conclusions previously held by the Administration.

We "happened to notice" the utter disregard of students' rights; partly manifested in our rigid dress code. We "happened to notice" the suppression of free and unconforming thinking. And—worst of all—we couldn't "help but notice" that this type of atmosphere was condoned by the Administration and employed by the majority of teachers.

Knowing that the Administration and faculty would never agree to our conclusions and resulting proposals, we decided to work among ourselves, the students. We decided that apathy about our situation had existed far too long, and that some action should be initiated immediately.

Here are a few examples of what has happened to us in our fight at D.C. Everest:

1. After months of "negotiations" with students, faculty, parents, and Administration, our new dress code completely disregarded most recommended changes which students had made;
2. Attempts to circulate materials resulted in threatened suspensions;
3. The creation of a civil rights bulletin board resulted in criticism ("Why are *you* interested in civil rights?");
4. The selling of underground newspapers and "Black Power" buttons resulted in a suspension;
5. Lockers were and are searched for "condemnable" materials;
6. The formation of a high school SDS group resulted in an Administration conference for every student in attendance at one of our meetings;
7. Students selling underground newspapers were sent to the school psychologist;

8. Students who wrote into newspapers criticizing the dress code were called into the office—if they had enough guts to sign their name;
9. A student was relieved of a Student Council pass, although activities that were supposed to have taken place under that pass were never proven;
10. Those leading the movement were and are subject to hours in the Administration's office;
11. And the writing of this letter will provide impetus for a headhunt that would be terribly funny if it wasn't so pathetic.

This middle class suppression has been allowed to exist far too long. They have done enough to us, but not quite enough. Those who continue the fight will subject themselves to the label "communist" (which we have been called), and to pressure and investigation not unlike the McCarthyism of the 1950's.

Their hostility is incredible. Their tactics are as dirty as ours are labeled to be. The searching of lockers and personal possessions, the tracing of out-of-school activities, the request for names in return for clemency—it's an endless list, all supposedly in the name of "the educational system."

Is it too much to ask—to be able to criticize our educational system without apologizing? Is it too much to ask that those who hold accepted norms be questioned?

Yes, we at Everest guess it is. So we're not *asking* anymore, *we're demanding!*

> By the Brothers and Sisters
> of D.C. Everest High,
> Schofield—Wausau.
> *Links*, Madison, Wisconsin

Leaflets are effective student mobilizers. Along with the underground papers, they present immediate issues that range from dress codes to capital-arrest students who cause disorders in the schools and the Board of Education is training plainclothes cops for permanent assignment to "troubled" schools. We'll have to show them that that ain't enough to stop us either. ONWARD THE STRUGGLE! STUDENT POWER!!

FOLD THIS UP AND CARRY IT WITH YOU

We're on the move in New York City. But the government is also moving—against us. The Black Panthers have been jailed, welfare demonstrators have been beaten up and high school students suspended. Arrests and harassment are increasing. Here are some basic rules for avoiding useless arrests and injuries and for handling it when you get busted.

COP-FRONTATION

Cops may stop you on the street even when you're not in a demonstration. They will question and frisk you. If you're alone, there is probably nothing you can do to stop them. You can, however, sometimes avoid a useless bust by acting respectful and giving innocuous answers to their questions instead of asserting your rights.

Don't Talk to Investigators!

Local cops and the FBI may question you. Don't answer! You have a right to remain silent. Don't try to argue with them or outsmart them. You never know what use they can make of what you say and lying to them can be a crime. If it's too hard to refuse outright to talk, you can say, "I don't want to talk until I speak with my lawyer."

Preparation for a Demonstration

Dress for action: women should wear pants and no earrings; wear shoes, not sandals; do not wear glasses unless absolutely necessary; wear a hat or a helmet and a heavy sweater to soften blows if it might be a rough demonstration.

If there is a possibility of tear gas and Mace: bring *plastic goggles* which can fit over glasses to protect your eyes from Mace and tear gas. Bring a *damp cloth* to cover your mouth and nose from tear gas. Cover your face with *vaseline* to protect yourself against Mace. Remove the vaseline as soon as you are Maced or you will get a slow burn.

Don't ever carry penknives or even a nail file to a demonstration; they can charge you with possession of a dangerous weapon.

Don't ever carry drugs to a demonstration.

Don't bring your address book; if you are busted, the cops will get the names of all your friends.

Carry the number of a lawyer or defense organization written on your arm or a piece of paper.

In a Demonstration

Stay with a small group of friends and decide what to do together.

Demonstrations are infiltrated with plainclothes cops who often look like us. If you spot a cop, expose him to other people. Never accept a brick, spray paint, or a package with undisclosed contents from someone you don't know. If you've done something for which you might be arrested, don't think you haven't been seen just because there are no uniformed cops around; you might not want to hang around.

When You're Busted

Don't try to talk the cop out of busting you or ask what the charges are. There is no chance of his releasing you and great chance that you will make admissions and get yourself and friends into trouble.

If there's no one around who knows you, shout out your name so that someone in the crowd can call a lawyer.

Try to get the badge and radio car number of the cop who busts you;

notice the circumstances of the arrest and write them down as inconspicu-ously as possible. All this information may be useful during your trial.

In Captivity

Especially if you are under twenty-one, your parents should come to the police station. They can be of great help in getting you released.

You have a right to make phone calls as soon as you get to the police station, and you should ask to do this. Often, however, they will not let you call for a while. First call a lawyer, then call a friend or relative who can come to your arraignment with cash for bail.

If a cop says, "There is an Attorney X on the phone, does he represent you?" you should answer "yes"; it means that someone has called a lawyer for you. The cops may be more cautious with you if they know you have a lawyer. You can always change lawyers later.

Only answer questions about name, address, age, occupation, and prior convictions. Give an address where there's someone who will say that you live there. Do not answer questions about drugs or about what you did. If the cops harass you, try to put them off but not antagonize them; say something like, "I don't want to talk until my lawyer gets here." DON'T TALK. DON'T TALK. DON'T TALK. DON'T TALK. DON'T TALK.

The cops have a right to search you once they arrest you, and they prob-ably will.

You may be able to get a summons, like a traffic ticket; it allows you to go home immediately and requires your appearance in court the next day. If they don't mention it, ask, "Can't I get out on a summons?"

Arraignment (for people sixteen and over)

After booking at the police station you will be taken to the courthouse and put into a cell called the bullpen. Probably you will feel isolated and scared as you get dragged around from one place to another. It will all be easier if you talk to the other prisoners.

A probation officer will ask you questions in order to advise the judge whether to release you without bail. Sometimes his recommendation in-fluences the judge; if you have nothing to hide you should answer the questions, although you don't have to.

Then you will go before the judge to hear your charge and have bail set. If you have no private attorney, ask the judge for a legal aid attorney. You can get your own lawyer after arraignment. If you are charged with a minor offense called a violation (disorderly conduct, loitering), you should plead "not guilty"; you can always change your plea later. If you are charged with a misdemeanor or a felony, you should enter no plea at all at this time.

Helping Your Friends

If you see someone arrested and you don't know his or her name, try to find it out. Then call a lawyer and tell him about the arrest and ask him to call the police station. Get as much cash as you can and take it to the arraignment. It is great to see friends in the courtroom.

Where the courts are located: Manhattan—100 Centre St. (City Hall or Canal St. subway); Brooklyn—120 Schermerhorn; Bronx—162nd St. and Washington Place; Queens—125–05 Queens Blvd.

If your friend was arrested before 3:30 in the afternoon or after 10:30 at night, he or she will be taken to Day Court in whatever borough the arrest occurred. If your friend was arrested between 3:30 in the afternoon and 10:30 at night, he or she will be taken to Night Court. (These hours are approximate.) The Manhattan Night Court is used for people arrested in Manhattan and the Bronx. The Brooklyn Night Court is used for people arrested in Brooklyn and Queens.

Lawyers: National Lawyers Guild: 962–5440; 227–0385; Emergency Civil Liberties Committee: 683–8120

Doctors: Medical Committee for Human Rights: 927–6073; 243–8686; 427–6499

High School Student Union: 799–2020

N.Y. Regional SDS: 674–8310

From a H.S. Student Union Leaflet, New York

The high school commune is the center for much of the organizing that goes on in New York City high schools. The students involved with it form programs and make demands constantly. The following article, "Troublemaker's Communique: 2," expresses the goals of the Student Union concerning the mobilization of New York City students:

TROUBLEMAKER'S COMMUNIQUE: 2

H.S. Committee

According to the newspapers, a small group of outsiders is responsible for the "disorders" in the schools. Talking about conspirators, outside agitators, and disruptive students allows the city government to ignore the real problems of a racist school system that has to be done away with. We, the students that must suffer through school every day, know that the only outside agitators in the schools are the police; that the only disruptive influences in the schools are the irrelevant classes we must attend; that the only conspiracy is a conspiracy to brainwash us and to control our lives.

By creating a conspiracy in the high school movement, Mayor Lindsay wants to make it seem like there's a small group of people leading a larger group of weak-minded, impressionable students. And by arresting this small group (which is a very real possibility at this time), he thinks that the disorders will cease. What he doesn't know is that this is no part-time recreation of a bunch of hippy-yippie! extremists—it is the full-time commitment of every aware student in the New York City Public School System.

The strength of our movement and the strength of our politics is not measured by how many people we can turn out of school. Three kids can close down a school. But just closing a school doesn't change anything. For one day, we stand around in the sun for a while and talk. Then we all have to go back to school—back into the same cesspool we broke out of.

We have to realize that we are not going to get our demands by demonstrating. A rally at the Board of Education or a picket or march at a school isn't going to force the system to get the cops out, or to open up the colleges or the trade unions, or to give us the good jobs and decent housing we need. The principals aren't going to stop suspending or expelling students. We have to realize that our demands strike at the foundations of the school system. They aren't going to "give" us what we need—and we aren't playing around. We *need* the things that the student unions demand. We will not get these demands until we get our brothers and sisters together. Demonstrations are not an end. They are a tool that we can use to get our people together. We cannot measure our success by the numbers we turn out. We measure our success by the number of people we change.

However, some of the muscle that has been most recognized by adults has been because of violence. The high school students in New York City, for example, have received much press coverage because they have employed violence. The mass media press realizes how large the High School Student Union is because the Student Union has, according to the press, been behind much of the violence in New York high schools.

The Student Union cannot really claim credit for all this violence. For the most part, violence in the high schools is not organized or initiated by the underground. It is not usually organized by anyone. The violence is usually an expression of justifiable frustration and anger on the part of the students.

In one case in particular, however, the Student Union, along with the Black Student Union and the Afro-American Students' Association, was behind violence. The date was April 21, 1969, and the violence was meant to enforce the demands of the students. It was planned and organized violence, something that doesn't appeal to me personally. The style was too SDS-like. It did not really represent the high school underground movement on the whole, but it was what was happening in New York, so it was important.

The disruptions that occurred in New York high schools between April 21 and May 19 did not have a marked effect on the high school underground, but they did show the city just how much muscle the New York City high school underground had acquired. The demands weren't met. But lots of fires were started.

From an H.S. Commune Leaflet, New York

The following articles give the stories of these disruptions—before and after.

SPRING OFFENSIVE

We've all been shit upon in one way or another. But what did we do about it? Some of us dropped out. Others tore up bathrooms and desks and broke windows to tell them how we see the schools. I heard about a couple of Molotovs going off at Brooklyn Tech. Most of the kids still in the school get out of it by using dope. Scag, coke, grass and hash are all over the halls. Then the teachers' strike showed us how to really fuck up the schools. The teachers went out together and closed down the schools. The city called it a "crisis." While they were at home or on picket lines we took the schools. We learned what it meant to move as a group. The student unions and the black groups all over the city went into the schools and ran them themselves. We know what it is to move against the school system. But we've always done it as individuals. As loners. Troublemakers who were considered anti-social. This year we did it together.

But there's not much you can do against the schools alone. Not much at all. There are thousands of us who are down to fight. But fighting alone hasn't done shit towards changing the schools. Last year there were twelve thousand suspensions. Twelve thousand kids had to bring their parents in to see the principal. Twelve thousand of us had to hassle with the dean or the principal and sit there while he told us that we ought to drop out and get a job—we're just not fit for school. Or told to "talk" to our guidance counselors. Like we were crazy. Damn, we know that it's these schools and our parents that are crazy, not us. But what could we do about it? Not a thing. Some kids put out papers, to let us know that the schools suck—and they got suspended for telling us what we know already. A couple of kids got lawyers to defend them—and they won, but so what. When they went back to school and acted alive again, they were suspended again, and had to do it all over. No change, just more hassles. And that's just suspensions. How many brothers and sisters were transferred out of their schools or districts because some teacher or administrator wanted to get rid of them? At Brandeis, the principal decided that he wanted a smaller student body. So he kicked out all the "troublemakers" he could. If you were over seventeen you could be kicked out for cutting a couple of classes, or for being a "nuisance" to teachers. They throw us out. Every kid in the school system catches shit. We all know that. Not a single kid reading this paper is learning what he could in school. Not a single one of us is going to be able to choose what he wants to do after high school. Not one of us learns the skills needed to get a good job; most of us won't even get into college. Anyone who loses his program card can be picked up for trespassing. Everyone has to sit through the same bullshit courses, the same boring classes. We are all treated like dirt by teachers who think that being a teacher gives them some sort of super power.

Everyone's been fucked over by the schools, but who catches the worst shit? The "troublemakers." The ones who cut classes because they're boring and meaningless. Those kids who told the teachers what we all really think of them. Those who are always "hanging around" in the halls, trying to get our brothers together. The ones who opened the schools in the fall, and the ones who closed them down in the winter. Anyone who passes out a leaflet, or sells the *Free Press*. The militants, radicals, bad cats, troublemakers, organizers, agitators. We're all being pushed around like we're babies who can't do shit to fight back. But the students are really the most powerful people in the schools. We're the ones that are ready to fight for what we should have. For what we want.

What we learned this year is that it's just not enough to be bad. We've got to be together. Bad cats get their heads kicked. Union members fought together and protected each other's heads. We have to build unions. Unions aren't bullshit organizations that give orders or that get "social functions" together. Basketball games and school dances are not what student unions will be about. And neither is sitting in offices, or monthly dues. Student unions are the banding together of all "troublemakers" and would-be "troublemakers" in schools. They help us keep on fighting for what we want, without getting screwed by the system. The High School Student Union, and The Black Student Union, and The Afro-American Students' Association (and any other groups like them) have to be built in every school. We can't afford to say that unions and politics are just for the middle class kids, or for the hippies, or for the militants, revolutionaries, radicals, or blacks. Every kid in the schools gets shit. And those of us who fight against that have to get together, or we're going to be squashed.

This spring we have a program to get together around. There's going to be a lot happening in the city. In Eastern District High School the students are already in the streets. At Lincoln Hospital the community and the community workers have taken the hospital for the community and are ready to fight to keep it. There were five fires set at Brooklyn Tech High School. There have been anti-social riots at Canarsie and Jackson. Welfare rights groups are getting together for a spring offensive. That was during winter. The temperature's going up inside. The temperature's going up outside. Last year 25 per cent of us were absent from school every day. Six years ago there were only 9 per cent absent each day.

This spring there may be more people outside the schools than inside. We have got to make sure that when we're "absent from school" this spring that we're not just wasting time and ending up screwed by the schools again. We want to use that time to make damn sure that next fall we're not in the same lousy position we're in now:

This spring we're going to begin the fight to make the buildings they call schools useful.

WE DEMAND:

1. NO MORE SUSPENSIONS, no involuntary transfers, no exclusion from classes, no detention, no discharges, no harassment of students. All the forms of discipline peculiar to schools are oppressive. They don't protect us; they protect a racist, oppressive school system.
2. NO COPS IN SCHOOLS. There are cops in every high school in the city. We want them out. No undercover agents or informers in the schools.
3. NO PROGRAM CARDS. No hall checks, lunchroom checks, bathroom

passes. The schools are there for us to use. The teachers have no right to tell us where we can or cannot go in the schools.

4. AN END TO GENERAL AND COMMERCIAL DIPLOMAS. The schools are made to separate us. They take white, middle class kids and put them into the IGC [intellectually gifted children] classes and SP [special progress] classes in grade and junior high school. Then in high school the white middle and upper class kids are put into "academic" courses. The black and Latin students, and the poor whites, are put into general and commercial courses. They say that we have freedom to choose which we're in, but that's bullshit. Students in the academic courses are encouraged to go into general courses, but the reverse never happens. Many students are put into general courses without being told. Others are told by their grade advisers that the general course is easier, and just as good for a student who "isn't capable" of going to college. A general diploma is a ticket to the army. Nothing else. In the commercial and vocational courses students are trained for jobs that don't exist any more. Nearly every student graduating from vocational school was put into a job after he graduated. Only one in ten was able to keep it. That's about how well they train us. When we get out of high school the good jobs are going to require college training. And we all want to be able to get those jobs. We all want the same diploma to have the same chance.

A high school diploma doesn't mean anything unless we can get somewhere with it, so we demand as well:

5. OPEN ADMISSIONS TO COLLEGE. A college education free for everyone, and support for all students who need it through college. Columbia University, New York University, the City University, the community colleges, New York State University, and all other colleges in New York must open up to any high school graduate who wants in. Let them take money out of the armed forces to build enough facilities to give every one of us a place in college. Students on all campuses will fight together with us in the spring. The colleges have always been to educate the elite and leave the rest of us with lousy jobs and low wages. No more middle class. We all want to get good jobs and enough money to live.

6. We demand that there be a JOB AND DECENT HOUSING AVAILABLE for every high school student who drops out or graduates and doesn't want to go to college. Our people desperately need more and better housing, food, transportation, education. There is a labor shortage in all of these areas. And still we can't find jobs when we have to. We can't find jobs because the people who run the big businesses and the trade unions in this city don't think it's profitable for them.

Well, they don't have to live in our communities and they don't have to work for a living. Let them be unemployed and let us go to work at decent wages to build our communities up.

7. NO MILITARY RECRUITMENT IN SCHOOLS. The army is not a substitute for a good job. We want no military assemblies, no names to the draft boards, no army recruiters in the schools, an end to the draft. All of us that can't get jobs or can't get away from our parents but we can "join the army; see the world; learn a skill." Bullshit. The only part of the world you'll see in the army is basic training camp and Vietnam. The only skill you can learn is how to survive in a jungle war, against our brothers and sisters of Vietnam. When you get back from the army, you still have to find a job on a job market that doesn't have room for us. The war we have to fight is here, for good jobs, housing, education and an end to racism. Not one of us can afford to be shot at in Vietnam for the rich.

8. We demand BLACK AND LATIN DEPARTMENTS, controlled by the students. Departments must be established, controlled by the Black and Latin students to eliminate racism in the textbooks, in the teaching, in discipline.

   There must be courses in Black and Latin history and culture set up in every school in the city. Black and Latin students must have the power to root out the racism that is forced on us.

9. COMMUNITY CONTROL of the schools and all other public facilities. That's what it's all about. The communities of this nation must take control of their own destinies. We must have power over the distribution of our own labor and money. We must control our schools, hospitals, police, welfare, and transportation. We are just as much a part of our communities as our parents. We must unite with them to take for the people the things that we and our parents have built up and paid for. We must control our own education. That education must serve the needs and wants of our community, not some rich men at the board or the Mayor's office. "We want the world, and we want it now!"

10. POWER. We want student power. The only way that students can gain power over their own lives is to organize. Therefore we demand the right to get ourselves together for our own needs. This means: the right to leaflet, the right to have assemblies, real student government, the right to have newspapers and literature of our own, the right to have politics and ideology and political action in our own interests in the schools or for distributing leaflets, or for smoking in the halls. We've been busted and alone for talking back or for being against the UFT and the principals. Everything we have been busted for is important—to us. Each rule must be gotten rid of, as well as each racist teacher, each lousy textbook, each bad program, each obstacle to college admissions. Each one has to go. But we can only get rid of each one by getting rid of them all. If some kids in Seward Park go down to get rid of the general diploma and nobody else in the city is ready to go down with them, then they can't win. The principal will

appoint a student-faculty committee, and transfer the "troublemakers" and that will be that. But the fight is not at Seward Park alone. There are students at every school in the city fighting against the schools. Even if for you that means fighting for Black and Latin courses or open admissions to college, we are still in the same fight as the Seward Park students. When the principal at Seward Park says no to their demands he is not saying no to the students at Seward, he is saying no to every student in the city. We must be prepared to support the struggles of high school students on every issue, in every school. If we support each other, we can win. If we only support ourselves, we will be fucked over like we never have been fucked before. The demands above are being made by the High School Student Union. The High School Student Union is pulling together all students who are fighting against the school system. We will defend each other when the need arises. The brothers and sisters in the Bronx will be working together; in upper Manhattan, lower Manhattan, eastern Queens, western Queens, Brooklyn. Groups of five to ten schools will be going down together when it gets warmer. We will be moving directly against the source of our oppression. We will move directly, and we will move together.

The Black students have declared April 21 as the day when we begin to move. The High School Students will stand by their Black brothers and sisters. They will move their own groups to support the Black students' movement and to take what the white students need for their community. We will use the spring actions to build strong groups in the schools that can move together, and a strong city-wide union that will bring us together for mutual defense.

The *High School Free Press* is being distributed in forty-seven high schools. Students who want to get it out where it is not yet available will be able to get copies. The *Free Press* will keep us aware of what is happening to our brothers and sisters around the city as they go out in the spring. The *Free Press* will also print as many leaflets as our organizations need to build and educate. All student groups that are moving against the repression we suffer can have material printed by the *Free Press*: 799–2020.

The Student Union will bring its people to support the actions of all students in the city. Students at any school can get in touch with the "troublemakers," black or white, at the schools near them through the Central Communications office: 799–2020.

Newsreel films are available through the Central Communications office. LAWYERS and legal advice are available at Central Communications: 799–2020.

There will be leaflets printed around each of the demands. There will be posters along with the leaflets. These too will be available from Central Communications.

The Central Communications office will serve to keep us in touch with one another, and to print for us what we need to work with. They will make available to students at each school the contacts we need to become effective and to support and defend each other in our struggle. It is not an organization. It is established to help all us troublemakers build the organizations we want.

FROM APRIL 21 TO MAY 19 IS OUR MONTH! THE STREETS, THE SCHOOLS, THE COMMUNITIES ARE ALL OURS, WE'RE GOING TO TAKE THEM BACK!

New York High School Free Press, No. 7, New York

POWER

The NY High School Student Union, the Black High School Student Coalition, the Afro-American Students Association, and the Black Student Unions called for disruptions in the citys' schools from April 21 through May 19 to back up demands presented to the administrations of various schools and to the Board of Education.

They started right on schedule, and are still going on.

Van Buren—300 members of the BSU took over the cafeteria and the auditorium. A few fires and no arrests.

Walton—1,000 kids join a group of Clinton students. Three arrested.

Clinton—500 kids walked out and set fire to the basement. Then they went all over the neighborhood doing things.

Erasmus—A peaceful demonstration outside the school became a melee when the cops charged the gathering. At the same time, a few fires and bombs went off in the school. As the school was closed immediately, several hundred students joined the demonstrators and engaged in a real live street battle with the cops for a few hours. About twenty-five arrested, with several injuries. The next day, a new battle in which another thirty were busted. In the middle of the battle, the kids held a small restaurant as a first-aid station.

Springfield Gardens—Three students and a dean arrested after the cops charged a peaceful demonstration. Two days later, the students held the auditorium in support of their demands.

Tilden—When the principal of the school refused to let Les Campbell speak, the students took to the streets. After fires appeared, the school was closed.

Jackson—Seventeen kids arrested when the students take the auditorium and the cafeteria, and 1,500 of their supporters walk out of school.

Brooklyn Tech—300 Black students took over the auditorium and presented their demands to the administration.

Jefferson—School evacuated as a fire starts early in the morning. 400 kids meet with the principal in the auditorium to discuss "non-negotiable" demands.

Julia Richman—A fire in the basement closed the school early one day.

Eastern District—Vandals set fire to the records in the offices and swept through the school.

Teddy Roosevelt—Students burned an American flag, and went on a rampage throughout the school.

Westinghouse Vocational—150 students denied entrance after arriving late try and break through locked doors. After failure, they went on a rampage in the immediate vicinity.

Bronx Science—The students occupied the offices for a brief time, causing confusion.

Bushwick, Lincoln, and Morris also reported fires and rallies. At Canarsie, the Black students took over the auditorium.

By the Staff, with the help of LNS and Howie Swerdloff and all the high school students in the streets, and, of course, the educational system, the cause for all this activity.

New York Herald Tribune, No. 5, New York

I repeat: The violence that occurred in New York does not represent the high school underground as a whole. However, since it is part of the movement, it must be represented.

My biggest objection to these actions is that it shows that some high school students are making some of the same mistakes as the SDS. And that was something I'd hoped to disprove completely. The following article expresses *Smuff*'s editorial stand on the SDS. (And we are not the only ones in the underground who feel this way.)

A Need for Change in Student Radicalism

An immediate change must take place within the structures of organized student radicalism. And if the change does not come, radicalism will fall.

Organized radicalism hit a high point last spring with the SDS. The students had a good cause—to stop Columbia University from building a gym in Morningside Park and to return the park to its West Harlem community. Columbia had previously ignored its duties to the West Harlem community in which it is centered, so the righteousness of the students' cause was emphasized.

Since the student demonstrations were successful (Columbia stopped the construction of the gym), students have gained political power. And the SDS has gained strength.

But now, the SDS and other radical organizations have changed their style. The new style is typified by pointless violence. Recently, for example, two SDS members beat up a Columbia professor with a club. There was no difference between this action and the actions committed by the Chicago "pigs" last summer. Yet, ironically, these students (who were probably the first to give the Chicago "pigs" their name) called the professor the "pig."

Nothing was accomplished by beating up this professor. If anything, the students' cause was hurt. This violence shows that the SDS has gotten so wrapped up in the means toward its end that they have actually forgotten the end. And a low point in organized student radicalism has been hit—by the SDS.

If organized radicalism is to survive this low point, it must undergo a radical change. The organizations must employ more effective means toward radical goals. They must begin to use such arts as diplomacy. In other words, radical actions should be carried out to accomplish an end, not simply to break up furniture.

Smuff, Vol. I, No. 1, Hackensack, New Jersey

D. Social Policy Restructuring

Reslicing the School Pie

JOHN E. COONS, STEPHEN D. SUGARMAN, AND
WILLIAM H. CLUNE III

State systems of taxing and spending for elementary and secondary education tend to combine misery and mystery in equal parts. Historically, the school money debates have been dominated by specialists on such complex questions as "subvention," "overburden," and "equalization formulas," effectively insulating the institution from the scrutiny of its victims. Today, however, in what may be the last shot in the skirmish on poverty, school finance is finally receiving serious public attention:

> ITEM. President Nixon has appointed a School Finance Commission. ITEM. The Supreme Court has twice in the past two years been asked to strike down as unconstitutional the methods by which public education is presently financed; it has not foreclosed the question, and may be forced to face the issue directly in its next term. ITEM. Governor Milliken of Michigan has proposed shifting from a shared state-local school finance arrangement to an essentially state funded one. ITEM. The Office of Economic Opportunity has announced its willingness to sponsor experimental tuition voucher programs; Governor Reagan of California has commented favorably on one form of the voucher plan. ITEM. Governor Rockefeller of New York has appointed a blue-ribbon commission to make a comprehensive examination of the quality, cost, and financing of elementary and secondary education for the coming decade.

All this may stimulate a large yawn; yet there may be surprises in store. A variety of hostile forces are beginning to converge on the old system. Lawyers, educators, and social scientists increasingly score the unfairness to students and taxpayers of our reliance upon local property taxes; voters (allegedly property owners) reject local bond issues, budgets, and property tax overrides at an alarming rate; striking teachers demand an even higher priority for education on our list of national commitments; school districts reluctantly

FROM *Teachers College Record*, Vol. 72, No. 4 (May 1971), pp. 485–93.

shorten the school year because of the money pinch; Catholic schools either close or stagger along, praying with their public counterparts for a governmental rescue that will keep parochial pupils from landing in the over-burdened public schools.

Ironically, this tumult comes as leading educational critics proclaim the utter irrelevance of current schooling, especially in our cities. The system is not diseased, they say; it is a corpse that more cash will simply cosmetize. Their hope—if hope they have—is integration, is accountability of teachers, is individualization or technology; it is not money. Even many of the most radical structural reformers, decentralizers, and political participators decline to engage seriously the question of economic support for their enterprises. Their know-nothing attitude is, to an extent, pardonable; financial reform will not itself revitalize education, and its pursuit lacks the allure of public combat over more visible and glamorous objectives. Regrettably, it is a precondition to improvement of any sort whatsoever.

Villains and Victims

However, even the idea of financial reform in education is as confused as the rhetoric of equal opportunity that confounds the debate. Lest we sin ourselves, an initial clarification is indicated. The issue is not quantity. Even conceding the onus of guilt borne by a curmudgeon federal government, *the critical need in school finance is not simply for more money.* The fundamental evil of the present system is reliance upon *local property taxation of unevenly distributed property wealth.* This is not so complex a matter as sometimes it is made to appear. Simply put the tragedy involves two villains and two victims, all four of which typically inhabit school districts with low property wealth per pupil. The villains are higher tax rates for education and lower spending in schools; the victims are the children and those who bear the taxes for their public schools.

Consider this example from Los Angeles County in California. Michael, a fifth grader, lives in the Walnut elementary district; in 1968–69 the cost of his public education was $500. His friend, Robert, lives in the Keppel elementary district; in that same year his fifth grade spent $786 per pupil. Each boy's family has the same income and owns a home of the same value (market and assessed). Michael's house is taxed at 3.28 percent of assessed valuation; Robert's at 2.33 percent. The California "system" thus provides substantially fewer school dollars for the children of those in the Walnut district who pay the higher tax rate. The example chosen is conservative. It is typical of our states.

Disaster of Form

The historical parent of this prodigy is the rough compromise that emerged from the struggle after 1850 between the public school enthusiasts and their individualist opponents. The victory of the schoolmen was never complete; education was made compulsory and universal, but the principle of state responsibility was never clearly accepted. Instead, the local community became the foundation of "public" education, a result which tempered individualist fears of a monolith, making the enterprise politically possible. In an agrarian economy with a fairly uniform distribution of wealth within most states, this parceling out to local units of the new duty to educate might have been seen as tolerable to both sides. After another quarter century of economic change, the nightmarish reality began to surface. What the individualist had surrendered in the establishment of public education was beyond recall; what the reformers had bargained for in equality had become a casualty of the industrial revolution.

By 1900, the clustering of wealth in urban foci already was well under way. Then, as now, school districts in most states depended for their principal support upon the power delegated to them to tax the value of real property located within their boundaries. As the disparities in taxable wealth widened among communities, education prospered in some districts and foundered in others for reasons unrelated either to local need or local enthusiasm. Balkanization of education had come to mean good schools in the rich cities and the virtual collapse of many rural districts. Public education has never recovered from this original disaster of form. The identity of rich and poor districts shifts and changes with time; in some cases cities favored through the first half of this century may now face the problem of corporate poverty. But for town and country alike the iron rule of the system is unaltered: the dollars spent for a child's education are a function of the wealth of his school district. Today in some states the taxable wealth per pupil in the richest districts is 100 times the wealth in the poorest.

State "equalization" programs of aid to poor districts have been the typical twentieth century response to this problem. From state to state there is considerable variation in these devices whose details are impenetrable to the amateur and deserve no attention here. Their principal effect is anesthesia for the outrage of the victims. State support for poor districts is made highly visible and thus politically effective in tranquilizing local indignation. However, the notion that the districts have been "equalized" is transcendent fiction. So far from reality is it that in California, Wisconsin, Illinois, and elsewhere millions in "state aid" have been identified which, under existing legislation, actually benefit only the wealthy districts. This aid is a bonus for being rich! The consequence of the system is disparity in spending, which in California districts ranges from well below $500 to $3,000 per pupil.

Seeing this helps to explain the durability of the local property tax despite the predictions and imprecations of politicians, property owners, journalists, and others prone to discover taxpayer revolts. Plainly, it survives because it is the basis of a highly effective system of privilege. Communities that enjoy high property values per pupil, either because of the presence of wealthy residents or of industry, can have good schools (and other municipal services) for a cheaper tax rate than their poorer neighbors. Such communities and their residents have a strong interest in preserving the discrimination.

The benefited class is a peculiar one: it is not distinguished simply by personal wealth. Rich families sometimes live in districts poor in taxable wealth, while some of the richest districts are industrial enclaves inhabited largely by blue collar or poor families. Overall, however, there appears to be a correlation between personal wealth and district wealth, and it is the children of the poor living in poor districts who are the most poignant victims. These families cannot afford to move or to choose private schools. By and large they are white families, at least in the North. Minorities tend to cluster in larger cities near or somewhat above average in wealth. This is not to say that such minority children are never victims of fiscal discrimination *inside* their district of residence, though that particular swindle itself is beginning to decline.

The problem, then, is not vicious motivation or conspiratorial purposes, but merely wild and arbitrary imposition of privilege and deprivation according to the accident of district wealth. The evil is blindly structural in the most primitive sense that the state has created a discrimination machine. Districts above the median in wealth naturally resist change, and they are politically vigorous; districts of roughly average wealth have no clear stake in reform and are apathetic or even turned off by the centralist rhetoric of most of the reformers. Only poor districts would clearly benefit, and their historic failure to move the legislatures is not surprising.

JUDICIAL INTERVENTION

Ironically, this chronic political impotence of the victims itself may assist reform by sanctioning judicial intervention. It is not fanciful to describe the projected relief for children of poor districts as another rescue of a (literally) disenfranchised minority. Who but the Supreme Court could brake this machine so insulated from ordinary majoritarian politics?

However, seen as a constitutional issue for the Court under the Equal Protection guarantee, the matter becomes complex. Three pointed problems of judicial role threaten to bar even threshold examination of the problem. First, to be effective in dealing with any issue of this magnitude, the Court must be able to articulate a clear and principled basis for condemning the system. The principle must permit reasonably accurate prediction of future decisions involving a variety of possible legislative responses. Second, sensitive to its nonelective and antimajoritarian character, the Court should shrink from imposing a uniform system upon the states. Its primary objective should be not to bind but to loose the legislatures from the existing log jam, sparing whatever is tolerable in the old order and permitting a wide variety of new state systems. Third, the Court will need confidence that its will can be enforced. However, the first is the key to all; the primary concern must be the discovery of a satisfactory standard by which to judge state systems. So far it is the failure of litigants to offer such a standard that has alienated the judges who have spoken on the issue.

Until this year two cases had reached the Supreme Court, one each from Illinois and Virginia. The three-judge federal panel in Illinois dismissed for lack of "discoverable and manageable standards" a suit which asserted a duty of the state under the 14th Amendment to spend for each child according to his individual needs. The Supreme Court affirmed without argument or opinion, and with but one dissent. Except for an additional dissent a similar complaint in the Virginia case met an identical fate in the following term of the high Court. Counsel in the several remaining cases are seeking a standard that will pass judicial muster and yet be effective. The problem is urgent, as crucial cases in California and elsewhere proceed to their final disposition. Thus far, the Court appears to have kept an open mind. A recent appeal in a school finance case from Florida presented an opportunity to seal off debate on the issue. Instead, the Court sent the case back for trial. This leaves the final judicial answer perhaps a year or more away.

The difficulty in this quest for principle is illustrated by the disunity of the critics, some of whose proposals have bordered on the extreme. For example, one formula—an analogy to the one man–one vote rule—asserts a duty to spend equal dollars per child throughout the state. The federal judges in the Illinois suit declared this "the only possible standard" and then rejected it. Only diehard egalitarians would quarrel with the court's assertion that a rule forbidding compensatory spending is the last thing we need. What then of the "needs" formula proposed by the Illinois and Virginia complaints? The primary flaw in such a standard is that it is really not a standard at all; indeed, it is the replacement of all standards by the purest nominalism, each child bearing his own "rule." This approach may be satisfactory for educational philosophers; its appeal to judges is less obvious. Finding and enforcing the dollar rights of each child according to his needs (whatever that may mean) is not an activity in which courts will be eager to engage.

Two other formulas contending for scholarly and judicial attention at least can claim status as bona fide principles. Each is simple and is cast in the negative—that is, as a proscription of particular state action, thus avoiding the problems raised by insisting upon a duty of specific legislative behavior. Under *Proposition One* the state would merely be forbidden to permit variations in district or family wealth to affect spending per pupil. *Proposition Two* would agree but would add a prohibition against variations in the number of dollars spent on any child by virtue of his place of residence. This difference is highly significant. *Proposition Two* (Professor Arthur Wise) is a centralizing principle satisfied only by statewide standards for spending. *Proposition One* would permit local decision resulting in the spending of more or fewer dollars per pupil from one unit to another, so long as those variations in spending are not in any degree the consequence of variations in wealth.

Together these two propositions draw the line of battle between the centralists and those favoring local incentive. The former are outraged that the quality of education could be affected by differing enthusiasm for education from district to district. On the other hand, the latter see in local decision a source of health, variety, and citizen involvement plus an insurance against the statewide mediocrity risked by centralization. In any case, one's policy preference in this regard should not be confounded with his view of the Constitution. Even centralizers should prefer *Proposition One* if the Court sees preservation of local choice as the condition of its intervention. Continued local choice, liberated from the effects of wealth variations, is a more attractive prospect than no reform at all; besides, who can say the legislatures will not be persuaded to centralize once the old order is invalidated under *Proposition One?*

POWER EQUALIZING: DISTRICTS

However, our own preference for *Proposition One* is not purely tactical. The use of relatively small units to determine important aspects of educational policy seems to us plausible; and it is quite feasible to make existing school districts substantially equal in their power to raise money for education. Even retaining the property tax as the local source (we would prefer a local income tax), such parity of power could be managed through a combination of state subsidies, redistricting, and other devices. The resulting system is called "power equalizing." Suppose, for example, the legislature provided that all districts might tax local real property at a rate of from 1 percent to 3 percent and that the district's own choice of specific tax level within that range would, in accord with a relation set by law, fix the district's spending level. The amount per pupil actually raised by the tax would be irrelevant. What would count is how hard the district chose to tax itself, not the wealth on which the tax was levied. The relation might be as simple as the following table:

LOCALLY CHOSEN TAX	PERMITTED SPENDING PER STUDENT
1% (minimum permitted)	$ 500
1.1%	550
2%	1,000
3% (maximum permitted)	1,500

Mechanically it might operate in a variety of ways. For example, if a district taxing at 2 percent raised $800 per student, it would be subsidized $200 per student from general sources by the state. If a district were wealthier and raised $1,200 at 2 percent, $200 of this would be redistributed as part of the subsidy for poorer districts. Alternatively all proceeds of the locally chosen taxes could be paid into a state pool with all disbursements made from that pool based solely upon the local tax rate.

Power equalizing formulas can be adjusted to take into account variations in the cost of educational goods and services from place to place. They can also be tuned to reflect subtler economic factors such as municipal over-burden and educational considerations such as the "needs" of disadvantaged (or, for that matter, gifted) students. In short, power equalizing formulas provide the base for any true "compensatory" scheme.

Power equalizing also is an answer to the central dilemma of the community control movement: how can an urban enclave like Ocean Hill–Brownsville achieve political autonomy without accepting economic prostration? Every district, irrespective of size or wealth, through power equalizing can be rendered both independent and equal in the power to educate its children. The poverty of a neighborhood's tax resources cannot by itself justify con-tinued subordination to a larger school district. If the state desires it, Ocean Hill–Brownsville can be economically as unfettered as Scarsdale.

Power Equalizing: Families

Some have suggested that power equalizing can satisfy both the centralist drive for equality and the objectives of local government by a further exten-sion to the family level. Imagine, for example, that each family with school-age children is a small school district that has been equalized in its power to tax itself and to spend for education. All parents would choose among schools, each of which operates at a set level of cost per pupil, say $500, $800, $1,100, and $1,400. The school would receive its income (for secular instruc-tion) from the state; it could charge no further tuition. The family's choice of a school cost level would fix the rate of a special tax upon its own income. The tax rates also would vary by family income class with the aim of equalizing for all families the economic sacrifice required to attend any school at a given spending level. For example, a welfare mother might pay $15 in tax for all her children to attend a $500 school; for that same school the tax price to a middle-class family might approach the full $500 cost, while the price to a rich family would exceed the full cost. A $1,400 school might cost these same three families $100, $1,000, and $2,000 respectively.

Schools in such a system could be all public, all private, or mixed. The con-straints on curriculum could be few or many, but any substantial limitation would frustrate at least some of the purposes for trying such a system in the first place. One important object is, after all, for the first time to give a true choice to all families—including the poor. Through family choice, it is argued, competition and experimentation would be stimulated and variety and quality thereby enhanced. Also better matching of schools and children would be effected by the judgments of parents and children than by an im-personal attendance boundary for the neighborhood or the judgment of an expert. In providing choice to the parent, an answer also would be given to the other dilemma in the community control movement: how to maintain a true "community" while respecting the interests of dissenting minorities. In a family based system, the community would be transformed from an artificial and inescapable community of geography to a community of interests, one freely chosen and freely abandoned.

Obviously the details of such a system would have to be carefully tailored if such ancillary policies as racial integration, fair competition, minimum standards, and job security for teachers were to be satisfied. The model "Family Choice in Education Act" which has been drafted to express these policies comprises hundreds of provisions. It encourages private schools with guaranteed loans but protects public schools against unfair competition by limiting the capitalization of private schools. For similar reasons it disallows contributions either from interested sources or for ideological objectives. The model act also puts pupil admission to a school on a random basis, thereby maximizing racial and social integration. To assist the choices of schools by parents, an elaborate system of information and counseling would be provided. Of course, free and adequate transport would have to be made available. In all respects, the complex provisions of the model act strive to assure the fullest measure of independent action and equality of opportunity for schools, parents, and pupils.

However, an interesting division recently has emerged between what may be viewed as the centralists and decentralists among family choice proponents. The schism is illustrated by a proposal for educational vouchers outlined by the Center for the Study of Public Policy at Cambridge, a proposal that conceivably will be supported by the Office of Economic Opportunity in a series of experiments. (*Teachers College Record*, February, 1971.) Though reflecting some of the aims of the model family choice act, the CSPP proposal specifically rejects it and offers in its place a striking contrast. Rather than provide equal access for all to schools of different quality, the CSPP model deliberately tends to equalize all schools in the voucher system at a level of quality to be centrally, not parentally, determined. This uniformity would be achieved by giving more money to schools with a higher population of disadvantaged children. It would not allow for variation in spending in accord with the tax effort families are willing to make for their education. Effectively, parents who are poor would be denied the opportunity to aspire to an education which is not merely different in style but qualitatively superior to the governmentally mandated minimum.

The CSPP model is the expression of a plausible—if, to us, mistaken—value choice in education. It is probably compatible with the constitutional test we have offered, since (depending upon its eventual details) it divorces quality in public education from variations in wealth. Along with power equalizing systems—both district and family—it nicely illustrates the boundless possibilities for experiment and change in the structure of American education. If the old order survives another century, it will not be for want of alternative models.

The Detroit School Decision *

STEPHEN J. ROTH

. . . The City of Detroit is a community generally divided by racial lines. Residential segregation within the city and throughout the larger metropolitan area is substantial, pervasive and of long standing. Black citizens are located in separate and distinct areas within the city and are not generally to be found in the suburbs. While the racially unrestricted choice of black persons and economic factors may have played some part in the development of this pattern of residential segregation, it is, in the main, the result of past and present practices and customs of racial discrimination, both public and private, which have and do restrict the housing opportunities of black people. On the record there can be no other finding.

STATE RESPONSIBLE

Governmental actions and inaction at all levels, federal, state and local, have combined, with those of private organizations, such as loaning institutions and real estate associations and brokerage firms, to establish and to maintain the pattern of residential segregation throughout the Detroit metropolitan area. It is no answer to say that restricted practices grew gradually (as the black population in the area increased between 1920 and 1970), or that since 1948 racial restrictions on the ownership of real property have been removed. The policies pursued by both government and private persons and agencies have a continuing and present effect upon the complexion of the community—as we know, the choice of a residence is a relatively infrequent affair. For many years FHA and VA openly advised and advocated the maintenance of "harmonious" neighborhoods, i.e., racially and economically harmonious. The conditions created continued. While it would be unfair to charge the present defendants with what other governmental officers or agencies have done, it can be said that the actions or the failure to act by the responsible school authorities, both city and state, were linked to that of these other governmental units. When we speak of governmental action we should not view the different agencies as a collection of unrelated units. Perhaps the most that can be said is that all of them, including the school authorities, are, in part, responsible for the segregated condition which exists. And we note that just as there is an interaction

* This decision rendered by U.S. District Court Judge Stephen J. Roth on September 27, 1971, pertaining to the Detroit Public Schools promised to have national import. It was precipitated by charges from the Detroit Chapter of the NAACP that the Detroit Public School System was segregated. In the above selection, Judge Roth provides the reader with both a sociological and legal rationale for his decision. Case citations and technical legal statements have been omitted for reading ease.

FROM Stephen J. Roth, "The Detroit School Decision," Integrated Education, Vol. 9, No. 6 (November–December), 1971, pp. 3–8.

between residential patterns and the racial composition of the schools, so there is a corresponding effect on the residential pattern by the racial composition of the schools.

SCHOOL BOARD SEGREGATES

Turning now to the specific and pertinent (for our purposes) history of the Detroit school system so far as it involves both the local school authorities and the state school authorities, we find the following:

During the decade beginning in 1950 the Board created and maintained optional attendance zones in neighborhoods undergoing racial transition and between high school attendance areas of opposite predominant racial compositions. In 1959 there were eight basic optional attendance areas affecting 21 schools. Optional attendance areas provided pupils living within certain elementary areas a choice of attendance at one of two high schools. In addition there was at least one optional area either created or existing in 1960 between two junior high schools of opposite predominant racial components. All of the high school optional areas, except two, were in neighborhoods undergoing racial transition (from white to black) during the 1950s. . . .

. . . The Board, in the operation of its transportation to relieve overcrowding policy, has admittedly bused black pupils past or away from closer white schools with available space to black schools. This practice has continued in several instances in recent years despite the Board's avowed policy, adopted in 1967, to utilize transportation to increase integration.

With one exception (necessitated by the burning of a white school), defendant Board has never bused white children to predominantly black schools. The Board has not bused white pupils to black schools despite the enormous amount of space available in inner-city schools. There were 22,961 vacant seats in schools 90% or more black.

The Board has created and altered attendance zones, maintained and altered grade structures and created and altered feeder school patterns in a manner which has had the natural, probable and actual effect of continuing black and white pupils in racially segregated schools. The Board admits at least one instance where it purposefully and intentionally built and maintained a school and its attendance zone to contain black students. Throughout the last decade (and presently) school attendance zones of opposite racial compositions have been separated by north-south boundary lines, despite the Board's awareness (since at least 1962) that drawing boundary lines in an east-west direction would result in significant integration. The natural and actual effect of these acts and failures to act has been the creation and perpetuation of school segregation. There has never been a feeder pattern or zoning change which placed a predominantly white residential area into a predominantly black school zone or feeder pattern. Every school which was 90% or more black in 1960, and which is still in use today, remains 90% or more black. Whereas 65.8% of Detroit's black students attended 90% or

more black schools in 1960, 74.9% of the black students attended 90%
or more black schools during the 1970–71 school year.

The public schools operated by defendant Board are thus segregated on a
racial basis. This racial segregation is in part the result of the discriminatory
acts and omissions of defendant Board.

In 1966 the defendant State Board of Education and Michigan Civil
Rights Commission issued a Joint Policy Statement on Equality of Educational Opportunity, requiring that

> "Local school boards must consider the factor of racial balance along
> with other educational considerations in making decisions about selection
> of new school sites, expansion of present facilities . . . Each of these situa-
> tions presents an opportunity for integration."

Defendant State Board's "School Plant Planning Handbook" requires that

> "Care in site location must be taken if a serious transportation problem
> exists or if housing patterns in an area would result in a school largely
> segregated on racial, ethnic, or socio-economic lines."

The defendant City Board has paid little heed to these statements and
guidelines. The State defendants have similarly failed to take any action to
effectuate these policies. . . .

The construction at Brooks Junior High plays a dual segregatory role: not
only is the construction segregated, it will result in a feeder pattern change
which will remove the last majority white school from the already almost
all-black Mackenzie High School attendance area.

Since 1959 the Board has constructed at least 13 small primary schools
with capacities of from 300 to 400 pupils. This practice negates opportunities
to integrate, "contains" the black population and perpetuates and compounds school segregation.

Segregation Maintained

The State and its agencies, in addition to their general responsibility for
and supervision of public education, have acted directly to control and maintain the pattern of segregation in the Detroit schools. The State refused,
until this session of the legislature, to provide authorization or funds for the
transportation of pupils within Detroit regardless of their poverty or distance
from the school to which they were assigned, while providing in many neighboring, mostly white, suburban districts the full range of state supported
transportation. This and other financial limitations, such as those on bonding
and the working of the state aid formula whereby suburban districts were
able to make far larger per pupil expenditures despite less tax effort have
created and perpetuated systematic educational inequalities. . . .

In conclusion, however, we find that both the State of Michigan and the
Detroit Board of Education have committed acts which have been causal

factors in the segregated condition of the public schools of the City of Detroit. As we assay the principles essential to a finding of de jure segregation, as outlined in rulings of the United States Supreme Court, they are:

1. The State, through its officers and agencies, and usually, the school administration, must have taken some action or actions with a purpose of segregation.
2. This action or these actions must have created or aggravated segregation in the schools in question.
3. A current condition of segregation exists.

We find these tests to have been met in this case. We recognize that causation in the case before us is both several and comparative. The principal causes undeniably have been population movement and housing patterns, but state and local governmental actions, including school board actions, have played a substantial role in promoting segregation. It is, the Court believes, unfortunate that we cannot deal with public school segregation on a no-fault basis, for if racial segregation in our public schools is an evil, then it should make no difference whether we classify it de jure or de facto. Our objective, logically, it seems to us, should be to remedy a condition which we believe needs correction. In the most realistic sense, if fault or blame must be found it is that of the community as a whole, including, of course, the black components. We need not minimize the effect of the actions of federal, state and local governmental officers and agencies, and the actions of loaning institutions and real estate firms, in the establishment and maintenance of segregated residential patterns—which lead to school segregation—to observe that blacks, like ethnic groups in the past, have tended to separate from the larger group and associate together. The ghetto is at once both a place of confinement and a refuge. There is enough blame for everyone to share.

Conclusions of Law

1. This Court has jurisdiction of the parties and the subject matter of this action under 28 U.S.C. 1331(a), 1343(3) and (4), 2201 and 2202; 42 U.S.C. 1983, 1988, and 2000d.

2. In considering the evidence and in applying legal standards it is not necessary that the Court find that the policies and practices, which it has found to be discriminatory, have as their motivating forces any evil intent or motive. Motive, ill will and bad faith have long ago been rejected as a requirement to invoke the protection of the Fourteenth Amendment against racial discrimination.

3. School districts are accountable for the natural, probable and foreseeable consequences of their policies and practices, and where racially identifiable schools are the result of such policies, the school authorities bear the burden of showing that such policies are based on educationally required, non-racial considerations.

4. In determining whether a constitutional violation has occurred, proof that a pattern of racially segregated schools has existed for a considerable period of time amounts to a showing of racial classification by the state and its agencies, which must be justified by clear and convincing evidence.

5. The Board's practice of shaping school attendance zones on a north-south rather than east-west orientation, with the result that zone boundaries conformed to racial residential dividing lines, violated the Fourteenth Amendment.

6. Pupil racial segregation in the Detroit Public School System and the residential racial segregation resulting primarily from public and private racial discrimination are interdependent phenomena. The affirmative obligation of the defendant Board has been and is to adopt and implement pupil assignment practices and policies that compensate for and avoid incorporation into the school system the effects of residential racial segregation. The Board's building upon housing segregation violates the Fourteenth Amendment.

7. The Board's policy of selective optional attendance zones, to the extent that it facilitated the separation of pupils on the basis of race, was in violation of the Fourteenth Amendment.

Illegal Busing

8. The practice of the Board of transporting black students from overcrowded black schools to other identifiably black schools, while passing closer identifiably white schools, which could have accepted these pupils, amounted to an act of segregation by the school authorities.

9. The manner in which the Board formulated and modified attendance zones for elementary schools had the natural and predictable effect of perpetuating racial segregation of students. Such conduct is an act of de jure discrimination in violation of the Fourteenth Amendment.

10. A school board may not, consistent with the Fourteenth Amendment, maintain segregated elementary schools or permit educational choices to be influenced by community sentiment or the wishes of a majority of voters.

11. Under the Constitution of the United States and the constitution and laws of the State of Michigan, the responsibility for providing educational opportunity to all children on constitutional terms is ultimately that of the state.

12. That a state's form of government may delegate the power of daily administration of public schools to officials with less than state-wide jurisdiction does not dispel the obligation of those who have broader control to use the authority they have consistently with the constitution. In such instances the constitutional obligation toward the individual school children is a shared one.

13. Leadership and general supervision over all public education is vested in the State Board of Education. The duties of the State Board and super-

intendent include, but are not limited to, specifying the number of hours necessary to constitute a school day; approval until 1962 of school sites; approval of school construction plans; accreditation of schools; approval of loans based on state aid funds; review of suspensions and expulsions of individual students for misconduct; authority over transportation routes and disbursement of transportation funds; teacher certification and the like. State law provides review procedures from actions of local or intermediate districts, with authority in the State Board to ratify, reject, amend or modify the actions of these inferior state agencies. In general, the state superintendent is given the duty "[t]o do all things necessary to promote the welfare of the public schools and public educational instructions and provide proper educational facilities for the youth of the state."

STATE MUST ACT

14. State officials, including all of the defendants, are charged under the Michigan constitution with the duty of providing pupils an education without discrimination with respect to race. Art. VIII, § 2, Mich. Constitution of 1963. Art. I, § 2, of the constitution provides:

> "No person shall be denied the equal protection of the laws; nor shall any person be denied the enjoyment of his civil or political rights or be discriminated against in the exercise thereof because of religion, race, color or national origin. The legislature shall implement this section by appropriate legislation."

15. The State Department of Education has recently established an Equal Educational Opportunities section having responsibility to identify racially imbalanced school districts and develop desegregation plans. M.S.A. 15.3355 provides that no *school* or department shall be kept for any person or persons on account of race or color.

16. The state further provides special funds to local districts for compensatory education which are administered on a per school basis under direct review of the State Board. All other state aid is subject to fiscal review and accounting by the state. M.S.A. 15.1919. See also M.S.A. 15.1919(68b), providing for special supplements to merged districts "for the purpose of bringing about uniformity of educational opportunity for all pupils of the district." The general consolidation law M.S.A. 15.3401 authorizes annexation for even noncontiguous school districts upon approval of the superintendent of public instruction and electors, as provided by law. Op. Atty. Gen., Feb. 5, 1964, No. 4193. Consolidation with respect to so-called "first class" districts, *i.e.*, Detroit, is generally treated as an annexation with the first class district being the surviving entity. The law provides procedures covering all necessary considerations. M.S.A. 15.3184, 15.3186.

17. Where a pattern of violation of constitutional rights is established the affirmative obligation under the Fourteenth Amendment is imposed

on not only individual school districts, but upon the State defendants in this case. The foregoing constitutes our findings of fact and conclusions of law on the issue of segregation in the public schools of the City of Detroit.

PROPER REMEDIES

Having found a de jure segregated public school system in operation in the City of Detroit, our first step, in considering what judicial remedial steps must be taken, is the consideration of intervening parent defendants' motion to add as parties defendant a great number of Michigan school districts located out county in Wayne County, and in Macomb and Oakland Counties, on the principal premise or ground that effective relief cannot be achieved or ordered in their absence. Plaintiffs have opposed the motion to join the additional school districts, arguing that the presence of the State defendants is sufficient and all that is required, even if, in shaping a remedy, the affairs of these other districts will be affected. In considering the motion to add the listed school districts we pause to note that the proposed action has to do with relief. Having determined that the circumstances of the case require judicial intervention and equitable relief, it would be improper for us to act on this motion until the other parties to the action have had an opportunity to submit their proposals for desegregation. Accordingly, we shall not rule on the motion to add parties at this time. Considered as a plan for desegregation the motion is lacking in specificity and is framed in the broadest general terms. The moving party may wish to amend its proposal and resubmit it as a comprehensive plan of desegregation.

In order that the further proceedings in this cause may be conducted on a reasonable time schedule, and because the views of counsel respecting further proceedings cannot but be of assistance to them and to the Court, this cause will be set down for pre-trial conference on the matter of relief. The conference will be held in our Courtroom in the City of Detroit at ten o'clock in the morning, October 4, 1971.

Schools for Scandal — The Bill of Rights and Public Education

IRA GLASSER

There are only two public institutions in the United States which steadfastly deny that the Bill of Rights applies to them. One is the military and the other is the public schools. Both are compulsory. Taken together,

FROM Ira Glasser, "Schools for Scandal—The Bill of Rights and Public Education," *Phi Delta Kappan*, Vol. 51 (December 1969), pp. 190–94.

they are the chief socializing institutions of our society. Everyone goes
through our schools. What they learn—not from what they are formally
taught but from the way the institution is organized to treat them—is that
authority is more important than freedom, order more precious than liberty,
and discipline a higher value than individual expression. That is a lesson
which is inappropriate to a free society—and certainly inappropriate to its
schools.

I. Procedural Rights

Walter Crump is a slim, 18-year-old, esthetic-looking Negro college
student. On first impression he is talented, articulate, and gentle, and
further meetings do not alter that impression. Until May 4, 1969, he attended the High School of Music and Art, a special school in New York
City, compiling a satisfactory academic and disciplinary record. With
graduation only a few weeks away, Walter Crump was looking ahead to
college in the fall and from there to a career in the theater. On May 4 all
that very nearly came to an end.

Early in the day, Mr. Crump was involved in a minor verbal altercation
with a teacher. The facts of the disagreement are unimportant; the incident
at worst appears to have involved an undetermined amount of rudeness and
discourtesy on both sides. No violence or threat of violence occurred. It
was the kind of a verbal flare-up that occurs daily in almost every imagin-
able setting, and which usually passes without damage to either party.

Later that afternoon, however, Mr. Crump was summarily suspended and
told to go home until further notice. (That procedure was unambiguously
in violation of the New York City Board of Education's own rules, which
require that a suspended student be kept in school until a parent is informed prior to sending the student out of the school.)

Further notice did not come until 12 days later, at which time Mr.
Crump's foster mother was told to come with Walter to a hearing—the
board called it a "guidance conference"—eight days later on May 22, at
the office of an assistant superintendent of schools. (That procedure also
was in violation of the board's own rules. The maximum period that a
principal may suspend a child is five days, and a "guidance conference" with
prior notification to the parent by certified mail must occur within that
period.)

Mr. Crump was unable to persuade his foster mother to attend the
hearing, so he went himself. When he arrived, approximately 45 minutes
late, he discovered that the hearing had been held without him. Before
the hearing began, two separate requests were made by parents of two fellow
students at the High School of Music and Art to attend the hearing in support of Mr. Crump. Both requests were denied, despite the fact that a
state law had been passed and signed by Governor Rockefeller that very
month granting the right of students to be represented—even by a lawyer

if they wished—at hearings arising out of suspensions of more than five days. The denial of these requests, therefore, was in violation of state law.

At the "hearing," Mr. Crump was summarily "convicted" (of what, nobody knows) and, just a few weeks short of graduation, dismissed from the school. On May 23, Mr. Crump's foster mother received a letter from the assistant superintendent curtly informing her that a "guidance conference" had been held in absentia and that Walter had been discharged from school, effective immediately.

The expulsion of Mr. Crump from full-time public education was totally lacking in even the minimal rudiments of due process of law. He never received a meaningful hearing; he was never informed of his right to be represented by counsel; he was never informed of the charges against him; and his supporters were not permitted to speak in his behalf.

But that was not the end of it. A few days later, Mr. Crump's foster mother received another letter, this time from the Bureau of Child Welfare. The letter informed her that since Mr. Crump was over 18 and now out of school (the Board of Education had been thoughtful enough to allow a bureau caseworker to attend the "guidance conference" and to send his supervisor a copy of the dismissal letter), board payments to his foster parents would soon end.

At that point, one of the High School of Music and Art parents who had been refused admission to the guidance conference arranged an appointment for Mr. Crump with an attorney from the New York Civil Liberties Union. NYCLU immediately informed the Bureau of Child Welfare that the dismissal from school was being contested, that in their judgment the dismissal was illegal, and that a federal suit was being prepared that very afternoon. To no avail: The Bureau cut off board payments the next day, also without a hearing and without even the courtesy of a reply.

Mr. Crump's attorney subsequently filed suit in federal court, obtained a new hearing (which he was allowed to attend), and, not surprisingly, Walter Crump was reinstated, more than a month after the initial suspension. He was graduated without incident three weeks later.

If what happened to Walter Crump had been an isolated instance, it would be no less outrageous; but at least one could not easily draw inferences about an entire school system. In fact, however, the procedures which governed Walter Crump's case govern other cases as well. The frightening thing about the procedures followed by school officials in the Crump case is precisely that they were *routine*. The independent experiences of several respected agencies in New York—the NAACP Legal Defense and Education Fund, Citizens Committee for Children, the New York Civil Liberties Union, the Metropolitan Applied Research Center, Mobilization for Youth, and several parents associations—suggest that what happened to Mr. Crump happens regularly and widely to anyone facing suspension. Two things may be said about the procedures governing student suspensions in New York (and there is no reason to believe that New York is unique; although some other cities may enjoy better procedures, cases raising the same issues have arisen all over the United States):

1. The procedures represent a gross denial of the constitutional right to due process, including the right to a fair hearing.
2. Even those inadequate procedures are regularly violated by school officials.[1]

If Mr. Crump had not had a friend knowledgeable enough and aggressive enough to seek legal help, it is difficult to say where he would be today. Certainly he wouldn't be in college. Other students, perhaps I should say other *children*, have not been so fortunate.

Even when legal redress is possible to obtain, it may not be possible to undo the damage inflicted in the meantime. Nothing illustrates that better than the mass expulsions that occurred at Franklin K. Lane High School in New York last January.

On January 27, 1969, 670 students, most of them black or Puerto Rican, were summarily expelled from Lane. They received no notice of, nor any opportunity to contest, the action taken against them. Letters were sent out on January 24 informing parents that they had a week to contest the expulsions, but only three days later all 670 were expelled and informed that there was no chance at all to reverse the decision. Moreover, January 24 turns out to have been a Friday and January 27 the following Monday, so actually parents received no notice whatsoever.

The alleged reason for the expulsion was to relieve overcrowded conditions at Lane by eliminating multiple sessions and by putting the school on a single session. Yet two-thirds of the 61 academic high schools in New York City were more overcrowded than Lane, some of them substantially so, and only one operated on a single session. The truth is that what happened at Lane was the result of severe pressures arising out of the bitter teachers' strike during the fall; those pressures finally resulted in an agreement by the powerful—teachers, administrators, and politicians—against the powerless—students and their parents. It is precisely to protect the powerless against the excesses of the powerful that the Bill of Rights was invented. Yet here that protection did not exist. It is ironic indeed that a city which was capable of being whipped into a frenzy over the issue of due process during the strike was conspicuously silent during what was surely the single most stunning denial of due process ever to have occurred in the New York City school system.

Once the decision was made to expel the students, a mechanical rule was devised: All students who were absent 30 days or more during the fall semester and who had maintained an unsatisfactory academic record in the fall semester were to be expelled.

---

[1] A startling fact in the Crump case was the extent to which school authorities broke even their own rules and regulations.

The decision to expel based on student attendance records and academic achievement during the 1968 fall semester seemed peculiar indeed. After all, it was during that semester that Lane was struck for 36 days as part of the city-wide teachers' strike. In addition, there were several brief boycotts by students and parents over dissatisfaction with the strike settlement. Finally, there was a severe flu epidemic in New York that fall, causing widespread absenteeism among both students and teachers. Hardly a typical semester by which to measure either attendance or achievement!

Although we hear much these days about procedures which supposedly protect the guilty, it is ultimately out of a concern for the innocent that fair procedures were developed. Consider what happened to a few of those caught in Franklin K. Lane's net:

1. *Arthur Knight.* Mr. Knight was expelled on January 27 as he attempted to re-register for the spring, 1969, semester. Prior to the fall, 1968, semester, Knight had maintained a satisfactory academic record. He was legitimately absent for the entire fall semester due to a serious kidney ailment. On his first day back he was expelled.

Later by more than a month, during which he was out of school entirely, he was directed to report to a special annex to continue his "education." (Inexplicably, some of the expelled students were ultimately assigned to this annex instead of being expelled completely.) But the "annex" offered no grades, no examinations, and no homework. There were few if any books, and only three teachers. The entire annex was only open from 9 A.M. to 12 noon. It was clearly a custodial institution, not an educational one.

What had Arthur Knight done to deserve such punishment? Why wasn't he allowed to contest the punishment at a hearing?

2. *Oscar Gonzalus.* Mr. Gonzalus was notified of his expulsion by mail. He had no chance to challenge it. Yet the criteria by which students were expelled did not apply to him, because he had been absent less than 30 days during the fall, 1968, semester. Furthermore, most of those absences were due to an attack of the flu. Finally, Gonzalus had maintained a satisfactory academic record before the fall semester. All these facts could have been proven at a fair hearing *before* expulsion. But no fair hearing was allowed.

3. *Marcine Chestnut.* Miss Chestnut was expelled because of an allegedly deficient attendance record. Yet despite her poor attendance, partly due to a severe case of the flu, she maintained a satisfactory academic record during the fall, 1968, semester, as she had during previous semesters. Like the others, however, she had no chance.

More than two months later, a complaint was filed in federal court in behalf of all 670 students. In late April, 1969, almost three months to the day after the initial expulsion, Federal Judge Jack B. Weinstein reinstated all 670 students and ordered the school to provide remedial work to make up for the lost time. Judge Weinstein found that the action against the 670 had denied them their constitutional right to due process.

Beyond the legal question, of course, is the larger morality of what happened at Lane. Though many students were innocently caught up in the action, and all were denied due process, many others were indeed absent for more than 30 days and did have failing academic records. For these students, the penalties were even greater, for these were students in grave trouble. For such students, the legal victory was meaningless because the educational damage was irremediable. At this writing (August, 1969), ongoing attempts to retrieve what was lost during the three months are reaching only a few of the 670, and helping even fewer. It says a great deal about a school system whose response to students hanging on by the slimmest thread is to cut that thread for reasons of administrative convenience.

II. 1st Amendment Rights

Procedural rights are not the only rights denied to students by public schools. Attitudes toward individual rights are indivisible; institutions that do not protect the right to a fair hearing are not likely to protect free speech either. The schools are no exception.

Indeed, the most publicized conflicts between school authorities and students involve First Amendment rights: free speech, freedom of the press, freedom of assembly. All across the country, from New York to Mississippi, from Iowa to Texas, from California to Alabama, courts are being asked, for the first time in many cases, to consider the demands of students for freedoms normally guaranteed to adults but traditionally denied to students. Like soldiers in the military, students are suggesting that the Bill of Rights applies to them.

In 1965, a group of black students in Mississippi were suspended for wearing buttons saying "Freedom Now." The suspension was challenged in federal court and eventually resulted in a landmark decision by the U.S. Court of Appeals for the Fifth Circuit. The court reinstated the students on the ground that no significant disruption of the educational process had taken place as a result of the wearing of the buttons, and that therefore there was no legal basis for suspending the students.

It is instructive to note that on the same day the same court decided a similar case *against* another group of suspended students. In that case, school officials were upheld because there was clear evidence that the students wearing the buttons harassed students who did not wear them and created a variety of other substantial disturbances.

Thus the court sought to limit the power of school officials to prevent the free expression of views, but nonetheless upheld the power of school officials to regulate disruptive conduct. In effect, the court constructed a factual standard which requires school officials to provide conclusive evidence of substantial interference with the educational functioning of the school before they may prevent political expression by students. In the absence of such a factual determination one way or the other, implied the court, we are simply granting public school officials a blank check to suppress political speech arbitrarily, a right no other civilian public official has.

Despite this decision, students all over the country have been regularly denied the right to peaceful political expression during the past few years, whether or not such expression involved substantial disruption. In 1967, John Tinker, then a 15-year-old high school student in Des Moines, Iowa; his sister Mary Beth, 13; and a friend, Christopher Eckhardt, 16, decided to publicize their opposition to the war in Vietnam by wearing black armbands to school. The form of expression seemed to fall well within the standard enunciated in the Mississippi case: What could be a more passive, less disruptive form of expression than the wearing of armbands!

The principals of the Des Moines schools responded by first banning the wearing of armbands and then suspending the Tinkers and their friend. Parents of the students filed suit in federal court, and the case eventually reached the U.S. Court of Appeals for the Eighth Circuit, which upheld the principals' action. That decision was in clear conflict with the earlier decision by the Fifth Circuit Court of Appeals in the Mississippi case, and no one could resolve the conflict except the U.S. Supreme Court, which agreed to hear the case.

On February 24, 1969, the Supreme Court reversed the lower court's decision and upheld the students' right to wear the armbands. The court made the following points:

1. The wearing of an armband for the purpose of expressing views is clearly within the protection of the First Amendment.
2. Both students and teachers are entitled to the protections of the First Amendment. "It can hardly be argued," said the court, "that either students or teachers shed their constitutional rights to freedom of speech or expression at the schoolhouse gate. This has been the unmistakable holding of this court for almost 50 years."
3. While actual disturbance which intrudes upon the work of the school or the rights of other students may be banned, the mere *fear* that such a disturbance might occur is not sufficient. As the court said, ". . . in our system, undifferentiated fear or apprehension of disturbance is not enough to overcome the right to freedom of expression. Any departure from absolute regimentation may cause trouble. Any variation from the majority's opinion may inspire fear. Any word spoken, in class, in the lunchroom, or on the campus, that deviates from the views of another person may start an argument or cause a disturbance. But our Constitution says we must take this risk; and our history says that it is this sort of hazardous freedom—this kind of openness—that is the basis of our national strength. . . ."
4. The standard of the Mississippi button case was upheld; that is, before an expression of views may be prohibited, school officials must show that the exercise of the forbidden right would "materially and substantially interfere with the requirements of appropriate discipline in the operation of the school."
5. Students are constitutionally entitled to freedom of expression not only in the classroom but also elsewhere in the school hours. Freedom

of expression, said the court, "is not confined to the supervised and ordained discussion which takes place in the classroom. . . . A student's rights . . . do not embrace merely the classroom hours. When he is in the cafeteria, or on the playing field, or on the campus during the authorized hours, he may express his opinions. . . ."

While the *Tinker* case appears to settle the problem of wearing buttons, armbands, or other symbols in school, other First Amendment rights are still in dispute, and some are currently in court. These chiefly involve the right of students to distribute political leaflets and other material such as unauthorized newspapers in the school. In one case in Jamaica High School in New York City, Jeffrey Schwartz, a senior, was suspended for *mere possession* of an unauthorized newspaper which in previous issues had been harshly critical of that school's principal, particularly with respect to students' rights.

When the suspension was challenged by the student's parents and their lawyer, the school decided to waive Jeffrey's remaining requirements and graduate him about six months ahead of time. When his parents went into court to contest the action, the Board of Education lawyers argued that the case was moot because the boy was graduated; his diploma was available to him anytime, they insisted. But after making that argument for six months, the principal refused to grant him his diploma in June on the grounds that he had not fulfilled the requirements which the principal had waived months before! Subsequently, after being out of school for an entire semester, Mr. Schwartz had to attend summer school in order to be able to get into college in the fall. Along the way, the principal caused a New York State scholarship, won by Mr. Schwartz in a competitive examination, to be revoked for failing to graduate on time in June!

The issues raised in the *Schwartz* case are typical of those being raised in high schools all over the country.

It is particularly difficult for students to reconcile what they learn in their social studies classes about James Madison and free speech and John Peter Zenger and freedom of the press with what they confront when they try to exercise those rights in school. It is even more difficult to reconcile what they learn about fair trials with what they are subjected to at "guidance conferences." In the end, students learn less about American values from formal classroom instruction than from the way the school is organized to treat them. Unfortunately, what they do learn is that where individual rights collide with discipline and authority, individual rights inevitably recede. That such lessons are taught by our public schools is an educational scandal of major dimensions.

III. Personal Rights

No discussion of students' rights is complete without mentioning the widespread attempt by school officials to regulate the dress and personal appearance of students. Nothing illustrates the repressiveness of public schools more. All across the United States, thousands of students have been suspended or otherwise excluded from classes for the style of their dress or the length of their hair. In almost all cases, questions of offensiveness, health, or safety were not present. Such cases have arisen practically everywhere and have been decided differently in different places. In New York, the Commissioner of Education has clearly upheld the rights of students to wear their hair or their clothes as they please within limits of safety. In Texas, the U.S. Court of Appeals has upheld the power of school officials to regulate the length of a student's hair, and similar rulings have occurred in Connecticut. In Wisconsin a federal court recently declared such actions by school officials to be unconstitutional. And in Massachusetts federal judge Charles Wyzonski has written an eloquent opinion in support of a student's right "to look like himself." The U.S. Supreme Court has so far considered the issue too trivial to deserve its attention.

Beyond the legal questions, however, consider the social significance of the attempt by school authorities to regulate personal appearance so closely. Consider the institutions of our society which insist on regulating dress: prisons, mental hospitals, convents, and the military. All these institutions depend for their existence on maintenance of a rigid system of authority and discipline. The slightest expression of individualism represents a threat to the structure of authority. These institutions recognize that the strict regulation of personal appearance is an important social mechanism to maintain control by creating a climate in which unquestioning obedience to authority will flourish. Whatever justification for such a practice may exist in prisons or in the military—or for that matter in political dictatorships whose first official acts usually involve the rounding up of "hippies"—what possible justification is there for such repression in the schools of a free society? In fact, the denial of personal rights must be seen as part of a pattern which includes the denial of First Amendment rights and procedural rights as well.

It is not the students who are radical. They seek completely traditional American rights, rights which are guaranteed in the Constitution but denied to them. Rather, I think, it is the principals who violate students' rights who are the radicals. They are the ones who deny the traditional protections of the Bill of Rights to students, and they are the ones who are subverting the traditional balance between freedom and authority by perpetuating rules which sacrifice individual rights at almost every opportunity.

As the U.S. Supreme Court said in the case of *West Virginia* v. *Barnette*:

> The Fourteenth Amendment, as now applied to the states, protects the citizen against the state itself and all of its creatures—boards of education not excepted. These are, of course, important, delicate, and highly discretionary functions, but none that they may not perform within the limits of the Bill of Rights. That they are educating the young for citizenship is

reason for scrupulous protection of constitutional freedoms of the individual, if we are not to strangle the free mind at its source and teach youth to discount important principles of our government as mere platitudes.

That was 26 years ago.

E.   Alternative Educational Patterns

Open Education: Its Philosophy, Historical Perspectives, and Implications

EWALD B. NYQUIST

I have stated that if I do not accomplish anything else as a new commissioner of education I want to do all I can to make the educational system more humanistic—more humane with respect to the curriculum, administration, governance, and, indeed, the whole teaching, learning process. To be humanistic is simply a way of looking at the world which emphasizes the importance of man, his nature and central place in the universe; which teaches that all persons have dignity and worth, and that man was made just a little lower than the angels; studies that provide joy in learning, pleasure in creating, and a sense of self; studies that make a critical examination of the quality of life and society in the United States and what can be done about it; programs that lead to a repair of our ravaged environment and solve our social malignancies; that satisfy one's emotions and aspirations in an age of feeling and of a sensate culture; that lead to the development of a personal life-style, celebrate spontaneity, and make one fully human.

Charles Silberman states unequivocally in *Crisis in the Classroom:* "Our most pressing educational problem is not how to increase the efficiency of the schools and colleges; it is how to create and maintain a humane society."

We are at a crossroads in American education and it has seemed to me that the concept of "open education" offers unique opportunities for humanizing and individualizing learning, making it relevant, meaningful, and personally satisfying. School must be a place to prepare young people to take their place in society—not a place where we isolate them from the main currents of life—and this can be done by making education at every age level person-centered, idea-centered, experience-centered, problem-oriented, and interdisciplinary, with the community and its other institutions a part of the process: this in contrast to the frequent educational experience with its information-gathering, fact-centered, course-centered, subject-centered, grade-getting, and bell-interrupted activity. To paraphrase Alfred North White-

FROM *Open Education*, edited by Ewald B. Nyquist and Gene R. Hawes. A Bantam Book, September 1972. Pp. 82–92. Reprinted by permission of the author.

head: Celibacy does not suit an educational institution; it must mate itself with action.

I first began studying about open education, as practiced in many of the British infant and junior schools, through the literature and was very impressed. Then I discovered that several of our staff in the State Education Department had been to England on study grants, and in every instance returned with high praise for the open classroom and all that it includes. They have also visited schools and classrooms in this country where the open education concept is being implemented.

What Is Open Education?

As explained in the May 16, 1970, issue of the *Saturday Review*, this kind of education refers to an approach to teaching that discards the familiar elementary classroom setup and the traditional stylized roles of teacher and pupils for a much freer, more informal, highly individualized, child-centered learning experience. Respect for and trust in the child are perhaps the most basic principles, with assumption that all children *want* to learn and *will* learn, if the emphasis is on learning and not on teaching, on each child's thinking processes and not rote skill acquisition, on freedom and responsibility rather than conformity and following directions.

Open education is based on the concept of childhood as something to be cherished; that it is not mere preparation for later schooling or life but a vital part of life itself to be lived richly each day; that learning is more effective if it grows out of the interests of the learner in a free, supportive, nonthreatening environment. Open education is based on the recognition that children are different, learn in different ways, at different times and from each other. There is little uniformity in an open education classroom. Children move about freely, talk with each other, make choices, work alone or in small groups, and peruse materials relevant to them. There is no sign of mere busywork, meaningless drill, or conformist activities. Materials in the open classroom include a wide, rich range of text, library books and reference books of varying difficulty, a multitude of audiovisual materials which children can and do use, quantities of materials for manipulation and experimentation and supplies for music, art, and creative pursuits. The open classroom is rich in living and growing plants and animals. There is an unending supply of interesting things to try and with which to experiment. There are provocative written and spoken questions posed by the teacher to stimulate children to think, test, describe, write, read, and figure. It is a happy, learning environment for children.

The purpose of open education is to provide a format whereby children are free to learn at their own pace and in their own way. The teacher serves as a facilitator of learning, providing an invitingly arranged environment, materials, motivation, guidance, and assistance. She works with individuals and small groups helping to set goals and achieve them, raising questions, intervening when necessary, observing children, and assessing their progress. Children's growth is evaluated on an individual basis with the teacher in terms of strengths and weaknesses and for the purpose of diagnoses and planning.

Students' feelings, interests, and needs are given priority over lesson plans, organizational patterns, rigid time schedules, and no-option structures. It must be noted that part of feeling good about oneself is being able to do, to exercise control over your own life. The learning of skills and development of understandings in the subject-matter areas when integrated around self-selected projects and activities help a child feel successful and are a part of his sense of fulfillment.

In an article for *Inside Education* Mrs. Jenny Andreae, a British educator who is developing a program using the open education approach in three New Rochelle elementary schools, describes a usual day:

> While the basic classroom routine varies, typically, children come in the morning, meet with the teacher, and discuss together the plans for the day; for instance, who the teacher would like to hear read. Then there is a period when the children are actively involved in assignments and projects, mostly working on their own, two children together, or with the teacher. They do math, reading, writing, studying, and make observations, for example, of plants and animals. We minimize the difference between work and play. All the subjects are interrelated. Students might learn about gerbils by watching them, about plants by recording their growth, or by reading books in the library.
>
> In the late morning the class gets together for discussion. The teacher selects children's work to be shared with the group—it might be reading a story written by a child, describing an experience, a puppet show, or a play.
>
> In the afternoon some teachers might have a math or reading class for specific skills. Others might use the period for completing projects begun in the morning. Then there is time to meet together, to listen to a story or poem, or a record.

In classrooms designed for open education, including those in Mrs. Andreae's program, you see many inviting nooks and corners for math, science, reading, writing, cooking, art, and dramatics—not rows of children's desks with the teacher up front. Corridors are used along with classrooms for carpentry, artwork, small- and large-group activities, displays of children's work, and stimulating questions posed by teachers and children. Doors are open and children go in and out freely. Teachers also move in and out of rooms and corridors, "pinching" ideas from one another, sharing exciting happenings, and helping each other.

Family or vertical grouping is another aspect of openness characteristic of many British primary schools. This organizational plan groups several age levels together in one classroom: 5s, 6s, and 7s; 5s and 6s; or 6s and 7s. Such multi-age grouping capitalizes on the fact that children learn from one another and realistically increases the number of "teachers" in each class-room. Five-year-olds are helped to "settle in" and younger children are motivated by a learning environment which includes models of older children who are deeply involved in reading, writing, and working with math materials.

The goals of open education, in England and in this country, are:

1. Happy children who feel successful and confident.
2. Self-disciplined children who have wholesome attitudes toward life and learning.
3. Independent thinkers who are self-propelled and continuing learners.
4. Readers who are increasingly fluent and who enjoy reading for purpose and meaning.
5. Children who write because they need to record and convey thoughts.
6. Competent students who are able to cope with fundamental math, science, and social science concepts because these are necessary to answer important questions and to solve problems.

Open education puts the learning where it belongs—squarely within the youngster. It is partly a matter of motivation. As Melvin Tumin of Princeton University says, "Motivation is not a boot in the tail." It is working on things you are interested and absorbed in, being free, feeling respected and worthwhile, having necessary jobs to do and purposes that are meaningful.

A headmistress of a British primary school who spent a few months recently working in our classrooms said that under a veneer of difference American children are very much like English children. American children have tremendous ideas and imagination but *no one* is tapping this resource. In fact, our educational system, as she saw it (though not representing all schools, of course) seems to be turning the children off through workbooks, drill, dull recitations, total group teaching, teacher domination, testing and pressure for academic achievement. "Mindlessness," Charles Silberman calls it.

WHAT ARE THE HISTORICAL PERSPECTIVES?

Dr. Mary Langmuir Essex, formerly of Vassar College and now at the Tavistock Clinic in London, told a conference of educators in White Plains not long ago that the trends in our two countries had become reversed. She said the United States in the 1920s and '30s under the influence of John Dewey had been moving toward a freer, more relevant kind of education, while the British were enmeshed in rigid, formal, cheerless, repressive training of the child, dominated by the specter of the 11-plus examinations. Now as *we* have become more rigid, structured, repressive, pressure-ridden, dominated by testing and the necessity to achieve, the British have been moving slowly, cautiously, gradually toward a freer, more childlike, humane, relevant, but by no means less hard-nosed form of education.

Therefore, as a basic philosophic approach, open education is not new. Its tenets were central to the progressive movement in American education and vestiges of their implementation are still to be found in many schools and individual classrooms throughout this country with the support of the philosophic commitment of countless educators. A recent conference gave evidence of this in its title: "Open Education: The Legacy of the Progressive Movement." But actually progressive education never really got off the ground, certainly not in the public schools. There was a great deal of rhetoric about growth, personality development, creative self-expression and the importance of the individual, but little basic change in methods of teaching or understanding of learning. As a matter of fact, the underlying principles of the philosophy were distorted in the implementation by classroom teachers. The important role of the teacher as organizer of the learning environment, manager of time, space, and materials, and guide in the learning experience was neglected or misinterpreted. Authority by virtue of mature understanding of human growth and development was equated with repressive control and self-discipline seen as a possible result of complete permissiveness.

In England, while the rhetoric is reminiscent of the progressive movement there is a difference—an important difference in pedagogy. While in the open education schools in England children are encouraged to help each other, work independently, work on their interests, move about and talk, there is no abdication of adult authority and responsibility. Teachers are fully in charge. They *expect* responsible behavior. Ground rules are clear cut. There is emphasis on teaching children to *think*. As Featherstone has pointed out, it is this deep pedagogical seriousness and the *attention paid to learning* that makes the British primary revolution so different from progressive education.[1]

Public education in this country faces the fact that even good traditional practices and theories have failed too many of our students. Educators talk glibly about "meeting the needs of the individual" and yet schools continue to foster competition, pass and fail children, and teach whole classes of children or three constant groups as though everyone were alike.

In a society which cherishes diversity, the least we can do now is offer these students, their teachers, and their parents another option, another approach to education: one in which students do no worse in the specific skills of reading and math but from which other significant values are derived as well.

As the Educational Development Center tells us, "Promising advances in curriculum, technology and knowledge of the learning process have scarcely begun to modify long established classroom practices and attitudes. Schools, for the most part, have absorbed 'innovations' without significant institutional change."[2]

We pour money into all kinds of instructional materials and yet many children are neither acquiring competence in reading nor the desire to read. New ideas in math and science in countless classrooms are taught in the same old ways. Innovations in curriculum, school architecture, instructional equipment are not necessarily improving the quality of education. While such innovations may be useful and good, their use is still dependent upon the human environment and the vital dialogue between children and teachers.

To be practical we must realize that education must prepare children for work that may not even exist today and whose nature cannot even be imagined 30 or 40 years hence. This can only be done by teaching children *how* to learn. For many youngsters we are doing a poor job of motivating them to work on their own, dig for information, and test out ideas. The child must be the principal agent in his *own* learning in order that he be a continuing learner.

It is for these and other reasons that I feel we must examine seriously what we are doing, why, and to what end result. It is for some of these reasons that I have spoken up in support of open education as an approach which offers us hope. It is not the only way, of course, but it is a promising way I would like New York State to investigate and promote.

What Are the Implications?

Implementation of the concept of open education presents danger and difficulty as well as tremendous opportunity. If educators, children, and parents do not understand it, open education, like progressive education, can easily degenerate into sloppy permissiveness, wistful romanticism, or shallow imitation. If our characteristic enthusiasm for whatever is "new," our predilection for attractive, mass-produced packages, and our craving for guaranteed success leads us to see the British primary school or open education as an importable mechanism for immediate educational improvement we will fail to understand the implications of the opportunity being presented.

If, on the other hand, we agree with Featherstone that "careful work on a small scale is the way to start reform worth having" we will avoid the "bandwagon" approach and build in the key elements essential for a dynamic, ongoing change process capitalizing on our own experience with progressive education and our British friends' experience in open education. Some of these elements are:

1. The involvement of parents, teachers, and administrators at every step.
2. Meaningful in-service education activities for teachers and other school personnel.
3. Built-in personal support for each teacher, including the approval and encouragement of the administrator, at least one other teacher who shares her attitude and goals, and hopefully, someone similar to a "teaching head" coming into the classroom as a coworker, not supervisor.
4. Patience to allow the philosophy to become actualized through gradual program development recognizing the individuality of the teachers' learning as well as the child's.

5. Tolerance of flexibility—even confusion at times—in regard to schedules, routines, use of space, etc.

The New York State Education Department, although swamped with work, will give top priority to provision of leadership for school districts throughout the state to do the careful planning necessary to develop sound programs using the open education approach. The response represented in the 2,000 attendants at a recent open education conference sponsored by the department is indication that districts in the state are ready to move and cooperate in securing consultant services and supporting one another through ongoing dialogues between individuals and staffs. A number of colleges, teacher training institutes, boards of cooperative educational services organizations, and regional centers are interested in providing help on a regional basis to individual schools or districts. Possibilities of working out exchange programs permitting American teachers to work in British schools and British teachers to share their experience with us are being investigated by a number of districts, in addition to plans for summer workshop activities under the leadership of visiting British educators.

Ideally, open education should start with the young child and permeate his entire career. The major thrust of local school districts might be to introduce this concept in the schooling of the 5s to 7s. It is here that the child is most ready for the freewheeling, episodic program of the open classroom since he may not have been so conditioned to traditional conforming. However, the philosophy and theory of open education are eminently appropriate for other age levels.

In approaching open education, especially with the older children, it is not necessary that the whole school or the whole day be immediately converted to this process. Rather the schools might move a piece at a time so that children and teachers could grow with the change. It takes a great deal of learning on the part of all involved, administrators, teachers, parents, and children, before open education can become a successful venture. Yet, even in the most traditional school building, on every level from prekindergarten through high school and college, this philosophy can help each of our youngsters become more of what he is capable of being.

In other words, we must make haste slowly. Administrators must redefine their role. Teachers need to be retrained. Parents need to be involved.

A few final comments:

1. Open education will flourish best when there is maximum decentralization of authority to local school building principals from central headquarters and when there is more independence for the individual school to do its own thing (given that the principal and the staff are capable of handling the increased freedom granted and assuming some means of central control over quality). I think it is now clear that the individual school is the crucial unit for change and that the principal is the key agent of change. If our schools are to change and to reform, it will

no longer be satisfactory for individual schools to receive per diem wisdom dished out from some centralized source.

2. It is probable that open education will flourish best and most promptly in smaller, rather than bigger, schools.

3. Having advisers from outside the school system working directly with teachers in implementing the open classroom is very important. Technical assistance from the State Education Department, roving specialists from the boards of cooperative educational services, use of the state-sponsored in-service regional training network, or assistance from Title III regional supplementary centers are sources of support.

In closing, let me draw upon the thinking of Roland Barth and Charles Rathbone:

> Open Education is a way of thinking about children and learning. It is characterized by openness and trust; by spatial openness of doors and rooms; by openness of time to release and serve children, not to constrain, prescribe and master them. The curriculum is open to significant choice by adults and children as a function of the needs and interests of each child at each moment. Open Education is characterized by an openness of self. Persons are openly sensitive to and supportive of other persons— not closed off by anxiety, threat, custom and role. Administrators are open to initiatives on the part of teachers; teachers are open to the possibilities inherent in children; children are open to the possibilities inherent in other children, in materials, in themselves.
>
> In short, Open Education implies an environment in which the possibilities for exploration and learning of self and of the world are unobstructed.[3]

[1] Joseph Featherstone, "The Primary School—Revolution in Britain," *New Republic*, August 19, September 2, September 9, 1967.

[2] *A Plan for Continuing Growth* (Newton, Mass.: Education Development Center, Follow Through Program, 1969).

[3] "Informal Education—the Open School: A Way of Thinking About Children, Learning, Knowledge," *Center Forum*, July 1969.

After Deschooling, What?

Ivan Illich

Schools are in crisis, and so are the people who attend them. The former is a crisis in a political institution; the latter is a crisis of political attitudes. This second crisis, the crisis of personal growth, can be dealt with only if understood as distinct from, though related to, the crisis of the school.

Schools have lost their unquestioned claim to educational legitimacy. Most of their critics still demand a painful and radical reform of the school,

FROM Vol. 2, No. 3 (September–October 1971), pp. 5–13 of *Social Policy*, published by Social Policy Corporation, New York, New York 10010. © Social Policy.

but a quickly expanding minority will not stand for anything short of the prohibition of compulsory attendance and the disqualification of academic certificates. Controversy between partisans of renewal and partisans of disestablishment will soon come to a head.

As attention focuses on the school, however, we can be easily distracted from a much deeper concern: the manner in which learning is to be viewed. Will people continue to treat learning as a commodity—a commodity that could be more efficiently produced and consumed by greater numbers of people if new institutional arrangements were established? Or shall we set up only those institutional arrangements that protect the autonomy of the learner—his private initiative to decide what he will learn and his inalienable right to learn what he likes rather than what is useful to somebody else? We must choose between more efficient education of people fit for an increasingly efficient society and a new society in which education ceases to be the task of some special agency.

SCHOOLS REPRODUCE SOCIETY

All over the world schools are organized enterprises designed to reproduce the established order, whether this order is called revolutionary, conservative, or evolutionary. Everywhere the loss of pedagogical credibility and the resistance to schools provide a fundamental option: shall this crisis be dealt with as a problem that can, and must, be solved by substituting new devices for school and readjusting the existing power structure to fit these devices? Or shall this crisis force a society to face the structural contradictions inherent in the politics and economics of any society that reproduces itself through the industrial process?

In the United States and Canada huge investments in schooling only serve to make institutional contradictions more evident. Experts warn us: Charles Silberman's report to the Carnegie Commission, published as *Crisis in the Classroom,* has become a best seller. It appeals to a large public because of its well-documented indictment of the system—in the light of which his attempts to save the school by patching up its most obvious faults pall into insignificance. The Wright Commission, in Ontario, had to report to its government sponsors that postsecondary education is inevitably and without remedy taxing the poor disproportionately for an education that will always be enjoyed mainly by the rich. Experience confirms these warnings: Students and teachers drop out; free schools come and go. Political control of schools replaces bond issues on the platforms of school board candidates, and—as recently happened in Berkeley—advocates of grassroots control are elected to the board.

On March 8, 1971, Chief Justice Warren E. Burger delivered the unanimous opinion of the court in the case of *Griggs v. Duke Power Co.* Interpreting the intent of Congress in the equal opportunity section of the 1964 Civil Rights Act, the Burger Court ruled that any school degree or any test given prospective employees must "measure the man for the job," not "the man in the abstract." The burden for proving that educational requirements are a "reasonable measure of job performance" rests with the employer. In this decision, the court ruled only on the use of tests and diplomas as means of racial discrimination, but the logic of the Chief Justice's argument applies to any use of an educational pedigree as a prerequisite for employment. "The Great Train Robbery" so effectively exposed by Ivar Berg must now face challenge from congeries of pupils, employers, and taxpayers.

In poor countries schools rationalize economic lag. The majority of citizens are excluded from the scarce modern means of production and consumption, but long to enter the economy by way of the school door. And the liberal institution of compulsory schooling permits the well-schooled to impute to the lagging consumer of knowledge the guilt for holding a certificate of lower denomination, thereby rationalizing through a rhetorical populism that is becoming increasingly hard to square with the facts.

Upon seizing power, the military junta in Peru immediately decided to suspend further expenditures on free public school. They reasoned that since a third of the public budget could not provide one full year of decent schooling for all, the available tax receipts could better be spent on a type of educational resources that make them more nearly accessible to all citizens. The educational reform commission appointed by the junta could not fully carry out this decision because of pressures from the school teachers of the APRA, the Communists, and the Cardinal Archbishop of Lima. Now there will be two competing systems of public education in a country that cannot afford one. The resulting contradictions will confirm the original judgment of the junta.

For ten years Castro's Cuba has devoted great energies to rapid-growth popular education, relying on available manpower, without the usual respect for professional credentials. The initial spectacular successes of this campaign, especially in diminishing illiteracy, have been cited as evidence for the claim that the slow growth rate of other Latin American school systems is due to corruption, militarism, and a capitalist market economy. Yet, now, the hidden curriculum of hierarchical schooling is catching up with Fidel and his attempt to school-produce the New Man. Even when students spend half the year in the cane fields and fully subscribe to "fidelismo," the school trains every year a crop of knowledge consumers ready to move on to new levels of consumption. Also, Dr. Castro faces evidence that the school system will never turn out enough certified technical manpower. Those licensed graduates who do get the new jobs destroy, by their conservatism, the results obtained by noncertified cadres who muddled into their positions through on-the-job training. Teachers just cannot be blamed for the failures of a revolutionary government that insists on the institutional capitalization of manpower through a hidden curriculum guaranteed to produce a universal bourgeoisie.

This crisis is epochal. We are witnessing the end of the age of schooling.

School has lost the power, which reigned supreme during the first half of this century, to blind its participants to the divergence between the egalitarian myth its rhetoric serves and the rationalization of a stratified society its certificates produce. The loss of legitimacy of the schooling process as a means of determining competence, as a measure of social value, and as an agent of equality threatens all political systems that rely on schools as the means of reproducing themselves.

School is the initiation ritual to a society oriented toward the progressive consumption of increasingly less tangible and more expensive services, a society that relies on worldwide standards, large-scale and long-term planning, constant obsolescence through the built-in ethos of never-ending improvements: the constant translation of new needs into specific demands for the consumption of new satisfactions. This society is proving itself unworkable.

SUPERFICIAL SOLUTIONS

Since the crisis in schooling is symptomatic of a deeper crisis of modern industrial society, it is important that the critics of schooling avoid superficial solutions. Inadequate analysis of the nature of schooling only postpones the facing of deeper issues. But most criticism of the schools is pedagogical, political, or technological. The criticism of the educator is leveled at what is taught and how it is taught. The curriculum is outdated, so we have courses on African culture, on North American imperialism, on Women's Liberation, on food and nutrition. Passive learning is old-fashioned, so we have increased student participation, both in the classroom and in the planning of curriculum. School buildings are ugly, so we have new learning environments. There is concern for the development of human sensitivity, so group therapy methods are imported into the classroom.

Another important set of critics is involved with the politics of urban school administration. They feel that the poor could run their schools better than a centralized bureaucracy that is oblivious to the problems of the dispossessed. Black parents are enlisted to replace white teachers in the motivation of their children to make time and find the will to learn.

Still other critics emphasize that schools make inefficient use of modern technology. They would either electrify the classroom or replace schools with computerized learning centers. If they follow McLuhan, they would replace blackboards and textbooks with multimedia happenings; if they follow Skinner, they would compete with the classical teacher and sell economy packages of measurable behavioral modifications to cost-conscious school boards.

I believe all these critics miss the point, because they fail to attend to what I have elsewhere called the ritual aspects of schooling—what I here propose to call the "hidden curriculum," the structure underlying what has been called the certification effect. Others have used this phrase to refer to the environmental curriculum of the ghetto street or the suburban lawn, which the teacher's curriculum either reinforces or vainly attempts to replace. I am using the term "hidden curriculum" to refer to the structure of schooling as opposed to what happens in school, in the same way that linguists distinguish between the structure of a language and the use the speaker makes of it.

THE REAL HIDDEN CURRICULUM

The traditional hidden curriculum of school demands that people of a certain age assemble in groups of about thirty under the authority of a professional teacher for from five hundred to a thousand times a year. It does not matter if the teacher is authoritarian so long as it is the teacher's authority that counts; it does not matter if all meetings occur in the same place so long as they are somehow understood as attendance. The hidden curriculum of school requires—whether by law or by fact—that a citizen accumulate a minimum quantum of school years in order to obtain his civil rights.

The hidden curriculum of school has been legislated in all the united nations from Afghanistan to Zambia. It is common to the United States and the Soviet Union, to rich nations and poor, to electoral and dictatorial regimes. Whatever the ideologies and techniques explicitly transmitted in their school systems, all these nations assume that political and economic development depend on further investment in schooling.

The hidden curriculum teaches all children that economically valuable knowledge is the result of professional teaching and that social entitlements depend on the rank achieved in a bureaucratic process. The hidden curriculum transforms the explicit curriculum into a commodity and makes its acquisition the securest form of wealth. Knowledge certificates—unlike property rights, corporate stock, or family inheritance—are free from challenge. They withstand sudden changes of fortune. They convert into guaranteed privilege. That high accumulation of knowledge should convert to high personal consumption might be challenged in North Vietnam or Cuba, but school is universally accepted as the avenue to greater power, to increased legitimacy as a producer, and to further learning resources.

For all its vices, school cannot be simply and rashly eliminated; in the present situation it performs certain important negative functions. The hidden curriculum, unconsciously accepted by the liberal pedagogue, frustrates his conscious liberal aims, because it is inherently inconsistent with them. But, on the other hand, it also prevents the take-over of education by the programmed instruction of behavioral technologists. While the hidden curriculum makes social role depend on the process of acquiring knowledge, thus legitimizing stratification, it also ties the learning process to full-time attendance, thus illegitimizing the educational entrepreneur. If the school continues to lose its educational and political legitimacy, while knowledge is still conceived as a commodity, we will certainly face the emergence of a therapeutic Big Brother.

The translation of the need for learning into the demand for schooling and the conversion of the quality of growing up into the price tag of a professional treatment changes the meaning of "knowledge" from a term that designates intimacy, intercourse, and life experience into one that designates professionally packaged products, marketable entitlements, and abstract values. Schools have helped to foster this translation.

Of course schools are by no means the only institutions that pretend to translate knowledge, understanding, and wisdom into behavioral traits, the measurement of which is the key to prestige and power. Nor are schools the first institution used to convert knowledge to power. But it is in large measure the public school that has parlayed the consumption of knowledge into the exercise of privilege and power in a society in which this function coincided with the legitimate aspirations of those members of the lower middle classes for whom schools provided access to the professions.

Expanding the Concept of Alienation

Since the nineteenth century, we have become accustomed to the claim that man in a capitalist economy is alienated from his labor, that he cannot enjoy it, and that he is deprived of its fruits by those who own the tools of production. Most countries that officially subscribe to Marxist ideology have had only limited success in changing this exploitation, and then usually by shifting its benefits from the owners to the New Class and from the living generation to the members of the future nation-state.

The concept of alienation cannot help us understand the present crisis unless it is applied not only to the purposeful and productive use of human endeavor but also to the use made of men as the recipients of professional treatments. An expanded understanding of alienation would enable us to see that in a service-centered economy man is estranged from what he can "do" as well as from what he can "make," that he has delivered his mind and heart over to therapeutic treatment even more completely than he has sold the fruits of his labor.

Schools have alienated man from his learning. He does not enjoy going to school. If he is poor he does not get the reputed benefits; if he does all that is asked of him, he finds his security constantly threatened by more recent graduates; if he is sensitive, he feels deep conflicts between what is and what is supposed to be. He does not trust his own judgment, and even if he resents the judgment of the educator, he is condemned to accept it and to believe that he cannot change reality. The converging crisis of ritual schooling and of acquisitive knowledge raises the deeper issue of the tolerability of life in an alienated society. If we formulate principles for alternative institutional arrangements and an alternative emphasis in the conception of learning, we will also be suggesting principles for a radically alternative political and economic organization.

Just as the structure of one's native language can be grasped only after he has begun to feel at ease in another tongue, so the fact that the hidden curriculum of schooling has moved out of the blind spot of social analysis indicates that alternative forms of social initiation are beginning to emerge and are permitting some of us to see things from a new perspective. Today it is relatively easy to get wide agreement on the fact that gratuitous, compulsory schooling is contrary to the political self-interest of an enlightened majority. School has become pedagogically indefensible as an instrument of universal education. It no longer even fits the needs of the seductive salesman of programmed learning. Proponents of recorded, filmed, and computerized instruction used to court the schoolmen as business prospects; now they are itching to do the job on their own.

As more and more sectors of society become dissatisfied with school and conscious of its hidden curriculum, increasingly large concessions are made to translate their demands into needs that can be served by the system—and thus disarm their dissent. As the hidden curriculum moves out of the darkness and into the twilight of our awareness, phrases such as the "deschooling of society" and the "disestablishment of schools" become instant slogans. I do not think these phrases were used before last year. This year they have become, in some circles, the badge and criterion of the new orthodoxy. Recently I talked by amplified telephone to students in a seminar on deschooling at the Ohio State University College of Education. Everett Reimer's book on deschooling became a popular college text even before it was commercially published. But this is urgently important: Unless the radical critics of school are not only ready to embrace the deschooling slogan but also prepared to reject the current view that learning and growing up can be adequately explained as a process of programming, and the current vision of social justice based on it—more obligatory consumption for everybody—we may face the charge of having provoked the last of the missed revolutions.

SCHOOLS ARE TOO EASY TARGETS

The current crisis has made it easy to attack schools. Schools, after all, are authoritarian and rigid; they do produce both conformity and conflict; they do discriminate against the poor and disengage the privileged. These are not new facts, but it used to be a mark of some boldness to point them out. Now it takes a good deal of courage to defend schools. It has become fashionable to poke fun at alma mater, to take a potshot at the former sacred cow.

Once the vulnerability of schools has been exposed, it becomes easy to suggest remedies for the most outrageous abuses. The authoritarian rule of the classroom is not intrinsic to the notion of an extended confinement of children in schools. Free schools are practical alternatives; they can often be run more cheaply than ordinary schools. Since accountability already belongs to educational rhetoric, community control and performance contracting have become attractive and respectable political goals. Everyone wants education to be relevant to real life, so critics talk freely about push-ing back the classroom walls to the borders of our culture. Not only are alternatives more widely advocated, they are often at least partially im-plemented: experimental schools are financed by school boards; the hiring of certified teachers is decentralized; high school credit is given for appren-ticeship and college credit, for travel; computer games are given a trial run.

Most of the changes have some good effects: the experimental schools have fewer truants; parents have a greater feeling of participation in the decentralized districts; children who have been introduced to real jobs do turn out more competent. Yet all these alternatives operate within predictable limits, since they leave the hidden structure of schools intact. Free schools, which lead to further free schools in an unbroken chain of attendance, produce the mirage of freedom. Attendance as the result of seduction inculcates the need for specialized treatment more persuasively than reluctant attendance enforced by truant officers. Free school graduates are easily rendered impotent for life in a society that bears little resemblance to the protected gardens in which they have been cultivated. Community control of the lower levels of a system turns local school board members into pimps for the professional hookers who control the upper levels. Learning by doing is not worth much if doing has to be defined, by pro-fessional educators or by law, as socially valuable learning. The global village will be a global schoolhouse if teachers hold all the strings. It would be distinguishable in name only from a global madhouse run by social therapists or a global prison run by corporation wardens.

In a general way I have pointed out the dangers of a rash, uncritical disestablishment of school. More concretely, these dangers are exemplified by various kinds of co-option that change the hidden curriculum without changing the basic concepts of learning and of knowledge and their re-lationship to the freedom of the individual in society.

BENIGN INEQUALITY

The rash and uncritical disestablishment of school could lead to a free-for-all in the production and consumption of more vulgar learning, acquired for immediate utility or eventual prestige. The discrediting of school-pro-duced, complex, curricular packages would be an empty victory if there were no simultaneous disavowal of the very idea that knowledge is more valuable because it comes in certified packages and is acquired from some mythological knowledge-stock controlled by professional guardians. I believe that only actual participation constitutes socially valuable learning, a par-ticipation by the learner in every stage of the learning process, including not only a free choice of what is to be learned and how it is to be learned but also a free determination by each learner of his own reason for living and learning—the part that his knowledge is to play in his life.

Social control in an apparently deschooled society could be more subtle and more numbing than in the present society, in which many people at least experience a feeling of release on the last day of school. More intimate forms of manipulation are already common, as the amount learned through the media exceeds the amount learned through personal contact in and out of school. Learning from programmed information always hides reality behind a screen.

Let me illustrate the paralyzing effects of programmed information by a perhaps shocking example. The tolerance of the American people to United States atrocities in Vietnam is much higher than the tolerance of the German people to German atrocities on the front, in occupied territories, and in extermination camps during World War II. It was a political crime for Germans to discuss the atrocities committed by Germans. The presentation of U.S. atrocities on network television is considered an educational service. Certainly the population of the United States is much better informed about the crimes committed by its troops in a colonial war than were the Germans about the crimes committed by its SS within the territory of the Reich. To get information on atrocities in Germany meant that one had to take a great risk; in the United States the same information is channeled into one's living room. This does not mean, however, that the Germans were any less aware that their government was engaged in cruel and massive crime than are contemporary Americans. In fact, it can be argued that the Germans were *more* aware precisely because they were not psychically overwhelmed with packaged information about killing and torture, because they were not drugged into accepting that everything is possible, because they were not vaccinated against reality by having it fed to them as decomposed "bits" on a screen.

The consumer of precooked knowledge learns to react to knowledge he has acquired rather than to the reality from which a team of experts has abstracted it. If access to reality is always controlled by a therapist and if the learner accepts this control as natural, his entire worldview becomes hygienic and neutral; he becomes politically impotent. He becomes impotent to know in the sense of the Hebrew word *jdh*, which means intercourse penetrating the nakedness of being and reality, because the reality for which he can accept responsibility is hidden from him under the scales of assorted information he has accumulated.

The uncritical disestablishment of school could also lead to new performance criteria for preferential employment and promotion and, most importantly, for privileged access to tools. Our present scale of "general" ability, competence, and trustworthiness for role assignment is calibrated by tolerance to high doses of schooling. It is established by teachers and accepted by many as rational and benevolent. New devices could be developed, and new rationales found, both more insidious than school grading and equally effective in justifying social stratification and the accumulation of privilege and power.

Participation in military, bureaucratic, or political activities or status

in a party could provide a pedigree just as transferable to other institutions
as the pedigree of grandparents in an aristocratic society, standing within
the Church in medieval society, or age at graduation in a schooled society.
General tests of attitudes, intelligence, or mechanical ability could be
standardized according to criteria other than those of the schoolmaster. They
could reflect the ideal levels of professional treatment espoused by psychiatrist, ideologue, or bureaucrat. Academic criteria are already suspect.
The Center for Urban Studies of Columbia University has shown that
there is less correlation between specialized education and job performance
in specialized fields than there is between specialized education and the
resulting income, prestige, and administrative power. Nonacademic criteria
are already proposed. From the urban ghetto in the United States to the
villages of China, revolutionary groups try to prove that ideology and
militancy are types of "learning" that convert more suitably into political
and economic power than scholastic curricula. Unless we guarantee that
job relevance is the only acceptable criterion for employment, promotion,
or access to tools, thus ruling out not only schools but all other ritual
screening, then deschooling means driving out the devil with Beelzebub.

THE NEED FOR POLITICAL OBJECTIVES

The search for a radical alternative to the school system itself will be
of little avail unless it finds expression in precise political demands: the
demand for the disestablishment of school in the broadest sense and the
correlative guarantee of freedom for education. This means legal protections, a political program, and principles for the construction of institutional
arrangements that are the inverse of school. Schools cannot be disestablished
without the total prohibition of legislated attendance, the proscription
of any discrimination on the basis of prior attendance, and the transfer of
control over tax funds from benevolent institutions to the individual person. Even these actions, however, do not guarantee freedom of education
unless they are accompanied by positive recognition of each person's independence in the face of school and of any other device designed to compel
specific behavioral change or to measure man in the abstract rather than
to measure man for a concrete job.

Deschooling makes strange bedfellows. The ambiguity inherent in the
breakdown of schooling is manifested by the unholy alliance of groups that
can identify their vested interests with the disestablishment of school:
students, teachers, employers, opportunistic politicians, taxpayers, Supreme
Court justices. But this alliance becomes unholy, and this bedfellowship
more than strange, if it is based only on the recognition that schools are
inefficient tools for the production and consumption of education and that
some other form of mutual exploitation would be more satisfactory.

We can disestablish schools, or we can deschool culture. We can resolve provisionally some of the administrative problems of the knowledge

industry, or we can spell out the goals of political revolution in terms of educational postulates. The acid test of our response to the present crisis is our pinpointing of the responsibility for teaching and learning.

Schools have made teachers into administrators of programs of manpower capitalization through directed, planned, behavioral changes. In a schooled society, the ministrations of professional teachers become a first necessity that hooks pupils into unending consumption and dependence. Schools have made "learning" a specialized activity. Deschooling will be only a displacement of responsibility to other kinds of administration so long as teaching and learning remain sacred activities separate and estranged from fulfilling life. If schools were disestablished for the purpose of more efficient delivery of "knowledge" to more people, the alienation of men through client relationships with the new knowledge industry would just become global.

Deschooling must be the secularization of teaching and learning. It must involve a return of control to another, more amorphous set of institutions, and its perhaps less obvious representatives. The learner must be guaranteed his freedom without guaranteeing to society what learning he will acquire and hold as his own. Each man must be guaranteed privacy in learning, with the hope that he will assume the obligation of helping others to grow into uniqueness. Whoever takes the risk of teaching others must assume responsibility for the results, as must the student who exposes himself to the influence of a teacher; neither should shift guilt to sheltering institutions or laws. A schooled society must reassert the joy of conscious living over the capitalization of manpower.

THREE RADICAL DEMANDS

Any dialogue about knowledge is really a dialogue about the individual in society. An analysis of the present crisis of school leads one, then, to talk about the social structure necessary to facilitate learning, to encourage independence and interrelationship, and to overcome alienation. This kind of discourse is outside the usual range of educational concern. It leads, in fact, to the enunciation of specific political goals. These goals can be most sharply defined by distinguishing three general types of "intercourse" in which a person must engage if he would grow up.

Get at the facts, get access to the tools, and bear the responsibility for the limits within which either can be used. If a person is to grow up, he needs, in the first place, access to things, places, processes, events, and records. To guarantee such access is primarily a matter of unlocking the privileged storerooms to which they are presently consigned.

The poor child and the rich child are different partly because what is a secret for one is patent to the other. By turning knowledge into a commodity, we have learned to deal with it as with private property. The principle of private property is now used as the major rationale for declaring certain facts off limits to people without the proper pedigree. The first goal of a political program aimed at rendering the world educational is the abolition of the right to restrict access to teaching or learning. The right of private preserve is now claimed by individuals, but it is most effectively exercised and protected by corporations, bureaucracies, and nation-states. In fact, the abolition of this right is not consistent with the continuation of either the political or the professional structure of any modern nation. This means more than merely improving the distribution of teaching materials or providing financial entitlements for the purchase of educational objects. The abolition of secrets clearly transcends conventional proposals for educational reform, yet it is precisely from an educational point of view that the necessity of stating this broad—and perhaps unattainable—political goal is most clearly seen.

The learner also needs access to persons who can teach him the tricks of their trades or the rudiments of their skills. For the interested learner, it does not take much time to learn how to perform most skills or to play most roles. The best teacher of a skill is usually someone who is engaged in its useful exercise. We tend to forget these things in a society in which professional teachers monopolize initiation into all fields and disqualify unauthorized teaching in the community. An important political goal, then, is to provide incentives for the sharing of acquired skills.

The demand that skills be shared implies, of course, a much more radical vision of a desirable future. Access to skills is restricted not just by the monopoly of schools and unions over licensing: there is also the fact that the exercise of skills is tied to the use of scarce tools. Scientific knowledge is overwhelmingly incorporated into tools that are highly specialized and that must be used within complex structures set up for the "efficient" production of goods and services for which demand becomes general while supply remains scarce. Only a privileged few get the results of sophisticated medical research, and only a privileged few get to be doctors. A relatively small minority will travel on supersonic airplanes, and only a few pilots will know how to fly them.

The simplest way to state the alternatives to this trend toward specialization of needs and their satisfaction is in educational terms. It is a question of the desirable use of scientific knowledge. In order to facilitate more equal access to the benefits of science and to decrease alienation and unemployment, we must favor the incorporation of scientific knowledge into tools or components within the reach of a great majority of people.

Insight into the conditions necessary for the wider acquisition and use of skills permits us to define a fundamental characteristic of postindustrial socialism. It is of no use—indeed it is fraudulent—to promote public ownership of the tools of production in an industrial, bureaucratic society. Factories, highways, and heavy-duty trucks can be symbolically "owned" by all the people, as the Gross National Product and the Gross National Education are pursued in their name. But the specialized means of producing scarce goods and services cannot be *used* by the majority of people. Only tools that are cheap and simple enough to be accessible and usable by all people, tools that permit temporary association of those who want to use them for a specific occasion, tools that allow specific goals to emerge during their use—only such tools foster the recuperation of work and leisure now alienated through an industrial mode of production.

To recognize, from an educational point of view, the priority of guaranteeing access to tools and components whose simplicity and durability permit their use in a wide variety of creative enterprises is simultaneously to indicate the solution to the problem of unemployment. In an industrial society, unemployment is experienced as the sad inactivity of a man for whom there is nothing to make and who has "unlearned" what to do. Since there is little really useful work, the problem is usually "solved" by creating more jobs in service industries like the military, public administration, education, or social work. Educational considerations oblige me to recommend the substitution of the present mode of industrial production, which depends on a growing market for increasingly complex and obsolescent goods, by a mode of postindustrial production that depends on the demand for tools or components that are labor intensive and repair intensive, and whose complexity is strictly limited.

Science will be kept artificially arcane so long as its results are incorporated into technology at the service of professionals. If it were used to render possible a style of life in which each man could enjoy housing, healing, educating, moving, and entertaining himself, then scientists would try much harder to retranslate the discoveries made in a secret language into the normal language of everyday life.

SELF-EVIDENT EDUCATIONAL FREEDOMS

The level of education in any society can be gauged by the degree of effective access each of the members has to the facts and tools that—within this society—affect his life. We have seen that such access requires a radical denial of the right to secrecy of facts and complexity of tools on which contemporary technocracies found their privilege, which they, in turn, render immune by interpreting its use as a service to the majority. A satisfactory level of education in a technological society imposes important constraints on the use to which scientific knowledge is put. In fact, a technological society that provides conditions for men to recuperate personally (and not institutionally) the sense of potency to learn and to produce, which gives meaning to life, depends on restrictions that must be imposed on the technocrat who now controls both services and manufacture. Only an enlightened and powerful majority can impose such constraints.

If access to facts and use of tools constitute the two most obvious freedoms needed to provide educational opportunity, the ability to convoke peers to a meeting constitutes the one through which the learning by an individual is translated into political process—and political process, in turn, becomes conscious personal growth. Data and skills an individual might have acquired shape into exploratory, creative, open-ended, and personal meaning only when they are used in dialectic encounter. And this requires the guaranteed freedom for every individual to state, each day, the class of issue which he wants to discuss, the class of creative use of a skill in which he seeks a match—to make this bid known—and, within reason, to find the circumstances to meet with peers who join his class. The rights of free speech, free press, and free assembly have traditionally meant this freedom. Modern electronics, photo-offset, and computer techniques in principle have provided the hardware that can provide this freedom with a range undreamt of in the century of enlightenment. Unfortunately, the scientific know-how has been used mainly to increase the power and decrease the number of funnels through which the bureaucrats of education, politics, and information channel their quick-frozen TV dinners. But the same technology could be used to make peer-matching, meeting, and printing as available as the private conversation over the telephone is now.

On the other hand, those who are both dispossessed and disabused of the dream of joy via constantly increasing quanta of consumption need to define what constitutes a desirable society. Only then can the inversion of institutional arrangement here drafted be put into effect—and with it a technological society that values occupation, intensive work, and leisure over alienation through goods and services.

Alternative Systems of Education
JESSIE E. WRAY

I would say in a common way of putting things, that I am not an educator. I went to school in Mississippi only four months a year, and got all the school that they would give me. I worked hard at the school in Mississippi and when I got to school as a boy in the upper grades, I had to go outside to get wood to make the fires. I had three books that had to be distributed between three families. The education that I got came from the lumps and the bumps against the head that I got in the street. Sometimes I wouldn't change it for the world—I don't think I would change it for anything in the world. I am also the father of ten children.

The people that developed this community school are people like myself—parents. And we had an input of educators. I'll tell you how we use educators, and I mean in no slight way: we use them as we need them as consultants; and we discard them as we don't need them as consultants. And I mean this as no insult. When we set up the school boards

FROM Jessie E. Wray, "Alternative Systems of Education," *Integrated Education*, November–December, 1970, pp. 39–45.

through some persuasion of my own, I asked that the controlling interest of those school boards be made of parents, like myself, because many problems have to be answered. Many times if a lawyer or doctor is sitting next door to a parent that cannot read and write so well, this parent becomes withdrawn and won't express what he feels. So we wanted that kind of situation to be far away from our planning and our setting up of the school board, because we wanted our parents to be fully satisfied with what they planned and what they implemented. So, we brought in the educators and we needed consultants. And that's where the Federation came in. Its job is to bring in educators from all over the country to sit down and plan with our parents. And that's what we are all about.

The Community School has a fifteen-member board, of which nine members are parents, three are teachers and three are teenagers—young adults. Each school has its own say about how many members it wants to have serve on its school board. Some have seven, some have eleven— they all gave an odd number, but they have to plan their own curriculum. One thing the school has to do is become a fair-rated school, as we call it, completing a cycle. When the Archdiocese could no longer fund this school, we could do two things: we could just sit idly by and watch our kids go into the public system—which we didn't feel related to them, and naturally so—because it really didn't. Or, we could plan our own alternate system, which we did. And that's how the Community School came into being.

In planning the system we were very careful to see to it that the power of this school stayed in the autonomous school. The Federation itself is designed and set up with three members that are sent to the Federation from each school, which means that those three delegates must take orders from their own school, and take that order to the Federation, so that the Federation doesn't become another over-all body that will take control like the public system does, and get to the point where it doesn't relate to the localized community.

We call our school, actually, a service center. It becomes a service center. That building sits there to serve the community—we don't feel that our kids should come to school at 8 o'clock in the morning, it's ten or fifteen below zero and stand outside in the cold. If he comes to school at six o'clock in the morning, he should come in and if he feels that he wants to have his nose wiped, that should also be done.

We are going to open the schools as soon as money is available for mothers, who don't have the money to pay baby sitters in these high cost day care centers, to bring their babies by and go ahead to work. And it doesn't necessarily mean that the woman or the family has a child at Boniface school. The same thing will apply at night. When a poor family wants to go out for recreation and they hardly got enough money to buy bread and meat, they can't go out for recreation because they don't have the money to get a baby sitter. We intend to make that school serve that need.

We had a fund-raising thrust about a month ago, right around the local communities, and we got about $20,000 from people who paid their money in 50 cents and 25 cents and to show you what kind of impact we had —one old gentleman who lives around the school sent in $3.00 and he said, "This is my last money. I'm on pension and I'm on welfare, but I believe in what you're doing so here's my last $3.00." We also got baby sitter's money from a little girl who got the money from baby sitting. So this is the kind of impact that's gone into the community schools in Milwaukee.

Now we are running into rejection from the public schools because they feel, number one—they feel threatened. For the first time in the history of, I would say Milwaukee, we've begun to put apathy on the run in parents, because they've begun to feel a part of things. They can come and have their say in the school. They can sit and talk about setting their policies. They can run their policies. They can set up the structure. We set up our own curriculum. We hire our own teachers. And we talk about that teacher! If he isn't doing right, then we put him out, if he isn't right. So that's the system, as we're set up here. It is relevant, we feel, to what the community needs. And we try to make a few of the classes in each school open to parents of children that just don't give a doggone where their kids go. Because, somehow somebody's got to start reaching those children. And we feel it's our responsibility to bring these kids in, because in one way or another, society is going to have to deal with them.

Now the community schools in Milwaukee are running into the same kind of predicament the black man ran into. And, you know, when you go talking in so many of these conventions and meetings, we hear the rhetoric: "We know that we're treating you wrong, but that's where it starts." Yet, they aren't willing to do anything about it. The same thing is happening in the system that we've started here. As we talk to educators, we hear, "It's a beautiful plan," but that's where they leave us. Nobody is giving us the support we need. We have, I think, a proposal into just about everybody all over the country, and we've had people come in and study this plan. People from Washington—they've been out to study this alternate system. To this day, we don't have any funds available to us. We just had some people from Atlanta studying the system. We've had people in from Chicago, the Woodlawn Organization (TWO) in Chicago. From all over the country, they've been in to study what Milwaukee has started. And we find that the rejection that has been here is based on the fact that the people don't really support the public schools, but they don't have the guts to get up and say it.

If, in education, what they say is, "Why should we then support the system? A system that's not doing a good job and take on another system that is doing good?" The reason is, the bureaucracy is so thick you couldn't cut it with a knife, and you've never been able to do anything with it. So, since you know you can't do anything with it, let's make something relevant and maybe by some way we can influence this system. If you can't, at least we'll have helped some children.

So, we have 2,200 kids next fall that sit on the threshold of not having a school to go to. Number one, because we can't get funds for it. And, the city tells us—the Model Cities agencies which we're trying to get funds through—tells us (only we've been closed off by them) that we can send our kids to public schools. In the area where we would send our kids to they already are busing out 56 busloads of kids a day because the school's overcrowded. Now, when you have these kinds of situations at hand—I'll tell you something else—we're going to keep those schools open come hell or high water. We got to fight to keep those schools open.

It's people like myself—I went home from my job (we just had money to pay, incidentally, a coordinator for two weeks ago)—I went home from my regular job with a 41 cent paycheck, because my time was spent developing and working with teachers and working with people to develop this system. All of our teachers were dedicated enough to sign their contracts, knowing full well that there might not be any money. Everyone of them that signed have gotten offers to work as far away as Louisiana, because they've been and seen what's going on in Milwaukee. We control our schools completely, and we intend to keep it that way. So, the community schools in Milwaukee are working. All I ask you to do is help us keep it moving, because the system is working beautifully.

Addendum on the Federation of Independent Community Schools [1]

Beginning October 1, 1970, he was employed fulltime as Federation coordinator with funds from a federal Office of Economic Opportunity one-year research and development grant of $102,000. The Federation is to set up a Curriculum Resource and Development Center under the terms of the grant.

Community control of schools was first suggested four or five years ago when the Milwaukee Catholic Archdiocese could no longer fund parochial schools. In 1969, three of Milwaukee's innercity parochial elementaries banded together and became the Federation. St. Boniface became Boniface Community School; St. Francis, Francis C. S. and St. Gaul's Martin Luther King C. S. Now there are four others in the Federation: Bruce Guadalupe C. S.; Harembee C. S. (Swahili for all together); Michael C. S. and Leo Community School.

The total enrollment in the seven Federation schools is 2,200 children

---

[1] Following is information gained from Mr. Wray by Integrated Education: RACE AND SCHOOLS on Milwaukee's Federation of Independent Community Schools.

taught by 90 teachers. Boniface is the only school with an all-black student body but its faculty is integrated. Francis is next, 85 per cent black, 15 per cent Spanish speaking; Harembee and King are 80 per cent black; Guadalupe is 90 per cent Spanish speaking, the rest white and black; Leo, 60 per cent white and Michael, 50 per cent white. All the schools have a waiting list of black and white children, some of the latter from suburbia. Applications are dated when received and children admitted on a first come, first serve basis. Wray explained the system in answer to a query about Federation views on integration. If integration eventuated from this admissions policy, so be it, he seemed to say, and no more.

The seven schools charge tuition based on family income and no child is refused for lack of money. A physician's family may pay as much as $500 but per family tuition is usually less—the Boniface average is $250—some families paying as little as $50. The amount is set by the local school board.

Each school has an autonomous board chosen in open election by the community. The size of the boards ranges from five to 15 persons, mostly parents, and all boards are integrated racially. The Boniface board, for instance, is composed of nine parents, three teachers, three teenagers and has three white members. Board elections are advertised in the newspapers and an individual representing a minority point of view who is not slated for election may offer his name and have it on the ballot, safeguarding dissident views.

Some nuns still teach in the schools but there is no longer any religious instruction during school hours. Nuns work for as little as $25 monthly and the community school board pays the entire amount.

At present, the Archdiocese provides no financial support although efforts are under way to encourage this. No federal educational funds are received either, except for Title I support of Head Start programs at a few schools.

Each school raises much of its own funds, through public meetings, auctions, raffles, etc. Federation leaders hope to add a high school to the group within a year or two.

Mississippi's Freedom Schools: The Politics of Education

FLORENCE HOWE

All education is political. In Mississippi, at least, it is impossible to find this trite. There, it is inescapable that the educational system furthers the political, that the kind of learning the individual gets depends completely upon the role he is supposed to live.

REPRINTED by permission from *Harvard Educational Review*, 35 (Spring 1965), 144–60. Copyright © 1965 by President and Fellows of *Harvard* College.

A thirteen-year-old Jackson, Mississippi, girl, sitting within a Freedom School circle this summer, described the events of the last day, the previous year, in her public (segregated) junior high school. Students in a high school nearby had asked the students in "Shirley's" school to join them in a protest-demonstration against local school conditions and procedures. "Shirley's" (Negro) teacher had threatened the class with failure for the year, should they walk out to join the demonstrators. Most of the class was intimidated, but not "Shirley" and several of her friends. She left, she said, because she knew that she had not failed for the year, she knew she had earned good grades, and she knew that it was right to join the demonstrators. As she and her friends reached the downstairs floor, they met, head on, the (Negro) principal "who was coming at us with a board." They turned, fled, back-tracked through the cafeteria and out the back way to join the demonstrators.

The Negro school child in Mississippi, like "Shirley," associates the school he attends, in spite of the color of his teachers and principal, with the white world outside him—the police, the White Citizens' Council, the mayor or sheriff, the governor of his state. And the school child's instinctive vision is perfectly correct. His teachers are either timid and quiescently part of the system or they are actively extra-punitive, dictatorial, hostile, vengeful, or worse. Sometimes his teachers are badly-trained, misinformed, but even when they know just that, they remain fearfully bound to the system that made them. The teacher with the ruler or iron chain or whip is himself caught in a power structure that allows him to teach only by rote to rote-learners. You learn this, he says, and you too can learn to get along. Get used to the violence, get used to being struck, get used to taking orders, for that is the way life is on the outside. You too can learn to follow the rules and get to sit up here, ruler in hand, ready to strike out at anything out of line.

It is possible to sympathize with the middle-class Negro teacher caught between his own desire to rise from the poverty around him and his fear of the white power structure that controls his ability to rise. For the Negro teacher and his Negro principal are directed by white school superintendents, themselves under the direction of other white political forces. In Negro schools, the intercom is used by the principal to intimidate and harass the teacher. The principal, in turn, is harassed by others. And only the "Shirley," finally, is able to stand up and sing, with her friends and associates in Freedom Schools:

> Before I'll be a slave
> I'll be buried in my grave
> And go home to my Lord and be free.

If the official public school system of Mississippi is geared and oiled to operate efficiently for the status quo, it is no wonder, then, that the civil rights movement should have conceived of the Freedom School. But would children for whom a school was an unpleasant training ground for a repressive society come, voluntarily, even to a "Freedom" school? Of course, voluntarily was the first cue. No one had to come, and once there, no "attendance" was taken. You came if you wanted to and you stayed if you were interested and you left if you felt like leaving. Your teacher, moreover, was "Tom" or "Leo" or "Gene," who shook your hand, called you by your first name, and said how glad he was to meet you. In your "class," your teacher sat with you in a circle, and soon you got the idea that you could say what you thought and that no one, least of all the teacher, would laugh at you or strike you. Soon, too, you got the idea that you might disagree with your teacher, white or black, and get a respectful hearing, that your teacher was really interested in what *you* thought or felt. Soon you were forgetting about skin colors altogether and thinking about ideas or feelings, about people and events.

As educators, we live in a fool's paradise, or worse in a knave's, if we are unaware that when we are teaching *something* to anyone we are also teaching *everything* to that same anyone. When we say we are teaching mathematics to Freddy, we also must admit that we are teaching Freddy what kind of person we are, how we live in the kind of world we control (or the kind of world that controls us), and how he can grow up to be one of the controllers or controlled. Teaching, we become, as so many people have said, a model for Freddy to learn from, quite apart from the mathematics or French or history we may be teaching him. And sometimes we are very "good" models. Sometimes, like "good" parents or "good" political leaders, we teach Freddy to love his neighbors, to honor honesty and integrity, to value the means as well as the ends, to abstain from using and controlling and killing human life. But sometimes we are not so inclined. Sometimes, at our worst, we educators resemble tyrants.

The idea of the Freedom School turns upside down particularly effectively the conventions of many public school systems that have to do with the role of the teacher. The teacher is not to be an omnipotent, aristocratic dictator, a substitute for the domineering parent or the paternalistic state. He is not to stand before rows of students, simply pouring pre-digested, pre-censored information into their brains. The Freedom School teacher is, in fact, to be present not simply to teach, but rather *to learn with* the students. In the democratic and creative sense that Wordsworth understood when he described the poet as "a man among men," the Freedom School teacher is a student among students. He does not have all the answers; his creativity is his ability to communicate with his students, to listen to them as much as they listen to him. The vitality of the teacher, as Freedom Schools would have it, lies in the student's and the teacher's mutual apprehension of life. A Freedom School teacher knows that education is the *drawing out* not of blood from stones, but rather of experience and observation from human beings. He knows that a thirteen year old who has survived his years in Mississippi understands, however fearfully or inarticulately, a great deal about the world he has survived in. The Freedom School teacher is there not as professional manipulator, but as concerned questioner—who really wants to hear what his companions will say, who really wants, himself, to be led by it. And thus he can turn the key to help the student break through the door that confines him—and all without recourse to the same means, authoritarianism, repression, violence, that have kept him locked in.

For much of the month of August, I coordinated and taught in one of Jackson, Mississippi's nine Freedom Schools. Opened on the fifth of August, these were in addition to the more than forty others that functioned through the summer in more than twenty different towns. Like most of the schools around the state, mine was located in the basement of a church. The basement room was acoustically difficult for a single voice and yet many voices together filled it uncomfortably. How to get attention, even briefly for announcements or for the start of some activity, perhaps the breaking up of the group into small discussion units? On the second day, when my voice had begun to hurt and when clapping my hands had begun to seem in-effectual, I hit accidentally upon the Quakerly method of raising your right hand. The children saw me standing before them, my right hand raised, and for communication's sake, my left index finger against my lips. They began to nudge one another, to raise their own hands, and to place their own fingers on their lips. And very quickly, the room grew quiet. I said, "All hands down," and delighted that the method had worked, added, "Isn't this a lovely way to get silence?" Of course the children responded all together to me and to each other, and we had to begin all over again, right hands raised. But the method did work.

Also on one of the very first days, in the hot afternoon, with the teachers uncomfortable because they had had no lunch, and the children restless because we had not yet solved the problem of outdoor play space, two little boys began to fight. They were small enough so that I could forcibly separate them, but even in the midst of my hot, hungry exasperation, I had a vision of other fights and bigger boys whom I would be unable to pull apart. And from somewhere came the words: "Now, look here, we have few rules in this school, but we do have one important one and that is we do not hit each other—we talk. Understand? We talk here. This is a school for talking. Whenever you feel like hitting someone, remember to talk instead." The children looked puzzled and I said it all again. And then I sat down—in the midst of chaos—to talk with the two little boys about their fight. There were more fights in the next several days, but my words had begun to spread so that some of the older children were repeating them to the younger ones. And while we were never entirely free from an occasional blow—it was virtually impossible, for example, to keep older brothers from "punishing" their younger siblings—there were few or no fights after the first week.

The Greater Blair Street AME Zion Church, under the direction of Reverend R. M. Richmond, gave us not only shelter and equipment but most of all moral support and friendly protection. We drew our students, regardless of church membership, from the neighborhood. The families in a six to ten block radius ranged from lower-middle class to very poor (incomes from close to nothing to four thousand). The people in the neighborhood, like most of Jackson, were nervous about the arriving Freedom School teachers and were especially loathe to give us housing, for that would signify open support. Reverend Richmond convinced the people next door to give their empty room to the two male teachers. They, Gene Gogol and Tom Timberg, in the company of friendly students-to-be, had been canvassing the neighborhood during the time I was spending getting acquainted with the minister. When they reported back that they had had several offers of spare cots that could be moved elsewhere as well as of food—signs, of course, of a desire to help but without the attendant danger of housing a summer volunteer—we were able to make arrangements to move the beds into the empty room in the house next door to the church.

Our first impressions of the community were not incorrect: the parents continued to be cautious. With few exceptions, we had no contact with parents. But the children, of course, were different. They turned up, they turned out, they were willing to do anything, to go anywhere with us.

As Staughton Lynd, professor of history at Yale and summer director of all Freedom Schools in Mississippi, said, it was "a political decision for any parent to let his child come to a Freedom School." And many parents, in Jackson at least, avoided making that decision. I had assumed that parents knew that their children were attending Freedom School—until the day when I took up the question of sending a representative from our school to the state-wide Freedom School convention in Meridian. Expenses would be paid and the weekend program would be entertaining; I felt certain, that morning, that it would be difficult choosing the one delegate we were allowed to represent us. But to my surprise no one was willing to make a nomination—it was as if they all understood something I did not. I asked for volunteers and got no response again. Then I asked a thirteen year old girl, who had been particularly articulate the day before in a discussion, whether she would like to go. She said, first, only an abrupt "No," but when questioned in disbelieving tones, she admitted to, "Yes, but I can't."

"But why not, then? All your expenses would be paid, and you know you'd enjoy it."

She finally said that her father would not allow her to go, that he disapproved of her association with "the movement" in general, and that he did not approve even of her attending Freedom School. She was deliberately vague about whether or not he knew she was attending. When I asked whether it would help if I went to see him, she first laughed and then urged me most seriously not to. The story repeated itself, with certain variations, around the room.

Two young mothers, both of them relatively new to the neighborhood, were sympathetic enough to the movement and interested enough to issue invitations to us. The mother of a six year old, who sent her daughter to Freedom School, sent word also that she would like to see "the teachers" after school, at which point she invited all of us to a hot dinner the following afternoon at three. Later, she asked to be included in our evening activities. Another mother of a teen-ager, whose own family disapproved of the student's attending Freedom School, also sent for the teachers, whom she then invited to accompany her to a jazz concert. Later, this mother held a party for the departing teachers and announced her willingness to be of service to Freedom Schools in the future.

Freedom Schools were planned originally with high school students in mind. In most places around the state, when Freedom Schools opened, *all* children turned up, regardless of publicity about high school students. Eventually, around the state, community centers were founded, first to take care of the younger children, later to function in ways that Freedom School could not or would not. When we opened our Blair Street doors on Wednesday, August 5, at eight A.M., "children," ages three to twenty-three, began to arrive. And of course we turned no one away. They came in twos and threes, sometimes several from a family, the teen-agers holding the hands of their younger brothers and sisters. Fifty-one students arrived throughout that first day and fifty more during the next several days. Some stayed awhile ånd left, never to appear again. Others stayed that day and came every day thereafter. Some came and disappeared, and then came again to stay to the end.

Nearly half of any total number of children present at the Blair Street School were under the age of ten. For these children we ran a combined school and community center in one of the two basement rooms of the church. Luckily, on the day before school had opened, I had met Leo Reese, a magically personable reading specialist from Gary, Indiana, the father of eleven children, who had volunteered to spend one week in Jackson. Leo, a native Mississippian and a Negro, had been born and raised in Pascagoula, on the Gulf. In the few days that Leo was present, he organized a program for the younger children, and because of his skills, freed three of the four assigned teachers for work with the older students. Later, after Leo had gone, two young women, Shirley Logan, a Jacksonian and a recent college graduate, and her cousin from Chicago, Superior Walker, came to the Blair Street School for a visit and stayed for two weeks to carry on the program with the younger children.

Mornings at Freedom School began slowly without opening bells. On some days we sang freedom songs until the group collected. On one day, August 6, Hiroshima Day, I told the students about what had happened nineteen years ago. On another day, I read from Langston Hughes' poems and then listened to reactions from the students. By nine-thirty, we were usually numerous enough to break into smaller discussion groups. Those children under ten went off to their room, generally for the rest of the day, unless there was to be a special activity in the afternoon. The older students separated sometimes into several age groups for a discussion that occupied most of the morning. The Citizenship Curriculum, about which I shall have more to say later, is the core of the program shared by all Freedom Schools in Mississippi. There was usually time, an hour before lunch and one after, for two hours of "electives." Negro history, chemistry, biology, English, French, and typing were the subjects settled on by the groups' desires and their teachers' abilities.

The afternoons were particularly hot, and more and more frequent were the noisy visits to the drinking fountain and the lavatories at the back of the church. There was no outdoor play space, but, eventually, teachers began to take groups of students to the playground of a nearby Catholic school that the sisters allowed us to use. One of the older boys organized a softball team and both boys and girls were eager to play ball regardless of the heat. Late in the afternoon (called "evening" in Mississippi) some of the teachers and students joined the regular COFO precinct workers for voter registration work.

The best afternoons at Blair Street were those filled with special events. On opening day, for example, Pete Seeger arrived at one-thirty in the afternoon to give us a private concert. With the whole school present, the very littlest ones asleep in any arms that would hold them, Pete talked first of his recent visit to twenty-seven countries around the world. He told us that all children were the same the world over and that music was a language that flew easily over even the highest walls. He demonstrated his statements by playing and singing Indian, African, Chinese, and Polynesian songs, in each instance allowing the rhythms to illustrate the emotion before offering a translation of the words. "Isn't this a happy song," he said, after singing, in African dialect, "Everybody Loves Saturday Night." He taught the children to sing the foreign words of several songs, and though we didn't know it then, that was the high moment for them. The Blair Street students had no idea that Pete was a famous man, but they wanted to hear more of him and happily turned up that evening to be transported across town to Anderson Chapel where Pete Seeger sang for a packed and overflowing house until his voice gave out.

Films were also a good afternoon activity. On the day we showed the full-length *Oliver Twist* to an audience of more than one hundred, I heard one boy of ten mutter to himself about Oliver, "He sho' is white, but he's a slave just the same." The film ran too late in the afternoon for discussion, but the following morning was filled with questions and talk about child labor. Another group of films were part of a special, state-wide program arranged by Paul Lauter, a professor of English at Smith College. All bearing upon the connections among the struggle for civil rights, non-violence, and the need for world peace, the four films were used by Paul to spark discussions. Two of these films were documentaries, one about Gandhi, the other about the Montgomery, Alabama, bus strike. The students were more interested in talking, however, about the other pair of films. One was a recent Polish film, *The Magician*. The other, an animated cartoon, *The Hat*, consisted of a dialogue between two soldiers (Dizzie Gillespie—whose music also filled the film—and the British comedian, Dudley Moore) who guard either side of a line, the hat of one falling onto the side of the other as they march. The students were quick to compare lines that divided nations with lines that divided people within nations. They remembered, during the discussion that followed, relevant details through which the film attempted to show that talking, in human terms, helps to erase lines.

Evening activities provided still other kinds of experience for the Freedom School student. Apart from concerts, there were mass meetings, at one of which, for example, A. Philip Randolph spoke along with leading Jackson ministers. Best of all was the Free Southern Theatre's production of *In White America*, which toured the state as part of a continuing program of special entertainment for Freedom Schools. Most of these students had never seen live theatre, and certainly not a play about themselves in history. Their response as audience was continuously energetic, especially since, as they reported the next day, they enjoyed recognizing incidents they had been reading of or discussing. One student, Kaaren Robinson, age fifteen, wrote the following as part of a review published in the *Blair Street Freedom Bugle*:

> It portrayed the brutal transportation of the Negro from his native Africa to a new country, the inhuman treatment upon his arrival, the confusing position of the political-minded white man with regard to his stand on the slave question and the continuous struggle of the Negro against overwhelming odds.
>
> . . . Because of his up-bringing, the new freedom put the Negro in a confusing state which naturally led him back into another kind of slavery. This slavery has lasted until now.
>
> The author achieved these points through narration and conversation. Through this medium the Negro of today can better understand why the white man feels as he does toward him. However, this does not justify his feelings nor his actions. *In White America* is a great and moving drama which should be seen by black and white alike.

Though questioned, Kaaren resisted any attempt to enlarge upon the play's effect. From her point of view, the play allowed her to understand the white man's confusion; it told her nothing about the Negro she did not already know.

Charles Cobb, a student at Howard University before he joined the SNCC staff, was responsible late in 1963 for suggesting the idea of Freedom Schools. He has written cogently of their *raison d'être*, in a piece called "This Is the Situation":

> Repression is the law; oppression, a way of life—regimented by the judicial and executive branches of the state government, rigidly enforced by state police machinery, with veering from the path of "our way of life" not tolerated at all. Here, an idea of your own is a subversion that must be squelched; for each bit of intellectual initiative represents the threat of a

probe into the why of denial. Learning here means only learning to stay in your place. Your place is to be satisfied—a "good nigger."

They have learned the learning necessary for immediate survival: that silence is safest, so volunteer nothing; that the teacher is the state, and tell them only what they want to hear; that the law and learning are white man's law and learning.

There is hope and there is dissatisfaction—feebly articulated—both born out of the desperation of needed alternatives not given. This is the generation that has silently made the vow of no more raped mothers—no more castrated fathers; that looks for an alternative to a lifetime of bent, burnt, and broken backs, minds, and souls. There creativity must be molded from the rhythm of a muttered "white son-of-a-bitch"; from the roar of a hunger bloated belly; and from the stench of rain and mud washed shacks.

There is the waiting, not to be taught, but to be, to reach out and meet and join together, and to change. The tiredness of being told it must be, "cause that's white folks' business," must be met with the insistence that it's their business. They know that anyway. It's because their parents didn't make it their business that they're being so systematically destroyed. What they must see is the link between a rotting shack and a rotting America.

The Citizenship Curriculum, the discussion of which filled most of our mornings, is frankly a response to the repressive society Charles Cobb has described. It is aimed at meeting two basic needs of students: first, a need for information; second, a need for identity and hence activity. The "facts" of history; in terms of dates, people's names, places, events, as well as the interpretations of history—all this has been denied to them, and denied particularly in relation to their own situation as American Negroes. Not only is Negro history unknown to them, but even the history of the current Negro revolution is known only in bits and pieces, largely through television, since their newspapers are notoriously uninformative. The second need, the need for identity and activity, is organically one with the need for facts. It has to do with what happens when an individual begins to know himself as part of history, with a past and a potential future as well as a present. What happens when an individual begins to assess himself as a human being? The aim of the Citizenship Curriculum here is to assist the growth of self-respect, through self-awareness, both of which lead to self-help. In this way, the curriculum at the center of the Freedom Schools is frankly and avowedly a program for leadership development.

In many different ways, the mimeographed curriculum makes clear the Freedom Schools' purpose: "to provide an educational experience for students which will make it possible for them to challenge the myths of our society, to perceive more clearly its realities, and to find alternatives, and ultimately, new directions for action." Or more briefly, "to train people to be active agents in bringing about social change." The curriculum itself, however, declares that "It is not our purpose to impose a particular set of conclusions. Our purpose is to encourage the asking of questions, and hope that society can be improved."

Because the chief tool is the question, the curriculum is hopefully "developmental," that is, one that "begins on the level of the students' everyday lives and those things in their environment that they have either already experienced or can readily perceive, and builds up to a more realistic perception of American society, themselves, the conditions of their oppression, and alternatives offered by the Freedom Movement." The seven units are as follows:

1. Comparison of students' reality with others (the way the students live and the way others live)
2. North to Freedom? (the Negro in the north)
3. Examining the apparent reality (the "better lives" that whites live)
4. Introducing the power structure
5. The poor Negro and the poor white
6. Material things versus soul things
7. The Movement

In addition, two sets of questions are to be constantly in the minds of the teachers and frequently introduced to the students:

THE BASIC SET OF QUESTIONS:

1. Why are we (teachers and students) in Freedom Schools?
2. What is the Freedom Movement?
3. What alternatives does the Freedom Movement offer us?

THE SECONDARY SET OF QUESTIONS:

1. What does the majority culture have that we want?
2. What does the majority culture have that we don't want?
3. What do we have that we want to keep?

Some of my own experience was with a relatively young group—eleven to fourteen-year-olds. After describing their own houses, they went on to describe the houses of whites in Jackson that they had seen, either because they had themselves worked as domestics, or because their mothers did. When asked what changes they would like made in their own houses, while their answers varied from additional rooms to more yard space, no one thought in terms as grandiose as the "white" houses they had described, and most of them thought of their houses as "comfortable." On the other hand, they were certain that their (segregated) schools were inferior, even when they admitted that the buildings were new. They resented their hand-me-down textbooks, they suspected the inadequacy of their teachers, and they complained particularly bitterly about the repressive atmosphere. In their schools, they reported that no questioning or discussion was allowed, except in rare instances when they and a particular teacher knew they were "taking a chance." Of course, they knew little or nothing of conditions in white schools, either in Mississippi or elsewhere, beyond their impression that these, somehow, were "better."

High school juniors and seniors were especially interested in the subject of going north to freedom. On the one hand, many of them expressed a wish to go north to college, in part because they suspected that Negro colleges in Mississippi were as inadequate as their public schools, but also because they wanted the experience of learning in an integrated group. They were articulate about the need for communication between black and white. The freedom songs they sang each day—"Black and white together/We shall overcome," for example—were not simply words to be mouthed. On the other hand, some of them had been reading with us from the works of Richard Wright and James Baldwin of the Negro in Chicago or Harlem; and they knew they were living through a summer which had brought riots to northern cities, though not to Jackson, Mississippi. They questioned the condition of Negroes everywhere, and many of them concluded that it was probably better to stay in Mississippi and work to improve things there than to imagine that things were better in another place.

The Freedom School curriculum's most substantial statement about values, "Material Things and Soul Things," takes as its central idea the society that is "humane" because it is "nonviolent." Negroes, of course, are no more naturally violent or nonviolent than any other group. But these students, brought up on the edge of a volcano, named as their heroes Martin Luther King and Medgar Evers, and, when they knew of him, Gandhi as well. At Blair Street, I asked the question about heroes because Paul Lauter had reported that when he asked the question at Freedom Schools throughout the state, those very three names occurred. It was also Paul's impression that as SNCC people became veterans at their jobs, nonviolence for them became not strategic manner but genuine conviction. For the veteran SNCC worker, Matt Suarez, who dropped in one afternoon at Blair Street for a visit and stayed for a discussion, nonviolence had become essential to life. Some of the students who listened to him had also experienced organized demonstrations within the discipline of the nonviolent movement. But their minds were far from decided. They questioned the theory; they suspected themselves of "violent feelings"; they talked about "strategy"; they asked for a "speaker"—and got more discussion!

Because the student needs to learn not only about the world he lives in, but also how to be free enough to live in it, the chief tool of Freedom Schools always was discussion. Ideally, discussion began with the question, "How do you feel about . . . ?" or "How would you feel if . . . ?" and moved on to questions about motivation ("Why do you feel this way?" or "Why would anyone feel this way?"). Once the discussion had begun, the questions could move on to students' reactions to each other's ideas. At first, of course, students were distrustful of the situation generally. Some were also shy before their peers as well as frightened of their teacher. But of course they all had feelings and they all had some words with which to describe them. And eventually the moment came, unnoticed and passed over, when a student could say easily to his (white) teacher or to a fellow student, "I disagree," and explain why.

The teacher's main problem was to learn to keep quiet, to learn how to listen and to question creatively rather than to talk at the students. He had to discard whatever formal classroom procedures he had ever learned and respond with feeling and imagination as well as with intelligence and good humor to the moods and needs of the group. Above all, the students challenged his honesty: he could not sidestep unpleasantness; he could not afford to miss any opportunity for discussing differences.

I have no crystal ball, but I can submit two aspects of my own experience that suggest that the Freedom Schools of '64 spread more than transitory ripples in a huge Mississippi sea. The first was a discussion that led directly to social action independently instigated by the students themselves. The second was an experiment that led directly to the students writing poetry.

The third week of Freedom Schools in Jackson was also the week of school registration for those Negro first-graders who were to attend previously white schools. Registration was scheduled for early Thursday morning; a mass meeting for interested parents had been called by thirty-six Negro ministers of Jackson for Tuesday night. This was Monday morning, and the group at the Blair Street School had begun, for some reason, to talk about the "myth" of Negro inferiority. At one point, when there was silence, I asked how many of the twenty students present (ages fourteen to twenty) knew some first-grader who was about to start school. Everyone did. Did anyone know any who were going to a white school? No one did. When I asked why, I got many different responses:

My sister thinks her son would be unhappy with white children.
My brother hasn't gone to kindergarten.
The white school is too far away.
My mother wants my brother to be with his friends.
My father says he doesn't like the idea.

None of the students had mentioned the word fear. They all looked uncomfortable and I felt my anger rise: "What am I going to say to my friends back North when they ask me why Negro mothers haven't registered their children in white schools? That they like things the way they are?" I could see the consternation on the face of Gene Gogol, my fellow teacher, who began, "I disagree, Florence, you just don't understand the situation." I felt that his rebuke was probably a just one, but then the students began to smile wryly and, one by one, they began to talk of the various fears that "perhaps" these parents were feeling. Personal safety. Economic security— the loss of jobs because they weren't being "good niggers." Failure in the white school—either because of social ostracism or because of poor training and possibly the alleged intellectual inferiority. But then suddenly, I don't know exactly what shifted the discussion, perhaps something about the white faces that Gene and I wore in the midst of the black ones, suddenly the students were talking about *positive* reasons for sending children into integrated schools. Then one of the sixteen-year-old girls suggested that perhaps we—meaning those of us in the discussion group—ought to go out into the neighborhood and talk with parents who were reluctant to send their children to white schools, that perhaps we were most suited for this job since we knew the value of good education and we knew there was really nothing to fear. When I suggested that we try one of the school's favorite procedures, role-playing, there were volunteers immediately for mother, father, child, and for two visitors from the Freedom School. The players were evenly matched so that the play-discussion rehearsed all the arguments we had heard. The role-playing father remained essentially unconvinced, but his wife assured the visitors that she had really changed her mind and that, after they had gone, she would "work on" her husband.

Gene and a crew of student-volunteers worked all the rest of Monday, Monday night, and all of Tuesday. They talked to more than seventy families and received from twenty-seven of these assurances that at least the mother would attend Tuesday night's mass meeting, perhaps would take advantage of the transportation we would provide. Disappointingly, only one mother kept her promise. But on Wednesday morning, Gene and some students began their visits again, and by Thursday noon, all of Blair Street's Freedom School were boasting that eleven of the forty-three Negro children in Jackson who actually registered to attend previously white schools had done so as a direct result of Gene's and the students' talks with parents.

Thus the students had direct evidence that their school experience had led them to create something that was lasting and profound. Additional evidence—this of a more personal nature—followed their reading and discussion of poetry.

We had begun with poems by Langston Hughes. They knew immediately that when Hughes, in a poem called "As I Grew Older," mentioned a "thick wall" and a "shadow" growing between him and his childhood "dream," he was talking about walls and shadows they knew everyday in Jackson: the barbed wire around the parks, for example, or the hate in white men's faces when they tried to go to a movie downtown. I didn't need to be a teacher showing the difference between literal meaning and what was "symbolized." There *was* curiosity about forms. Do all poems rhyme? What is rhyme, anyway? Can poets use any words they like? The students, who had never heard of Langston Hughes, were surprised by his slang, by his use of jazz expressions. They listened to the occasional irregularity that made rhythms interesting, especially in a Hughes song-poem like "The Weary Blues"—which they never tired of.

One day, when discussion had flagged, I suggested a "game." Let's divide into four groups of five and try writing a "group" poem. I even offered a subject: try writing about yourselves and Jackson—we had just been reading about Hughes and Harlem. When I returned, half an hour later, cries of "Listen to this" greeted me. With one exception, the poems were not group products—the groups had stayed to watch individual members create. The best poem came from a sixteen-year-old girl, a visitor to Jackson from Pascagoula, who had just come for the first time to Freedom School, and who was to continue attending thenceforth. This is Alice Jackson's poem called "Mine":

> I want to walk the streets of a town,
> Turn into any restaurant and sit down,
> And be served the food of my choice,
> And not be met by a hostile voice.
> I want to live in the best hotel for a week,
> Or go for a swim at a public beach.
> I want to go to the best university
> And not be met with violence or uncertainty.
> I want the things my ancestors
> Thought we'd never have.
> They are mine as a Negro, an American;
> I shall have them or be dead.

In the days that followed, we read poems by Sandburg and Frost, two poets the students had heard of, but the greatest excitement came from their introduction to e e cummings, especially to the poem "Anyone Lived in a Pretty How Town." One day, after two hours of a discussion of cummings' poems, I asked the eight or nine students present—ages fourteen to seventeen—whether they wanted to try writing again. When I asked whether they wanted a suggested subject, I heard an overwhelming series of no's. No subject . . . let us write what we feel like writing.

Within twenty minutes, Shirley Ballard, age seventeen, was reading aloud to me a poem called "Time." She read it slowly, emphasizing the individuality of certain words and phrases. Its feeling was clearly fragmentary. But then she showed me the page on which she had written the poem: four long lines, resembling her reading not at all. She had read it in a manner that suggested something else, and I showed her cummings' page. She caught on instantly, took her page, and returned in several minutes with the following version:

> Times goes by so slowly
> my mind reacts so lowly
> how faint
> how moody
> I feel,
> I love not
> I care not.
> Don't love me.

> Let me live.
> > Die
> > Cry
> > Sigh
> All alone
> > Maybe someday I'll go home.

Another seventeen year old, Sandra Ann Harris, quickly produced a cummings-like poem—even to the elimination of all capitalization:

> why did i my don'ts
> why did i my dids
> what's my didn'ts' purpose
> is to fulfill my dids
>
> what isn'ts have i proclaimed
> what ises have i pronounced
> why can't i do my doings
> my couldn'ts do renounce
>
> my wouldn'ts are excuses
> my couldn'ts couldn't be helped
> my wern'ts were all willful
> my words of little help
>
> the haven'ts were just there
> my didn'ts did believe
> that all my won'ts are daring
> my wills to receive

If it is startling to consider how much these students learned so quickly, it is also instructive to consider that in Freedom Schools all over Mississippi this summer students were becoming both social activists and poets. An impressive volume of poetry (which may soon be published) appeared in Freedom School newspapers. And a Mississippi Student Union has been formed. The connection between poetry and politics should surprise no one who has read the Romantics or, more recently, the poets of the Irish Renaissance. What is surprising is that, in some ways, it took *so little* to accomplish so much in the Mississippi Freedom Schools.

Consider the discussion circle, the union of teachers and students in a status-free ring. Consider too the position of these students—blacks in a white culture—as outsiders who were now, in 1964, *conscious* outsiders, youngsters seeing new possibilities ahead of them and, at the same time, young adults with the wisdom to see what Negro slavery has been. Under these special new conditions, one could talk and think about what it was like to be a slave and what it might be like to be free. One could even try *being* free. Under these special conditions—the consciousness of being suppressed combined with the proffered opportunity to base education on that consciousness—creativity was the natural response.

What have we to learn from Freedom Schools? The politics of education.

That our schools are political grounds in which our students begin to learn about society's rules. That, therefore, if we wish to alter our students and our society, we must alter our schools. That if we would have strong and creative minds we must remove chains both from bodies and spirits. That we as adults and educators have to listen and respond rather than preach. That we need to share with our students a sense of being open to what each uniquely experienced companion can reveal. That this perspective of equality is itself a revolution that goes far beyond the surface movement of Negroes into white society. And that if Freedom School teachers in Mississippi society know themselves as unwelcome and harassed outsiders, not unlike the Negro students, then authentic teachers anywhere must face a similar knowledge.

The Freedom School students and teachers who heard Langston Hughes' "As I Grew Older" understood that Hughes' prayer was theirs too—for strength and wisdom to break through all spiritual prisons of self and society and so to reach freedom:

> My hands!
> My dark hands!
> Break through the wall!
> Find my dream!
> Help me to shatter this darkness.
> To smash this night,
> To break this shadow
> Into a thousand lights of sun,
> Into a thousand whirling dreams
> Of sun! *